THE
PSYCHIC EXPLORER

JONATHAN CAINER & CARL RIDER

A FIRESIDE BOOK
PUBLISHED BY SIMON & SCHUSTER INC.
NEW YORK LONDON TORONTO SYDNEY TOKYO

Acknowledgements

The authors and publisher would like to thank the following organizations for supplying illustrations and photos for this book:

Barnaby's Picture Library: p. 30 (top); Century Rider Limited: colour insert p. 7; Jean-Loup Charmet, Paris: p. 37; Mary Evans Picture Library: p. 29, colour insert pp. 3–6, colour insert p. 9, and colour insert pp. 11 and 12; Editions Grimaud, Paris: colour insert p. 8; by Gracious permission of Her Majesty the Queen: p. 30 (bottom); Images Colour Library, Leeds: p. 14, p. 44, colour insert pp. 1 and 2; Museo Fournier, Vitoria: colour insert p. 7; by courtesy of the trustees of The National Gallery, London: p. 63; Royal Greenwich Observatory: p. 15; Thames & Hudson Limited: p. 189.

A Fireside Book
Published by Simon & Schuster Inc.
Simon & Schuster Building
Rockefeller Center
1230 Avenue of the Americas
New York, NY 10020
Originally published in Great Britain by
Judy Piatkus (Publishers) Limited, 1986
FIRESIDE and colophon are registered trademarks of Simon & Schuster Inc.
Special photography: Helen Pask

Manufactured in the United States of America

10 9 8 7 6 5 4 3 2 1 Pbk.

Library of Congress Cataloging in Publication Data
Cainer, Jonathan.
    The psychic explorer.

    Reprint. Originally published: London : Piatkus, 1986.
    "A Fireside Book."
    Bibliography: p.
    Includes index.
    1. Occultism.   2. Psychical research.   I. Rider, Carl.   II. Title.
BF1411.C23   1988   130   87-23479

ISBN 0-671-65945-6 Pbk.

Contents

Do You Believe in Magic?

Welcome to a world that exists on the fringes of so-called reality.

Welcome to a world where dreams come alive, wishes come true – and science must surrender to sincerity.

Welcome to the world of Magic.

To be a psychic explorer, you needn't believe in magic. You can remain as cynical, sceptical and suspicious as you like. To be a magician, however, you must first become a psychic explorer.

Every chapter in this book is designed to provide a tangible experience. Follow our simple guidelines and see for yourself where they lead you.

There is nothing to be afraid of. This is a book about magic, but no sinister secrets lurk within its pages. It will not cause you to accidentally unleash a demon from your subconscious – or from anywhere else. Every chapter has been written with love, care and understanding. Nineteenth-century mumbo-jumbo and mediaeval superstition have been carefully removed – and what remains is our rightful heritage. The pure, original, esoteric arts.

The traditional rules of Palmistry, Astrology, Telepathy, Auric Perception, Tarot, Divination, Aromatics and Ceremonial Magic are now, finally, gathered together and clearly explained. The authors are not journalists, eccentrics or occultists. They are two sane, rational human beings who have actually practised the techniques they describe and who recognize their value, even in our modern, technological world. They are 'Psychic Explorers' not magicians although, as you will see, it's a borderline definition.

Once you have made these techniques work for yourself, and recognized that they are all related to a hidden power that lies within you, you will understand the true origin and purpose of magic, and you will develop faith in your own ability to manipulate time and space for the good of others.

Then you will see that whether you call yourself a 'Magician' or a 'Psychic Explorer' is irrelevant. You will simply be a human being, engaged in the process of discovering every ounce of your true potential.

By then you will be ready to enter the final chapter – the only section of this book that begins by asking you to try another chapter first.

With this exception, you are invited to delve and dabble as you please throughout the pages. The final chapter has nothing to hide. It contains no unspeakable secrets. It merely houses the most controversial material in our collection. Ceremonial Magic has become synonymous with witchcraft and satanism. Abandoned by science and adopted by fools, its innocent history has been corrupted by a long procession of maniacs. Rambling poets (like Aleister Crowley) and greedy dreamers (like Eliphas Levi) have stamped a harmless tradition with the mark of fear. Sensationalist writers of cheap fiction have managed to seal its fate. Magic, it seems, must always mystify and terrify the public. That is why you are asked to leave this volatile subject till last.

Before you can successfully enter the realm of Ceremonial Magic, you must leave behind the fantasies and lies you have learned to associate with its nature. The best way to do that is to gain your own experience of what *really* constitutes magic, and to know for yourself that magic is a force that lies within you and not in some lofty realm of mythical gods and vain superstition.

By the time you have learned to dowse, or read

palms, or see auras you will not need this explaining. By then, you will have your own experience of inner power. You will know how to contact it, how to use it successfully, why it is harmless, and just how rewarding it can be to become a Psychic Explorer.

The Father and the Mother of all understanding, the Stars, that measure out the
destiny of all; while underneath, the children
of the Earth look up and seek to know. Wise
are they who gaze upon the heavens as in a
looking glass and neither blame nor boast at
what they see. For Father Sun and Mother
Moon and every light would share their
deepest secret as an open book, and shine that
each may know his place under the starry
firmament.

An Introduction to Astrology

Mortal as I am,
I know that I am born for a day.
But when I follow
The serried multitude of the stars
(In their circular course),
My feet no longer touch the earth.
I ascend to Zeus himself
to feast me on
ambrosia
the food of the gods.

Claudius Ptolemy, astrologer, c.AD150

Nothing exists, nor happens in the visible sky,
That is not sensed
in some hidden manner
by the faculties of Earth
and Nature.

Johannes Keppler, astronomer, c.1600

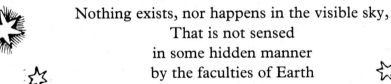

When the Moon is in the 7th house...
And Jupiter aligns with Mars
Then Peace will guide the planets
And love will rule the stars.

Hair, A Rock Musical, c. 1967

Somewhere in the depths of infinite space there is a tiny ball of rock. It hurtles through the heavens at breakneck speed, circling a faint yellow star. As it travels, it spins like a top. Somewhere on its surface are you and I, and approximately 4,000,000,000 other human beings.

Most of us are too engrossed with the earth beneath our feet to spare a second throught for the sky above our heads. However, to be a successful 20th-century magician it is necessary to disturb this state of ignorance. An understanding of the principles of astrology is vital to almost every magical pursuit – as is an understanding of your own inner motivation. For these reasons I have divided the chapter on astrology into two sections.

PART ONE is dedicated to the moon. When most people think of astrology they think of the sun and their sun signs. But for a magician, the moon is far more important. The sun may be King of the Day, but the moon is Queen of the Night, and night is traditionally the time for magic. The Queen of the Night is like the Queen on a chessboard. She has the power to go almost anywhere and do almost anything. The magician who wants to be more than just a pawn moving from square to square in pedestrian fashion, must learn to watch the moon, and learn not just to follow but to predict her movements. Also, the magician must learn to recognize and manipulate her power *within his (or her) own being*. A knowledge of 'the moon within you' is vital to a magical understanding of the universe.

PART TWO introduces the tradition of celestial symbolism. It explains how a horoscope is made and covers the use of astrology as a tool for forecasting and divination.

I hope that, between them, these two sections will stimulate your interest in the oldest and most rewarding magical art in the whole world.

PART ONE

How to Discover Your Moon Sign

**S**UN sign astrology is very popular. Hundreds of magazines, newspapers and radio shows feature a regular horoscope. Few people can resist a quick peep at what the stars foretell, even if they don't take it very seriously. A pinch of salt is a sensible thing to add to most popular astrology, for, as you will soon see, the real thing is considerably more complex and personal. But we all have to begin somewhere, so let's start with a summary of what you may already know.

According to the columnists, the world is divided into 12 different types of person. As far as sun signs are concerned, everything depends on the four-week period in which you were born.

If you were born between:	*They say you will be:*	
March 21–April 20	an active, assertive	**Aries**
April 21–May 21	a tenacious, tactile	**Taurus**
May 22–June 22	a gregarious, gullible	**Gemini**
June 23–July 23	a careful, cautious	**Cancer**
July 24–August 23	a loud, lordly	**Leo**
August 24–Sept 23	a versatile, vulnerable	**Virgo**
September 24–October 23	a leisurely, likeable	**Libra**
October 24–November 22	a strong, sexy	**Scorpio**
November 23–December 21	a sporting, surprising	**Sagittarius**
December 22–January 20	a capable, constructive	**Capricorn**
January 21–February 19	an arrogant, affable	**Aquarius**
February 20–March 20	a poetic, poignant	**Pisces**

While it is true that someone with a trained eye and a bit of astrological expertise can often spot a Scorpio or point out a Pisces, it is obviously not true to say that everyone born in the same 30-day period has an identical personality! The sun sign normally reveals only a vague impression, and sun sign astrology alone is really rather superficial and limited.

Real astrology requires the exact time, date and place of birth, not just the month. It is not as instant as sun sign astrology, but the extra information it reveals can be staggeringly accurate. In Part Two, I give an outline of how it works and explain how, using a computer service or a set of mathematical tables, you can obtain a unique, personal horoscope. For the moment I want to concentrate on the power of the moon in astrology as it has a very special relevance to magic.

Introducing The Moon

Some parts of astrology have to be taken on trust, at least to begin with. It is not always easy to see why the movements of a tiny planet such as Pluto, which is 3,578 million miles from Earth and invisible to the naked eye, should have a bearing on our daily lives. The power of the sun and the moon, however, are obvious to everyone regardless of their interest in astrology.

To appreciate the effect of the sun you only have to compare how you feel when the sun is shining with how you feel when it is not. If you are a farmer or a gardener the effect of the sun is paramount; it can make your crops grow or scorch them before they can be harvested. The power of the moon is not always so obvious, particularly if you happen to live in a crowded city where the streetlights and neon signs can detract from the awesome darkness of a moonless night. (A full moon, by the way, gives roughly the same luminosity as a 15-watt lightbulb on your bedroom ceiling.) Even so, if you are a sailor or a coastguard, you won't need me to remind you of the vital link between the moon and ocean tides.

The moon, in astrological terms, is the great mother figure in the sky. She rules the night, the seas, and the process of childbirth. In psychological terms she symbolizes the deeper, more private and more emotional side of human nature. If you like, the sun is yang (male, outgoing, obvious and active), while the moon is yin (female, introverted, subtle and passive). Since the dawn of time, almost every race and culture has considered the sun to be a masculine force and the moon to be a manifestation of feminine energy. One reason for this, of course, is that the moon waxes and wanes in a regular pattern, echoing the process of birth, maturity, old age and

Whether the moon is full or new, waxing or waning, she still only shows one of her two faces to those on Earth. Her mysterious, hidden side perhaps reflects the darker aspects of human nature.

reproduction, while the sun remains constant in its appearance. Another reason is the long-proven link between the monthly journey of the moon and the female menstrual cycle.

Our modern world is very *solar*. Despite recent advances in the feminist cause, we still live in a society dominated by male energy—and perhaps that is one reason why masculine sun signs have become so popular! There is a strong tendency for most of us to accept glib, generalized information and simplified scientific truisms. The sun rules 'simplicity', and it also speaks of 'material growth and self interest', two very characteristic 20th-century ideals. The lunar principles of compassion, sympathy and understanding *do* exist in our world, but most of us would agree that they normally play a muted second fiddle in the process of human motivation.

For the aspiring magician—and indeed for anyone who wishes to push against the limitations of their environment—it is crucial to recognize that people of either sex have two sides to their personality. Inside every macho man is a soft, poetic, sensitive individual trying to get out. Inside every soft woman is a strong, capable and ambitious person waiting for an opportunity to express herself. However, most women, at least on a superficial level, find it easier to identify with the lunar side of their character, while most men have more affinity with solar energy. In other words, women are often more in touch with their moon signs and men with their sun signs.

If you can accept the notion that each individual is not just a one dimensional personality with a cardboard cut-out façade but a complicated, sensitive mixture of differing (and sometimes opposing) inclinations, you are ready to enter the world of real astrology and begin a fascinating journey of self exploration.

What is a Moon sign?

Although you rarely hear about them in magazines and newspapers, everybody has a moon sign as well as a sun sign. We also have a Mercury sign, a Venus sign, a Mars sign, and so on (see pages 31–34). So what exactly is a moon sign?

The sun, the moon and the planets all move through the sky at different speeds. However, they all follow the same circular route, and astrologers chop that route into 12 equal sections to get our 12 signs of the zodiac.

On the day you were born each planet was in one or another of those 12 signs and as astrologers always work with the day of birth, we call the sign which the sun was in on that day your sun sign, and the sign which the moon was in on that day your moon sign.

The sun takes about 30 days to move through each sign of the zodiac, and as the route doesn't vary much from year to year it is easy to work out what sun sign you are.★ The moon, on the other hand, takes about 52 hours to move through each sign of the zodiac. It doesn't follow the same pattern each year so you can't look up your moon sign in a short simple list.

To find out whether you were born with the Moon in Aries, Taurus, Gemini, etc., all you have to do is look up your date of birth in the table at the back of the book. The list is long but easy to use. If you discover that you were born on a day when the moon changed signs, read Born on the Cusp (opposite).

★ Actually, although the sun doesn't vary much – it does vary! (It is odd how most newspaper columnists conveniently forget this!) If you were born within 48 hours of one of the change-over dates on page 13 you really should give your exact date and time of birth to an astrologer who can tell you on which side of the cusp you are.

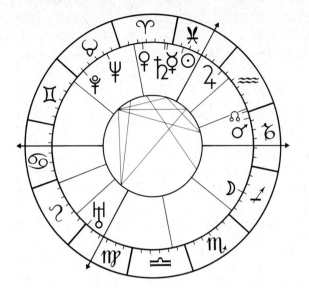 

Born on the Cusp?

If you were born on a day when the moon changed signs, or if you were born close to a sun sign change-over date, you'll need to know your exact time of birth in order to be sure which sign you are.

There is really no such thing as being born on the cusp. That's just an invention of lazy astrologers who couldn't be bothered to explain about Greenwich Mean Time; they simply created the notion of a grey area between two adjacent signs of the zodiac, where someone might be a bit of both. No serious astrologer would suggest this. If you don't know your time of birth (and can't find out), you'll simply have to read both relevant definitions and choose between one or the other.

The horoscopes of two famous scientists. Albert Einstein (left) was born on 14th March 1879 in Ulm, Germany, at 11.30 am local time. Marie Curie (right) was born on 7th November 1867 in Warsaw, Poland, at 1.30 pm local time. The visual appearance and 'shape' of a horoscope can be interesting. Both these people have planets in two tight bunches, suggesting a highly focused mind.

If or when you establish a birth time, refer to pages 307 to 318 to find your sign. The figures given in the charts are GMT (Greenwich Mean Time), so if you were born during a period when the clocks had been put forward (such as British Summertime or International Daylight Saving

Time), you'll need to deduct an hour from your time of birth. If you were born outside the UK, you'll also have to add or subtract the relevant difference in Time Zone (see page 306).

What Your Moon Sign Means

I am assuming that you will by now have turned to the back of the book, discovered your moon sign (or at least narrowed it down to one of two), and will be very keen to dive straight into the juicy section: 'What does it say about me?'

HOLD THAT FEELING FOR A MOMENT. It's a very moon-y thing to want to know about yourself in this way, so holding the feeling for a minute will help you identify which part of yourself the moon is describing.

In personal astrology, the moon is about feelings more than anything else. It's the way you can know, if somebody holds back a lot, worries a lot, is easily frightened, or tends to ignore his feelings. When the moon is not describing emotions, it's describing emotionally-related things, such as how you feel about your mother and father, how you react to children, and so on. The moon describes the ways in which you are likely to seek reassurance, and therefore, not surprisingly, it also describes your sense of need, the areas in your life where you are likely to feel lacking or dissatisfied. Put another way, the moon is about the vulnerable side of your nature, your soft underbelly where things can get to you.

It is, of course, this sensitive aspect of your character which is most responsive to magic. When you feel bright, rash and sun-ny there is little room to appreciate and tune into the subtler nuances of life. It is when you feel deep, dark, mysterious and moon-y that you'll find it easiest to develop your inner magical skills.

It is quite possible that you may not enjoy reading about your moon-y side. I have dwelt, quite deliberately, on some of the more painful or difficult manifestations of each moon sign. If you feel insulted by what you are about to read... so much the better! The psychic explorer must be able to face all aspects of himself – or herself – not just the complimentary! If, after reflection, you still feel that I've been unduly harsh, you can find out more about the positive qualities of your moon position by reading about the appropriate zodiacal sign on pages 37–41 and filtering what is said there through your own understanding of the moon sign characteristics. I rather hope that you will do this, for then you will be forming your own interpretations instead of taking them from a textbook. That act of independence is, in a nutshell, what separates an astrologer from a client, a writer from a reader, and a psychic explorer from an ordinary person.

The final thing I must explain before I let you dive in and find out about yourself is that each sign of the zodiac works at several different levels. How your moon sign behaves in you will depend on how old you are, what sex you are, how intelligent you are*, your cultural background, and so on. Please remember that these are things I cannot possibly know. The following 12 statements are drawn (a) from the basic character traits associated with the moon in each sign and (b) from the way I have observed people with these moon signs react to life's problems and difficulties. It is at times of stress that we are all most likely to show the moonier side of our character – and if I succeed in putting you under a little stress by being somewhat harsh, at least I'll be helping you to notice the way your 'moon' responds when you feel under threat or attack!

The 12 Moon signs

MOON IN ARIES

People with the moon in Aries find their emotions characterized by outbursts of passion. It's hard for them to repress their feelings, and it's also hard for them to separate a gut reaction from a logical assessment. When under pressure they are towers of strength and can be quick to find solutions. When life is slow, they champ at the bit, creating tension where none needs to exist simply for the sake of satisfying their need to get things moving. They have a volatile and frightening temper which can flare up suddenly – but it subsides just as quickly and these people don't hold grudges. They tend to have little patience with those who feel vulnerable or anxious, but perhaps this is just as well because their quiet confidence is infectious (even though it's a confidence that might also be seen as arrogance!).

MOON IN TAURUS

Taurus is a sign notorious for its love of luxury. The moon is equally infamous for stimulating self indulgence. Not surprisingly then, people with the moon in Taurus are normally sensual in the extreme, placing comfort and stability very high on their list of priorities. Whether their favourite pleasure is sex, food or art, or some combination of the three, you can be sure they will linger for a long time over the things they enjoy. It

* Sorry, but raw intelligence is not shown by astrology alone – only how you are likely to use it.

also takes them a long time to change their hearts (and their minds), their anger is slow to arouse, but it's harder still to shake off. They can cling stubbornly to a point of view or a belief – and seem to gain a sense of security from the fixedness of their opinions. In fact, emotional stubbornness and the refusal to give way are both their blessing and their curse.

MOON IN GEMINI

'Busy doing nothing, nothing the whole day through – trying to find lots of things not to do!' might well be the motto of those with the moon in Gemini. Not that they're lazy, they're actually hyperactive and never seem to stop worrying about the most inconsequential things. As a result, it's rare to find someone with this moon position sitting still and relaxing. They love to analyze every feeling, assess every emotion and discuss every situation – often taking a controversial or antagonistic point of view for the sake of it. On the positive side, it makes life interesting, but on the negative side it means that there's always a crisis to be dealt with or something traumatic about to happen. The temptation to talk about everything that occurs on their 'inside' makes these people a little like the boy who cried wolf. No one knows when they really mean what they say they feel.

MOON IN CANCER

Whether male or female, there is something very maternal about people born with the moon in Cancer. They have a powerful desire to nurture, cherish and protect – and if this isn't directed towards the people they love, it will be channelled inwards, making them rather too keen to look after what they consider to be their own interests. Fortunately, this is a fairly rare development because one of the hardest things for them to do normally is to decide where *their* interests end and those of others begin. They are too sensitive by far to the pain and suffering of the world and find it almost impossible to dissociate themselves from another person's need. This, in turn, makes them a sucker for a sob story and therefore rather vulnerable and weak-willed.

MOON IN LEO

Whenever the moon is in Leo you can expect to find a bit of a show off: somebody who likes to be the centre of attention and cannot bear to feel overlooked or unimportant. Needless to say, this attitude goes hand in hand with a strong sense of self worth, which it takes a great deal to shake. They can be very generous, sociable and friendly but – even so – it's normally tied up with a desire to obtain support and admiration from the people with whom they come into contact. There's quite a strong fear of failure underlying all this, which is one reason why people with moon in Leo are normally quite high achievers – even though they all share an abhorrence of hard work. Instead, they make the little they can bring themselves to do go a long way! When they feel threatened or put upon they can become extremely aggressive.

MOON IN VIRGO

More than anything else, these people fear chaos. A place for everything and everything in its place would be their motto – although that doesn't necessarily mean that they like their physical environment to be tidy. It's more to do with their understanding of the world around them; they like to feel that they *know* what's going on, and are happiest when they are in charge of organizing things. When they aren't applying their minds to the niggling little details that other people won't touch, they become ridiculously self critical and can disappear into a morass of self inflicted pain. Moon in Virgo people find it very hard to deal with their own emotions. They normally consider their feelings an annoyance and try too hard to intellectualize and compartmentalize their fears.

MOON IN LIBRA

Two opposing traits come together here. On the one hand, a person with the moon in Libra will always have a keen aesthetic sense and know exactly what they like and don't like in terms of music, art, and all forms of wordly beauty. On the other hand, they will always find it hard to know exactly how they feel about how they feel(!), particularly in relation to other people. Their own desire to avoid confrontation at any cost stops them from expressing the few strong opinions they hold, with the result that they are always saying one thing and doing quite another! They like to subject their every emotion to a process of leisurely deliberation and contemplation and thoroughly hate having to face up to difficult issues, waiting instead until someone else makes a decision for them.

MOON IN SCORPIO

People with the moon in Scorpio are never quite sure of themselves. They have intense passion, deep longing and an overwhelming need for reassurance. They are very afraid to admit any of this and spend much time trying (and failing) to hide the depth of their feeling. They are easily hurt, and rarely understand that this is because of their own hypersensitivity and not because of a conscious campaign by other people. As a result, they will often shoot first or put up a heavy guard and allow no one through. While all this makes them very difficult to live with (and hard for them to live with themselves), it is also the reason why they often become very successful in their chosen fields – channelling all their nervous and frightened energy into proving themselves sexually or materially. (Often both.)

MOON IN SAGITTARIUS

The moon in Sagittarius bestows an emotional make-up that might be compared to a punchbag. No matter how hard they are hit, these people simply wobble for a while and bounce right back. This means that they find it hard to learn from their experiences and will often repeat the same mistakes throughout their lives. Indestructible positivity *does* bring forth a special form of wisdom, but the benefits are normally more theoretical than practical. Often, their infectiously cheerful faith in humanity leads more vulnerable individuals into trouble and when reproached for this, lunar Sagittarians may simply shrug their shoulders or grin glibly. They also have a terrible fear of mundanity and cannot bear to be committed to a person or a project unless there is a strong element of challenge.

MOON IN CAPRICORN

Here is the person who carries the weight of the world on his (or her) shoulders. Admittedly, few people are more responsible, mature and practically minded than those with the moon in Capricorn, but it should also be said that no one is more prone to over-seriousness, inflexibility or pomposity. There is an almost religious reverence for the past and a tendency to cling to outmoded or old-fashioned ideals and attitudes. They hate to break agreements and tend also to hate those people who break theirs. Needless to say, this doesn't exactly encourage spontaneity, although people with this moon position can manage a calculated impersonation of this quality if pushed. Generally, though, they are best left alone to pursue their natural inclination to take control of every situation – for then they are happy and pleasant to be with!

MOON IN AQUARIUS

Nobody understands a person with the moon in Aquarius, least of all the person with moon in Aquarius. These people are quirky, eccentric and

unpredictable individuals who find it very hard to come to terms with their emotions. They find it hard to laugh, hard to cry and hard even to know which of the two responses they ought to be manifesting. Instead, they prefer to maintain a healthy disinterest in their own feelings and the feelings of those around them, and to hold lofty intellectual discussions on obscure and seemingly irrelevant subjects. Occasionally, something that to the rest of us would appear inconsequential pierces their armour and they become passionate proclaimers of the oddest causes – unable to understand why the rest of the world fails to share their inspired enthusiasm.

MOON IN PISCES

Pisces is the sign of the Martyr and people with the moon in Pisces will have no difficulty in empathizing with martyrdom in any guise. They simply adore agony, worship worry and deify disappointment! Whether or not this is simply a form of inverted selfishness is open to argument. Certainly these people are more than ready to listen to anyone who is sad or suffering – but in a funny sort of way they seem to do it in order to add to their own burden. They have an almost morbid fascination with raw deals, and can't hear enough about the darker side of life! When faced with a tricky situation or a pressing problem their favourite solution is to retreat, escape, run away, get drunk, change the subject, write poetry, go to the doctor or, as a last resort, collapse in a flood of tears and beg for help.

How do you feel, now that you have read about your moon sign? If you think it was a little too close for comfort, don't feel bad. Remember, this is a book about psychic exploration and one of the principal aims of astrology is to make you feel better about yourself and more capable of dealing with the world around you. One of the best ways to do this is to face up to these things.

If I hit the nail on the head, don't feel that this is the only way you will ever be. Astrological labels are not an excuse ('Oh I can't help it – I've got moon in bladibla'), they are a method of encouraging self growth. Diagnosis, as they say, is half the cure. If you can recognize your tendency to be a certain way you can begin to do something about it.

The more you can turn your negative moon sign characteristics into positive ones, the more conscious you will have become of your subconscious. This, in turn, will help you recognize and tune into psychic signals from nature. In other words, the better you know yourself, the more effectively you will be able to work magic.

If you're still absolutely convinced that the interpretation was way off beam, try asking someone who knows you well for a second opinion. In the unlikely event that they agree with you and not me, the paragraph below might explain why.

To understand your moon sign fully, you have also to think about your sun sign. If you are a soft, soppy moon in Pisces but your sun is in tough, uncompromising Capricorn, only a few people will ever see how gentle you really are – and you may even hide it from yourself. Conversely, if your moon is in cool, distanced Aquarius but your sun is in hot, passionate Aries, people may be surprised to discover how dispassionate you can be in times of turmoil, even though most of the time you're the first to lose your temper.

If you want to sink your teeth right into the subject (and right into the true story of your inner self) there's an awful lot more to consider, understand and place in perspective. Before we move on to Part Two where all will be revealed, there are a few final words I want to say about moon signs.

1 **Watch your Moon sign** The moon is the most changeable factor in astrology, which is fitting when you consider that it rules the most changeable factor in human beings – their emotions. Whether you are male of female, you may find that you have one regular time of the month when you feel particularly vulnerable. It's very often the time when the moon in the sky *today* passes through the sign it was in when you were born. Using the list on page 307, you can look for the next time the moon is in *your* moon sign and see what happens during those two days! It should prove very revealing. Astrologers call this a 'lunar return' because the moon returns to the same place it was in when you were born. When the sun does the same thing it's called a 'solar return' – and you'll always have one of these within 24 hours or so of your birthday. (Hence the expression 'many happy returns')

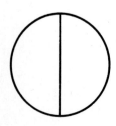

Full moon

2 **Full Moons and New Moons** The full moon brings out the moon sign in everyone – which is why the whole world often goes a little 'loony' at these times. When the full moon occurs in the same sign as your moon sign you will be particularly likely to have an intense (though not always unpleasant) experience.

The sign that the full moon is in is always the *opposite* sign of the zodiac to the sign that the sun is in at the time. To find out which signs are opposite signs, read Part Two. (Logically-minded readers will realize that by using the list of sun signs on page 13 and the list of moon signs on pages 307 – 318 they can work out the date of the next full moon.)

By the same token, a new moon always occurs in the same sign as the one that the sun is in. When there is a new moon in your moon sign, you should find it an excellent time for making new beginnings and fresh starts.

First quarter

3 The Dance of the Sun and Moon   If your moon sign is the same sign as your sun sign, each new moon and full moon in that sign will be particularly noticeable. It also indicates that your parents were probably quite close to each other and that you are relatively well equipped to deal with traumatic events in life.

If your moon sign is in the *opposite* sign of the zodiac to your sun sign, the chances are that there was a lot of family tension in your childhood. Normally, this implies that the sun (father) was opposite to (or at loggerheads with) the moon (mother).

The list on pages 31–34 contains the planetary rulers for each sign. If your moon and sun signs share the same ruler, you will have a very strong tendency to live out the qualities of that ruling planet. For example, if your moon is in Aries and your sun is in Scorpio (or vice versa), you will be very Martian, for the planet Mars rules Scorpio and Aries.

Although the moon changes in shape from day to day, astrologers always use this symbol to depict the moon in a horoscope.

4 The Moon and the Daily News   The list on pages 37–41 contains some of the day-to-day items, as well as the psychological qualities ruled by each sign. It's interesting to note how often they come into the news when there is a full moon in the sign that rules them.

By now, I hope you are beginning to see just how magical astrology can be. If it seems a little complex – well, the next section is guaranteed to boggle the brains of everyone except a nuclear physicist or an ardent crossword puzzle solver! I've done everything I can to explain things clearly without over simplifying, but, as you'll see, there's a lot of detail to get through. I hope you'll give it a whirl because it's extremely useful to have an understanding of how astrology works even if you don't want to become an astrologer. Amongst other things, you'll understand why so many people with an interest in magic have taken up Tarot or palmistry instead. Both those subjects are a lot simpler!

PART TWO

How to Read a Horoscope

The sun, the moon and five planets trace endless circles through the sky. Since time immemorial, our ancestors have gazed at this celestial dance and attributed meaning to its steps and rhythm. Today, we know that the Earth is itself part of a cosmic cavalcade, racing through space around a central sun.* Despite the fact that we have discovered that we share our path with three other planets, invisible to the naked eye, the essence of the ancient art of astrology remains unchanged. Events in the sky above our heads reflect events on the Earth beneath our feet. The macrocosm reflects the microcosm. As above . . . so below!

Trying to understand someone's character, or predict their future, from a sun sign alone is a bit like trying to play a piano sonata with just one finger! Working with the sun and moon together is like playing the sonata with one hand! There's a lot more music to hear and appreciate in the complex symphony of celestial spheres and to help you understand more of real astrology I've made the following pages a guided tour of an astrologer's inner chamber. I hope you will join me on it, even if your interest is casual. A psychic explorer needn't know a T-square from a Disassociate Quincunx, but he ought to know a Fire sign from an Earth sign! I'm about to explain both – but I don't expect you to soak it all in! Just read the chapter with an open mind and an inquiring spirit. You will instinctively know which information you need to learn and which information you ought simply to be aware of. If you find something you can't easily understand, feel free to gloss over it. When you are ready to go deeper, return to the details.

* The sun itself is slowly moving in orbit around a far-flung arm of our galaxy. The journey takes billions of years to complete, but if we translate the co-ordinates of this distant point into zodiacal longitude, it equates (at least for this century) with approximately 26 degrees of the sign Sagittarius. Therefore, people born on or around December 18th each year can claim a very special connection to the cosmos. The sun in their horoscope will be on what astronomers call the Galactic centre!

A Potted History of Astrology

Astrology began many thousands of years ago as a system of omens. The meeting of two planets might herald a famine; an eclipse might signify the onset of a flood. Later, people began to chart the entire sky positions for a given day.

They used these charts to predict the outcome of a battle or the death of a king. Eventually astrology became a complex system of divination, capable of answering a host of specific questions. The rules we use in the 1980s are little different in essence to those laid down in Babylonia, 2,000 years BC. Ever since then – until the early 18th century – healers, philosophers, mathematicians, magicians and soldiers referred constantly to charts of the heavens in their work. Today, the political, medical and magical branches of astrology are largely, sadly and mistakenly, forgotten. Most people think of astrology only as a form of character analysis. Surprisingly, this sort of personal astrology is fairly new: it only began in about 300 or 200 BC! Nonetheless, we must begin with personal astrology, if only because its complex rules are still the easiest to explain! Later in the chapter I'll talk about the other, more exotic, branches on the astrological tree.

This classic medieval woodcut represents the heavens as a series of cosmic wheels. The idea is that our lives are controlled by a form of celestial clockwork – and that the workings of this astral machine will become apparent to anyone who is humble and determined enough to peer through the heavenly veil.

How to Obtain Your Own Horoscope

Drawing up a horoscope is a fiddly, time-consuming and difficult process. Fortunately, you will never need to do it because being a 20th-century psychic explorer means that you can take advantage of 20th-century technology. There are many excellent home computer programs on the market which will calculate a horoscope for you. If you don't have a computer, you can still obtain a computer chart from one of several quick, cheap and reliable mail order companies to be found in the back of any horoscope magazine.

I thoroughly recommend that you obtain a copy of your own chart, plus the charts of your friends and loved ones. Although you won't need it to make sense of the rest of this chapter, having your own horoscope in front of you will certainly enhance your enjoyment! On first sight, your horoscope can look daunting and formidable. It needn't be. All you need to understand it is a basic grasp of astrological symbolism – and a little patience. You will have to supply the patience yourself (although there is a spell for it on page 297), but I can help you with the symbolism . . .

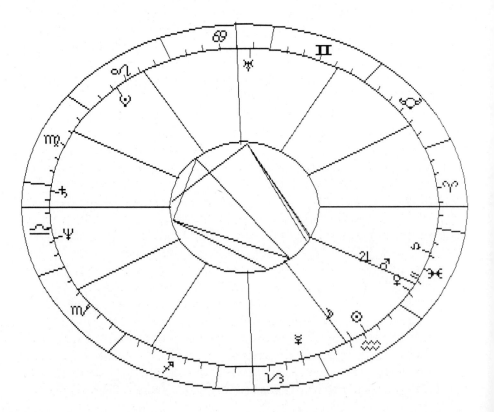

This horoscope has been calculated and drawn by a small home computer.

The Meaning of Symbols in Astrology

Astrology is often called the study of symbols and cycles. Symbols, because each planet symbolizes an aspect of human life; cycles, because each planet has a cycle, or period of revolution, which echoes the rhythm of growth and change on Earth.

Let's look at symbols first. They are a kind of shorthand code for things that are difficult to express in words, and as all forms of magic involve perceiving the universe at a level deeper than words, symbols have a very special significance in magic.

Carl Jung, the great psychologist, wrote:

C. G. Jung.

. . . A word or an image is symbolic when it implies something more than its obvious and immediate meaning. It has a wider, 'unconscious' aspect that is never precisely defined or fully explained. Nor can one hope to define or explain it. As the mind explores the symbol, it is led to ideas that lie beyond the grasp of reason.

Within each one of us, there is a deep well of fears, hopes and desires. They are the things we dream about. The things we feel but can't express. We may try to ignore them, we may try to suppress them, but they refuse to go away. Instead, they leak out into our lives. This is one reason why, from time to time, we all find ourselves doing things we can't fully explain, or saying things we don't fully understand.

Poets, artists, musicians and religious visionaries are able to tap in to this deep well. They can only hint at what it contains, but we know when they have done so for their work strikes a chord within us and we are moved by it. This is because – to some extent – we all share the same deep well! Although these dreams, yearnings and desires seem very personal, they are shared by all the human race. Throughout history, totally different cultures have produced myths, stories, pictures and images with astonishingly similar themes. Each civilization has left behind symbols of their most profound experiences.

Today, because of the work of people like Carl Jung, it has become easier and more acceptable to talk about such things. We have all heard a Rolls Royce described as a 'status symbol' or a movie star described as a 'sex symbol'. We understand that our need for sex – and for status – is almost too strong to be put into words. The movie star and the Rolls Royce are stereotypes, or symbols. On to them we can project, and so express, some of the basic urges that lie in our deep well of fears, hopes, dreams and desires. Psychology has coined a word for this deep well. Perhaps the fact

Sex symbols: ancient and modern!

that this word has become so popular proves how much we all want to explore our inner selves. The word is *sub*conscious.

You must be wondering what this lecture on psychology has to do with astrology. Please bear with me for one more paragraph and your patience will be rewarded! You see, the subconscious existed long before Mr Freud and Mr Jung gave it a name. And, of course, Mr Rolls and Mr Royce did not invent the first status symbol. There were even sex symbols before Marilyn Monroe! It's just that – in those days – we didn't have the wisdom of psychology to explain it all away. Symbols of the subconscious were treated much more seriously. People didn't even call them symbols. They called them gods.

Astrology is chock full of gods. Greek gods, Babylonian gods, Roman gods, Mesopotamian gods. But now, you will understand that they aren't really gods at all. They're symbols: archetypal images that have served to express the human subconscious since the dawn of time!

Each planet is called by the name of a different god. Or, if you prefer, each planet symbolizes a different aspect of our subconscious. There is a planet of sex (Venus), a planet of status (Saturn) – and there is even a planet of symbols (Mercury)!

The signs of the zodiac and the planets are universal symbols. They represent urges and inclinations that are common to the whole human race. You will find *all* 12 signs of the zodiac and all 10 planets within your own horoscope.* You will also find them in every horoscope you ever see. What makes your horoscope unique is the special *relationship* between these symbols. Your horoscope is a chart of the heavens as they were at the exact moment of your birth. The pattern made by the planets as they journey through the sky never repeats itself exactly.

The Ten Planets in Astrology

Before I explain the planetary cycles I want to introduce the planets themselves. I want you to get a feel for the nature of the planets. You don't need to learn that Mars rules iron and Saturn rules lead, but it would be helpful if you could form a picture of Mars as a warrior and Saturn as a stern teacher. Perhaps you would like to meditate a little on each of the following descriptions.

* When astrologers use the word planet, they mean it in the original Greek sense as heavenly wanderer. The lights that move in the sky above our heads are planets for astrological purposes and it makes no real difference that the sun is technically a star and the moon is technically a satellite.

THE SUN *The sun rules the sign of Leo.*

The power of the sun it self evident. It gives us light, warmth and energy. It has been worshipped, revered and respected. It's not surprising that almost every culture associates the sun with a strong, dominant and confident personality.

In a personal horoscope the sun describes your simple, childlike nature; what you're like when you are not pretending to be responsible, important or impressive. The way you naturally respond to life and the things you'd like to get out of it.

In general astrology the sun rules children, citrus fruit, coins, daytime, emperors, fatherhood, gambling, gold, health, jewellery, laughter, lions, peacocks, pomp, popularity, pride, prosperity, royalty, simplicity, spotlights, stardom, Sundays, the colour orange, and the heart.

THE MOON *The moon rules the sign of Cancer.*

The sun is King of the Day and the moon is Queen of the Night. She pulls the oceans and her movements govern the reproductive cycles of all living things. For this reason most cultures have ascribed to her the personality of Mother Goddess.

In a personal horoscope the moon describes your emotional nature. The way you respond to problems, threats and difficulties. The things you yearn for and the way you yearn for them. Your attitude towards your mother and towards your progeny.

In general astrology the moon rules boats, breasts, childbirth, the common people, dairies, fermentation, fluids, insanity, mariners, Mondays, nursing, plumbers, public, reproduction, silver, stomach, tears, water.

MERCURY *Mercury rules the signs Gemini and Virgo.*

Mercury travels so close to the sun that it is often very difficult to see (the sun's light outshines it at dawn or dusk). Perhaps this is why many cultures gave Mercury the personality of a trickster and ascribed to it the rulership of commerce and trade. In Greek mythology, Mercury was Hermes, winged messenger of the gods.

In a personal horoscope Mercury describes the way your mind works. Your thought patterns. The way you communicate. The subjects that interest you, the way you approach them and your attitude towards information in general.

In general astrology Mercury rules advertizing, air travel, authors, bargaining, books, clerks, clothing, computers, editors, history, hygiene, intellect, lectures, logic, messages, mercury (metal), nerves, post, respiration, signals, talking, telephones, typewriters, Wednesday, wit, writing, youth.

VENUS   *Venus rules the signs Libra and Taurus.*

Venus is the closest planet to Earth, which makes her the brightest in the sky. So bright that she almost 'twinkles' like a star. Like Mercury, she can always be seen close to the Sun, rising and setting just behind or ahead. In Greek mythology Venus was Aphrodite, goddess of love.

In a personal horoscope Venus describes the things you are attracted to. Your artistic and romantic inclinations. The way you feel about the people in your life and the way they feel about you. Your love life, your creative (and procreative) aspirations all are ruled by Venus.

In general astrology Venus rules all forms of art, entertainment, music and beauty, adornment, amusement, boudoirs, brass, confectionery, dance, desire, dimples, doves, emeralds, fashion, feminity, flowers, grapes, immorality, intimacy, justice, lingerie, love, marriage, money, partnership, relaxation, sexual intercourse, social centres, societies, style.

MARS   *Mars rules the signs Aries and Scorpio.*

Mars is further from the sun than the Earth. It glows red in the evening sky, and, not surprisingly, almost every culture associates this colour with a bloody, battle-minded personality. In Greek mythology Mars was Ares, god of war.

In a personal horoscope Mars describes your desires and your determination. Your will to succeed, to conquer and to achieve your ambitions. Mars also describes your temper and your temperament.

In general astrology Mars rules armour, armies, blood, butchers, cars, controversy, disease, engineering, executives, garlic, guns, heat, heroes, incense, inflammations, iron, knives, locks, murder, passion, penetration, pipes, pirates, radiators, razors, sarcasm, stamina, sport, surgery, tobacco, virility, wrestlers.

JUPITER   *Jupiter rules the signs Sagittarius and Pisces.*

Jupiter is the largest planet in the solar system and is often personified as a large, humorous and benevolent uncle. In Greek mythology Jupiter was Zeus, king of the gods.

In a personal horoscope Jupiter describes your optimistic outlook. The luck you allow yourself to have, the opportunities you allow yourself to take. The extent of your aspirations and your desire to reach beyond yourself.

In general astrology Jupiter rules amplification, capitalism, celebrations, college, courts of law, doctors, feet, foreign countries, furry animals, glory, gluttony, law, legality, luck, ceremonial magic, merchandize, merit, millionaires, monasteries, orthodoxy, over-indulgence, philanthropy, philosophy, preachers, prestige, professors, profit, pulpits, religion, science, ships, splendour, success, thighs, tin, Thursday, travel, truth, wisdom.

SATURN   *Saturn rules the signs Capricorn and Aquarius.*

Saturn is famous today for its rings. Previously, its main distinguishing feature was the slow pace at which it moves through the heavens. It marks time for the other planets and is often considered the harbinger of old age or death. In Greek mythology Saturn was Kronos, god of Time.

In a personal horoscope Saturn describes your 'inner braking system'. Your limitations, fears and barriers. The things you are afraid of, and the way in which you seek to provide structure, discipline and restraint in your environment.

In general astrology   Saturn rules agriculture, archaeology, architecture, bones, cattle, civil service, death, fatigue, history, land, leather, minerals, monogamy, monotony, obstacles, old age, perseverance, Saturday, self control, time, twilight, underground, widows, yesterdays.

THE THREE NEW, OUTER PLANETS: URANUS, NEPTUNE AND PLUTO

In 1781, a revolution took place in the world of astronomy – and in the world of the occult, too! It had always been believed that there were seven heavenly bodies moving through the sky. The number seven was significant, special and magical. A complex but highly efficient system of astrology had evolved – and at its heart was the sure and certain knowledge that there were seven planets.

The revolution began quietly enough. In the city of Bath, an amateur astronomer called William Herschel was sitting in his back garden, scanning the sky through a home-made telescope. As an invention, the telescope itself was less than 200 years old. Already it had revealed (to Galileo) the rings of Saturn and the moons of Jupiter and had shaken the foundations of both scientific and occult knowledge. It had brought the planets closer, and thus stripped them of their distant mystery. At first, Herschel thought he had merely seen a new comet, but gradually the truth began to dawn. It was a brand new planet!

This planet became known as Uranus. Sixty-five years later its discovery was followed by a further planet, Neptune. In 1930, one more planet, even more distant than the others was spotted. This was Pluto. At the time of writing, scientists are discussing the possible discovery of yet another member of our solar system – provisionally called Persephone. Whether or not she is found, we can be sure that the skies themselves will go on changing their message as the human race continues to evolve and grow.

The discovery of Uranus coincided (roughly) with the dawn of the Industrial Revolution, and with the American and French revolutions. Not surprisingly, Uranus soon came to be associated with both new technology and sudden, dramatic action leading to change.

The discovery of Neptune coincided (roughly) with the development of film, photography, petrol, the internal combustion engine, and man's first steps in analytical psychology. Neptune is felt to have a special influence and effect in these areas.

The discovery of Pluto coincided (roughly) with a world-wide recession, the rise of fascism and World War II, and the discovery of nuclear power. Pluto is therefore felt to be a 'dark' planet and is watched by most astrologers with some consternation.

Because these three outer planets take so long to move through one sign of the zodiac there is nothing very special about having Pluto in Leo or Uranus in Cancer, etc. Everyone born within a few years of each other has them in the same part of the sky. The outer planets become personal through the aspects they make to your inner planets and through the house they are in (see pages 46 and 50).

In magic, you can pretty much forget the outer planets unless you specifically want to achieve a very modern thing. A spell to make a successful film might include Neptune; a spell to help an anti-nuclear campaign might include Pluto; a spell involving computers or technology might require Uranus.

It should be stressed, however, that no astrologer doubts the power and influence of Uranus, Neptune or Pluto. They may be new and we may not yet have learned *all* their secrets, but we do know that there is a definite link between Uranus and Aquarius, Neptune and Pisces, and Pluto and Scorpio.

Some astrologers say that the planets are 'co-rulers' of these signs. I for one would not disagree.

Signs of The Zodiac

Now that you've been introduced to the planets, it's time to meet the signs of the zodiac. The signs of the zodiac are not constellations of stars; they are areas of sky through which the planets pass at different times. *Even if you don't learn anything else about astrology* I recommend that you find out about all 12 signs. There is a poetic beauty in the way that each one complements the others, and there is something very magical about the way they fit together.

A Mnemonic

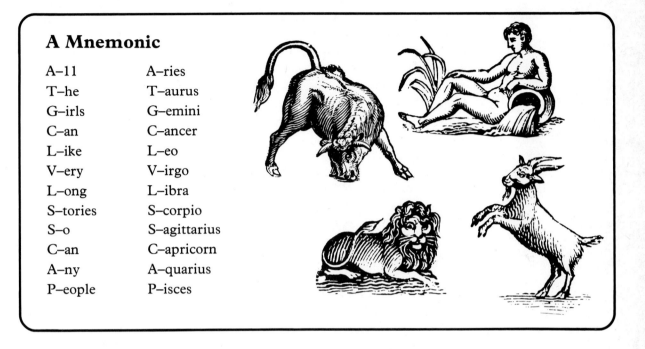

A–11	A–ries
T–he	T–aurus
G–irls	G–emini
C–an	C–ancer
L–ike	L–eo
V–ery	V–irgo
L–ong	L–ibra
S–tories	S–corpio
S–o	S–agittarius
C–an	C–apricorn
A–ny	A–quarius
P–eople	P–isces

Signs are divided into three different, overlapping groups. The most famous of these groups is the Elements – Fire, Earth, Air and Water.

1 Fire, Earth, Air and Water signs

To understand fully the concept of Fire, Earth, Air and Water you need to sit and meditate for a while. In ancient times it was felt that these four things were the basic elements of nature, the building blocks of creation.

Earth is perhaps the easiest to understand. We live on the earth. It provides our food, our shelter, and, ultimately, our burial ground. The earth is practical, frutiful, solid, reliable and sometimes a little 'dry'.

Air is almost as easy to grasp. Each breath we take confirms and enhances our life. The air contains the sky. It holds our future, our philosophy, our aspirations and our desire to know more about ourselves. Human beings are only just beginning to conquer the spacious but sterile element of air. Only in the last 100 years have we learned to fly, and to put a man on the moon.

Water is just as vital to our being as earth and air. Every human being must drink, as they must eat and breathe. Water symbolizes our feelings, our needs, our insecurities and our desire to merge with something that has no beginning or end. If you've ever been out at sea in a small boat, or if you enjoy going swimming, you'll know all about that feeling of being consumed by a vast, powerful and overwhelming element.

Fire is probably the hardest element to understand. The sun, of course, is a ball of fire and without its heat we would perish. Nonetheless, it is an inner fire which is most vital to the health and success of every human being. The will to live, the inner passion, the hidden flame of life itself. Raging forest fires and exploding volcanoes are nature's external allegories for these essential internal qualities. Fire provides heat, warmth and power – but it lacks direction, discrimination or compassion.

Fire signs share an impulsive, excitable and buoyant approach to life.

Earth signs share a sensual, practical physical outlook on life.

Air signs share an analytical, intellectual, unemotional attitude.

Water signs all share a sensitive, emotional and mysterious quality.

2 Cardinal, Fixed and Mutable signs

Cardinal signs share a basic need to initiate action. They like to get things going, take a dominant role and act as catalysts, forcing ideas into action!

Fixed signs share a certain stubbornness. They are keen on commitment, persistence and dedication.

Mutable signs share a certain adaptability. They like to hop from one thing to another, and thrive on the challenge of change.

3 Active and Passive signs

Active signs are all, in some way, assertive, outgoing and independent.

Passive signs are all, in some way, receptive, introverted and dependent.

The 12 Signs of the Zodiac

Zodiac is Greek for 'circle of animals', a reference to the main symbolic image in each sign. In fact, not all the signs are represented by an animal. Aquarius, Gemini and Virgo are human figures, and Libra is a machine. As you can see in the illustration, each sign has an opposite both in position and in temperament (see page 46). Signs are also grouped by Element (see page 35) and by Quality (see above).

This ornate carving depicts the Greek 'circle of animals' surrounding the gods which traditionally ruled them.

ARIES

Sign:	**Aries**
Symbol:	**Ram**
Polarity:	**+**
Quality:	**Cardinal**
Element:	**Fire**
Ruling planet:	**Mars**
Opposite sign:	**Libra**
Phrase:	**I am**
Colour:	**Scarlet**

Aries brings a quick, impulsive and confident quality to whichever part of the horoscope it rules. There is little time for the past or future here. Just an overwhelming sense of the urgency in the present moment. Arian energy can make you: brash, bossy and brave, strong, certain and straightforward; passionate, powerful and pugnacious; unsophisticated, uninhibited and unstoppable; explosive, excitable and exasperating.

TAURUS

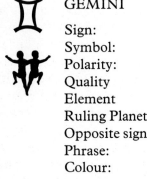

Sign:	**Taurus**
Symbol:	**Bull**
Polarity:	**–**
Quality:	**Fixed**
Element:	**Earth**
Ruling planet:	**Venus**
Opposite sign:	**Scorpio**
Phrase:	**I have**
Colour:	**Pale green**

Taurus is a sensual, physical and steady sign. It brings a patient, determined and indulgent quality to whichever part of the horoscope it rules. Taurus is concerned only with the things it can feel, see and touch. Abstract concepts and lofty ideals have little value here. Taurean energy can make you: acquisitive, adamant and artistic; lethargic, lazy and lascivious; greedy, grumpy and guarded; slow, sluggish and insensitive; robust, radiant and reliable; tenacious, tactile and tedious.

GEMINI

Sign:	**Gemini**
Symbol:	**Human twins**
Polarity	**+**
Quality	**Mutable**
Element	**Air**
Ruling Planet:	**Mercury**
Opposite sign:	**Sagittarius**
Phrase:	**I think**
Colour:	**Grey tints**

Gemini is a busy, nimble and intellectual sign. The part of the horoscope it rules will be spoken about often, worried about constantly and subject to sudden changes. Gemini is fascinated by ideas, facts and fancies. There is little interest here in commitment or practicalities. Gemini energy can make you: nervous, nefarious and nifty; bright, breezy and bubbly; sociable, slap happy and superficial; intelligent, intellectual and inconsiderate.

CANCER

Sign:	**Cancer**
Symbol:	**Crab**
Polarity:	**–**
Quality:	**Cardinal**
Element:	**Water**
Ruling planet:	**Moon**
Opposite sign:	**Capricorn**
Phrase:	**I care**
Colour:	**Silver**

Cancer is a soft, vulnerable and emotional sign. Everything in the zodiac which it rules will be loved, protected and cherished. Cancer is about close relationships, deep feelings and strong attachments. It doesn't care much for material, intellectual or spiritual values. Cancerian energy can make you: warm, winsome and worried; helpful, hearty and homeloving; cautious, careful and cuddly; soft, soppy and over-sensitive; possessive, pensive and panic-stricken.

LEO

Sign:	**Leo**
Symbol:	**Lion**
Polarity:	**+**
Quality:	**Fixed**
Element:	**Fire**
Ruling planet:	**Sun**
Opposite sign:	**Aquarius**
Phrase:	**I protect**
Colour:	**Gold**

Leo brings a proud, steady and certain quality to whichever sign of the zodiac it rules. It's a haughty, uninhibited and attention-seeking sign. Leo is about ruling the roost, calling the shots and leading the pack. Any other interests must lead to this or they will have no future. Leonine energy can make you: vivacious, voracious and vibrant; hot tempered, hot headed and hot blooded; effervescent, elegant and elitist; jovial, jocular and jolly; popular, personable and pretentious; dynamic, debauched and determined.

VIRGO

Sign:	**Virgo**
Symbol:	**Harvest goddess**
Polarity:	**−**
Quality:	**Mutable**
Element:	**Earth**
Ruling planet:	**Mercury**
Opposite sign:	**Pisces**
Phrase:	**I perceive**
Colour:	**indigo**

Virgo is a perceptive, incisive and practical sign. It brings a logical, intelligent structure to whichever part of the horoscope it rules. Virgo is about making sense of things, understanding how they work and getting the most out of them. Only items that are clever and practical attract it. Virgoan energy can make you: sharp, sensitive and subtle; incisive, intelligent and inscrutable; deep, diligent and dependable; wise, wealthy and witty; clean, careful and self critical.

LIBRA

Sign:	**Libra**
Symbol:	**Scales**
Polarity:	**+**
Quality:	**Cardinal**
Element:	**Air**
Ruling planet:	**Venus**
Opposite sign:	**Aries**
Phrase:	**I harmonize**
Colour:	**Pale blue**

Libra brings a peaceful, smooth and airy quality to whichever part of the horoscope it rules. It's an analytical, dreamy and distanced sign. Libra is about balance and compromise and anything that may lead to confrontation or commitment is viewed with extreme distaste! Libran energy can make you: placid, poetic and pliable; charming, cheerful and choosy; buoyant, blithe and bland; vague, vacuous and evasive; artistic, aesthetic and agreeable.

SCORPIO

Sign:	**Scorpio**
Symbol:	**Eagle or Scorpion**
Polarity:	**–**
Quality:	**Fixed**
Element:	**Water**
Ruling planet:	**Mars (and Pluto)**
Opposite sign:	**Taurus**
Phrase:	**I desire**
Colour:	**Opals**

Scorpio brings an intense, deep and unsettled quality to whichever part of the horoscope it rules. It's a penetrating , truth-seeking and explosive sign. Scorpio is about sensitivity and desire. Anything that fails to fulfil on a sensual or emotional level is easily dismissed. Scorpionic energy can make you: perceptive, passionate and paranoid; aggressive, angry and agitated; uncertain, unsafe and unpredictable; secretive, shy and sexy; fearful, frightening and furtive.

SAGITTARIUS

Sign:	**Sagittarius**
Symbol:	**Centaur with bow**
Polarity:	**+**
Quality:	**Mutable**
Element:	**Fire**
Ruling planet:	**Jupiter**
Opposite sign:	**Gemini**
Phrase:	**I seek**
Colour:	**Reds and purples**

Sagittarius is an adventurous, excitable and optimistic sign. It brings a happy-go-lucky, lively and philosophical quality to whichever part of a horoscope it rules. Sagittarius is about freedom and exploration. Anything that may stand in the way of these aspirations is ignored. Sagittarian energy can make you: restless, rash and reckless; enterprising, energetic and enthusiastic; natural, nimble and naïve; instinctive, innocent and impish; outgoing, outlandish and outspoken.

CAPRICORN

Sign:	**Capricorn**
Symbol:	**Sea goat**
Polarity:	**–**
Quality:	**Cardinal**
Element:	**Earth**
Ruling planet:	**Saturn**
Opposite sign:	**Cancer**
Phrase:	**I make use of**
Colour:	**Matt tones (black)**

Capricorn brings a serious, considered and practical quality to whichever part of the horoscope it rules. It's a measured, careful and mature sign. Capricorn is about discipline and structure. Anything that threatens an ordered existence is shrugged off. Capricornian energy can make you: rigid, wry and restrained; sturdy, strong and sensible; hearty, hale and hardy; dry, dour and diligent; perspicacious, practical and penny pinching; grouchy, gruff and geriatric.

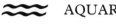

AQUARIUS

Sign:	**Aquarius**
Symbol:	**Water bearer**
Polarity:	**+**
Quality:	**Fixed**
Element:	**Air**
Ruling planet:	**Saturn (and Uranus)**
Opposite sign:	**Leo**
Phrase:	**I differ**
Colour:	**Electric blue**

Aquarius brings an altruistic, idealistic and lofty quality to whichever part of the horoscope it rules. It's an eccentric, unpredictable and intellectual sign. Aquarius is about high goals and individualism. Life's more sensual or emotional aspects pass by unnoticed. Aquarian energy can make you: quick, quirky and quizzical; friendly, fearless and fanatical; aloof, analytical and anarchic; tireless, tiresome and trustworthy; odd, obnoxious and outrageous.

PISCES

Sign:	**Pisces**
Symbol:	**Two fish**
Polarity:	**−**
Quality:	**Mutable**
Element:	**Water**
Ruling planet:	**Jupiter (and Neptune)**
Opposite sign:	**Virgo**
Phrase:	**I merge**
Colour:	**Deep values**

Pisces brings an open, loving and hypersensitive quality to whichever part of the horoscope it rules. It's a watery, dreamy and deep sign. Pisces is about mystery and escapism. Mundane matters are of little interest and are avoided at all cost. Piscean energy can make you: mysterious, misdirected and misunderstood; wild, woolly and weak willed; poetic, prophetic and pathetic; happy, humorous and hopeless; inventive, ingenious and intoxicated.

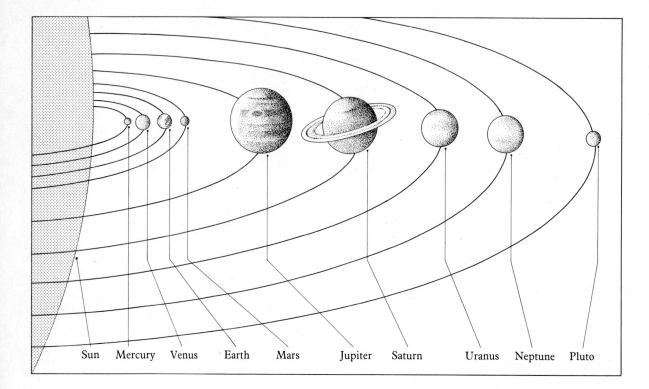

Sun   Mercury   Venus   Earth   Mars   Jupiter   Saturn   Uranus   Neptune   Pluto

The Meaning of Cycles in Astrology

In order not to bore you to tears with technical sidetracks, I'm about to simplify the cosmos somewhat. I doubt if this will offend many readers but, just in case, let me say that while I am about to simplify, I am not going to mislead.★

★ I doubt whether many astronomers will be reading this. Most of them are jealous of astrology's rich symbolism. They feel that its very existence threatens the scientific respectability of their work. Conversely, too many astrologers keep their interest in astronomy to a working minimum and miss the fascinating and inspiring implications of new discoveries. Fortunately, the state of cold war which has effectively drawn an iron curtain between these two subjects since their separation in the 17th-century is beginning to thaw. Recent scientific advances have shaken the foundations of the dry, empirical tradition and made it less easy to dismiss an instinctive rapport with the cosmos as mere superstition. It's about time too! After all, Johannes Kepler, the Father of Modern Astronomy, spent just as long exploring mystical symbolism and refining astrological techniques as he did proving that the planets move in ellipses and establishing the rules that govern their velocity. Perhaps one of these days some lofty academic will take a look at the other half of his work!

We live on a little planet that's speeding through space on an egg-shaped race track! Once, every $365\frac{1}{4}$ days we complete one circuit of the course. Ours is not the only car on this track. On the inside lanes, moving more quickly than us, are Mercury and Venus. On the outside lanes, moving more slowly, are Mars, Jupiter, Saturn, Uranus, Neptune and Pluto. As we look through the window of our racing car (into the sky) we can see our fellow travellers faintly in the distance and plot their progress.

From where we're sitting in our racing car it *looks* as though we're standing still and they're all going around *us*. Even the sun appears to be moving in a circle round the Earth, and the illusion is so good that hardly anyone even questioned it until 400 years ago. Although today we know the true situation, astrologers and astronomers alike still have to use a system of measurement that places the Earth at the centre. After all, it's the *view* from Earth that everyone's interested in.

All this means, very simply, is that I'm about to talk about the time it takes for certain planets to go round the Earth. You know and I know what's *really* happening, but that doesn't alter the way things *look*, and it doesn't alter the way we read messages in the movement of planets.

Are you still with me? Good! Now let's get down to something interesting!

How Astrologers Tell The Future

When an astrologer first looks at your horoscope, he will want to know two things.

1 What sort of person you are.
2 What kind of things have just happened, are happening or are about to happen to you.

Question **1** can be answered partly from noticing whether you have sun in Pisces, or moon in Virgo, or Mercury in Sagittarius, but mainly from noticing the exact positions of each planet and any special relationships between them. (More on this later.)

Question **2** can't really be answered until Question **1** has been sorted out, but I can show you the way it works in principle.

In the section on moon signs I explained the idea of a lunar return. This is what happens to you once every 28 days or so when the moon in the sky overhead hits the sign of the zodiac it was in when you were born. The return of the moon to its natal (birth) position marks the beginning of a new emotional cycle in your life. The same thing goes for every other planet. Each time Mercury (planet of intellect) gets back to its natal position you begin a new intellectual cycle. Each time Jupiter (planet of luck) returns to its natal position you begin a new cycle of luck, and so on.

Now you can see how an astrologer peeks into the future. We simply work out when the next cycle is due to begin.

Very roughly speaking, the pattern goes like this:

Emotional cycle (Moon)	Once every 28 days.
Intellectual cycle (Mercury)	Once a year (approx).
Energy cycle (The Sun)	Once every year (exactly).
Creative cycle (Venus)	Once every one and a bit years.
Ambition cycle (Mars)	Once every two years (approx).
Luck cycle (Jupiter)	Once every 12 years.
Learning cycle (Saturn)	Once every 28 years (approx).

As you can probably guess, the longer a planet takes to complete a cycle, the more eventful things will be when it happens. Just to keep matters interesting, astrologers also divide each cycle up into sections – making a note, for example, of when Saturn is half way through its cycle or a quarter of the way through. You must remember that each person's cycle is different. These figures in the chart are averages and, sticking with our example, Saturn could take between 27 and 30 years to complete a cycle of the zodiac, *depending on when you were born*.

I want to stay with the Saturn example for a while longer. It's a good planet to look at, because it tends to stir up the most trouble in people's lives.

Saturn rules old age, death, discipline and structure. By looking at the state of Saturn in someone's birth chart you can tell a lot about where a person's limitations lie. The things they are afraid of, the things they don't think they're capable of, and (most important of all) the kind of hard lessons they're likely to learn in the course of a lifetime. Mathematically minded readers will have already worked out that if Saturn takes an average of 28 years to complete a cycle of the zodiac, it must spend about two and a half years in each sign. This means that there's nothing very special about being born with Saturn in Aries or Saturn in Taurus, etc. Everyone born in a two and half year period will have Saturn in the same sign. To read the state of somebody's Saturn, you have to know which *house* it's in, and also what special connections it makes with the other, faster-moving planets. These special connections are called *aspects* and I talk about them (and houses) in more detail on page 46. For now, all we need to know is that an astrologer looking for difficult periods in the future would want to know exactly when Saturn in the sky was next going to meet up with Saturn in the birth chart. They'd also be very interested in when Saturn was a quarter or three quarters of the way through its cycle, and by looking up dates in a special *Ephemeris* they could pin things down to an exact day.* The quarter, halfway and threequarter marks in any cycle have always been considered important. The halfway point is easiest to understand if you think about the moon. Half way through its 27·5 day cycle, the moon is full. Before half way it is *waxing* (growing bigger), after half way, it *wanes*. Thus, half way is a turning point. The quarter and threequarter marks are clear visual measuring aids too, and they are also connected with numerology and the concept of dividing a circle by four, the *number of form*.

That exact day when Saturn entered his birth sign would mark a turning point in somebody's life. A time when some niggling problem might be sorted out or when a deep, inner fear might be confronted. From that day onwards, the person would be a little older, wiser and more mature (all Saturn qualities). In the weeks leading up to that day, the person would be experiencing stress, anxiety or difficulty (the darkest hour comes before the dawn). An astrologer could then give some very specific and helpful advice about what to expect and how to cope with it.

You can check what I'm telling you by thinking back over your own life. What happened to you when you were roughly 7, roughly 14, roughly 21, roughly 28, and so on? Most people remember these periods as times when they had to grow up a little. If you decide to go more deeply into astrology, you'll find it easy to trace the exact dates when Saturn was one quarter, one half and threequarters of the way through its cycle – and I'll bet you can still remember what happened to change you at that time.

That's the Saturn cycle. Similar principles apply to the Jupiter cycle, the Mars cycle, etc. If, or when, you get the hang of them, you could move on to discovering how the cycles interact with each other. That's a book in itself – but I will just mention in passing that at around the age of 35 or 36 most people get their third Jupiter return at around the same time as Saturn reaches the quarter mark of its second cycle. When a new phase of optimism (Jupiter) coincides with a turning point in maturity (Saturn) amazing changes take place particularly in the area of personal confidence.

All this may seem rather technical and it may help if you bear in mind that you don't have to memorize any of this stuff. I'm just trying to show

---

* An *Ephemeris* is simply a great big book containing the sky position of every planet at noon or midnight for every day in 100 years.

you how astrology can be used to predict the future. Some parts of astrology are easier to grasp than others.

Before we return to familiar territory there are two more terms I want to explain. They are Aspects and Houses.

What are Aspects?

Everybody's horoscope contains at least some planets in *aspect* to each other. (If an astrologer or a computer has given you a horoscope you'll probably find your aspects in a special list below the chart wheel.) Any planet may be in aspect with any other planet. For our purposes, there are five main kinds of aspect, each with a distinct and special meaning (explained on pages 48–49). Aspects speak volumes about your character.

Opposite is a diagram of the zodiac. It contains all you need to recognize: Conjunctions, Oppositions, Sextiles, Trines and Squares. In other words . . . all you need to understand aspects.

To show you how this system works I'll pick a sign at random and use it as an example. . . . VIRGO!

What's the opposite sign to Virgo? A quick look at the diagram should show you it's Pisces. So, if you had a planet in Virgo and another planet in Pisces, the two planets would be (roughly) *opposite* each other. In other words, in Opposition.

Right. Now, what's the sign next door but one to Virgo? Your answer should be Cancer or Scorpio, depending on which way round the circle you went. A sign next door but one to another sign is called a *Sextile*. (Sextile is Latin for dividing a circle into six). So, if you had one planet in Virgo and another in Scorpio or Cancer, the two would be (roughly) Sextile to each other.

And so it goes on. **Which sign is next door but two to Virgo?** The answer is Sagittarius or Gemini, depending again on which way round the circle you went. Signs next door but two to each other divide the circle into four. We call them *Squares*. If you had one planet in Virgo and another in Sagittarius or Gemini, they'd be (roughly) in Square.

Finally, which sign in next door but three to Virgo? The answer is Taurus or Capricorn. Signs next door but three to each other are said to be in *Trine*. (Tri is Latin for three, and this division chops the zodiac into three!) So, if you had one planet in Virgo and another in Capricorn or Taurus, they'd be (roughly) in Trine.

I hope all this is making sense. The meanings of oppositions, sextiles, trines, etc. are given on pages 48–49. The whole thing is a way of labelling

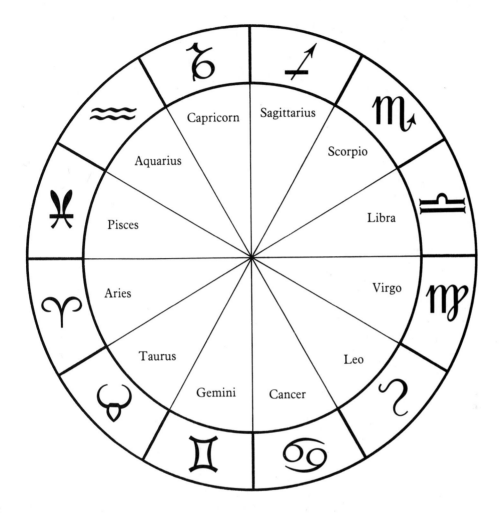

the relationships between different signs. The same principle applies no matter what sign you look at. In other words, if we had picked Aries, the Opposite sign would be Libra, the Sextile signs would be Aquarius and Gemini, the Squares would be Cancer and Capricorn and the Trines would be Leo and Sagittarius.

That's almost all there is to it *except* you may have noticed that I keep putting the word (roughly) in brackets. That's because *real* astrology is more precise. An astrologer needs to know not only what sign each planet is in but what *part* of that sign it's in. I don't want to dwell too long on this, but I should explain that, like any circle, the zodiac can be chopped up into 360 degrees. If this brings back painful memories of school geometry lessons, you may be amused to know that geometry was actually invented to measure the sky. (Even dusty old Pythagoras was an astrologer – and a celibate, vegetarian mystic too, for that matter!) Twelve (signs) divided into 360 (degrees) gives 30, and that's the number of degrees in each sign of the zodiac.*

Whether you were born when the moon was at 3 degrees of Libra, or at 28 degrees of Libra, you'll still have the moon in Libra. Knowing the exact degree won't change the extent to which, say, you find it hard to make up your mind about your feelings. *But* . . . knowing the degree will help you tell how near or far another planet in Libra might be from your moon. In other words, whether or not that other planet is in *conjunction* with your moon.

A Conjunction occurs when two planets are in the same part of the same sign. Planets need to be within 7 degrees of each other to qualify for the title Conjunction.

By the same token, it's not quite enough to call two planets in opposite signs *in opposition*. They both need to be in the same part of the opposite signs. And it's the same with Sextiles, Trines and Squares.

If you've managed to follow all that – congratulations! You now understand the theories of angular relationship, harmonic division and orbs of intensity. These are all posh words for things to do with aspects!

The Meaning of Each Aspect

To understand an aspect fully, you have to think about the planets involved and whether or not they get on with each other. The following explanations should prove useful as a basic guide.

A Conjunction: Means that two planets are literally fighting for the same space within a horoscope. If they are the sort of planets that get on well with each other (e.g. Moon and Venus), they'll merge their influence and give you extra strength. If they don't get on (e.g. Saturn and Mars), they'll still give you strength but they'll make you an extreme sort of character.

A Sextile: Means that two planets are harmoniously linked to each other. They will complement each other's influence and work smoothly to make your life easier and luckier.

A Square: Suggests tension between the two planets involved. It's normally the sort of tension that spurs you into action – but it also gives a restless, never-satisfied quality.

* Just to confuse things, the 30 degrees in each sign are actually numbered 0–29, not 1–30!

There are two ways to show aspects in a horoscope. They can be depicted as angular lines, linking each planet in the centre of the wheel, or they can be shown in an 'easy reference' diagram as a series of symbols.

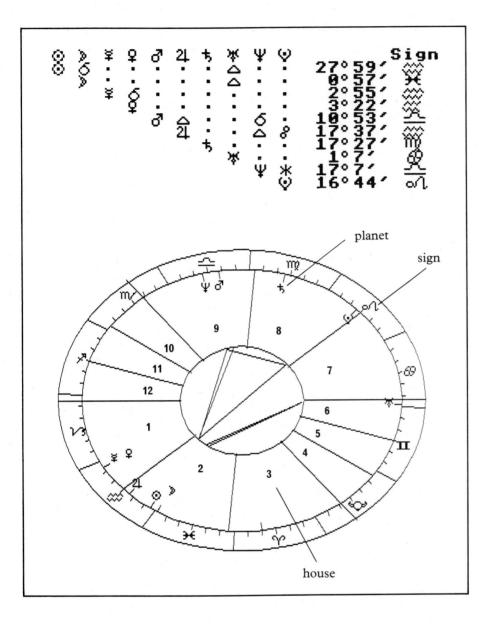

planet

sign

house

A Trine: Represents an easy-going, relaxed rapport between two planets. So easy-going, in fact, that you may take the talent given by a Trine completely for granted and even forget you have it until someone reminds you!

An Opposition: The sign of a tug of war between two planets. Each pulls in a totally different direction, leading to inner stress and (often) a deep sense of purpose.

If you are still a little unsure about where the diagonal lines in the centre of the wheel on page 49 have come from, perhaps these diagrams will explain the principle.

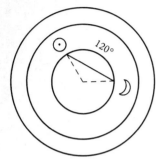

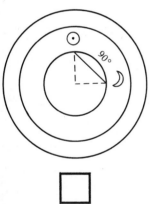

Interesting Things About Aspects

Normally every planet in your horoscope will make at least one aspect with another planet.

Very rarely, people are born with unaspected planets. A planet with no aspects stands alone in the horoscope. The things it rules will be hard to come to terms with. An unaspected planet shows someone whose personality is not fully integrated. If you've got one, it means you'll have to work harder than most people to understand yourself.

The planets in your horoscope can also form aspects with the planets in somebody else's chart. Correctly interpreting these aspects takes a lot of skill but it can be very revealing indeed, providing valuable clues about how the two of you will get on together!

The planets in the sky today (and every day) are making aspects with the planets in your horoscope. Astrologers read these aspects to find out what's going on in your life.

Signs of the same Polarity, Quality or Element are linked by different aspects. (See page 36.)

I am sure by now you will understand why it takes a fairly complex kind of person to become proficient in astrology. There's a lot of detail to mull over. And there is one other enormous area still to explore. You may have noticed that so far nothing I've mentioned has had very much to do with the time and place of birth . . . .

Houses

The moon is the only thing that moves fast enough in 24 hours for anyone to notice, and a matter of two hours or so is enough to make a small but significant difference to its position within a sign. Otherwise, apart from the odd occasion when a planet changes signs in the middle of a particular day, nothing in the sky changes quickly enough to distinguish somebody born at 5 a.m. from somebody born at 9 p.m.

Nothing in the sky . . . but the sky itself!

If you've ever stayed up to watch the sunrise, you'll know what I'm talking about. One moment, the sky is black as coal and only twinkling stars pierce the darkness. A few moments later, a glow can be seen over the eastern horizon. Moments later, the glow increases. The sun comes slowly into view, heralding the dawn and turning the heavens from black to blue.

This spectacular beginning to each new day is caused by the turning of the Earth itself. With each passing hour, as the sun rises higher and higher in the sky, it grows harder to believe that the sun is standing still. But it is!

Noon occurs at a different time throughout the globe. Sunrise in Cincinnati happens when it's sunset in Saigon.

A horoscope is not just a map of the sky frozen in time at the exact moment of birth. It's also a diagram of the view from a particular place. In other words, everyone born on 10th September, 1953 would have had Mercury at 17 degrees of Virgo. But only those born at night on that date will have Mercury above the horizon. Those born during the daytime will have Mercury below the horizon. How far above or below the horizon will depend on the time (and therefore the place) of birth.

The horizon is therefore very important. It acts as a dividing line in your horoscope.

A new sign of the zodiac rises over the eastern horizon (roughly) every two hours. A new degree of that sign rises every four minutes. A matter of a few minutes or a few miles can make a small but significant difference to your rising sign. The phrase 'rising sign' is commonly used by people who are aware that astrology is about more than just sun signs. They know that the rising sign describes the kind of person you like the world to think you are. And so it does. The rising sign is a very important part of a horoscope.

But more important still is the degree of the rising sign. Using that, we can work out how to divide your horoscope into 12 houses, each with a very special meaning.

The Meaning of Houses

Each of the 12 houses describes a very specific and different part of your life:

The 1st house describes:
Your external personality. The face you wear to greet the world.

The 2nd house describes:
Your need for material security. Money, wealth and comfort.

The 3rd house describes:
The way your mind works. Your ability to communicate. The hands.

The 4th house describes:
Your need for emotional security. Close family, home life. Left side of the brain.

The 5th house describes:
Your need to have fun (and take risks). Children, competitive sport.

The 6th house describes:
Your need to be responsible. Duties, obligations, work and health.

The 7th house describes:
Your need for a partner. Marriage, relationships, enemies.

The 8th house describes:
Your attitude to sex and because sex is linked to birth and birth to death, your ability to deal with the transience of existence.

The 9th house describes:
Your spiritual and philosophical outlook. Religion, university and travel.

The 10th house describes:
Your status. How important you want to be and in what way.

The 11th house describes:
Your social life. Friends, peer group, social conscience.

The 12th house describes:
Your secret dreams, fears, hopes and wishes!

Needless to say, the above list is very abbreviated. There are entire dictionaries dedicated to the things ruled by each house. For example, the 3rd house also rules books, telephones, schools, short journeys, brothers and sisters and even . . . the secret enemies of your father! Actually, it's all quite logical once you get the hang of things and if you ever do get into serious astrology you'll have lots of fun exploring each house and deciding which house rules fish and chip shops or left-handed tennis players.

How Astrologers Use The Houses

Put very simply, each planet describes a *part* of your personality.

The *sign* of the planet tells you what's happening to that part of you.

The *house* of the planet tells you in what area of your life those attitudes will show up.

In other words, having a planet in a particular house can greatly alter the meaning of having a planet in a particular sign.

The best way to explain this is by example. Let's go back to our old friend the moon. In the first half of this chapter I gave a series of definitions for the moon in each sign. I'm now about to do the same thing for the moon in each house. Any thorough astrologer would then simply add the two factors together and come to a considered conclusion.

However, if you haven't had a horoscope drawn up, there's no way you can know which house your moon is in. The following list is provided on the assumption that if you don't know now, you'll be finding out soon! After all, even if you don't want to become a fully fledged astrologer, as a psychic explorer, you'll need to know all you can about your moon sign and moon house.

The moon in the 1st house:
Someone who wears their heart on their sleeve. Hard to hide their feelings. Shy and moody.

The moon in the 2nd house:
A materialist. Someone who needs to feel the reassurance of possessions around them.

The moon in the 3rd house:
A busybody. Someone who can't resist finding out new information, swapping ideas and chatting away.

The moon in the 4th house:
A homelover. Not happy unless tucked up by a cosy fire with one or two loved and trusted people.

The moon in the 5th house:
A funlover. A gambling, reckless adventurer who hates to be tied down.

The moon in the 6th house:
A workaholic. Carries the cares of the world on his or her shoulders and never ceases to serve other people's interests.

The moon in the 7th house:
A romantic. Loves to love. Believes in the ideal relationship, and strives relentlessly to achieve it.

The moon in the 8th house:
A sensualist. Deep, dark and dusky. Has to get to the bottom of everything.

The moon in the 9th house:
A philosopher. Loves to explore and expand own horizons. Strong spiritual or religious outlook.

The moon in the 10th house:
A patriarch. Fusses and frets over other people's problems, tries to mother the world.

The moon in the 11th house:
A socialite. Can't resist an opportunity to make new friends, host a party or share an event.

The moon in the 12th house:
A dreamer. Lost in a world of colourful, fanciful visions. Out of touch with own feelings.

The meaning of the moon in the first house is obviously different to the meaning of Mercury in the first house or Mars in the first house, in the same way as the moon in Aries is different from Mars or Mercury in Aries. There are, of course, some similarities, but so much depends on the planet itself.

A Special Complicated Point

Perceptive readers may have noticed a certain similarity between the meaning of certain signs and the meaning of certain houses. If so, let me put you out of your misery and say that, yes, the 1st house is a bit like Aries and the 2nd a bit like Taurus (and so on in order). But the connection ends there. The two are totally separate and, at least for the time being, you'd be as well to store them in different compartments of your brain.

You should by now have got a pretty good feel for what's involved in astrology. If I've managed to whet your appetite for further study – GOOD! If I've simply clarified a few mysterious things about the subject that had been bothering you – also good! I'd better say, though, that I had another objective in mind. I wanted to give you, as a psychic explorer, an understanding of the principles of astrology, because astrology and ceremonial magic are inextricably linked. I can guarantee that you will be coming back to this chapter time and time again throughout your mystical, magical career.

Consulting an Astrologer

I told you that astrology was complex, and I'm sure that even if you didn't believe me then you do now! Maybe you feel that you'd like to ask a professional to do the job. It's not a terrible idea, but I must stress that if you persevere with astrology, you'll soon get the hang of it and you could have the satisfaction of knowing not only how to read your own horoscope but also how to read other people's. By all means go ahead and see an astrologer if your really want to, but make sure you choose one who is genuine. The following tips and comments should help you choose.

Computer Horoscopes   It's one thing to have your horoscope calculated by a computer and another to have it interpreted by one. Sometimes computer interpretations can be fun, but never forget that the computer has no 'overview'. It can't really weigh up differing factors in your chart and make allowances for contradictory influences. All it can do is spew out from its memory a bunch of textbook definitions. These may be more interesting and appropriate than a reading by a bad astrologer, but they can't begin to touch on the intimacy and accuracy you would get from a good one.

Written, Postal, Taped Consultations   Avoid them! When you've chosen your astrologer, you should expect to meet him or her in the flesh – even if it means travelling! If they object, they're running a factory not a consultancy.

Cheap Fees, Bargain Prices, Discounts   You get what you pay for! Simply interpreting the character of someone from a chart can take an hour or two's work for a professional astrologer. Calculating and interpreting the future in any depth at all takes a long time. There are ways of cheating – and if someone offers you a cheap service you'll be getting very shoddy advice.

Outrageously High Prices   Only if you can afford it! A chart reading with one year's major predictions and a brief look at the next five or 10 years' trends should cost you about the price of dinner for two with wine at a medium-priced restaurant. If the fee is higher, you're paying for the astrologer's name/reputation/prestige as much as for the advice. (Most astrologers have a strong code of ethics and will lower their fee in cases of genuine hardship.)

Mrs Jones from down the road   No! No! No! Unless Mrs Jones has really studied astrology over a period of years she will know little more than you do. Her advice may be confidently delivered, but it may well be wrong, wrong, wrong!

Look in the back of a horoscope magazine for the words 'Qualified Astrologer'. Write a letter or phone asking for full details of what they are offering. It's a shame that charlatans and sincere astrologers are allowed to advertize side by side, but if you don't have a word of mouth recommendation to go on you'll have to trust your instincts.

Other Sorts of Astrology

Finally, although there isn't the space to go into detail, I ought to point out that a thing can have a horoscope – just as a person can. Also, not all astrologers specialize in character analysis and personal prediction.

Mundane Astrologers use the horoscopes of nations (drawn from the time a certain treaty was signed or battle was won) to predict future political, sociological or economic developments.

Electional Astrologers specialize in choosing the right moment to sign a contract, get married, launch a book or commence a meeting. It's quite a lengthy process – you couldn't do it for trivial matters like which bus to catch or what time to go to the shops – which is just as well or we'd all be very neurotic!

Horary Astrologers invite you to ask them a question. They then draw up a chart for the moment you asked the asked the question and read a very definite, specific answer from that chart. Good horary astrologers are few and far between, but there are some with a staggering success record!

The rules involved in these other branches of astrology are quite different to the rules of natal astrology, although the basic principle remains the same. If you do decide to study the rewarding, fascinating and exciting field of astrology for yourself, I'm sure that sooner or later you'll want to investigate them.

Fascinating Facts

★ Many people know that the Emperor Augustus of Rome had Capricorn the Goat engraved on the back of his coinage. Few know that Capricorn was his moon sign – not his sun sign. (Augustus had the sun in Libra.)

★ Although the three wise men were led to the infant Jesus by a Star, the Church has never been officially keen on astrology. However, there have been many famous Christian astrologers (such as William Lilly) and an astrologer pope (Pope Sylvester 11 – around AD100 – wrote the first original, European astrological textbook).

★ William Lilly, a 17th-century Horary astrologer, predicted the great fire of London in a famous woodcut depicting the Gemini Twins (which rule London) engulfed in flames above the River Thames. After the fire, he was hauled before Parliament and accused of starting it himself! He was acquitted, protected by a long-standing reputation for accuracy.

★ The prophecies of Nostradamus are known all over the world. He timed many of his predictions with astrological references and he was a skilled reader of horoscopes. Nonetheless, it seems his inspiration came as much from a visionary gift as it did from astrology.

★ In AD150 Cladius Ptolemy spent many years in the library at Alexandria, researching scrolls about astrology and writing a definitive textbook called *The Tetrabiblos*. It is still used today as a basis for modern horoscope interpretation.

★ Chinese astrology is not very different in principle to Western astrology. There are 12 major figures and, although in the West we only hear about Chinese years, they also have special months, days and hours.

The seer must learn to see with more than the external eyes, for there is much that may be missed. Myriad are the waves that break upon the shores of the senses, but for many the sands remain dry. Without the heart, the eye is as dumb crystal. Light may fall and the heavens blaze forth, but who is to know? When the inner eye is open, and the heart is still, light abundant surrounds and fills all things.

How to See
The Human Aura

EVERYONE has an aura. As you leaf through this book standing in a bookshop or sitting quietly at home, you are giving off your own unique aura. You are shining with your own personal energy field. Every day of your life you spend at the centre of a radiant and often revealing halo of light. This light is the expression of the life force within you – and the life force within you is as real and perceivable as magnetism is in a magnet.

Sceptical? Then read on:

Ever since I can remember, I have seen colours in connection with people. I do not remember a time when the human beings I encountered did not register on my retina with blues and greens and reds gently pouring from their heads and shoulders. It was a long time before I realized that other people did not see these colours. It was a long time before I heard the word aura, and learned to apply it to this phenomenon which to me was commonplace. I do not even think of people except in connection with their auras; I see them change in my friends and loved ones as time goes by – sickness, dejection, love, fulfilment – these are all reflected in the aura and for me the aura is the weathervane of the soul. It shows me the way the winds of destiny are blowing.

Edgar Cayse, eminent American healer, from his book *Auras*, 1945.

Sometimes, fountains of light would pour towards me from luminous centres merging into all the irridescent splendours on their way. Sometimes, radiations would flow from me and become lost to view in the distance. More generally, flashing streams of light would move to and fro in straight lines, though sometimes fluidic emanations would sweep around in the curves of a parabola. What was more marvellous than anything else was the infinite millions of radiations, emanations and luminous currents which at times I would see streaming from and into and through all things, and filling all the surrounding space with coruscations and lightning activities.

Dr Edwin Babbit (1829–1905), *Principles of Light and Colour.*

It [the aura] is an object of great beauty, the delicacy and rapid motions of its particles giving it an aspect of living iridescent light and this beauty becomes an extraordinary radiance and entrancing loveliness as the intellect becomes more highly evolved and is employed chiefly on pure and sublime topics. As we shall see . . . every thought gives rise to vibrations in the mental body, accompanied by a play of colour described as like that of the spray of a waterfall as the sunlight strikes it, raised many degrees in colour and vivid delicacy.

Annie Besant and C. W. Leadbeater, *Thought Forms*, 1905

When a person stands against a homogeneous background, either very light (sky blue) or very dark (midnight blue), and with certain arrangements so that there is a softness and a uniformity in the light, one can clearly see, with the aid of coloured filters (cobalt blue) or with the unaided eye, a most thrilling phenomenon. From the periphery of the body arises a cloudlike, blue grey envelope which extends for 2–4 feet where it loses its distinctness and merges with the surrounding atmosphere. This envelope is brilliant and illuminates the periphery of the body in the same way as the rays of the rising sun light up the fringes of dark mountains. It swells slowly for 1–2 seconds, away from the body until it forms a nearly perfect oval shape with fringed edges. It remains in full development for approximately $\frac{1}{4}$ of a second and then, abruptly, it disappears completely. It takes about $\frac{1}{5}$th to $\frac{1}{8}$th of a second to vanish. Then there is a pause of 1 to 3 seconds until it re-appears again to repeat the process. This process is repeated 15–25 times a minute in the average resting person.

Dr John C. Pierrakos, American psychiatrist and researcher, 1974.

All quite specific and very spectacular stuff. I don't for one second think that these eminent people are lying. But how many of us could say that we see anything even remotely resembling phenomena like these? Not many. But we are humans too. We have the same eyes. We inhabit the same human bodies with the same senses. Why must we be blind? Surely we can at least begin to see this fascinating phenomenon of the aura that Cayse and the others describe so vividly.

Of course we can if we try. The aura is visible to everyone, and in this section of the book I will be describing some steps you can take in order to open your eyes. If you've never seen an aura, its not surprising. All our life, our focus of awareness is trained to be very physical. This physical way of looking at things is forced on us so strongly that we have forgotten that there are other ways of seeing. Actually, the situation is even worse than that. Nowadays we all go to great lengths to *discourage* each other. We are not allowed even to mention our finer perceptions – let alone use them. I'm sure we've all had the experience of making an intuitive – or, on the face of it, unsupportable – statement, and then been immediately attacked and ordered to justify ourselves. If we can't, we are labelled 'emotional' or 'illogical' or, worse still, 'mad'. It seems, even in our so-called enlightened times, there remains a taboo on any enthusiasm for self discovery. I am certainly no great psychic, but I have seen auras and there is absolutely no reason why you shouldn't see them too, with a bit of encouragement.

Seeing is believing

What are these elusive auras? What secrets can we learn from the theories and explanations behind them?

As with all things, seeing is believing. We are all aware that our physical bodies radiate physical energies. Heat, infra red light waves, chemical pherenomes, and so on. In fact, modern science has evolved machinery so sensitive that it can detect the presence of the minutest particles of any physical energy you care to mention. We can now look at ourselves in terms of the amount of electrical energy we give off, how much heat we emanate or even how radioactive we are! In physical terms, it is well established that we do not stop at our skin. In Russia, the researcher Kirlians proved the point further by capturing on film an impression of what scientists have since called 'Bioplasmic' energy – a halo completely encompassing the outside of all living things. 'If we can measure it, it exists' is the scientists' cry, and in those terms at least there is no doubt whatsoever about the existence of some sort of a human aura. As for what kind, no one is sure exactly.

For a more complete answer, we must look to older and much more intuitive ways. The instruments of science, sensitive though they are, are not adequate for the task of understanding all the mysteries of the human body. The electro-encephalograph (lie detector) can register the physical effects of emotions and thoughts (changing electrical resistance, heart rate,

A Kirlians photograph of the human hand gives insight into the owner's health and state of mind. Here the strong black flaring round the fingers suggests an excess of willpower.

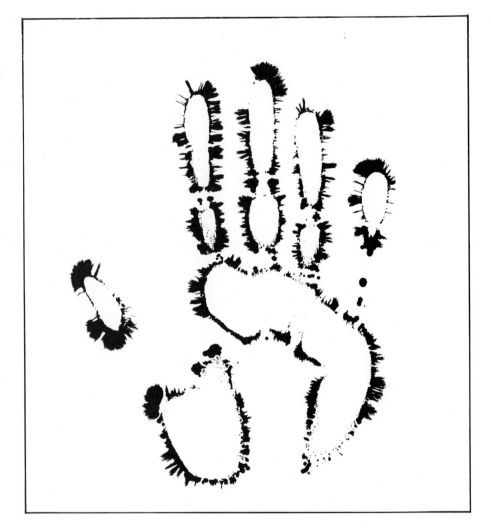

brain activity) but only the human personality itself can actually feel the feelings of them.

To a great extent, the magic of the experienced aura lies in the act of perceiving it. To see an aura is to feel another human presence with your eyes and it is very much a mystical experience. The existence of the aura will never be 'proved' as such, though it is a visual experience that seems to occur on the retina and contains light and colour like any other physical experience. Yet somehow its source seems to be within the beholder. Although it surrounds, follows and expresses another person, the aura exists in some strange way in the awareness of the viewer, and it is the inner understanding of the viewer that greatly affects what is actually seen. Therefore, to perceive an aura you must first find a certain state of mind.

The Halo Symbol

The idea that the body of a saint or divine being glows is well established. For centuries, the halo has been regarded in art as a sign of purity. Christian artists evolved a whole code of symbolism to confer different ranks of spiritual awareness on their subjects. A plain disc around the head showed latent or potential saintliness. Little lines extending around the disc showed an awakening spirituality. Radiating straight lines symbolized great power of the soul. Curved lines showed the lunar forces of the lower self! The idea of religious art without halos became unthinkable. How could a painting be regarded as religious if the people in it were not seen to be saints and holy men, and how was anybody to know this unless the artist painted them with halos?

The halo became a mere symbol. With the decline of Christianity as a source of sincere inspiration for painters (c. 17th century), the halo eventually degenerated into a mere artistic cliché – a sort of compulsory saint's hat. And the possibility of the actual existence of halos faded away from the Christian mind. And I must admit that the existence of halos had faded away from my mind, too, until the day I saw one. I was sitting in a rather bored and sleepy state in a lecture theatre, and I became aware of a kind of golden light all around the head of the man who was speaking. The light shimmered there for about 10 seconds and then faded. I was surprised – but no longer bored or asleep! This man in front of me was certainly no saint. And yet, for a few seconds, I had definitely seen his head and the whole top half of his body surrounded with golden light. It was all too much for me, and I went back to sleep!

This detail from a painting by the Italian Renaissance painter Masaccio shows how much halos can vary according to the spiritual rank of the person concerned.

Energy Fields

Talking about auras has always been something of a problem. In order to communicate the idea better, it seems that people (including many who haven't actually seen an aura themselves) have often had to resort to interpreting their experience in terms of various forces or energy fields.

The idea of one universal all-pervading energy is as old as philosophy itself, and considering the theories of cosmic energy is as constructive a way of beginning to come to terms with the human aura as any. There is a popular school of thought which believes that the aura is an interaction between this universal energy field and the energy field of the individual person. The universal energy field has been called many things in many cultures – among them, God, Prana, the Ether, the Od, and, more recently, the Force.

The world, and in fact the entire cosmos, is a vast mosaic of constantly changing energy. Everything is energy, even matter is energy. Feelings are a form of energy, and so are thoughts. We humans are swimming in a universally present sea of energy. If you think about the idea sympathetically, it may conjure up a vision of the human body surrounded by an ever-moving, swirling field of shifting and changing patterns. The basic concept of the aura is that, as the human being flows through the pervading mist of energy, his own personal energy field becomes visible in it. But since a human being's energy field does not stop at the skin, there exists a whole area of interaction and vibration between the two fields and this becomes visible as the aura.

But enough of cosmic theories for now. What of us, the humans in the story? What is this individual energy field that emanates from us?

Resonances

There is evidence which proves that the energy field/aura has been noticed throughout history, going back to the times of the cavemen. Cave art clearly shows pre-historic man's awareness of the aura. Many figures drawn on cave walls and rock faces are surrounded by halo-like areas or radiating lines projecting from the body. Some show the aura around the head, while others show it round the whole body. It seems that awareness of these fields was universal, as pictures of people with auras appear in prehistoric art the world over.

Some of the most expressive prehistoric cave art in the world is to be found in Australia, and it is here amongst the aborigines that there are some interesting traditions. One of these traditions speaks volumes in support of the theory of a universal awareness of the human aura, an awareness which we seem to have lost over the millennia. Our English word 'aura' comes from the Greek word 'auria' meaning a breeze. When an aborigine wants to gather information from the environmental aura around him, he speaks of 'leaning on the wind'. This poetic phrase expresses very pointedly the whole subtle and gentle process of tuning into the life field of nature and blending the human aura with it in one, natural, wholeness. The resultant state of resonance, we are told, gives the hunter a unique sense of relationship both physically and spiritually with everything that is around him. I am sure that there are precious moments in everyone's life when we could say the same.

This 'environmental aura', with which primitive man was so in tune, is still with us today, although sadly it is somewhat polluted. Basically, it consists of anything that has not been made by man. All life forms – birds, animals, flora and minerals – constantly interact with each other in subtle energy exchanges and give rise to what is, in effect, a vast data bank of resonances. With sensitivity, this data bank can be tapped into.

Auric Personalities

WE have been told by psychic experts that an aura is beautiful and revealing, and we have been reassured by art historians that it exists. But what about us? How can we come to understand it?

As with all matters of intuition, auras can only be approached in a friendly way. You must be nice to your subconscious or it won't help you. You have a huge reserve of built-in understanding which is quite capable of seeing an aura. Be kind to it and give it the benefit of the doubt and it will come to your aid. We have all, I'm sure, had experiences like the three I am about to describe:

You meet someone and you feel an indefinable sense of discomfort in their presence. Or perhaps you know another person who always leaves you feeling that you've been drained. Yet another person you know makes you feel warm inside (no, not a sexual feeling). Three common everyday situations. Yet imagine for a second that you had the eyes of a gifted reader of auras. How would these experiences appear then?

If you were to picture the scene through clairvoyant eyes for a moment, it would take on a very different perspective. The first thing an aura reader would know is that what shows on the outside is what is on the inside. The aura is a true expression of the spiritual heart of the individual, and as such it can only be looked on with compassion and with no hint of criticism. The seer of auras would look at you and simply see you as you are. Your aura would appear either predominantly one colour or another, large or weak, clear or fuzzy, depending on your emotions, your physical health and your 'purity of soul' (for want of a better phrase). He/she would also see you against a background of considerable auric pollution. Radio waves, overcrowding, environmental damage, all the so-called technological advances, leave their mark on the natural energy field through which we move and in which we exist. There you would stand, with your aura radiating outward about two feet all around, perhaps a bit more around the head.

Suddenly, into your auric picture comes your uneasy friend. The colours of his or her aura are not in harmony with your aura. They resonate against it. Your auras mingle and interact. At a conscious level you are both saying and doing the right things to get on with each other: your faces are going through the correct motions. There are no obvious reasons for discord, and yet you have disharmony! And so you part. Your aura will be affected for a while and will resonate (maybe for days). Then it will return to its former comfortable state. Remember, the aura is a natural phenomenon. Like the sea or the seasons, it has its own pace and cannot be hurried. You will have absorbed another's auric impression and it will be with you until it wants to go.

Now imagine the next situation I mentioned, the one where you meet the person who leaves you feeling depleted after ten minutes' conversation. We all know such people. (I wonder if one of them is reading this book now, sublimely unaware that they are being written about!) These people are 'drainers'. They mean well, but they have the unique ability to plug into your aura and syphon off energy at an alarming rate. They are harmless and you can learn a lot about the feeling of your own aura from your dealings with them because they operate so completely in the field of 'personal energy'. Because encounters with such people are so instructive (probably on the principle that you don't notice a thing – in this case your aura – until it's taken away from you), I will dwell on them for a while. Please don't get me wrong. Drainers are often pleasantly friendly people. They simply provide a good starting point for learning how to feel the flow of one's own personal auric energies.

Drainers can be slightly neurotic people, but their neurosis is well masked. They are often a bit depressed. Generally they have quick nervous movements, are fast talkers and fix you with their eyes. They get you in resonance with them, usually by means of some emotive topic of conversation, and as soon as you resonate in sympathy with them – wham! The tap is turned on and it's "goodbye energy" for you! Don't worry, though, they are quite harmless and you will soon recover! Try feeling this drain aurically next time it happens and you will learn a lot about your identity as an energy from your inter-reactions with these people.

Not all drainers act in the way I have just described. Some come at you with their voices and their eyes, talking quickly and scanning your face, urging you to meet their eyes. Because they are working at a subconscious level, they are probably very sincere and this makes them hard to deal with politely. If you register their approach you can resist them easily, although they are deeply motivated and very persistent. They become highly agitated the moment you frustrate their attempts to link up and start syphoning. What a game it is! They will use any trick in the book to distract you and to get you in resonance with them. A favourite is to make some pointed and perhaps barbed remark about you. The simple way to deal with them is to remain unsympathetic and detached. Bring down a complete psychic shutter between you and them. Your next encounter with such a person should provide you with some fascinating and, I hope, friendly games to play.

I hope that you are now beginning to get a slight feel for your aura. So far you have had it jangled and you have had it drained. Now let's give it a bit of a lift. I think it needs one! In fairness, it must be said that your aura doesn't get elevated very often.

Consider your aura again, through a seer's eyes. It's probably light gold, shot through with grey and a hint of blue. Around its edge is a hard grey line. There is a good reason for this. You live an ordinary life in the ordinary world, which means that you are open to all sorts of impressions and frantic patterns of energy surround you. The very buildings and even the streets you walk in have the memories of previous generations imprinted into their physical fabric. To survive, you have developed this character armour – a kind of brittle, desensitized edge to your precious aura. This protects you. Suddenly you come into contact with another aura. This aura has a softer edge. It is calm, with a blue appearance and perhaps a hint of violet. Your auras mix. Your hard edge is cushioned, and instead of being a necessary barrier it begins to feel like a hinderance and to be blocking you from something good – so you let it go. Immediately your own energy field expands and you start to feel good. The other person, because of his or her own natural awareness, does not try to steal or syphon off any of your expanding energy. They just continue to be as they are. They simply resonate. Soon, both auras are reverberating in sympathy. Your energy is flowing and there is harmony.

People who have this kind of effect on you are rare, I must admit. But they do exist, and it is so refreshing when you meet one.

Let's come down to earth. All that you have seen so far is what you have imagined through another person's eyes. What of your own eyes? Can you see auras? The answer is most definitely yes. Yes, yes, yes, and again yes! The following section is for you if you want to try.

How to See Auras

First, let me say that there is absolutely nothing I can tell you about how to approach this subject. You are your own master in these matters. Your way is the best way, whoever you are.

First Step – Believe

How many times have you said of a woman, 'Why does she wear that colour? It does not suit her at all.' How many times have you said, 'How beautiful she looks in that dress. The colour is just right for her. She was made to wear it.' In both cases, you have been reading an aura. The first woman was wearing a colour that clashed with her aura; the second woman was wearing a colour that harmonized with her aura.

'But,' you say, 'I haven't been reading an aura at all, I simply looked at the colours of her clothes and decided whether they suited her or not.' And who would disagree with you? Certainly not me.

But think again. If that is your final reaction, then that is as far as you can go. Don't you remember why you picked up this book in the first place? You were curious. You wanted to learn something new. You had a small feeling that you could find out something extra about yourself. So – try again. This time be in sympathy and take a step towards the idea. Perhaps the reason that the girl's clothes suit her *is* simply because the colours she wears are in harmony with her aura. Perhaps it *is* true that your subconscious perceived something about her, then judged her choice of colour against that. Maybe you *did* somehow sense something first and then looked at her clothes later. Talk yourself into it. Try to accept the idea. Why not? You don't have to answer to anyone if you are wrong. And who knows? You might be right!

Seeing With Feelings

Next, an exercise you can do anywhere where there are people to look at. It's an extension of the one above.

I assume that you have now admitted that there *is* some inner quality that a person gives off and that their appearance is (or isn't) in harmony with it. Now look at a complete stranger. Look at everything about his or her clothes. The colours, the materials they are made of. Are they tight or flowing? Are they symbolic of anything? Look at their clothes closely from every way you know how. Now look at the face and just 'feel'. That's all, simply sense them. What do you get? Are you left with any impressions? Are your two perceptions of this person in harmony? You may have felt that they were sad but wearing happy bright colours. Perhaps they were dressed in dark leather, and yet somehow looked 'innocent'. Only you know best. Whatever answers you may have to these last questions, treasure them. They are yours!

A Magnet in the Dark

Now it's time to do an actual 'seeing' exercise. This is one recommended by a clairvoyant called Ousley. It involves looking at a magnet in complete darkness. The best place to do this, I have found, is under the bedclothes at night. (If you get caught, boldly explain *exactly* what you are doing! Don't give an inch!) Another good reason for doing this exercise in bed is that it is one of the few places where you can relax properly. If you're going to be a seer of auras, you're going to have to relax. You are never going to see anything – let alone an aura – if you sit there rigid, staring at where you expect it to be. Try falling asleep or something. Drift off somehow.

Stare into the blackness. It is pitch dark. You should see a faint glow, shimmering around the poles of the magnet. As you become more sensitive, the faint glow will intensify into a white light with a hint of blue and green in it. You may see ray-like streaks of light coming from the magnet. At first, you will probably find it hard to concentrate in the darkness, but after a few minutes something will happen: you will either have seen your first aura or you will be fast asleep! Either way, you must agree it will have been worth it.

Your Own Aura

For the next exercise, hold your hands about one foot (30 cms) from your eyes against a dark background or a white wall in shadow. Spread your fingers apart and touch your left-hand fingertips against your right. Now, concentrate on visualizing energy flowing into your fingers. Hold them there together for a minute, then draw them apart, keeping your eyes focused on the gradually widening space between them. You will see minute radiations of energy issuing from your fingertips, bridging the gap between your two hands.

It may help if you rub your hands vigorously together before you do this exercise. Alternatively, try this as a warm-up. Hold your hands close together (not in front of any particular background this time) and imagine the space between them filling with energy. Then move them slowly together and apart again in a gentle pulsing movement. As the energy builds, you may sense a tingling in the palms of your hands, and eventually this charge may become so strong that you have the impression you are squeezing an invisible sponge. Now put your fingertips together and look for the auric radiation in the same way as before.

Perceiving The Human Aura

Finally, how to see another person's aura. For this, you are going to need a volunteer. If it's the first time you have tried it, there is going to be some giggling, hilarity and general embarassment involved.

Find a friend – someone with whom you feel in harmony – and ask her (or him) gently, if she would kindly help you and be your 'subject'. If she says 'Yes' and is curious and sympathetic – good! If not – never mind. You'll just have to leave it. Do not try to persuade her, simply find someone else or wait till she changes her mind and brings up the subject again of her own accord (a thing that happens a lot in these matters).

When you have got a sympathetic subject, ask her to sit in front of a plain dark background – perhaps a large piece of cloth hung on a wall, or even a wall itself as long as it's featureless and dark coloured. The lighting in the room must be soft – not dim – without harsh shadows. An average room lit by daylight through a window without beams of sunlight streaming in is the kind of thing I mean. If it's night-time, keep the light level bright (i.e. comfortable reading level), but shade the bulbs and, once again, go for a bright, soft effect. Avoid spot lights and fluorescent tubes.

If it's daytime, gaze at the sky (not the sun) for about half a minute. If it's night, look at a lamp. Then, sit down, close your eyes and make yourself very comfortable. If you know how to meditate, do so. If not, no problem! Simply relax and listen to the clock ticking or the sound of the traffic or something. Just be there.

Now open your eyes and look casually straight past your subject (as if you didn't want to see her). Let your gaze wander, then let it rest. Let it wander again, then concentrate it again. Let it flit around – then hold it still. Remember, the idea is to look hard, straight past your subject and then move on. This way, you pick up impressions out of the corner of your eye and forget them quickly.

Eventually, your brain will become so confident about these impresions that it will inadvertently let some through. Suddenly, you will *see* something! Almost immediately, though, your brain will shut it off. Thoughts like, 'Oh it was nothing' or 'My eyes are playing tricks on me' will flood into your head and you will start to wonder and doubt yourself. (And probably smile.) Simply carry on as long as you feel comfortable and see what else you can see. Congratulate your intuition for getting through. Keep looking at the space all around your subject in a gentle, unforced way and casually notice out of the corner of your eye any changes or patterns in the light fields. Notice them and move on.

Soon, you will be seeing an aura! After a while, have a rest and do something completely different. Turn on the TV. Go and feed the cat. Do anything. Then come back, and if you want to, try again.

The Colours of The Aura

The aura is a very individual thing. It is made up of many different colours, and not all colours are present in all auras. Here is a list of colours and what they are said to mean when seen as part of an aura. This list is a compilation of the general view of many psychics and you had best regard it as a guide and starting point. Even if you don't see colours in your auras, it is still fascinating because it gives an idea of the emotional meanings of colours. Why do you choose to wear the colours you do? Why do you paint your house the way you do? Is your favourite colour telling the world something about your inner feelings?

Red

A very physical colour. It shows force, strength, energy and passion. Light red in an aura suggests a highly strung, hyperactive type, whereas dark red can show temper or a love of the sensual. Red can mean nervous problems and over-concern about self. Pride, greed and selfish affection are to be seen in the aura as red. People with a lot of red in their aura are often physically strong, wilful, with a rather materialistic outlook.

Orange

Bright orange shows a healthy and vital person. It indicates a strong, positive personality. Consideration, self-control, thoughtfulness and intellectual development. On the negative side, pride, ambition and selfish goals. It is a most wholesome colour. (If an aura is exposed to the colour orange, its owner will experience a feeling of increased vitality.)

Yellow

Indicates intellectual ability. Wellbeing, optimism. Pale yellow can suggest a weak willpower, indecisiveness and timidity. According to Edgar Cayse, people with yellow in their aura usually take good care of themselves, are happy, helpful and friendly and not inclined to worry. Yellow is a sign of clear mental processes, and a golden yellow can indicate a developing spirit. Yellow is very refreshing to the nervous system. It invigorates not only the physical body but the mind and the emotions too, giving a feeling of optimism.

Green

The colour of nature and healing. Green in an aura is a sign of health, but dark green can suggest dishonesty. Green people are usually lively, versatile and adaptable. Green governs the mental levels and suggests a versatile brain. It is the colour of rebirth, new life, prosperity and Spring.

Doctors and nurses are said to have a lot of green in their auras. Green tinged with brown and red denotes jealousy. Sympathy and adaptability show up as green.

Blue
According to Cayse again, this is the colour of high-mindedness and great thoughts. It denotes idealism, devotion, spiritual feelings, self reliance and confidence. Other qualities associated with blue are integrity, sincerity and loyalty. Dark blue is a sign of wisdom and saintliness representing meditation. Pale blue indicates an, as yet, unfulfilled potential. As it gets darker, it shows a realization of the inner self. Blue can be a sign of 'the blues', and if shot through with black is a sign of religious vanity.

Violet
Love, wisdom, knowledge. The colour of enlightenment.

Indigo
The colour of the seeker and the aspirant. It also represents benevolence, calmness and the possibility of psychic qualities. According to some, it can represent changing relationships or internal poisoning.

Black
The colour of ignorance. In severe cases, it appears with crimson red. When associated with great anger, it can appear as a kind of 'smoke' in the aura.

Grey
Depression, torpor, sadness and gloom. When strong, grey can indicate fear. Greenish-grey is a sign of deceit.

Brown
Associated in the aura with avarice. In nature, brown appears with green, symbolizing wholeness and solidity.

Rose Pink
The colour of the emotions, romance and sincere friendship. Often the sign of a modest and refined person. If the aura is exposed to pink, the effect is vitalizing, dispersing feelings of lethargy.

Auras . . . Myths and Facts

★ 'The majority of people do see auras, they just don't realize it.'

Edgar Cayse

★ John Keely (born 1837), a worker of techno miracles, allegedly tapped the auric 'dynaspheric force'. With a note from a violin, he could fly a model Zeppelin weighing 8 lbs (3·6 kg) around the room, run a 25 hp electric motor, turn a 72 lb (32·5 kg) fly wheel, and float an iron ball on water. Mankind, it seems, was not ready for this kind of unlimited power and somehow Keely could never seem to develop or complete his inventions.

★ In 1930, Saxton Burr, an American embryologist, invented a supersensitive voltmeter for measuring minute electrical currents. Applying it to human beings, he discovered that we are all surrounded by an electromagnetic field, the life field, he called it. Monitored over a period of years, this human 'L force' varied in patterns that were directly related to the seasons, the lunar phases and even sun spot activity. Eventually, he was able to predict the forthcoming reactions of mentally unstable people to distant magnetic storms in space.

★ Try this and feel better. Sit comfortably in a chair. Think of a nice, natural shade of green. (Lettuce?) Breathe steadily in for the count of 6 (roughly – you don't need a stop watch) and imagine you're breathing in the colour you have visualized. Hold for about 3 seconds (guess it), then breathe slowly out. As you exhale, imagine green flooding through your aura. Done gently, in a relaxed way, this can perk you up no end!

The language of words is not enough. The spirit speaks in pictures, and let whoever would listen hark to the cards! In their mirror the past and present lie as one, and from that story told, the future takes its form. Who would read a picture book may know as a child the secrets of the ages. Shapes and patterns, colours and signs whisper their message. The wise gaze deep and listen from within.

Reading The Tarot

TAROT? The very word has a ring of magic to it. The cards of the Tarot pack strike a chord of mystery in the heart of everyone. One glimpse through the 78 pages of this ancient picture book reminds even the most hard-headed of us that there is a part of everyone that is truly ancient. The Tarot pack provides a way of reaching past the details of our day-to-day selves and touching on our very intuition. By means of a deep intuitive response to the visual stimulus of the cards, we can learn to speak directly from our own subconscious. After a short period of study of the cards, many people feel a sense of growing inner understanding. The awareness takes on a clear magical quality and the undercurrents and motivations of daily life somehow become more obvious. Such is the power of the Tarot.

The history of the Tarot pack is a mystery in itself. The 22 picture cards, known as the major arcana, are said to be derived form the pages of the oldest book in the world – allegedly written by Hermes Trismegistus, counsellor to Osiris, king of Egypt, at a time when the magical arts and symbolic writing were in their golden age. Other theories maintain that the cards were introduced by the Chinese. And some say that they were brought over from India by the gypsies. The Tarot is also frequently related to the Hebrew Kabbalistic law and a correspondence is often pointed out between the cards of the major arcana and the letters of the Hebrew alphabet.

One more interesting theory of the origin of the cards states that after the destruction of Alexandria in 641 AD, the city of Fez became the spiritual capital of the world and it was to Fez that sages and seers of many different countries travelled to exchange ideas. In order to facilitate communication between so many philosophers speaking so many different languages, they set about creating a universal language which they embodied in a book of pictures and from that they have handed down to us the Tarot. Amid all this theory, the Tarot remains inscrutable. The earliest known date attributed to an actual Tarot pack is 1390. The deep psychological responses that the symbolism of the cards provokes seem to demand an historical explanation and justification which in the case of the Tarot simply does not exist. The cards are best accepted as magic, and like all magic they are timeless.

Getting a Feel for The Cards

If you have a pack of Tarot cards, now would be a good time to dig it out. If you haven't, you can easily buy one from a major bookstore or games outlet. When you take your pack and flip through it for the first time you will probably be left with quite a confused impression. Images of Kings and Queens in strange positions, surrounded by curious decorations. Patterns and symbols. Disturbing figures. A skeleton and a man hanging upside down. Batons, cups, flowers, faces, birds, dogs, swords. What do they all mean? How can anyone begin to comprehend all this?

Indeed, at this stage many people feel a slight aversion to the cards. They feel somehow uncomfortable about them. There is a good reason for this, and it is very understandable, for the symbols of the Tarot are designed to reach deep into the subconscious. A large part of the enduring value of the cards has lain in the fact that the images cannot be fitted into any hard-and-fast dogma. They can never be completely comprehended by the conscious mind. To a person educated only in the ways of the rational, the awakening of the innocent power of our magic selves can come as a surprise, and some people don't like surprises. Not even nice ones! The cards touch us, but we don't know how. The pictures stir a response, but we are not sure what. They are an enigma – and that is what they are supposed to be. The Tarot does not speak to the logical side of the brain. It calls, with pictures, directly to a much deeper part.

Pick up your pack again and simply browse through it. Look at whatever card catches your interest. Who are the people? What are they doing? What are they wearing? What are they holding? Where are they seated or standing? Read each card (or page, for the Tarot is really a book) for as long or as short a time as you like. This is the principle of the Tarot. Each card is a symbol and each card contains symbols. These symbols filter through and by-pass your conscious mind, and thus become a means of getting in touch with and awakening your unconscious mind.

The Packs

There is no standard Tarot pack. All packs have been drawn at some time or other by someone, and as such they are all of equal worth. Generally, they conform to the guide given here, but it must be said that Tarot packs can vary. The card names are often in different languages; the suits have different labels; and there are various differing titles and pictures to some of the main themes of the 22 major arcana. Some packs have more decoration and pictures than others, particularly in the minor arcana. However, let me say now that all this is unimportant. If you feel inspired to go out and buy a Tarot pack and you are uncertain which pack to get, don't be. Buy whichever pack attracts you. Problems of labelling, numbering and naming disappear after the first few minutes of handling anyway, and within a very short time the words and titles, numbers and labels will cease to be relevant.

The secret of the Tarot magic lies not in the cards themselves but in your understanding of them. This understanding will grow of its own accord as you get used to using your pack and very soon your pack will become your pack.

A Word About Symbols

A few basic shapes form the building blocks of all the complex forms of Nature.
air
fire
water
earth
Each shape inspires a different emotion.

Magic cannot be put into words. The feeling of magic is best expressed in images and associations, and by symbols and shapes. The star, the sword and lightening are universal magical images common to every branch of the magical arts and they have the power to call forth a deep response in the human mind. By means of a wide range of symbols drawn from the mists of antiquity, the Tarot cards beguile the intellect almost involuntarily into letting go of a fraction of its grip on the wealth of intuition and understanding that lies beneath.

The power of symbols is only superficially understood in our modern world. It seems that the media and advertizers are the only people who do go to any length to understand them, and their objective is almost entirely mercenary. First, they grab your unwilling attention and force it on to one of their products. They then unleash upon you a whole arsenal of heavy-duty emotional and sexual symbols and associations in order to goad and bamboozle you into parting with your money. No wonder we have become de-sensitized to symbols!

This was not always the situation, however. There was a time when a simple, static image could be an irresistible reminder of something friendly, familiar and profound. In other words, a simple human emotion. It is to this naïve state that we return when we begin to read the Tarot. We are all primitive beings. We have our roots in an ancient past where the forces of nature and the elements were supreme. These roots are still with us today; they are in every one of us, no matter how civilized or advanced we may profess to be. This urge to respond to certain symbolic shapes and ideas is an important constituent of our mental and emotional make up. Unfortunately, it is one that for generations we have been led to overlook.

In the words of Carl Jung:

As scientific understanding has grown, so our world has become de-humanized. Man feels himself isolated in the cosmos, because he is no longer involved in nature and has lost his emotional 'unconscious identity' with natural phenomena. These have slowly lost their symbolic implications. Thunder is no longer the voice of the angry god, nor is lightning his avenging missile. No river contains a spirit, no tree the life principle of a man, no snake the embodiment of wisdom, no mountain cave the home of a great demon. No voices now speak to man from stones, plants and animals. Nor does he speak to them believing they can hear. His contact with nature has gone, and with it has gone the profound emotional energy that his symbolic connection supplied.

That is the bad news! But don't worry – all is not lost forever. It's a bit like a person who, after being asleep for a while, wakes up to find that he can't quite remember where he is. Happily, a few reminders and gentle memory jogs will soon restore the situation.

The Major Arcana

Let's jolt the prehistoric memory a bit and take a closer look at the cards of the Tarot pack. You should do this in two stages. First, come to an inner understanding of some of the cards. Second, based on this intuitive grasp, learn how to lay out the cards and read the fortunes of yourself and others.

The Tarot pack consists of 78 cards – the *major arcana* of 22 cards and the *minor arcana* of 56. It is the major arcana that we are going to concentrate on first. Each card of the major arcana has a roman numeral, a picture and a title.

The cards are:

0	The Fool	XI	Fortitude (Strength)
I	The Magician	XII	The Hanged Man
II	The High Priestess	XIII	Death
III	The Empress	XIV	Temperance
IV	The Emperor	XV	The Devil
V	The High Priest	XVI	The Tower
VI	The Lovers	XVII	The Star
VII	The Chariot	XVIII	The Moon
VIII	Justice	XIX	The Sun
IX	The Hermit	XX	Judgement
X	The Wheel of Fortune	XXI	The World

A Word to the Puzzled Reader

Before going any further, I want to remind you of one thing. If you can remember this it will save you a lot of time and Brain Strain. Tarot is simple, visual and intuitive. You do not need a massive understanding of numerology, astrology, mythology, Egyptology and a degree in philosophy in order to understand the cards. In fact, any person is free to make their own Tarot pack using symbols for which they have a feeling and to which they have ascribed personal experience of their own. So do not, therefore, be awed by authority or get lost in references to 'Apollonius of Tyana' or 'The Hindu wheel of Sansara' or 'The Hebraic concept of Sacrifice', or any other such academic confusion so often found in Tarot guides. The cards of the major arcana will make themselves clear to you without any struggle or book learning on your part. Your inner experience (which you already possess in huge quantities) is what you are trying to get in touch with. It will respond to the suggestion of each card and will project itself on to the card in its own way, giving you your own personal feeling for that card. Trust your responses. Your intuition is usually right.

Take the 22 cards of the major arcana and lay them out according to the illustration. It is a good idea to keep the cards lying around in that form for a few days while you assimilate their meaning.

You have, in fact, laid the cards down in the symbol of infinity. This is the map of a journey made by every consciousness (including yours) from infancy to the state of complete awareness. As you can see, the journey is divided into two parts, with a turning point in the middle. The 22 cards of the Tarot represent the 22 different energies which act upon us growing humans as we make our journey.

Identifying The 22 Energies

As we go through life, we pass in and out of many different situations, and in every situation we have a particular feeling. (This may seem very obvious when written down in front of you like this, but the reality of it is something that very few of us seem to grasp.) The fact is simple: our lives are a series of feelings. You might therefore conclude that in order to understand ourselves and our lives all we have to do is understand this flow

of feelings. This is true, but there is one major snag. If you stop at any one point in the day and ask yourself 'What am I feeling now?' (give it a try sometime), the answer you get back as you scan through your thoughts, emotions and aspirations is likely to be extremely complicated and time consuming. So complicated, in fact, that once you have stopped and asked such a $64,000 question, you will probably be out of action for the rest of the day, pondering on the answer! Consequently, we have given up asking ourselves this simple question because the answer is more complicated than the basic thing we want to know. Eventually we avoid questioning and looking at ourselves altogether.

However, imagine for a second that instead of asking the question of your superficial conscious brain, you had a means of speaking to your deeper, intuitive self. What would be the answer then? The answer would be much, much simpler. Instead of the host of words, emotions, attitudes, concepts and moral judgements that are the stock in trade of the mundane mind, the answer would come back strong and clear. You are experiencing one of your 22 basic, inner energies. And these basic energies are all represented on Cards 0–21 of the major arcana of the Tarot pack. In understanding this you now have a good basis on which to start learning.

The Journey

Look back at the cards. They are laid out in the figure of eight, each card representing one of your 22 inner motives. Now consider this. *Although they are numbered in sequence, they do not occur in you in any particular order. All of them are in you, and in any situation equally at any time.* It's important to try and get your mind around this idea, however abstract it may sound. (The seeds of everything are present in everything else, is another way of putting it.) After a bit of Tarot study you will soon see what I mean.

Let us begin by looking at the unfolding of these 22 inner qualities in terms of a journey or an evolution of a human spirit. The journey is in two parts. The first part from the Fool to the Wheel of Fortune is directed towards the physical world and the establishment of the personality in it. It is an outward-looking phase, when the individual is concerned with a world *outside* himself. The Wheel of Fortune to The World represents the second stage of growth. During this stage, perspective is reversed and the individual seeks to establish links with his inner self and to confront the unknown mysteries of his psyche. You will notice if you look at the layout of the cards that the first ten face outwards and the second ten face inwards. All of us have these two stages to our growth, and anyone who feels any sympathy for this book is probably well into the second stage. (But remember, folks, all the qualities are present in all people all the time!)

I want to tell the story of the journey quite briefly here, and later examine the symbols in much more detail.

You start off as **The Fool**. You are literally a baby. Pure, innocent and unaware of yourself as a separate person. (You still possess this quality, even at this moment.) You have no number. Out of this unformed innocence emerges an identity. A feeling of 'I exist, I can manipulate things around me'. This is card number I, **The Magician**: the wielder of the tools of consciousness and the symbol of the human and his craving to discover his limits and purpose. This fragile being is subjected to four huge forces in its little life – **The High Priestess** (II), **The Empress** (III), **The Emperor** (IV) and **The High Priest** (V). These are the powerful currents of female and male sexuality, spiritual and material tendencies. Then comes card number VI, **The Lovers**, carrying with it the feeling of adolescent rejection of one's family in preference for a mate; a time of choice and of becoming responsible for one's own life. The story unfolds with **The Chariot** (VII). Here, the self is picking up momentum in the world and rolling confidently along in its self-made vehicle. But wait! You have achieved an identity and your affairs are definitely rolling in the world . . . but where are you going? As you cruise along, you feel there is something else you need to know. Some other part of you that is yet unfulfilled. You start to weigh it up. The card **Justice** (VIII) is the voice of this feeling. **Justice** suggests that so far your growth has been a bit one-sided. Inevitably, this process of self examination leads to the **Hermit** (IX). As the **Hermit** you stand alone (not necessarily a recluse – still very much in the material world). You are determined to find your happiness in the fulfilment of those unknown feelings first brought to your attention by **Justice**. You take your simple desire to conquer the spiritual world, just as you did the physical one, and you lay it on the table.

The **Wheel of Fortune** (X) spins and you're off again on a new voyage. But this time – to who knows where. The next card is **Fortitude** (XI). For the first time, you can see what you're up against in your other self. You sense that only by fearless confrontation can the primeval forces within you be understood. You are confident and feel no fear. And so to **The Hanged Man** (XII). Here, you willingly and deliberately throw your life into a state of topsy turvy. As far as you are concerned, up could just as well be down (and vice versa). Any differentiation between the two you are quite prepared to sacrifice in the cause of your growth. And sure enough . . . **Death** (or as it's sometimes called, **Transformation**) (XIII). This is your first moment of spiritual success. You are in a position to see how your old, small self is dying away. Yet you do not mourn it.

Temperance (XIV) is next. You're on the path and you know you're getting the measure of it. The imbalance hinted at all those cards ago is beginning to be evened out. This is the feeling of the card **Temperance**. But it's not over yet. What should arise from your subconscious now but **The Devil** (XV). **The Devil** is a force that has to be seen for what it is if growth is to continue. And sure enough, like a bolt from the blue – and with shattering consequences – your progress does continue. You arrive at **The Tower** (XVI). Here, you see that you are involved in a process of unlearning those things you thought were certainties. You now really know something about the powers that lie within. Your journey is not yet over but you are no longer wandering blindly. **The Star** (XVII) is there to reassure you and guide you towards your ultimate goal.

Between you and it lies one final adventure – **The Moon** (XVIII). The supremely attractive, fascinating and ultimately deceptive lunar forces must be tested, tasted and understood. It is a risky business and it involves faith. Then, at last, after the dark night of **The Moon** . . . **The Sun** (XIX)! Showing attainment, victory, success and enlightenment, but still very much to do with the separate, enlightened individual. All very well but inevitably the journey must proceed yet further. **The Judgement** (XX) symbolizes willingness to let go of all individuality no matter how spiritual or deep and no matter how hard won. **The Judgement** is the pay-off. After this card, the being can experience freely the perfection of the final state, expressed so beautifully as **The World** (XXI). From this card, to the innocence of **The Fool** (where we started all those cards ago) is now just one simple step. And so the cycle repeats itself.

There it is! It's quite a story and you are not expected to swallow it in one sitting. If any of the feelings in this story are familiar to you, then take the card in question and focus on it. It will provide a starting point from which you can gain valuable insight into your own inner state and also enable you to develop a good working knowledge of the forces at work in the Tarot.

A Closer Look

Let's take a more detailed look at the 22 cards of the major arcana and some of their associations. These are not the lighter divinatory meanings of the cards for fortune telling – those are listed later on pages 108–110. Note that each card has a positive and a negative aspect to it.

THE FOOL

THE FOOL

This card has no number. He is an innocent spirit, about to embark on incarnation. His clothes are often ragged and a dog is often seen harassing him as he walks with complete unconcern towards a precipice. He is the vagabond who lives on the outside of organized society. He cares nothing for the laws and rules by which he is supposed to abide, and is perhaps considered a lunatic. Yet within him are the seeds of genius and enlightenment. He can be seen either as the beginning or as the end of the 22-card sequence. His heart is open and carefree and his mind is open too. But there is a hint of pitfalls and trials lying before him. On his back, he carries a staff with a bag tied to it. What does it contain? All his worldly goods? Memories of the innocence that he is about to lose? Who can say? Who can see through the eyes of the fool? He is the pure impulse. . .

. . . If he is not, then he is just a joker chasing after extravagent diversions, indifferent to the chaos he leaves behind him. A laugh at any price might be his motto.

THE MAGICIAN

THE MAGICIAN

Number I. The number of positive action. The magician is the first stage of existence – the emerging self awareness of a child as it starts on the voyage of life. He stands before a table on which lie the tools of his trade. In some packs they are the tools of a cobbler. He is no longer a fool. The rest of the Tarot will tell of the trials of his journey back to his lost innocence. With one hand he reaches to the heavens. With the other, he controls the things of the Earth. His is a divine Hero/Heroine armed with confidence and his four senses. He is the master who appears when the pupil is ready, to instruct fools in the ways of knowledge. Is he the Magus? The Chosen One?

. . . If he is not, he is a manipulative trickster whose sole pleasure is to conjure with others and dupe those slower than himself. Power is his goal, his will is his only solace.

THE HIGH PRIESTESS

Papess or Juno. 'The great feminine force controlling the very source of

THE HIGH PRIESTESS

THE EMPRESS

THE EMPEROR

life, gathering into herself all the energizing forces and holding them in solution until the time of release.' She is known as a wise woman, crowned and seated on a throne. She is assigned the number II, the number of duality. She is the primeval female element, present in both man and woman. Intuitive revelation and inspiration are at her command. Passive and all wise, she speaks and the fool must learn to hear her. She is often shown holding a book. What mysteries are written in her book?

. . . Scorn or ignore her message and The High Priestess becomes the Queen of the Night. An alluring witch whose delight is to ensnare in illusion and destroy.

THE EMPRESS

The Empress has the number III. The number of harmony and synthesis. The tensions of I against II are resolved in her. The Empress is full and abundant. She is the Mother Goddess, generous and creative, who rules the paradise of creation. She is often shown as a pregnant woman. The throne is in the wide open air. Her power is passive, expressed in emotion and feeling and she can know everything in a moment. She rules with warmth and compassion, comforting and giving forth abundantly from her realm of Nature. The fool may eat fully of her fruits . . .

. . . But he must not indulge or exploit her generosity. He must understand the true nature of his benefactress, or else one day she may well turn around and eat him! The Mother Goddess can also be a monster.

THE EMPEROR

The Emperor is the male counterpart of The Empress. Seated firmly on his material throne, he rules the physical world with his will and his logic. His is the number IV, the number of structure and organization. He makes himself felt on the material plane, exerting a benign and strong influence. His creative energy builds and sustains whatever he wants it to and he perceives his empire with his senses. The Emperor is the father figure and wielder of authority and raw power. . .

But what will he do with his power? On some cards, he is depicted enthroned in a barren landscape. Did he destroy it to prove his strength? If he did, he is not a father but a bully and an oppressor.

THE POPE

Hierophant or Jupiter. The traditional representative of God on earth, The Pope is the male aspect of the High Priestess. His number V was traditionally seen as being made up of 1 (god) + 4 (matter), so The Pope symbolizes spiritual teachings and moral codes of behaviour in the world. His wisdom is practical and he teaches his flock the ancient mysteries in their daily lives. He is a profound thinker with an understanding of the physical, emotional and mental worlds. He is the good shepherd who teaches that which can be learned by word and example. The Pope is orthodox and directs the intellect to its highest goal. He instructs in the ancient formulae, and the world must come to him if they want to know them . . .

THE HIEROPHANT

. . . Those who don't, or who make light of his message, can be his downfall. In a second, he leaves his throne to carp, and harass anyone who dares question his dogma. The Pope in his negative aspect can be the intellectual oppressor, the inquisitor, or the professional liar.

THE LOVERS

The fledgling spirit is about to fly the nest. A man stands between an older woman and a younger one (the mother and the bride). Though it is a man on nearly all packs, the spirit it represents is neither male nor female. He is making his choice between his old way and his new one. But are they not just two versions of the same theme? If he not merely substituting one woman for another? That is not how he sees it at this time. He is making his first solo decision. He is separating himself from his origins and choosing himself a new identity. Cupid – the symbol of harmony – hovers overhead to ensure he makes the inevitable choice. How could he stay with the comforts of the old and the familiar, with his new identity and Eros himself goading him on to pastures new. The number of this card is VI, which like II carries a hint of tension and a need for resolution. A choice must be made, destiny demands it. . .

THE LOVERS

. . . If it is not, if he cannot bear to leave his mother, there will only be stagnation, or, at best, futile and sad vacillation.

THE CHARIOT

The number is VII. The number of progress and independent action. The decision of the preceding card has been firmly made and the show is on the road. And what a show it is. Confident and effective, the integrated ego moves smoothly through the material world. He needs no reins to guide his two horses. The power of his personality controls all he comes into contact with. He knows where he is going and his role his clear. Through mastery of will, he has concentrated his faculties and he uses them well to the benefit of himself and of those outside his golden chariot. . .

THE CHARIOT

. . . But there's the rub. Do not stand in the path of his triumphant

journey or you may have to be run down – in the interests of progress, of course.

JUSTICE

This card depicts the traditionally female figure of Justice. She holds a balance and a sword, and she is *not* blind. She has the power to assess, and if necessary demand redress. VIII is her number, the number of justice as it is made up of equal portions of even numbers. She is impartial, and only manifests to settle disputes and restore an imbalance. Why has she come now? Justice takes the broad view, and the charioteer of the previous card must hear her caution. If he does not, a sword will fall. Justice weighs up the individual whether he thinks he deserves it or not. The law of life is best understood and obeyed in order to avoid frustration. The voice of the psyche must be heard. Justice is a goddess . . .

. . . If she is less, she will use her sword wilfully to justify her scales and her judgements will have no mercy.

THE HERMIT

Do you remember The Fool? Setting out naïvely on a journey. His exterior journey is complete. Now we see him as the hermit, setting out again on the final stage of a journey towards a new dark land. He is number IX, the last of the single numbers. The Fool finds his fruition in the world as The Hermit. He no longer has a bag, a crown or a chariot. He bravely holds his tiny light towards the darkness before him and leans on his simple staff. He knows that all his former wealth and understanding will not help him on his coming journey. He is alone, uncertain, but he knows that he wants to go on. He has no comfort except his sense of purpose. The Hermit is the 'wise old man' who dreams. But does he know what he's up against this time?

. . . If asked, he might have a theory. He is capable of clinging stubbornly to theories. Perhaps the past has made him too used to knowing all the answers. The Hermit can be a fixed and dogmatic old fool.

THE WHEEL OF FORTUNE

The Wheel is a mandala, a round, unified symbol that speaks of wholeness and perfection. The Wheel brings an awareness of the rightness of things, and for a moment The Hermit sees his position on the whole journey. This cosmic perspective brings him serenity, and that reassures him. He is not alone. Forging his own part he is part of a greater plan. The perils of the coming new journey are unknown, but the journey itself has been run many times. All things must pass. This card has many different symbols on different decks. Some are rising up, some are going down. Is it the wheel of fate? The cycle of death and rebirth? The drawing up of the unconscious into the light of day? The descent of the beast? The wheel is a mystery to be enjoyed. Its number is X, the first of the double numbers symbolizing the perfect start of a new cycle . . .

. . . If it is not, it is an interminable merry-go-round of action and action on which the distracted traveller must ride forever, overwhelmed by his senses. The wheel offers perspective and momentum to go on – except for those who hang on and get dizzy.

FORTITUDE (STRENGTH)

The numbers hold the key to this card. Traditionally, two-digit numbers like 11 are viewed as $1 + 1 = 2$. So, 11 is an extension of the qualities of 2. Fortitude, calmly battling the lion, symbolizes brave confrontation with the other self. At last, the enemy has stepped out from the shadows and the true nature of the conflict to come is clear. The Hermit confronts his opposing self, the wild man within, who is as much himself as the wise old man of card IX. The expression on the face of Fortitude often shows serenity and faith. She is strong but not severe. How can she overcome such a ferocious beast without a sign of savagery herself? The Hermit must reconcile himself to his other self through fortitude. This is the theme of his new quest. Fortitude gives the strength of inner purpose. She recognizes and subdues the lion, she does not destroy it completely.

. . . If she does, she will be alone, like the charioteer – triumphant in a small way but incomplete. The power of fortitude is great and can hold back the instincts to maintain a superficial and over-civilized status quo.

THE HANGED MAN

A strange image, full of meaning. Don't be afraid of this image. This man is not being punished or tortured. He has put himself voluntarily into this helpless position. What else could he do? His journey is well under way. He has seen his lower self; he cannot return to that, nor to his charioteer days, for on this journey the direction is not his to decide. He cannot go forward or backwards. He is caught, yet he feels he must do something. He does the only possible thing. He grasps and admits his helplessness. The Hanged Man acknowledges and demonstrates his inability to make any conventional move. His world is upside down. He has sacrificed the luxury of all values, and the concepts of progress. He hangs voluntarily motiveless and disorientated. His head now points towards Mother Earth where he hopes his future lies and he awaits his rescue with faith. The Hanged Man adopts this precarious position with sincerity and his reward is bliss.

. . . To assume this posture for any other reason is to become a crippled idealist, hamstrung by an obsession with spiritual concepts. A lunatic ascetic. The number of the Hanged Man is XII. 12 breaks down into $1 + 2 = 3$. 3 contains the idea of all. Perhaps that is what the hanged man has given?

DEATH

Once again, this is not an image to be afraid of. On the face of it, it is a gruesome picture of a living skeleton, scything and dismembering parts of a human body. He bears the number XIII and 13 reduces to 4, the number of order. Death, though he comes out of chaos is also the bringer of new life. The Hanged Man made an offering of himself. His reward is the breaking up of his old personality, and with the fragmentation of the burden of his old ego he is free to proceed in any direction. Death has brought release. The parts of the body that lie scattered about seem somehow alive and active; they exist, but they do not adapt to an identity. Death has removed the problems of personality, so much the bane of The Hermit, and now new energy is released. . .

. . . To those who are frightened of the new, Death is a terrible reminder of the inevitable pain of stagnation. Death knows no mercy.

TEMPERANCE

Temperance balances the drama and energy of the two previous cards. The number is XIV (14) which equals 5, symbolizing the reconciliation of parts in a unified whole. The seeker has rejected everything that he once knew. He no longer values his ego or his old identity. The angel of temperance descends to soothe this disorientated new spirit and grants it a new balanced perspective with which to function in the new dimension into which Death has cast it. She is female and bears the waters of life and measures them passively and reassuringly. Her passive presence softens the drama of the cards that surround her. Temperance mediates and restores the extremes of the emerging self and regulates the unfolding of the past.

. . . Temperance gone wrong is an irritant. Someone who constantly burdens the weak with unwanted help, forcing flowing, unresolved situations into negative conclusions.

THE DEVIL

Another powerful image. Temperance has put the seeker in touch with his higher self. He is now a 'spiritual grown up'. It is his time to look even deeper than ever before. The useless identity that Death cut down at card

XIII had a root. And this is the root. The Devil himself must be confronted. A potentially deadly encounter, for The Devil only fights battles he knows he will win. For the first time, there is a very real possibility of failure. This is the turning point of magic, for defeat may bring great worldly power to the loser and victory is unimaginable. The seeker confronts not only his own devil but the negative energies of the whole world. He must comprehend and integrate his wildest and most profound chaotic energies if his evolution is to continue. The card's number is XV (15) reducing to 6, the number of resolution. The darkness of his shadow is only as strong as the brightness of the light that causes it! But does he know this? This is the battle he has longed for. The forces at stake are the primal energies that turn the world itself. There can be no defeat.

THE TOWER

Number XVI (16) reduces to 7, a number that denotes power. A thunderball blasts off the top of a solid stone tower. The battle with The Devil ceases in one profound moment of understanding. The light of true perception devastates the edifice of understanding on which the seeker stood so confidently. At last, the light breaks through. It is an awesome light that strikes all ignorance and cares nothing for the concepts and frailties of the individual. The Devil is seen for what it is – neither good nor bad – and the effect of this realization is shattering. A gateway leading to the ultimate goal suddenly opens. The battle against the will is over. No material structure can stand before the raw power of the full glare of the divine light . . .

. . . Some cannot accept the realization of the Devil's true nature and become trapped in a cage of inflexible dogma and neurotic compassion.

THE STAR

The seeker is no longer guided from within. He is given a sign, a hint of the sustained enlightenment of which he has so far only tasted a flash. In due time, The Star tells him, he will reach his destination. It is the call of destiny that grants hope of fulfilment after the devastation of The Tower. Stars were believed to be gods. After the realization of The Tower, God can be the seeker's last and only aspiration. The Star hints at immortality and pours forth new water on the Earth in a symbol of gentle encouragement. Hope of ultimate fulfilment and the most natural and gentle motivation are the mood of this picture. After the storm comes peace, refreshment and new hope. The number is XVII (17) = 8, the number of renewal and rebirth. The Star has no prejudices, expectations or morals

and she beckons continually. It would be hard to avoid seeing such a bright celestial light or, having seen it, fail to respond. . .

. . . Complacency and ignorance are the prerogatives of those who cannot see the purity of her light.

THE MOON

The Moon is the last obstacle the Hero must overcome. The lesson of The Hanged Man and The Devil have been understood. Now, the all-attractive Moon must be experienced. XVIII $(1+8)=9$, the last of the single numbers. The card carries a strange, lonely and disturbing image. Sanity and every perception of reality are at stake. This is not the benign lunar mother of popular astrology. The fatal pull of the lunar will passively threatens to envelop and extinguish life itself. Is The Moon the home of the dead? What lies on its terrible darker side? Who can resist the subtle and insidious magic of The Moon? She is the great illusion, bland and powerful: devouring and unstable, she fascinates and hypnotizes even the purest soul. All the secrets of the night are revealed beneath her watery second-hand light. On the card, she seems to pull the crayfish, the dogs and all things upwards and towards her. All is illusion and in her realm nothing fits with anything else. The Hero must resist without will; understand without reason; and proceed without direction or effort. Anything less and he will be left, drained and deluded, in the lunar night . . .

. . . The Moon is the nightmare before the dawn. The nightmare cannot be fought. The soul can only hope to wake up.

THE SUN

Its number is XIX, and $1+9=10$, which equals the symbol of unity out of multiplicity. The Sun dawns and the night of deception is ended. Even The Star is eclipsed. The seeker has true understanding at last. He has achieved the highest attainment. The Sun contains the ultimate power of the soul as it shines down on the new-born hero. His being is in a garden, dancing and basking in the glory of his innocence. The card is in two halves with a barrier in between. The sun shines benignly down, showering all the gifts of life on the infant who is safely enclosed by the walls of the garden. The Sun child will grow to even greater understanding in time . . .

. . . But at a worldy level, this card can be a reminder of those who refuse to mature beyond their senses.

JUDGEMENT

At last – the final call. Until now, the seeker has striven and achieved, struggled and overcome. On this card he is called. The number of the card is XX (20) – meaning the duality of 2 on a higher level. The judgement is the moment when the seeker is invited to let go of all his attainments, including the path itself. He has taken many forms and has won much knowledge on the path. With the Judgement, he is summoned to dissolve his individuality. The journey is at an end. He has knocked on the door and now it is being opened. When he enters, his self will disappear.

. . . At a mundane level, the negative side of this card speaks of lost opportunity and unheeded calls.

THE WORLD

A mandala; the symbol of perfection. A being dances blissfully within it. Outside it are symbols of protection (traditionally a lion, a bull, an eagle and an angel). The card's number is XXI, 21, which reduces to 3, the number of synthesis and creation. There is a suggestion of the foetus in the womb. The World is the culmination of the journey of the Tarot.

So there you have it. A guide to the feel of the symbols behind the major arcana. The best way to get to grips with each one is to leave the cards lying around in the figure 8 shape I demonstrated earlier. Pick them out, one at a time, then read the appropriate section. If you find any discrepancies or irregularities or any gaps in your understanding at all, try not to let them worry you. Just like the evolution of the soul in the Tarot, your learning will unfold in its own time, spurred on by the excitement of discovery. Anyway, too tight an understanding early on may actually block you from opening up to new and wider understandings.

Reading The Cards

I'm putting off the business of telling fortunes with the Tarot pack until later in this chapter. Frankly, until you have developed a grasp of at least some of the major arcana, the process of reading a spread probably won't work for you. Bad news, but true. You simply will not trust yourself to say what the cards are telling you to say!

So look at the cards on your own for a while. First put your own conscious mind in touch with the cards and let them stimulate your inner feelings. Believe me, they will, and when the moment comes for you to open your mouth and speak you will be amazed by what a lot you've got to say! Thoughts like 'Did I know all that?' or 'Where did that come from?' will doubtless cross your mind after the reading.

After you've read about a card, here is an exercise you can do to increase your understanding of individual cards of the Tarot. It takes the form of a period of gentle meditation on the card of your choice. As some people find the word meditation a bit daunting or off-putting, let me put it this way: instead of sitting thinking about the bills, or your lost lover, you should sit quietly down and try to focus your mind from time to time on the symbols of the Tarot. It's called scrying – give it a try.

1 Sit down comfortably and prop up the card at reading distance in front of you, slightly to one side. Place it in such a position that you have to turn very slightly in order to concentrate on it. When setting this up, try to avoid the temptation to rush round the room making adjustments to things in an effort to make your environment perfect.

2 Get comfortable. Relax. Look straight ahead of you and totally ignore the card. Let your thoughts run, or try to meditate, if you know how. Listen to the neighbour's lawn mower or the sound of the TV downstairs. Count your own teeth with your tongue. Mentally do anything you want, but don't look at the card – and keep facing forward. The idea is to be relaxed and mentally concentrated on something simple and immediate.

3 Now take a glance at the card. Hold your glance for a very short time, then quickly go back to ignoring it again. A glimpse is all you want. Now go back to your meditation/daydream/counting.

4 Repeat this process for as long as you can stand it! (1–2 minutes?)

5 Move the card to the other side of centre so that you have to turn your head the other way to catch a glimpse of it. Ignore it completely for a while (stare at a point on the wall straight in front of you), as before. Then begin the glancing. Once again, do this for as long as you feel comfortable (or sane!).

6 Now put the card directly in front of you and imagine that it is a huge picture and you are going to walk into it. As you enter it, let it come to life. Stand in your new kingdom and look around you. Stretch your imagination like you used to as a child. Have a look round, behind and inside things. What is there? Speak to the characters. What do they say? Let the events of the card unfold. What happens next? Take something into the picture with you and ask the character on the card what they think about it. What do they tell you? Perhaps take a walk into a part of the card that is not actually depicted. What is there? Let your imagination rip.

These are some of the ways your imagination may go. They are merely suggestions.

The process may only last a few seconds, and it's not one that you will be able to force in any way. So take it easy on this last visualizing step of the exercise or you will bore yourself to death, staring at a piece of card!

7 When you've had enough, don't leap up and start tidying up. Tidy your imagination up first. Be slow. Take it very easy at this point. Shrink the card back to its original size in your imagination. Climb out of it (mentally) and have a stretch and a yawn. Clap your hands or whistle the national anthem or do anything to wake yourself up from your little daydream. Now tidy up.

That's all there is to it. Believe it or not, results will come in their own time and in their own way.

If you find it hard to set aside some time and space, here is an alternative. Read the exercise through once to get the gist and then make up your own version. Perhaps stick the card you want to understand on your mirror or put it by the telephone or somewhere where you will see it. Over the course of a few days you will catch its meaning, or some feeling will be evoked. However, withdrawing to a quiet place on your own and looking at the card in a concentrated way will probably give a clearer and quicker result.

Fortune Telling with The Tarot

At last – the juicy bit! I'm sure there's a part of every one of us that wants to know the future. As with all magic, even if you've only skimmed through the previous section and had one go at the visualization exercise you qualify to try to read the Tarot. So pluck up your courage and have a go. There are – literally – hundreds of traditions to be observed if you want to be correct about it. If your temperament inclines you towards learning the time-honoured way, or if you want to know exactly which direction to face, or what type of incense to burn – if all these things help you keep in touch with a past where somehow there is inspiration for you – well, then I'm afraid it's another trip to the library or a bookstore. None of these extras in themselves will affect your ability as a diviner in any way. Magic is already in you, so use anything, any ritual or any absence of ritual to help you explore your own powers. If you want to fulfil your pre-conceived ideas, I'm afraid you will need to find another book. If you want to experience magic – read on!

The method I am about to describe is a guide. It contains elements of profound magic and psychic common sense, and it will provide a simple basis for an exciting voyage of discovery for both participants in the reading.

The two participants are the querant (the one who is asking the question) and the diviner (that's you! – the Tarot magician).

What to Do (and What Not to Do)

Find some time (one hour at least) and find some privacy. (Extremely friendly spectators might be OK; others will definitely distract and disperse your concentration.) Though you may be excited about your new-found understanding and naturally want to demonstrate it, you had better resist the temptation to make Tarot reading your party piece. There are two simple, good earthly reasons for this. (a) Because you're putting a strain on your intuition at an early phase when you can least afford to, and (b) because you can't win! Think about it. If you make an inaccurate reading in public you may be considered at best a kind of buffoon. But worse still! Make an accurate reading and you'll probably be considered a sort of *threatening* buffoon. Who wants to be either?

1 Form a Bond With Your Cards

Traditionally, it is recommended that your keep your cards in a silk cloth (dark coloured) and spread them out on it to stop them touching anything except your hands and the cloth. No one else should handle the cards except perhaps the querant. If you can do this, without going absolutely beserk when someone else *does* touch them (or even merely tries to in some cases), do so. It is a good ritual and it engenders a feeling of purity and concentration. If not, just leave them in the box and simply try to stop the kids from building houses out of them.

2 Ask The Querant To Give You His Attention

As the diviner you are the guest speaker and it's your show – but you do need a willing and attentive audience to spur you on. Remind him or her that he/she must try not to giggle too much. As the reading progresses, you will find that the querant will be only too keen to listen to you. Once you're rolling you'll be as interested and amazed by what you're saying as he is.

Use any ritual or absence of ritual to make yourself comfortable. When people meet for any purpose there are certain small rituals that we can use to break the ice and generally make people feel more at ease with each other. A Tarot reading is no exception. Do whatever makes you comfortable in terms of lighting, incense (if any), cups of tea, etc.

It is much easier to be relaxed when doing a Tarot reading than the beginner might expect. The reason is simply that you've got something to concentrate on – i.e. the cards themselves. The cards will provide a meeting point and a common ground for you and the querant, and they will be a resting place for both of you in the silences. This is a good thing and if possible you should try to heighten this gentle concentration in any way you can. When you handle your cards or turn them over, try to do it in a flowing sort of way. Use your hands as gracefully as possible as your querant will be affected by the feel of your movements. You'll probably find it strange at first, having someone looking so closely at your hands and listening so attentively to your voice, but you will soon pick up confidence. By the end of your first reading you will have learned how to keep your querant's attention by simply trusting your intuition, being yourself and letting the cards set the pace.

3 A Golden Rule

You are about to read another person's destiny. They have come to you, albeit in a light-hearted way, to gain some insight into themselves and their problems. In a word – they want you to help them. They are relying on you not to use your understanding of the cards to abuse or hurt them. So please let me give you a golden rule. BE VERY GENTLE.

Inevitably, during a reading, you will say something that the querant has felt deep inside for a long time, but has never been able to put into words. When you suddenly express the very thing that they have been only vaguely feeling for years, they will react. This reaction will make you feel powerful, and somehow wise. You will sense that you have influenced them and taught them something. It is at this time that *you* must learn *your* lesson. Be humble, be wise and learn to be very gentle. Remember, your readings are at first not a lot more than experiments. Be positive to your querant. The Tarot symbols will give even the novice a tremendous intuitive advantage over a person who has never reflected on them, and they will also put the querant in a very receptive mood indeed. Do not abuse the situation. Conduct your reading humbly, like a student. Tell your querant what you are learning from the cards and let him come to his own conclusions. Be specific and positive, trust your intuition and be firm if you like. But remember – be very gentle.

How to Lay Out a Tarot Spread

All the following spreads use the major and the minor arcana. (i.e. all 78 cards.)

The minor arcana is made up of 56 cards divided into four suits. The suits are *Batons* (rods, wands, etc.), *Cups* (coups), *Swords* (épées, espadas), *Coins* (pentacles, deniers, discs).

Each suit has four court cards – the King, the Queen, the Knight and the Knave. It also has ten small cards labelled from ace to 10. Once again, don't be put off by discrepancies in labels. Get used to your own pack.

The minor arcana has a feel of its own. It is generally used for fortune telling, rather than for meditation and self-awareness purposes. If your minor arcana has pictures on it, you can use it for meditation in the same way as the major arcana. As there are so many cards to understand, I think the best way to get to know the minor arcana is by repeated reference and experience. After a while you will get feel of each of the four separate suits and from that point you will eventually begin to learn the meaning of each individual card (see pages 112 to 115).

The court cards of each suit are usually interpreted as humans rather than influences. See them as actual people who exist in the life of the querant and who are particularly relevant (or who will become relevant) to his situation, problem or personality. For divinatory meanings, see pages 110 to 112.

Cards that are upside down from your position as the reader of the spread are called 'reversed'. They take on a negative or delayed feeling.

The Celtic Cross

1 The first thing the diviner must do is to choose the significator. This is a card chosen from the court cards of the minor arcana. The significator is a pictorial representation of the person who is asking the question. Either a King, Queen, Knight, Knave or one of the suits. The purpose of this card is to get the querant to form a relationship with it and for it to be a visual point of concentration within the spread of cards before him. Choose a card that you think is suitable, but if the querant has a preference accept his or her choice. Use your judgement confidently along the following lines:

For a man, choose a King or a Knight according to maturity and general bearing.

A woman – a Queen.

Children and young people of either sex – traditionally Knaves.*

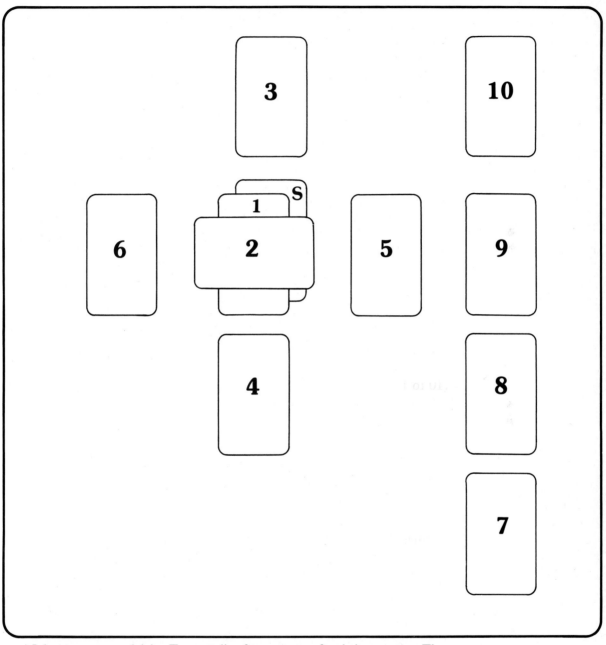

* I do not recommend doing Tarot reading for youngsters for obvious reasons. They are unformed and very prone to taking even the most gently expressed opinions of older people as unchangeable facts. Similarly, strongly held adult insights about a child's personality can easily be projected on to the child by the adult and thus actually contribute to forming the innocent child's nature. Whole areas of potential growth could be prematurely blocked off for the child this way.

The choice of an appropriate suit is very flexible. Either read the descriptions of the males and females of each suit and choose the one that is the closest fit, or choose according to the colouring and feel of the person, along these lines:

Batons – medium colouring and a good intellect.

Cups – fair and friendly.

Swords – darker and stern.

Coins – very dark and down-to-earth.

If you're still not sure, choose according to the Element of the querant's moon sign (see page 307). Air = Batons; Water = Cups; Fire = Swords; Earth = Coins.

Once you have chosen a significator, place it face up in front of you.

2 Shuffle the cards yourself. Then ask the querant to shuffle the pack thoroughly. Let him do it in his own way and reassure him that he is doing it right. Ask him to jumble the cards as much as he wants and cut the pack as often as he likes until he feels happy. He does not need to speak aloud any question he might have. In fact, the querant does not have to have a question as such at all. General feeling will do.

3 Pick up the deck, face downwards. Turn over the top card (side to side, not top end to bottom) and place it, face upwards, right on top of the significator. Say to yourself (mentally) as you do this, 'This covers him (or her)'. This is card number 1. Now lay out the following nine cards one at a time, face upwards, according to the illustration. As you put each card down, say to yourself the appropriate thought for each card. Save the interpretation until all the cards are down.

Card 1 'This covers him (or her).' It represents the circumstances and general atmosphere that surrounds the question. It is the aura of the question.

Card 2 (laid sideways but always read right way up): 'This crosses him (or her).' This card shows the influences working against the querant. Opposing forces good or bad.

Card 3 'This is beneath him.' Shows the basis of the matter. The root or hidden subconscious background to the situation or person. It is a thing that exists already as part of the matter or the querant.

Card 4 'This is behind him.' This card shows the broad events and influences which existed in the past.

Card 5 'This crowns him.' This card represents an influence that *may* come into being. It is a possible outcome if the present trend continues.

Card 6 'This is before him.' This shows the influence that will operate in the near future.

Card 7 'He fears.' This card represents the fears and negative feelings that the querant has on the matter.

Card 8 'He is in the house of.' This card represents the situation as it appears to others. The opinions and influence of the querant's friends and family.

Card 9 'He wishes.' Represents the hopes and ideals of the querant. What he would like to happen in the situation.

Card 10 'This is how it will be.' The outcome of the effects of all the other cards. It contains, in essence, the answer to the question.

The lay-out of the cards is complete. The spread is in front of you, ready to be read in more detail. You will be glad that you went to the trouble of saying to yourself the thoughts for each card as you put them down as this will act as a guide and general reminder to your memory.

4 Look up each card, one at a time, in the reference section. As you progress through the cards you may start to see causes and possible connections between the elements before you. Point them out to the querant. Talk openly and tell him (or her) of the influences you see in the cards. Ask the occasional question. Guide him through the map of his life, using your understanding and intuition as the key. Let the querant speak if he wants to. Querants can often help when your inspiration has dried up. And one final thing – don't be afraid to start sentences when you don't know how they are going to finish.

5 Sometimes the final card can be one from which no conclusion can be drawn. It will take a little experience and courage to decide this, but sometimes – not often – you just know that the final card is out of place. If this happens, take the final card and use it as a significator for one more reading. Do the whole process again, including shuffling and cutting as before. This should throw some light on the subject and can often help. If it doesn't, simply put the cards away and try again another day.

Tarot divining – like any other form of divination – is not a guaranteed thing. It's like using the phone. All you can do is pick it up and call the right number. If there is no reply – well, that's the end of it. You'll just have to try later on. There's no question of blame or failure.

Circular Spread

This reading can be used to get an idea of the general direction of things to come on the individual days of the coming week. It can also be employed, using 12 cards, to divine the trend of the months of the coming year. Shuffle the cards yourself, then ask the querant to do so in the usual way (see page 100). Starting at the 9 o'clock position, lay out the appropriate number of cards (seven or 12) in an anti-clockwise direction. They can be laid face up or face down. Now place the next card in the middle of the circle. This middle card is the most important and should be read first. It gives the overriding flavour of the coming week or year.

Read the cards one at a time in the order in which you put them down (turning them sideways to face up if necessary, of course!).

Imagine the cards as standing on a circle. The centre of the circle is *down*. So cards with their base inwards are the right way up and those with their base outwards are reversed.

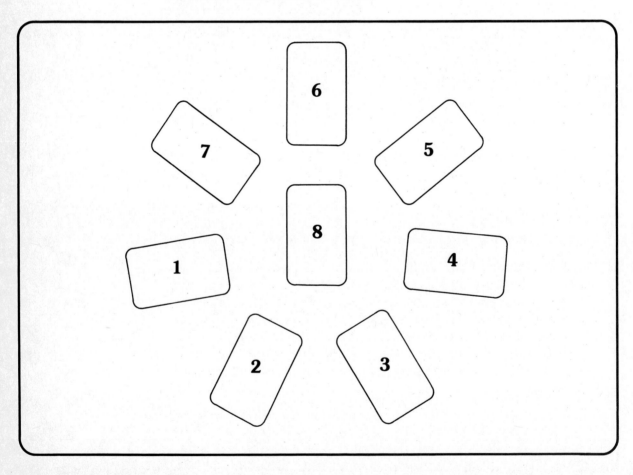

The Horseshoe Spread

This is a good spread to use when you require an answer to a specific question (as opposed to an understanding of a personality or complex situation). Shuffle the cards yourself, then ask the querant to shuffle them in the usual way. Take the pack and deal out the top seven cards face up as in the diagram.

Card 1   Past influences.
Card 2   Present circumstances of querant.
Card 3   General future conditions.
Card 4   Best policy for querant to follow.
Card 5   Opinions and attitudes of others.
Card 6   Obstacles standing in the way of a solution.
Card 7   The probable final outcome.

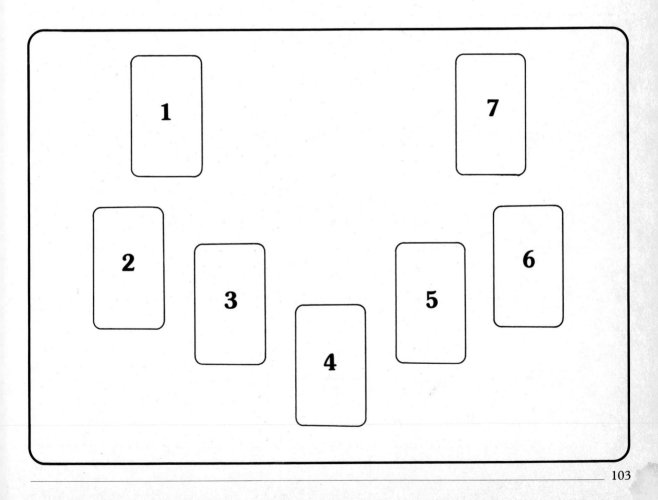

The Nine Card Spread

There is an element of suspense in this spread. Shuffle the pack in your usual way and ask the querant to do the same. Take the deck and deal out the top nine cards. Lay them out *face downwards* as in the diagram. Turn them over and interpret them one by one. (Once again, be sure to turn them over side by side, not end over end or you will be reversing them as you turn them over!)

Card 1   The most salient feature of the querant's present circumstances.

Card 2   The highest that the querant can attain at this time.

Card 3   The background to the situation. Matters that are hidden or subconscious.

Card 4   Past causes of the present situation.

Card 5   What may happen if everything carries on as it is going.

Cards 6, 7, 8, and 9   The probable direction of the immediate future, card 6 being the events nearest the time of the reading, and card 9 more distant events. The time scale is in weeks or months – not years.

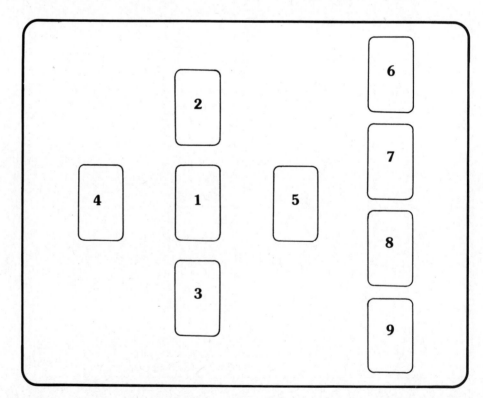

The Tree of Life

This is, in a way, the opposite of the Horseshoe method mentioned earlier. The Tree of Life is best used when a general picture of the complexities of an individual personality is required, rather than a specific answer to a specific question. In its oldest from the Tree of Life is a very complex spread requiring considerable experience, as it needs the interpretation of

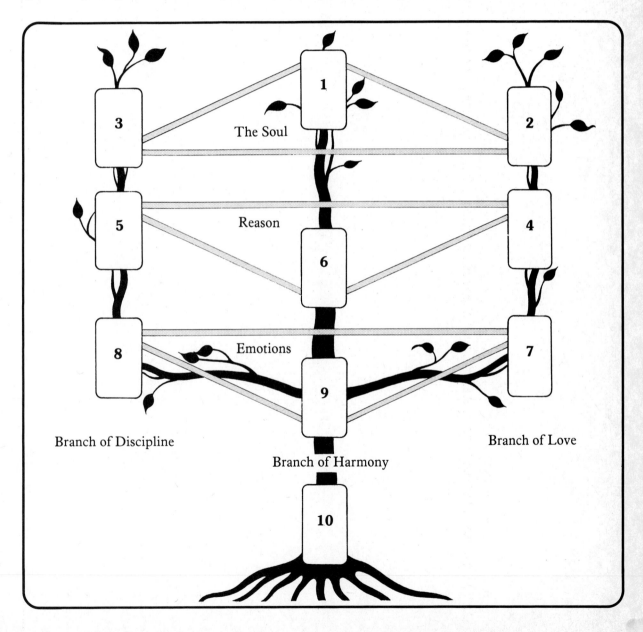

The Soul

Reason

Emotions

Branch of Discipline

Branch of Harmony

Branch of Love

all 78 cards. Given here is a perfectly valid miniaturized version of the original. Notice that the spread is made up of three triangles, a root card and a 'qualifying pack'. Triangle 1, pointing upwards, represents spirituality, the highest ideal of the querant. Triangle 2, pointing downwards, represents the intellectual and normal nature of the querant. Triangle 3, pointing downwards also, represents the querant's subconscious; his intuition, inner desires and motives.

When using this method, try to respond to the cards as they affect each other in their groups. Though each card tells a story in itself, the group of three cards weaves a much more subtle tale. Let your intuition play lightly on the individual cards of the group until a strong composite picture builds up for that triangle.

1 Choose an appropriate significator and shuffle the cards in your usual way. Place the significator high at the top of the table. Now lay out the first ten cards from the top of the pack face upwards as in the diagram.

Card	**1**	The querant's highest nature.	
Card	**2**	The creative force. The father card.	THE SOUL
Card	**3**	Wisdom. The mother card.	

Card	**4**	Virtues. Good qualities.	
Card	**5**	Conquest. Intellect or physical force.	REASON
Card	**6**	Spirit of sacrifice. Health.	

Card	**7**	Love, lust, the qualities of Venus.	
Card	**8**	Procreation, arts and crafts.	EMOTIONS
Card	**9**	Imagination, creative mental and physical force.	

Card	**10**	This card represents the body of the querant or his home.

2 Now deal the next seven cards face downwards and place them to the left (as in the diagram). This small pack of seven cards is called the qualifying pack. Put the remainder of the pack to one side.

The cards in the qualifying pack refer to the future and to the aspects of the querant's personality which are about to unfold. The story contained in these seven cards should not be read until the other cards have been interpreted as fully as possible. As you can see from the diagram, the Tree of Life has three branches. The cards on the branch of 'discipline' should be read uncompromisingly and fairly literally.

The cards on the branch of 'harmony' should be read in a spirit of moderation and compromise. The cards on the branch of 'love' should be read in a spirit of love and compassion.

A Few Points on Reading The Cards

I am deliberately not giving these points in any order of importance or priority. They are simply for you to bear in mind when you are reading a Tarot spread. Interpreting the Tarot cards is a highly individual process and things like how to talk to your querant, what to say, when to say it and what to look for are almost impossible to write about with any sincerity, as they depend on so many millions of variable factors. To the beginner, they may seem like vital questions which must be answered conclusively before he/she can start. They are not. Simply go straight ahead and do your version of what you think is right, based on your understanding at that moment. This is the easiest way to gain experience in Tarot reading as in all the intuitive arts. If you read this section every now and again you will probably find that you have learned many of the points, without realizing that you have already read about them.

★ The question, if one is expressed, may only be a starting point. You do not have to answer it. Each reading goes its own way.

★ Look at the cards in relation to each other. The meanings of some cards are heightened or lessened by being next to others.

★ Cards of the major arcana in a spread are of extra significance. Interpret them at the level that you think is suitable.

★ Notice a predominance of one suit or another in the spread. Also look for patterns of suits.
  Batons are about enterprise, action, possibilities and change.
  Cups are about emotions, higher feelings, good news.
  Swords are about conflict, intellect and struggle.
  Coins are about money and material matters.

★ Feel free to refer to books and references and to look up meanings. It is not a sign of ineptitude but of interest.

★ Feel free to disagree with written interpretations and rules. If your feeling for a card goes against what you see in print, simply follow your feeling and ignore the written guide. Ultimately, your experience will guide you.

★ Be careful when telling people about the future. Remember – *absolutely nothing* is definite in this world until it actually happens!!

★ Avoid giving personal advice. Simply speak what the cards tell you.

★ Be gentle and positive with people who come to you for readings. They are often much more interested in what the cards say about them than they pretend to be.

★ Avoid the temptation to do the cards over and over again until you get a result that you like.

★ Batons and Swords are male, Cups and Coins are female.

★ You do not have to interpret reversed cards as negative. If you prefer, just treat every card as though it were the right way up. You'll find the true story still gets told.

★ Sometimes a card simply 'looks right' or perhaps 'looks wrong' for no justifiable reason.

★ Don't be in a hurry to finish the reading. Even when it seems to be over, leave it spread out for a bit longer and see what happens.

The Major Arcana – Divinatory Meanings

These fortune telling interpretations should be strengthened and modified by the reader's own personal understanding of the deeper meanings of the major arcana. Refer to the earlier part of the chapter if you feel you need clarification.

The Fool   Unexpected influence of some significance needs dealing with. Handled well, it can lead to success. In a weak context, it can warn of the possibility of error. Also the start of a new cycle, or the influence of a 'creative dreamer'. *Reversed*: Recklessness and lack of forethought will cause major problems. Instability.

Magician   Self confidence and willpower. Expansion and initiative. A willingness to adapt and take risks all lead to success. The start of the new cycle. *Reversed*: Loss of nerve and hesitation. Failure to confront the situation.

High Priestess   Revelation and new insight. Intuitive possibilities. A new perspective comes to light. Inspiration. Also perhaps, the presence of a wise woman in the situation. *Reversed*: Emotional instability. Negative female influences. Problems resulting from lack of good advice.

Empress   Fruitfulness. Domestic ability. Pleasures of the senses and satisfaction connected with nature. Growth and the establishment of a firm footing. *Reversed*: Domestic disturbance. Negative maternal energies. Paranoia and isolation. Poverty.

Emperor   Willpower, authority, creative energy. The weight of experience. An influential person with power to assist. *Reversed*: Weakness and subservience. Failure of ambition.

Pope   Morality. Good advice. Disclosure of facts. The comfort of established religion. A person who throws light on the subject. *Reversed*: Bad advice. Deliberated half truths. Chicanery and sophistry.

The Lovers   Time to choose. A time for an instinctive decision. Sudden insight. *Reversed*: Temptation and difficult decisions. Vacillation.

The Chariot   Successful solutions to problems and obstacles. Progress through personal initiative. *Reversed*: Inconsideration, oppression and egomania.

Justice   An appraisal. A verdict. Just deserts. Arbitration and negotiation. *Reversed*: Injustice, legal wrangling and delay. Unfairness. Bias and prejudice.

Hermit   A time to withdraw and weigh matters up. A warning against unpredictable actions. Consider and be cautious. Wise advice from a competent counsellor. Discretion. *Reversed*: Rejection of sound advice and much-needed help. Unjustified suspicion.

Wheel of Fortune   Benign act of destiny. A sense of inevitable and fruitful unfolding. The beginning of a new cycle. Reaping what has been sown (usually good). *Reversed*: A turn for the worse which must be endured until the wheel has turned full circle. The end of an era.

Fortitude   An opportunity is there for the taking. A risk may pay off. The subduing of negative tendencies. Reconciliation with an enemy. *Reversed*: Loss of will. Letting go to negative urges.

The Hanged Man   Willingness to surrender to conscience and intuition. Adaptive abilities. Sacrifice. *Reversed*: Over-reliance on material consideration.

Death   Renewal. A major change – often positive but requiring a clearing away of the old situation. *Reversed*: Inertia. Unexpected change. Forced removal of something that should have been abandoned willingly.

Temperance   Success through patient harmonizing of restless forces. A partnership or friendship. *Reversed*: A poorly handled opportunity.

The Devil   Integration of wilder energies into constructive uses. *Reversed*: Release from bondage. Unhealthy repression of feelings.

The Tower   Sudden change. The apparent indifference of fate in handing out misfortune. *Reversed*: Continued oppression. Unnecessary suffering. An ongoing rut.

The Star   Optimism. Bright futures and promise of fulfilment. Broadening horizons. *Reversed*: Frustration. Narrow-mindedness. Resistance to opportunity and change.

The Moon   A caution against error caused by self-deception or trickery. A crisis calling for personal integrity. *Reversed*: A minor crisis easily avoided. Loss of nerve. Exploitation of another.

The Sun   Accomplishment and success against all odds. Acclaim at last. Warmth, sincerity, contentedness. *Reversed*: Miscalculation and failure. Ill-gotten success unmasked. Imagined success.

Judgement   Rebirth. An outcome in one's favour. A restoring of health. A pay-off in a situation. *Reversed*: Guilt. Reproach. Delay. Alienation of affection.

The World   The final culmination of success. The end of a cycle of destiny. Completion and fulfilment at all levels. *Reversed*: Disappointment, failure of will and misdirection of energies.

The Minor Arcana – The Court Cards

Batons

The King of Batons   Heroic, just and brave. A noble family man with a virile and passionate side. He is a tower of strength and a good mediator. Quick to act but sometimes indecisive. He can be autocratic, cold and intolerant.

Queen of Batons   A creative, outgoing woman. Intelligent and loving. She protects her home and the natural world. She has authority, charm and popularity. She can be over-bearing and clinging, given to unprovoked venom.

Knight of Batons   Intuitive and fast-acting. He does the right thing though it may look doubtful at the time. He is charming and attractive. He can be a hell-raiser and a stirrer, given to provoking arguments.

Knave of Batons   An able and ambitious representative. A bringer of good news and exciting information. Willing and active in the service of his masters. He can be slanderous – a 'big mouth' with ideas above his station.

Cups

The King of Cups   Worldly wise and sharp witted. He negotiates himself expertly into positions of power. His agile mind grasps changing situations and turns them skilfully to fulfil his ambitions. He is discreet, self contained and inscrutable. He inspires respect rather than affection. He can be treacherous and amoral – callously leading others astray.

Queen of Cups   Artistic and imaginative. She has an ethereal beauty about her. Her intuition is faultless. She has a romantic and affectionate outlook. She is very receptive to those around her. She can be fickle, frivolous and vapid, exploiting her fatal fascination.

Knight of Cups   Enthusiastic and congenial. He brings new ideas and opportunities. He is open, refined and artistic but bores very quickly. He is highly motivated but weak. He can be carried away by his own enthusiasm, making wild and empty promises. He is a fraud.

Knave of Cups   A young introvert. Highly aware and articulate. He has a deep understanding of himself and his advice often turns out right. He can be a dilettante, given to intellectual hoarding and private scheming.

Swords

King of Swords   Mental, rational yet inventive. An advocate of order and organization. Authoritative yet still versatile, sometimes too versatile. Young in spirit. He can be cruel and calculating in pursuit of his intellectual roles.

Queen of Swords   She is intelligent and perceptive and she misses nothing. Artistic and meticulous, she is quick to see any opportunity to further her cause. She can be devious with a cutting tongue. Subtle and insidious.

Knight of Swords   A warrior and man of action. Forceful in crisis and confrontation. Where he appears there is a battle to be fought and won. He can be headstrong, impulsive and lacking in staying-power.

Knave of Swords   Shrewd and alert. He is a gifted diplomat and negotiator on others' behalf. A clear thinker and an eloquent tongue. He can be sycophantic, subtle and treacherous.

Coins

King of Coins   Steady and solid. Skilled in practical and down-to-earth matters. Material and positive, he attracts the things of the world. A loyal man of few words. Devoted and cautious in love; implacable in hatred. He can be ignorant and dull. Blind to refinement and resentful of any change. Money can buy him and he can be led.

Queen of Coins   Generous and compassionate. She is the wise and practical woman with a love of comfort and the good life. She has no need for fine words and ideas. She rules her ample domain with warmth and generosity but she can be grasping and aquisitive, protecting her self indulgent narrow-mindedness with excess and display.

Knight of Coins   A man of practical virtues and protector of conventional morals who will defend them to the end. His code of honour can make him stern and smug – or even set him tilting at windmills.

Knave of Coins   Worthy and steadfast in his duty, he is proud of his responsibility. He has good business and administrative sense. He can be pompous and dull witted, getting lost in details and small matters.

The Minor Arcana – Ace-10

Batons

Ace of Batons   Primal energy – positive power. Origination. New beginnings. Inspiration. Strength and enthusiasm. *Reversed*: Over confidence and arrogance. Barrenness. Impotence.

2 of Batons   Dominion. A firm will brings authority and honest success. Power used responsibly. Courage and initiative. *Reversed*: Relentless determination. Power at any price. Corruption and futility.

3 of Batons   New ideas put into practice. Inspiration is rewarded. Dreams become reality. *Reversed*: Crippling idealism. Frustration, resulting in pipe dreams. Disregard for practicalities.

4 of Batons   Intellectual achievement. Beauty, elegance, refinement. Creative brilliance. *Reversed*: Superficial decadence. Snobbery. Artistic emptiness.

5 of Batons   Challenge demanding great mental agility. A battle of wits. Necessary conflict requires struggle to succeed. *Reversed*: Loss caused by deceit. Unnessary conflicts.

6 of Batons   Victory. A major triumph. Good news. Skill and diplomacy bring success. *Reversed*: Delay. Uncertainty of outcome. Suspicion and circumspection.

7 of Batons   Courage required to fulfil potential. Victory against all odds through individual effort. *Reversed*: Hesitation and indecision resulting in lost opportunity. Embarrassment and unmasking.

8 of Batons   Events are moving. Delays are ended. It is time to act. Opening negotiations. Travel abroad. *Reversed*: Projects rashly undertaken. Impetuousness spoils the opportunity.

9 of Batons   Great strength. Nothing can stand against you. Your position is impregnable. Stability. *Reversed*: Dogma and inflexibility. Unnecessary delay.

10 of Batons   Oppression. Overbearing will. Repressive and negative use of resources. Power as an end in itself. *Reversed*: Deliberate and destructive dishonesty.

Cups

Ace of Cups   The female nurturing force. Fruitfulness. Creation and protection. Faithfulness and feelings. *Reversed*: Stagnation and heartbreak.

2 of Cups   Love and harmony. Reconciliation and affinity. Arguments are resolved and peace reigns. *Reversed*: Disagreement and separation. A sincere offer rejected. Jealousy and indiscretion.

3 of Cups   The fruits of love. Joy from a birth or a marriage. Confidence. Abundance. *Reversed*: Selfish gratification. Emotional excess. Emptiness. Want.

4 of Cups   Happiness that has reached its peak. Now what? Enjoyment of the fruits of earlier achievement. Taking for granted. *Reversed*: Excess. Over-indulgence brings a bad situation.

5 of Cups   It was all going so well until now. Worry and loss. Reappraisal and a major adaptation can still bring success. *Reversed*: Fate strikes a blow and leaves you powerless. Unexpected complications.

6 of Cups   Well-earned fulfilment. Enjoyment of the fruits of past effort. A long dormant seed is awakening. *Reversed*: Indulgent nostalgia. Inability to adapt causes loss.

7 of Cups   Time of decision. A time for careful scrutiny. Great potential in the right choice. Introspection. Inspiration. *Reversed*: Wishful thinking. Inertia. Deception in love.

8 of Cups   Redirection of the affections. Altering of loyalties. A new perspective leading to growth. *Reversed*: Fecklessness. Unreasonable rejection. Abandoning a good thing simply out of impatience to move on.

9 of Cups   Contentment and inner joy. Goodwill and emotional well being all round. Affection and generosity. *Reversed*: Vanity and complacency. An over-indulgent attitude causing the holder to be exploited.

10 of Cups   A happy and secure situation. Perfect enjoyment and harmonious order. *Reversed*: Disruption. Perversity, cynical manipulation of moral values.

Swords

Ace of Swords   Success. Victory against all odds. Progress. Removal of obstacles. Power of intellect. *Reversed*: Uncontrolled destruction. Misuse of power. Enforced restriction.

2 of Swords   Peace restored. Equilibrium. Reconciliation of forces. A helping hand in times of strife. *Reversed*: Aggravation and deliberate disharmony. Betrayal. Deceit. Lack of self control.

3 of Swords   Necessary sorrow. Upheaval, separation and discord – for the purposes of improvement. *Reversed*: Quarrels and hostilities. Chaos and disorder. Loss of trust.

4 of Swords   Rest from strife. Harmony and order re-established. Recuperation and refreshment. *Reversed*: Loss of nerve. Fear of conflict. Enforced withdrawal.

5 of Swords   Defeat. Facing an inevitable loss. The swallowing of pride. Abandonment of a futile struggle. *Reversed*: Problems caused by dishonesty. A warning against deceit.

6 of Swords   A solution. The battle is won – but the war may continue. Retreat to a safe place? *Reversed*: False victory. The true problem must be confronted at its root and overcome.

7 of Swords   Avoid head-on confrontation. Success will come from steady planning and cunning strategy. *Reversed*: Giving up when success is in sight. Playing too safe.

8 of Swords   Difficulties and obstacles. Fate appears to be against you. Patient action and attention to detail bring success. *Reversed*: Wasted effort. Hard work and no reward. Frustration.

9 of Swords   Despair; disappointment. Cruelty; blind passion. Only acceptance brings strength and victory. *Reversed*: Misery, suffering, isolation.

10 of Swords   Downfall; disruption. A group or community setback. Things can get no worse; they can only get better! *Reversed*: False hope. An apparent solution turns out to be unworkable.

Coins

Ace of Coins   Sensual pleasure. Material security. Wealth, possessions and comforts. Stability. Endurance. *Reversed*: Greed. Indulgence. Materialism. Lack of imagination. Inflexibility.

2 of Coins   Harmonious change. Enlightened planning. Communications, good news, travel. Inspired material success. *Reversed*: Inconsistency. Wild optimism. Short-sighted indulgence in immediate pleasure.

3 of Coins   Business acumen rewarded. Success and approval. Sowing the seeds for a fruitful outcome. *Reversed*: Failed effort and valid criticism. Stubborn refusal to stop and listen.

4 of Coins   Total material success. Power and influence from wealth. Money smoothes the way. *Reversed*: Inability to let go. Over-cautious use of resources. Too much power in one place. Beaurocratic and uninspired.

5 of Coins   Poverty; financial worries. Money restrictions lead to growth elsewhere. Empty pockets but fuller friendships. *Reversed*: Present path cannot succeed. Past problems that could have been handled better.

6 of Coins   Well balanced accounts. Charity, philanthropy and money put to good use. *Reversed*: Extravagance. Careless use of money.

7 of Coins   Financial matters come to fruition. Avoid inaction or the opportunity will be lost. *Reversed*: Loss. Imagined financial worries. Hope that fizzles out.

8 of Coins   A material improvement. A chance to invest energy and reap great benefits. *Reversed*: Living for today at the expense of tomorrow.

9 of Coins   Prosperity and comfort. Intelligence and application bring unbegrudged rewards. *Reversed*: Wealth founded on others' misfortunes. Unstable and potentially dangerous.

10 of Coins   Material gains from family. Inherited wealth. Family traditions bring prosperity. *Reversed*: Oppressive family traditions. Entitlement disputes. Breaking up of an estate.

All things are held in all things. Let he who
would seek an answer look no further than
the end of his nose or the tip of his little
finger. Let him ask the earth beneath his feet
with understanding, and, as a tree, draw
forth life-sustaining knowledge from far and
wide. Ask with a pure heart and by your very
hand can the answer be returned, for the
innocent may know the way by pointing his
own finger!

The Art of Dowsing

WHY, oh why, should such an interesting subject have been given such an awful name? It reminds me of eccentric yokels with twigs in their hands searching for hidden waters.

And it seems that I'm not the only person who has reacted in this way over the years. In the early 20th century, someone coined the name radiesthesia for the same subject. This is an even more terrifying word, sounding like a kind of nuclear age disease. Then came rhabdomancy. Somehow that doesn't appeal either.

Dowsing is a pyschic tool which is not only used to discover secret wells on remote hillsides but to answer any question you care to pose, or to find anything from an aura to your lost car keys. Dowsing is simple and totally practical and anyone can do it. It works as well indoors as it does out, and you don't need to use the sacred willow or the mystic hazel twig – a home-made dowsing rod is fine. In fact, you don't need a rod at all – a pendulum will do. However, what you will need is a means of sensing the force of nature which contains the answer to your question. And that is your brain.

Dowsing – A Psychic Tool

There is a much more basic human principle involved in dowsing than at first meets the eye. The rustic in the field with his forked stick is simply one expression of a quality that everybody possesses. That is the God-given ability to send out thoughts and questions into the universe and to request answers back from it.

The idea seems very far-fetched to the modern mind, steeped as it is in the belief that information is stored in books or computer files. The possibility of the universe being in some way an enormous memory bank is a bold suggestion, but it is worth sympathetic consideration. Certain natural phenomena and simple laws have come to be misunderstood and to be regarded as 'supernatural.' The ordinary person no longer appreciates the fact that every tiny atom or event is connected to every other particle or event. However, separation is something only perceived by the rational mind – that 'clever dick' tip of the iceberg that receives so much attention in our modern world. The subtler mind sees no separation. It is, and always will be, aware that everything is a part of everything else. When this sense of oneness dawns on a person, they see absolutely no reason why they should not gently send out a few probes into the oneness that surrounds them and see what comes back.

We are so surprised when we accidentally charge into our larger nature and inadvertently score a bullseye with our intuition that we become frightened by it. We think that we have stepped into some dark area where we should not have gone. We feel that we have somehow cheated the system and had better keep quiet about it, or it will be the worse for us. Yet all around us in nature there are endless examples of miracles, simple acts of will that produce the most spectacularly accurate and inexplicable results. Salmon return to breed in the exact tributary where they were hatched. The golden plover can fly non-stop from Alaska to the Hawaiian islands with no landmarks to guide him. At a microscopic level, the simple amoeba (a one-cell, jelly-like animal) can extend a leg of itself from any point on its body to reach out for food – yet it has absolutely no muscle tissue! How are these things done? They are not rehearsed or worked on, nor are they explicable. They are done by simple life forms that have no need of any identity or overbrain, but are instead locked in perfect harmony with the whole natural order.

I'm sure you have heard a story similar to this one:

In October 1978, a cat in Australia walked over 1,000 miles in 12 months to reach its home. It happened when Kirsten Hicks, about to leave Adelaide with his parents on a long sea journey, arranged for his grandparents – 1,000 miles away on Queensland's gold coast – to look after his Persian cat while he was away.

When the family returned home, the grandparents had to tell Kirsten that his cat had disappeared and all their efforts to find it had failed. Kirsten and his parents made numerous inquiries themselves, but, after several weeks with no word or sign of the cat, Kirsten gave up all hope of seeing his pet again. A year after the cat had been taken to the grandparents it turned up on the doorstep of its old home.

Kirsten Hicks said at the time that although the cat's white coat was matted and filthy and its paws matted and bleeding, the cat was purring when he found it. Kirsten's father pointed out that to reach its home, the cat had travelled more than a thousand miles, crossing rivers, deserts, and a vast wilderness in the process. 'Not surprisingly,' he adds, 'it is still a little nervous. No wonder it doesn't stray more than a few yards into the garden.'

> Reported by Peter Hicks in *The Complete Book of Dowsing and Divining*.

This animal 'psi-awareness' is not a fact that *defies* explanation, it simply *needs* no explanation. It is quite normal! Humans, if they gave less attention to being excited or amazed by it, could regularly do just as well themselves and wouldn't have to walk the length and breadth of Australia to prove it! All of us have intuitive flashes when our subconscious breaks through. When you are dowsing, you merely make use of an external instrument to assist in penetrating the veil. Instead of one mighty, unexpected flash of intuition, dowsing expresses your psychic understanding through millions of tiny unconscious muscle contractions which affect the pendulum or dowsing rod you are holding. Experience then tells you what the rod is saying. If you care to try the exercises mentioned later, you will be able to feel for yourself. It is very exciting to watch yourself controlling but not controlling at the same time! Pretty soon, you will want to start asking questions about what is going on.

The Scientific Line

Scientifically, what is going on has been pretty well investigated. From Christopher Bird's book *Divining* comes this account of an experiment. I think it goes a long way towards clearing up any feelings of nervousness that a first-time dowser might have as he imagines magnetic forces taking control of the dowsing rod or pendulum and giving it a life of its own.

Dr Jan Merta constructed an electronic measuring instrument called an accelerometer which, when attached to a pocket-sized Y rod held in his hands in the dowsing mode, could record the rod's every movement through an extremely sensitive built-in crystal, including movements so slight or minimal that observers, unable to measure or detect them visually, believed that the rod was motionless. When the rod was under tension and moving in the hands of the dowser, its imperceptible motion was recorded on a strip chart as a wiggly line. When it lay still on a table, the record on the chart flattened out into a perfectly straight line. This was clear proof to Jan that the dowser's muscular contractions could move the rod even before he went searching for a target.

Merta next reasoned that one of the principal muscles involved in the rod's movement might be the *carpi-radialis flexor* in the wrist area of the forearm. To test this idea, he electrically wired this muscle to his apparatus to allow any contraction in it to be recorded on the chart together with any motion in the rod.

He began his experiment by having a technician pass a vial of water in front of his face that he could see it. This produced a reaction in both the muscle and the rod. The pen graph revealed clearly that the muscle contracted well before the rod responded to the same contraction. Since two squares on the tape's grid were the equivalent of a second of time, he concluded that the interval between the muscle's contraction and the rod's movement was about half a second. Merta was then blindfolded by the technician and the above experiment repeated with exactly the same result. The only difference being that he could not see the vial of water and thus had to be recording its presence in front of his line of sight extra-sensorily.

As a result of these and many other tests, Merta believes he has proved absolutely that dowsing devices react only after people operating them pick up a signal which stimulates a physiological reaction.

Success Stories

In dowsing we have a situation where our unconscious muscle movements are magnified and expressed in the movements of a stick or pendulum. But where is the magic in that? Well, think about it. Your pendulum or rod is giving you a direct, visible link to your subconscious and contained in your subconscious is the potential to move in time and space to any dimension. If you tune in to the movements of your dowsing rod or pendulum you are opening yourself up to the possibility of tuning in to information on anything in the whole universe. The number of successful dowsings suggests that this is true.

As a means of finding the unfindable, dowsing is an indisputable fact of life. The success stories are endless. The many cases I have come across all have the ring of truth and follow a similar pattern.

Person A cannot find something that he needs to find, either oil, buried treasure, enemy landmines or his own lost uncle. He tries all the modern, scientific means at his disposal but he gets no result. Finally, often by accident, he hears of Person B. Person B is a dowser. At this stage Person A thinks that he has nothing to lose and requests the help of Person B.

Usually with great humility and confidence, Person B locates whatever was being searched for and then quietly leaves. Person A is left with the object of his quest, a tremendous feeling of gratitude – and dozens of angry and resentful 'experts' to deal with.

How to Dowse with a Pendulum

'What are you looking for, dear?'

'Oh, er – nothing really – just a coat hanger.'

'There are plenty in the wardrobe.'

'Ah yes, but I need a wire one.'

'A wire one? Why do you need a wire one?'

'I, er, well, um, ah, – well actually – I, er – I want to make something out of it.'

'That's nice, dear. What?'

'Gulp-' Long pause while brain and stomach freeze solid. Much self appaisal and wondering if you really are mad, etc., etc. Finally, in a voice as casual as you can make it, you squeak, 'A dowsing rod. I'm making a dowsing rod.'

'YOU'RE WHAT?!?!? etc., etc.'

So forewarned is forearmed. As an adventurer into the realms of magic, you are going to have to ask for any kindness that you may want. People will want to pressure you before you even get started. All you'll have to do in return is to realize that you are your own boss. You are not a paid performer, you don't have to come up with any results. This is not a circus, it is you, very delicately sensing the limits of your intuition and awareness. And intuition and awareness do not run to rules or timetables. They never have done and they never will. If magic fascinates you, you have every right to be fascinated and to join in in your own way if you want. If you want to do some dowsing dowse away to your heart's content.

The first thing you'll need is something to dowse with. There are two types of dowsing instruments – rods and pendulums – and sooner or later you must get your hands on one or both of these. I strongly recommend that you make your own dowsing tools and do as much improvising as possible in the process.

L Rods

So called because of their shape. Easy to make, and in no way an inferior or amateur tool. Two wire coat hangers, clipped at appropriate places and

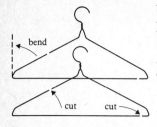

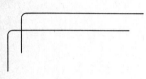

bent into an L shape make a basic L rod. The smaller part of the L is the handle.

The idea is that you hold the rods parallel in front of you, and when you detect something the rods either cross over each other or point outwards. To make them more free-moving, put the handles into some sort of tube – half a biro casing or something similar. Now, when you hold the tubes the wire rods should swing about very easily.

I am deliberately keeping these instructions a bit on the vague side for a good reason. I want you to get the general idea of what is needed and then go and make it in your own way. As long as you end up with two rods that flop easily about in your hands in front of you, it doesn't matter how you make them or what they're made of.

The Pendulum

The same principle applies here, too. Start on the understanding that anything on the end of a piece of string is a pendulum, and as such will dowse for you. This way, you can't go wrong. You only need to know the answers to the following two deeply spiritual and much-asked questions. (1) How big should the bit on the end be? (2) How long is a piece of string?

You are going to have to hold the string for quite long periods, and as it is supposed to be a sensitive instrument, the bit on the end should be kept quite small. I chose a brass jet from a carburettor because it was a shiny gold colour with a nice shape and no potentially confusing spiritual associations. It seems to dowse perfectly for me.

Between 4 inches (10 cm) and 10 inches (25 cms) is ideal for the length of string. Use thin string or cotton as they both dangle better than rope or wire. To learn how to experiment for length, see page 123.

The Y Rod

This is the traditional hazel divining rod, much beloved of yokels in days of yore. The principle is that you hold the two top bits of the Y with the single bit pointing away from you. You then stretch the two top bits very slightly apart, make the whole thing slightly unstable and quivery in your hand. The single end is now very responsive to changes in pressure and movement in your body and will move up or down very easily.

The Y rod is not as simple for a beginner as L rods or a pendulum because it demands a sensitivity of touch that only comes from experience. But if you want to, go out and cut a branch and experiment with it. Hazel and ash are the favourite woods, though anything will do as long as it is flexible and won't split when you gently tension it. Entire books have been written on the subject of how, where and when to cut a good divining rod. If this interests you, I recommend a trip to the library. If you want to avoid the traditions and conventions of the ancients but still would like to use the Y rod principle, try this:

Take two long pieces of flexible material (two large knitting needles or short plastic curtain rails). Fix them together at one end (jam them into a cork, tape them, bolt them, arc weld them), then hold your creation out in front of you and stretch the two free ends gently apart, one in each hand. You now have in your hands a perfectly good, home-made, ready-to-dowse, Y rod. You may have to hold such springy devices in a unique, delicate way, which I'm sure you will discover if you've gone to the trouble of building such a rod. It may involve a lighter grip, or using only your thumb and a bit of light bending.

There you have your basic dowsing hardware – L rods, pendulums and Y rods. Just to allay the usual doubts people have in their own creations (the 'if I made it, it won't work' attitude), let me reassure you by pointing out the following simple truth. It is impossible to build a dowser that isn't right for you. There are on record expert dowsers who use nothing more than a stick or a pair of old pliers and some who simply point with an arm or a finger.

Pendulum Exercise (1)

Unless you're a raging extrovert superperson, you will probably want to experiment in private or maybe with one or two sympathetic friends. Start with the pendulum because you can use it safely indoors.

Assuming you have your personal pendulum, with about 10 inches (25 cms) of string on it, sit or stand in front of a convenient work surface. Hold the string between your thumb and forefinger, about 4 inches (10 cms) above the weight, and let it dangle. You will find it most convenient if you hold your forearm roughly parallel to the ground. And relax!

1 Let the string untwirl so the pendulum is not swinging on its axis.

2 Swing the weight gently and get it to move back and forward and in circles – clockwise and anti-clockwise – using only the minimum amount of movement of thumb, forefingers and forearm.

3 Adjust the length of the string from time to time. As you get the feel of the movement of the pendulum you will discover what length of string suits you best. You'll have found the ideal length when you get the feeling that the pendulum is swinging of its own accord.

4 Look closely at the movements of the pendulum. It will move in many different ways and it will change from one direction to the other in its own time.

This first pendulum dangle can be quite tiring! There's so much to be aware of, and concentration when you're not used to it can give a feeling of tiredness. Clockwise, anti-clockwise, length of string, diagonal, straight line or circle, feel of the string, tension, am I doing it deliberately?, etc., etc. All these thoughts and more will run through your head. If you add to that mix any feeling of self-doubt or 'Oh God – I'm new to this – it won't work for me – I'm sure I'm doing something wrong' then you can see why it's so important to be as relaxed as you can.

Pendulum Exercise (2)

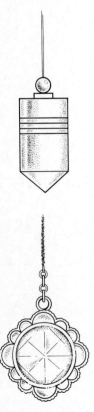

The next exercise is fascinating, and to many people even a bit uncanny. Take three coins. Two should be the same – same size and same date – and the third should be different. (For example, two 2 pence pieces and a 5 pence piece or two cents and a nickel.) Put the two similar coins on the table in front of you, one in front of the other, about 4 inches (10 cms) apart. Take your pendulum and hold it at your ideal length, a couple of inches above and in between the two coins. Watch the pendulum and allow it to oscillate from one coin to the other. Gradually, it will set a rhythm and it will seem to be drawn alternately to one coin and then to the other.

When the rhythm is clearly established, have someone replace the 2p piece furthest away from you with the 5p piece. (It's a bit tricky to do this on your own without jogging the pendulum). So now you have a 2p piece and a 5p piece and your pendulum swinging above from one to the other. But look! Something unexpected is starting to happen. Even though you are holding the pendulum exactly as it was before, the pattern of the swing is changing. The new coin is affecting the swing of the pendulum. Soon it will be swinging in a completely different way. Perhaps a diagonal or left to right or a circle. In any case, it will be a completely different oscillation from the one that happened over the two similar coins. Do not try to affect the pendulum. Just watch it as casually as possible.

Once it has settled in this totally different rhythm, change the coin back again to the original 2p piece. Now see what happens. Sure enough, your pendulum reverts to the first rhythm and oscillation.

This exercise is likely to set you wondering about all sorts of things. But it gets worse, unbelievers. Try this! Get someone to change the coins without your knowledge – when your eyes are closed or you are blindfolded. You may both be very surprised at the results!

Pendulum Exercise (3)

Hold your pendulum in front of you, steady it and just let it hang. Concentrate on it and imagine it swinging in a clockwise direction. Be patient, and sure enough it will start to swing in that direction. Now, without any great effort, imagine it going in an anti-clockwise direction. Sure enough it will slowly change the pattern of its swing to fit your imagination. All you have to do is hold it as casually as possible and concentrate on it and watch it change direction.

Are you aware of something? A kind of feeling that you are doing it but not really doing it. That is your starting point. That is the point where your conscious and unconscious meet. It is an uncertain area – a place of yes and no – yet it is a very definite feeling. Think of the sea shore. On one side there is the solid dry land you know so well; and on the other, the deep and mysterious ocean. Yet the shore itself is not a clearly defined edge at all. You're standing on land but a couple of hours later the tide comes in and the point where you were standing is ocean. How do you mark it on a map? Is it land or sea? It's both! This is the feeling of magic.

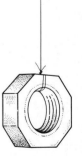

Pendulum Exercise (4)

Now that you've dangled and sensed something about what is going on, pluck up your courage and have a go at *using* your new found sense. Here's how to dangle the answer to some questions.

Your inner self knows a lot more than you do, and it's quite happy to talk to you through your pendulum. What you've got to do next is to find out when it's saying 'Yes – positive' or 'No – negative'. Get it to speak your language.

Hold your pendulum in one hand and place your other hand underneath it. Now ask yourself a question to which the answer is Yes. ('Is my name ...?' or 'Am I in my own house?') It doesn't have to be a deep question and there's no harm in asking a question to which you already know the answer. Soon, the pendulum will start to move in a certain way. If it doesn't, ask it to be a bit clearer (don't be embarrassed to talk to your pendulum!). Keep asking it positive-answer questions until it shows a definite, clearly defined movement. This movement is your own personal Yes movement.

Now ask it a No question and wait and see what happens. It should start to swing in a different pattern. Ask another No question and then another if you want. Ask it Yes and No questions until you see a clear difference of swing between the two. Spending a lot of time dangling and observing can make you a bit stiff, which will result in the pendulum giving a weak response (ie. not a very wide swing). It is possible to trick yourself into letting go and relaxing a bit. If you're right handed, simply use your left hand, and vice versa.

Soon, you will have your own personal code with which to read the pendulum. In my case, 'Yes' is a circle anti-clockwise and 'No' is clockwise. Left to right shows me that I'm not really concentrating on what I'm doing. The time will come when you will feel ready to ask a question to which you don't know the answer. Let me mention a few ways in which your pendulum can be a guide.

Dowsing to Find The Answer

1 Dowse over a map of the room/area if you are searching for something or someone.

You will need to fix your concentration lightly but firmly on the object you are looking for.

It will help you if you can have a physical reminder in your hand of whatever it is – perhaps a lock of hair, or, failing that, a person's name on a piece of paper. If it's an object you're looking for – say a stolen car – hold something strongly connected with it (e.g. a log book or a picture of a similar model car). Remember, the answer is in you. It's not impregnated on the map that you are dowsing.

2 You can pendulum dowse outside to find your way to an objective, e.g. a source of water or a hidden object. This takes a bit of skill and patience – and some nerve as you're working in public! Choose a direction and then ask the pendulum 'Is this the way I should go?' or 'Does X lie in this direction?' If the answer is negative, point a different way and repeat the question.

3 You can dowse over objects to see if they are positive or negative, suitable or unsuitable, working or not working.

4 You can diagnose by dowsing, and heal by dowsing. However, here is a word of warning. If you must be a healer and you want to use pendulum dowsing, then find a teacher and work patiently on your art under his or her guidance. To put it bluntly, I don't think it is fair to experiment with your dowsing skills on sick people.

5 Use your imagination. You can dowse for auras; you can dowse Tarot cards; diagnose and cure plants; choose presents and much more. It's up to you. You'll soon get the swing of it.

How to Dowse with L Rods

NOW for the L rods and how to use them. These are great fun, very mysterious, and everyone gets a result. L rods are best used outside and are ideal for locating water, though you can use them to seek out anything. You will need to tune yourself in mentally to the thing you are looking for. If it's a copper pipe, holding a piece of copper in your hand will help. If it's buried treasure, visualize it as best you can in your mind's eye and keep returning to your mental image. Again, perhaps hold a piece of precious metal as you dowse. If it's water you are looking for, simply visualize water from time to time.

If you've already made your rods, I'm afraid you've got no excuse for delaying any longer. This is the moment when you go outside into the wide world, armed only with a pair of L rods and a feeling of 'I hope nobody's going to notice me!'

Start by simply wandering about and seeing what the rods do. Hold them lightly, parallel in front of you, about the width of your body apart, and with your elbows tucked in at your sides. They will respond either by crossing in front of you (the most usual) or swinging very clearly outwards or to left or right. You won't need to do anything. Merely walk casually about, holding your rods in front of you.

If you've got a lawn or garden with water pipes running underneath, see if you can locate them. You could check your accuracy from the house plans, if you have them.

The organized way of dowsing for underground objects is to divide the area into squares and cover each square thoroughly, marking any response you get with a peg in the ground. When you find the point on the surface underneath which your objective is buried, you'll need to know how far down it is. There is a good method for doing this, which with experience you will be able to modify to your own needs. Stand on the spot you have found. In your mind (or out loud if you feel bold), ask 'How deep is it?' Now walk forwards slowly. Your rods should react at some point. The distance between this reaction point and the point where you started is the depth at which the object is buried.

I have deliberately avoided recommending any ideas for special tests or for finding objects that have been deliberately hidden. Of course, you're very welcome to try and find a bottle of water or a coin hidden by a friend. However, I have found that the test situation can create a very strong desire to succeed, and this desire for success can often be stronger than any other response that the dowser may have. The result is often loss of confidence and general deflation all round.

Dowsing Facts

Water veins beneath the Earth's surface are alleged to affect the health of those above. In 1976, on 55 different occasions, Herbert Douglas dowsed and located underground veins of water that intersected under the sleeping places of people who were being treated for arthritis. Every one of those who began sleeping in a new location experienced a substantial reduction or a complete disappearance of pain after periods ranging from a few days to three months.

Dowsing can also be done by rubbing and there is an African tradition of using rubbing boards. Anthropologist Edward Evans tells how a Zande witch doctor made a small wooden disc with a handle on it and another disc with two little legs and a supporting piece. Squatting on the ground, the witch doctor steadied the lowered disc with his foot and rubbed the upper disc over it with his right hand. He asked questions as he rubbed. If the disc stuck in mid rubbing, the answer to the query was yes.

There are reports of people successfully rubbing answers on any convenient surface using only their index fingers.

The search for buried gold? Or a burst water-main? Either way, this 17th-century German woodcut shows the dowser's art at its most practical.

On every hand the line of destiny is written. Though men may change their faces, thinking to deceive, who can falsify one line upon his palm? The tracks that trace the course through valleys deep and over hills, what journey is recorded there, and what history retold! What promises of days and nights to come lie in those simple veins! For those who would search with diligence the story is completed, and on the open hand the hidden secrets of the heart lie plain to see.

How to Read Palms

'Beyond the obvious facts that he has at some time done manual labour, that he takes snuff, that he is a freemason, that he has been in China, and that he has done a considerable amount of writing lately, I can deduce nothing else.'

'How, in the name of good fortune, did you know all that, Mr. Holmes?'

'Your hands, my dear sir . . .'

Taken from *The Red-headed League*, Sir Arthur Conan Doyle

 IN A WAY, we are all Master Detectives. Whenever we meet someone, we measure and compare their eyes, lips, nose, hair and ears. We assess the size of their body, weight up the sound of their voice, check their stature, notice their clothes . . . and so on. The whole process takes place in a matter of seconds and most of it is so automatic that we don't give it a second thought. Often, all we register in our conscious mind is a vague impression – whether we like the person or not; whether we are attracted, repelled or ambivalent; whether they remind us of someone we like, or of someone we distrust.

This, in itself, is a form of divination. It is a method of reading complex, natural signals. Nobody taught us how to do it. We learned by experience. It's worth bearing this in mind as you make your way through the rest of this chapter. You are about to encounter technical terms in abundance. Your head will soon be spinning with mounts and lines, chains and islands, stars and grilles, etc. There is no need to feel daunted. Only the names are unusual; the ideas they represent are simple and quite familiar. You may not yet know the rules of palmistry, but you do have a knowledge of something else which is going to be a tremendous help. This something else is your own ability to judge character.

Palmistry is therefore an *extension* of a talent you already possess. Once you've achieve the feel for where things are on the palm, and what areas of life they cover, your common sense and intuition will do the rest. You certainly shouldn't need to keep referring back to specific points in a textbook.

Bearing this perspective in mind, we might as well dive in straight away, because the sooner you've read, digested and memorised the basic rules of palmistry, the better! But first I want to tell you what you are *not* going to find in this chapter.

You're *not* going to find out when you will die. Nobody can tell you this – and if you don't know why, please take a few moments to read the section marketed Fortune Telling on page 165.

You are *not* going to find out how to read fingers, thumbs and hand shapes, which, technically speaking, belong to Chirognomy, the art of reading whole hands and not just palms. My own experience show that the extra factors in Chirognomy simply retreat and confirm messages contained on the palm itself, and I'd rather provide a thorough introduction to one subject than a skimpy outline of two.

Neither will you find out how to read skin ridge patterns or fingerprints. However, if you do feel an affinity for the subject, I'm sure that later you'll want to explore a fascinating new development in palmistry which is called Dermatoglyphics.

Finally, if you're hoping to have a quick read and then go straight out and amaze your friends, please accept my apologies. Things just don't happen that quickly. However, if you spend some time practising, experimenting with and absorbing what you have read, I guarantee that you soon *will* be able to impress your friends – and even complete strangers, for that matter.

How To Get Started

To begin with, you'll have to do a lot of peering, poking, staring and measuring. Most of it will be on your own hand, but before you can be sure whether you have high or low mounts (for example) you'll have to see what other people's palms look like and make comparisons. The trouble with this is that when you ask someone to show you their palm, the first thing they'll do is expect you to tell them their whole life story in intimate detail! 'What can you see?' will be the cry. 'Nothing!' is not much of an answer – but it's the best one to give.

Explain that you're just beginning to study palmistry, that you haven't really got the hang of it yet and that you don't want to say anything that you might have to take back later! Would they mind very much if you could just take a look at their hand and made a few notes? People may still try to draw a comment out of you, but as long as you reassure them you're keeping quiet because you *don't know* and not because you're keeping back some terrible secret, everything will be fine.

This kind of honesty may surprise those who think palmistry is a con trick – and if it does, so much the better! Sincerity and humility are the most efficient tools a student can possess, and they are also far more likely to stimulate a meaningful dialogue with the person who lends you their hand. Instead of telling them things, you can ask questions. Often, they will open up to you and there'll be a chance to see the stories they tell you are reflected by the markings on the palm. This is how you will obtain confidence, experience and eventually fulfilment from your chosen art. Even when you *do* have something to say, you'll find the joy comes not from showing off your knowledge but from using it to help someone talk freely about difficult or worrying aspects of their life.

So, be humble, be honest and be genuine. You'll need to look at as many palms as possible, and before long people will be queueing up to help you with your research.

Left Hand or Right Hand?

Which hand do you write with?

The hand you write with is your *main* hand. It's the one you use most to express yourself. The hand you don't write with is your *other* hand. It represents the more private, undeveloped or latent side of your personality. You may have heard that the main hand can be read as what you have done with your life and the other hand as what you might have been expected to do with your life, but as the lines on both hands are subject to change over a period of time this is a rather over-simplified idea. Both hands are important. But while you are learning you'll have more than enough information to deal with on your main hand and should forget the other hand. (Any palmists or psychologists who would like to argue this point are cordially invited to see the footnote below.)*

* I don't deny that the subconscious or repressed hand contains more vital psychological clues than the main hand. But (and it's a big but) we all have to walk before we can run. The information on the main hand is easier to verify. It represents manifest as opposed to potential energy and is consequently less subject to nebulous interpretation or suggestive response.

If you meet anyone who claims to be ambidextrous, ask them to point to a picture on a nearby wall. The hand they instinctively use to point with can be safely read as the main hand at least while you're learning.

Astrology and Palmistry

Long, long ago, somebody named the parts of the hand after the planets in the sky.* Nobody knows who did this, but as it's a very good system and works extremely well, almost every palmist uses it. On pages 31–34 there is a list of the planets and their meanings which will give you extra information on certain points.

Although both subjects use the names of planets to describe facets of life, they are quite separate. A birth chart reading will normally confirm a palm reading (and vice versa), but otherwise it's a bit like the difference between learning to play a wind or a keyboard instrument. Both require you to read musical notation but a piccolo doesn't sound very good if you hit it, and you won't get far trying to blow down a piano! In astrology, the 'condition' of a planet is decided by the sign it's in, the house it's in and the aspects it makes. In palmistry, the 'condition' of a planet is decided by the length, texture and pattern of various points on the hand. Whichever system you use, you can expect to come to similar conclusions.

The only other similarity between astrology and palmistry worth noting is that they are both forms of divination, and as such they share certain ethical considerations. For an outline of these, I would refer you once more to the section on Fortune Telling (page 165).

The Mounts

The mounts are pads of flesh which occur all around the edge of your palm. Later we will talk about how to read them, but for now they are important as geographical markers. To see them clearly, curl and relax your hand slightly, as if you were about to catch a tennis ball. I'm going to introduce each mount in turn so that you can get a general description of where things are and what they're called.

---

* This was done before the discovery of Uranus, Neptune and Pluto. Although attempts have been made to incorporate these three outer planets into palmistry, I have not yet seen a satisfactory system and have therefore explained only the traditional correlations in this book.

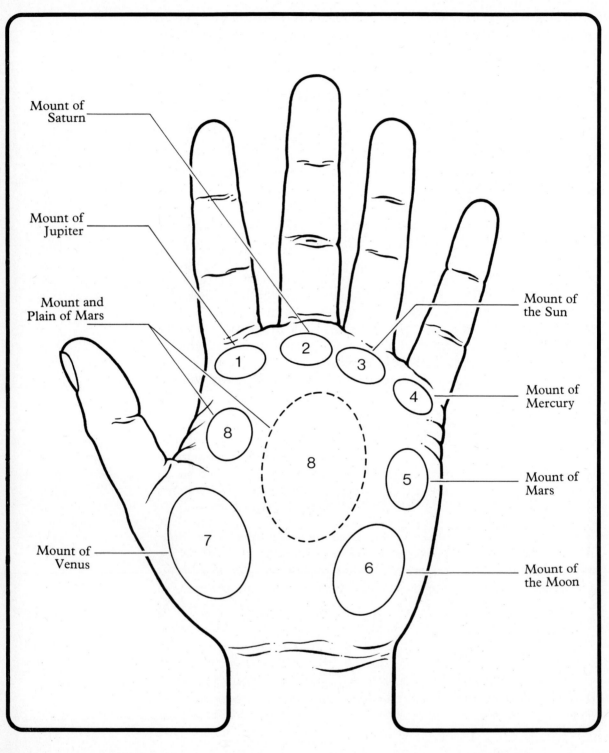

Mount of Saturn

Mount of Jupiter

Mount and Plain of Mars

Mount of the Sun

Mount of Mercury

Mount of Mars

Mount of Venus

Mount of the Moon

1 Counting from your thumb, your first finger is the Jupiter finger. The fleshy area just below it is your *mount of Jupiter*. This is the area of your hand that deals with optimism, faith, enthusiasm, positivity and good fortune. How much of all that you've got, we'll look at later!

2 On to the second or Saturn finger. Underneath this is probably a dip rather than a mount, but, whatever it is, the area just below your Saturn finger is the *mount of Saturn* and speaks of your strength, self discipline, career prospects, ability to be realistic and sense of responsibility.

3 Your third finger is called Apollo. In Greek mythology Apollo was the god of the sun. The mount below is the *mount of the Sun* and it symbolizes solar qualities such as health, vitality, talent, wealth and charm.

4 Last is your little finger. It's named after Mercury (messenger of the gods) and the *mount of Mercury* below it will speak of your ability to communicate, express yourself, think clearly, analyze, rationalize and generally apply your intellect.

5 Under the mount of Mercury is the first *mount of Mars*. See the diagram opposite if you aren't quite sure where it is. We'll come back to Mars in a moment, because there are three Martian areas that must be considered together. Meanwhile, those readers who know their astrology will see that there are two planets we haven't mentioned yet – the moon and Venus.

6 The moon, which symbolizes the unconscious, dreamy, private, emotional and protective side of human nature, rules the large mount at the bottom left of your right hand and the bottom right of your left hand. Some people, who think that palmistry isn't complicated enough already, use Latin and name this area the mount of Luna. I prefer to call it the *mount of the Moon*.

7 Venus, planet of love, peace, harmony, beauty, music and attraction, governs the area directly opposite Luna and below your thumb. You can see the *mount of Venus* quite clearly in the diagram.

8 Finally, look down on the main body of the palm. You can see that it dips in the middle. The area of dip is called the *plain of Mars*. Mars is the planet of determination, aggression, willpower, anger and strength. To the left and right of the plain of Mars are the lower and upper *mounts of Mars*. Once again, the diagram will make this clear. You'll find a full explanation of the difference between the three mounts of Mars on page 159.

If you are serious about palm reading, sooner or later you'll have to learn the name of each area off by heart. If and when you actually want to do this, the following little rhyme may help. It may sound a bit moronic but it should help things stick in your brain. Beginning with the mount of Jupiter and following the route we have just taken, point to each mount in turn and say . . .

> Jupiter Sat on the Sun,
> Mercury mars the Moon,
> Venus is under my thumb
> and Mars plays the rest of the tune.

Markings on The Mounts

It's still too early to read the mounts themselves (you'll need more experience) but you can look at them to see if they bear any special markings. Most people have at least a few of these, and once you know what to look for they should be easy to see. The old-fashioned palmists and gypsy fortune tellers considered them highly significant.

With a few exceptions, any of the markings shown in the diagram can be found on any mount. The marks can be as deep as the lines on your palm, but they don't travel in one direction. Instead, they form tiny patterns. It's quite simple to distinguish them from the fine network of fingerprints which cover your whole hand. The marks are noticeably deeper, but at first you may confuse them with the crossing of two or more minor lines, particularly if those lines are broken. If you're not sure, give yourself the benefit of the doubt for now. Later, when you've read more about the lines, it will be an easy matter to decide which you have.

Meanings of The Marks

The shape of each mark has a special meaning, which is modified somewhat by the mount on which, or close to which, it appears.

The Circle
This is quite rare. The person who bears this mark is likely to spend at least some part of his or her life wandering round in circles unable to learn from previous mistakes and failing to make progress. The mount it appears on will tell you which part of their life will be subject to this problem.

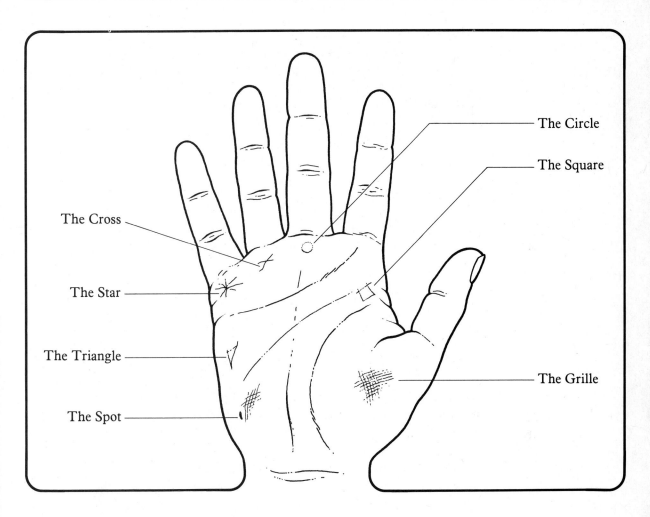

The Circle

The Square

The Cross

The Star

The Triangle

The Spot

The Grille

The Square
The Square is a symbol of protection. Wherever it appears, the owner of a square can expect to find themselves sailing smoothly through troubled waters. It's not that troubles won't occur. It's just that, when you do, you can expect an unseen hand to come to the rescue.

The Cross
This is basically a warning. It implies a powerful, external force which (or who) is likely to have too much influence in the area where the Cross appears. Only if the bearer of a Cross can develop wisdom and foresight will they be able to resist the frustration or confusion that this influence may bring. A Cross on the plain of Mars or the mount of Jupiter has a somewhat different meaning (pages 139–140).

The Star
The Star is simply a sign of excellence, dramatic success and brilliant achievement. It is considered fortunate on every mount except Saturn. Here, it used to be seen as a warning of violent death but experience has shown this to be untrue. Instead, it seems to be evidence of a talent for phenomenal discipline, restraint or self control (which, in excess, can be quite problematic!).

The Grille
The Grille, wherever it appears, shows extremism. There will be a strong tendency for you to take the things ruled by the relevant mount to excess. This is not always bad news – but it's not always good news either. If you want to know *which*, think about the consequences of taking certain things to their limits and decide for yourself!

The Triangle
The Triangle is the mark of a practical, level-headed talent. Ease, success and common sense will all meet and merge in the area of life shown by the mount on which the Triangle appears.

The Spot
Although, you are more likely to find a Spot on a line than on a mount they do sometimes appear. When they do, you can expect to find a blockage in the path of progress that only concentrated effort will clear. This may show up (especially on the main hand) as a refusal to talk about certain issues or face certain facts. Probe gently when covering subjects ruled by the mount on which the Spot appears.

What they mean

I am now going to give specific interpretations for a spot on the mount of Mars or a grille on the mount of Saturn. I would be lying if I said that it was an infallible list of definite meanings, and I'd also be depriving you of a chance to use palmistry as a springboard for your intuition. The meanings of the marks vary from person to person and you should try to add your understanding of a mark to your understanding of a mount and draw conclusions of your own. If you must use these definitions, don't take them too literally. Remember that nobody is cast at birth into a cruel fate, and it is quite possible for someone with the luckiest of markings to abuse or ignore their talents completely. It's also quite possible for someone with the most miserable or doomy set of markings to overcome the problems and flourish as a direct result of fortitude in the face of adversity.

JUPITER

Star: Success, good fortune, joy.
Triangle: Application brings excellent results.
Cross: Luck through a partner or lover.
Spot: Lack of self confidence.
Grille: Insecurity breeds great determination.
Square: Indestructible optimism.
Circle: Blind faith.

SATURN

Star: A 'bloody minded' streak.
Triangle: A deep, probing, thoughtful mind.
Cross: Self sufficiency.
Spot: Lack of caution.
Grille: Over serious attitude can prove problematic.
Square: Natural wisdom safe progress through life.
Circle: Plagued by unnecessary fear.

THE SUN

Star: Fame and/or prestige.
Triangle: Public recognition (well deserved).
Cross: Fortunes rise and fall dramatically.
Spot: Often unsure of 'direction'.
Grille: A show off.
Square: Stable finances and health.
Circle: Fascination with fame.

MERCURY

Star: Ingenious wit and intelligence.
Triangle: Brainy but lazy.
Cross: Gullible and vulnerable.
Spot: Can't put ideas into practice.
Grille: A bit *too* clever (!)
Square: Common sense prevails.
Circle: Lost in a dreamworld.

♂ **MARS**
Marks on any of the three mounts of Mars are rare. I have included some definitions, but you'll find them in the section on reading the mounts on page 159.

☽ **MOON**
Star: Vivid imagination.
Triangle: Strong, reliable intuition.
Cross: Always finding something new to worry about.
Spot: Out of contact with own feelings.
Grille: Terrified of facing reality.
Square: A protective 6th sense.
Circle: Over-protective of others.

♀ **VENUS**
Star: A desperate need to be liked.
Triangle: Popularity.
Cross: Unconventional love life!
Spot: Excessive vanity.
Grille: Worry!!!
Square: A bullet-proof heart.
Circle: Creativity knows no bounds.

Contradictions

You may already have discovered that many markings appear to contradict one another. If you haven't, don't worry – you soon will! Part of the fun in character analysis is weighing up how two opposing pulls affect each other.

Never forget that most people are, in themselves, contradictory. People who appear to be outgoing can be very shy under the surface; people who appear to be fond of accumulating money can, in their own way, still be very generous. A good palmist should weigh the hand up very carefully, be brave, and try to make specific rather than sweeping statements.

The Lines on the Palm

Lines are probably the most famous part of palmistry, and there's no denying that they contain plenty of nitty gritty information. Roughly speaking, there are three types of line.

1 Major Lines   These are the main crease marks on your palm. The Life line, the Head line and the Heart line. Everyone has them and (not surprisingly) they have most to reveal.

2 Minor Lines   These are sometimes a bit fainter or less distinct and they include the Fate line, Mercury line and Sun line. Almost everyone has each of these, and their conditions (or absence) will tell you a lot.

3 Oddities   Although no fainter than the other minor lines, only certain people have a Girdle of Venus or a Ring of Solomon, etc. Most of these uncommon lines are listed on pages 154–157. Also in this category, but less unusual, are Marriage lines.

A Word About Normality

Most people have lines of average length. If this includes you, please don't think it makes you an average person. It certainly doesn't, although it does indicate that you have a healthy balance between two extremes and are therefore less likely to encounter specific problems. For this reason you will find no comment about average-length life lines, head lines, heart lines or any other lines.

How to Read The Lines

The nicest thing about learning palmistry is that (nearly) everything means what you think it means. There are no tricky sideways formulas to catch you out! Each line describes a different aspect of your personality. Whether it is long, short or average is a direct indication of how much *emphasis* you are likely to place on that area of your life.

The *direction* of the line (the mount it begins at and the mount it ends up pointing towards) shows how you are likely to *direct* that part of your personality.

The *quality* of the line (i.e. straight, bent, clear, islanded, broken or faint, etc.) describes the quality of that part of your personality (whether it

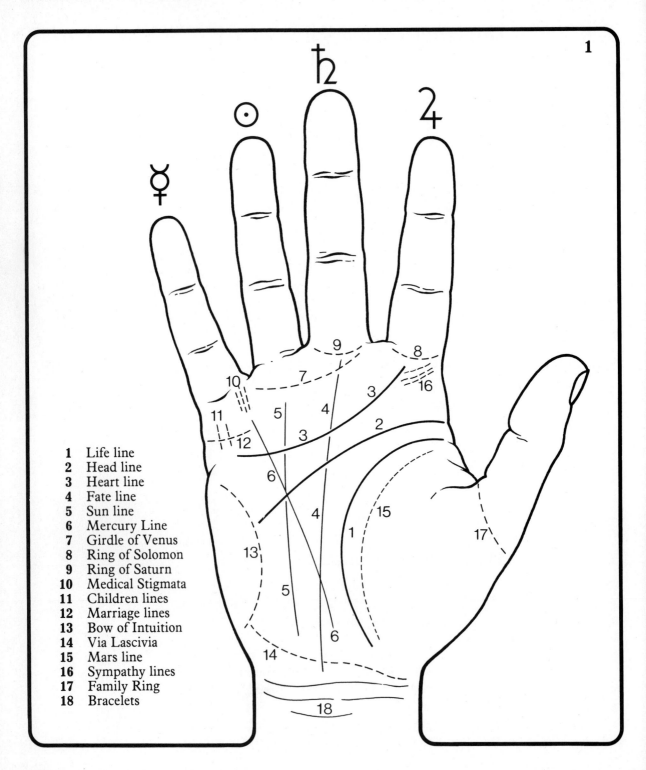

1 Life line
2 Head line
3 Heart line
4 Fate line
5 Sun line
6 Mercury Line
7 Girdle of Venus
8 Ring of Solomon
9 Ring of Saturn
10 Medical Stigmata
11 Children lines
12 Marriage lines
13 Bow of Intuition
14 Via Lascivia
15 Mars line
16 Sympathy lines
17 Family Ring
18 Bracelets

makes you happy or sad, causes you problems or gives you a talent).

If you grasp these basic principles, it will make everything much easier, but as with everything simple there is always someone who wants to complicate it and I could tell you about a whole host of variations that different people have dreamed up. But I won't! The only potentially confusing thing that must be mentioned is how to time a line – and even that can safely be avoided until you arrive at page 160.

The Major Lines

THE LIFE LINE

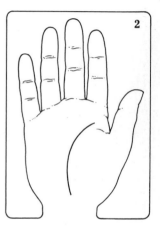

I often meet two sorts of frightened people – those who have been told by an amateur palmist that they have a break in their life line, and those who are scared of seeing a palmist in case this is what they are told! Although, technically, this comes under Timing and Fortune Telling (see pages 160–166), I want to say here and now that plenty of people with long, clear life lines have died at an early age, and many people with more holes in their life line than a piece of Swiss cheese have lived to be a hundred. The life line describes the strength, not the length, of your life. It relates to the amount of energy you have at your disposal; your sense of vitality, urgency, motivation and physical strength. It runs around the edge of your mount of Venus and begins somewhere above your thumb (diagram 2).

Beginning . . .

A life line is considered *high* if it begins close to or even on the mount of Jupiter. A *low* life line begins very near the thumb. On most palms, the line starts midway between these two points.

A high life line implies a particularly energetic, ambitious, optimistic and successful life.

A low life line suggests someone who finds it hard to achieve their chosen goals – or, for that matter, chooses no goals!

. . . and Ending

Most life lines finish near the base of the palm, roughly in the centre. This shows a healthy balance between the following extremes.

(a) The life line takes a very clear route under the ball of the thumb, showing a strong need to retreat and feel safe. It could indicate a love of home comforts and a need for a secure physical base, or just a general sense of caution.

(b) The line 'forks' towards the end, with one prong moving off towards the base of the thumb and the other out across the palm towards the mount of the Moon. This second prong indicates a desire to cast off family ties and reach out for new horizons. The fork implies a dilemma occurring from this pull, and the stronger of the two lines shows the most likely outcome.

(c) The line runs a long way down on to the wrist and merges with one of the bracelets, (see page 142). It suggests someone who is very self sufficient.

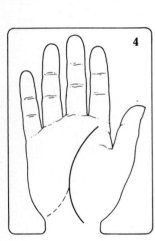

Short and Long

A *very short* life line might begin close to the mount of Mars, create room for only a slim mount of Venus and tail off rapidly at the base. (See diagram 3.)

A *very long* life line would start higher up, sweep further out and either curl a long way under or branch right out across the palm. (See diagram 4.)

Don't, however, make the mistake of assuming that a life line that begins low is automatically short or that a high life line is always the same as a long one.

The shorter the lifeline the greater the tendency to cram as much experience as possible into every day, giving rise to impatience and a great sense of urgency.

The longer the life line the more life will be taken at a leisurely pace, encouraging long-term plans and sympathy with the idea of deferred gratification.

The State of The Life Line

A *deep* line reflects positivity and determination. A *shallow* or *weak* line shows a tendency to let fate take its course and indicates less ability to resist illness and disease.

Breaks in the line show turning points or moments of crisis. Perhaps one reason why breaks were once associated with death is that the stress created by such an incident (divorce, redundancy or illness, for example) can cause a weakening of the spirit. If a break exists on your life line, it means that either you have not recovered from a traumatic event in the past, or you have a deep sense of foreboding about something in your future. The section on Timing (page 160) may help you decide which. A break, therefore, normally indicates the need to face an unpleasant or disturbing truth. Once you do this, the event can be dealt with successfully and the break itself may even heal up on your palm.

Sometimes, a small line will be found next to a break. It's like an alternative route, or a solution which may present itself at a critical time –

often in the form of outside help. It may also form when you are overcoming a personal fear, or taking brave new steps after crisis or disaster.

Islands on the life line have similar meanings to circles on the mounts. They represent moments in life when you are liable to be stuck in a rut – mentally or physically. You may have a general tendency to this. If you have an island you may find that until or unless a strong motivating force arises you'll wander over the same old ground, unable to make progress.

BRANCH LINES

There are several relatively faint but fairly lengthy lines that may branch out from the life line and head off towards various fingers or mounts. These are distinct from little influence lines which cross the life line (see page 147), and also distinct from a fork in the life line itself (see page 143). Diagram 5 should help you see what to look for. Don't worry if you haven't got any branch lines. It doesn't mean that you don't possess the qualities mentioned below, simply that they aren't strongly emphasized at the moment. Branch lines are not always one solid line. They can sometimes be formed by two or three lines that overlap (diagram 6), or by one broken line which implies they are in a state of formation.

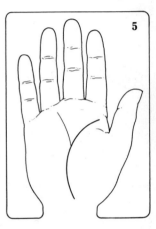

Ambition Line

This line leads up towards the Jupiter mount. It shows that you have one or, if the line is made up of overlaps, several burning ambitions. The stronger the line, the more confident you'll feel about your ability to fulfil them. The higher up the mount of Jupiter the line rises, the more confidence – and the more success. As to *what* the ambition is . . . if you want to find out, you'll have to play detective and use a combination of logic and intuition. Look for signs of a lack elsewhere on the hand. For example, someone with a broken heart line might well aspire towards a stable relationship through their ambition line – and successfully achieve it too!

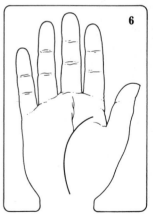

Effort Line

This line rises up and out towards the Saturn mount (although it rarely gets that far). It shows, quite simply, the capacity to move mountains. It may be there because a mountain has already been moved – or it may be there because a mountain is going to be moved. In either case, you can be sure, if you have one, that the capacity for intense, serious, dedicated and determined hard work will be shown strongly in your personality. (Though it may take a problem or an upheaval to bring it out.) Don't confuse it with the *fate* line that can sometimes emerge from the life line – but from a point much lower down the palm (see page 152).

Success Line

This line goes towards the mount of the Sun. It shows a Midas touch – although not necessarily with money. Unlike an ambition line, the good fortune, opportunities and luck seem to come to you whether you want them or not – particularly at the period of time indicated by the point on the life line where it begins. (See Timing, page 160.) During the rest of your life, the successes may be intermittent or sporadic – but they will certainly be noticeable. It's not quite the same as a Sun line (see page 153) but as its meaning is pretty much identical it won't matter if you get them confused!

Travel Line

Some palmists use this term to describe the fork at the bottom of the life line, heading off towards the mount of the Moon. As outlined above, it suggests that you have a predisposition towards long-distance travelling and a need to explore. This may not, of course, be physical. It could imply a great, soul searching journey into the inner self.

Mars Line

This is not strictly speaking a branch line. It runs parallel to part of the life line along the inside (on the mount of Venus). It is, if you like, a large bridging line implying strength in adversity, protection from harm and inner fortitude. When particularly long, it can be considered a *double* life line, meaning, quite literally, a double life – an alternative course of activity or identity into which you may choose to escape when the main course of events proves hard to take.

Worry Lines

It is very common to find the mount of Venus covered in a network of parallel and/or vertical lines. They're called worry lines and, not surprisingly, most people have them! You need only worry about your worry lines if they are particularly heavy or if they actually cross the life line itself. This suggests a tendency to greatly over-dramatize trivial concerns. Things get out of perspective too easily and anxiety replaces commonsense. On second thoughts, *don't* worry if you have extended worry lines – it will only make things worse! Instead, see them as a message from your body that you need to be more relaxed.

Influence Lines

Similar in appearance but different in meaning to extended worry lines are influence lines. These are usually somewhat longer and tend to follow the shape of the life line (see diagram 7). An influence line represents another person who has had or will have a profound (and normally positive) influence your life. Probably this will be a friend, lover or partner – but unlike a *relationship* line (page 157), it doesn't have to be someone you've actually met. It *could* be a hero (or heroine) or perhaps a distant relation who bequeathed you some money that changed the direction of your life. The length of the influence line shows the extent and duration of the influence.

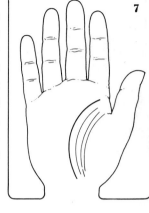

THE HEAD LINE

While the life line shows the vitality, stamina and energy available to you, the head line shows how that energy is translated into thoughts, attitudes and the acquisition of information. In a nutshell, it describes what sort of a mind you have.

Beginning . . .

The head line may begin in the same place as the life line, or some way above it on the mount of Jupiter. The higher the starting point, the more mentally confident and self assured you will be.

When the line begins further down, it doesn't deny intellectual confidence, but suggests that it will be learned – not taken for granted. If the life and head lines begin together, tied above the thumb, it suggests that childhood experiences may have left you unsure of your abilities and that you may have to shake off a lot of early doubt before you gain faith in your own intelligence.

. . . and Ending

Most head lines end underneath the mount of Apollo (about three quarters of the way across the palm). As a rough guide, you could say that any head line reaching further than the mount of Apollo is *long* and any failing to reach this point is *short*.

The length of a head line does not reflect *size* of intellect. It reflects the *breadth* of it. In other words, someone with a long head line may find it easier to encompass a lot of attitudes, viewpoints and ideas. Conversely, someone with a short head line is more likely to concentrate their mind on one particular subject. When considering the length of the head line, it's also important to see if it's . . .

Sloping or Straight

Some head lines take a fairly horizontal path across the palm. Others slope downwards, heading towards the mount of the Moon. Regardless of length, the straighter the head line, the more matter of fact or scientific your thoughts. You should find it fairly easy to separate intellectual responses to life from physical ones – making you quite analytical but perhaps rather dry. The further the line slopes down towards the mount of the Moon (again regardless of length), the more intuitive, artistic, creative and illogical you'll be.

A *short* head line shows a lack of intellectual confidence.

When *short* and *straight* reassurance is sought in physical status items (such as possessions, wealth and or qualifications).

When *short* and *sloping* reassurance is sought in emotional status items (such as friends, lovers or partners).

A *long* head line implies independence of thought, born of greater self confidence.

A *long, sloping* head line can be the sign of a born eccentric who disappears into the realm of ideas – rarely to emerge! With one of these lines, you may often be accused of having impractical or far-fetched ideas, but you may also find they come to fruition and gain acceptance because intuition breeds luck!

A *long, straight* line shows much more fixed, practical and commonsense mentality. A natural talent for planning and organizing is shown here – though some might call it a bossy streak!

A *wavering* line (long or short) simply shows a butterfly mind, interested in many subjects but unable to get to grips with any of them.

The State of The Head Line

As a general rule, the *deeper* the line, the greater the ability to study, absorb new information and apply discipline to the mental processes. A noticeably *faint* line implies a short attention span.

With an *Island* on your head line, every so often you may enter a period of intellectual uncertainty. It may be a deep depression or perhaps a conflict of identity produced by some new information or discovery which attacks the foundations of everything you previously believed to be true. Although not exactly comfortable, an Island isn't such a bad thing to have. Times of intellectual self-doubt inevitably lead to re-appraisal and renewed strength. Those without Islands may be spared the pain of seeing their whole outlook on life crumble and fall, but they are also denied the pleasure of coming to a deeper, more profound understanding of the way things are and growing wiser, more experienced and more nature in the process.

A *Dot* on the head line suggests a big mental block in some area. A difficulty with words, numbers, music or something less specific like social conventions, for example.

One or a series of little *diagonal lines* that cross the head line are obstacles presented not by the mind itself but by external circumstances, i.e. lack of money to pursue a course of study, or the need to do a certain sort of job that stops you indulging a favourite hobby. When the line breaks up or goes faint by a crossing line, the obstacle is major and will require great fortitude to overcome. When the line remains clear and strong – surging through the crossing line – there is every likelihood that the problems can be easily taken in hand and dealt with. These are character building developments – don't worry about them!

A *Chained* head line (or part of the head line) suggests you have often come under mental pressure (such as exams) or that people look to you for advice (intellectual responsibility). The chain proves that you can cope under stress – but it's an effort which you try to keep secret.

A *Fork* at the end of the head line shows an intellect capable of great diversification, imagination and application. It implies an ability to visualize and communicate ideas and is sometimes called a writer's fork, although not everyone who has one is a writer of words. It's more truly an indication of creative ability with a practical bent and as such could also show a sculptor, painter, musician or even inventor. When the fork is particularly pronounced (with the lower or creative branch going steeply down to the mount of Luna while the upper or analytical branch heads straight for the mount of Mars) there is less harmony between the two talents. You may find yourself torn in opposing directions, unable to reconcile a desire to remain at a distance with the temptation to get really involved in a project.

Very occasionally a three-pronged fork is found, implying even greater versatility.

Even more rare is a double head line. It implies a unique ability to see both sides of an argument and leads either to great wisdom or to great indecisiveness.

Final Note

When the life and head lines are so close together that they cannot be properly distinguished and the head line appears, to all intents and purposes, to be a late fork from the life line, you may expect to find a very bad-tempered personality who simply cannot separate their intellectual experience from their physical experience. They will be impulsive, rash,

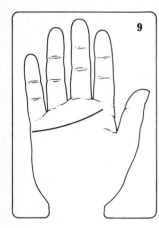

low on cool clear rational thought, and often prone to express intellectual dissatisfaction in a physical way (stamping of feet, hurling of books or even fighting).

THE HEART LINE

Above the head line and below the finger mounts is the heart line (diagram 9). It's mainly concerned with the poetic or romantic idea of a heart (although some say that you can also read the condition of the physical heart on this line). The heart line describes the way we feel about the people around us. Whatever and whoever we love will show up in the heart line – as will those people who love us.

Beginning . . .

The heart line will begin on your hand under either the Jupiter or the Saturn finger, or from a point midway between the two.

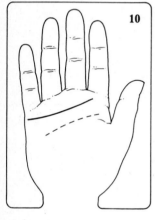

. . . and Ending

It's rare to find a heart line that doesn't end at the very edge of the palm – so length is normally decided by where the line begins, not where it ends.

Some heart lines slope downwards, others are straight, and a further division can be drawn between high- and low-lying heart lines (see diagrams 10 and 10a).

Long and Short

A heart line which begins below the Jupiter finger carries with it the optimism and enthusiasm that Jupiter endows. It makes for a demonstrative, outgoing and giving personality – but also one who can be a little too extreme in their emotional expression. High ideals, great expectations and a tendency to disappointment and disillusionment – although if your line starts here you'll probably also have a natural resilience which protects you from too much sadness for too long.

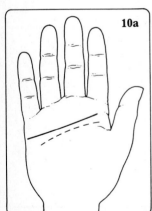

When the line begins *midway* between the Jupiter and Saturn mounts, a less idealistic approach to matters of the heart is shown and there is a more equal balance between give and take in inter-personal relationships. The closer to Jupiter, the more generous the heart but also the less able to receive the love of others. The closer to Saturn, the more protected the heart and therefore the more likely to take without giving. The nearer to midway, the more freely sensual and indulgent you'll be, with a consequently happier and more realistic outlook on love.

When the line begins very clearly under the Saturn mount there is a strong emphasis on commitment and the need to see things proven time and time again. If yours begins here, you may tend to hold back your feelings and be slow to accept love.

As a general rule, the *longer* your heart line, the easier it is for you to channel your emotional needs into creativity rather than procreativity.

High and Low

The further the heart line is from the head line, the less importance will be placed on a physical and mental involvement in love. The closer they are together (in some cases they may actually meet) the more thoughts and feelings combine.

Long and *low*: Extreme sensitivity, possessiveness, unrealistic needs.

Long and *high*: The traits above are modified by the ability to see them for what they are and deal with them.

Short and *low*: Strong physical desires tempered (or aggravated?) by intellectual sensitivity.

Short and *high*: Ability to draw a very clear line between physical desires and emotional needs.

Merged Head and Heart Lines

Sometimes called a *Simian line*, the appearance of only one line across the top of the palm (see diagram 11) indicates someone with a ruthless streak who sees clearly what they want, knows how it will affect their feelings and goes unceasingly in search of it, maybe at the expense of other people's feelings.

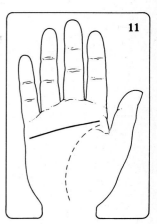

11

The State of The Heart Line

A *break* in the heart line means exactly what you'd expect. A broken heart! It should be seen as a warning – that something or someone will not be able to supply the fulfilment and happiness that you require. If you've got one, you'd better learn to be more self sufficient and want less from the world around you. Traumatic times may be in store unless you can learn to 'let go' a little of a treasured but unrealistic aim.

If you have a *thin*, uninterrupted line, you may surprise people with how emotionally self sufficient you can be.

Islands represent many deep, powerful and usually short-lived emotional entanglements.

A *Chained* line indicates changeability of the affections. If your line is made up almost entirely of Chains and Islands, you may be fickle in the extreme!

The Minor Lines

The following lines are often found, but by no means every palm has them so don't be too surprised if one or more is missing!

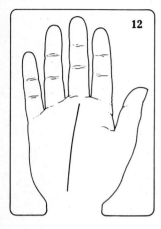

THE FATE LINE

This is sometimes called a *Career line*. Whatever you call it, it's a line that occurs most strongly in the hands of people who take destiny into their own hands, making the most of their talents and recognizing where their limitations lie. The fate line speaks of self control, discipline, determination, application, will power and sense of purpose. The stronger the line, the more of these qualities you can expect to find.

Beginning . . .

This line will run from somewhere on the base of the palm (normally around the middle) towards the Saturn mount. You can't read too much into the beginning of a fate line unless it clearly comes from the mount of Luna (a strong desire to influence the public) or it begins as an upward fork from the life line (suggesting that you are either living out the dreams of your parents or that you feel born to a certain task).

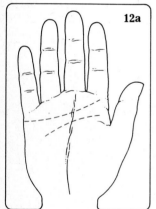

. . . and Ending

Although the fate line always heads towards the Saturn mount, it won't always arrive there. It may be short and finish at the head line, or be longer and stop near the heart line. Don't expect it to be one solid line. It's common to find it a series of little lines, or a double line, or as one long line that stops and then continues after a gap (see diagram 12a).

A fate line that stops at the head line is an indication of a sudden, unexpected change of direction. An intellectual realization has stopped you being motivated purely by gut feelings.

If it stops on the heart line you may get your sense of purpose confused with your need for emotional stability. It implies commitment in long-term relationships but often at the expense of personal self expression.

If the Fate line does extend beyond the heart line, it simply means that something very powerful drives you towards fulfilling a personal goal – and whatever stands in your way had better look out!

The State of The Fate Line

Remember that a broken fate line is not necessarily a weak one and a solid line isn't always strong. These can be indications, but it's also important to consider the depth and length of the line. (Experience and comparison will help here.)

If the fate line is very *strong*, you'll have a dogged, inflexible quality leading to success at the expense of freedom or to failure born of an inability to bend with the winds of change. To find out which, you'll have to consider the rest of the hand.

If it's *weak* (or non existent) you may lack a sense of direction or purpose. This might not be such a problem. Many people thoroughly enjoy drifting on the wings of fate, even though others accuse them of being underachievers.

Although you shouldn't read too much into a broken or disjointed line it's fair to say that it shows a strong sense of purpose which disappears suddenly for a while and then re-emerges in a different guise. Perhaps, with one of these you have learned to be flexible through some hard lessons.

If a strong, separate *parallel* line appears between the fate line and the life line for at least some of its length, you can expect to experience more than your fair share of frustrated effort. Unless you also have a strong, philosophical Jupiter mount you must be careful that it doesn't make you bitter instead of wise.

When the fate line itself does not begin on the mount of Luna but is joined by an upward fork that does, expect to find added strength from your intuition – or from a female influence.

THE SUN LINE

This line shows success, fulfilment of ambition, recognition, fame and the creative use of talent for good ends. It also speaks of financial prowess and wealth in general although its absence need not mean poverty. It may exist simply as a series of small lines below the sun mount, or these lines may extend down the hand towards the mount of Luna (see diagram 13). It's hard to say what a normal sun line looks like because they can vary so much from person to person. What you can look for with more certainty is clarity and depth. Traditionally, a sun line that begins above the heart line – and is not found elsewhere – indicates that success will be found later in life; consequently, the lower down the palm the sun line emerges, the earlier success will arrive. Look to the sun line as confirmation (or denial) of other symbols in the hand. Don't read it on its own.

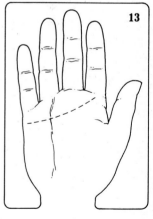

13

THE MERCURY LINE

The sign of a clear, powerful communicator is a line rising up to the Mercury mount from anywhere in the palm. It is very unlikely to be a continuous line and may well be made up of a series of overlapping little

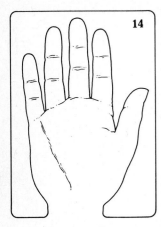

lines all heading in the one direction (see diagram 14). It shows a talent for commerce, business or dealing with information in general. If it starts from the heart line it will be a material talent; if from the head line, an intellectual talent; if from the life line, an emotional talent; and if from the mount of the Moon, a talent for manipulating the dreams and subconscious wishes of others.

Oddities

The Girdle of Venus
Immediately above the heart line and below the mounts, you may find a girdle or curling line which runs between the Saturn finger and the edge of the palm (diagram 15). It probably won't be one unbroken line but a pattern of smaller lines. The fuller the girdle, the more sensitive you'll be to the needs and hopes of others. This is a fine talent when put to practical use – but if you aren't careful it means that you may over-empathize too much with other people's pain, even when there's little you can do to help them.

The Bow of Intuition
Similar to a Mercury line, but long and forming a definite curve around the outer edge of the palm (see diagram 16), this line is the mark of someone with a real talent for knowing what's going on around them – instinctively!

The Via Lascivia
If you've got one of these lines curling round the bottom of your palm (diagram 17), be careful with drugs and alcohol. On some people, it's a sign of allergy to these things. On others, it's a sign of trouble arising from over-indulgence in them!

The Medical Stigmata
Three little vertical lines crossed by one little horizontal line on the mount of Mercury (diagram 18). The sign of healing hands.

The Ring of Solomon
A clear semi-circle around the base of the Jupiter finger (diagram 19). If you've got one of these, you'll be very wise.

The Ring of Saturn
A clear semi-circle around the base of the Saturn finger (diagram 20). If you've got one of these, cheer up and you'll find it'll clear up!

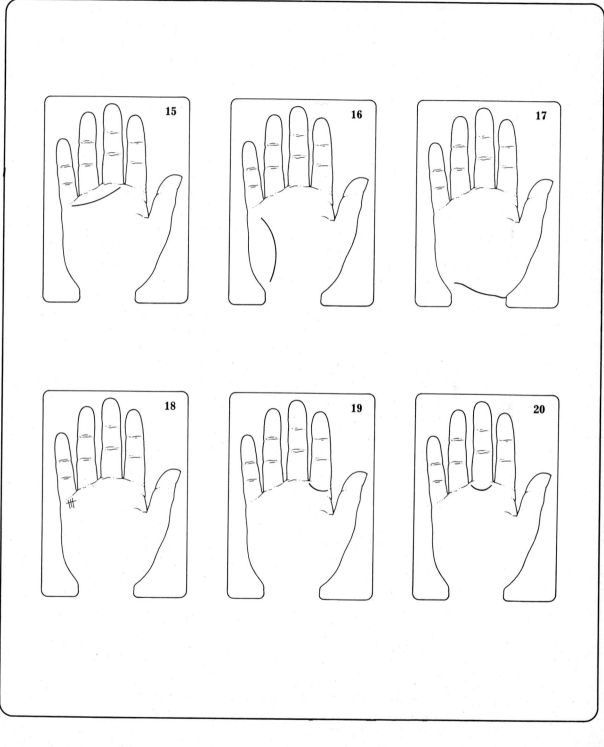

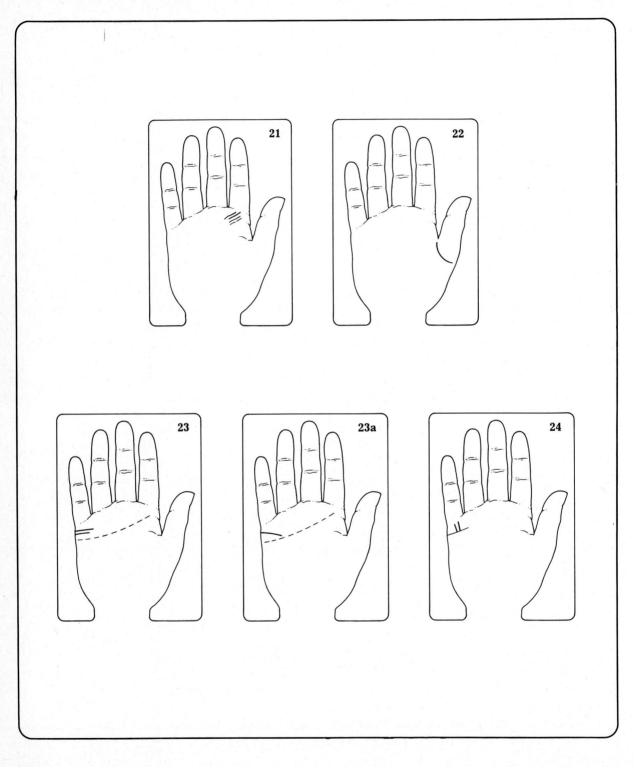

Sympathy Lines
Small diagonal lines on the mount of Jupiter (diagram 21) show a warm heart.

The Family Ring
A clear line closely hugging the base of the thumb (diagram 22) suggests close family ties that create emotional problems in later life.

Marriage Lines
If you turn your palm so you can see the edge of it, below the Mercury finger (see diagram 23), you'll see one, two or several lines of varying depth above the heart line. In this day and age, it's probably a lot more realistic to call these *relationship lines* than Marriage lines. Each one represents a particularly close emotional bond, and in terms of time you should read them from the heart line up.

Whether all or any of these lines will result in a formal marriage can only be decided by other factors in the hand that imply a respect for the traditional ceremony. It also depends on how you define a marriage. It's fairer to say that a deep partnership will be felt with each line and that the deepest partnership will be shown by the deepest line. Forks, breaks, islands and other marks on a relationship line mean exactly what you'd think they would! Traditionally, if a relationship line droops down towards the heart line it's a sign of an unhappy alliance, or one that will contain more than its share of sadness (see diagram 23a).

Children Lines
A line that drops down on to a relationship line (diagram 24) used to be considered a sign of children. If faint, a girl would be indicated, if deeper, a boy. It may once have been a hard and fast rule, but it's not any more. Take it as a sign of fertility within a relationship, although it could imply a partnership that produces other things besides children!

A Sermon on The Mounts

Now that we've covered all the major markings and lines it's time to go back to the subject of mounts. I've left them until last because I know from my own experience how hard it is to read them before you've had a chance to look at a lot of different palms and compare.

If and when you feel ready, the best way to investigate mounts is to feel for them. Ask the person who is going to lend you his (or her) hand to relax – or, better still, grip his hand firmly by the wrist and gently shake it two or three times to relax it. Then, hold his hand with one of yours and ask him to curl it slightly while you prod their mounts softly with your other hand. Don't be afraid or embarrassed to do this. It's a necessary part of palmistry and only a stupid hangover from Victorian England makes so many people nervous of physical contact.

You're trying to find out whether the mount is developed or under-developed. In other words . . . is it high or low? This depends partly on the type of hand. Some people have skinny hands while others are more padded. It is not necessarily anything to do with the weight or build of the rest of the body. Of course, a tubby person will tend to have a tubby hand, but even then the mounts may not stand out much in comparison to the rest of the palm. On a relatively skinny hand, it will be even more necessary to press, poke or feel the area of the mount to help you decide.

Although the difference between a high and a low mount can often be measured in millimeters, it's not as tricky as I'm probably making it sound! If you are at all in doubt, reserve your judgement until you've had more experience. Simply make a mental note of what you feel to be the situation and check it again later. You'll probably find that your intuition is right.

The higher or fatter the mount, the more of a certain quality your subject will possess. (And, of course, vice versa.) For this reason, high mounts (with the exception of a Saturn mount) are considered good. However, it is not quite so simple, and a few moments' thought and deliberation will help you see why. For some people, too much Saturn may, indeed, imply a sombre, self-righteous and dour personality – but for others it may simply indicate a disciplined, concentrated and sensible outlook on life. To a degree, the two things go together, but you must be careful not to dismiss a talent as a curse.

Here are some stock definitions for high and low mounts. They come with the usual reservations about being only a general guide.

THE MOUNT OF JUPITER
High: Self importance, arrogance, extravagance and over-confidence.
Low: Lack of faith, nervousness, feelings of inferiority, inability to let go and enjoy life.

THE MOUNT OF SATURN
High: Lonely, serious, dour, hardworking, conservative, pessimistic.
Low: (Most Saturn mounts are low. Here we are talking about positively concave.) Inability to concentrate, lack of application, no sense of caution or restraint.

THE MOUNT OF THE SUN

High: Big headed, insensitive. Power and status fixations.
Low: Uncertain and shy. Easily led. Lacks spontaneity.

THE MOUNT OF MERCURY

High: Over-active mind. Talks for the sake of talking and can be argumentative, and/or waffling and/or even deliberately deceptive.
Low: Slow to grasp issues, uncommunicative, gullible and self conscious.

THE MOUNTS OF MARS

In palmistry, Mars, which rules energy, ambition, determination, will power, vitality and strength, is divided into three sorts of energy.

The *upper* mount is passive – it reflects how you respond to the challenges life throws down to you.

The *plain* of Mars is neutral – it shows the amount of stamina, staying power and strength you can muster in everyday living.

The *lower* mount is active – it shows how much of a temper you have, how determined you are to get your own way and how interested you are in winning.

Of course, these three areas overlap somewhat in meaning. They should always be considered together and will normally produce a coherent picture. Occasionally, an anomaly will show up (such as a low upper mount and a high lower mount). Then you know you are dealing with an unusual character who desperately wants to be brave (high lower Mars) but cannot bear the idea of taking a risk (low upper Mars.) A little thought on your part will help you sort out what the combination infers.

The upper mount is the little area directly below the mount of Mercury. It takes some experience to spot this at all, let alone decide if it's high or low!

High: A dogged insistence that suffering is a cross to be born, and a refusal to take soft options.

Low: A big softy, afraid of the slightest physical or mental pain or conflict – to the point of total obsession.

The plain of Mars is the dip in the middle of the palm. You would normally expect it to be quite thick and firm but it can be flabby or thin.

Flabby: Someone who prefers to take it easy and is only motivated by greed.

Thin: An energetic dreamer, who is more interested in hoping than actually making the dreams come true.

The lower mount of Mars

High: A go-getter who can't stop. Perhaps a mental or physical bully.

Low: A meek, lethargic, passive and easily cowed personality.

Marks on the mount of Mars

I have kept these separate from the other markings because it is necessary to see them in the light of which mount of Mars they appear on. They are quite rare.

Square: Strong will power, well directed.

Star: A high achiever.

Cross: Tendency to make enemies.

A cross on the plain of Mars is reputedly a sign of exceptional psychic ability and the mark of a born magician.

THE MOUNT OF THE MOON

High: A tendency to live completely in the world of feeling, at the expense of rational thought or realistic action. Over-thrusting, over-caring, too sympathetic and sensitive.

Low: Lack of sympathy, hard, inflexible and unimaginative.

THE MOUNT OF VENUS

High and *firm*: A love of life and a desire to live it to the full.

High and *flabby*: Giving, loving, kind and creative, but also indulgent, soft and lazy!

Low: Afraid of love, afraid of people, afraid of life.

Timing and Fortune Telling

Up until now we have mainly discussed palmistry primarily as a way of judging character and perhaps you feel a little cheated. After all, doesn't everyone know that palmistry is about telling the future?

Well, everyone may know it, but that doesn't mean it's true! Throughout this chapter you will have seen references to the section on Fortune Telling. This is the last one. If you haven't got the message by now at least it's not for lack of trying on my part!

So here, for what they are worth, are the most popular methods of reading time on the lines of the palm. I make no apology for including contradictory systems. Each was supplied by a respected, practising palmist who swears it works for him. I can't help but feel that this underlines what I have been saying all along. The key to success in palmistry is your own ability to understand and expand the basic rules. It

The Earth as seen from space. It's easy to forget that we live on a tiny ball of rock which hurtles around the sun. The planetary positions which we read and interpret in a horoscope are their positions *as seen from Earth*. If, or when, a baby is born on the moon, it will be the planets *as seen from the moon* which are important to an astrologer.

The four elements in nature. In this picture it is easy to see the power and splendour of the sky (air), the setting sun (fire), the earth and the sea. Each element has a distinct quality, which astrologers see reflected in the qualities of different human personalities.

Scientists long to capture the aura on film. In this photograph, taken by the Russian researcher Kirlians, an auric outline of the whole leaf persists, even though a large section of it has been physically taken away. Eventually this outline fades away.

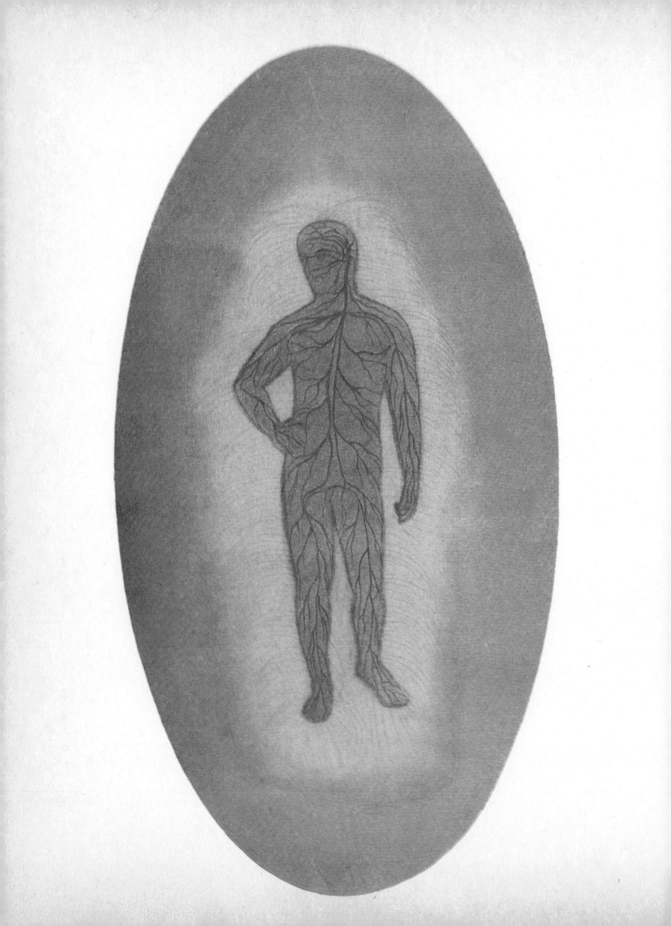

As a person's spirit grows, their increased vitality shows in the aura. The natural state for all of us is an expanding rainbow mixture of colours which mingles all the human feelings in harmony. More commonly, the pressures of the modern age lead to negative thoughts and emotions which limit the aura's colour range.

To psychic eyes, all expressions of thought and emotion are visible as light. Here, a phrase of the music of Gounod is shown as it appeared to the famous clairvoyant Annie Besant.

I

THE MAGICIAN

XVII

THE STAR

XVI

THE TOWER OF DESTRUCTION

XII

THE HANGED MAN

Selecting your Tarot pack is entirely a matter of choosing what appeals to you personally. Many people like the traditional 'medieval woodcut' style of the Marseilles Tarot.

The larger cards are from a pack designed by A. E. Waite. Their soft romantic feel contrasts with the brighter 'ecclesiastical' images on the smaller two cards, selected from The Spanish Tarot.

TESTING CANDIDATES FOR THE POSITION OF WATER DIVINER ON
THE METROPOLITAN WATER BOARD

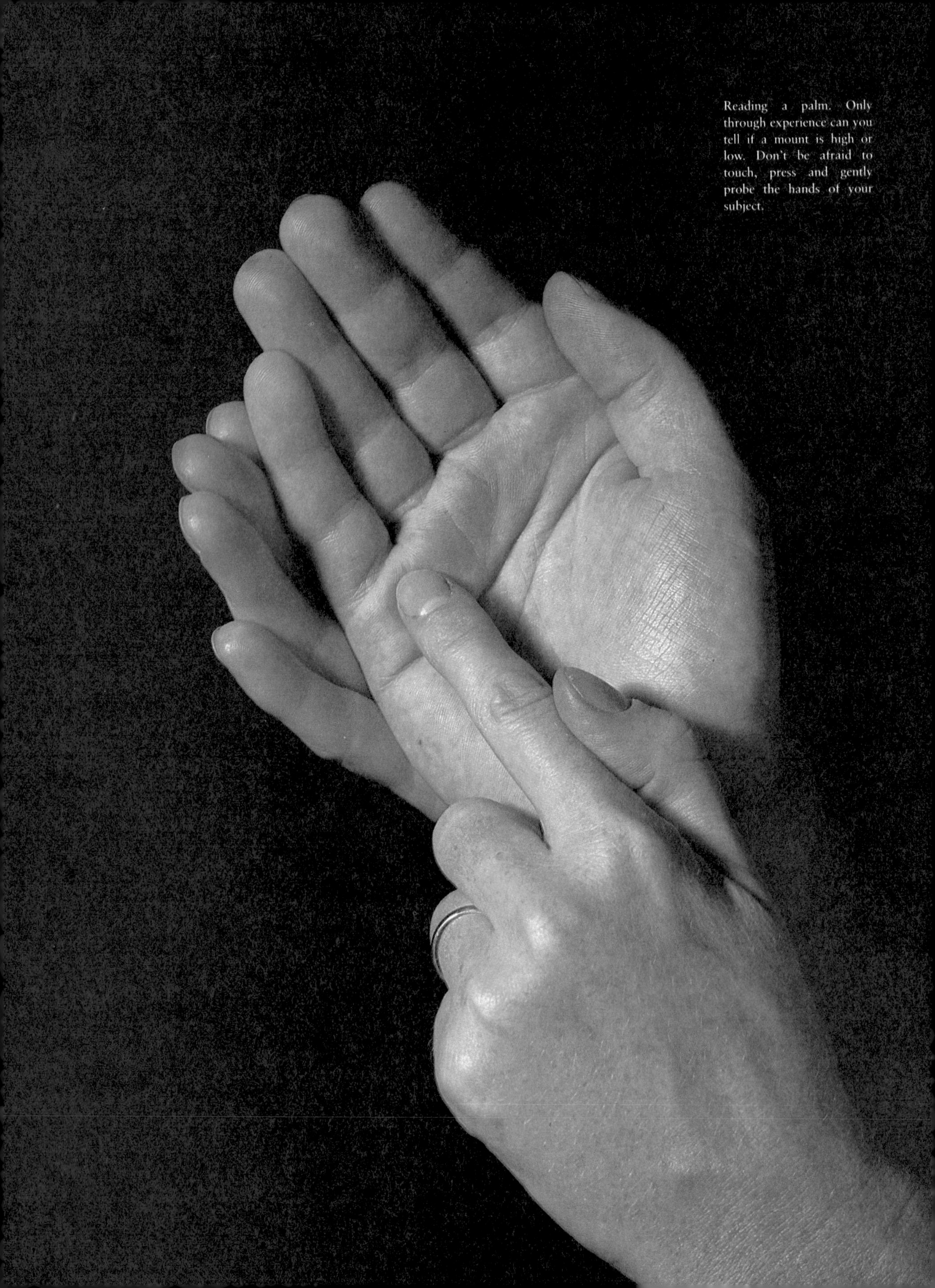

Reading a palm. Only through experience can you tell if a mount is high or low. Don't be afraid to touch, press and gently probe the hands of your subject.

LANGUAGE
35

A NEW SYMBOLICAL HEAD AND PHRENOLOGICAL CHART,
WITH THE NAME AND DEFINITION OF EACH ORGAN,
by R. B. D. Wells, Phrenologist, West Bank, Scarbro.

The common idea of the brain is of a glorified filing cabinet—'a place for everything and everything in its place.' This point of view is no longer adequate to explain our full human potential.

Chakras are our psychic energy centres. These spinning wheels of light are present in us all. Surprisingly, in people from the East the chakras are in line. The Western emphasis on the rational has slightly displaced them in many of us.

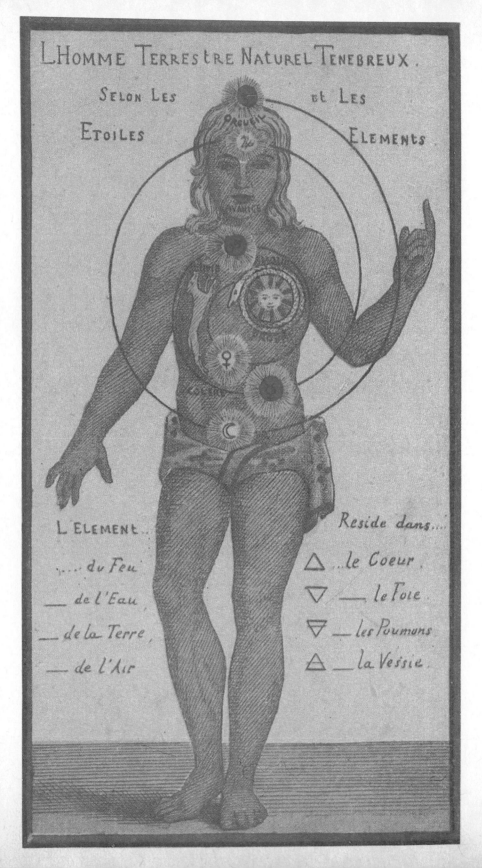

In aromatherapy, healing essential oils are mixed with a base or carrier oil and massaged into the body. Treatments can also be given by inhalation and bathing.

A collection of oils, herbs, loose incense, joss sticks and flowers. Also shown is an evaporator and a thurible, the top of which is being used as a joss stick holder.

Burning loose incense. In the background is a traditional, shop-bought thurible. In the foreground, a homemade equivalent. Silver foil is placed over a metal ashtray, charcoal is then lit and covered with herbs, and an empty can with holes punctured in the top is used as a cover.

A magical tool kit—all the materials needed for a traditional spell are kept in one safe place, partly for convenience and partly for psychological effect.

doesn't matter which traditional system you adopt for making predictions, as long as you use it as a springboard for your intuition.

Experiment. Watch and wait. Ask questions. Don't commit yourself until you feel confident. Rome wasn't built in a day, and you won't become a great seer simply because you have read the following instructions. It will take a little time and patience. There is just one final thing. Have a little fun. Don't concentrate too hard or take things too seriously. If you spend all your time staring intently at your palm you may miss the tall, dark, handsome stranger when he actually arrives!!!

Timing The Lines

Some palmists insist that you can only make precise timings if you take a print of the palm and make measurements from it. Others don't!

If you want to take prints, the section on page 163 tells you how to do it. If you don't, you can work by rule of thumb (literally!) instead.

Every technique employs one basic principle, as you will see. The line to be timed is divided into sections. If the line in question is forked, work with the clearest, deepest branch of the fork.

Timing the Life Line

Method One   The Bible gives the average life expectancy as three score years and ten. These days, at least in our part of the world, it's not unheard of for people to live into their nineties.

This technique requires that you simply divide up the lifeline into seven, eight, nine or ten equal sections (depending on whether you feel the average lifespan is 70, 80, 90 or 100 years), beginning at the top and working down towards the base of the palm. Each section represents a ten-year period of your life!

Method Two   This method suggests that the age of 20 can be established by drawing a straight line from the inside edge of the Jupiter finger, down the palm until it crosses the life line. The point of intersection will be age 20 and from there you can work forwards and backwards using the scale of one millimetre per year (or 5 mm per 5 years if you prefer). Advocates of this system say that the millimetre guide is not exact and should be made a little bigger or smaller depending on the length of the line – so in a way perhaps this technique is not too different from Method One.

Timing the Fate line

In this area, it seems that no one has challenged the old idea that life normally ends at 70.

Method One   Measure the palm from the top rascette (or lined bracelet around your wrist) to the base of the Saturn finger. Divide the line in half to find age 35 and work backwards or forwards from there.

Method Two   This suggests that age 35 can be found where the fate line crosses or hits the head line – regardless of how high or low the head line is.

Method Three   Simply suggests you divide the fate line into eight equal sections (10 years each).

Timing the Head line

Method One   This method suggests that youth, adulthood and old age are each shown by three equal divisions of the head line. Begin at the thumb edge of the palm for youth and move across.

Method Two   This suggests that the 35-year point can be established by drawing a line down from the inside edge of the Saturn finger until it reaches the head line and that you should then work backwards and forwards using the 1mm per year rule.

Method Three   Hardly a method, but at least one very eminent palmist swears that it is *impossible* to measure time on the head line!

Timing the Heart line

Almost every palmist agrees that there is no method of measuring time on the heart line.

Timing the Sun and Mercury lines

It should be said that most palmists *don't* consider it possible to time on these lines – and they consider that the few who have put forward methods are either very silly or are holding something back!

This is because they normally suggest that you divide the palm into eight equal portions from the base to the tip of the finger in question. Each portion represents a 10-year period of life, beginning at the base of the palm. The area(s) where the line is strongest show the years of most success. The trouble with this principle is that it is very common to find Sun lines (in particular) that are only really strong towards the top of the palm – even on the hands of those who find fame, recognition or success early in life.

Another technique suggested for the Mercury line is to read it as an indication of general health – with the area below the head line representing youth, the area between head and heart lines showing adulthood and the area above the heart line symbolizing old age.

Timing – A Summary

I've given these techniques because, as I've said, there are many people who swear by them. As you can probably guess from the tone of my writing I'm not so sure.

I do think that it's possible to time the hand up to a point but, perhaps because I am primarily an astrologer and used to very complex methods of timing the past and future, I find it difficult to accept such apparently illogical and simple methods.

If you are at all interested in the subject, I want to encourage you to experiment. Ask the owner of the hand you are looking at to tell you about one or two crucial events that occured in his or her life. They ought to show up on the relevant line, and perhaps by finding the corresponding marking you can develop your own system of timing or confirm one of the three methods outlined above.

Taking Prints

I have deliberately left the business of taking hand prints until the end of the chapter. If you intend to get serious about palmistry, you'll find that it is an absolutely invaluable way to study the subject. If on the other hand (pardon the pun), you just want to play with palmistry and use it to get a general idea of the character of a person then I think you will be able to see all you need to by holding the hand and looking at it closely, possibly with the aid of a magnifying glass.

If you do want to take prints you'll need some washable lino printing equipment which can be bought from an art shop. It's a slow, messy business – at least to begin with.

Many student palmists like to work with a print of the palm. This has the advantage of allowing you as much time as you need to make decisions – without the embarrassment of being watched all the time by your subject. There are, however, three main disadvantages.

The first is that you lose the personal contact which can make a palm reading come alive. It's undoubtedly true that the physical act of touching and holding someone's hand makes it considerably easier to establish a psychic bond between reader and subject. The art of Palmistry is not as scientific or 'rule bound' as astrology. With a horoscope, the planets speak for themselves. With a palm print, you are in the same position as the person who tries to do a long distance Tarot reading or I Ching consultation for somebody else. It's perfectly possible, but requires more confidence in your own telepathic and intuitive skill.

The second disadvantage is that palm prints are rather messy.

The third is that it feels a little odd. If you've ever had the misfortune to be arrested, or been burgled and obliged to give the police your fingerprints so they can distinguish your marks from the robbers', you'll know what I mean. There's something a little odd about having a part of your body manhandled, covered in ink and pressed firmly against a sheet of paper – no matter how worthy the cause. It's a bit like the feeling of being caught undressed in a changing room. Your subject can't help sensing a physical invasion of their personal privacy.

For this reason, I suggest that if you really want to take palm prints you make a point of doing it as sensitively, lovingly and carefully as possible. Try and make a few jokes or ask your subject actively to help you in the process. It will help keep the relationship between you sweet.

You can make a palm print with almost any form of ink or polish. Lipstick, boot polish and beetroot juice have all been used by friends of mine when they couldn't find anything else! Needless to say, none of these substances is recommended. Something instantly washable is far preferable. That's why many palmists recommend water soluble lino printing ink. You should be easily able to find this at a good art shop. You will also need a little ink roller, to make sure that the colour is evenly spread.

1 Find an old mirror, or a large sheet of glass.

2 Squeeze a dollop of ink onto it.

3 Spread the ink about with the roller till you have a nice, fairly thick, even coat of ink.

4 Now run the roller all over the subjects' hands, till they're nice and inky. Be sure to go down on to the wrist a bit too.

5 Before taking the print, get your subject to shake their hand in the air. This is nothing to do with drying ink. It's because, by now, their hand will have become tense and stiff. It's far preferable if you can get a print of a relaxed hand.

6 Get them to stretch out their fingers, then hold their hand over a large, clean and absorbent sheet of paper and place the wrist end down firmly. Then push the rest of the hand on to the paper. A sort of rolling effect is what you're after.

7 Now take a pencil and trace the shape of the outer edge of the palm, taking in the fingers if you like.

8 Now you will encounter the great disadvantage! Unless you've got the hand of someone with underdeveloped mounts, you'll find that there's a large dip in the middle, the Plain of Mars. You'll need to push the

paper gently up to meet this area – which will require lifting the hand with the paper still stuck to it and rubbing a soft ball of cloth or the handle of a knife over the hollow.

9 Now peel away the paper with one quick movement and study your result.

The chances are that your print will be blotchy, rather unpleasant – and possibly unreadable.

This is where only trial and error can help you.

It is perfectly possible to take a good palm print using the method I have just outlined, but there are factors like thickness of ink, vigour of rolling and pressure on paper, which vary from hand to hand and from palmist to palmist.

My best advice would be to practise on your own hand until you are fairly confident you can do it without too many retakes. If you happen to have a willing friend who will let you experiment on them, so much the better.

I shouldn't need to say this, but once you have mastered the art of palm printing, make a point of writing your subject's name on the paper and keep a record of which is the left and right print. It won't be long before you've built up a valuable reference library.

You may also like to date your prints so you can watch how people's hands change over the course of a few months or years.

I think it's safe to assume that if you are interested enought to take prints, you will also be interested enough to explore the other aspects of chirognomy such as hand shape, finger length, finger shape, and so on. In that case, you'll need to refer to a specialist book anyway, and as they all contain detailed instructions for taking prints I'll leave it at that for the time being – except to say that there are some very good books on palmistry and some very bad ones. A list of my favourite good books can be found in the bibliography on page 305.

Telling The Future – or Fortune Telling

I want to state, quite categorically, that no form of divination can tell you the future for sure. Whether you employ palmistry, astrology, Tarot, the I ching, tea leaves, market research or statistical analysis, you can only predict how things are most likely to turn out in times to come. The issue of Fate v. Free Will is a hoary one, and I don't believe anyone really knows the answers. It certainly seems as though some things are predestined, but it's also pretty clear that in many respects we all have the power to change and control the things that happen to us. To a degree, it's even as though the more you *believe* that your life is fated the more you will allow outside influences to affect you and thus confirm your own belief. And vice versa. The people who believe that there is nothing they cannot achieve are much more likely to change their own destiny.

Whatever you feel about fate and free will, it remains true that both magic and science only deal in possibilities. Those old stories about the gypsy lady who could look at a palm and predict a client's death to the hour and minute are simply rubbish. They may be true, but they are only true because the person having their hand read took the prediction to heart and *made* it come true. Even if death occurred by accident, the gypsy lady could not have seen it for sure. She was only taking a lucky guess based on a vision of the likely future. A little knowledge can be a dangerous thing, and too often those of us who have not studied a subject are at the mercy of those who claim they have. For every prediction of death or disaster that has come true there are hundreds on record that have been wrong.

No matter which field of divination you explore, given time, patience, study, discrimination and experience it certainly will be possible for you to make educated guesses about the future, and you may achieve a very high success rate. But please, never fall into the trap of believing that you – or any other forecaster – is infallible.

Having said all this, you will now understand why the information on palmistry given in this book does not go into great depth about how to read the future. As with astrology and Tarot, you cannot expect to dip your toe into a subject and find yourself submerged in its deepest secrets. Sometimes this happens, but usually it's necessary to spend many hours of study, becoming familiar with the basic tools of the art. Throughout the book you will find that we have tried to spell out the ground rules for each subject, rather than giving a potted, simplified and ultimately useless collection of fancy tricks which you could never hope to perform! The techniques given are simpler, but more reliable, and they will at least give you the confidence to get started. When you have found a subject that you feel an affinity for, you will be able to further your knowledge through any of the books in the bibliography on page 305.

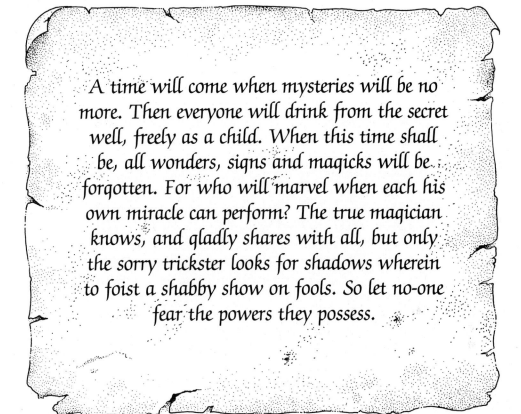

A time will come when mysteries will be no more. Then everyone will drink from the secret well, freely as a child. When this time shall be, all wonders, signs and magicks will be forgotten. For who will marvel when each his own miracle can perform? The true magician knows, and gladly shares with all, but only the sorry trickster looks for shadows wherein to foist a shabby show on fools. So let no-one fear the powers they possess.

ESP
and How to Develop It

**B**EFORE setting off on this particular magical adventure, let me explain some of the words you will be encountering. Firstly, ESP. ESP is the well-known abbreviation for Extra Sensory Perception, which over recent years has been the subject of considerable scientific research. According to formal definitions ESP is a label for four distinct phenomena: telepathy, clairvoyance, precognition and telekinesis. But because it is a word surrounded by so many scientific associations it is not a word that I am going to use. ESP is an observer's word, a laboratory label. The distinction between the phenomena of telepathy, precognition and clairvoyance is unimportant when it comes to magic. This chapter is a practical guide to making things happen, so who cares if your experience is labelled telekinesis or telepathy, as long as you experience something. The 'something' you are going to develop I shall call psi. Psi is that magical psychic feeling that knows the phone is going to ring, three seconds before it actually does. Psi is that quiet voice which tells you that the million-to-one coincidence of meeting your long-lost friend is no coincidence at all. Psi is that sudden impulse which makes you turn your head to look at the right part of the sky in time to see a shooting star.

Let's get this chapter off to an entertaining start. The following is a list of well documented, witnessed and attested to facts about certain people and their amazing experiences.

Jeanne Manlet, a 22-year-old French girl, could be struck with a 20 lb hammer without sustaining any injury whatsoever.

Gabrielle Maler, age 17, could stand sharp spikes being pushed against her body with the strength of four men without it doing her any harm at all.

In 1925, an Egyptian called Rahman Bey jabbed long knives into his body and cut himself all over without bleeding. He then healed the resultant wounds in a matter of minutes.

In 1934 at Calcutta University, before no less a witness than Nobel prize winner Sir C. U. Raman, a yogi drank a dose of sulphuric acid, some carbolic acid and nitric acid, then washed it down with broken glass. He immediately put himself into a trance for a while and emerged completely unaffected by his deadly meal.

There is an order of Tibetan holy men called Respas who live through the cold Tibetan winters in caves, clad only in one light cotton garment. The test for any aspiring initiate is that he should sit naked on the shores of the lake in midwinter, then, using only his body heat, dry out several large sheets of material which are first dipped in the ice-cold waters and placed on his body. This test is regularly passed and the order flourishes!

Daniel Dunglas Home (1833–86) is on record as having levitated in front of no less than 100 witnesses, some of whom were hanging on to his legs. He could also induce an accordion to float around the room, playing tunefully as it went. Not only that, but he could (and we are reliably told often did) stick his head into a blazing fire without suffering the slightest ill effect.

Al Herpin of Trenton, New Jersey, never slept from the day he was born until his death 20 years later.

Valentine Medinia, a Spanish farm labourer, had the same unique ability. He didn't sleep for 50 years. When his doctor suggested that he visit a specialist, Medinia walked to see him, covering the distance of 140 miles in four days and nights.

Carl Gustav Jung, the famous psychologist, could cause mysterious explosions and detonations to occur. He once caused two very loud ones to take place in Sigmund Freud's bookcase, much to the alarm of the great professor.

A 12-year-old schoolboy known as Andrew G twisted a single large crystal of aluminium out of shape at a distance of 30 feet. The experiment took place in controlled conditions, and the force being exerted on the metal was electronically monitored by no less than four stress gauges.

If the list were to continue, it would probably sound like this: Mrs X, a medium from Wye, successfully predicted disasters A, B and C, Z years before they actually happened. Or perhaps like this: 'At 4.30 last night, I woke up with the strangest feeling. I looked towards the foot of the bed and there was Granny and she did look sad. When I asked her what she was doing out of hospital at this time of the night, she simply said, "I must go" and then completely disappeared! The next day I got news that she had passed away in her sleep at the infirmary over 100 miles away. The time of death was given as 4.31 am!' And so on.

I am not mocking any of these tales, nor am I suggesting they are untrue. In fact, quite the reverse. They could be very true indeed and I am not alone in being quite prepared to accept that there are people in this world who have the power to blast the rules of normality to pieces.

When you read through lists of strange facts and amazing phenomena and learn of the regular breaking of human limitations, are you left with the following overriding feeling: 'That's great. But what about me? How can I fulfil some of *my* psychic potential? I don't want to fly or walk on water, but can't I come up with at least something, some small experience of the paranormal?'

Those were my questions and happily I learned that the answer to them was a big YES! Anyone can expand their awareness to the limits of the so-called normal order of things. Perception can be tuned to enable so-called 'extra sensory' events to occur. It does become possible. Your normal can become para, and your perception can become extra sensory. And surprising as it may sound, it will all feel very normal and totally sensory.

First you must stop marvelling at the ESP miracles of a tiny freak few. Instead you must look at your own life, your own senses and abilities. Then you can most definitely enter the realms of the miraculous.

Reading about the amazing power of other people can be very entertaining but it can be a great blockage to your own progress. Expectations can be raised so high that you become forced to remain a spectator and it becomes impossible to entertain even the thought of participating in such strange things. Scale your expectations down and you will soon feel the force of your own psi power. Then you will realize that there is nothing strange about psi – it is simply another dimension which everyone can enjoy. This point is very important and I'd like to go into it a bit further in order to make sure that you get as much as possible from the exercises and development games given later in the chapter.

Discovering the Real Power Within You

We live in a world where the other man's grass is always greener. We are regularly encouraged, even pressured, to imitate and aspire to be certain simple types of person, e.g. the perfect wife, the bread-winning husband, the extrovert performer, the sensitive artist. 'Be like me!' says the man on the beer advertisement hoarding. 'Be like me!' simpers the actress in the soap opera. 'No, be like me!' struts the rock star on the record cover. Eventually, we all become convinced that our lives would be so much better if only we could become a bit more like somebody else. People spend whole lifetimes walking around wishing 'If only I could be a star – then I'd be happy', or 'If only I were a millionaire – then I'd know what to do.' And there lies the great misunderstanding that robs us of so much. Is it so wonderful to be a star? Isn't is rather our imagination of what it would be like to be a star that is so attractive? Ask a star what it's like being one and he or she will probably answer along the lines, 'Well, it feels quite normal really. People think it's glamorous but it's just my job. It's what I do. It's hard work, etc., etc.'

Speak to a millionaire. Has his money made him happy? He'll probably say he's too busy working on his second million and trying to keep track of his first to worry about how happy he feels. Speak to a famous psychic about his paranormal powers. He'll probably give you a very normal answer.

So this then is the point. Do not be guided by your imagination of what you think an extra-sensory psychic experience should be and what it could do for you. If you do, I'm afraid you will get very frustrated. Trying to be a psychic wonder or hoping to discover and unleash some mighty inner power with which to conquer a new world will block off your real power. Psi is in you. It doesn't need to be invented. Start your investigations by gently experimenting with what you've already got. You'll be surprised at how deep your awareness is.

What is Normal?

The experience of psi is, to a great extent, caused by changing our attitudes to what is possible and what is normal. Normal and possible are very important words. For example, there is an account of a certain primitive tribe of Indians where the concept of writing on paper was completely unknown. When exposed to the written word for the first time, they showed amazement and disbelief. How, they asked, could one man know exactly what another man had seen and even spoken, down to the exact words, by simply holding in front of him what appeared to be a flimsy piece of cloth. To them, writing was not normal, and so reading seemed impossible. They thought it was magic.

We are in a very similar position today. Anything that happens to us that is not immediately explicable scientifically makes us uneasy. We have grown to have great faith in our scientists and we look to them for clear-cut answers and explanations for everything. If something happens for no reason that science can explain, we are quick to conclude that there is trickery or even black magic afoot! The possibility that there are other perfectly normal explanations apart from scientific ones is the last thing that occurs to us.

Well, times are changing. And in the very front ranks of this change are the scientists themselves. A very brief look at some of the scientific attitudes that we have inherited may help to put things into perspective.

In the 17th century the science responsible for investigating the human being was biology. However, studying the human being as a biological specimen was limited. Certainly, to reach any understanding of human perception or potential was out of the question. Physics, the study of matter in general, not just human matter, took over the task. The physicist of the time trusted his senses implicitly. He made notes and measurements, invented clocks to measure time and generally observed everything. His brain operated in the middle ground of basic, everyday, sensory experiences, finding a pattern in what appeared to be chaos.

Sir Isaac Newton (1642–1727) was perhaps the greatest exponent of this objective and rational view of life. He made the possibility that the universe ran like clockwork seem so convincing that for over 200 years any deviation from his theories was simply ignored. The world was one separate solid unit made up of bits and the theory was that if you kept chopping the bits in half and in half again you would eventually find the ultimate, unchoppable 'bit' out of which the whole universe was made. As the scientists concentrated on atoms and molecules they became more detached from the very thing they were looking at.

Heisenberg's Principle of Uncertainty

However, in 1931 Werner Heisenberg was given the Nobel prize for his Principle of Uncertainty. Like all Nobel prize winners, he supported his theory with more than the required amount of incontestable laboratory experimentation and the usual, irrefutable, brain-stretching mathematics.

In the opinion of the scientific world, if Heisenberg was uncertain, then *everyone* ought to be uncertain.

His uncertainty came about as the result of watching the behaviour of elementary sub-atomic particles. They were doing alarming things. For a start, even though they were moving, he couldn't measure their position and speed at the same time. He could measure one or the other, but not both simultaneously. Put another way, he could get a reading for them on his 'speedometer', but when he got a reading the particles didn't appear on his map of the usual paths along which they travelled. On the other hand, when they could be seen on the map, the 'speedometer' said they weren't moving. If the thing is moving, surely it must be somewhere. But it wasn't.

Eventually, Heisenberg concluded that these particles were doing what they were doing as a result of the simple fact that he was watching them! Therefore, you couldn't observe a thing without somehow altering it by observing it.

Einstein's Theory of Relativity

Heisenberg was not alone in generating doubt about the solidity of the universe. Another man who considerably loosened up the general view of what was possible and normal was Albert Einstein. He took the idea of time – which up to that point everyone had assumed was constant wherever and whenever you looked at your watch – and he pointed out that it was, in fact, a completely stretchable and variable phenomenon. Until Einstein, it was assumed that clocks went faster or slower while time itself always went at the same pace. After Einstein, time depended on how you looked at it – just like everything else in the universe.

Whatever happened to certainty? According to Einstein's theory of relativity, time was very much to do with (among other things) how fast you were travelling and there was nothing absolute about it at all. This theory has, in recent years, been put to the test and shown by practical demonstration to be true.

In the 1970s an interesting experiment took place to test the practical effects of the relativity of time. It was basically a very simple test, requiring two fast jet aircraft and four atomic clocks. The atomic clock is the most accurate time-measuring device known to man. It is accurate to within one ten millionth of a second per year (which is more regular than the movements of the stars or the planets). Two atomic clocks were placed on each of two jets. The jets then flew at high speed around the world in different directions, one flying east and one flying west. All four clocks were synchronized with each other and showed the same time when the jets set off. When the jets arrived back after their lightning, non-stop trip around the globe, the two clocks on one jet told a different time to the two clocks on the other jet! Somehow, it seems, motion through space had an effect on time. 'Space time' had come into being.

The implications of this experiment are fascinating from a psi point of view. Think about it again. You take two atomic clocks, start them simultaneously, put them on a table and leave them – and they both say the same time. They will both continue to say the same time as each other for as long as you leave them there.

Take one clock and hurl it around the world at high speed, and when it comes back put it next to its twin. Now they no longer say the same time. The travelled clock is running slightly slower – not because it has gone wrong in the journey or anything like that, but because it has been measuring a different sort of time. Time for the moving clock has been going past at a different rate. It is therefore clear that time and space are not separate things. There is a connection between the two. Events that are separate in time do not have to be unconnected with each other. Neither do events which are separate in space have to be considered unconnected.

The possibility of being able to communicate with another event, distant in time, becomes scientifically quite acceptable. Similarly, the likelihood of being able to connect with another person completely separate in space also becomes well within the realms of possibility. The psi labels for these two phenomena are precognition (for the time connection) and telepathy (for the connection between humans in space).

It seems that even scientifically, events do not have to be seen as before or after each other. They simply take place in the time-space continuum where before and after, cause and effect are not separate things. Effects can now happen before causes. Carts can happily precede horses!

Similarly, in the world of matter, the inescapable scientific conclusion is that there is some kind of magic afoot which rules and laws cannot encompass. Let's look at one more example in this area before we move on to the more personal, do-it-yourself part of the chapter.*

Bell's Theorem

Imagine you are standing outside with a pistol in each hand. You raise both arms outwards and fire the pistols simultaneously to the left and the right of you. The right-hand bullet hits a rock and ricochets wildly off at an angle. The left-hand bullet doesn't hit a rock, or anything else for that matter, but it too richochets wildly off at an angle!

If this happened to you, you would certainly regard it as a miracle, yet, on an atomic level, it is exactly what happens. Einstein, Podelsky and Rosen proposed the theory of it. Dr J.S. Bell than proved it mathematically. And recently, in repeated experiments, it has been observed as an irrefutable, if mind-boggling, fact.

The laboratory experiment which made this amazing discovery can be set up like this. A particle gun is arranged to fire out two streams of atomic particles in opposite directions. Not only does it fire them out, but it also makes each particle spin in an anti-clockwise direction as it flies forward. One of the streams of particles is aimed to pass through an electromagnetic 'spin reversing' device, which when switched on will change the direction of the spin of the stream passing through it from anti-clockwise to clockwise. Now this is where the fun begins. When the spin changer is turned on, not only do the particles passing through it change their direction and speed, but so too do the particles in the other stream.

Likewise, when the spin changer is turned off, the particles passing

---

* The only reason I am giving you this scientific and abstract information is to make you more confident in your own personal experience. You must forget any idea that you are trying to go against commonsense or the laws of nature. The laws of nature have been seen by great scientific minds to be in need of expanding. So go ahead and expand them.

through it revert to their anti-clockwise spin – and so do the particles in the other stream, instantaneously.

Physics finds this phenomenon hard to explain. How can one thing affect another thing which is completely unconnected with it? The answer is clear. There is a connection between the two separate particle streams, *and the connection is the mind of the observer*.

And so we have a situation where scientists are the first to admit that there is a lot more going on than anyone ever suspected. Their relentless precision and desire for explanations have in a sense backfired on them. Intense scientific curiosity has lifted a veil on a whole new era of understanding where, much to the disappointment of the professional scientist, scientific attitudes have no authority.

To quote 20th-century physicist Rodney Michael Heisenberg: 'The common division of the world into subject and object, inner world and outer world, body and soul is no longer adequate.'

Or on a more apologetic and slightly plaintive note, Erwin Schrodinger. 'The world of physics is a world of shadows. We were not aware of it; we thought we were dealing with the real world.'

This scientific confusion and rethinking is very reassuring. It puts the business of exploring human potential and awareness firmly back in the hands of the individual, the common person, us! Ordinary mortals do not need to take degrees in quantum physics or build billion dollar particle accelerators in order to prove that there is some X factor waiting to be explored. We are all born perfectly equipped to carry out our own personal research into the subject, using the ideal tool for the job – our own awareness. Space, time and matter have many dimensions and they are all interlinked. The way to investigate them is no longer by observing with microscopes and clocks from some supposedly detached point of view. We should participate and learn from the inside just what the human mind is capable of.

The Mind (And How to Get at It!)

The human mind is an unexplored region. We have all got one, and you are using yours at this very moment to read these words.

The trouble with the mind is that it is very hard to pin down. To most of us, the mind is inextricably associated with the brain and firmly locked away inside the head. From this citadel of bone it peers out via our senses at the world around us, and at other people peering out of their equally impregnable fortresses. Our senses make their connection with events and objects and send the information back to headquarters. And that is about all we understand of it. Once the information has been brought in from the outside world, what happens next remains to this day very much a mystery.

When it comes to facts about the human mind, science hasn't got any. Science has absolutely *no idea* where the mind is to be found. It has always assumed, as the rest of us do, that the mind is in the brain, and in its usual scientific, logical way science has chopped up and catalogued as many different aspects of the brain as possible. Meanwhile, the true human potential of the mind, the 'I' inside, has gone completely unnoticed. Science admits that large areas of the brain are completely unmapped and has no theories as to what these areas are for.

As for the sections of the brain that science has labelled, even these careful delineations have come under very close scrutiny in recent years. It used to be thought that isolated parts of the brain controlled specific and separate functions of thought and action, one area for speech, another area for movement, etc. Recent research has shown that this only holds true for the most basic aspects of human function, such as motor actions and reflexes. All the higher 'personality' or 'mind' qualities totally defy being pinned down to any one area of the brain. The higher functions seem not only to be concentrated in specific sections but to be equally present in every other part of the brain as well. The brain, it seems, is more like a hologram than a glorified filing cabinet.

Let me explain. A hologram, as every schoolboy knows, is a 3D picture made by laser light on a glass (or plastic) plate. What every schoolboy probably doesn't know is that if you break a hologram image plate in half down the middle and then look at the separate pieces under laser light, much to your surprise, you won't see half the picture on each piece. No. You will see, on each separate piece, a complete version of the original image. Break the pieces again into four, or indeed smash them to smithereens, and this process will continue. On each separate smithereen you will see a complete likeness of the original image.

If we look at the brain in a similar way, adopting a holographic viewpoint, it becomes quite reasonable to propose that the whole of the mind, or 'I', might be present in every separate part. This would be quite in keeping with modern biological evidence and would at least go some of the way towards loosening the idea that a human being's being is somehow rigidly located in the brain, which in turn is fixed firmly in the head, which is bolted solidly on to the shoulders.

The holographic idea of the brain is gaining support. *The Times*, on December 30, 1980, published an account of a student at Sheffield

University who had an honours degree in maths, and an IQ of 126. What this student didn't have was any cerebral cortex! That is the part of the brain which has always been assumed to be responsible for the higher thinking functions. What he was thinking with remains a mystery to this day. The suggestion that the mind has the ability to shift around, at least within the brain, seems a reasonable hypothesis in the circumstances.

If we are going to try to get to grips with this mind, this sense of 'I am here' which seems to exist somewhere between our ears and behind our eyes, then we're going to have to look beyond science for our answer. In short, the only way to come to terms with the mind is from inside. And this means a total change of perspective.

The Feeling of Me

What we have to do as aspiring 20th-century psychic explorers is to develop an inner way of looking at things. We must start the journey back from the colours and sounds and events of the world around us, back via our senses, past our opinion of it all, to arrive at the subtle yet powerful feeling of *me*. We need to change our perspective and loosen the monopoly that our senses have on us. If we are to develop psi, we must no longer be solely concerned with events around us and how they relate to each other, but rather with how those events affect us. We should not care about winning or losing, giving or taking, going fast or going slow, rather we should care about how it *feels* to win, how it *feels* to lose, what feelings giving inspires and what feelings we get when we take.

This may sound a little daunting when written down in stark black and white, so remember that it is only a tendency or trend that we are trying for. The senses will always dominate, but what we want to do is to create the possibility of swinging the balance between senses and inner intuition a little bit more in favour of intuition. To do this, we must look inside rather than outside. We must take our concentration back from the world around us and redirect it on to the experience that the world around us is inspiring within us.

The First Exercise
(or How to Prove You Exist!)

This is a pleasant exercise and a good example of what we are up against once we start trying to listen to the tiny little cosmic experiences that lie behind our overwhelmingly normal day-to-day sensory experiences.

With this exercise, you are being, quite literally, thrown in at the deep end – either to feel a complete idiot or to have a hint of a feeling about something. I can promise no more at this stage. Try it.

Next time you have a bath, fill the bath a bit fuller than usual. If you are a quick bathing sort of person, change your routine and take your time. Lie there in your deeper-than-usual bath for a ridiculously indulgent length of time. If this is what you normally do, stay there even longer! When you've finished your soak, instead of pulling out the plug and getting out, pull out the plug and stay in. Simply lie back with your arms by your side and let the water slowly drain away.

As the water runs out, what do you feel? Obviously, as you haven't done the exercise yet, you won't know! Let me tell you some of the reactions that others have reported. These are the reactions of people who have just done a totally mundane thing like staying in the bath after the plug has been pulled out.

I felt frightened. I thought my life energy was draining away. I had to do something quickly.'

'When the water had gone, I felt I was trapped in someone else's body. I knew it was my body but it was as if I was locked in something that didn't belong to me.'

'For the first time ever, I felt my body for what it was. I could feel its limits. I felt I was inside every part of it.'

'I felt cold, wet and dirty and I wanted to get dry, so I did. What a stupid thing to ask me to do.'

This last reaction is a very common and perfectly valid one, both when felt in yourself or when expressed by other people. In any psi experiment, as in all magic, there can be no element of force or coercion.

We have to listen willingly to what the gentler subconcious part of the mind is saying and we only hear what we want to hear. After decades of living in the 20th century, the inner voice has had most of its life kicked out of it. It is not going to stand up and shout or compete with the powerful input of the senses. But it is there and it can be heard. I hope that you will try this experiment and see what happens. As with all psi games, it can go one of two ways. Either you will end up stark naked, wet and freezing and covered in scum; or perhaps you will feel a sense of 'Here I am in my body'. This is a very simple, yet very magical, awareness.

A Tuning-in Exercise

To keep the ball rolling, here is another very simple psi experiment which you can do anywhere. But first, let me tell you a story.

A great magician was sitting in a Paris street café, talking to a friend. His friend was sceptical about magic and about psi power in general. So the magician agreed to give him an on the spot demonstration. He asked his sceptical friend to point to a passer-by who he wanted to be the subject of the demonstration. When a man was pointed out, the magician immediately leapt up and began walking in step behind him. The magician walked slowly closer and closer to the man, keeping perfectly in step. Soon the magician and the man were separated only by inches, with the magician, unbeknown to his subject, completely tuned in to his breathing, rhythm and gait, walking along behind him in step. To the casual observer, they must have looked a comic pair, doing the music hall 'ducks' routine on the street. Suddenly, the magician threw himself to the ground. Immediately, the unsuspecting man did exactly the same – collapsing in an extremely surprised heap on the pavement.

I do not recommend that you try that exercise as it could have some very embarrassing consequences for everyone concerned. However, here is a simpler one to do which is on the same lines.

Whenever you are out in public in a stationary situation (i.e. on the bus or train, in a queue or sitting in a waiting room), find someone who has got their back turned towards you. The object of the exercise is to get them to turn round. Obviously, you don't say anything to them or wave at them, you simply 'tune in' and 'will' them to turn around. It is quite possible to achieve, and gives a slightly exhilarating feeling when you manage it, as if you'd just worked a great miracle. It is a normal, everday human ability, yet scientifically and rationally it is inexplicable. This a good exercise for giving yourself confidence in your natural psi potential as it very rarely fails.

PSI and Relaxation

Let's take a look at the whole subject of relaxation. It is undoubtedly true that the human mind performs its psi function best when it is relaxed. If you are going to make any progress in awakening your psi powers, you must take stock of yourself in this area. Are you relaxed? If the answer you give yourself is 'Yes', then I'm afraid you are probably lying! Tension is normal, so normal that you don't even notice it. The reasons why we have come to accept such a high level of anxiety in our lives are unimportant,

Pushing back the psychic thresholds in deepest Carshalton, Surrey, circa 1937. Mr. D. C. Russell throws respectability to the wind to prove once again that 'it's all in the mind'.

because knowing the reasons for anxiety and for tension does not release us from them. As 20th-century psi aspirants, we are not concerned with the complexities of how the problems came into being. They do not matter. All we know is that we have a tremendous amount of tension flooding our being and jangling our responses, and we would like to get rid of it. Knowing reasons and labelling causes only *creates* tension. This is an admission we must all make if we are to open our psi channels.

So referring back to the original question – 'Are you relaxed?' the anwswer must be No, unless you've taken some specific steps to learn how to relax yourself. Anyone who is leading a 'normal' routine in a 'normal' day-to-day situation, having 'normal' relationships with 'normal' people cannot possibly be relaxed and the first thing you'd better do is admit it. When you have admitted that you are not perfect, and you are prepared to accept that there may be one or two little knots in your personality that could perhaps be holding you back in some way, then you can set about the business of finding out the source of the blockage. I mentioned change of perspective earlier. Here again, the source of the problem does not lie outside, in your life around you or in your friends and family. It lies in you. Let me illustrate this point with rather an extreme example – firewalking.

Firewalking is not a myth or a possibility. It is a scientifically witnessed and attested fact. Although it seems impossible, many people are able to stroll across beds of hot coals unharmed. Even relatively 'unqualified' Western people can walk on red hot cinders with no ill effect and with apparently only their state of mind to protect them. Look at it like this. If anyone had good reason to put the blame for their discomfort on something outside themselves, then it must surely be a person standing barefoot on a red hot cinder! But they do not. Firewalkers pay no attention to the fire. It seems that their state of mind goes beyond responding to scorching feet. Indeed, it goes so far beyond responding that it is able to influence and control the situation outside. The magical mind is actually capable of changing a normally flammable substance like skin into something temporarily fireproof. The key to the whole situation is not in the feet or the fire. It is in the mind.

Let's take the first steps, not towards performing great firewalking miracles, but towards looking inwards into our own minds.

Meditation

Meditation is relaxation. It is a technique, or a course of action, or a thing to do which has the sole purpose of directing this inaccessible thing called the mind. The mind loves to be concentrated and is at happiest when it has something to do and its energies are all focused in one place. Concentration through meditation brings about relaxation.

Here is a true story that happened to me. It took place many years ago when I was aspiring to be an actor. I had made an appointment with a drama teacher to see if he would accept me as a pupil. I arrived at his studio on time and we sat down, he behind a desk and me in front, and we talked about my potential as an actor and about drama in general. After about five minutes he asked me to get up and go and stand facing him at the other end of the room. I willingly did this as I assumed that it was some kind of appraisal of my height or posture or something. I stood in my best casual actor's posture, trying to look composed and relaxed. This was when it began to get difficult. The trouble was that having asked me to go and stand at the end of the room, he stopped talking altogether. He said nothing at all and just sat behind his desk looking at me. The seconds ticked by very slowly indeed. My 'relaxed' posture began to feel extremely unrelaxed as if it had been hung on me like a suit that was two sizes too small. As the minutes went by, I cracked altogether. I started to shuffle stiffly, to scratch my head and jerkily put my hands in and out of my pockets. I finally ended up nervously wringing my hands together, biting my lip and awkwardly darting glances around the room or out of the window. At that point the good man had mercy on me.

'How many books are there on the shelf behind me?' he said.

Immediately, without realizing it, I was saved. I had something to concentrate on. I started enthusiastically to count the books. By the time I had got to ten, I felt at ease. My shoulders dropped and my body began to lose its tension. I stopped twitching and shuffling. My hands also stopped flapping and dropped naturally to my side and my gaze became steady. By the time I had counted the books, I was standing relaxed, alert and unselfconscious – feeling fine. Where there had been a tense, confused and distracted person (me!), a single act of concentration of mind had produced a relaxed and happy individual whose being was functioning in the natural and spontaneous way that it was made to.

There is a phrase in English, beloved of sensational fiction writers. It is 'tense with concentration'. It could not be further from the point. Concentration brings relaxation, QED, concentration is what meditation is all about.

Meditation is a very spiritual and rather daunting word. Put simply, meditation is a deliberate attempt to concentrate the mind. In fact, in its simplest form meditation can be said to be no more than simply watching the television or listening to a record. For 'watching' and 'listening' substitute 'meditating on'. It's as straightforward as that. The idea is that by putting your concentration on something, and keeping it there, the rest of you simply drops into place while you're not looking. There are literally millions of people throughout the world who do meditation and it is to be thoroughly recommended.

The techniques of meditation, i.e. what you do, vary enormously. So much in fact that it is impossible to do justice to the subject in this one short chapter. So what I have done is to choose three very simple methods of meditating, which can be easily understood from a book. If these techniques interest you and you feel you want to know more about meditation, then you should find a teacher. However, for the purposes of relaxation and psi development, these meditation techniques will work for anyone, regardless of temperament. Use them as it suits you and feel free to adapt them in any way that makes you feel comfortable.

Candle Meditation

This is a very calming and slightly romantic thing to do. I recommend it as an introduction. It is best done at night and requires only some time, some quiet and a nightlight or candle. With this exercise, there is no substitute for a relatively quiet environment and a bit of privacy, so you'll have to wait till the kids are in bed and the neighbour's stereo breaks down. If this is your first experiment with meditation, you will need to do it in a place that is as distraction-free as possible. The exercise should last for about ten minutes.

Sit down comfortably, either in a chair or on a cushion on the floor. (The idea is to get your body in as relaxed a position as possible. Just because you are about to meditate does not mean that you have to assume some great yogic posture with your legs crossed and your back as straight as a ramrod. Don't lie down, though, or you'll fall asleep.) When you've chosen a comfortable position, get up, light the candle and turn out the light. Place the candle securely about 6 feet (2 metres) in front of your chair. Return to your pre-prepared, comfortable position.

Concentrate on the candle flame. That's all you have to do. There is nothing else to this exercise. Simply concentrate on the candle flame. Let it hypnotize you, if you can. Stare at it. Gaze at it. Focus on it. That's all you have to do.

I think you will soon see that these are deceptively simple requests! Obviously, like the bath exercise earlier, you won't be able to know exactly what it feels like to do this experiment until you have done it, and there is not a lot I can say in the way of guidance without prejudicing you. But here are a few points that may help and be of interest. Remember, though the thing that counts is *your* experience. You are not trying to imitate something you have read in a book.

★ Although you are trying to focus your eyes on the flame, they keep wandering off after a few seconds at the most.

★ You suddenly become aware of your thoughts talking to you – apparently inside your head.

★ Your body, which can sit motionless for hours watching the telly, becomes extremely restless.

★ Sometimes your mind comes to rest on the flame and you have a feeling of peace and your body feels relaxed.

★ When you close your eyes, you can still see the image of the flame on your retina. You continue to concentrate on it.

★ Your thoughts drift off to some event of the past or some imagination of the future.

★ You suddenly notice your other senses hearing minute or distant sounds and rustles or new smells.

★ You notice your breath coming and going.

The list of possible experiences could go on and on. For every person who does this exercise there would be a different catalogue of sensations and impressions. The idea of the exercise is to draw your attention to the wealth of subtle inner feelings and tendencies that are present all the time within. For only when we start to concentrate in a subtle and reflective way do the workings of our mind become apparent. In the silence of a quiet room, against the simple background of one hypnotic candle flame, the thoughts and feelings of daily life can be clearly seen for what they are. This is the beginning of meditation. Simply by concentrating a large part of our awareness in one place, we have created some space for the remainder of our mind to unfold in its unique way. The impressions that filter through are not ours to control; they come from a deeper part, a part that with practice we can learn to trust.

Candle meditation is an introduction to meditation and is not intended to be an exercise to repeat regularly.

A Relaxation Exercise

The following relaxation exercise can make you feel very good indeed if it is done with the mental awareness of the previous exercise. The basic principle is very simple. You concentrate on different areas of the body, one at a time, first tensing up all the muscles and then relaxing them suddenly. This exercise can be done anywhere – in the bus, at the office, at home. For the first few times, do it lying on your back on the floor, with your head gently supported by a pillow. Wear loose clothing and no shoes.

Start with the feet, one at a time. Tense the muscles in your feet, and as you do so count slowly to five. 'One, two, three, four, five.' Then release all the tension and mentally count to five again. Feel the relaxation in your feet for these five seconds and enjoy the feeling. Now repeat the process.

Next, treat the calves in the same way. Tense for a count of five; relax for a count of five; twice. Then do the thighs.

Now tense the entire left leg and then the right, only this time hold the count for ten, then relax for ten. Obviously the counting side of the exercise doesn't have to be exactly right, as if you were counting seconds on a clock. If you prefer, you can count your breaths instead. Breathe slowly and gently, if possible making the sounds of the in and out breaths the same. Count in 'one', out 'two', in 'three', out 'four', etc. The idea of the count is to set a gentle steady pace at which you can cover all the sections of the body.

Here is a running order for the entire body. Do every section twice and hold the tension/relaxation on the group sections for longer.

1 Feet	9 Stomach
2 Calves	10 Back
3 Thighs	11 Stomach and back together
4 Legs	12 Neck
5 Hands	13 Face
6 Lower arms	14 Neck and face together
7 Upper arms	15 Everything! (i.e. the entire body)
8 Arms	

For this final stage – the tensing/relaxing of the entire body – breathe as follows. Take a deep breath (not a huge one) and hold it. Then tense the entire body for a mental count of five. As you relax, gently and slowly breathe out. Phew!

After you've done this exercise a few times, you might like to lengthen the number of cycles of tension/relaxation from two to three or four. Also, feel free to lengthen the holding count, once you've done a few sessions at the given rate.

'Internal' Meditation

If the above exercise is a little on the physical side for you, try the following meditation technique.

In this exercise, most of the 'action' takes place in your brain. Electronic brainwave scanners (EEG machines) have shown that there is often an increase in the brain's alpha rhythms during meditation. These slow brain wave patterns occur when a person is relaxed, maybe with their eyes closed, still attentive and alert. It is not like an 'awake and active' wave or like an 'asleep or passive' wave. It is somewhere half way between the two and is similar in many ways to sitting contentedly in a sunny country garden with no particular thoughts or problems, occasionally hearing a bee droning by. Or perhaps lying on a remote beach with no worries, listening to the waves. It is in this alpha state that the psi can grow if it wants to. NB: Psi can never be forced.

By practising meditation regularly, you will increase the chances of your psi potential coming through enormously. Obviously, after one session of meditation you cannot expect to be able to predict the future or to walk on water. But after a few sessions, the increased awareness brought about by your inner concentration will spill over into your day-to-day life. Psi will begin to show. Researchers in America have found that the people who practise meditation (in this study it was Transcendental Meditation, an excellent form of meditation which I recommend but which depends on being taught orally so is therefore impossible to learn from a book), are better in psi tests than non meditators. In another experiment, it was found that ESP scores of a small group of students increased significantly after an Indian yogi had given brief instruction on meditation. Similarly, the ESP scores of the renowned and respected psychic Lal Singh Harribance were best when the EEG recording his brain waves showed the most alpha waves.

In the last two meditation techniques, you placed your concentration on something outside yourself – a candle flame and different parts of your body. This time, you are going to concentrate on something internal. Something in your own mind. All meditation must have an object. In this meditation exercise you are going to choose an idea to focus on and this idea you must choose yourself. It is going to provide you with an anchor and a point of reference from which you can experience clearly the impressions and thoughts of your own mind while remaining poised in an uncritical and compassionate position. The thing you choose to meditate on should be something for which you have an affinity and be something which you like. (Meditating on people is not recommended.) For example only, here is a list of some of the things that I have known people to meditate on.

- ★ My favourite colour – blue.
- ★ The nature of astrology.
- ★ The shape of a leaf.
- ★ The word love.
- ★ The word desire.
- ★ Things I like about tennis.
- ★ Music.
- ★ Simple, positive and natural ideas or shapes are best as there seems to be a tendency for the mind to rest more easily on objects that are not man-made. Having chosen what you are going to meditate on, you are ready to begin.

Sit down comfortably in as peaceful and private a place as you can find. You are experimenting with a very delicate and receptive thing – your own mind – so keep distractions to a minimum. If necessary, darken the room. It is often a good idea to wear a light blanket or a bedspread, wrapped around you like a cloak or robe. This is in no way a necessity, but it does make you feel snug and somehow more concentrated.

Close your eyes, shuffle about if necessary till all your itches are scratched. Take a deep in-breath, then have a deep, loud sigh. Have another if you want. Shake the tension from your shoulders and roll your head about on your neck to ease any tightness. Now relax. Feel your breath coming and going quietly. Count your breaths from ten down to one. In out (ten); in, out (nine); in, out (eight); etc. When your reach one, allow your attention to focus on the subject of your meditation. In this example, I am going to describe how to meditate on the word 'psi'.

See it in your mind – the word psi. (If you want to, write down the subject of your meditation on a piece of card before you start and prop it up clearly in front of you.) Hear the word in your head, or if necessary say it once or twice quietly to yourself.

What you must do is think only of psi and of nothing else. Psi is your main interest and you are going to consider all the meanings and associations it has for you. Hold psi at the centre of attention in your mind – then *watch what flows past*. Don't get carried away by it. Simply observe it. It is a bit like watching a rock with a fast stream running past it. Your attention will leave the rock and fix on the flowing water and be swept away a bit. You may return to the rock as soon as you notice that you are not looking at it. You must suddenly find that you are thinking of something completely different. Try to trace it back to what you are meditating on. There is usually some connection. Return to the object of your meditation. It may be that some image connected with psi starts a whole chain of associations and you may wander off into your imagination for minutes at a time. Don't get frustrated, simply re-focus your thoughts on your subject. Be aware of your thoughts as they flit about, taking your concentration with them. Observe them but always return to the object of your meditation. Explore the flow of your mental processes.

Your Psychic Energy Centres

The traditional scientific view is that the brain is the seat of awareness. The right-hand side is alleged to concern itself with the more spiritual, artistic and intuitive functions, and the left-hand side with the logical, rational and deductive functions. If you think about it, this piece of information, however impressive it may be to scientists, is not really of very much practical help to the rest of us. Knowing that your psi faculty lies somewhere buried underneath the right-hand side of your skull is not going to help you to develop it. When it comes to looking at and understanding your own consciousness, it is not enough to look only to the brain. You must look to the East and learn from the Indian philosophers.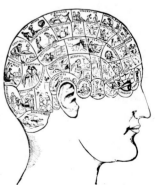

Before going any further with the exercises, I want to tell you about the other 'brains' or psi centres that you possess, and which you probably don't know anything about. There are seven of these centres, all equally as

Mantras

If this were a talking book, I would be able to direct and help you to a greater extent. Instead of asking you to focus your mind on a subject of your own choice, I would be able to recommend a suitable mantra. A mantra (there is no equivalent English word) is a word or phrase that has the right sound – a sound which is considered by the meditation teacher to be suitable for the particular temperament of the student. The student would then take the word and make it the object of meditation, repeating it inwardly with the coming and going of the breath.

If you want to understand the principle of what I'm saying, try this word as a mantra: 'IN-OUT'. When you breathe in, say in your mind the first part of the word 'IN-'. And when you breathe out, say the last part '-OUT'. This is just an example to help you understand the basic principle of meditating on mantras. Try it by all means, but if you want to study it more deeply I recommend that you go to a meditation teacher for personal, face-to-face, instruction.

After only a few sincere attempts at meditation your mind will get more used to dealing with what is immediately in front of it, instead of flitting about all over the place, raising fears and doubts and dissipating itself. It will get used to its new habit of dealing with one thing at a time. You will experience greater simplicity and clarity in all your affairs. Energies normally wasted and mental activity hitherto needlessly expended will be available for deeper understanding and perception, while energy that has for so long formed blocks and barriers will be concentrated, leaving the channels open for the more spontaneous psi powers to pass through.

important to you as the centre called the brain. Let me explain. As I have said, people today, particularly in the West, are conditioned to think of their head as the centre of their being. This is not so. The consciousness or being of the human being is spread out (remember the bath experiment?) over the entire body. Everybody, whether they believe it or not, has seven centres or focuses where their consciousness is concentrated, each one in its own way as powerful as the brain. The cerebral cortex (the brain) is the home of only one out of our seven psychic powerhouses.

While Western scientists have not even managed to discover the existence of one psychic energy centre, Hindu occultists have managed to confuse the issue by discovering 88,000 of them! However, readers will be relieved to know that for the purposes of 99·9999% of the human race, there are only seven of these centres to be experienced. But as these centres have been ignored in the Western world for thousands of years, no English word is available to describe them. I shall refer to them by their Indian label – the Chakras.

7 Crown Chakra
6 Brow Chakra
5 Throat Chakra
4 Heart Chakra
3 Stomach Chakra
2 Loin Chakra
1 Root Chakra

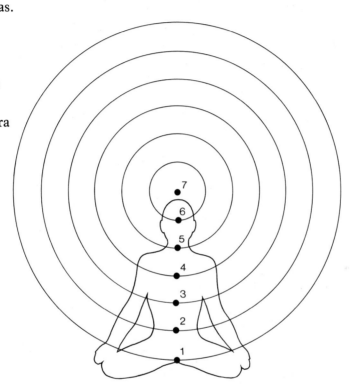

The energy centres of the chakras work together in harmony. The combined energies lead the individual upwards, to their highest awareness.

Crown Chakra   God awareness, entrance point for highest human potential, harmonizes and controls entire being.

Brow Chakra   Idealism, high intent, purity, personal magnetism, energy and attractiveness.

Throat Chakra   Highest creative feelings, imagination, voice, breath and communication.

Heart Chakra   Compassion, feeling for others, self as part of groups, sympathy.

Stomach Chakra   Needs and appetites, pleasures, lower emotions and fears.

Loin Chakra   Sexual motivation and reproduction.

Root Chakra   Survival and crisis reaction.

The Chakras are an integral part of our spiritual geography. To the average Westerner they sound outrageous and unlikely. However, with a little bit of awareness and subtlety, they are easy to feel. Each Chakra represents a different level of consciousness – which, put simply, means a different type of feeling. Every feeling or thought we have has its seat in one of our Chakras and can be physically felt there. Everyday language unwittingly acknowledges the existence of Chakras with such phrases as: 'Gut reaction', 'My heart went out to him', 'Highbrow, lowbrow', and more colloquially, the survival expression: 'To save your butt'.

The Chakras are not on the surface of the body; they are within it and they are best imagined as tiny, bright lights, inside the body, each one having a gentle round glow around it radiating outwards.

More about Chakras

There is a whole esoteric science associated with the Chakras and Chakra meditation. At the risk of offending, may I say it is about as relevant and comprehensible to normal human beings as is the mathematics behind Heisenberg's Uncertainty Principle! But in the pursuit of enlightenment, according to the science of Chakras, Chakras are 'opened', 'closed', 'blocked' and 'cleared', rather in the manner of a complex hydraulics system. When you get all the pressures right, in the right sequence, with the right valves open, and you're sitting in an appropriately complicated position, after years of study, *then*, one golden day when you least expect it, the cosmic force at the base of your spine will suddenly wake up and rush up your spinal cord, zipping past all your precariously balanced Chakras like a rabbit through a minefield, and blow out of the top of your head – taking you with it to Nirvana (heaven). Personally, I don't recommend it!

For our purposes, we simply need to be aware of the existence of our Chakras. Nature will do the rest.

Chakra Exercise

The purpose of introducing you to the Chakras is to get you used to feeling in different parts of your body. This is not as strange an idea as it might sound, as you are, in fact, already doing it. Whether you admit it or not at this stage, your feelings are already to be found in these different areas. This very simple exercise is intended to draw your attention to what is already going on. It will heighten your awareness quite considerably and go some way towards loosening the psi-numbing grip of logic and intellect. Do the exercise now and again, over a period of weeks.

1 Look at the diagram on p. 189 and see which, if any, of the Chakras and its associated feelings sticks in your mind.

2 Next time you feel that feeling, instead of being swept away by it, detach a bit of yourself and concentrate it on the appropriate Chakra area.

There is no more to the exercise than that. You will be surprised how comfortably certain states of mind can be traced to certain areas of the body.

Loosening Up The Brain

In our attempts to increase our psi powers, we must never let ourselves become bored. Psi ability is a completely spontaneous event with a will of its own and it will only show itself where there is a feeling of interest and excitement. Routine and boredom are killers. But it only takes a fraction of a second to get bored. Every minute, the mind files millions of unique and varied impressions into standard, humdrum little boxes in the brain. This is what it is trained to do and there is no way or even need for us to try and stop it. What we can do is to cultivate a kind of mental looseness and encourage a certain amount of enlarging of the mental boxes into which we put things. Also, we can allow the contents of one box to spill into the other boxes wherever possible. This is great fun, very childish and very good for ESP. The idea is to start thinking in general impressions rather than through specific, accurate ideas. In the following anti-boredom games mistakes do not exist. Neither do winning or losing, for that matter. These games, if played in a light-hearted way, can help you to loosen up your rational side and let your psi awareness come through.

The Hints Game

This game has to be played by two people. Play it with a friend with whom you have recently shared a common experience, for example, someone with whom you have just been shopping or on a journey. The idea of the game is for you to describe one particular event, scene or moment of your shared experience in as imaginative and indirect a way as possible. You must give them a hint of the thing you are describing and let them guess what you mean. Here is an example.

The other day, I went with my children to an amusement park. On the way home we played the hints game. When it was my turn, I chose a tiny moment in the day when we had stopped and watched people sliding down a huge communal slide. At the very top of it this slide dropped vertically about 10 feet (3 metres). The slide was very crowded. My hint for this one moment out of the day's millions of little moments was: 'People fallling over a cliff.' After a few seconds, my son came up with the exact moment for the event. 'The Hell Slide! We stopped and watched the people on the Hell slide!

Do you get the idea? Simply choose a moment or scene that you know your friend saw or felt and drop very evocative hints. Be as fanciful and obscure as you like. If you both stopped and asked a policeman what time it was, you could say something like, 'We spoke to a blue man about the height of the sun.' Let your imagination run riot and don't be afraid of sounding a little mad.

Nearly Touching

Here is another mad game that also requires two people. It is a totally stupid little exercise if looked at logically, but it does have a unique mind-stretching quality. It is a good warm-up to telepathy as it inspires a considerable rapport between the two players.

The two players stand or sit opposite each other, their right index fingers pointing towards each other about a foot (30 cms) apart. They then concentrate on the gap between the tips of their fingers. The object of the game is not to touch each other but to get as close as possible, as slowly as possible. As you inevitably get closer and closer, you say out loud, 'Nearly touching, *Nearly* touching, *Neee--arly touching*,' etc. Whoever makes the final touching move – i.e. the person who covers the final millimetre that actually makes contact – is the loser!

This is not a game to be hurried or 'won'. It can bring about quite a build-up of laughter and the feeling of the two of you deliberately going to all that trouble to nearly-but-not-quite touch each other is both entertaining and slightly excruciating. Remember the feel of this game for later psi experiments.

Bad Writing

A lot of time and effort went into all of us at a very early age in order to teach us how to read. Here is an exercise to teach us how not to read. Scholarly types who regard the written word as sacred may find this game hard to play, but with a little letting go and perseverance, even the cleverest person should eventually be able to sound like a complete lunatic. This game is best played with another person or in a group as it involves speaking out loud and laughing. Find a person with bad handwriting and get them to write a few sentences very quickly and scruffily on a piece of paper. (Alternatively, find a doctor's prescription or an Italian waiter's restaurant bill!) What you are looking for is a specimen of normal, slightly illegible handwriting.

Now, without studying it in advance, read it straight through, out loud and at speed. You must not pause or falter at the bits you can't decipher. Instead, you must continue loudly and confidently and say the first sound, word or made-up word that the indecipherable squiggles on the page suggest. Keep going, boldly losing the thread of what is written, never faltering or pausing for a moment.

The following passage from a friend's notebook makes a good example. When read aloud without any effort to resolve the handwriting, it could sound like this:

'Ears have a muck of proletarian refrigerator. Pupils contact in bright searchlight, shortly out exercise light that may be demagogues.'* With practice, one can become almost poetic.

Remember – no stopping!

* What was actually said: Eyes have a number of protective reflexes. Pupils contract in bright sunlight shutting out excessive light that might be dangerous.

Visuals

Here are a couple of visual games. One for your outer eyes and one for your inner eyes! First, the outer one. I call it Jigsaw.

Jigsaw

You can play Jigsaw alone, anywhere. Simply do as follows. Wherever you are, or whatever you are doing, *stop*. Stop and look at what is in front of you. Look at it as if it was a picture painted on a huge piece of card propped up before you. Now, instead of looking at the objects that make up the picture, look at the shape of the space around those objects. Mentally, cut out the pieces of card with the main objects on them and look instead at the shape of the card that is left. This is quite a tricky thing to do because after a few seconds your eyes will go back to looking at the objects themselves. But keep playing.

Start by selecting one simple object out of the many and look carefully at it. Once you can see its outline, then cut it out with your mental scissors. Now you should be able to see the shape of the space around it. As I say, this is a tricky sort of game. Your mind, you will find, will be very keen to fill the hole – like a child itching to put in the last piece of the jigsaw.

Imagine

The game is an indulgence, requiring you only to sit down, relax and see pictures in your head. Remember, though, it's actual pictures that you want to conjure up – images as in a dream and not just thoughts. To get you going, try this series of images.

Close your eyes and imagine in your mind's eye a sea stretching out before you. It reaches the horizon where it meets a beautiful sky. Pause for a while. Now some birds fly into the scene, flapping past from left to right. Follow them as they fly away out of the right-hand side of your head! Pause again. Some more birds appear. This time they flap past the other way. From right to left. Watch them as they disappear.

From now on, you're on your own! Play with the scene. The sea, the sky and the flying birds. Make them do whatever you want them to. Let the birds change colour and dive into a stormy sea. Let the sky turn green. Let an aeroplane or an island appear. Who knows what will happen? Just try to see it in your mind's eye as you make it happen.

Alternative titles and settings for your inner movie could be:

'In the desert.'   'Under the ocean.'
'Flying.'   'Out in space.'
'In the jungle.'

Don't be limited by this list. The object of the exercise is to see events inside your head and then, if possible, to control them.

Things Not to do to Increase PSI Power

- Don't do crosswords.
- Don't play chess.
- Avoid Baroque and modernist music (e.g. Scarlatti and Stockhausen).
- Keep away from long numbers.
- Avoid nuclear physics and advanced calculus.
- Don't eat fried foods.

Overdoing It!

The key to this game is to do something to excess! Perhaps a better way of putting it would be to say do any small, harmless thing to excess. Remember, you're only playing. You are not trying to develop super powers or bend your own mind.

Here is an example of an excess game. You can find millions of different versions for yourself. Pick up a pencil, then drop it on the desk again. Pick it up and drop it again. Pick it up, and drop it again. Continue to do this. Pick it up and drop it. There will come a point when you will want to stop. There will seem to be absolutely no point in what you're doing and something inside will say very firmly: 'OK, that's enough. Stop now.' Ignore this inner advice. Soon, your mental advisor will get quite cross and *insist* that you stop this futile action immediately. Continue to ignore it. Keep picking up the pencil and dropping it again. Soon, boredom will set in. Ignore the boredom barrier and carry on with the action (if you can!). This is where it starts to get really interesting. Remember, it's excess that you're going for, so you *have* to keep going.

One word of caution about this game. Sooner or later, you're going to have to stop. Overdo it by all means but don't hurt yourself on the way by getting a real obsession.

Negative Listening

This is the hearing equivalent to seeing the spaces around things. In this game you listen to the silences between things and focus on the gaps.

At first you may find it hard to find any gaps in the general noises that go on around you. So first of all let your ears wander round and pick out every sound that is going on. A good way to do this is to start with the sounds that are physically closest to you and then move on to the more distant ones. Once you have a good idea of the general noises that are going on, simply focus on the spaces between them. Listen to the gaps.

Try the same approach when listening to music. Never mind the notes, concentrate on the time between the notes. You'll find this exercise very tricky, so don't get impatient with it.

Answer Back

This is an easy game and very good fun for a few seconds, or a minute at the most. Turn on the radio and tune to a station where someone is talking. Now simply disagree with absolutely everything that the person is saying. Disagree, out loud, on every point and detail they mention. If they say it's 1.15 on a Wednesday afternoon – deny it immediately. Insist that it's 2.16 on a Thursday morning. If they say that the traffic's moving freely and the weather is sunny – refuse to believe it and state loudly that the roads are jammed to standstill and the rain is falling harder than it has ever done in recorded history. Find as may different ways of disagreeing as possible and argue loudly and relentlessly!

The Will Game

One final mind game. This game is a bit hard to describe as it involves your *will* to do something and this is a difficult thing to talk about and define on paper. Anyway, see what you make of this one.

Sit at a table. Put a small object on the table (say, a glass or a book). Rest your hands on the edge of the table and look at the object in front of you. Now decide to reach out and pick up the object but, instead, *don't move an inch*. Mentally, go as far as you can towards reaching out and picking up the object; physically, don't move, don't even tense your muscles. Simply concentrate on the *will* to pick it up and remain completely relaxed and unmoved.

Obviously you can do this exercise with any action. You don't need tables and objects. The idea of the game is to isolate the will to do the action and to separate your will to act from your actual action. This feeling of will is a vital part of your psi potential. Some people say that finding the feeling gives them a kind of tickly feeling in the stomach – remember it. It's the key to your psychic ability.

PSI Games

This is the section for the head-on miracle seekers amongst us. No rituals to savour here, simply experiments. This is raw, 20th-century psychic exploration. With these games, you will be pitting youself against the laws of chance, and hoping, with the help of your natural psi ability, to swing the odds in your favour. It's exciting stuff, adding up your score after a run of these games, and the realization that you could be causing something supernatural to happen can keep you playing for hours.

Played in a lighthearted spirit, these exercises will provide you with considerable entertainment and will be a good background against which any natural psi talent you possess will clearly show itself. Try them and see how much of your psi you can unleash on the unsuspecting world!

Clairvoyance Exercise Using Playing Cards

For this game you need an ordinary pack of playing cards. In any pack of 52 cards, half the cards are red (diamonds and hearts) and half are black (clubs and spades). The object of the game is to predict which are the red ones and which are the black ones – without looking at the faces, of course – and to place them in two appropriate piles. After a reasonable number of tries add up your score and check it against the chart. This will tell you if you have been able mentally to influence the results and whether your score shows that some force other than chance has been brought into play. Obviously, the more attempts you make, the more proof you're going to have. If you only tried ten cards and guessed nine of them right, it would merely show a flash of good luck. If, however, you had 100 tries and 65 of them were correct (the chance expectation of correct guesses is in the region of 40–60), you could safely assume that you had brought some extra factor other than coincidence into play. The word that decribes that factor is MAGIC!

1 Shuffle the pack very thoroughly.

2 In order to avoid mental dullness and bad shuffling, guess the cards in groups of ten. Take off the top ten cards and place them face downwards on the table or floor.

3 Look at the back of the top card. Is it going to be red or black? If you think it's a red, put it to the right (still face down). If you think it's going to be black, put it to the left. (R-ed = R-ight) Do this with all ten cards.

4 Now turn the two piles over. Count the number of red cards in the right-hand pile. These are the ones you've guessed right and put in the correct pile. Likewise, count the number of blacks in the left-hand pile. Add the numbers together and find your total number of correct guesses.

5 Write the number down. Put the ten cards back in the main pack, reshuffle and repeat the process.

6 Check your score against the chart.

It is easy to get into a rhythm with this game and as you make your guesses and tot up your scores it's possible to feel lots of different emotions. Sometimes, you're sure you scored ten out of ten, and you turn the cards over only to find you've scored your lowest ever. Other times, your mind wanders and much to your surprise, you find you've scored nine! Sometimes, again, you simply can't decide which pile to put the card in, or you suddenly become wildly certain that you've got seven reds in a row coming up!

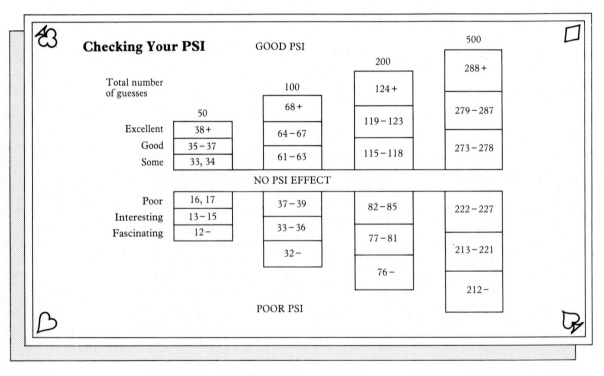

Checking Your PSI

GOOD PSI

Total number of guesses	50	100	200	500
				288 +
			124 +	
		68 +		279 – 287
Excellent	38 +	64 – 67	119 – 123	
Good	35 – 37			273 – 278
Some	33, 34	61 – 63	115 – 118	

NO PSI EFFECT

Poor	16, 17	37 – 39	82 – 85	222 – 227
Interesting	13 – 15			
Fascinating	12 –	33 – 36	77 – 81	213 – 221
		32 –		
			76 –	212 –

POOR PSI

Remember that if you get a very low score it's just as significant as a high score — if not more so!

Playing this game can reveal a lot. Anyone who scores consistently higher than the mathematics of the statistics predict can definitely award himself or herself the title of clairvoyant or psi star or whatever. The proof is there in front of you. You have psi power.

Try doing the exercise at different times of the day or when you're in different moods. Try deliberately inducing different feelings and states of mind as you guess, and see if you can influence your score this way. I think you'll be amazed by your results.

Telepathy Exercise

This is similar to the previous game, but with an extra person involved. I score very highly in this game with one particular friend. The effect is eerie. The odds against the totals we get being simply due to coincidence are millions to one, yet it happens, and often. Telepathy must be experienced to be believed.

One of the participants is going to look at the cards, one at a time and without showing them to the other person, who is going to try to pick up what is being 'transmitted' and say if the card is a red or a black.

1 Sit one behind the other. The one at the back is the sender, the one at the front is the receiver.

2 The sender (imagine it's you for the sake of this example) shuffles the pack then takes off the top ten cards.

3 Turn over the top card and look at its face. Think red or black. The sound of the card being turned over will alert the receiver to the fact that a card has been turned and that you are transmitting.

The receiver now speaks out loud whatever colour he thinks the card is.

5 If he says 'red' put the card to the right (even if it is in fact black). If he says 'black', put it to the left (even if it is red). (It's easy to get your piles wrong at first and it may help if you write guessed red and guessed black on to postcards and use them to label your two separate piles.)

6 Guess in runs of ten as in the previous game, and do as many guesses as possible. Talk to each other as little as possible and try to get into a rhythm.

7 Evaluate your results on the chart.

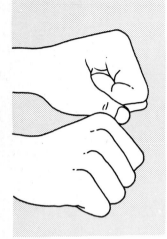

Telepathy with Coins

Here is a less scientific telepathy game. There is a high comedy and bluffing side to this game which can lead to a very high level of empathy and some high scores.

1 Stand facing each other at a comfortable distance. Both of you must hold a coin – preferably of the same denomination.

2 Both of you put your hands behind your backs. The sender (imagine you are the sender for the sake of this example) now places his coin in one of his hands (taking a few seconds to decide which one). He then holds out both his clenched hands in front of him.

3 While you (the sender) were deciding behind your back which hand to put your coin in, the receiver was doing the same. Now he holds out his hands in front of him. You both look at each other.

4 The sender opens his hands.

5 The receiver opens his hands.

Are the coins in the same hand?

There is good opportunity for eye contact in this game and this helps build up a good telepathic rapport. Once again, the less you say and the more you slip into a rhythm, the better will be the affinity between you. As a rule, laughter and fun mean high scores.

The 'Ganzfeld' Technique

(Sensory deprivation for beginners)

A good way to increase your psi awareness is to pay less attention to the senses and instead to try to concentrate more on the feelings *inside*.

Early experimenters in *para*-psychology invented a sensory deprivation tank in order to find out what the human mind would do if it was cut off from any sensory input whatsoever. Volunteers were placed in total blackness with their ears sealed. They lay in a bath of water kept exactly at body temperature. Many subjects reported total disorientation, complete loss of perception of time ('Have I been in there for five hours or five days?') and vivid auditory and visual hallucinations.

Depriving the mind of anything external to concentrate on obviously has a profound effect on its ability to function rationally. It was observed in this experiment, however, that some of the subjects felt that the impressions and images their minds had thrown up while they were in sensory deprivation were meaningful in an unspecifiable way. As total sensory deprivation experiments with large numbers of people was an expensive and difficult thing to achieve, researchers developed a more convenient and flexible way to examine the ESP implications of sensory deprivation. In psi research, this technique became known as the Ganzfeld. (*Ganzfeld* in German means uniform field.) The theory behind Ganzfeld is as follows. The mind's main function is to respond to perceptions of change in the outside world. Therefore, if the input of the outside world is kept constant and unchanging (uniform), after a while the mind will stop attending to its sensory input and be released to focus on other potentially deeper parts of itself.

All the equipment required to achieve a Ganzfeld is available in most homes, so if you would like to experience an 'altered state' of consciousness have a go at it.

The idea is that the subject's sensory input should be kept constant. To the mind totally geared to detecting changes, *no* change will eventually trick the brain into thinking that nothing is happening. With the brain no longer busy handling the five senses, the subtler sixth sense is able to come to the fore. The technique of Ganzfeld is to bathe the subject's vision in a soft, warm, constant orange light. Their hearing is soothed by a continual gently hissing sound – rather like the noise of a distant waterfall. They lie down, comfortably cushioned, in a friendly, relaxed environment where they stay for anything up to an hour.

Ganzfeld is a relaxing, pleasant and often interesting experience both physically and mentally. Some people report feelings of floating and tingling, or a deep, relaxed sensation. Others hear inner noises – water running, voices, music, surf, rain. Some experience strong visual imagery. It is as well to have someone else present at your Ganzfeld session as this will make it much easier for you to relax and enjoy it. When a person's sense of sight and (particularly) sound is removed, they can suddenly become plagued by the idea that the phone might be ringing and they can't hear it, or that the cat has got in and is about to jump on them. Someone around who can set up and look after the session makes all the difference.

To start, do Ganzfeld simply as an experience in itself. Later, do it as part of a telepathy exercise (see page 204).

What you Need and What you Do
This is an experiment for two people. Let us assume that you are the helper. For the visual part of Ganzfeld you will need a pair of ping pong balls, some cotton wool and some adhesive tape. Cut the ping pong balls in half, throw away the halves with the maker's name on and smooth down

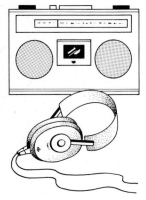

the edges of the remaining two halves. Gently place half a ping pong ball over the subject's right eye, making sure it is comfortable. (Contact lenses should be removed.) Now gently pad round the eye with cotton wool in order to obscure the field of vision completely. Gently tape the whole thing in place. The subject should not be aware of the tape on his (or her) skin. Repeat the process for the left eye. You should now have a happy subject who is wearing a pair of translucent but totally blinding white goggles.

Place a red light source next to the subject so that he perceives a soft red glow through the ping pong goggles. An anglepoise lamp with a red 60 watt bulb in it, positioned 1 or 2 feet (30–60 cms) away from the face is ideal. Turn the main lights down or draw the curtains. Err on the side of too bright rather than too dim when choosing the intensity, because often after a few minutes of Ganzfeld the light will appear to get dimmer.

For the ears you will need a pair of headphones and a radio/cassette recorder. What you are trying to achieve is a hissing sound known technically as 'white noise'. White noise is a hiss that contains all frequencies of sound spread out equally across the whole sound spectrum. Don't be daunted by this description. It is easy to achieve a very close and completely adequate approximation in one of the following ways.

The Radio Way

1 Buy a long running cassette.
2 Tune your radio to a space between stations where there is a steady hiss.
3 Record one hour of hiss on to the cassette.
4 Play the tape back to the subject through headphones (filtering out any rumbling bass or harsh treble by using the tone controls on the amplifier).

The Noisy Amplifier Way

1 If you have an *old* amplifier, use its internal noise as a source of hiss by turning the volume well up when there is nothing playing through it.
2 Filter unpleasant bass and treble (as above).
3 Record the hiss on a cassette.

The Cheap Cassette Way

Simply buy a very cheap blank tape and play it back at high volume. (NB: Make sure that all your connections are good and crackle free.)

These are three ways of getting a constant *shhh* noise that is neither too shrill nor too muffled. Aim to get a sound rather like walking on shingle or a distant waterfall. Don't worry about getting it exactly right. It's not that important. If in doubt, simply get a source of uninterrupted hiss, listen to it with full treble, then listen with full bass and then finally set it half way between the two. After the subject has put on the headphones, adjust the volume to a distant but clearly audible level.

The idea *above all else* is for the subject to be comfortable. Audio Ganzfeld is intended to be a distant, gentle and constant distraction for the ear to come to rest on. The idea is most definitely not to blast the subject's brain into submission with the application of high decibel levels of white noise. Enough said, I hope!

Let's assume that you are the subject. Imagine a distant waterfall and set the loudness to about that level. Have pen and paper beside you. Now you are all set for a gentle trip into the unknown. You're going to be in Ganzfeld for anything up to an hour so get comfortable – preferably lying down. The person who is looking after your session should be very much in the background at first in order to let you settle in and overcome the self consciousness of lying there with a pair of ping pong balls over your eyes! The carer's function is to be around to reassure you that the outside world is not going to do anything drastic while you are cut off from it.

When you've settled down, say after five or ten minutes, you can start to write down anything you may want to speak out loud – some visual impression or train of thought. These scribbles will make fascinating reading after a few sessions. The loosening up exercises will, I hope, have helped you in this. Often perceptions while in Ganzfeld are not logical, and a normally logical mind will often resist expressing exactly what it experiences while in this state. So, loosen up and speak freely to yourself or to your friend. It is amazing how connections and themes begin to appear after a while in what at first seem to be unrelated mental impressions. Drift for a while in Ganzfeld and mention all the things that come into your mind. There is no need to comment on them or to try to make them sound important or spectacular, and certainly no need to make them sound sensible. If you suddenly see a pink elephant and get a strong feeling that it should really have been turquoise, then speak it out without hesitation. Reality is unimportant. In Ganzfeld, it is your impressions that matter. Relax and let whatever wants to float pleasantly to the surface. Safe in your orange/red light by your distant waterfall, Ganzfeld is a thoroughly enjoyable experience that leaves you refreshed and stimulated.

Another way of noting any insights or mental impressions you may perceive during the session is to leave a tape recorder running. This is a good way of reducing self consciousness and easier than scribbling. It is best to wait until a little while after the session before playing the tape back. This will give you a clearer perspective on the insights you have spoken about.

Telepathy Experiment

This experiment, using picture guessing and Ganzfeld, is a modified version of a full-blown ESP test as conducted in many para-psychological research laboratories. When performed in these conditions, there are many rigid controls and restrictions applied to ensure that the results obtained cannot be argued with. When done by friends for simple curiosity and as an opportunity for testing one's own personal psi powers, it can be conducted in a much freer, more lenient and enjoyable way. Use your own judgement when it comes to evaluating your rate of success. There are ways of evaluating whether the picture has been more or less correctly guessed but the preparation for these methods takes too long.

In this exercise, the carer plays a greater part than in the simple Ganzfeld exercise. Once the subject has been settled in Ganzfeld conditions, the carer becomes the sender and tries to transmit a picture for the person in Ganzfeld to receive.

Before the experiment begins, the sender should choose four pictures from old magazines. The pictures should be cut out and put in identical envelopes. (Obviously, the sender should do all this snipping and choosing in secret.) The choice of picture is very open but avoid strongly negative, or sexy or surreal images for the simple reason that concentrating on them for any length of time will have an adverse effect on the sender and may produce confusing responses in the receiver. Almost any other sort of picture will do: drawings, paintings, cartoons, photographs.

The sender, with the four pictures in their envelopes, should withdraw to a different room. By shuffling them in his hands behind his back, he should randomly select one of the four envelopes and take out the picture. This is the picture he is going to transmit. This last-minute random choice avoids the possibility of the sender subconsciously giving hints or indications about it in advance. The sender should now sit quietly and comfortably in the other room and concentrate on the picture. After a comfortable length of time (say half an hour or so) he should stop transmitting and go and find out how the receiver has got on. It is a very good idea to have a short break of five to ten minutes (and perhaps a cup of tea) before listening to any tape recordings that the receiver might have made, or discussing any impressions he might have had. During this time avoid all mention of the experiment. Then let fly!

Evaluating the results of this experiment is a very personal thing. Scientists would probably regard it as too subjective, but a good way of weighing up and discussing the results is as follows:

The sender says nothing at all and keeps the chosen picture a secret. The receiver does all the talking for about five minutes, mentioning impressions or sensations which stick in the memory. Then he draws a sketch of any shapes or colours that he received during his spell in Ganzfeld. Still the sender says absolutely nothing. Next, both sender and receiver listen to the tape, using the fast-forward button wherever necessary. The sender then goes to the other room, fetches the four pictures and places them, as casually as possible, in front of the receiver. The receiver now chooses the one he thinks it is. By this time he should have a fairly clear idea and will probably point to the correct one without any hesitation.

The whole experiment can take quite a long time, but it is a very rewarding and intriguing process. During the course of your post-picture-guessing discussion, you may discover all sorts of coincidences, connections and possibilities which, on the face of it, may seem irrelevant. Do not overlook them. Very little that comes from the subconscious is irrelevant.

Dreams

Most people claim that they don't dream but we all do. It's a fact. What most of us can't do is remember our dreams when we wake up. Try this exercise for a few days. Keep pen and paper by your bedside, or alternatively a tape recorder ready to roll. As soon as you wake up – that is the very second you become conscious – write down or record your immediate memories. You'll be surprised how much you've got to say. Just like the mental images that surface during Ganzfeld, the elements of your dreams can give you fascinating psi insights. The apparently random quality of the dream is not as random as we might think. The colours, objects, people and particularly the odd little details can often provide evidence of pre-cognition and clairvoyance. It's amazing what turns up in the future that has featured in some unlikely way in the dreams of the past. Keep a note of your dreams and you may develop a valuable link with the future.

Magic, Healing and Faith

I have two friends called Fred and Christine. When Gus, their little boy, was almost three they bought him a model car which was controlled by infra red rays from a handset. I once watched him play with it. The tiny child who had hardly begun to walk and talk saw no difficulty in pointing the remote at his toy and directing its movements. Suddenly, I realized that his generation have already learned to perceive time and space in a different way. The relationship between an object and its buttons, knobs or controls is now almost totally abstract. When Gus wants to change channels on his parents' TV set he looks for the remote control. It may be anywhere in the house and will work from anywhere in the room. When Gus wants to move his toy car from behind the sofa to under the bookcase, he again looks for the remote.

If I present Gus with a device of any kind he will never automatically assume that the means to control it lies somewhere on its body. He has been born into a wire-less world. Just as his parents take for granted that their radio is capable of receiving programmes broadcast in another country, he will think nothing of exerting invisible power over a distance. As Gus grows older – and technology grows smaller and more simple – he will learn to use remote controls that look like a ring, sit on his finger and are powered by tiny batteries, or even just the light of the sun. Sooner or later, a psychic scientist will develop a toy car that runs on thought waves alone. Gus will have no difficulty in adapting to the kind of mental posititivity necessary to channel his own mental energy in this way. If one tiny button can move his car over a great distance, why can't one tiny thought send it there instead?

The science fiction writers who flooded the world with far-fetched ideas in the early years of this century have made a greater contribution to our modern world than they probably realize. What kind of person devours Sci-Fi paperbacks? Any publisher will tell you that impressionable, science-minded adolescents make up a significant part of their market. A large proportion of these people go on to university. They end up working in the laboratories and research centres of our world.

What defines their ideas about the things that can and can't be achieved? Their imagination. And what defines the limits of their imagination? Why – the books they read in their childhood.

I hope by now, the analogy is clear. If you feel in your heart that a thing is possible, you make the possibility a thousand times greater. If you speak to other people of your dream, and convince them of your sincerity, the thousand becomes a million. If they, in turn, pass your wild hopes on to others in conversation, you have created a popular folk story. Each popular folk story contains an element of truth. Once an idea is in the hearts and minds of many, it takes on weight. People remember it. Consciously or unconsciously, it will affect the decisions they make. These include judgements about what is or is not possible.

Magic involves pushing back the frontiers of belief. It involves opening up the imagination, sifting through the treasure house of ideas there – and selecting a favourite vision. It then involves taking that vision and concentrating on it. Wishing, hoping, praying, acting, moving, thinking and existing as if that vision were a reality. Eventually, if you do this, it cannot fail to happen. It may take longer than you want it to. It may not take the exact shape you want it to – or it may take the exact shape but have repercussions you did not quite foresee, but happen – it will.

The art of a good magician includes discretion and discrimination. The skill is not in transforming dream to reality – but in choosing the right dream – and carefully shaping the exact WAY in which it comes true.

In this respect, Magic is similar to the creative process – and also to the healing process. Indeed, every musician, artist and painter, and every true healer draws on exactly the same source as the magician. Creative Inspiration from the heart of their being.

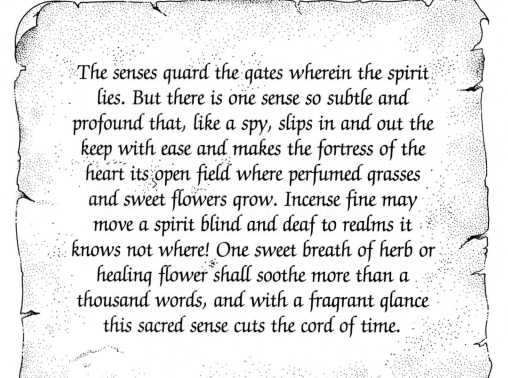

The senses guard the gates wherein the spirit
lies. But there is one sense so subtle and
profound that, like a spy, slips in and out the
keep with ease and makes the fortress of the
heart its open field where perfumed grasses
and sweet flowers grow. Incense fine may
move a spirit blind and deaf to realms it
knows not where! One sweet breath of herb or
healing flower shall soothe more than a
thousand words, and with a fragrant glance
this sacred sense cuts the cord of time.

The Secrets
of Incense and Oils

Open your lungs and take a long, slow, deep breath. What do you notice about the air you breathe? How does it feel to you? What can you smell in it?

The nose is a magnificent and sensitive device, capable of deeply refined discrimination and yet the very words we use to describe it (snout, conk, beak, snozzle, hooter, etc.) say something about our attitude towards it. A curious mixture of indifference and disdain. Despite the copious attention that we lavish on other sense organs, the nose is too often overlooked. It is a sad omission because in the right circumstances the nasal passage can give tremendous pleasure and introduce us to a vast range of evocative experiences.

Dogs, cats and most other animals have a much keener sense of smell than humans. It seems that we possess the potential but lack the inspiration to develop it. We are all quick to respond to an unpleasant odour but find it hard to appreciate fully an attractive one. Perhaps it's because sweeter smells are relatively subtle sensations, or perhaps it's to do with our preference for instant gratification. After all, when something tastes nice – we can *eat* it; when something feels pleasant – we can *touch* it; when something looks appealing – we can *gaze* at it; and when something sounds interesting we can *listen* to it. But when something *smells* good – it's hard to know quite what we can do to prolong our pleasure.

The short answer is that we can *savour* it – but that's a short answer! It would be fairer (and more true) to say that a pleasant smell can be a gateway to the world of fantasy. An invitation to indulge in the leisurely exploration of sensual beauty. A key to release the mysterious forces that dwell in our imagination.

Magicians, mystics, alchemists and people of an inspirational nature have known this for thousands of years, which is one reason why we have such a rich tradition of aromatics and incense to draw on. They recognized, long ago, that everything in nature has a special fragrance or aroma. Each can provoke a unique and powerful response within the human psyche. There are smells that make us feel aroused, excited or inspired; smells that make us feel secure and smells that make us feel alarmed, smells that whet the appetite and smells that depress it; smells that evoke memories and smells that dispel them. There are esoteric smells, exotic smells and, of course, erotic smells!

It can sometimes be hard to know whether we react to a smell because of something in it or because of the associations it holds, but react we do. Every emotion from overwhelming revulsion to ecstatic delight can be triggered by the briefest exposure to an aromatic source. More than any other organ, it seems, the nose can bypass the process of analytical thought and speak directly to our animal nature. When we encounter a delightful fragrance the brain says, 'Hmmm yes . . . very nice but so what?' While the body says 'Wow! I can *feel* this!' Our moods change, emotions come to the fore and our inner chemistry reacts strongly to the sensory stimulation.

Despite this, there is a widespread social taboo against admitting to primal urges. We tend to play them down or even deliberately repress them. Can you remember ever being encouraged to explore your sense of smell? The world is full of artists, writers, musicians and sculptors – yet how many perfumers have you met? Of course they exist, but mainly as paid professionals employed by cosmetic companies and food manufacturers. Who on earth would sniff for a hobby? The answer is that you and I would – if we knew what we were missing! Not only would we sniff for a hobby but we would sniff for a way of life because a keen sense of smell doesn't just make life more interesting – it actually makes it more fulfilling. You'll find, as you explore the world of natural aromas, that there is a smell for every occasion and that certain smells create occasions of their own! There are smells that create an atmosphere, smells that promote healing and even smells that get you high. They all occur in Nature as byproducts of plants, flowers, herbs and trees. A variety of time-honoured techniques allow us to capture and concentrate their essence. As essential oils, infusions, extracts and incense, these delightful aromas are readily available and relatively inexpensive.

The rest of this chapter will deal with how you can enter the secret world of aromatic indulgence. We will talk about how to obtain and how to use a host of exotic fragrances. But we had better begin by exploring the equipment we must use to appreciate them . . .

Getting to Know Your Nose

Unless the publishers can be persuaded to print this book on perfumed paper (a doubtful proposition, I'm afraid), I will have to start this section by suggesting that you put down the book and go on a tour of your home. First stop should be the bathroom. Wander in as if you owned the place and open up every jar, bottle, tube and packet you can see. Gently waft each opened package beneath your nose and let the fragrances seep through your nostrils. Try the shampoo, the toothpaste, the bath salts and even the tube of burn cream from the back shelf of the bathroom cabinet. If it helps, pretend you're about two years old and that every item is a source of potential fascination.

Close your eyes and let your mind wander where it will as you imbibe each fragrance. See what the smells remind you of. How do they make you feel? There are two reasons for doing this. The first is to make you familiar with certain fragrances that you'll be encountering later on in their raw or pure form. The other is to start getting your nose in training, straightaway!

Once you've sorted gently through the contents of the bathroom cabinet, soap dish and window ledge, wander into the kitchen and repeat the process. Open the food cupboards, the jars in the spice rack and in the refrigerator. Take your time, and apply your rapidly sharpening sense of smell to every item of food you can find. The peanut butter, the cheese, the bread – everything! You could even open a can or two if like. You'll probably find that the smells in the kitchen make much more vivid impressions than the ones in the bathroom. You'll also probably start feeling rather hungry. That's OK. Food smells send a very direct message to your brain. The mouth starts to salivate, the stomach starts deciding how much room it's got, the throat muscles get ready to do some serious swallowing and your whole body gears itself up for a mammoth eating session as soon as it smells something tasty.

Food aromas definitely generate the most obvious and measurable response. But see if you can resist the temptation to succumb to them right now. Instead, go to the window and take in a few deep lungfuls of good, fresh air.

If you feel up to it, there is one more source of interesting aromas I'd like you to investigate. It's still in the kitchen, but this time it's a collection of smells that definitely won't make you feel hungry. Open up the cupboard under the sink and begin to work your way through the disinfectant, washing-up liquid, floor cleaner and pan scrubbers, etc. Go very gently as some of these smells are very strong and quite unpleasant. Don't suck them in – just open the lids and catch a very brief whiff of the contents.

Invite anyone who walks in and asks you what you are doing to help you by playing a game. Take it in turns to pop on some sort of blindfold (or simply close your eyes) and get the other person to waft a random selection of items beneath your nose. See how many you can identify. You'll probably find that you both do very well on the food, but when it comes to bathroom items, things get a little more vague. We can all tell toothpase from soap – but can you tell one shampoo from another? You may find that you recognize an aroma but you can't put a name to it. Or you may find that you know the brand name rather than the active ingredient. For example, you may be able to identify a familiar, high-pitched, penetrating, lingering, hospital smell as a jar of 'Bloggs ointment' – but what you are really noticing is the smell of menthol.

Don't worry about guessing wrongly. The ability to discriminate between smells will increase automatically as you develop an interest in aromatics. Consequently, you shouldn't need to make the above exercise a regular discipline. Instead, you can enter the next phase of aromatic appreciation and encounter some extracts, essences, infusions and oils. Pure and beautiful fragrances, undiluted by chemicals, your nose is about to receive the treat of a lifetime . . .

Concentrated Fragrance

Nature is bursing with beautiful aromas, from pine trees to pineapples and from garden herbs to gardenias. No one would deny that scents are at their best when fresh and alive, but since time began we have been successfully refining techniques to capture the fascinating odours of creation. We learned long ago how to dry the leaves of aromatic plants and extract the fragrant oils from flowers. The methods in use today differ little from those in use a millennium ago.

Although, technically speaking, there are hundreds of subtly different ways to preserve a smell, we will concern ourselves here with the two most interesting, exotic and magical methods. The first is essential oils, the second incense (see page 225).

Essential Oils

With the current rise in popularity of aromatherapy, essential oils are becoming less rare and difficult to obtain. This is tremendous news for us because there can surely be no better, or purer, way to indulge in aromatic exploration.

Essential oils are exactly what they sound like. The 'essence' of a plant or flower extracted in the form of a highly concentrated and fragrant oil. Almost any aroma can be captured in this way and the oils are used in perfume manufacture the world over. At some point I hope you will have the chance to compare an essential oil with a perfume created from it. You will find, no matter how expensive the perfume, that it becomes a pale imitation when you encounter the oil on which it is based. Commercial perfumers use only a tiny amount of the fragrance and they dilute it with everything from alcohol to pig fat. It's particularly sad, because the oils themselves are not even that expensive in their pure state, as you will discover. In fact, you could well afford to experiment with some creative blending of different oils to make your own, exclusive perfume or cologne.

Aromatherapy

Aromatherapy is simply the science of applying particular essential oils to particular illnesses. The patient is encouraged to inhale the oil by heating it on an evaporator, adding a few drops to a bath, or (best of all) having it massaged into the body. It's a modern branch of complementary medicine, based on ancient principles, and there are special schools for those who wish to learn it. If you've got a serious complaint and you'd like to try aromatherapy for a cure you should see a *qualified* aromatherapist but if you've got a headache, or cold or are suffering from various other minor symptoms you could safely treat yourself. Oils can be particularly effective if you need an instant pick-me-up or calm-me-down and you don't want to fill your body with spurious chemical preparations. A few lungfuls of pure peppermint oil, for example, will swiftly dispel lethargy, tiredness and even exhaustion. On the other hand a gentle breath or two of lavender will rapidly soothe away aches and pains and help you relax or sleep.

You'll find a list of symptoms and cures on page 223. Remember, though, that the oils are not to be taken internally. Remember also, that if you're not used to aromatherapy there is a tendency to misjudge the tiny quantities needed and overdose yourself. You won't do any real harm if this happens – but you may end up getting too perked up by a stimulating oil or too wound down by a relaxing oil.

Finally, remember that in this book we are setting out to explore the experience of each aroma and not its specific healing property. By all means investigate that side as well and if you think you'd like to go further into medicinal aromatherapy you'll find some excellent recommended reading in the bibliography (page 306).

Herbs, Healing and Magic

In this book we have mainly focussed on the more esoteric areas of magical tradition. It should be stressed, however, that even our clinical, modern world is chock full of magic. This includes, of course, the magic of herbs, plants and flowers.

There are millions of different kinds of flora and fauna in our world. There are hundreds of different wants in which we can apply them to the process of healing. The Bach Flower remedies, the homoeopathic doctrines, the herbal folklore of mediaeval Europe – they are all branches of one, magical, medical tree. One simple belief lies behind them all:

Where there is illness, there is also a cure.

It is generally felt that a herb exists to cure every form of human sickness.

Some say you can actually see the part of the body that the plant cures in its shape, size or size or style.

Some say that if you are ill you will always find the herb you need growing within a few feet of your door. Nature, they argue, is surely wise enough to know in advance when we may be ill and to arrange for spores of the necessary plant to start growing nearby in plenty of time.

Some say the healing link between herbs and people can be found through astrology. Different diseases come under different planets. Find a plant ruled by the same planet – and you also will find the cure.

Others say that only scientific, statistical research can provide a reliable method of healing. The influence of this belief has been strong enough to divide the world of medicine into two camps. Those who believe in science –and those who will accept what they feel in their hearts. It's impossible to assess who is the most successful.

Response to a treatment depends, at least partially, on what a patient believes. Those who distrust modern medicine find that hospitals make them feel more ill; doctors make them nervous. Those who distrust alternative or complementary medicine will subconsciously fight a natural healer's touch.

If you wish to heal through herbs you must choose your system and study it well. You cannot look up a list, select a herb and always expect to apply it with instant results. The philosophy, attitude and approach must be understood. If your desire to learn is sincere, and you study hard, it will work for you. to this extent, the actual method you choose is irrelevant. You will pick the one which feels right – and it will be right.

Because human bodies are precious, vulnerable and fragile, we have not felt it right to say any more than this. There is no doubt that natural medicine works, or that it is safe. It's just that it's one thing to experiment with palm reading or dowsing and quite another to dabble with just a few of the rules in a complex, physical subject. Please feel free to read about and venture into the world of complementary medicine. As you do this, however, remember the importance of learning from someone who is wise, experienced and sincere. Not every book on the subject is honest. Not every writer or teacher is experienced.

In this book, we will only explore the safest and gentlest form of alternative healing – aromatherapy. As you will see, it is both effective and a subject with which you will be safe to experiment.

Vegetarian Diet

I cannot stress strongly enough how important it is for anyone seriously attempting to discover the world of magic – or wanting to become a psychic explorer – to give up eating meat, and preferably fish and eggs too. It's nothing to do with humanitarianism. It's a pure, simple matter of consciousness. Animal flesh in your body will directly impede your sensitivity and the ability to focus your mental energy. If you don't believe me, try it. Gently and slowly wean yourself off meat for a period of 6–9 months. Eat a balanced, natural vegetarian diet. Watch your consciousness grow, change and expand. No further explanation is necessary.

Where to Get Essential Oils

At the time of writing, stockists of essential oils are thin on the ground. You may have to travel or use a mail order service to make your purchases. However, I strongly suspect that as each year passes, more and more stores will be selling them and the advice below will become redundant.

Begin the search in your local health food shop. The chances are that they will stock a small range. Even if they don't, the owner will know where to direct you, or offer to get them for you. In the unlikely event that your local health store can't help you, try one in the student area of any large town. There you will not be disappointed.

Other possible stockists are herbalists, alternative health centres, some pharmacies or enlightened gift shops. Be careful, though. Not all oils in tiny bottles are pure essential oils. Some are essential oils mixed with alcohol or a base oil to make them go further. These are usually a little cheaper and more professionally packaged. If in doubt, look for the words 'pure, *essential* oils' – and use your intuition (and your nose) to help you decide if what you are smelling is pure.

It's worth hunting around until you find a knowledgeable supplier with a large selection of oils to choose from. At the end of your quest is a highly rewarding, deeply sensual, exciting and provocative experience. So make a little effort and ask around.

Which to Choose

It probably doesn't matter which oils you select to begin with. They are all delightful. If you've been lucky enough to find a shop or store that stocks them you'll be able to smell each one before you buy it and decide on your own preferences. People who trade in essential oils are very aware of their intoxicating and morish effect and they won't think it at all strange if you ask to sniff your way through their entire stock. In fact, they'll probably be delighted to see someone who shares their passion for delicate and mysterious fragrances. You'll find yourself inundated with suggestions and recommendations and wind up making a friend as well as a purchase.

Some smells will be immediately attractive while others will grow on you. Try not to dismiss a scent immediately, just because you aren't too keen on it on first encounter. If it reminds you of something you don't like there's probably a good reason to buy it (see Associations on page 220). If it simply smells a little odd, ask yourself if you think you could grow to like it over a period of time. If you have to shop by mail order, you won't have the benefit of a test run, but this doesn't matter really – you'll just have to take my advice to begin with! However, the choice of essential oils is very much a matter of individual taste and you can tell a lot about someone's personality from the essential oils they like. At the risk of giving away some personal secrets, I've listed a few of my favourites on page 219.

As well as giving a brief description of each oil and its effect, I've included the name of the planet which rules it. The rulerships were decided, many years ago, by a general consensus of astrologers, healers and magicians.* It's easy to see why. There is a definite correlation between certain smells and certain planets that you can feel or sense if you shut your eyes and imagine . . .

The astrological references are also here so that (a) you can select one that complements your own moon sign, and (b) you will know which oils to bathe in if you choose to perform the spells in the Ceremonial Magic section of this book.

Seven Recommended Essential Oils

I would really have liked the above heading to read **70 Recommended Essential Oils**, but after much thought and heartsearching here are seven to represent a cross-section of style and flavour and to make a fair introductory selection.

Ylang Ylang

An exotic name for an exotic smell. It's a little sweet in the bottle but when exposed to the air it takes on a very desirable 'attack'. A musky, sensual oil, distilled from the flowers of *Cananga odorata* which grows mainly in hot places like Manilla. Ruled by the planet Venus, it can be a powerful aphrodisiac.

Orange

A bright, cheerful and uplifting oil which smells exactly like a fresh orange. Why, you may ask, should I buy the oil? Wouldn't a trip to the fruit shop be simpler? The answer is, try it and see! It is ruled by the sun, and like the sun it gives a warm, happy glow.

---

* A general consensus, of course, is not the same as a unanimous decision. It seems you can always meet someone with a point to prove or a case to argue and it should be said that not all astrologers and magicians agree about the rulership of every oil. It is ultimately a matter of personal understanding, but for now at least you will be quite safe to take the rulerships I have given here.

☿

Sandalwood
This, like Ylang Ylang, has a musky smell – but it's much more 'contemplative' in its effect. It seems to appeal to the intellect, which is maybe why this heady oil, taken from the heartwood of mature Indian Sandalwood trees, is attributed to Mercury.

♂

Peppermint
Although you'll immediately recognize this sharp, clean smell, you'll be surprised how much sharper and cleaner it is without toothpase or chocolate around it. It's a vibrant, bright and piercing experience and although mint in general comes under Venus, the stimulating, active oil of peppermint is definitely a subject of Mars.

☽

Jasmine
This subtle yet deeply moving fragrance is ruled by the Moon. The best Jasmine is terribly expensive, but only a minute amount is needed and a good supplier should sell you a tiny bottle. Even the cheaper Jasmine oils are effective though. It will bring out the soft, sensitive and sweeter side of your nature.

♃

Lemongrass
Sniff it and feel your heart lighten and your thoughts cheer up. It's an expansive, optimistic, exuberant aroma extracted from the leaves of the lemongrass and ruled by Jupiter.

♄

Vetivert
A slow, ponderous, calming experience seeps from this particularly thick essential oil. It is extracted from the root of an Indian grass called Khus-khus, which explains its earthy smell and its connection with Saturn.

Note: If you want to use the oils as perfume or massage oils, buy a bottle of Sweet Almond Oil which is a neutral base for mixing.

You should be able to obtain all these oils quite easily, but sometimes supplies fluctuate and you may have to wait for a new crop!

The combined cost of buying a small bottle of each of the seven oils listed above should come to no more than the price of dinner for two at a mid-price restaurant. It's a very worthwhile investment and you won't regret the expenditure. Remember, the oils are extremely concentrated – and potent! A tiny bottle will last for months, even if you use it heavily. If your wallet can stand the pressure, you might also care to add some of the following to your shopping list:

Oil	Description	Planet
Lavender	cheerful, clingy and pungent	Jupiter
Spearmint	bright sweet and frivolous	Mercury
Patchouli	deep, dark and dusky	Venus
Khus-khus	light and sharper than Vetivert	Mars
Lemon	refreshing and intriguing	Mercury
Gardenia	sweet, fragrant and strong	Mercury
Honeysuckle	gentle, sweet and mysterious	Moon
Cloves	sharp and penetrating	Mars
Wintergreen	clean, clear and crisp	Moon
Cinnamon	sharp, warm and stimulating	Sun
Amyris	West Indian sandalwood	Saturn
Geranium	soft, slow and seductive	Venus

If you've arrived at this section via the Ceremonial Magic chapter and are looking for a certain oil to aid a certain spell and it is not available you could always substitute another oil with the same planetary ruler.

How to Use The Oils

1 **You can wear them**   As a perfume, cologne or aftershave they will make an unusual and sophisticated change. I must stress, though, that they are *very* concentrated. Don't put them straight on to sensitive skin – even in small amounts. Instead, mix a few drops with a neutral unflavoured base such as almond oil. Use about 10 drops of the flavoured oil to about 40 drops of the base oil.★ A mixture like this is still very concentrated (you won't need to splash it on) but safe to wear.

2 **You can 'evaporate' them**   As oils are heated they are quickly absorbed by the air. Try putting a tiny drop of oil on a lightbulb or warm radiator. The whole room will soon be alive with pure fragrance. The only trouble is that oils leave a sticky residue. For this, there are two solutions. (a) Put some aluminium foil between the oil and the source of heat, or (b) buy an evaporator – a raised metal or ceramic bowl with room to place a nightlight or small candle underneath. As the candle burns, the bowl is heated and the oil is dispersed into the air. Evaporators are inexpensive, practical, decorative and almost certainly available from your oil supplier. They also make it easy to use the oils as

★ If you want to use an oil for massage, make this mixture twice as weak.

air fresheners. Remember once again that only the tiniest drop is needed to fill your room with an aroma that will linger for hours.

3 You can bathe in them   This is by far the most effective way to experience an oil, and the method most suited for 'magical practices'. Simply add one or two tiny droplets of oil to your bathwater while it is running. The oil will spread out and cover the whole bath with a microscopic layer. While you soak in the bath, the oil will soak into your skin, and, as it rises in the steam, you can inhale glorious fragrance with every breath. Towel dry in the usual way. The oils are very pure and they won't make you greasy!

Associations (1)

When you first encounter an essential oil, your emotional, mental and physical reaction will depend – to some extent – on where (or if) you've come across the fragrance before. Peppermint, for example, will almost certainly make you think of toothpaste. The idea of bathing in it may seem quite laughable at first. Lavender, if you're above a certain age, will conjure up images of old ladies' wardrobes. You may literally turn your nose up at the idea that it can be a mild aphrodisiac.

I had a problem appreciating Jasmine at first. When I was young, my aunt used to clean her bathroom with a Jasmine-scented disinfectant. Before I could fully enjoy the moody, dreamy and mysterious qualities of Jasmine, I had to exorcise that memory from the smell. It's easily done. If there is a fragrance that you like but can't shake off the associations, make a point of using it or wearing it every day for a while. Then stop and leave it alone for about the same length of time. When you return to it, you'll find that it has lost much of the older associations and developed new ones. Some particularly powerful smells may require you to repeat this procedure two or three times before they become totally 'cleared'.

Associations (2)

Sometimes the new associations you build with an aroma can be more troublesome than old ones! During a particularly turbulent love affair, my partner and I got into the habit of wearing and evaporating Ylang Ylang to heighten the pleasure of our romantic encounters. When we parted, I found it almost impossible to smell Ylang Ylang without unleashing a flood of memories. This is probably one good reason to vary the oils you use. It's easier said than done! Familiarity may breed contempt, but it can also give a very desirable sense of security. It's quite common to find people getting hooked on a particular fragrance. If it happens to you – don't worry too much. There are some advantages in building up psychological associations with a fragrance. If you ever want to break a habit or forget something, you'll find that changing your regular oil is a powerful way to banish old memories and usher in a new phase of your life.

Essential Oils and Magic

In the chapter on Ceremonial Magic I have tried to explain that *real* magic is not about becoming immersed in mumbo-jumbo. It's about coming to terms with the hidden powers in yourself – and in Nature – and learning to use them. Essential oils represent an intense distillation of the 'active' forces within a plant or flower. They are, all on their own, a form of natural magic.

For thousands of years, people have bathed in essential oils, worked with them, worn them and used them as offerings to the gods. Each oil has an astrological correlation which in turn connects it with the hidden forces (or gods) within our unconscious mind. The list on page 219 will give you some idea of the attributes of each oil. More than that, you will not learn from reading. Magic is very much a personal thing and there is no single correct way to practise it. Your own experience and a process of trial and error must guide you. All I have done (and all I can do) is draw your attention to the principles involved and offer some suggestions. I cannot give you definitive rules, for though I can tell you that oils are fabulous, potent and able to stir up emotions, images and powers from deep within you, I cannot tell you which will be most effective for you as an individual. As you experiment and explore you will discover that for yourself. You cannot do yourself any harm by experimenting – but you could deprive yourself of a valuable opportunity to learn and grow if you were to take your information and ideas exclusively from the pages of a book.

Finally, I should say that even if you don't want to practise Ceremonial Magic, and are only interested in Tarot, astrology or dowsing, you'll find essential oils a valuable aid. In much the same way as a party is not complete without the right music, so the Magical Arts require a harmonious and inspiring atmosphere. The oils will provide this and I heartily recommend them.

Exercises with Essential Oils

The art of successful magic lies in environmental manipulation. You need to create an atmosphere that is evocative, exotic and inspiring. That's why

I've lingered so long on my introduction to aromatics. I cannot stress strongly enough the need for at least a passing knowledge of the ins and outs of essential oils.

Before you go on to the Ceremonial Magic section of this book you really must travel at least some way on a journey of aromatic exploration.

It may be enough to purchase a few bottles of oil and surround yourself with a series of attractive fragrances. Or:

★ You could start blending your own perfumes to create particular moods and environments.

★ You could play more blindfold guessing games in order to sharpen your sense of smell.

★ You could experiment with the idea of *classification*. Some aromatherapists compare essential oils to music. They speak of fragrances having a Base, Mid Range or High frequency. I have deliberately refrained from telling you which (they say) is which. It's far better that you reach your own conclusions, for your own feelings about a particular oil will be far more valuable than those of the so-called experts. (Though if you do want to compare conclusions you can obtain one of the books listed on page 306.)

Aromatherapy

This section has been mainly about the effect of aromatics on the mind. The following list is very incomplete, but it deals with the affect of essential oils on the body. It doesn't represent all the oils available and it certainly doesn't cover all the things they cure. Nevertheless, it should prove useful as a 'dabblers' guide'.

Feel free to try your hand at healing with essential oils. It's quite safe and very effective as long as you take the following precautions.

★ Use only a tiny, tiny drop!

★ Never take an essential oil internally without the advice of a trained aromatherapist.

★ Internal disorders are best treated by inhalation. External problems (skin disorders, etc.) by bathing or massage.

★ Don't go on for hours. A few minutes, twice a day, is plenty for treatment purposes.

★ Don't try to treat serious illness without a fuller understanding of aromatherapy (see page 306 for recommended reading).

Aniseed   Asthma, migraine, palpitations.
Basil   Bronchitis, coughs, respiratory disorders.
Benzoin   Arthritis, gout.
Bergamot   Eczema, skin diseases.
Cajuput   Rheumatism, dysentery.
Camphor   Flatulence, constipation.
Cedarwood   Cystitis, gonorrhoea, dysuria.
Chamomile   Loss of appetite, stomach ulcers, sunstroke.
Cinnamon   Wasp stings and insect bites.
Clary Sage   Tension, hysteria, convulsions.
Clove   Toothache, measles.
Elder   Insect repellent, as sunscreen.
Fennel and Sweet Fennel   Hiccups, kidney stones.
Geranium   Sore throat, diabetes, glossitis.
Jasmine   Angst, post natal depression.
Labdanum   Skin tonic.
Lavender   Boils, dyspepsia, nausea, insomnia and hypertension.
Lemon   Thrush, warts, verrucas.
Lemongrass   Aids digestion, vertigo.
Melissa   Flatulence, stomach cramps.
Myrrh   Haemorrhoids, ulcers.
Neroli   Depression, tension, nerves.
Niaouli   Tuberculosis, enteritis.
Oakmoss Resin   Expectorant.
Orange   Diarrhoea, worms.
Patchouli   Anxiety, dry skin.
Peppermint   Indigestion, lethargy, headache.
Pine   Colic, pneumonia.
Rose   Conjunctivitis, insomnia.
Rosemary   Jaundice, influenza.
Sage   Period irregularities, laryngitis.
Sandalwood   Acne, urinary infections.
Sweet Almond   Base or carrier oil.
Thyme   Anaemia, fatigue.
Vetivert   Head pains, hangovers.
Wintergreen   Muscle pain.
Ylang Ylang   Impotence, frigidity, hypertension.

Aphrodisiacs

I have mentioned that ylang ylang and lavender oils have aphrodisiac qualities. They do – and they aren't the only ones! Aromatically speaking, there are some herbs and spices that will very definitely heighten desire! The question is – which ones? And the answer is that it varies from person to person. Different people respond to different stimuli – and that's what makes the world go round! Ylang ylang, khus khus, and patchouli are normally the most likely to produce an effect, but I know some people who show no response to these but become aroused when confronted with lavender, geranium, honeysuckle or even orange. It should also be noted that while some people are turned on by an oil, others prefer the smokier incense. I'm afraid only trial and error will reveal the ideal combinations, but I can console you with a guarantee that somewhere in the range of oils and incenses there is an aroma that will speak directly to you or your lover's reproductive organs!*

Important If the right chemistry between two people is absent, there is nothing you can do but give up. You must be prepared to face this, for neither science, psychology, Nature or magic can provide a wonder recipe for sexual arousal. Only when mutual attraction exists, but is in some way restrained or inhibited, will an aphrodisiac be effective.

* Needless to say, in your quest for the ideal sensual aromatic, you shouldn't forget the importance of other things such as wine, music, candlelight, sensitivity, massage, clothing and travel. All or any of these may also bring you closer to the fruits of Venus.

Natural Highs

Certain smells can get you 'high' and a familiarity with essential oils will heighten your perception. Perhaps you think that these words are beginning to sound a bit like the language used by a drug taker. After all, incense makes many people think of hippies, and the idea of using healing oils for sensual exploration seems to echo the practice of taking therapeutic drugs for fun. Your concern may be further increased because this is a book on magic and we all know that magic has long been associated with

weird and wondrous eccentrics who have (to say the least) loose morals!
If this *has* been worrying (or interesting) you, read on.

1 The oils and incenses recommended and referred to in this book are not
narcotic, hallucinogenic or illegal. They are subtle, natural and very
safe.

2 It all depends on what 'getting high' means to you. If you think it
means losing your discrimination or disappearing into a morass of
psychedelic dreams and hallucinations, then I'm afraid you will find
essential oils and incense disappointing. But if you think of getting high
as having a good feeling when you wake up in the morning, or basking
in a glow of happiness, or having a sense of warmth, security and
comfort, or gently expanding your perspective on life – then you
certainly *can* get high with aromatics.

Of course, there *are* chemical smells (such as dry cleaning fluid and
particular makes of glue) that carry dangerous intoxicants in their fumes.
There are drugs refined from natural sources, such as cocaine and heroin,
which can be taken through the nose. (Add to this tobacco and marijuana
smoke, if you wish.) You will find no other reference to these intoxicants in
this book. They haven't been left out just because they aren't, technically
speaking, aromatics. Neither have they been left out because of a desire to
make the book respectable or socially responsible. They have been left out
of the book because they have no place in modern magic.

The 20th-century magician doesn't need to resort to such gross and
uncontrollable inebriants. By the creative and sincere use of Nature's more
subtle intoxicants, a series of beautiful, colourful and meaningful revela-
tions may be enjoyed at a pace which allows you to benefit fully from them.

Incense

A Brief History

Aromatic oils have been used to heighten the senses for thousands of
years, but the use of incense is even older. It began with the discovery
of fire. If you've ever spent an evening round an open hearth, you'll know
that everything, when burnt, gives off a special aroma. The difference, for
example, between the smell of an oak tree and the smell of a pine tree is
greatly emphasized when a branch of each is consigned to the flames.
Throw on some dried leaves, or an orange peel and the air will immediately
fill with a unique, penetrating aroma. It's easy, as you stare into the flames
and breathe in the smoke, to see why our ancestors believed they were

freeing a spirit when they ignited certain herbs. The effect of suddenly unleashing a blast of unexpectedely fragrant smoke can be quite devastating.

Early civilizations were quick to incorporate the effect of this incense in their festivals and rituals. From Egypt to China and from India to South America there began a tradition that is still followed today in mosques, churches and temples. At around the same time, there also began a longstanding association with Ceremonial Magic.

Plants, herbs and spices (especially from distant lands) soon became much-prized and highly desirable commodities. For many years they were a currency more valuable than gold or silver. In almost every religion, aromatic oils, leaves and powders were considered a gift from God, symbolic of divine grace. The New Testament tells of three wise men bringing Frankincense and Myrrh as gifts for the baby Jesus.

Today, although essential oils have been neglected, the burning of incense remains popular throughout the world. It's not such a 'pure' way to enjoy an organic smell because the fragrance is carried by smoke, which has an odour of its own. Nonetheless, incense is very evocative, and in spite of (or perhaps because of) its smokiness, the most effective way to release the mood or feeling behind a particular aroma.

Buying Commercial Incense

Incense is simply a general term to describe the aromatic smoke that arises from burning any herb or plant. For magical purposes, loose incense is normally preferable to commercial (see page 229), but a piquant, poignant or provocative atmosphere can still be generated by commercially-made cones and joss sticks. In both cases, a mixture of gums, oils and powders, drawn from one or from several plants, is combined with charcoal to produce a slow-burning resin.

★Joss sticks are long pieces of wood that have been dipped in this mixture.

★Cones are simply the mixture itself, fashioned into a cone shape for easy burning.

Cones and joss sticks can be bought from novelty shops, specialist ethnic stockists (such as Indian shops) and health stores. They come in a wide variety of flavours, shapes and sizes. The more expensive makes are usually worth the extra money because they burn much longer and give a much purer smell. Cheaper brands often contain artificial, chemical ingredients.

If you have never bought incense before, you may be able to find a 'variety pack', containing half a dozen different flavours. If not, just make a selection at random from the shelves. (Sniffing a packet in the shop won't really help you get a true indication of the smell as most incense changes its character quite radically when set alight.)

Burning Joss Sticks and Cones

You don't need any special equipment to burn commercially-made incense. Purpose-built holders are available, but they are normally more decorative than practical. Cones and sticks are quite safe. They won't spark, flash or fizzle, but they will turn to ash and this can be a little messy unless you are well prepared.

Joss sticks will deposit a trail of ash beneath themselves so you should place them over a surface you can wipe clean afterwards. Stand them upright with the bottom of the stick held in place by a piece of plasticine, or by poking it into a plantpot of earth.

Cones don't spread their ash, but they do get very hot so you must put them on a fireproof surface (like an ashtray), and even that should not rest on anything that may be damaged by heat.

Both sticks and cones can be lit by holding a lighted match to the top. After a few seconds the cone or stick will catch fire. Once this happens, let it burn freely for a few seconds, then blow out the flame. The cone or stick should begin to glow and give off a thin plume of aromatic smoke. If it doesn't glow, you haven't let the incense flame long enough and you'll need to repeat the above steps.

Once your cone or stick is smouldering, it will carry on for somewhere between 20 minutes and an hour, depending on its size. If you need to extinguish a joss stick, pick it up, then turn it upside down and plunge the lit end into a pot of earth or sand. You can then relight it later. Extinguishing a cone is also simple. Pour on a few drops of water. (Unfortunately, you can't re-light cones!)

Preference in incense, as with all aromatics, is a matter of individual taste. If you find that you've purchased some incense that has a pleasant flavour in the packet but is too strong, sweet or sickly when you burn it, you needn't feel you've wasted your money. You can pop an unlit cone or stick in your linen drawer, airing cupboard or laundry basket. It will gently permeate everything in there with a subtle, pleasing aroma.

Choosing and Using Incense

Unless you're purchasing incense for use in Ceremonial Magic, you'll be buying it for the sheer pleasure of an olfactory experience so you can go

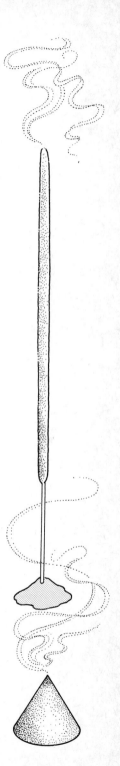

entirely by your own preferences. Common flavours include sandalwood, musk, rose, lemon, vanilla, patchouli, ylang ylang, etc.* It can be quite interesting to compare them with essential oils of the same plant. You'll soon decide which flavours suit which moods and which activities. After a while, you'll find it becomes a matter of habit to 'put on a smell' in the same way as you might 'put on a record'.

Incense and Magic

If you simply want to surround yourself in a pleasant smelling, evocative environment, cones and sticks will more than suffice. If you want to conjure up primal forces from deep within your subconscious you are ready to enter the realm of magic. Read on!

Incense has always played an integral and possible pivotal part in Ceremonial Magic. The burning (or suffumigation) of certain herbs has long been considered a way of releasing magical energy. Traditionally, the magician would use *loose* incense, although these days many use the pre-packaged commercial kind. It would have been gathered fresh in the woods, fields or garden, dried in the sun and then burnt over a small charcoal fire at the allotted hour. The loose incense would be chosen by astrological correlation – i.e. if the spell was designed to conjure up a Mercurial force (for example, a spell to persuade or deceive) plants governed by Mercury would be selected. If a spell involved two or more planets (Mercury and Saturn for a learning spell, or Venus and Mars for a love potion) the appropriate incense would include plants of each planet.

The same principle is still valid for 20th-century magic, although not for quite the same reasons as our ancestors would have given. They might have said that a particular incense had the power to attract or banish a god or demon. We would say that it evokes certain qualities we already possess and helps us bring them to the surface where they can be exploited. Whatever the reason, it's important to be aware of the astrological rulerships of herbs and plants if you are planning to undertake magical work.

The remainder of this chapter concentrates on the use of traditional, loose incense, but I must stress that the power of your spells will be much more likely to be affected by your sincerity than by whether you use cones,

---

* When I first started buying incense, I discovered some delightful Indian joss sticks called *agarbathi*. For some mysterious reason, no two packets by this name ever smelt exactly the same. Eventually I discovered that *agarbathi* was merely Hindi for incense!

sticks or loose incense burnt over charcoal. The following descriptions and instructions are provided in case you'd like to try them and not because they are in some way vital to the practice of magic. It's just that it can be quite romantic and expressive to do things the old-fashioned way. If you would prefer to be a magical modernist you can simply consult the list on pages 232–234 and buy the incense you use in cone or stick form.

How to Obtain Loose Incense

You won't find loose planetary incense in your local shops! You'll almost certainly have to make it yourself, or go to a supplier of Magical Paraphernalia (see page 304).

Making it yourself does not necessarily mean going out and actually picking the relevant plant. Whether the herbs you burn are hand-picked by Tibetan monks from the foothills of Himalayas or gathered fresh from the shelves of Safeways will make no difference to their efficacy!

Here are seven highly effective forms of incense, using materials you probably have in your own kitchen.

SUN	Dried orange peel.
MOON	Demerara sugar.
MERCURY	Caraway seeds.
VENUS	Cardamom pods.
MARS	Whole peppercorns.
JUPITER	Sage.
SATURN	Dried yeast/cinnamon.

In all cases, simply place a tiny pinch or a few pieces on hot charcoal. (See Burning Magical Incense, page 230.)

The older texts on magic often call for obscure plants with esoteric names like 'hound's wort' or 'dragon's blood'. The only point in using rarer plants is that tracking them down may force you to concentrate harder on obtaining your incense and consequently increase the energy you are putting into a spell. Other than that, there are no advantages.

The older texts often suggest that you should mix several plants ruled by the same planet to make your planetary incense. This is not such a bad idea because it allows you to create an incense which is unique and personal. If you'd like to try it out, feel free to mix and match ingredients with the same ruler from the list on pages 232–234. If you do this, I recommend giving your mixture a trial run before using it in a spell to make sure that the quantities and ratios you've chosen give a pleasant effect. (You may also like to try adding a drop or two of an appropriate essential oil to your home-made incense.)

Burning Magical Incense

The technique I'm about to describe is not exactly renowned for its subtlety and finesse! It creates a thick, heady and pungent environment which is excellent for bouts of intense mental concentration (as in magic) but more than a bit overpowering for everyday use!

The simplest way to burn loose incense is to place it on hot charcoal, bought from your nearest hardware store as barbecue charcoal. Buy the easy-to-light sort that's been impregnated with chemicals to make it quick to ignite. All you need is one small piece of charcoal and something to put it on. A ceramic tile or ashtray will do. As with the burning of incense cones, you should make sure that the table top below will not be damaged if the tile gets too hot. Hold the charcoal with an old pair of tweezers and place a lighted match next to it. It should soon start fizzing and giving off tiny sparks. Let the match go out and gently blow the charcoal to help the sparks spread across it. As they do, the side you began with will start glowing as you blow it. Soon, the glow will spread (though you may only be able to see this when you blow). As soon as a third or more of the charcoal is glowing, you can put it down on the tile or ashtray.

Now it's time to put on a small piece of incense. As soon as you do this, a lot of aromatic smoke will rise, and the smell of chemicals and hot charcoal will be replaced by the herbal smoke. It will last for up to 20 minutes, though you may need to add more incense before that time has elapsed.

If you want to, you can make a lid to place on top of the incense. An empty can will do splendidly. Just puncture a good few holes in the side and top to allow the smoke to escape and air to circulate.

Alternatively, you can be very sophisticated and buy a thurible from your nearest magic supply shop (see page 304). Despite the exciting name, it's only a more decorative version of the ashtray and tin can device I have just described. (A thurible is what used to be used to burn incense in churches, but it has now been replaced by a perforated vase.)

If you *do* use a lid, and then wish to add more incense, remember that your lid will get hot so keep a cloth or oven glove handy.

Table of Incense and Astrology

HERBS AND PLANETS

Mystics have long believed that everything on earth has a heavenly ruler. As above – so below. There is an astrological correlation for every part of the human body, for every building, every piece of music and every part of the creation. Normally, the connection is obvious. Bricks, mortar, dark woods and graveyards all come under the dominion of Saturn, planet of limitation. Art, music, sweet herbs and confectionery all come under the rulership of Venus, planet of sensual indulgence.

Sometimes, the connection is less clear. It all depends on what aspect of the item you are considering. Herbs, plants and flowers are not always what they seem. The bright petals of a rose come under Venus, but the sharp thorns belong to Mars. The dock leaf, as a weed, is Mercurial, but its healing properties bring it under the umbrella of the nurturing, caring moon. To this extent, dual or even triple rulerships are common, and although I can tell you the traditional ruler of a plant, its aroma could well belong to a totally different planet.

Let us take peppermint by way of example. Mint, traditionally, belongs to Venus. Mint is attractive, clean and refreshing. Peppermint toothpaste, sweets and tea all reflect the attractive nature of the goddess of love. Peppermint oil, however, is sharp and stimulating. Put some on your tongue and it will burn, not soothe you. Inhale too much and you will be excited not calmed. As such, there is a distinctly Martian, aggressive quality to be found in peppermint oil. Sandalwood is mercurial when distilled to an essential oil, but undoubtedly seductive and Venusian when burnt as incense.

You may feel you know little about astrology, planets or herbs. You may feel too inexperienced to reach your own decisions. You are, however, eminently qualified. In magical work at least, this kind of ignorance has a great advantage. It means that you lack preconceptions and have an automatically open mind. I suggest that you gradually form your own opinions about what is ruled by which planet through a process of trial and error, experimentation and contemplation. If you do not let pride get in your way – and remain prepared to change your mind as your understanding grows – you will be performing a valuable service to yourself. If you think that a herb belongs to a certain planet, you have every right to use it in magical activity connected with that planet. If you later feel differently, it will not affect the outcome of anything you have previously done – as long as at the time your intentions were sincere.

Having said all this, I now present a list of traditional, herbal affiliations. Planets in brackets are *secondary* rulers.

Mint

Marigold

SUN
The sun rules plants which resemble it in colour and/or shape, and medicinal plants which affect the heart.

Angelica, lingwort (Venus)
Ash (Jupiter)
Bergamot
Black mustard
Blue weed
Calamus
Celandine (Jupiter)
Chamomile
Cinnamon, Ceylon cinnamon
Cinquefoil, five leaf, finger grass
Clove tree
Common rue
Common scarlet pimpernel (Jupiter)
Dittany

Elecampane
Eyebright
Gentian (Jupiter)
Ginger
Grape vine (Jupiter, Moon)
Ground ivy (Venus)
Juniper (Jupiter, Mercury)
Laurel (Jupiter)
Lemon balm (Jupiter)
Lemon tree
Lesser centaury
Marigold
Marshmallow (Jupiter, Venus)
Mistletoe (Jupiter, Moon)
Olive tree (Jupiter)

Orange tree
Passion flower
Pepper
Plantain (Mars)
Peony
Ribwort (Mars)
Rice
Rosemary
Saint John's wort
Sundew
Sunflower
Walnut tree (Mercury)
White mustard
Wild strawberry (Jupiter)

MOON
The moon rules plants of similar shape or colour, and plants which have a high water content or live mainly on or near water.

Acanthus
All willows
Brassica (all types)
Cabbage lettuce
Chickweed
Corn poppy (Saturn)
Cuckoo flower
Cucumber
Daisy
Duckweed
Florentine iris (Saturn)
German iris (Saturn)
Goose grass

Hawkweed
Hyssop
Lime tree (Venus)
Moneywort
Monk's pepper
Moonwort
Notchweed
Nutmeg
Opium poppy (Saturn)
Orpine
Pale iris (Saturn)
Papaya
Periwinkle

Privet
Pumpkin gourd
Saxifrage
Sedum
Speedwell
Turmeric
Wallflower
Water chestnut
Water lily
Watercress
White lily

MERCURY
Mercury rules plants with fine or divided leaves, medicinal plants affecting the brain or speech.

All acacias
Anise
Azalea
Bitter sweet
Bryony
Buckbean

Endive, chicory
Fennel
Elacampane
Calamint, mountain balm, wild
    basil
Caraway

Carrot
Celery
Coltsfoot
Dill
Garlic, hedge mustard
Germander

Hazel
Honeysuckle, woodbine
Hopclover
Horehond, white
Hound's tongue (Jupiter)
Lavender (Jupiter, Sun)
Licorice
Lily-of-the-valley (Moon)

Maidenhair
Marjoram (Sun)
Mandrake (Saturn, Moon)
Mint, calamint
Mulberry tree
Myrtle
Oats (Jupiter)
Oregano

Parsley
Parsnip
Red foxglove
Savory
Southernwood
Valerian
Wormwood (Venus)

VENUS

Venus rules plants with especially pretty flowers, red fruits and apples and plants of an aphrodisiacal nature.

Alba (type of birch)
Apple (Sun)
Artichoke
Blackberry
Bugle
Burdock
Catnip
Chestnut (Jupiter)
Chickpea
Columbine
Elder (Saturn, Mercury)
Garden thyme (Sun)
Geranium (Mars)
Goldenrod

Gromwell
Ground ivy (Sun)
Groundsel
Lady's mantle
Marshmallow
Mint (all types)
Morello cherry
Motherwort
Mugwort
Navelwort, cotyledon
Orchids (all types)
Peach
Pear
Primrose

Red foxglove (Mercury, Saturn)
Rose (Jupiter)
Runner bean
Soapweed
Sorrel
Tansy ragwort
Teasle, Fuller's thistle
Vervain
Violet (Moon)
Wheat (Jupiter)
Wild strawberry (Sun, Jupiter)
Wild thyme (Sun)
Wood sorrel, clover sorrel
Wormwood (Mercury, Mars)
Yarrow

MARS

Mars rules plants with thorns or prickles and plants with a strong, bitter taste. Also medicinal stimulants.

All aloe (Saturn)
Anenome
Avens, blessed thistle
Barberry (Uranus)
Basil (Jupiter)
Black radish
Bloodwort, rootwort (Sun)
Box
Bryony
Catnip
Chinese rhubarb (Jupiter)
Common figwort
Common onion
Coriander (Venus)
Cuckoo pint, wake robin
Daisy (Moon)

Dogrose (Jupiter)
Dwarf elder
Dyer's broom
Flax (Jupiter, Saturn)
Garlic
Gentian, yellow
Geranium, herb Robert (Venus)
Gold flower
Hawthorn (Saturn)
Hedge hyssop
Honeysuckle (Mercury)
Hop
Horseradish
Madder (Jupiter)
Marsh crowfoot (Venus)
Mustard (all types)

Oak (Jupiter)
Paprika, red pepper various kinds
Pine (all types)
Pineapple
Plantain (Sun)
Poison nut, emetis nut
Red cedar
Sasparilla
Sea onion
Senna
Spurge laurel
Stinging nettle (Pluto)
Tobacco
Thorny harrow, restharrow
Wormwood (Venus, Mercury)

JUPITER
Jupiter rules highly nutritious food, large plants, quick growers and medicinal plants which affect the liver or arteries.

Agrimony
All poplars
Almond (Sun)
Anise (Mercury)
Apple tree
Apricot tree
Ash (Sun)
Asparagus
Balm (Sun)
Basil (Mars)
Bilberry
Borage
Celandine (Sun)
Carnation
Centaury
Chicory
Cinquefoil
Coltsfoot (Mercury)
Comfrey
Dandelion
Dog grass
Dogrose (Mars)

Edible chestnut (Venus)
Endive
Fennel (Mercury)
Fig (Venus)
Flax (Saturn, Mars)
Garden chervil
Genetian, yellow (Sun)
Ginseng
Grapewine
Henbane (Saturn, Neptune)
Horse chestnut
Houseleek
Hyssop (Moon, Mars)
Irish moss
Jasmine
Juniper (Sun, Mercury)
Laurel (Sun)
Lavender (Sun, Mercury)
Licorice (Mars)
Lime tree (Venus)
Liverwort
Lungwort (Mercury)

Madder
Marshmallow (Sun, Venus)
Mistletoe (Sun, Moon)
Mullein
Myrrh (Sun)
Nutmeg (Moon)
Oak (Mars)
Oats (Mercury)
Olive (Sun)
Peppermint (Venus)
Poplars (all types)
Raspberry
Red sandalwood (Venus)
Rose (Venus)
Sage
Scarlet pimpernel
Sorrel
Sugar cane
Sycamore
Tansy
Tomato
White sandalwood (Venus)

SATURN
Saturn rules poisonous, narcotic and dark plants.

Alder, buckthorne
Aloe (Mars)
Barley
Beech tree
Beetroot
Belladonna (Mars)
Bittersweet nightshade
Black elder (Mercury, Venus)
Blackthorne
Burdock (Venus)
Caraway (Merury)
Chickweed
Christmas rose
Comfrey (Jupiter)
Corn poppy (Moon)
Cowbane
Elm (Mercury)
Fenugreek
Flax (Jupiter, Mars)

Foxglove (Mercury, Venus)
Fumitory
German iris (Moon)
Hawthorn (Mars)
Hemlock (Neptune, Uranus)
Hemp (Neptune)
Henbane (Jupiter, Neptune)
Horsetail
Ivy
Jew's ear
Kitchen onion (Mars, Moon)
Maize
Male fern
Mandrake (Mercury, Moon)
Medlar
Monkshood (Mars)
Mullein
Opium poppy (Moon)
Pale iris (Moon)

Pansy
Periwinkle (Moon)
Plantain
Poplars (Jupiter, Sun)
Quince
Rye
Scots pine
Sea holly
Sea onion (Mars)
Senna
Shepherd's purse
Silver beet
Solomon's seal
Tamarind
White Hellebore
Wild masterwort, Goatweed
Willow herb
Wintergreen
Yew

Let the wise magician learn the power of
actions and of deeds, of gesture and of words
done in solemn consecration. Of all the
pathways to the heart this is the most direct,
treading with lightness and with gentleness.
Who would seek to change with spell and
ritual uses the will of life itself to gain their
chosen end. In silence let the innocent
withdraw, and in their stillness see the subtle
power of word and deed that the world, with
noise, debate and quantity, would obscure.

Ceremonial Magic

WE ARE about to explore the world of Ceremonial Magic. The following pages contain instructions for spells, incantations, rituals and ceremonies. This material has been left to the end of the book because, quite frankly, you might have found it hard to follow or hard to swallow if you hadn't studied the earlier chapters first. Now that you have had your own, very real, experiences of dowsing, auras, ESP, palmistry, etc., I'm sure you'll have no difficulty with it. Ceremonial Magic is, after all, simply an extra way to tune into and channel the secret powers of nature which you have already explored in the earlier chapters.

Before we go any further, it must be said that Ceremonial Magic has nothing to do with the kind of satanism, witchcraft, voodoo, devil worship or virgin sacrifices that you read about in books and newspapers and see in horror films! Nor, for that matter, is it connected with ouija boards, poltergeists, Flat Earth societies, UFOs, or heavy metal rock music! The behaviour of one or two eccentric individuals and the sensationalism of the media have combined to taint an ancient, respectable art with a host of unpleasant or bizarre associations. Ceremonial Magic is, if you like, White Magic as opposed to Black Magic, but I'd rather not use those terms for reasons that Marian Green has expressed very well in her book *Magic for the Aquarian Age*.

You may have heard of black and white magic; in fact, there is no such thing as black or white magic. Only black or white magicians. If you set out to work magic for selfish reasons, using cruel or ancient methods, that is black magic. If you work for the benefit of others, using your knowledge and skills wisely, trying to make the world a better place, albeit in a small way, that is white magic.

That, in a nutshell, says it all. (Needless to add, if you *do* have insidious or unpleasant motives for studying magic, you will find Nature has her own ways of keeping you in check.)

What is Ceremonial Magic?

Ceremonial Magic is not really something you can describe, debate or discuss. It has to be experienced. The best I can tell you is that Ceremonial Magic is about placing mind over matter. It's about the triumph of belief over logic. It is, if you like, a very ancient and very beautiful form of positive thinking. The symbols and the ceremonies are part of a tradition that stretches back the dawn of time itself. Some might argue that they are too ornate for our streamlined technological age, or that it is possible to assert mind over matter without employing so much mumbo jumbo, ritual or symbolism. They may be right. Certainly, if you want to cure warts, you'll find it quicker to visit the pharmacist than cast a spell. But there are still some ailments, medical or psychological, that 20th-century technology cannot cure. And there is plenty of documented evidence to prove the power of faith and belief in the face of the impossible, the incurable or the unachievable.

This chapter contains instructions for seven magic spells. Each has been tried and tested and will do what I have said it will do. They have been borrowed and adapted from various sources – from ancient grimoires (French word for a book of spells), from the notes of other magicians, and from my own experiences and successes. Once you have performed one or two of them, you will find your own understanding of magic grows much quicker than it ever would from merely reading about the theory. You will automatically start to understand the value and the limitations of magic, and the ways in which the spells provided can be adapted to more specific purposes.

However, if you are looking for instant tricks, magic words or obscure recipes that will turn your friends into kings, your enemies into frogs and your wallet into a goldmine, you should look elsewhere. Such things may be possible through Ceremonial Magic, but you will not achieve them through repeating words in a book. First, you will have to sharpen your own awareness. Then you will have to become supremely confident of your own understanding and of your own ability to manipulate Nature. Magic is very much an individual process. I have simply done my best to help you take the first steps on your own path to magical accomplishment.

Magic, Mysticism and Alchemy

If you are only reading this chapter and not actually performing the exercises, you may find that some of it sounds terribly dry and serious. The experience of magic is not like that at all. At the heart of all magical practice must be joy, happiness and laughter. No magician, past, present or future, would disagree with that. Even the great, mystic Kabbalah – one of the weightiest and most ancient philosophies on magic – places laughter and happiness firmly at the centre of its tree of life.

The kabbalistic tree has its roots firmly in ancient Hebrew tradition. The Kabbalah itself is not really a book – it is a mystical philosophy, about an esoteric, spiritual search. I wouldn't like to draw a strong line between the words magical and mystical, but I might pencil in a very faint, provisional, one!

I should also mention magic's other sister subject – alchemy. Once again, the division is a bit hazy. Most people who have tried to define them have taken refuge behind a pile of long words and complicated statements. I can't say I blame them . . .

★ **Mysticism** is part of the philosophy behind magic. It's about a search for the spiritual principles of Nature; a quest for the hidden meanings in creation. Mysticism is an intellectual pursuit that doesn't necessarily need to be expressed in rituals, ceremonies or any formal physical action. A mystic may be quite happy to sit, look, listen, learn and meditate.

★ **Alchemy** is not just about turning lead into gold. Like mysticism, it concerns a quest; in this case, for something called the philosopher's stone. This is not really a stone at all, but a state of understanding, which, once gained, gives the power to change the elements themselves. In some ways, modern chemists, physicists and biologists are all successful alchemists. However, the philosopher's stone, in its real sense, is as elusive as ever. Nobody has fully grasped the hows and whys of our universe. Each of us receives an occasional glimpse, and scientists and magicians alike agree that these come at least partly from an inspired state of mind.

There you have it. I've laid myself on the line, and given two definitions. I hope they help. But if you are looking for a definition of magic itself, I'm sorry. Even I daren't go that far! As soon as you wrap words around a subject you begin to limit it, and I don't want to limit magic.

This brings me to a question that I suspect you may be asking. Do you need to do some serious studying before you can become a magician? Should you read up on the Kabbalah or the Emerald tablet of Hermes Trismegistus or the collected works of John Dee or even Aristotle?

It's not really for me to say 'Yes, you should' or 'No, you shouldn't', but I will say this. All these people were wise and sincere, they had experiences that they felt were worth writing about. However, magic is not a literary subject. It's the inspirational birthright of every human being and the only way to understand it is to experience it. And as you will find when you have tried the next few exercises, this experience is freely available, regardless of how many (or how few) books you have read on the subject.

Magical Techniques

I have deliberately kept the ceremonial side of things to a minimum. I have worked hard to remove as many of the superstitious trimmings and unnecessary rituals as I can. Still, we cannot begin by leaping straight into a spell. There are a few magical techniques to master first. Let's begin by meditating upon and then making a mystic pentagram . . .

How to Make and Use a Mystic Pentagram

Certain signs and shapes have always had a very special meaning in magic. In times when few people could read or write one magical symbol would be worth a thousand words. By drawing that symbol on parchment, carving it in stone or simply inscribing it in the air, a magician could give formal expression to a deeply held desire or intention.

Today, many of the old symbols have lost their magical potency. The cross, an ancient sign of spiritual unity, has become inseparable from Christianity. The swastika, for thousands of years a symbol of the quest for enlightenment, simply reminds us of Hitler and World War II. Today, we only know the hexagram as Judaism's Star of David. But there is one particular magical symbol that hasn't been borrowed by too many other vested interest groups. This is the pentagram or 5 pointed star. It is a rather beautiful image and has always been used to express the union of the human spirit with the four elements of nature.

In this first exercise, I would like to show you how the pentagram can be used to experience some of your own spiritual nature. When you've tried it, you'll understand why almost every magician works with a pentagram in one form or another. I hope you'll find that it takes on a very special significance for you personally.

Pentagram meditation

1 To appreciate fully the meaning of the pentagram, you will need to understand the concept of the four elements. This is the idea that everything in life can be divided into Fire, Earth, Air or Water. A full explanation of this can be found in the Astrology section on page 35. Perhaps, even if you've already read it, you should begin this exercise by re-reading that section. You'll find it's worth the effort because the four elements and all they stand for keep cropping up in Ceremonial Magic and you won't get very far without them! As you go back over those pages, try to see how each element is related to the others.

Imagine the effect of fire on water (steam) or water on fire (extinguishing). Spend a few minutes doing this with each element in turn. Let your imagination have free rein.

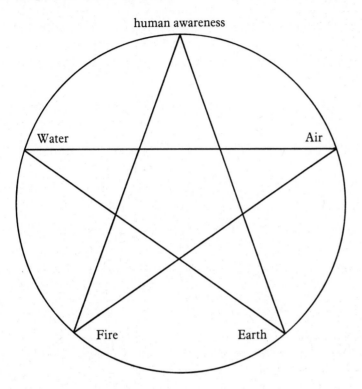

2 Once you are confident that you have a 'feeling' for the meaning of each element, it will be time to meditate on the pentagram itself. The best way to do this is to draw one for yourself. Copy or trace it from the picture above. As you draw, you'll notice that the five points are connected by one continuous, non repeating line. Although you don't have to do it this way, the fact that a pentagram can be drawn with a continuous movement is meaningful in itself.

3 Sit back and look at the pentagram. Relax, open your mind and see what comes into it. Try also to think about the following ideas:

★ The uppermost point on a pentagram represents human awareness.

★ The four lower points symbolise the four elements.

★ The continuous line is the energy of life itself, unifying and connecting all things.

★ The pentagram symbolizes our basic human desire to be in harmony with the forces of Nature through an experience of the pure life energy that flows through everything in creation!

4 Try imagining yourself as the top point of the pentagram – connected to all the elements by a universal thread. Now spend a little while thinking about each element in turn, as a part (or aspect) of your own personality.

★ When you think of Fire, think of the things that get you excited or enthusiastic.

★ When you think of Earth, consider the way you go about dealing with your bodily needs. How you feel about having a roof over your head, money in the bank, or a healthy body.

★ As you contemplate Air, think of yourself thinking about the things you are thinking about! Notice the way you can detach yourself from your activities and see life from an intellectual perspective.

★ Finally, consider Water. What makes you happy, and what makes you sad? What are you afraid of? What do you yearn for? What do you *feel* about yourself?

5 As you continually visualize yourself at the top of this pentagram, connected to each of those elemental facets of yourself, notice how the real you is greater than the sum of its parts. You feel (Water), you think (Air), you respond to the challenges of your environment (Fire), you take responsibility for your human body (Earth), and yet . . . There is something more. Something that sits outside all this and just quietly observes. This is your spiritual nature.

By meditating on the pentagram you have begun to use its unique shape as a launch pad for a journey of self discovery. The next exercise serves a similar purpose, although it is more physical. The idea is to project a pentagram into the air, using your whole body as a tool.

Inscribing a Mystic Pentagram

Inscribing a pentagram is very simple. There are five points on your body that correspond with the five points on the pentagram. All you have to do is stand up and use your arm to trace a connecting line in the air between these points. You can do it almost anywhere, at any time and although by

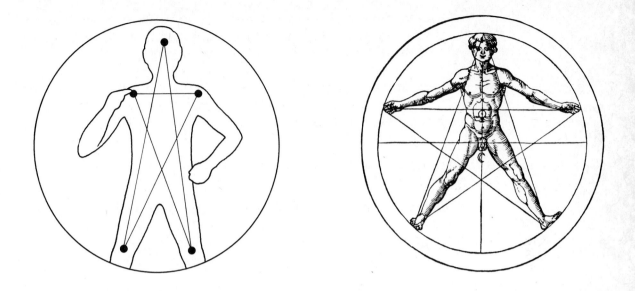

tradition you should face towards the East, if you haven't got a compass handy it doesn't really matter.

1 Stand with your legs apart, and your head held high.

2 Hold out your right arm,★ and stretch out your first and middle fingers together, as if you were pointing with them.

3 Bring them up to touch your forehead. Hold this position for a brief moment.

4 Now bring them down across your body in a diagonal line, to touch your left knee.

5 Next, bring them across to your right shoulder.

6 Now move them over to your left shoulder.

7 Now down again to your right knee.

8 Finally, bring them back to up to your forehead.

★ It doesn't matter *which* arm you use. Some people have theories about the cosmic significance of the left and right sides of the body, but once you begin bothering with that sort of thing it's the start of an endless spiral of symbolism that leads to nothing but confusion. Certain famous magicians have driven themselves (and their followers) quite potty with all these layers of meaning. It turns the whole art of magic into a kind of chess game for neurotics where the winner is the person who can invent the most complicated rules. It certainly doesn't make the magic itself any more powerful.

That's it. You've inscribed a mystic pentagram. Congratulations. You're becoming a genuine magician. Quickly, before you start asking what the point of it is, do it again.

It's easier the second time, isn't it? Keep on inscribing the pentagram until you can do it without thinking about it. Five or six more attempts should see you to this stage.

OK. Now we can start considering the point of it all. Do you recall the first exercise? The one where you saw yourself at the top of the pentagram, with all the different facets of your personality symbolized by four elemental points. Remember this while you inscribe the pentagram. Technically speaking, your left knee is Earth, your right shoulder is Water, your left shoulder is Air and your right knee is Fire. Practically speaking, it doesn't really matter. All you need to be aware of is that you are bringing together the four elements of your inner self in a gesture of unification. You are acknowledging the existence of your inner spirit – the top of the pentagram – and you are expressing a fundamental desire to be in harmony with creation itself. There's no need to think of anything quite so specific while you do it. Just be generally aware of the significance, and let the actions speak for themselves. This is the ritual of the pentagram. It is very ancient, very beautiful and very magical. You have just completed your first, fully fledged magical ceremony.

Now that you know how, you can perform the ritual of the pentagram at any time you choose. It can be a gentle prelude to all your magical activities. You can also inscribe it whenever you feel the need to be reminded that you are more than the sum of your parts. It can help you regain your calm after hectic day, or inspire you to stand back from your problems, summon up your inner perspective and see things in a positive, uncomplicated light.

Beams of Magical Light

This is an exercise in visualization and it involves using your imagination. Before you close the book saying 'I see, so magic is just imaginary', please remember that your imagination is a very powerful tool. We all like to pretend that our world is cut and dried. We like to think that the divisions between reality and fantasy in our lives are very clearly drawn. In fact, it's not so simple. Try telling someone who has just bought hotels on the best street of the Monopoly board that it's only a game. It is 'only a game' in one sense, but there is still a very real, very powerful experience attached to playing that game. And so it is with magic. The techniques are personal and private. They take place *inside you*, but they can have very noticeable, measureable repercussions in the real world around you as well. With this understanding in mind, I'd like to invite you to do something that might seem a little odd or childish. If you don't want to do it, that's fine. But you can't expect to get very far with Ceremonial Magic if you aren't prepared to stretch your imagination a little . . .

1 As with inscribing a mystic pentagram, the first step involves standing with feet apart and one arm outstretched, the first two fingers extended as if they were pointing.

2 Imagine that the tips of your fingers are glowing with a bright golden light.

3 Try and see that light actually streaming like a torch beam across the room. Make the beam quite thin and direct. Just keep looking at your fingers and into the direction they are pointing. Let the light come rushing out as far as it can go. When it reaches the wall or whatever is in the way, imagine that the light is extending beyond it, travelling right through all barriers and obstacles, just shining endlessly into the distance.

4 Hold your arm there for as long as you feel comfortable and keep imagining the light. If you start thinking things like 'This is really silly' or 'What a waste of time' that's quite OK. Try to ignore that negative voice and concentrate instead on letting your imagination go to town. After a few moments, stop and relax. Don't try too hard or for too long. Nothing is supposed to happen. Whether you've really seen a brilliant light, or whether you've just felt slightly foolish is irrelevant. What's important is that you've made your first attempt at magical projection. You've made a symbolic gesture. You've extended the limitations of your mental and physical field of influence.

When you feel ready, try it again. It should be easier each time you do it. By easier, I mean that there will be less interference from the Doubting Thomas in your mind who spoils the fun by saying you're only pretending. Although the Doubting Thomas never really goes away, you can learn to keep him quiet long enough for you to have a rather enjoyable, visionary experience. Keep practising this exercise every few hours for a few days. *Don't* think about it when you're not doing it. And don't think too hard about it when you are doing it either! Just make a point of, every now and then, reaching out your arm, extending your first two fingers and projecting a beam of pure white imaginary light into the surrounding universe. That's all there is to it.*

You know how to create a beam of magical white light, so why haven't you tried the exercise yet? What's stopping you? It's that Doubting Thomas, isn't it? Now you can begin to see what we're up against and what the value of this exercise really is. It's a way of overcoming your superficial intellectual outlook on life and letting your subconscious dream instincts have a chance to come out and play. It's an exercise in overcoming the resistance that we have all been brought up to feel against anything wonderful, magical or even just plain unusual.

There is one other very valid point about this exercise. When you have tried it, you will be a little more certain that practising magic is not going to cause a sudden personality change or turn you into a raving eccentric. You'll understand that being able to project imaginary, magical beams of light simply gives you a heightened sense of perception.

So . . . are you going to do it? If and when you do, you will be ready to go on to the next exercise and the rest of this chapter. Until then, you might as well go back to one of the less esoteric subjects in the book like astrology or dowsing. You can always come back to this section when you feel ready to have a try.

Drawing a Magical Circle

To help themselves concentrate, most magicians like to be surrounded by a closed energy field when they are working. A circle (which has no beginning or end) is the traditional shape of this field and there are various ways to make a magical circle. Some people draw one in chalk on the floor. Others take a length of silken cord and lay it in a circle around their working area. In my opinion, the fewer physical props a magician uses the better. I create a magical circle by using the imaginary beams of light I described above.

1 Inscribe a mystic pentagram. This will clear the air and help you adopt a relaxed, carefree state of mind. When you've done this, stay in the same position and begin to project a magical beam of light in the usual way.

* If you've watched a lot of movies where people are shown practising magic, it may take some effort to reconcile yourself to the difference between what you see on the screen and what you see in your own magical imagination. The special effects departments have become so good at creating dramatic images that it's easy to forget they are just artists' impressions of what a real magician experiences. The real thing is considerably more subtle, but it is the real thing and it's also considerably more powerful.

2 This time you are going to trace the light in a full circle around your body. Line your arm up with something that will act as a marker (a picture on the wall or a tree in the distance) so that you'll know when you've traced a complete circle. Point your beam of light in the direction of the marker.

3 Slowly shuffle your feet around in a clockwise direction. As your feet move, keep your arm still and imagine the beam of light flooding out from your outstretched fingers. Carry on turning slowly, until your arm has described a complete circle in the air. Take your time

4 Slowly lower your arm until it hangs by your side. As you do this, imagine that the beam of light has stopped (you have turned off the switch).

Creating a circle in this way is a gesture of magical intent. It's a way of confirming the link between your inner self and the rest of creation. It's a very natural prelude to any actions designed to harness or draw on the elements of Nature. These elements are within you (as you found when you explored the pentagram), and yet they are also the fundamental building blocks of the physical universe. That's why this light which you have imagined flooding out of your body is so symbolic and so relevant. By drawing it around you in a circle you have created an extension to the limits of your being. The light which you send streaking out into infinity takes a part of you with it. It illuminates the connection between you and the furthest corners of the universe. The whole world is now your oyster and you are the pearl in its shell. If you think I'm being a little poetic or woolly, then I bet you haven't actually tried the exercise for yourself yet! Please do. It is quite harmless and can bestow you with a deep sense of confidence and strength.

Well, there you are. That is your very first magical circle. A beam of light from the innermost depths of your being has traced a grand circle in the air around you. How do you feel? When I first did this exercise, I felt rather odd. I knew that I had traced the magical circle and yet there was still a part of me that said, 'Nothing has happened – you're just kidding yourself'. I still don't have an answer to that. I might be kidding myself and so might all the other magicians throughout the ages who have done a similar thing. But I do know this. It feels really good, and when I do it the question of whether the sense of power, strength, comfort and protection I feel is real or imaginary becomes irrelevant. Instead of entering the old debate on where reality begins and fantasy ends, let's just say that, if you are prepared to enter into the spirit of the thing, all sorts of wonderful things can happen in the name of Magic.

Undoing a Magical Circle

First of all, no harm will come to you if you don't undo your magical circle. All that will happen is that you'll start to take the nice feeling it produces for granted and sooner or later you'll forget that it is even there. The trouble is that the next time you want to make a magical circle you'll remember that you already have one. Should you try and revive it? Or should you trace a new one in its place? As you can see, if you don't undo your magical circle things can get a little messy and cause a certain amount of confusion and doubt. That's why, if only for the sake of tidiness, it is a good idea to undo your magical circle at the end of each operation.* So, when you've completed your magical work and want to pack things away and get back to normal, here's how to go about it.

1 Line yourself up with the same marker you used when you began to create the magical circle. Extend the same arm you used to draw it, but this time don't extend your fingers. Instead, raise your whole hand as if you were signalling *halt* to an approaching car.

2 Keeping this position, begin to imagine that the same beam of light you sent streaking out into the air is flooding back to you through the palm of your hand. It's not so important to see it this time. Try to feel it coming in through your palm, up through your outstretched arm, across your shoulder, and down towards your solar plexus. Remember, you're not looking for a physical feeling, just a general sense that you are pulling back the energy you sent out earlier.

3 Once you feel comfortable that this is happening, begin to move slowly round in an anticlockwise direction. All the time you should try to be conscious of the light energy flowing back into your body.

4 When you return once more to your original marker position, pause for a second and then slowly lower your arm. Now that all that light energy has been gathered back to your solar plexus, it's time to make a final symbolic gesture. Take a deep breath, hold it for a second and imagine it mingling with the light energy you have collected within you, then exhale the whole lot with one, quite forceful, out-breath.

That's it! Your magical circle is undone. Everything is back to normal. It's time to relax. You can (and should) forget everything mystical and

---

* In case you're wondering, it's not necessary to do the same thing with the mystic pentagram where the gesture does not involve you projecting anything out of yourself.

magical for a while and get involved in the most trivial pursuit available. Watch TV, read the paper, or best of all, make yourself a well-earned cup of tea. Even the most accomplished and experienced magician needs to put his feet up occasionally!

Magical Paraphernalia

Most magicians like to work by candlelight, and burn incense while they work. Technically, there is no reason why you could not perform a spell under fluorescent light, using cans of airfresh, but obviously it's not as atmospheric! For this reason – and as long as you promise to remember that the candles and incense are trimmings not essentials – I suggest we go about things the olde worlde way.

A Magical Tool Kit

Here is a checklist of items you'll be needing regularly throughout your practice of magic.

---

4 candles
4 candlesticks
1 incense burner (see page 230)
charcoal
a selection of planetary incense (see pages 232–234)
. a white square of cloth (silk is best) approx 12″ × 12″ (30 × 30 cms)
a clean table to work on

You are welcome to invest in silver candlesticks, seek out beeswax candles or even arrange to import a few thousand silkworms so you can oversee the quality of the cloth, but it won't make your magic any more (or any less) effective.

It is a good idea to keep all the paraphernalia together, and it can also be helpful to set aside a special place where you can perform your magical activities. Just as a mechanic would say that his job becomes easier in a garage with a good tool kit, or a secretary might prefer to work in a proper, well-equipped office, magicians are generally happier if they can set up a permanent magical workshop. If you don't have the space though, it doesn't really matter.

Note: In the 'olde worlde' books on magic these workshops are sometimes referred to as temples and the tool kits called altars. Traditional magic is full of apparent religious parallels. This is because, in its infancy, Christianity borrowed a lot of terms and customs from older traditional ceremonies. They have been on loan for so long now that their new connotations are hard to shake, and (in my opinion) it's simpler and easier to adopt new words than try to clean up the old ones.

Magic Spells

The remainder of this chapter contains seven traditional magic spells, each dedicated to a specific planet. The first spell is a lunar or moon spell. Before you read it, you may wish to return to the astrology chapter and check your moon sign. You will also need to know how to read the lunar ephemeris on page 307.

1. MOON SPELL
A Spell for Increased Sensitivity
(Ceremony of Self Awakening)

The Ceremony of Self Awakening is designed to transform you, the aspiring student, into a confident practitioner of magic. It is a gesture of readiness and of awareness. Performing this spell will heighten your sensitivity, your responses and your consciousness in general. Once you have performed it, you will be able to approach any of the other spells or ceremonies in this book with full understanding and insight. It is not (and should not be confused with) a gesture of allegiance to any group, philosophy or school.* It is your very own, personal declaration to

---

* It is a popular myth that somewhere there are groups of wondrously high magicians who know all there is to know about everything, and who (if you are lucky) may accept you into their midst and teach you their secrets. Somewhere in the back of your mind may be a feeling that what you are doing will not be real unless or until you have joined such an elite. In truth, there is no such thing as a definitive school of magic. How could there be? The whole subject is deeply personal. Of course, there are people who pretend to be part of some superior organisation, but then there are some people who would turn eating cornflakes into an exclusive activity if they thought they could do it convincingly!

yourself that you want to experience and benefit from all the potential and wisdom that lies inside your very own being.

There are reasons why you may not wish to perform certain other spells in this book until you have a specific need for them. There is, however, no reason why you shouldn't perform the Ceremony of Self Awakening as soon as you can.

When to Perform The Ceremony

Good timing is essential in all magical work. If you've read the section on astrology, you'll understand how the movements of the planets create periods when certain activities will be very fruitful – and certain other activities will not. For magic in general, and for this spell in particular, it is important to ensure that the moon is in the right place. After all, it's the moon that traditionally rules magical work, and the moon that symbolizes the hidden depths and secrets that you want to discover in this spell.

Because the Ceremony of Self Awakening is a ceremony of rebirth and renewal, the best time to do it is when the moon is new! Many diaries and calendars give details of the monthly phases of the moon, or alternatively you can easily work it out from the moon sign tables in back of this book. Symbolically, the very best time to do this spell would be when the moon is new in the same sign as your own moon sign. As this only happens once a year you may not want to wait that long. You could also do it when the moon is in your moon sign at any phase (your personal lunar return).

The ceremony doesn't have to take place at the actual moment of the new moon, or lunar return. Any time in the preceding or following 24 hours will do. Neither does it have to take place at night. There's no reason why you shouldn't do the ceremony in broad daylight.

You can, in theory, perform this or any other ceremony out of doors. In practice, though, you'll probably have to avoid wind, rain, extremes of temperature and neighbours, so unless you live in the heart of the country or own an enormous mansion with secluded grounds I don't really recommend it.

I realize that the above list of pre-conditions means that you may have to wait up to 25 days before you can perform the ceremony. However, patience is a virtue, particularly when it comes to magical workings. We live in a push-button age, but magic is not a push-button thing. It is an organic process and as such is dependent on the ebbs and flows of Nature. Sometimes you *can* snap your fingers like Mary Poppins and see instant results. At other times, you may have to wait for days or months before you begin to see your magical workings take effect. So, be patient!

While You Are Waiting

One good thing about having to wait until the time is right is that you will have plenty of time to prepare for it. The ceremony itself will not take more than a few minutes of real time to perform, but it is quite an intense activity and you would be well advised to put aside a few hours on either side of it when you won't be disturbed. You can also prepare for it by making sure that you have all the items you need in your magical tool kit (see page 249). If you know which room you're going to perform the ceremony in, it's not a bad idea to give it a spring clean in advance – but that's a question of atmosphere, nothing more.

The other useful thing you can do while you are waiting is to read up on and rehearse the ceremony. Run through the whole thing in your mind several times and even have a sort of dress rehearsal, if you like. The more prepared you are when the time comes, the smoother everything will be. If you can commit it all to memory so much the better, but there is no reason why you can't keep this book to hand and refer to it during the ceremony. The thing that will bring the ceremony to life is your own enthusiasm – not my instructions. On balance, it would be better to get things out of sequence confidently than follow everything to the letter nervously!

When The Time is Right

★ Lay out your work table as shown opposite.

★ Place the four candles at the corners of your silk cloth and the incense burner in the centre. Place the incense on a saucer to the side of the cloth, and keep a box of matches handy.

★ The incense you require for this spell depends on your own personal moon sign. Select the incense that represents the ruling planet of your own moon sign (see pages 232–234). For example, if your moon sign is Aries you will need Mars incense, and if it is Taurus you will need Venus incense, etc.

★ If you are using charcoal incense (as opposed to a joss stick) it would be a good idea to practise with it before you do this ceremony. It's not always easy to get going and you don't want all your concentration to end up going into a piece of coal! (See Aromatics.)

★ Once you've got everything ready, it's time to prepare yourself. The nicest possible way to relax and concentrate yourself for a ceremony like this is to take a long hot bath. Better still, if you can scent the bath with an essential oil . . . and if the essential oil is of the nature of your own moon

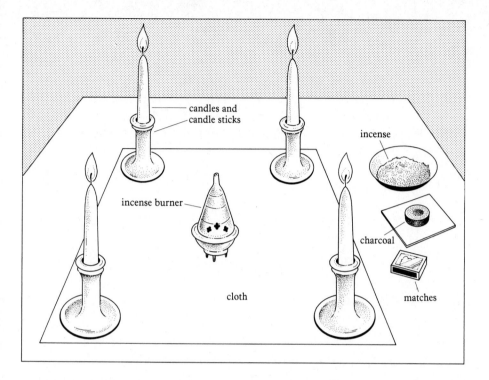

sign's ruling planet, well that's even more evocative, but not (if you'll excuse the pun) essential!

★ While you're taking your hot bath, don't particularly think about the ceremony you're about to perform. Instead, let your mind wander and try and relax and feel as comfortable about yourself and life in general as you can. Count your blessings!

★ When you've dried yourself off, dress in some clean, loose fitting clothes and retire to the room in which you have set up your table. If you want to, you could make yourself a special robe to wear. I always wrap myself up in a clean white sheet, toga fashion. It makes me feel like an Indian sage when I wear it. However, I have been known to perform magical ceremonies in baggy trousers and a T shirt, or even in my dressing gown!

★ If it's daytime, or if you've got windows that face on to a busy street, you may want to close the curtains. It makes things a little more private and the dimmer light adds to the atmosphere, but once again it's not essential. You may also like to turn off any electric lights.

Once you've sorted everything out, you're ready to perform the ceremony itself.

The Ceremony of Self Awakening

1 Begin by lighting the four candles. Traditionally they represent Fire, Earth, Air and Water – the four elements. If you want to, you could make things more symbolic by placing a little card in front of each one with the symbol for an element drawn on it. If you do this, then you should know that – by tradition – Fire would be top right, Earth top left, Air bottom right, and Water bottom left, as you face the table. Even if you don't identify with them you may still want to light them in the order given above.

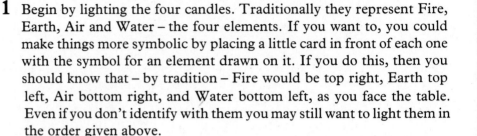

2 Once you've lit the candles it's time to inscribe the pentagram. Pause for a few seconds before you do it and make the gestures slowly. Relish the experience. It's not every day you get to participate in one of the oldest ceremonial activities known to humankind.

3 Now create your magical Circle. Once again, do it slowly and carefully. Surround yourself with that beam of brilliant white light and feel the essence of your being reaching out and joining forces with the universe itself.

4 Stand for a few moments inside the magic circle and relax. Just let your mind go blank. There is no rush and no hurry.

5 Now light the incense. If you're using a joss stick, light in the usual way and place it in the holder. If it is charcoal, then you may need to lift the burner from its place in the centre of the table in order to get it lit. When its fizzing nicely, pop it back in the middle and drop a small handful of incense on the top of it. You should get a nice, aromatic 'fug' wafting away merrily. Leave it for a few seconds and then pop the top on the thurible.

6 Once again, it's time to sit back and relax. This is the point where you are going to make your very own, personal gesture of self awakening. You could do all – or any – of the following things, or you could think up something of your own instead.

(i) Crouch down on the floor and curl yourself up into a little ball. Very slowly, stretch up and up and up until you are standing with your feet apart and your arms outstretched. Hold this position for a few moments, then inscribe a mystic pentagram and relax.

(ii) Stand very still and close your eyes. Imagine that you are on a beautiful hillside watching the sun come up over the horizon. Imagine a dark sky, slowly filling with a golden glow as the first rays of sunlight begin to appear. Slowly, the sun is rising and the sky is turning a beautiful shade of pale blue. Try to hear the birds beginning to wake up and sing. When all is light and clear in your vision, open your eyes and inscribe a mystic pentagram. A minute or two is the longest you should spend in this visualization.

(iii) Think of yourself as a tiny child. Imagine that you are no longer a self sufficient adult but a small baby discovering the universe and everything in it for the first time. Notice how unfamiliar and interesting the things around you are. Everything you can see appears to contain a wealth of exciting new information about your environ- ment. Spend a few moments just standing still but letting your eyes wander over everything you can see as if you didn't know what anything was – or even who *you* were. After a little while, stop doing this and inscribe a mystic pentagram.

Once you've done one, all, or any of these three things (or done your very own personal exercise designed to symbolize re-birth) . . .

Whisper your own name. It will sound a little odd as it pierces the silence.

Now say it a little louder.

Once you feel comfortable speaking in your magical ceremony you can say the words below. They don't have to be exactly what's printed here. Anything will do as long as it catches the spirit of the moment.

'I am alive – I am awake – I am aware.'

'I am (say your name) – and yet I am more than (say your name again).'

'I am a tiny cog in the wheel of the universe and yet I am also a part of the centre of all things.'

'I call upon the loving spirit of life that lies within my heart to guide me to true wisdom and understanding.'

7 With this, you can inscribe the mystic pentagram again and relax. It might even be a good idea to sit down for a little while and imagine all the tension and anxiety you have ever felt in your whole life flood through your body into the floor below you.

After a short while, stand up again and undo your magic circle.

8 It's a good idea to retire to another room. If this is possible, extinguish the candles and leave the incense to burn itself out.

If you can't vacate the room then you can leave the candles burning but you should always open the curtains if it's daytime, or turn on the light if it's night. Either way it's time to relax and forget the ceremony you have just performed. There is no need to remember it – for you have called on a part of you that is much deeper than your conscious mind and it needs no help from your thoughts. In fact, the more distraction you can provide the better. Watch television, listen to the radio, read a book, play a record or just curl up and go to sleep.

The results of this ceremony will be with you for the rest of your life in the form of a subtle change of attitude and outlook. Don't look for a sudden realisation of cosmic wisdom. That will come gently – in its own time. Make yourself a cup of tea and relax. Your first full magical ceremony is complete.

A Magical Diary

Now that you've performed your Ceremony of Self Awakening you can consider yourself firmly on the path to magical mastery. Whether you never perform another ceremony in your whole life or whether you go on to become a great Caster of Spells, you have opened up a door inside yourself that will subtly alter the way you look at the world around you. From now on you'll find it much harder to look at your situation and say 'There is nothing I can do about this.' The voice of inner wisdom you called on will always be there to guide you gently through the stickiest problem and – somehow – you will always know what to do.

This is why, if you are at all interested in developing your new-found skills, it is a good idea to start keeping a magical diary. It doesn't have to be particularly detailed, or even written up daily. Perhaps once a week you could sit down and put your thoughts on paper. They can be quite abstract, especially at first. You may find yourself writing half-formed notions that don't quite seem to make sense. You may find yourself breaking out into little bursts of poetry. Or you may just write down a series of mundane activities like 'paid the milkman' or 'mended the hall table'. The actual words are not important. Whatever you write, the diary will serve as a good way of looking back and assessing how your life is slowly becoming more 'magical'.

There is another good reason for keeping a special diary. The process of writing things down can help you consolidate your magical understanding. Eventually, it will become your very own Magician's Work Book – or, if you like your magic continental style, your *grimoire*. Traditionally, every magician has one of these and no two are ever the same. One reason that the world is not full of published spell books is that each magician keeps his other own personal (and usually private) records. As there is no such thing as a definitive way of doing anything in magic and as each magician must find the approach that best suits his or her own personality, you will eventually find yourself designing your own techniques and writing them up in this work book. Indeed, you may have to for there are plenty of things that you may want to do for which I have given no instructions.

The Morals of Magic

If you are finely enough tuned to your inner nature you can make almost anything happen in the world around you. Magical workings allow you to clarify exactly what it is that you want to happen, and help you concentrate on achieving it. This sort of power is all very well if you want to do spell to make yourself healthier or wiser, or even generally wealthier. It becomes a little tricky if you want something that has to come at the direct expense of another individual. In view of this, there are two golden rules that I must stress:

1 No matter what form of magic you practise, you must never do anything that could possibly harm another human being.

2 The only way that you can harm *yourself* through magic is if you try to harm somebody else.

A classic example of this would be a love spell. The idea of a magical spell that will cause one person to fall hopelessly in love with another is very evocative, but think for a moment. Even if it were possible, nobody in their right mind would ever want to perform it. Imagine that such a spell *was* available to you and let us suppose that there was one particular person whom you deeply longed for but who didn't reciprocate your feelings. All you would have to do would be to draw a magical circle, mutter a few magical words, perform a few magical gestures and hey presto – they would be yours for eternity!

How would it feel if you performed such a spell? Could you possibly enjoy your lover's embrace, knowing all the time that they had been 'bewitched' into giving it? Would they even be the same person you loved, once their individual freedom of choice had been stolen away from them by your enchantment?

Even if you thought you could learn to live with those disconcerting doubts (because of the strength of your own selfish feelings), ask yourself this: If they could respond so fully to your magical charm, what is to stop them from responding to another spell cast by another magician? What would you do? Practise your magic desperately until you were the strongest magician in the whole world? Devote your entire life to a desperate battle for power and control?

You can see what I'm driving at. Any apparent gain you might make from using the love spell would be overshadowed a thousand times by devastating repercussions on your own sanity. The object of your affection might conceivably not even suffer. They need not even know you had cast a spell on them – but you certainly would. Your one simple spell, no matter how strongly inspired, would lead you to spend the rest of your life in a state of perpetual anxiety. You could not even share your problems with the person you love so dearly. You could hardly tell them that your every waking moment was spent worrying that something might break the spell you had put on them.

I don't think I need to spend much more time discussing this hypothetical love spell. It must be obvious that it is vital to think fully and deeply before you embark on any magical working. I also don't want to appear too negative or offputting. There is, after all, a much easier magical solution to the problem outlined above. In fact, there are several.

1 A Spell to Make Yourself More Attractive (see page 261). This sort of spell is very effective. It works by adapting something in *you* – not the person you have designs on. There is still a chance that they will resist your charms, but the odds in your favour are considerably increased. If it fails, their resistance runs very deep indeed and you had better face it. If it works, there is nothing you need feel guilty about. You have simply used magic to make yourself more attractive in the same way that you might use make-up or clothes.

2 A Spell of Determination. Using the Spell of Determination on page 277 you would cure yourself of your infatuation. You only need to gather up the strength and certainty to use it and you will be free of the agonizing need you feel – for ever. (Ironically, by freeing yourself from your feelings in this way you are quite likely to render yourself more attractive to the person you are trying to forget!)

3 A Spell for Perspective and Patience (see page 297). This is perhaps the most useful spell you can employ. It provides you with the strength to do nothing at all about your desired purpose. Once you have cast it you can simply sit back and see what happens with a feeling of genuine indifference to the results. In other words, you make a gesture designed to cast your fate to the winds and agree to accept Nature's solution, regardless of whether it is the one you 'think' you'd prefer. If you think back over your life, you may well decide that some of the best things that have ever happened to you were either not what you were expecting or not what you thought you wanted at the time. This is the least dramatic of your potential solutions, but if you can summon the resolve to do it, it's almost bound to be the wisest.

The above examples refer to possible solutions to a love problem. There are similar solutions to any other problem, if you think about it. Once you've performed the Ceremony of Self Awakening, you'll find it easy to know instinctively which spell to use.

The Responsibility of Power

By taking your first steps in magic, you are beginning to realize and elevate your true potential as a human being. This brings with it what could almost be called a duty to the rest of humanity. As someone who has seen the deeper levels of possibility in life, you owe it to yourself in life, you owe it to yourself and to those you love to be pure and irreproachable in your actions. This doesn't mean that you need become a Goody Two Shoes but you'll certainly have to be answerable to your own conscience so you had best stay within the limits of what you know is right! (I should also say that the more you develop your magical understanding the clearer it will become that you have only your on conscience to answer to. This, in turn, may lead to your rejecting some – but not all – conventional morality and replacing it with your own higher and more exacting standards.)

Magic and Discretion

There is no reason at all why you shouldn't tell other people about your developing interest in magic, but at the same time you probably won't want to go broadcasting it from the rooftops. Unless they, too, have read this book, most people are likely to have formed a host of strange impressions about the subject and may even start worrying that you're about to begin sacrificing virgins or raising demons. There's also nothing to stop you forming a magical group or partnership with another person or other people you feel you can trust and who share your interest, but be discreet.

Elemental Weapons

You may be surprised that there has been no mention yet of four traditional tools: the Chalice, the Sword, the Wand and the Pentacle. The idea is that these four objects should represent the four elements and be used in magical ceremonies. Personally, I feel that magic, a mainly internal process, becomes debased by an over-emphasis on exotic paraphernalia. To gain empathy with and power over the elements you need to understand how they operate with your own personality. After that, four candles is more than enough physical symbolism.

Magical Words

You may also have been expecting to encounter a long list of magic words. It was once very fashionable to create spells with a verbal patchwork quilt of Greek, Hebrew, Latin, Sanskrit and Babylonian phrases, stitched together with plenty of biblical English (thees, thous, and so mote it be's). Using olde worlde language may add a sense of elitist mystique but it detracts from the relevance of magic to everyday life. It gives the magician a sense of false power based on the ability to bandy obscure phrases rather than the ability to tune in to the forces of nature. The choice of words you use in magic is important, but it must depend on which words *you* consider to be important. There would be no point in asking you to say (for example) 'Abracadabra' when trying to express the concept of infinity. It may once have been an evocative word (it's a palindrome with special numerological qualities), but today (at least in England) there are few people who can hear Abracadabra without thinking of Sooty and Sweep.*

* Sooty is a glove puppet TV star who performs amazing feats of apparent power by waving a wand, sprinkling 'oofle dust' and inviting the children to incant 'Izzy wizzy let's get busy' and 'Abracadabra' on his behalf.

2. VENUS SPELL
A Spell to Make Yourself More Attractive

There are two ways you can make yourself more attractive. The first is to alter your physical appearance in some way. The second is to adjust your personality. Actually, the two things are very closely linked. If you really have (for example) an extreme weight problem you might want to use the Spell of Determination (pages 277–284) to deal with that problem separately. Even so, you should begin by doing this one. It will make things noticeably better – no matter what you *think* is wrong with you!

Timing

Attraction comes under the rulership of the planet Venus. Venus rules two signs of the zodiac – Libra and Taurus. You can do this spell whenever the moon is in either of these two 'aesthetic' signs (you will find the dates you need on page 307). The only exception to this rule is that you should not do the spell when Venus herself is in what the ancient astrologers used to call a 'bad condition'. Once every couple of years or so Venus goes retrograde, or backwards through the sky. At this time her influence is impeded and you would be wise to wait until she starts moving 'forwards' again. Here are the dates in the next few years when you should avoid doing this spell.

Venus in retrograde

From . . .		. . . *Until*
1986	15th October	26th November
1988	22nd May	4th July
1990	29th December (1989)	8th February
1991	1st August	13th September
1993	11th March	22nd April
1994	13 October	23rd November

As in the spell for Increased Sensitivity (the Ceremony of Self Awakening), the spell does not have to be cast at any particular time of night or day. As long as the moon is in the right sign you can do it whenever it is convenient.

While You're Waiting

1 Find a photograph of someone whom you consider to be particularly attractive. Ideally it should be full face (i.e. not a profile).

2 Stare at the photograph for a while. If you want to you could use the same technique (scrying) that you employed in the Tarot section to explore each card (see page 94). The only difference with this photograph is that you should try to project yourself behind the eyes in the photograph. Try and imagine what it feels like to *own* that face.

3 Whether you're scrying or simply staring, stop after a little while and ask yourself: 'What can I see?' 'What is it that makes this person so "attractive"?' 'Is it really their physical appearance?' 'Is there *really* something terribly special about the proportions of their face?'

4 The more you look, the more you will see that they have two eyes, a nose, a mouth and a fairly standard issue human body attached to these fairly standard issue features. So what is it that's so attractive about them? It's something deeper. An inner charm or poise that shines through their eyes, lightens their features and turns a relatively ordinary face into one that is a pleasure to gaze upon.

5 Now try something even more interesting. Take a piece of plain card and cover up the left-hand side of the photograph. Leave yourself looking at one eye, half the nose and half the mouth. Look long and hard. Notice the expression on the face. Try and get a sense of what this person is feeling. Are they hiding anything? Are they trying to project something?

6 Now move the card again. Cover the side of the face you've just looked at and do the same for the other half. Once again, look long and hard and ask the same questions. Do you notice something different? It's interesting, isn't it? The left and right hand sides of almost everyone's faces give out totally different impressions. If you've never done this sort of thing before, I won't be surprised if you want to leap up and grab every photograph you can find. By all means do so. Rustle through old colour magazines and newspapers. Try the technique on as many pictures as you want. You should now be getting a much clearer perspective on how this business of attraction really works. It's very definitely an *inner* thing.

If you still need convincing, think about some of the famous film stars who are described as having 'rugged good looks' or a 'unique charm'. Often, these phrases are euphemisms for 'not classically good looking'. And yet – these people are very popular and successful in the business of attracting people to them. Why? Because what they have on the inside shines through.

Finally, just to drum the point home, think of some people you know who are very attractive at first sight – until you get to know them . . .

7 Now, ask yourself what you *think* is so wrong with your physical appearance. Obviously if you're seriously interested in doing the spell that follows you must be worried about something. That worry is actually the root of your problem, whether the 'defect' in your appearance is real or imaginary is irrelevant. You will find that in the game of attraction, charm, poise, and confidence are far more crucial than mere looks. (If you're just doing this spell to make yourself more attractive to one particular person it is just the same. Even if your heart's desire told you that he/she couldn't love you unless you were six inches taller, it's not true. I guarantee that the real barrier is the way they sense your own lack of self confidence. Once you've learned to be proud and pleased about who and what you are, you'll have the psychic equivalent of an extra six inches and more besides!)

8 Sit down in front of a mirror. Look at the image you see reflected. Stare at it, scry it, cover up one half and then the other. Be merciless. Peer and peer. As you hear yourself thinking things like 'Oh God, I'm really ugly' or 'Look at my awful expression/eyes/ears/nose/spots/or whatever', just keep looking. Criticize yourself until it really hurts, if you must, but still don't stop looking. Just keep staring and staring until you've run out of negative thoughts.

Now, keep staring and start to think about the good points. Go on – admit it – there are some! In fact, the more you keep looking, the more you will find what there is to like. There's a certain unique quality about that person in the mirror which is rather irresistible. They do have a certain charm. When you bear in mind that you know for a fact that behind that certain charm is a warm and wonderful human being – well, actually, they're rather fanciable. Can you imagine being hugged by this person? Wouldn't it be rather pleasurable? In fact, wouldn't it be extremely desirable? You can trust this person completely. You could fall into their arms and know that they'd really know how to love you, look after you and introduce you to a world of sensual and intellectual delight that is exactly what you'd like to experience! Come to think of it, this person just has to be one of the most attractive people you've ever seen! In fact, the *most* attractive! How can you bear to tear yourself away from the mirror? Don't you want to keep on looking and admiring?

9 Once you get to this point (and don't worry, you will!), it is probably time to stop looking at yourself! After all, the idea is to render yourself more attractive – not totally narcissistic!

10 Go straight out to the local shops. Notice how people look at you. Notice how – even if you're only wearing some tatty old clothes – they appear to be staring at you as if you were some glamorous film star. It really does work! As long as you remain confident that you are an attractive person your whole body will reflect this. And as soon as you start to lose your confidence, this too will show.

You can do this exercise as often as you feel you need to. Try to get into the habit of feeling good about yourself. If you want, indulge in a good haircut and some new clothes. They will help you get used to feeling new and different, but they are only props. The real art of making yourself attractive is to change how things are on the inside, not the outside – as we shall see in the course of the spell itself . . .

Final Preparations

The structure of this spell (and almost all the others) closely follows the Ceremony of Self Awakening. Certainly the same sort of preparations and basic equipment are called for. Rather than repeat myself, let me just refer you back to that ceremony for general notes. Specifically, though, you'll need your usual magical kit *plus*:

1 small, hand-held mirror
some Venus incense (see page 233)
some essential oil of a plant ruled by Venus (see page 219)

In ancient times the magician would summon the goddess Aphrodite and exhort her to bestow great beauty and charm upon him or her. In this spell we are going to do something rather similar, but with deference to our more sophisticated understanding of how magic actually works.

The goddess Aphrodite was a Greek name for Venus who gave her name to the planet. There is no doubt in the mind of any practising astrologer that she (or it) *can* bestow the gifts of attraction and charm. You have only to look at the horoscopes of some of the world's most beautiful people to see how prominent the planet Venus is in all their horoscopes.

By waiting until there is a strong Venusian influence in the sky, and then burning the herbs of Venus, we are going to create an environment that is rich in her qualities. We are then going to invoke the spirit of Venus. Remember, though, that Venus is not actually a goddess hovering around on some mystical cloud waiting to be summoned by a magician. Venus is a quality within you that you wish to bring out and increase. The invocation is directed at a part of your own psyche (although we are going to take a bit of magical artistic licence in the instructions below).

At The Allotted Hour

1 Make all your preparations exactly as you did for the Self Awakening Ceremony. Lay out your work table with candles, candle sticks, cloth, incense, incense burner and the hand-held mirror.

2 Take what is going to become your usual pre-spell bath and add a tiny drop of your essential oil to it before you climb in.

3 Put on your magical garments and light your candles as you did in the previous ceremony.

4 Inscribe a Mystic Pentagram (page 242) and draw your magical circle around you (page 246).

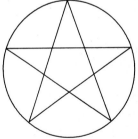

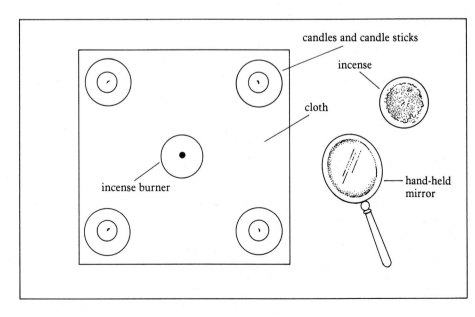

candles and candle sticks

incense

cloth

incense burner

hand-held mirror

5 Light the incense and relax. You are now ready to invoke the spirit of Venus.

6 Breathe slowly and deeply. Try and let all tension flood away from your body. Stand in silence for a few moments.

When you feel ready, begin to say the following, in a calm, even voice:

Venus.   Venus.
I call upon the spirit of Venus.
Hear my call and come to me.
Venus.   Venus.

Now stare into the smoke of the incense. Imagine that every wisp and vapour is the spirit of Venus, merging with the air around you. Listen to the sound of your own breath for a moment. Try to feel the sweet smell of the Venusian herbs filling your lungs. Each breath is awakening the sleeping spirit of Venus, the mythical enchantress within you.

You may begin to feel a little weak and slightly more conscious of your own body. Possibly your skin will start to tingle. These are the symptoms of a Venusian experience. The awakening of the senses.

After a few moments you should lift up the mirror and begin to look into it. The image you now see before you is the image of *you* – being transformed by an overwhelming experience of sensuality and sensitivity.

Keep looking at yourself until you feel that you are looking at the most beautiful and the most lovable person you have ever seen. Don't be ashamed or inhibited. Allow yourself to indulge in a few moments of unashamed self adoration. You deserve it!

(If you feel at all inhibited, or feel that it is somehow wrong to be quite so self indulgent, remember this. You are a child of creation. Behind your personality and behind your human body is pure and perfect energy. The essence of life itself. It is perfectly natural for you to respond to the beauty of creation, manifest in your own physical body. After all, you would not hesitate to admire a flower, or a tree, or a beautiful blue sky.)

Keep looking into the mirror until you are totally delighted with the image you see there.

Slowly remove your gaze, place the mirror back on the table and relax.

Now say:

> Venus is within me now.
> Venus is within me always.

Stand still for a few moments longer and then inscribe a Mystic Pentagram.

Sit down for a few moments and imagine all the tension you have ever felt flowing through your body into the floor below you. With the tension, send the last remnants of self doubt and the last feelings of physical inferiority you will ever experience. Just let it all sink into the floor.

7 After a few moments, you can undo the magical circle and extinguish the candles. Let the incense burn itself out. Your spell is complete and from now on it will be working for you. You need never think of yourself as unattractive again.

As always, you should now do something completely trivial or undemanding. Put on the kettle, put on some music, or put on your dancing shoes and go to a disco!

The spell will begin to take effect immediately and will grow stronger with every passing day. It doesn't necessarily mean that you will be immediately swamped with offers from the opposite sex (or the same sex!), but you will find that it won't be long before people begin to be drawn to you. You may also like to start wearing a tiny drop of the bath oil you used as a perfume – it can act as a subtle reminder of the spell.

Two Last Words of Advice

1 Remember, it's one thing to draw people to you and another to hold their interest. Just as you learned to love yourself in this spell, you must now learn to appreciate other people with similar enthusiasm. After all, a popular person is one who makes other people feel good by being sensitive to their needs. Learn to sense when someone needs support, when they need warmth and when they need to be left alone. The spirit of Venus that you invoked in the spell will naturally help in this area, but if you do find that you are drawing people to you but not getting through to them you may also need a Spell for Increased Sensitivity (the Ceremony of Self Awakening).

2 If you did this spell to make yourself more attractive to one particular person, don't expect them to leap all over you the next time they see you, particularly if there is a history of rejection. It will take a little while before you new-found attraction can seep under their strongly guarded defence mechanism. Play it cool, and if necessary perform the Spell of Indifference to help you.

3. MERCURY SPELL
A Spell to Increase Your Understanding

You can use this spell to counter any problem that involves your intellect, your powers of analysis or your ability to receive or transmit information. In fact, anything that has its roots in your mind. If you wanted to be sure of passing an exam, winning an argument, making a sale or writing an interesting book, this is the spell you'd need!

The Mercury spell also has some less competitive applications. If you were having difficulties communicating with a loved one it would grant you greater perspective and insight into their point of view. If you were unsure of the extent of your own talents or were at some sort of creative crossroads in your life, the same spell would help you gather together all the salient information and come to an enlightened decision.

Although the spell itself, like all spells, should only be performed if and when you feel you have an outstanding need for it, the pre-spell exercise can be performed as often as you like.

Timing

Mercury rules two signs of the zodiac: Virgo and Gemini. You can do this spell whenever the moon is in either of these two signs (see page 307). The only exception to this is if Mercury is retrograde. Therefore, you can select any date when the moon is in Virgo or Gemini unless it falls within the dates below.

Mercury in retrograde

From . . .		. . . Until
1986	2nd November	22nd November
1987	18th February	12th March
	21st June	15th July
	16th October	6th November
1988	2nd February	23rd February
	31st May	23rd June
	28th September	19th October
1989	16th January	5th February
	12th May	5th June
	11th September	3rd October
1990	30th December (1989)	20th January
	23rd April	17th May
	25th August	17th September
	13th December	3rd January (1991)
1991	4th April	28th April
	7th August	31st August
	28th November	18th December
1992	17th March	9th April
	20th July	13th August
	10th November	1st December
1993	27th Febuary	22nd March
	1st July	25th July
	25th October	15th November
1994	11th February	5th March
	12th June	6th July
	9th October	30th October

Although Mercury goes retrograde more often than any of the other planets, it doesn't stay retrograde for anywhere near as long. This is because its proximity to the sun makes it the fastest-moving planet in the solar system. Every time Mercury goes retrograde anything to do with communication seems to suffer a setback of some sort. If you want to impress your friends, pick one of the periods and predict for it delays in the post, faulty phone lines, bad business deals or just a general spate of misunderstandings. You're almost bound to be right!

While You're Waiting

To prepare for this spell, I'd like you to give up talking for a while! You'll find that silence can be a tremendous aid to concentration and awareness. The length of time you should remain silent depends on how much of a talker you are. If, like me, you can't keep your mouth shut for more than a few minutes you may find that a couple of hours is all you can take! If, on the other hand, you're naturally a taciturn sort of person you may need to keep quiet for a whole day.

People who have gone blind often say that although they miss their sight their other senses become much clearer. This exercise is based on a similar notion. If you can make yourself go dumb for a while you'll find that you start using parts of your brain that you didn't previously know you had!

The time you pick to perform this experiment is important. There's no point in doing it when you're alone. (Most people can manage not to talk to themselves!) There's also no point in trying to do it when you're at work. (How would you answer the telephone or speak to your boss?) Ideally, you should select an occasion when you'll be (a) in company, and (b) in an informal, relaxed environment. For example, this could be a night at the pub or an afternoon picnic in the park.

The trickiest part will be getting started. If you were to announce to your friends (by way of a written note) that you'd given up speaking for a while you'd probably find yourself becoming the centre of attention. This can be very distracting, particularly as some clever character is almost bound to try and trick you into slipping up and saying something! On the other hand, if you just turn up and give no explanation at all for your sudden loss of voice people may take it personally. 'Why aren't you speaking to me?' they will ask.

The simplest way around this problem is to pretend that you've actually lost your voice in a medical sense. That way, you'll get a certain amount of sympathy at first and once all the usual jokes have been cracked your friends will stop bothering about why you're keeping quiet and just get on with entertaining themselves.

'Fibbing' in this way is quite a fitting prelude to a Mercury spell which rightly places a lot of value on honesty. Most of us feel very guilty about telling even the smallest of lies. A few people break the rules almost compulsively, and the rest of us are so innocent and credulous that we let them get away with it. If you are one of those people who doesn't mind bending the truth in your own interests you will find that performing this exercise will give you a valuable insight into your own psyche which allows you to change for the better. On the other hand, if you normally feel uncomfortable about even telling a little lie, you'll find that having your own, controlled experienced of being deceptive will give you a much keener ability to spot deception in other people. By indulging in a bit of harmless play acting, you can broaden the scope of your own experience in the field of communication and discrimination.

Alternatively, don't pretend. Simply make your conversation absolutely minimal. Restrict yourself to as few words as possible. Compensate by providing plenty of friendly facial expressions. You'll soon find that even your closest friends won't mind you being quiet as long as you appear to be giving them plenty of attention!

So one way or another you're ready to begin. Exactly what is going to happen to you and what you will learn from the experiment is not for me to say. It will depend on the kind of person you are – and the kind of person you want to become! However, I can tell you that the longer you can remain in your state of silence the more surprising things you are likely to discover.

It might also be a good idea to write up an account of your experiences in your magical diary. I did this, and below are a few (edited) excerpts from my notes.

. . . I never realized how much energy I use up talking. It's much easier to listen to other people if I'm not always trying to think of a ready answer or a witty reply. Watching people talking to each other reminded me of those TV interviewers who never listen to the answers to their questions. Everyone's competing to be heard.

. . . It's interesting how much more concentration I have. I just beat two of my friends at pool and I don't even know how to hold a cue properly. I think it happened because I was channelling my energy more directly than they were. Also, I think my silence unnerved them. For one thing – I wasn't able to tell them that I didn't know how to play . . .

. . . I became a lot more conscious of the power of body language. I was only allowing myself to communicate with gestures and grunts. It's amazing how much you can get across to someone without saying anything . . .

. . . For the first time I understood something about B........ that I'd never seen before. Because I was being so quiet, he started talking to M......... as if I wasn't there. I felt like a fly on the wall and it was fascinating to observe their rapport together. I think I'll have to make a point of shutting up more often . . .

My diary went on like this for several pages but much of it is a bit too personal to share with you here. All I really want to point out is that I had a wealth of profound realizations while performing this experiment. I really did thrash two reasonable players at pool – and whilst I'm not trying to imply that simply keeping your mouth shut will turn you into superman (or superwoman), I'd like to bet that you discover some very exciting new talents when you try this for yourself.

If possible, do it several times before you do the spell. As you'll see, the spell itself is simply an affirmation of mental prowess. Its success depends, to a great extent, on how flexible and open-minded you are prepared to be. If you are determined to stick to the same old pre-conceived ideas and fixed notions that you have held all your life, about who you are and what you can do, then there is no magical ceremony that will instantly change it. But if you are prepared to push back the boundaries of your own limitations and try out a few different perspectives, you'll find that the spell allows you to consolidate these new discoveries and apply them most successfully (and satisfactorily) in your everyday life.

Final Preparations

As usual, you'll need:

your spell kit
Mercury incense
Mercury essential oil

. . . and in addition, you'll need:

your magical diary
a pen

(Books, and the act of writing in general, are ruled by Mercury.)

As the spell requires you to do a certain amount of magical writing you may want to have something available to rest on, or you may want to perform the spell sitting on a chair with the magical work table acting as a desk.

If you are unsure about how to write the sigils called for in the spell, by all means practise as much as you need to.

As always, I would advize you to read the spell carefully before you commence and if possible memorize it. This is particularly fitting for a Mercury spell because Mercury rules memory.

I should also like to make my usual point that Mercury is only a symbolic name for a power that lies within your own subconscious. In ancient Greek mythology Mercury was known as the god Hermes. The Egyptians used to speak of this power as Thoth. Some magicians say that Thoth, Mercury or Hermes is the power that rules all magic. They may be right. Nonetheless, I must stress that although we are invoking Mercury, (or Hermes or Thoth) in the process of this spell, we are not summoning up an entity or personality from any mystical, imaginary domain. We are calling upon Mercurial energy from the place where it really lies – the very depths of our own being.

At The Allotted Hour

1 Lay out your work table with candles, candlesticks, cloth, incense, burner, magical diary and pen.

2 Enjoy a relaxing pre-spell bath, to which has been added a tiny drop of Mercurial oil.

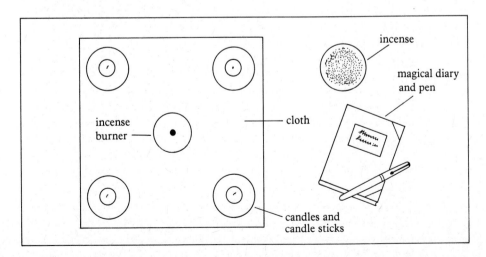

incense

magical diary and pen

cloth

incense burner

candles and candle sticks

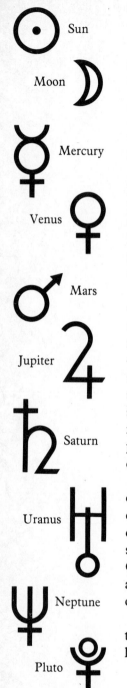

Sun

Moon

Mercury

Venus

Mars

Jupiter

Saturn

Uranus

Neptune

Pluto

Sigils, Glyphs and Signs

Each planet, and each sign of the zodiac, has a magical symbol attached to it. In the days when few people could read or write these simple markings were widely used – for each encapsulates a host of ideas and associations. At school, you may have learned about the Chinese alphabet. Each letter is really a picture, telling the complicated story. Magical symbols work in much the same way. Once you have the 'key' to a symbol, you can begin to explore its meaning – and once you begin, you may never finish. The planetary symbols can be also found on pages 31–33, but we have repeated them here for ease of reference. As you can see, they are mainly comprised of circles, half circles and crosses. A circle is essentially a female symbol of fertility and 'openness'. A cross is basically a masculine symbol of power and assertion. A half circle represents the yearning of the human spirit to discover universal truth and is really neither male nor female.

In thousands of years the basic symbols have hardly changed, but the way they are drawn has become a little stylized. Thus, the cross on the end of Mars has become an arrow – and the right hand half of a circle which meets an elongated cross for Jupiter has begun to look rather like a number 4. Don't worry about this. You are free to make your own drawings of the symbols as artistic as you please. The important thing is that you make some effort to trace or copy them. By expressing the character of each symbol in your own free hand you will be fulfilling an ancient ceremonial rite, and also allowing your subconscious to express itself by driving your pen to put the sum total of your own understanding into each symbol you draw.

There are other symbols in traditional magic besides the astrological ones you have already encountered. At one time or another magicians have created simple line drawings to represent happiness, sadness, despair, death, sex, power – and a host of other basic human experiences. Some are self explanatory – others are a weird mixture of Hebrew, Roman and Greek figures. All are irrelevant in contemporary magic. They belong, by and large, to an era when most people were illiterate. Today, a symbol need only be used when there is no simple verbal or written equivalent.

Symbols of this nature are often call sigils or glyphs. Some have argued that there's a difference in meaning between these two words. If so, it's largely semantic.

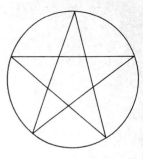

3 Put on your magical garments and light the candles.

4 Inscribe a Mystic Pentagram and then draw a magical circle around you.

5 Light the incense and relax. You are now ready to invoke the spirit of Mercury.

6 Breathe slowly and deeply. Stare into the incense smoke and imagine that you are controlling the flow of the smoke with your own mind. Keep watching the smoke and keep trying to control its movement with your thoughts.

—☆—

After a few moments, repeat the following in a calm clear voice:

All that I think
and
All that I hear
and
All that I see
and
All that I smell
is
Mercury Mercury Mercury.

Mercury emerge from within me
Mercury surround me
Mercury fill me with intelligence.

—☆—

Remain standing still and calm. Stare once more at the incense and simply watch the smoke rising and merging with the air. You may begin to feel as if your brain is actually growing in size. As if your conscious mind is suddenly very sharp and very powerful. As if there is no problem you cannot solve and no limitation to the power of your own intellect.

—☆—

Slowly, unhurriedly, reach forward and pick up your diary. Open it at a blank page.

—☆—

Now pick up your pen and pass it through the incense smoke.

In your best handwriting, write down the thing you most want to be able to achieve with your intellect. Try to restrict yourself to a few words. You may want to write 'memory' or 'understanding' or 'concentration' or all three things.

Underneath this list, write your own name in full. If for some reason you have more than one name, write the name that you feel most comfortable with in your heart of hearts.

Underneath this write the date and the word Mercury.

Underneath this draw the sigil for the moon and the sigil for the sign of the zodiac the moon is currently in (Gemini or Virgo).

Take your time with this writing. Once you have done it slowly replace the pen and book. Put them back in the same positions you picked them up from.

Now sit down, relax and stare into the incense smoke once more. Imagine all the tension you have ever felt in your whole life flood into the floor below you.

The spell is cast.

7 Undo the magical circle, extinguish the candles and restore the room to a normal state.

From now on, you will find that your mind is open to new ideas and inspiration, that you are capable of greater retentive memory, that you have the capacity to see right to the heart of your own and other people's problems and that, in general, the power of Mercury is alive and alert within your intellect, driving you on to greater and higher goals of intellectual attainment.

Once agin, it is time to relax and unwind. Resist the temptation to put your head straight into a complicated book. Give yourself at least an hour of enforced frivolity. Watch the most vacuous television show you can find; make a cup of tea or find a children's story book and read that. Your newly awakened intellectual strength will be with you for the rest of your life. It will grow and flourish over the following days, weeks, months and years. For these first few moments it is important, as with all spells, that you 'Earth' yourself with some mundane activity.

Two Last Words of Advice

1 You may well find yourself growing interested in all sorts of topics and subjects that previously held little interest for you. You may find yourself spending a lot of time in the local library, or you may find yourself just lying back and thinking a lot more deeply and carefully than you previously did. You will soon discover that what goes into your brain has a strong effect on what comes out of it, and you will find that your own ability to communicate becomes much stronger and more direct. Do remember that nobody can be an expert on everything and that the roots of wisdom are found in humility.

2 Give the spell at least a few weeks or even months to work on you before applying for membership of Mensa!

4. MARS SPELL
A Spell for Determination

This spell is designed to give you strength, certainty and willpower. It will allow you to channel your enthusiasm and direct it towards a chosen goal. Regardless of what you require, if it is at all possible to achieve it, this spell will allow you to do so. It is just as good for giving things up as getting things. I know people who have used it to help them learn a difficult skill, and others who have used it to help them give up smoking, drugs or helpless romantic infatuations! It can be an intensely powerful spell and you shouldn't enter into it lightly.

Everything I have previously said about the mortality of magic applies particularly strongly here. It may seem very tempting to apply this spell towards gaining direct power over another person. I can only stress, once more, the blind folly of doing this. It will ultimately be you who suffers. By aiming your magical power away from yourself you will in effect be passing your own energy into someone else. The very act of naming or visualizing another person in a spell like this would have the opposite effect to the one you want. It would bestow the other person with more strength and substance than they already have. You would effectively be making an acknowledgement of their power instead of an assertion of your own.

I am sorry to harp on like this, but this spell is very powerful.

There is one more thing I should stress and this is to let your determination be tempered by wisdom. Don't channel your new-found strength and certainty into a goal that is unworthy of you. If you are at all in doubt about the sense of your proposed actions, perform the Spell to Increase your Undertanding too (see page 268). This will help you decide clearly.

Timing

The spell is of the nature of Mars. It summons the qualities of ambition, assertion and dynamic energy associated with the fiery red planet and brings them to life within the magician. Mars rules the signs of Scorpio and Aries and this spell should therefore be performed when the moon is in Scorpio or Aries. It may be performed at any time when the moon is in either of these two signs except when Mars itself is retrograde.

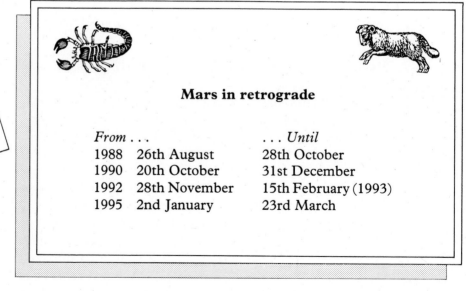

Mars in retrograde

From . . .		. . . Until
1988	26th August	28th October
1990	20th October	31st December
1992	28th November	15th February (1993)
1995	2nd January	23rd March

While You are Waiting

At the time of writing, a particular motto has become very popular in the English language. It is used by a special army division which undertakes difficult and demanding tasks involving much courage and daring. The motto is 'Who dares – wins'. Whilst you may not wish to develop your courage in order to go storming embassies or freeing hostages, there may well be situations in your life which present an equivalent sort of challenge to you as an individual.

The idea of a motto, such as 'Who dares – wins' or 'I can and I will' is a very valid one. It forms a quick, simple channel between the conscious and the unconscious mind. It can serve as a trigger for the willpower and strength. Therefore, I'd like to suggest that you adopt such a motto. It can be one that already exists (such as the two above) or it can be a short phrase of your own invention. If it sounds slightly silly or glib on first hearing that's probably an advantage. Often such phrases stick more firmly in the memory because of their very awkwardness.

Decide on your motto ('I'm going to do it' or 'Nothing will stop me' or whatever. . .) and practise saying it to yourself. Already you will begin to feel more confident and assertive. Now imagine the most difficult thing you could ever be called upon to do (within reason – don't select something that you would never *want* to do). Make it something that you feel slightly afraid of or incapable of. When I first did this exercise, I thought of climbing a mountain – difficult because I don't like the cold and I am nervous about heights, even though I'm attracted to the sense of achievement.

Imagine yourself going through the motions of this imaginary challenge. Consider as many details as you can. Every time you feel yourself getting stuck or losing your nerve, clench your fists firmly together and say your motto. Then carry on, in your imagination, with the task in hand. See it through to a successful conclusion.

You may well argue that there's a world of difference between having courage in your imagination and having courage in real life. In fact, the two are closely linked. If you can anticipate a problem or a state of fear and overcome it mentally, it will be easier when you have to experience such a situation.

You will be relieved to hear that I am not about to suggest that you go out and put yourself to the difficult task you just imagined yourself going through. Nor am I going to suggest that you go out and find all the little things you're afraid of and systematically conquer them one by one. That's bravado not bravery. Most people find that life brings them plenty of challenges without having to go out and seek them. If you don't agree you probably already posses most of the qualities this spell is designed to imbue and don't really need to do it anyway!

What I am going to suggest is that, over a period of days or weeks, you repeat this exercise with a variety of things or situations you feel afraid of in your mind. You should also keep an eye out for situations that occur in your life naturally and which appear to threaten or unnerve you. As they arise, watch yourself handling them. Begin making a conscious effort to take a more direct approach. Become a little braver or a little more adventurous each time an opportunity presents itself. Measure your success in small degrees and you will build your confidence up. If you set yourself too high a goal too quickly, you are likely to set yourself back.

Practise saying or remembering your motto every time you are presented with a challenge. Gradually it will take on more meaning for you and come to symbolize your own inner link with a source of strength and determination.

Finally, it will help you prepare for this spell if you can do something about your own physical fitness. It is amazing how much more powerful you can feel if your body is strong and healthy. Take to running round the block each day, or doing a spot of weight lifting, aerobics or general physical exercise. Even just a few minutes every day will begin to increase your physical strength and teach you something very valid about the power of mind over matter.

When you have won a few imaginary battles, made at least some progress in the field of daily life and achieved a certain amount of new-found physical energy, you will be ready to perform the spell itself.

Final Preparations

This spell can be quite noisy. It contains an opportunity for you to shout something out at the top of your voice. For this reason, it would be sensible to do it somewhere out of earshot. You wouldn't want to worry the neighbours! If this proves difficult, you'll have to practise saying things quietly but with a lot of force.

By now you should be quite familiar with the basic pattern of a ceremonial magic spell. Besides the usual spell kit, you will require:

Martian incense
Some essential oil of a 'Martian' nature
A sharp clean needle

The needle is required for a part of the ceremony that is definitely optional. Traditionally, the needle would be used to draw a tiny droplet of blood from your fingertip with which you would then annoint your forehead. It's a powerful, symbolic gesture of determination (as you won't need to be told if you are already experiencing discomfort at the idea!) but it is *not* essential to the success of the spell. If you find the idea of drawing your own blood abhorrent (or if you have a family history of haemophilia!) it will be more than sufficient to mime this action.

As with all spells, it will help if you are rehearsed and clear about what you are going to do in advance. Read the instructions carefully first and make notes if you want to.

The spell involves summoning the spirit of Mars. As with the other spells, I must take one final moment to define terms. Mars is not a god floating on a cloud, waiting to be summoned by certain words or fragrances like a genie in a bottle. Mars is, if you like, a component of our own psyche that we wish to emphasize and gain control of. With this is mind, it will also help you to re-read the description of Mars in the astrology section.

At The Allotted Hour

1 Lay out your work table with candles, candlesticks, cloth, incense, incense burner and needle.

2 Take a leisurely pre-spell bath (having added a tiny drop of Martian oil while it's running).

3 Put on your magical garments and light the candles.

4 Inscribe a Mystic Pentagram and then draw a magical circle around you.

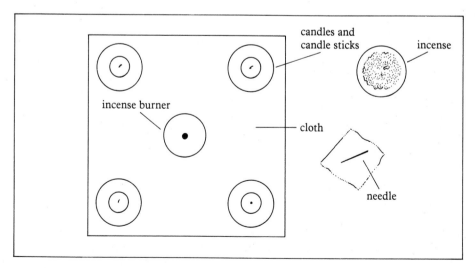

candles and candle sticks

incense

incense burner

cloth

needle

5 Light the incense and relax. You are now ready to invoke the spririt of Mars.

6 Breathe slowly and deeply. Remaining relaxed and calm, begin to imagine the whole room flooding with a brilliant, bright red light. When you feel ready, repeat the following in a calm, clear voice:

The spirit of Mars is within me
The spirit of Mars is around me
I feel the strength
I feel the power
I am the strength
I am the power

Remain standing still and calm. Imagine the red light that you visualized flowing through your body. You may begin to feel very charged as if a powerful electric current was racing round your body. This is the spirit of Mars inside you, flooding into your conscious mind.

After a few moments, lift up the needle and pass it through the incense smoke.

If you wish to, you may push it into the tip of your first finger (either hand) and draw a tiny drop of blood. Otherwise, hold the needle over the tip of your first finger and imagine a tiny charge of energy entering your body from it, and a tiny drop of your own life energy emerging on to your fingertip.

Replace the needle on the table.

Now press your fingertip against the middle of your forehead. If you drew blood, you would now be 'smearing it' on your forehead. If your gesture is symbolic only, simply imagine the tiny droplet of life energy being absorbed back into the centre of your conscious mind through the 'third eye'.

Stand relaxed for a moment, with your arms hanging loosely at your sides.

☆

Imagine yourself as a living 'powerhouse', full of raw determination and certainty. There is now *nothing* you cannot do if you so choose.

☆

It is time to speak your motto.

☆

Say it quietly to yourself at first.

☆

Now say it louder. Now, if circumstances permit . . . SHOUT IT OUT AS LOUDLY AS YOU CAN. (If this is not possible, simply whisper it with plenty of force!)

☆

Relax once more, and breathe deeply. The spell is cast.

As you breathe, imagine that you are absorbing all the red light you visualized earlier.

7 Sit down, relax and imagine all the tension you have ever felt in your life flooding into the floor below you.

8 Undo the magical circle, extinguish the candles and draw the curtains or turn on the light. From now on, you will always be able to find the power and strength you need to achieve your goals. You have made contact with a vast reserve of courage and confidence within you and you will now be able to tap into it whenever you choose.

There is no need to think any more about what you have done. It is time to relax and indulge yourself in the usual post ceremony wind-down. Besides the usual cup of tea, book reading or TV watching, you may also like to change into some running clothes and go for a long, energetic race around the block. This will help you work off any surplus energy or excitement you may be feeling. It is very important to wind down completely after a spell of this magnitude.

NB: If you did draw blood in the spell, it might be a good idea to wash it off your forehead before you go into the street!

Two Last Words of Advice

1 Remember that courage and determination are relative things. If you have spent your whole life as meek as a mouse you can hardly expect to turn into a raging lion overnight. You will have to start by being a 'raging mouse' and over a period of weeks or months from performing the spell you will gradually become more Leonine!

2 Some people find themselves affected by outbursts of hot temperedness after performing this spell. If you do find yourself snapping at people, or getting hot under the collar, don't worry, it will soon wear off and you can warn your loved ones that you might be feeling a bit on edge for a few days and suggest that they try not to cross you!

5. SUN SPELL
A Spell for Health, Confidence and Vitality

As magicians, we are able to bring about some very real changes in our own state of health. The more we understand and empathize with the forces of nature within our own body, the more we can recognize our own physical problems and know instinctively how to deal with them. I must stress though, that becoming a healer (in any school of medicine) requires a lifetime's dedication. No magician can expect to replace all that knowledge and experience with a single spell. So this is definitely a spell for health, not a spell for healing. It is a form of magical preventative medicine.

If you are the kind of person who suffers from weakness or illness a lot, you should find it very useful indeed. Even if you're normally strong, it won't harm to do it; if you are actually ill, it should help you recover some strength. If, however, you perform this spell when you are sick and you don't return quickly to perfect health, your body is telling you that you also need the aid of a professional. Specialist knowledge and skill can then combine with the power of the spell to return you to a state of wholeness and vitality.

Timing

You can do this spell at any time. It involves summoning the energies of the sun. As centre of the solar system and focus for the cosmic cavalcade of planetary motion, the sun is available every day, and to everyone.

The sun symbolizes the basic life force within you in its pure state. All the other planets symbolize aspects or variations on the sun's primal theme. Therefore, the only concession you need make to timing is to try to perform this spell as close to noon or midday as you can. Then the sun will be directly overhead and its energy can be felt and seen most clearly.

Pre-Spell Exercise

If you've ever browsed through a medical textbook, or one of those encyclopaedias on the human body, you'll know that you live inside a very complicated and fascinating machine. Thousands of signals and messages are racing around your body at breakneck speed, every minute of every day. Right at this moment, your heart is pumping blood, your stomach is digesting food, your bowels are breaking down waste, your lungs are drawing in air and your brain is processing the information in this book. Meanwhile, your body is preparing to embark on a series of finely-tuned mechanical operations involving muscles, nerves and blood supply. The whole complex network is ready to spring into beautifully coordinated action as soon as you decide to lift up your hand and turn the next page of the book!

Fortunately, for the sake of our sanity, the entire system functions automatically. If you had to oversee every operation in your body you'd never have time to think – let alone get on with your life! This is one reason why when you feel ill, you become less capable of getting on with your life. Your body then has to draw more of the energy normally available to your brain just in order to keep the life support system going. As a result you become sluggish, tired and much more conscious of the things that are happening within your body.

Spells for Other People

You will find no mention in this book of spells you can do on someone else's behalf. Such things are possible, but there are many practical disadvantages and sometimes the morality of such magic is questionable. I recognize that if you know someone who is very sick you might want to do this spell for them. Even so, I would advize against it. If your friend or loved one is seriously ill, it is better that they consult an expert. If their condition is not that bad, they will be better off performing this spell themselves than having you do it for them.

The more familiar you can become with the incredible piece of bio-chemical engineering that comprises your body, the more you'll be able to channel the power of your conscious mind to its aid in times of sickness or stress. The exercise below is designed to increase this familiarity. You can begin the exercise at any time, in any situation (unless you are ill already – in which case you should not do it without proper medical advice). You should not do this exercise within 24 hours of taking *any* drugs.

The exercise involves not eating for at least 24 hours.

During this time you can drink as much water and/or fruit juice as you like. I recommend though, that you avoid tea and coffee. Alcohol is definitely out. This is not particularly for spiritual reasons, it's because by the time you've been fasting for 12 hours or more you'll be as high as a kite, quite naturally!

The first 12 hours are the hardest. You'll probably experience hunger on a colossal scale. You may feel as though you haven't eaten for half a year, not half a day. You may find yourself getting irritable, bad tempered, depressed, or just very dizzy. You may start to come up with all sorts of reasons for changing your mind and starting to eat again. You'll begin to hunt for a set of extenuating circumstances. Tomorrow will suddenly sound like a much better time to try the experiment. RESIST ALL THIS!

The best way to resist is to make sure that you spend your first 12 hours in an environment where there's plenty to do. Go to work or find yourself an interesting project that you've been meaning to embark on for ages. What about a mammoth knitting spree, or try sewing, painting, drawing, or writing? Clear out the cupboard under the stairs or sort out the bottom drawer in the office. Just keep yourelf busy and interested. If you do feel as though you may faint from hunger, drink some more water or fruit juice. As much as you like. It won't do any harm, and in fact it will help to flush your system out. (One of the main physical benefits of a liquid diet like this is the way that it gives your body a chance to burn up impurities in the system.) Another good idea is to drink spring or mineral water rather than ordinary tap stuff. After a few hours of nothing else, you'll find there's a world of difference between one sort of water and another!

Going without food for a limited period of time can be a joyous, cleansing and delightful experience. You won't be depriving your body of anything it needs and you'll be giving it a rare and much-needed rest. Try not to think of it as a self-imposed prison sentence (even though it may seem like one in the beginning). *Don't* start counting the hours or thinking thing like 'Technically, I've already been without food since my last meal the night before.' Your 24 hour period should run from waking up one morning to waking up the following day. In fact, once you've got through the first 12 hours, you'll find things get easier and easier. You may even start losing your appetite altogether and be rather appalled at the whole idea of eating. Even so, you should try to avoid the kitchen – and if anyone else in the house is preparing a meal I suggest you go for a walk in the fresh air until they've finished cooking and eating it.

As each hour passes, you'll notice new and more wonderful things about how your body works and what's going on inside you. If you have any specific ideas or realizations, write them down in your magical diary. You may well find yourself getting quite creative and poetic!

When it comes to your normal bedtime you may find that you are not tired. Don't worry. This is a natural side-effect of fasting. Your body is lighter, and is making less effort than usual. It's used to coping with a deluge of unwanted material. Most of us eat far more than we need to keep us alive. The Western world has made gluttony into a virtue and you are experiencing the liberating sensation of intelligent restraint. Put your extra energy into something enjoyable. Read a good book or catch up on all those letters you've been meaning to write.

Sooner or later you *will* feel sleepy, and when you do you'll find you drift into a much more refreshing and enjoyable sleep than you've been used to.

When you wake up the next morning, you may well feel as though the last thing you want to is eat. Even if you feel hungry, you'll find that it takes far less food than you'd expect to satisfy you. There will be no harm in extending your fast if you feel like it. You could carry on with water and fruit juice for another 24–48 hours with no potential harm to your body (as long as you are relatively healthy when you begin). You could start eating some fresh fruit and raw vegetables. You may even decide to spend the next seven days eating only crisp, raw carrots, ripe juicy pears and sweet, fresh oranges. If you do, you'll find yourself just getting higher and higher – without any harmful effect! (More than a week, and you'd have to check with a good book on nutrition and make a few modifications.)

Even if you decide to stop after 24 hours and return to your old diet, you will have established a new, deep and profound awareness of your physical body and the way it works. You will have found yourself drifting into all sorts of pleasant and attractive states of mind, and you will also have found yourself much more sensitive to smell, touch, sound and colour. The memory of these discoveries will stay with you, and you will find that you have a much more positive and rewarding relationship with the living organism that we so glibly call the body. This relationship will make it much easier for you to understand what's going on inside you – and much easier for you instinctively to know what your body needs, and when it needs it. This will make you much more able to enhance, nurture and control your own state of health. It will also make you much more conscious of what you don't need. If you normally smoke (for example), and you try to smoke while not eating, you will find that soon each cigarette tastes more unpleasant than the one before.

I have refrained from calling this exercise a fast. That's because the word 'fast' implies some sort of deprivation. This exercise is technically a fast, but it would be better described as a 'slow' – a gentle awakening of your senses! If at all possible you should fast (or slow, if you prefer) on the day you do the spell itself. It can help to concentrate your mental energy in a very wonderful and effective way.

Final Preparations

You won't need your spell kit for this particular endeavour, but you will need some solar incense, a drop or two of solar oil and a glassful of fresh water (bottled spring water is best).

If possible you should perform the spell out of doors. However, if it's cold, wet or windy you'd better do it inside. (It wouldn't do to catch a cold performing a spell for health!)

This is one spell where 'direction' is important. Whether you do it indoors or outdoors – you'll need to know:

(a) Where the sun is in the sky above you at the moment of the spell.

(b) Which way is East.

The idea of the great solar 'provider' of energy is perhaps the most ancient magical concept known to humanity. Although, as with all spells, we are primarily concerned with summoning a source of energy from inside ourselves, it is quite acceptable to imagine yourself drawing down the energy of the sun itself.

At The Allotted Hour

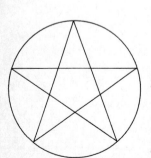

1 Hopefully, you will have fasted for 24 hours before performing this ceremony. If you haven't, it would be a good idea to begin by going back over the pentagram meditation on page 240 as a symbolic gesture of purification.

2 Prepare by bathing in the usual way. Don't forget to add a drop or two of solar oil to the bath water.

3 When you are ready, light the solar incense and then face the East.

4 Inscribe the pentagram and then draw your magical circle around you.

5 Begin to breathe very slowly, deeply and regularly. Listen to your own breath, to your own heartbeat, and to your own human life beating away within the walls of your body.

6 Become as relaxed as you can. If you know how to meditate, do so. If you don't, simply sit or stand within your circle and let yourself become as peaceful as you can.

Raise the glass of water in your right arm and hold it up towards the sun. Hold it there for as long as you can comfortably, and imagine the life-giving rays of the sun pouring down into the water, as they pour down continuously on to the face of the Earth, giving energy to the plants, the animals and the people.

Still holding the glass of water, turn back to face the East.

Dip one of the fingers of your left hand into the water and anoint your forehead with a drop of it. As you do so, say: 'The strength of the sun before me.'

Dip your finger back into the water and then anoint the crown of your head with a drop of water. As you do so, say: 'The strength of the sun above me.'

Dip your finger one final time into the water and then anoint the back of your neck with a drop of it. As you do so, say: 'The strength of the sun behind me.'

Now, hold the water to your lips and drain the glass.

After you have done this, say: 'The strength of the sun within me.'

Take several more deep breaths, and as you do so you should feel a very warm, positive and healthy glow begin to creep through your body. This is the beginning of a new-found radiance, confidence and healthy vitality that will be with you in increasing quantity from this day forward.

7 When you are ready, undo the magical circle. Relax in the usual way. Go and do something lighthearted, simple, trivial or amusing. And if you have been fasting, go and eat something light. It's time to break your fast and celebrate!

6. JUPITER SPELL
A Spell for Good Fortune

This is a spell for good fortune. Nothing more – and nothing less. Good luck, as a quality, can be isolated and vitalized. Traditionally Jupiter embodies this quality, so the spell is designed to harness and channel the spirit of Jupiter within you. It's a practical way to let the energy of the largest, brighest planet shine in your life.

Key words for Jupiter are optimism, enthusiasm and expansion. This last word counts for a lot. Luck and spiritual expansion are closely linked. Jupiter is the part of your spirit which wants to be in all places at once and to fill the world with wide eyed, innocent joy. Jupiter knows no bounds and, for this part of you, nothing is impossible.

Before you perform the spell you must be honest with yourself. Is your luck really bad – or are you simply failing to perceive good fortune and miserably turning your back on a cornucopia of opportunity. In either case, you should feel free to perform the ceremony – but Jupiter is also the planet of philosophy. It will help you enormously if you have thought about and considered the true nature of your apparent problem. The more you understand about luck – how it works and how you would like it to work – the more successful your magical endeavour will prove.

Timing

Jupiter rules Sagittarius and Pisces. You can do this spell at any time when the moon is in Sagittarius or Pisces (see page 307) unless it happens to be during a period when Jupiter is retrograde. Below are the dates in the next few years when Jupiter will be apparently moving backwards through the heavens.

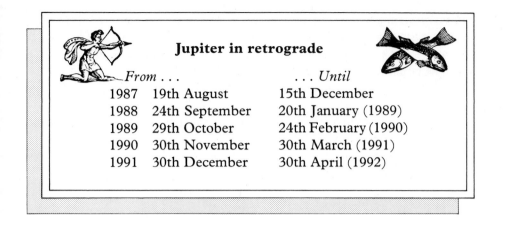

Jupiter in retrograde

From . . .		*. . . Until*
1987	19th August	15th December
1988	24th September	20th January (1989)
1989	29th October	24th February (1990)
1990	30th November	30th March (1991)
1991	30th December	30th April (1992)

Even if you feel an overwhelming need to change your luck during one of these periods, it will not be appropriate to perform the spell. You'll simply have to do the best you can with your own sense of hope and willpower. The power of Jupiter can still be felt and channelled during the time when the planet itself is retrograde – but you shouldn't perform a fully fledged ceremony at such a time. One other point about timing. As you will see, the spell for hope and good luck should be performed a long way from your home. This means you may need to prepare it some while in advance.

While You're Waiting

A lot of people think that luck has something to do with gambling. Popular mythology tells us that luck is contained in a throw of the dice, the turn of a wheel or a cut of the cards. Not so. Gambling is about losing! All gambling situations are set up to make losers out of the participants. Even if you win in gambling situations, it's no true indication of how lucky you are. Try the following experiments and see for yourself.

The Fruit Machine
Set aside an amount of money you can afford to lose (say the price of a drink) and find a fruit machine which takes the smallest possible stake. (*Hint*: Travelling fairs, old museums and country pubs sometimes have machines which accept copper instead of silver coinage.) Stand in front of your chosen fruit machine and stuff coins into it. Keep pulling the handle (or pressing the buttons) until one of two things happen. Either you will reach a point where you are richer than you started – *or* you will have no coins left.

If you manage to lose all your money quickly – well done! You have achieved the vital experience and can safely move on to the next paragragh but one.

If you manage to win, you must stop *as soon* as you are ahead. It's important that you walk away from the machine clutching more money than you had when you approached it. As you savour this experience of beating a system, ask yourself if it's what you really wanted. The answer you give yourself is significant. It's bound to be a variation on No! The reason for this is that what you've really enjoyed is playing the game. Winning is important only in as much as it allows you to carry on.

Whether you feel elated because you have apparently won – or depressed because you have apparently lost, you will be suffering from the same syndrome. All you really want to do is play the game – and feel the excitement of involvement. Watching luck in action in your life is a different thing from winning and losing.

Bake Yourself Lucky

As you prepare for the spell, make a point of reading this next section several times. Memorize it if you like. Drum home the message to yourself.

Some people are naturally attracted to the feeling of risk. It's just the way they are. Open-ended situations make them feel comfortable. Therefore, they wind up involved in a higher number of risky scenarios. Consequently, more unexpected opportunities arise for them.

Luck, for these people is the cherry on a cake. No cake – no cherry. If you expect luck to come tumbling out of the sky at random, you are missing the point. Luck comes to all of us, equally. It's just that some people seem better able to take advantage of it. These people know that the more cakes you bake – the more cherries you will need. They don't expect every cake to receive its cherry. They simply know that if you make a cake with enough sincerity, put a little indentation in the top and then place a sign over it saying 'Cherry here, please' – something sometimes happens. They also know, however, not to hover anxiously over the cake waiting till the cherry appears by magic. Like waiting for a kettle to boil, this is a frustrating waste of time. Instead, they leave their specially prepared, cherry-awaiting cake to sit quietly on its own – and go off to bake another and another and still another cake. They know that cakes attract cherries – in the same way that gardens attract rainfall. Left all alone, a natural process will normally occur. The Jupiterian forces in this world will not be able to resist all those cakes. Plop, plop plop – from out of the blue, cherries will start to cascade down. Soon, there will be more cherries than cakes. That, however, is not your department. The essential trick is to forget all about cherries and just keep on making cakes.

Something For Nothing

Next time you are in a café, or sitting down somewhere, reasonably at ease, try this little trick. Mentally, get out of your body . . . walk across the room . . . turn around . . . and look back at yourself. Now take every item of clothing you are wearing, every accessory and every piece of jewellery and scrutinize it. Ask yourself: 'What's the story behind that shirt?' 'How did I come by those shoes?' 'Why did I choose these glasses?', etc. As you answer yourself, go into detail. Was it a gift? If not, where did you get the money to buy it? Did anything else happen on the day you bought it? Was it bought for you?

Somewhere in your wardrobe there is bound to be something which you got for nothing. This feeling of something for nothing ties into the experience of Jupiter. Jupiter often supplies good fortune in embarrassingly large quantities. Learn to understand the true nature of good luck, and with care and sincerity use it.

Final Preparations

This spell requires you to travel in order to perform it as you should be as far away from home as possible. If you can time it to coincide with your annual trip to Hawaii or Torremolinos, so much the better. Otherwise make the distance as far as you can practically manage or afford.

An anonymous room in a large hotel is ideal (leave the window open to let the incense escape). If the weather is fine you could always find a sheltered corner of moorland or park and do it there.

There is nothing to stop you performing *any* of the spells in this book with a partner – as long as you both do each gesture separately. The Jupiter spell is certainly more fun with a partner or friend to share the experience, and this could be one way to help you overcome the anxiety of performing an odd ceremony hundreds of miles from home.

Remember that you are about to perform a series of symbolic gestures that will change your luck for the better *for ever*. That's worth a little effort in preparation, and it's also worth overcoming a little nervousness for!

To perform the spell, you'll require:

your spell kit

Jupiter incense

Jupiter essential oil

a balloon (an ordinary child's balloon)

a glass of mead (or white wine, spiced with cinnamon and sweetened
    with honey; serious teetotallers may substitute grape juice)

a pin

As usual, it would help to memorize or at least rehearse the spell in advance.

At The Allotted Hour

1 Lay out your work table with candles, candle sticks, cloth, incense, burner, balloon, glass of mead and essential oil.

2 Enjoy a relaxing pre-spell bath, to which has been added a tiny drop of Jupiter oil.

3 Put on your magical garments and light the candles.

4 Inscribe a mystic pentagram and then draw a magical circle around you.

5 Light the incense and relax. You are now ready to invoke the spirit of Jupiter.

6 Breathe slowly and deeply for a short while and then say as firmly and as loudly as you can . . .

☆

Jupiter!
Jupiter!
Hear my cry!
Jupiter!
Jupiter!
Don't pass by!
Jupiter!
Jupiter!
Come to me!
Jupiter!
Jupiter!
Let me see!

☆

Relax again and continue to breathe slowly and deeply. You may begin to feel a light, warm and joyous feeling or 'presence'. The feeling may only be very slight – but it will be there. Now it is time to toast the king of joy, hope and good fortune.

☆

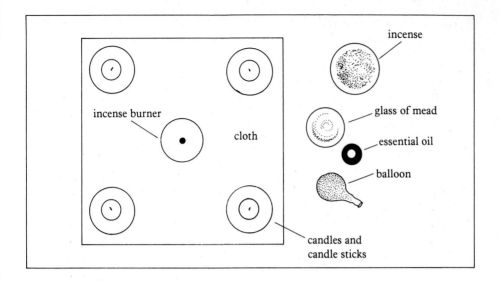

Raise the glass to your forehead. Pass it slowly through the incense smoke. Raise it once more to your forehead. Now drink it all.

Place the glass on the table and as you do so, simply say;

Jupiter.

Jupiter.

Relax again for a few seconds.

It is now time to inflate the balloon. (In ancient times this would have been a 'bladder', or else simply a breathing technique.) Simply hold the balloon and begin to slowly blow it up with your lips.

With each breath, try to imagine a part of your 'bad luck' or 'blockage' flowing into the balloon.

Let every breath contain your 'negativity', your 'need' and your 'lack of fortune'.

Keep blowing and blowing. Ideally, if you have the courage it will burst itself. Otherwise tie a knot in the balloon, hold it above the incense smoke and burst it with a pin. (If the balloon bursts with a bang, you can expect your fortunes to change overnight. If the air escapes slowly, the process may take a little longer.

Relax once more.

It is now time for the final part of the ceremony.

If you are wearing shoes – remove them.

Take the essential oil, open it and place a tiny drop of oil on the end of your finger. Say:

My feet will now carry me
to fortune's bounty.
Jupiter will guide them
I will follow.
I will trust.

Anoint each foot with the oil (gently stroking an oiled finger along the tips of your toes on each foot in turn). Replace the cap on the oil, stand still and breathe slowly and deeply once more.

Now sit down, relax and imagine all the tension you have ever felt in your whole life flood into the floor below you.

The spell is cast.

7 Undo the magical circle, extinguish the candles and restore the room to a normal state.

From now on, you will find that fortune, hope and optimism combine to present you with a 'lucky' life – and you'll soon start reaping the benefits of your new-found confidence in the Jupiter within you.

Once again, it is time to relax and unwind. Resist the temptation to run straight to the nearest casino! (Remember what you discovered earlier about gambling and luck!)

7. SATURN SPELL
A Spell of Indifference
'All things come to he who waits'

Cast Your Fate to the Wind

This spell is for when it seems as though you can't move forwards, backwards, left, right, up or down. Nor can you stay where you are! It is designed to harness and manifest the energy of Saturn. You might think this relentless planet is hardly likely to make you more flexible. No so! In hard times, the force of Saturn is what we all require. If you feel abandoned by fortune – and unable to control or influence your situation – you need inner strength. Develop this, and you will soon find patient acceptance leads to inspiration. By 'surrendering' or 'letting go of' of your problem, you can be freed of pain – and problems. With a fresh perspective – and a sense of 'from here it can only get better' – miracles can always be achieved. But first you must be genuinely prepared to relinquish control.

As a grass stalk will bend before even a light breeze, so Saturn will bend. The only force to which it will respond, however, is true humility – and sincerity. If you can 'wait on destiny's threshold', you may suddenly discover the doors of opportunity thrown open before you. Approach this spell without specific expectation. Carry only the seeds of hope in your heart. Be prepared to accept what it brings you. Only good can come of it.

Timing

Saturn rules Capricorn and Aquarius. You can perform this spell at any time when the the Moon is in Aquarius or Capricorn (see page 307). When Saturn moves retrograde through the sky there are certain undertakings that should be avoided or postponed. This spell is *not* one of them. If anything, a retgrograde Saturn will actually 'help' the spell. Below is a list of dates in the next few years when Saturn will be retrograde.

Saturn in retrograde

From . . .		*. . . Until*
1987	31st March	19th August
1988	11th April	30th August
1989	22nd April	11th September
1990	1st June	23rd September
1991	17th May	16th October (1992)
1993	10th June	28th October
1994	23rd June	9th November
1995	6th July	21st November

While You Are Waiting

The Universe doesn't run like clockwork. Nor is it a place where people are treated according to their merits. Lightning strikes, lotteries are won and wishes are granted in a seemingly random way. By making effort, and by directing your desires, it is possible to increase the odds – but life is still very much a gamble with unknown factors.

Much of the satisfaction you receive from having your fortune told is in hearing of a possible and completely unexpected new future. We are all creatures of habit, but our habits rob us of much hope. As we juggle our way along the high wire of life, it's the safety net of routine which makes us feel secure. If your net was taken away there'd be a pleasant surprise. You would not fall to your doom! Beneath you would be Nature's very own safety net, especially designed for your needs. Not a huge rigid and clumsy web of hard old ropes, but a very small, one-person size, silk cushion that hovers beneath you, moving wherever you go.

The following exercise may seem small, undemanding or apparently trivial. Don't be fooled! Pulling a trigger or lighting a fuse are small actions in themselves but can give rise to some very big bangs!

The idea is to break a few long-standing habits. You needn't set out to completely transform your life. It will be enough to have one small, positive experience of habit breaking. This will create another opportunity to break out, and this in turn will create another, and so on.

Important Note: The habit you decide to break should be something which time and change have turned into a blockage. Select a personal tradition which has become like a callous and is desensitizing you. Don't stop at breaking routine. It is not so much a change of habit that matters, but that you appreciate the new experience which comes in its place.

Once you've allowed yourself to stop smoking for a day – or missed your favourite soap opera, or given up a few sensual indulgences for a while – it will be time for you to explore the next habit-breaking exercise. The section below may seem blindingly obvious, but you should read it anyway – and do the exercise. Even if you think it's all too clear and simple, make the effort. After all, if you need to do this spell, you must be unhappy with your current position. One reason you are unhappy, and why things are not changing naturally for you, is because you are being subconsciously stubborn in a negative, retentive way. To break this habit you need to break a more obvious, superficial habit. And you also need to become humble, flexible and open to help. So do as you're told!!!

The Day Off Work
If you regularly attend work, or college, or a meeting of some sort, I suggest you take some illegal time off!

As you travel to work, save the decision for a day off until the last minute. Is there any real reason why you *have* to get off at the usual station bus stop? NO! Get off 10 stops later. Or ride to the end of the line. Or drive to a different town. Do this – and you will have physically broken the mould.

At first, you may be filled with a sense of terror! 'What have I done?' But hold on. Are terror and fear the just desserts of someone who simply sat on a train one stop longer than usual? Is the train about to enter some terrible forbidden zone where all will be lost? Is the bus about to come under attack and explode? No. There is nothing wrong at all anywhere. Life is carrying on perfectly.

Look around you. None of the people on the train or bus got off at that last stop and they're not terrified. Why should they be? There is nothing terrifying going on. Let go of the fear. You're riding along to an unknown destination with a whole new list of possibilities ahead of you. Leave the fear. The sun is shining (or the rain is falling). The world is still turning and you are part of it. Isn't that what you wanted?

Now repeat the formula. Choose an unexpected option and then appreciate the result. Remember, it's not necessarily a pattern for a whole new life. Your routine will still be there if you choose to return to it. You can make excuses for your absence and feel suitably guilty if necessary. By then at least you will have had one small positive experience. You will know the beneficial effects of stepping out of your own order into a broader, more chaotic order. This can have a huge effect. It will show you that there *is* a place for you no matter where you choose to put yourself. So try it and see – and enjoy yourself.

Once you have done this, you will be ready to perform the spell itself.

The Final Preparations

Besides your usual spell kit, you will require:

Saturn incense
Saturn essential oil
a calendar for the months or years ahead
a small plant pot, two-thirds full of earth from a garden
2 small saucers

The calendar should be printed (or written) on paper. It should cover at least the next few months – but if it were to cover the next few years (such as the year planners you find printed in the back of some diaries), so much the better.

In the spell that follows we will be calling upon the force of Saturn. In Ancient Greek mythology, Saturn was Kronos, god of time. Saturn symbolizes the part inside each one of us that must face the fact that life on Earth is only temporary. Kronos is sometimes called the god of Death, although a more proper title would be 'the god of awareness of death's inevitability'. This is a hard lesson to face, which is why Saturn is often thought of as a stern teacher. Once again, I must stress that Saturn is a tendency within you, not a god who lives in the sky (or anywhere else for that matter!). The planet and the word merely symbolize a part of you that wants to face reality and be sensible and practical in the face of adversity. This is the part of you that you need to awaken in order to cultivate protective detachment.

At the Allotted Hour

1 Lay out your work table with candles, candle sticks, cloth, incense, burner, calendar, plant pot and 2 saucers.

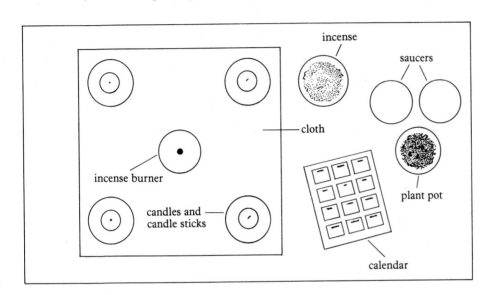

2 Place half the earth from the plant pot on one saucer, leaving the rest in the pot.

3 Take a leisurely pre-spell bath, having added a tiny drop of Saturn oil while it was running.

4 Light the candles.

5 Inscribe a mystic pentagram and then draw a magical circle around you.

6 Light the incense and relax. You are now ready to invoke the spirit of Saturn.

7 Your nose will soon begin to fill with the heady and slightly musty aroma of Saturnian incense. You may feel a little odd or unnerved, as if in the presence of something much greater or more powerful than you. This is the spirit of Saturn, the part of you that has an inexorable link with the forces of birth and death. It is the voice of experience, old age and wisdom within you.

Relax and stare into the incense smoke. Imagine that a sage old and benign figure has entered the room through the incense smoke. Sense the experience and wisdom of that person.

After a few moments, recite the following in a respectful tone of voice:

Darkness to light
Wrong to right
Birth to death
Breath to breath
Saturn, I call upon your firmness, your wisdom and your guidance.

Remain standing still and calm for a short while.

Now, unhurriedly, pick up your calendar and pass it through the smoke of the incense. Do this gently and at your leisure.

Now start to tear the calendar into small pieces and place each piece on the empty saucer. While you do this, say:

Saturn, Saturn
I call on you
to guide each coming day
and give me the strength
to face my destiny
secure in the knowledge
that I will be happier
with whatever unfolds
than with whatever
I desired.

(If you are casting the spell in order to free yourself from a very specific attachment or association, you should substitute the name of the person or situation in place of the final three words above.)

Take the saucer and empty the torn calendar into the plant pot. Cover the pieces of paper with the rest of the earth from the second saucer. As you do this, say:

> Into the earth
> I place my own desire
> and from the earth
> will spring nature's
> new gift for me

☆

Relax once more, and breathe deeply.

☆

The spell is cast.

☆

8 Sit down, relax and imagine all the tension you have ever felt in your life flooding into the floor below you.

9 Undo the magical circle, extinguish the candles and draw the curtains or turn on the light.

10 Within 24 hours of performing this spell, you should take your planted calendar to a remote spot (a quiet corner of a park or field, or the very bottom of the garden) and bury it, pot and all. Nothing untoward would happen if it were to be accidentally dug up – but it's important to complete the ritual in this way for symbolic reasons.

11 Before and after you do this, unwind in the usual way – cups of tea, TV, books, distractions and relaxation are vital after every spell and this one is no exception. If you drink alcohol, it might be a good idea to pour yourself a cold beer or a glass of white wine and celebrate. After all, now that you are no longer going to spend your time worrying about whatever or whoever, you are going to have a lot more time to do other things. Start thinking about some of them and see where that train of ideas takes you.

Final Word

Do not expect instant results. You can only be pleasantly surprised and delighted if you get them. Saturn is a slow-moving planet and notorious for dealing in reality rather than attitudes. It is possible that while at first your infatuation or determination or frustration seems as strong as ever, forces are working in the background. Something or someone else is about to present an alternative that you can't resist. This unexpected but attractive turn of events will slowly but surely begin to take your attention further and further away from the situation you were trying to resolve. And then, without your energy to bother it, chances are that things will sort themselves out pretty quickly, and probably to your advantage.

Useful Addresses

If you're new to magic, contacting a so-called specialist may not be such a good idea. These suppliers, while normally sincere, are in business to sell a lot of unnecessary equipment and promote their own fixed ideas about how things should be done. If you do want to check them out, they are easy to find. Go into your local newspaper shop and pick up a magazine that specializes in astrology or the occult—the adverts for magical supplies will be somewhere near the back.

Normally these companies work by mail order and offer an Aladin's cave of weird and wondrous substances. Most of them are useless, but hidden in their catalogue between the 'crystal balls', 'touchstones', 'genuine lucky charms' and 'rare books telling *all* the ancient secrets of witchcraft' will be a list of planetary incenses and their prices. The incenses themselves are a mixture of herbs and spices (hopefully) ruled by the planet in question, and packed in a plastic bag.

Here are some bookstores that carry a variety of products in the field.

Compendium Bookshop
234 Camden High Street
London, UK NW1
011-441-267-1525
Retail store with mail-order catalogue.

Sphinx Metaphysical Bookstore
1510 Piedmont Avenue
Atlanta, GA 30324
404-875-2665
Retail store, no mail order.

East West Books
78 Fifth Avenue
New York, NY 10011
212-243-5994
Retail store with mail-order service.

One Books
302 Old Main Street
Bradenton, FL 34205
813-747-1066
Retail store with mail-order catalogue.

Samuel Weiser Bookstore
132 East 24th Street
New York, NY 10010
212-777-6363
Retail store with mail-order service.

Peralandra Books and Records
790 East 11th Street
Eugene, OR 97401
503-485-4848
Retail store with mail-order service.

Yes! Bookstore
1035 31st Street
Washington, DC 20007
202-338-7874
Retail store with mail-order service.

Bodhi Tree Bookstore
8585 Melrose Avenue
Los Angeles, CA 90069
213-659-1733
Retail store with mail-order catalogue.

Bibliography

Although there are thousands of books about the intuitive arts, they vary dramatically in quality and approach. You will find some that are informative but badly written. You will find others which are lucid but nonsensical. If you approach the libraries and specialist book stores with a large pinch of salt in your hand—you will find plenty to fascinate you—and occasionally, will stumble across a real treasure—often privately published or in some sort of limited edition.

Below are some of the more readily available and recommended books on each of our psychic subjects.

Astrology
Derek & Julia Parker are a husband and wife team who have written several clear books on astrology. 'The Compleat Astrologer' contains all you need to construct your own horoscopes from scratch and is published by Mitchell Beazley. 'A History of Astrology' is published by Andre Deutsch.

Debbie Kempton Smith is a lighthearted American astrologer and her 'Secrets From a Stargazers Notebook' is published by Bantam books.

Arthur Koestler was one of this century's most intelligent writers on esoteric subjects. Any of his books will be rewarding reading, but 'The Sleepwalkers', published by Penguin, cannot be recommended highly enough.

Liz Greene is a psychologist who works in the Jungian tradition and whose books on astrology contain deep, valuable insights into personality and relationships. 'Relating', published by Conventure, is perhaps her most famous—but she is quite prolific and all her books are worth a read.

Claudius Ptolemy is the man who, in 150 AD, compiled most of the rules we still use today in astrology. A translation of his book, 'Tetrabiblos' is published by Heinemann and, while heavy going, is quite fascinating.

Jeanne Avery is a wonderfully spiritual astrologer whose deep insights will shed new light on your horoscope. Her newest book, 'Astrology and Your Past Lives' is published by Fireside Books; Doubleday publishes her two previous books, 'The Rising Sign: Your Astrological Mask' and 'Astrological Aspects.'

Auras
Annie Besant, a turn of the century clairvoyant, collaborated with C. W. Leadbeater on an informative and visual book called 'Thought forms' which is published by Adyar, part of the Theosophical publishing house.

Edgar Cayce, another famous and gifted psychic explorer who lived in the U.S.A. wrote 'Auras', published by A.R.E. press in 1945.

Tarot
There are many different Tarot packs to choose from—and even more 'definitive guides to the Tarot!'. As in the choice of packs, the choice of books is very much a matter of personal taste, and almost every pack you can buy contains its own instructions. We do not recommend that you become over reliant on any written work about the Tarot.

Dowsing
Tom Graves is one of the more modern school of Dowsers. 'Needles of Stone', and 'Dowsing Techniques and Applications' (Turnstone Press 1978) are helpful and practical.

Palmistry
David Brandon Jones has written several books on hand reading and gives succinct, informative help. Try 'Practical Palmistry' published by Rider.

ESP

Hans J. Eysenck and Carl Sargent's 'Explaining the Unexplained' (Wiedenfeld and Nicolson) presents a cool scientific view. As does Arthur C. Clarke's 'World of Strange Powers' (Collins). 'Supernature' by Lyall Watson (Hodder and Stoughton) is another fascinating survey. 'Occult Exercises and Practises' by Gareth Knight (The Aquarian Press) contains some good starting material for the practically minded.

For a thorough overview of the world of psychic phenomena, Bernard Gittelson's tome 'Intangible Evidence' can't be beat.

Aromatics

Robert and Maggie Tisserand are a husband and wife team who work with and import aromatic oils. Maggie has written 'Aromatherapy For Women' published by Thorsons and Robert has written 'The Art of Aromatherapy' published by C. W. Daniel. Both are excellent.

Shirley Price is a practising English Aromatherapist, and wrote 'Practical Aromatherapy', published by Thorsons.

Manfred M. Junius is the consultant editor of the International journal of Indian Medicine. His book, 'Practical Handbook of Plant Alchemy' is magical, fascinating... and a little odd! It's published by Inner Traditions International—of New York.

John Lust is the author of a Bantam publication called 'The Herb Book'—which is a fascinating guide to the healing qualities of plants and flowers.

Ceremonial Magic

Without exception, every book on ceremonial or ritual magic is flawed and/or misleading. Even this one has its limitations! It's vital to remember that ceremonial magic is personal, and that no author can speak about anything more than his or her own experience. I really can't feel happy about recommending a single book on the subject—although you should feel quite free to read as many as you like.

How to
Obtain Your Horoscope

If you have difficulty finding a horoscope calculation service, if you would like to be referred to a reliable consultant astrologer, if you were born close to the end of one sun sign and the beginning of another and want to know which sign you belong to, or if you need help converting your time of birth to GMT in order to establish your moon sign (see page 307)...FREE help is available from: Jonathan Cainer's ASTRO-CONNECTION'S ADVICE SERVICE, PO Box 265, London WC1N 2NR. Just write a brief letter, explaining your query or problem and including any relevant birth data—and, if possible, enclose a large stamped addressed envelope for the reply.

Moon Charts

The list below may look daunting, but it is simple to follow. The times given in the chart are Greenwich Mean Time. If you were born on standard time in the Eastern zone, add five hours to your birthtime; Central, six hours; Mountain, seven hours; Pacific, eight hours. For daylight time, subtract one hour from that result.

Suppose you were born on 10th May 1926 in the Eastern zone at 5:30 am. Add five hours to your birthtime (10:30 am adjusting to GMT) and look up the corresponding time on the chart. The list shows that the moon was in Aries from 8:55 am on 8th May until 11:36 am on 10th May. That's all there is to it. Free help is available, if you need it, on page 306.

January 1925
1st 3:01 am Aries
3rd 11:36 am Taurus
5th 10:54 pm Gemini
8th 11:34 am Cancer
11th 0:14 am Leo
13th 11:51 am Virgo
15th 9:31 pm Libra
18th 4:08 am Scorpio
20th 7:29 am Sagittarius
22nd 8:20 am Capricorn
24th 8:11 am Aquarius
26th 8:50 am Pisces
28th 12:05 pm Aries
30th 7:03 pm Taurus

February 1925
2nd 5:35 am Gemini
4th 6:11 pm Cancer
7th 6:49 am Leo
9th 5:60 pm Virgo
12th 3:05 am Libra
14th 9:51 am Scorpio
16th 2:24 pm Sagittarius
18th 5:00 pm Capricorn
20th 6:21 pm Aquarius
22nd 7:37 pm Pisces
24th 10:22 pm Aries
27th 4:07 am Taurus

March 1925
1st 1:29 pm Gemini
4th 1:37 am Cancer
6th 2:22 pm Leo
9th 1:24 am Virgo
11th 9:42 am Libra
13th 3:36 pm Scorpio
15th 7:51 pm Sagittarius
17th 11:07 pm Capricorn
20th 1:51 am Aquarius
22nd 4:34 am Pisces
24th 8:06 am Aries
26th 1:39 pm Taurus
28th 10:09 pm Gemini
31st 9:44 am Cancer

April 1925
2nd 10:33 pm Leo
5th 9:52 am Virgo
7th 6:02 pm Libra
9th 11:04 pm Scorpio
12th 2:06 am Sagittarius
14th 4:33 am Capricorn
16th 7:25 am Aquarius
18th 11:04 am Pisces
20th 3:46 pm Aries
22nd 10:01 pm Taurus
25th 6:35 am Gemini
27th 5:47 pm Cancer
30th 6:35 am Leo

May 1925
2nd 6:35 pm Virgo
5th 3:24 am Libra
7th 8:19 am Scorpio
9th 10:27 am Sagittarius
11th 11:32 am Capricorn
13th 1:11 pm Aquarius
15th 4:26 pm Pisces
17th 9:35 pm Aries
20th 4:42 am Taurus
22nd 1:53 pm Gemini
25th 1:07 am Cancer
27th 1:59 pm Leo
30th 2:34 am Virgo

June 1925
1st 12:24 pm Libra
3rd 6:17 pm Scorpio
5th 8:31 pm Sagittarius
7th 8:45 pm Capricorn
9th 8:56 pm Aquarius
11th 10:41 pm Pisces
14th 3:06 am Aries
16th 10:19 am Taurus
18th 7:58 pm Gemini
21st 7:38 am Cancer
23rd 8:30 pm Leo
26th 9:19 am Virgo
28th 8:11 pm Libra

July 1925
1st 3:29 am Scorpio
3rd 6:50 am Sagittarius
5th 7:22 am Capricorn
7th 6:51 am Aquarius
9th 7:10 am Pisces
11th 9:59 am Aries
13th 4:10 pm Taurus
16th 1:39 am Gemini
18th 1:35 pm Cancer
21st 2:33 am Leo
23rd 3:15 pm Virgo
26th 2:28 am Libra
28th 10:51 am Scorpio
30th 3:50 pm Sagittarius

August 1925
1st 5:42 pm Capricorn
3rd 5:39 pm Aquarius
5th 5:24 pm Pisces
7th 6:50 pm Aries
9th 11:24 pm Taurus
12th 8:00 am Gemini
14th 7:40 pm Cancer
17th 8:41 am Leo
19th 9:12 pm Virgo
22nd 8:03 am Libra
24th 4:42 pm Scorpio
26th 10:49 pm Sagittarius
29th 2:17 am Capricorn
31st 3:40 am Aquarius

September 1925
2nd 4:02 am Pisces
4th 5:03 am Aries
6th 8:31 am Taurus
8th 3:43 pm Gemini
11th 2:36 am Cancer
13th 3:29 pm Leo
16th 3:55 am Virgo
18th 2:14 pm Libra
20th 10:17 pm Scorpio
23rd 4:16 am Sagittarius
25th 8:34 am Capricorn
27th 11:27 am Aquarius
29th 1:19 pm Pisces

October 1925
1st 3:06 pm Aries
3rd 6:21 pm Taurus
6th 0:34 am Gemini
8th 10:34 am Cancer
10th 11:09 pm Leo
13th 11:40 am Virgo
15th 9:56 pm Libra
18th 5:09 am Scorpio
20th 10:09 am Sagittarius
22nd 1:56 pm Capricorn
24th 5:11 pm Aquarius
26th 8:14 pm Pisces
28th 11:22 pm Aries
31st 3:30 am Taurus

November 1925
2nd 9:47 am Gemini
4th 7:07 pm Cancer
7th 7:15 am Leo
9th 8:06 pm Virgo
12th 6:48 am Libra
14th 2:01 pm Scorpio
16th 6:10 pm Sagittarius
18th 8:38 pm Capricorn
20th 10:48 pm Aquarius
23rd 1:38 am Pisces
25th 5:32 am Aries
27th 10:48 am Taurus
29th 5:53 pm Gemini

December 1925
2nd 3:19 am Cancer
4th 3:13 pm Leo
7th 4:12 am Virgo
9th 3:48 pm Libra
12th 0:04 am Scorpio
14th 4:20 am Sagittarius
16th 5:58 am Capricorn
18th 6:37 am Aquarius
20th 7:55 am Pisces
22nd 11:01 am Aries
24th 4:28 pm Taurus
27th 0:19 am Gemini
29th 10:29 am Cancer
31st 10:25 pm Leo

January 1926
3rd 11:24 am Virgo
5th 11:42 pm Libra
8th 9:13 am Scorpio
10th 2:56 pm Sagittarius
12th 5:05 pm Capricorn
14th 5:06 pm Aquarius
16th 4:51 pm Pisces
18th 6:07 pm Aries
20th 10:17 pm Taurus
23rd 5:59 am Gemini
25th 4:33 pm Cancer
28th 4:52 am Leo
30th 5:48 pm Virgo

February 1926
2nd 6:08 am Libra
4th 4:35 pm Scorpio
7th 0:02 am Sagittarius
9th 3:46 am Capricorn
11th 4:34 am Aquarius
13th 3:57 am Pisces
15th 3:50 am Aries
17th 6:14 am Taurus
19th 12:28 pm Gemini
21st 10:29 pm Cancer
24th 11:01 am Leo
26th 12:00 pm Virgo

March 1926
1st 12:02 pm Libra
3rd 10:28 pm Scorpio
6th 6:37 am Sagittarius
8th 12:03 pm Capricorn
10th 2:37 pm Aquarius
12th 3:02 pm Pisces
14th 2:53 pm Aries
16th 4:11 pm Taurus
18th 8:44 pm Gemini
21st 5:33 am Cancer
23rd 5:37 pm Leo
26th 6:36 am Virgo
28th 6:25 pm Libra
31st 4:16 am Scorpio

April 1926
2nd 12:06 pm Sagittarius
4th 6:02 pm Capricorn
6th 10:00 pm Aquarius
9th 0:03 am Pisces
11th 1:02 am Aries
13th 2:32 am Taurus
15th 6:25 am Gemini
17th 1:59 pm Cancer
20th 1:07 am Leo
22nd 1:58 pm Virgo
25th 1:53 am Libra
27th 11:11 am Scorpio
29th 6:19 pm Sagittarius

May 1926
1st 11:34 pm Capricorn
4th 3:30 am Aquarius
6th 6:31 am Pisces
8th 8:55 am Aries
10th 11:36 am Taurus
12th 3:50 pm Gemini
14th 10:54 pm Cancer
17th 9:22 am Leo
19th 9:54 pm Virgo
22nd 10:01 am Libra
24th 7:40 pm Scorpio
27th 2:14 am Sagittarius
29th 6:23 am Capricorn
31st 9:19 am Aquarius

June 1926
2nd 11:54 am Pisces
4th 2:47 pm Aries
6th 6:30 pm Taurus
8th 11:44 pm Gemini
11th 7:18 am Cancer
13th 5:31 pm Leo
16th 5:49 am Virgo
18th 6:16 pm Libra
21st 4:38 am Scorpio
23rd 11:31 am Sagittarius
25th 3:15 pm Capricorn
27th 5:01 pm Aquarius
29th 6:15 pm Pisces

July 1926
1st 8:16 pm Aries
3rd 12:00 pm Taurus
6th 6:00 am Gemini
8th 2:21 pm Cancer
11th 0:50 am Leo
13th 1:08 pm Virgo
16th 1:52 am Libra
18th 1:02 pm Scorpio
20th 9:07 pm Sagittarius
23rd 1:27 am Capricorn
25th 2:47 am Aquarius
27th 2:47 am Pisces
29th 3:16 am Aries
31st 5:51 am Taurus

August 1926
2nd 11:30 am Gemini
4th 8:11 pm Cancer
7th 7:14 am Leo
9th 7:39 pm Virgo
12th 8:26 am Libra
14th 8:15 pm Scorpio
17th 5:35 am Sagittarius
19th 11:17 am Capricorn
21st 1:25 pm Aquarius
23rd 1:12 pm Pisces
25th 12:33 pm Aries
27th 1:30 pm Taurus
29th 5:43 pm Gemini

September 1926
1st 1:49 am Cancer
3rd 1:03 pm Leo
6th 1:41 am Virgo
8th 2:23 pm Libra
11th 2:15 am Scorpio
13th 12:17 pm Sagittarius
15th 7:33 pm Capricorn
17th 11:21 pm Aquarius
20th 0:05 am Pisces
21st 11:19 pm Aries
23rd 11:12 pm Taurus
26th 1:50 am Gemini
28th 8:38 am Cancer
30th 7:11 pm Leo

October 1926
3rd 7:47 am Virgo
5th 8:27 pm Libra
8th 7:57 am Scorpio
10th 5:52 pm Sagittarius
13th 1:46 am Capricorn
15th 6:58 am Aquarius
17th 9:25 am Pisces
19th 9:55 am Aries
21st 10:04 am Taurus
23rd 11:54 am Gemini
25th 5:11 pm Cancer
28th 2:31 am Leo
30th 2:43 pm Virgo

November 1926
2nd 3:20 am Libra
4th 2:34 pm Scorpio
6th 11:51 pm Sagittarius
9th 7:09 am Capricorn
11th 12:38 pm Aquarius
13th 4:20 pm Pisces
15th 6:26 pm Aries
17th 7:54 pm Taurus
19th 10:10 pm Gemini
22nd 2:56 am Cancer
24th 11:14 am Leo
26th 10:36 pm Virgo
29th 11:12 am Libra

December 1926
1st 10:38 pm Scorpio
4th 7:28 am Sagittarius
6th 1:48 pm Capricorn
8th 6:20 pm Aquarius
10th 9:44 pm Pisces
13th 0:32 am Aries
15th 3:23 am Taurus
17th 7:02 am Gemini
19th 12:23 pm Cancer
21st 8:18 pm Leo
24th 7:03 am Virgo
26th 7:29 pm Libra
29th 7:24 am Scorpio
31st 4:45 pm Sagittarius

January 1927
2nd 10:49 pm Capricorn
5th 2:09 am Aquarius
7th 4:06 am Pisces
9th 6:01 am Aries
11th 8:59 am Taurus
13th 1:33 pm Gemini
15th 8:01 pm Cancer
18th 4:32 am Leo
20th 3:10 pm Virgo
23rd 3:26 am Libra
25th 3:51 pm Scorpio
28th 2:18 am Sagittarius
30th 9:06 am Capricorn

February 1927
1st 12:17 pm Aquarius
3rd 1:05 pm Pisces
5th 1:22 pm Aries
7th 2:54 pm Taurus
9th 6:57 pm Gemini
12th 1:51 am Cancer
14th 11:14 am Leo
16th 10:17 pm Virgo
19th 10:31 am Libra
21st 11:08 pm Scorpio
24th 10:29 am Sagittarius
26th 6:51 pm Capricorn
28th 11:12 pm Aquarius

March 1927
3rd 0:05 am Pisces
4th 11:18 pm Aries
6th 11:07 pm Taurus
9th 1:30 am Gemini
11th 7:33 am Cancer
13th 4:55 pm Leo
16th 4:23 am Virgo
18th 4:50 pm Libra
21st 5:21 am Scorpio
23rd 5:04 pm Sagittarius
26th 2:37 am Capricorn
28th 8:34 am Aquarius
30th 10:48 am Pisces

April 1927
1st 10:28 am Aries
3rd 9:39 am Taurus
5th 10:31 am Gemini
7th 2:48 pm Cancer
9th 11:01 pm Leo
12th 10:21 am Virgo
14th 10:53 pm Libra
17th 11:19 am Scorpio
19th 10:49 pm Sagittarius
22nd 8:32 am Capricorn
24th 3:40 pm Aquarius
26th 7:34 pm Pisces
28th 8:42 pm Aries
30th 8:29 pm Taurus

May 1927
2nd 8:54 pm Gemini
4th 11:51 pm Cancer
7th 6:42 am Leo
9th 5:05 pm Virgo
12th 5:28 am Libra
14th 5:51 pm Scorpio
17th 4:56 am Sagittarius
19th 2:09 pm Capricorn
21st 9:15 pm Aquarius
24th 2:01 am Pisces
26th 4:36 am Aries
28th 5:51 am Taurus
30th 7:05 am Gemini

June 1927
1st 9:56 am Cancer
3rd 3:42 pm Leo
6th 0:55 am Virgo
8th 12:50 pm Libra
11th 1:16 am Scorpio
13th 12:14 pm Sagittarius
15th 8:50 pm Capricorn
18th 3:03 am Aquarius
20th 7:25 am Pisces
22nd 10:28 am Aries
24th 12:54 pm Taurus
26th 3:28 pm Gemini
28th 7:06 pm Cancer

July 1927
1st 0:50 am Leo
3rd 9:31 am Virgo
5th 8:48 pm Libra
8th 9:16 am Scorpio
10th 8:35 pm Sagittarius
13th 5:03 am Capricorn
15th 10:28 am Aquarius
17th 1:42 pm Pisces
19th 3:59 pm Aries
21st 6:25 pm Taurus
23rd 9:47 pm Gemini
26th 2:33 am Cancer
28th 9:04 am Leo
30th 5:45 pm Virgo

August 1927
2nd 4:45 am Libra
4th 5:16 pm Scorpio
7th 5:10 am Sagittarius
9th 2:18 pm Capricorn
11th 7:43 pm Aquarius
13th 10:04 pm Pisces
15th 10:58 pm Aries
18th 0:13 am Taurus
20th 3:10 am Gemini
22nd 8:23 am Cancer
24th 3:42 pm Leo
27th 0:57 am Virgo
29th 12:05 pm Libra

September 1927
1st 0:37 am Scorpio
3rd 1:08 pm Sagittarius
5th 11:28 pm Capricorn
8th 5:45 am Aquarius
10th 8:11 am Pisces
12th 8:17 am Aries
14th 8:06 am Taurus
16th 9:32 am Gemini
18th 1:53 pm Cancer
20th 9:15 pm Leo
23rd 7:04 am Virgo
25th 6:32 pm Libra
28th 7:07 am Scorpio
30th 7:54 pm Sagittarius

October 1927
3rd 7:10 am Capricorn
5th 3:01 pm Aquarius
7th 6:45 pm Pisces
9th 7:13 pm Aries
11th 6:18 pm Taurus
13th 6:15 pm Gemini
15th 8:52 pm Cancer
18th 3:09 am Leo
20th 12:45 pm Virgo
23rd 0:26 am Libra
25th 1:09 pm Scorpio
28th 1:48 am Sagittarius
30th 1:19 pm Capricorn

November 1927
1st 10:25 pm Aquarius
4th 3:51 am Pisces
6th 5:50 am Aries
8th 5:37 am Taurus
10th 5:06 am Gemini
12th 6:18 am Cancer
14th 10:54 am Leo
16th 7:15 pm Virgo
19th 6:41 am Libra
21st 7:26 pm Scorpio
24th 7:51 am Sagittarius
26th 6:58 pm Capricorn
29th 4:04 am Aquarius

December 1927
1st 10:33 am Pisces
3rd 2:16 pm Aries
5th 3:44 pm Taurus
7th 4:11 pm Gemini
9th 5:13 pm Cancer
11th 8:32 pm Leo
14th 3:27 am Virgo
16th 1:57 pm Libra
19th 2:30 am Scorpio
21st 2:56 pm Sagittarius
24th 1:35 am Capricorn
26th 9:51 am Aquarius
28th 3:57 pm Pisces
30th 8:17 pm Aries

January 1928
1st 11:14 pm Taurus
4th 1:20 am Gemini
6th 3:28 am Cancer
8th 6:55 am Leo
10th 12:57 pm Virgo
12th 10:17 pm Libra
15th 10:25 am Scorpio
17th 11:04 pm Sagittarius
20th 9:44 am Capricorn
22nd 5:23 pm Aquarius
24th 10:22 pm Pisces
27th 1:47 am Aries
29th 4:42 am Taurus
31st 7:49 am Gemini

February 1928
2nd 11:24 am Cancer
4th 3:55 pm Leo
6th 10:10 pm Virgo
9th 7:06 am Libra
11th 6:41 pm Scorpio
14th 7:29 am Sagittarius
16th 6:49 pm Capricorn
19th 2:44 am Aquarius
21st 7:01 am Pisces
23rd 9:08 am Aries
25th 10:44 am Taurus
27th 1:10 pm Gemini
29th 5:07 pm Cancer

March 1928
2nd 10:39 pm Leo
5th 5:53 am Virgo
7th 3:08 pm Libra
10th 2:31 am Scorpio
12th 3:23 pm Sagittarius
15th 3:30 am Capricorn
17th 12:25 pm Aquarius
19th 5:15 pm Pisces
21st 6:51 pm Aries
23rd 7:06 pm Taurus
25th 7:55 pm Gemini
27th 10:43 pm Cancer
30th 4:06 am Leo

April 1928
1st 11:55 am Virgo
3rd 9:47 pm Libra
6th 9:29 am Scorpio
8th 10:20 pm Sagittarius
11th 10:53 am Capricorn
13th 9:05 pm Aquarius
16th 3:16 am Pisces
18th 5:37 am Aries
20th 5:35 am Taurus
22nd 5:11 am Gemini
24th 6:17 am Cancer
26th 10:16 am Leo
28th 5:30 pm Virgo

May 1928
1st 3:36 am Libra
3rd 3:39 pm Scorpio
6th 4:32 am Sagittarius
8th 5:07 pm Capricorn
11th 3:55 am Aquarius
13th 11:30 am Pisces
15th 3:25 pm Aries
17th 4:23 pm Taurus
19th 3:56 pm Gemini
21st 4:01 pm Cancer
23rd 6:20 pm Leo
26th 0:08 am Virgo
28th 9:39 am Libra
30th 9:41 pm Scorpio

June 1928
2nd 10:37 am Sagittarius
4th 11:00 pm Capricorn
7th 9:38 am Aquarius
9th 5:51 pm Pisces
11th 11:13 pm Aries
14th 1:45 am Taurus
16th 2:24 am Gemini
18th 2:36 am Cancer
20th 4:06 am Leo
22nd 8:33 am Virgo
24th 4:46 pm Libra
27th 4:18 am Scorpio
29th 5:14 pm Sagittarius

July 1928
2nd 5:23 am Capricorn
4th 3:30 pm Aquarius
6th 11:23 pm Pisces
9th 5:02 am Aries
11th 8:47 am Taurus
13th 10:60 am Gemini
15th 12:21 pm Cancer
17th 2:10 pm Leo
19th 5:56 pm Virgo
22nd 1:04 am Libra
24th 11:50 am Scorpio
27th 0:34 am Sagittarius
29th 12:43 pm Capricorn
31st 10:33 pm Aquarius

August 1928
3rd 5:33 am Pisces
5th 10:32 am Aries
7th 2:18 pm Taurus
9th 5:23 pm Gemini
11th 8:05 pm Cancer
13th 10:59 pm Leo
16th 3:10 am Virgo
18th 9:59 am Libra
20th 7:59 pm Scorpio
23rd 8:28 am Sagittarius
25th 8:58 pm Capricorn
28th 6:52 am Aquarius
30th 1:26 pm Pisces

September 1928
1st 5:25 pm Aries
3rd 8:08 pm Taurus
5th 10:44 pm Gemini
8th 1:54 am Cancer
10th 5:53 am Leo
12th 11:05 am Virgo
14th 6:16 pm Libra
17th 4:06 am Scorpio
19th 4:24 pm Sagittarius
22nd 5:14 am Capricorn
24th 3:57 pm Aquarius
26th 11:01 pm Pisces
29th 2:30 am Aries

October 1928
1st 3:59 am Taurus
3rd 5:10 am Gemini
5th 7:24 am Cancer
7th 11:21 am Leo
9th 5:17 pm Virgo
12th 1:15 am Libra
14th 11:32 am Scorpio
16th 11:46 pm Sagittarius
19th 12:50 pm Capricorn
22nd 0:34 am Aquarius
24th 8:45 am Pisces
26th 12:60 pm Aries
28th 2:14 pm Taurus
30th 2:13 pm Gemini

November 1928
1st 2:43 pm Cancer
3rd 5:17 pm Leo
5th 10:42 pm Virgo
8th 7:07 am Libra
10th 5:55 pm Scorpio
13th 6:20 am Sagittarius
15th 7:25 pm Capricorn
18th 7:38 am Aquarius
20th 5:15 pm Pisces
22nd 11:14 pm Aries
25th 1:30 am Taurus
27th 1:23 am Gemini
29th 0:43 am Cancer

December 1928
1st 1:30 am Leo
3rd 5:20 am Virgo
5th 12:56 pm Libra
7th 11:46 pm Scorpio
10th 12:30 pm Sagittarius
13th 1:29 am Capricorn
15th 1:33 pm Aquarius
17th 11:48 pm Pisces
20th 7:10 am Aries
22nd 11:20 am Taurus
24th 12:37 pm Gemini
26th 12:17 pm Cancer
28th 12:10 pm Leo
30th 2:18 pm Virgo

January 1929
1st 8:11 pm Libra
4th 6:11 am Scorpio
6th 6:50 pm Sagittarius
9th 7:49 am Capricorn
11th 7:30 pm Aquarius
14th 5:19 am Pisces
16th 1:04 pm Aries
18th 6:34 pm Taurus
20th 9:42 pm Gemini
22nd 10:52 pm Cancer
24th 11:16 pm Leo
27th 0:48 am Virgo
29th 5:23 am Libra
31st 1:60 pm Scorpio

February 1929
3rd 1:58 am Sagittarius
5th 2:58 pm Capricorn
8th 2:32 am Aquarius
10th 11:39 am Pisces
12th 6:39 pm Aries
15th 0:02 am Taurus
17th 4:00 am Gemini
19th 6:44 am Cancer
21st 8:42 am Leo
23rd 11:02 am Virgo
25th 3:20 pm Libra
27th 10:54 pm Scorpio

March 1929
2nd 10:03 am Sagittarius
4th 10:53 pm Capricorn
7th 10:39 am Aquarius
9th 7:40 pm Pisces
12th 1:50 am Aries
14th 6:03 am Taurus
16th 9:22 am Gemini
18th 12:24 pm Cancer
20th 3:28 pm Leo
22nd 7:05 pm Virgo
25th 0:11 am Libra
27th 7:52 am Scorpio
29th 6:28 pm Sagittarius

April 1929
1st 7:02 am Capricorn
3rd 7:14 pm Aquarius
6th 4:48 am Pisces
8th 10:53 am Aries
10th 2:13 pm Taurus
12th 4:11 pm Gemini
14th 6:04 pm Cancer
16th 8:51 pm Leo
19th 1:04 am Virgo
21st 7:16 am Libra
23rd 3:37 pm Scorpio
26th 2:16 am Sagittarius
28th 2:44 pm Capricorn

May 1929
1st 3:18 am Aquarius
3rd 1:46 pm Pisces
5th 8:48 pm Aries
8th 0:16 am Taurus
10th 1:21 am Gemini
12th 1:44 am Cancer
14th 3:04 am Leo
16th 6:35 am Virgo
18th 12:56 pm Libra
20th 9:55 pm Scorpio
23rd 9:05 am Sagittarius
25th 9:34 pm Capricorn
28th 10:17 am Aquarius
30th 9:36 pm Pisces

June 1929
2nd 5:53 am Aries
4th 10:29 am Taurus
6th 11:54 am Gemini
8th 11:35 am Cancer
10th 11:28 am Leo
12th 1:25 pm Virgo
14th 6:42 pm Libra
17th 3:34 am Scorpio
19th 3:05 pm Sagittarius
22nd 3:45 am Capricorn
24th 4:23 pm Aquarius
27th 3:57 am Pisces
29th 1:16 pm Aries

July 1929
1st 7:29 pm Taurus
3rd 10:12 pm Gemini
5th 10:20 pm Cancer
7th 9:38 pm Leo
9th 10:12 pm Virgo
12th 1:55 am Libra
14th 9:49 am Scorpio
16th 9:02 pm Sagittarius
19th 9:48 am Capricorn
21st 10:20 pm Aquarius
24th 9:37 am Pisces
26th 7:12 pm Aries
29th 2:24 am Taurus
31st 6:40 am Gemini

August 1929
2nd 8:13 am Cancer
4th 8:12 am Leo
6th 8:27 am Virgo
8th 11:02 am Libra
10th 5:27 pm Scorpio
13th 3:45 am Sagittarius
15th 4:20 pm Capricorn
18th 4:48 am Aquarius
20th 3:44 pm Pisces
23rd 0:46 am Aries
25th 7:53 am Taurus
27th 12:60 pm Gemini
29th 4:02 pm Cancer
31st 5:27 pm Leo

September 1929
2nd 6:29 pm Virgo
4th 8:54 pm Libra
7th 2:22 am Scorpio
9th 11:42 am Sagittarius
11th 11:44 pm Capricorn
14th 12:14 pm Aquarius
16th 11:06 pm Pisces
19th 7:28 am Aries
21st 1:43 pm Taurus
23rd 6:24 pm Gemini
25th 9:52 pm Cancer
28th 0:29 am Leo
30th 2:53 am Virgo

October 1929
2nd 6:14 am Libra
4th 11:45 am Scorpio
6th 8:21 pm Sagittarius
9th 7:52 am Capricorn
11th 8:26 pm Aquarius
14th 7:38 am Pisces
16th 3:59 pm Aries
18th 9:27 pm Taurus
21st 0:54 am Gemini
23rd 3:23 am Cancer
25th 5:56 am Leo
27th 9:11 am Virgo
29th 1:42 pm Libra
31st 8:05 pm Scorpio

November 1929
3rd 4:50 am Sagittarius
5th 4:00 pm Capricorn
8th 4:34 am Aquarius
10th 4:28 pm Pisces
13th 1:42 am Aries
15th 7:15 am Taurus
17th 9:51 am Gemini
19th 10:53 am Cancer
21st 12:00 pm Leo
23rd 2:35 pm Virgo
25th 7:24 pm Libra
28th 2:41 am Scorpio
30th 12:11 pm Sagittarius

December 1929
2nd 11:26 pm Capricorn
5th 11:59 am Aquarius
8th 0:28 am Pisces
10th 10:53 am Aries
12th 5:45 pm Taurus
14th 8:47 pm Gemini
16th 9:03 pm Cancer
18th 8:35 pm Leo
20th 9:23 pm Virgo
23rd 1:03 am Libra
25th 8:15 am Scorpio
27th 6:13 pm Sagittarius
30th 5:56 am Capricorn

January 1930
1st 6:30 pm Aquarius
4th 7:03 am Pisces
6th 6:24 pm Aries
9th 2:56 am Taurus
11th 7:29 am Gemini
13th 8:31 am Cancer
15th 7:38 am Leo
17th 7:01 am Virgo
19th 8:51 am Libra
21st 2:30 pm Scorpio
23rd 11:56 pm Sagittarius
26th 11:53 am Capricorn
29th 0:34 am Aquarius
31st 12:58 pm Pisces

February 1930
3rd 0:23 am Aries
5th 9:45 am Taurus
7th 4:05 pm Gemini
9th 6:52 pm Cancer
11th 6:58 pm Leo
13th 6:15 pm Virgo
15th 6:54 pm Libra
17th 10:46 pm Scorpio
20th 6:52 am Sagittarius
22nd 6:13 pm Capricorn
25th 6:55 am Aquarius
27th 7:11 pm Pisces

March 1930
2nd 6:07 am Aries
4th 3:16 pm Taurus
6th 10:15 pm Gemini
9th 2:33 am Cancer
11th 4:25 am Leo
13th 4:54 am Virgo
15th 5:46 am Libra
17th 8:51 am Scorpio
19th 3:27 pm Sagittarius
22nd 1:40 am Capricorn
24th 2:03 pm Aquarius
27th 2:22 am Pisces
29th 12:56 pm Aries
31st 9:22 pm Taurus

April 1930
3rd 3:40 am Gemini
5th 8:08 am Cancer
7th 11:06 am Leo
9th 1:10 pm Virgo
11th 3:19 pm Libra
13th 6:47 pm Scorpio
16th 0:49 am Sagittarius
18th 10:10 am Capricorn
20th 9:57 pm Aquarius
23rd 10:20 am Pisces
25th 9:08 pm Aries
28th 5:05 am Taurus
30th 10:22 am Gemini

May 1930
2nd 1:51 pm Cancer
4th 4:30 pm Leo
6th 7:10 pm Virgo
8th 10:29 pm Libra
11th 3:07 am Scorpio
13th 9:42 am Sagittarius
15th 6:41 pm Capricorn
18th 6:05 am Aquarius
20th 6:34 pm Pisces
23rd 5:52 am Aries
25th 2:09 pm Taurus
27th 7:03 pm Gemini
29th 9:24 pm Cancer
31st 10:44 pm Leo

June 1930
3rd 0:36 am Virgo
5th 4:04 am Libra
7th 9:33 am Scorpio
9th 4:58 pm Sagittarius
12th 2:21 am Capricorn
14th 1:41 pm Aquarius
17th 2:11 am Pisces
19th 2:11 pm Aries
21st 11:36 pm Taurus
24th 4:56 am Gemini
26th 6:54 am Cancer
28th 7:06 am Leo
30th 7:30 am Virgo

July 1930
2nd 9:51 am Libra
4th 2:59 pm Scorpio
6th 10:50 pm Sagittarius
9th 8:50 am Capricorn
11th 8:24 pm Aquarius
14th 8:57 am Pisces
16th 9:24 pm Aries
19th 7:49 am Taurus
21st 2:33 pm Gemini
23rd 5:17 pm Cancer
25th 5:17 pm Leo
27th 4:36 pm Virgo
29th 5:22 pm Libra
31st 9:07 pm Scorpio

August 1930
3rd 4:27 am Sagittarius
5th 2:37 pm Capricorn
8th 2:27 am Aquarius
10th 3:02 pm Pisces
13th 3:31 am Aries
15th 2:34 pm Taurus
17th 10:45 pm Gemini
20th 2:59 am Cancer
22nd 3:56 am Leo
24th 3:15 am Virgo
26th 3:00 am Libra
28th 5:15 am Scorpio
30th 11:09 am Sagittarius

September 1930
1st 8:37 pm Capricorn
4th 8:27 am Aquarius
6th 9:06 pm Pisces
9th 9:19 am Aries
11th 8:17 pm Taurus
14th 4:58 am Gemini
16th 10:38 am Cancer
18th 1:15 pm Leo
20th 1:45 pm Virgo
22nd 1:46 pm Libra
24th 3:13 pm Scorpio
26th 7:38 pm Sagittarius
29th 3:52 am Capricorn

October 1930
1st 3:10 pm Aquarius
4th 3:48 am Pisces
6th 3:51 pm Aries
9th 2:13 am Taurus
11th 10:26 am Gemini
13th 4:27 pm Cancer
15th 8:18 pm Leo
17th 10:26 pm Virgo
19th 11:44 pm Libra
22nd 1:34 am Scorpio
24th 5:28 am Sagittarius
26th 12:33 pm Capricorn
28th 10:55 pm Aquarius
31st 11:24 am Pisces

November 1930
2nd 11:34 pm Aries
5th 9:34 am Taurus
7th 4:55 pm Gemini
9th 10:04 pm Cancer
12th 1:44 am Leo
14th 4:41 am Virgo
16th 7:28 am Libra
18th 10:39 am Scorpio
20th 3:04 pm Sagittarius
22nd 9:45 pm Capricorn
25th 7:27 am Aquarius
27th 7:35 pm Pisces
30th 8:05 am Aries

December 1930
2nd 6:30 pm Taurus
5th 1:31 am Gemini
7th 5:30 am Cancer
9th 7:52 am Leo
11th 10:05 am Virgo
13th 1:07 pm Libra
15th 5:21 pm Scorpio
17th 10:55 pm Sagittarius
20th 6:15 am Capricorn
22nd 3:48 pm Aquarius
25th 3:37 am Pisces
27th 4:29 pm Aries
30th 3:49 am Taurus

January 1931
1st 11:30 am Gemini
3rd 3:17 pm Cancer
5th 4:31 pm Leo
7th 5:08 pm Virgo
9th 6:51 pm Libra
11th 10:41 pm Scorpio
14th 4:52 am Sagittarius
16th 1:04 pm Capricorn
18th 11:05 pm Aquarius
21st 10:57 am Pisces
23rd 11:56 pm Aries
26th 12:06 pm Taurus
28th 9:16 pm Gemini
31st 2:09 am Cancer

February 1931
2nd 3:24 am Leo
4th 2:58 am Virgo
6th 2:57 am Libra
8th 5:07 am Scorpio
10th 10:27 am Sagittarius
12th 6:41 pm Capricorn
15th 5:16 am Aquarius
17th 5:24 pm Pisces
20th 6:20 am Aries
22nd 6:52 pm Taurus
25th 5:10 am Gemini
27th 11:42 am Cancer

March 1931
1st 2:21 pm Leo
3rd 2:20 pm Virgo
5th 1:35 pm Libra
7th 2:07 pm Scorpio
9th 5:34 pm Sagittarius
12th 0:38 am Capricorn
14th 11:04 am Aquarius
16th 11:26 pm Pisces
19th 12:22 pm Aries
22nd 0:44 am Taurus
24th 11:16 am Gemini
26th 7:02 pm Cancer
28th 11:29 pm Leo
31st 0:58 am Virgo

April 1931
2nd 0:49 am Libra
4th 0:51 am Scorpio
6th 2:54 am Sagittarius
8th 8:25 am Capricorn
10th 5:42 pm Aquarius
13th 5:48 am Pisces
15th 6:46 pm Aries
18th 6:47 am Taurus
20th 4:53 pm Gemini
23rd 0:41 am Cancer
25th 6:00 am Leo
27th 9:07 am Virgo
29th 10:34 am Libra

May 1931
1st 11:27 am Scorpio
3rd 1:18 pm Sagittarius
5th 5:40 pm Capricorn
8th 1:38 am Aquarius
10th 1:04 pm Pisces
13th 1:57 am Aries
15th 1:51 pm Taurus
17th 11:24 pm Gemini
20th 6:23 am Cancer
22nd 11:24 am Leo
24th 3:04 pm Virgo
26th 5:49 pm Libra
28th 8:07 pm Scorpio
30th 10:47 pm Sagittarius

June 1931
2nd 3:09 am Capricorn
4th 10:28 am Aquarius
6th 9:03 pm Pisces
9th 9:44 am Aries
11th 9:53 pm Taurus
14th 7:17 am Gemini
16th 1:33 pm Cancer
18th 5:34 pm Leo
20th 8:32 pm Virgo
22nd 11:21 pm Libra
25th 2:35 am Scorpio
27th 6:27 am Sagittarius
29th 11:38 am Capricorn

July 1931
1st 6:59 pm Aquarius
4th 5:11 am Pisces
6th 5:40 pm Aries
9th 6:12 am Taurus
11th 4:09 pm Gemini
13th 10:28 pm Cancer
16th 1:40 am Leo
18th 3:21 am Virgo
20th 5:07 am Libra
22nd 7:58 am Scorpio
24th 12:20 pm Sagittarius
26th 6:24 pm Capricorn
29th 2:26 am Aquarius
31st 12:48 pm Pisces

August 1931
3rd 1:09 am Aries
5th 2:02 pm Taurus
8th 1:00 am Gemini
10th 8:05 am Cancer
12th 11:26 am Leo
14th 12:24 pm Virgo
16th 12:46 pm Libra
18th 2:13 pm Scorpio
20th 5:50 pm Sagittarius
22nd 11:58 pm Capricorn
25th 8:40 am Aquarius
27th 7:28 pm Pisces
30th 7:56 am Aries

September 1931
1st 8:57 pm Taurus
4th 8:39 am Gemini
6th 5:10 pm Cancer
8th 9:46 pm Leo
10th 11:03 pm Virgo
12th 10:44 pm Libra
14th 10:41 pm Scorpio
17th 0:40 am Sagittarius
19th 5:52 am Capricorn
21st 2:21 pm Aquarius
24th 1:28 am Pisces
26th 2:09 pm Aries
29th 3:06 am Taurus

October 1931
1st 3:00 pm Gemini
4th 0:37 am Cancer
6th 6:46 am Leo
8th 9:31 am Virgo
10th 9:49 am Libra
12th 9:20 am Scorpio
14th 9:57 am Sagittarius
16th 1:24 pm Capricorn
18th 8:42 pm Aquarius
21st 7:35 am Pisces
23rd 8:20 pm Aries
26th 9:10 am Taurus
28th 8:46 pm Gemini
31st 6:24 am Cancer

November 1931
2nd 1:35 pm Leo
4th 6:05 pm Virgo
6th 8:02 pm Libra
8th 8:22 pm Scorpio
10th 8:41 pm Sagittarius
12th 10:54 pm Capricorn
15th 4:44 am Aquarius
17th 2:37 pm Pisces
20th 3:09 am Aries
22nd 3:58 pm Taurus
25th 3:10 am Gemini
27th 12:07 pm Cancer
29th 7:03 pm Leo

December 1931
2nd 0:16 am Virgo
4th 3:43 am Libra
6th 5:43 am Scorpio
8th 7:07 am Sagittarius
10th 9:22 am Capricorn
12th 2:16 pm Aquarius
14th 10:52 pm Pisces
17th 10:52 am Aries
19th 11:46 pm Taurus
22nd 10:56 am Gemini
24th 7:20 pm Cancer
27th 1:16 am Leo
29th 5:39 am Virgo
31st 9:16 am Libra

January 1932
2nd 12:24 pm Scorpio
4th 3:17 pm Sagittarius
6th 6:39 pm Capricorn
8th 11:46 pm Aquarius
11th 7:54 am Pisces
13th 7:10 pm Aries
16th 8:02 am Taurus
18th 7:45 pm Gemini
21st 4:21 am Cancer
23rd 9:37 am Leo
25th 12:46 pm Virgo
27th 3:08 pm Libra
29th 5:45 pm Scorpio
31st 9:08 pm Sagittarius

February 1932
3rd 1:40 am Capricorn
5th 7:53 am Aquarius
7th 4:19 pm Pisces
10th 3:19 am Aries
12th 4:06 pm Taurus
15th 4:25 am Gemini
17th 1:58 pm Cancer
19th 7:47 pm Leo
21st 10:25 pm Virgo
23rd 11:23 pm Libra
26th 0:22 am Scorpio
28th 2:40 am Sagittarius

March 1932
1st 7:09 am Capricorn
3rd 2:03 pm Aquarius
5th 11:16 pm Pisces
8th 10:37 am Aries
10th 11:19 pm Taurus
13th 12:01 pm Gemini
15th 10:45 pm Cancer
18th 5:53 am Leo
20th 9:15 am Virgo
22nd 9:56 am Libra
24th 9:37 am Scorpio
26th 10:12 am Sagittarius
28th 1:14 pm Capricorn
30th 7:33 pm Aquarius

April 1932
2nd 5:06 am Pisces
4th 4:53 pm Aries
7th 5:43 am Taurus
9th 6:26 pm Gemini
12th 5:45 am Cancer
14th 2:17 pm Leo
16th 7:19 pm Virgo
18th 8:58 pm Libra
20th 8:34 pm Scorpio
22nd 7:60 pm Sagittarius
24th 9:18 pm Capricorn
27th 2:06 am Aquarius
29th 10:59 am Pisces

May 1932
1st 10:47 pm Aries
4th 11:45 am Taurus
7th 0:20 am Gemini
9th 11:32 am Cancer
11th 8:45 pm Leo
14th 3:10 am Virgo
16th 6:29 am Libra
18th 7:13 am Scorpio
20th 6:49 am Sagittarius
22nd 7:17 am Capricorn
24th 10:37 am Aquarius
26th 6:02 pm Pisces
29th 5:11 am Aries
31st 6:04 pm Taurus

June 1932
3rd 6:29 am Gemini
5th 5:18 pm Cancer
8th 2:13 am Leo
10th 9:02 am Virgo
12th 1:37 pm Libra
14th 3:57 pm Scorpio
16th 4:45 pm Sagittarius
18th 5:34 pm Capricorn
20th 8:16 pm Aquarius
23rd 2:28 am Pisces
25th 12:38 pm Aries
28th 1:09 am Taurus
30th 1:33 pm Gemini

July 1932
3rd 0:06 am Cancer
5th 8:15 am Leo
7th 2:30 pm Virgo
9th 7:10 pm Libra
11th 10:27 pm Scorpio
14th 0:37 am Sagittarius
16th 2:35 am Capricorn
18th 5:47 am Aquarius
20th 11:39 am Pisces
22nd 8:53 pm Aries
25th 8:55 am Taurus
27th 9:26 pm Gemini
30th 8:03 am Cancer

August 1932
1st 3:54 pm Leo
3rd 9:13 pm Virgo
6th 0:56 am Libra
8th 3:50 am Scorpio
10th 6:32 am Sagittarius
12th 9:40 am Capricorn
14th 1:57 pm Aquarius
16th 8:15 pm Pisces
19th 5:19 am Aries
21st 4:57 pm Taurus
24th 5:33 am Gemini
26th 4:47 pm Cancer
29th 1:03 am Leo
31st 5:55 am Virgo

September 1932
2nd 8:30 am Libra
4th 10:07 am Scorpio
6th 12:03 pm Sagittarius
8th 3:14 pm Capricorn
10th 8:18 pm Aquarius
13th 3:32 am Pisces
15th 1:02 pm Aries
18th 0:32 am Taurus
20th 1:13 pm Gemini
23rd 1:12 am Cancer
25th 10:28 am Leo
27th 4:03 pm Virgo
29th 6:20 pm Libra

October 1932
1st 6:44 pm Scorpio
3rd 7:05 pm Sagittarius
5th 9:02 pm Capricorn
8th 1:44 am Aquarius
10th 9:30 am Pisces
12th 7:37 pm Aries
15th 7:23 am Taurus
17th 8:03 pm Gemini
20th 8:24 am Cancer
22nd 6:54 pm Leo
25th 2:02 am Virgo
27th 5:13 am Libra
29th 5:29 am Scorpio
31st 4:42 am Sagittarius

November 1932
2nd 4:58 am Capricorn
4th 8:11 am Aquarius
6th 3:11 pm Pisces
9th 1:26 am Aries
11th 1:34 pm Taurus
14th 2:13 am Gemini
16th 2:31 pm Cancer
19th 1:34 am Leo
21st 10:02 am Virgo
23rd 3:02 pm Libra
25th 4:35 pm Scorpio
27th 3:59 pm Sagittarius
29th 3:21 pm Capricorn

December 1932
1st 4:53 pm Aquarius
3rd 10:10 pm Pisces
6th 7:39 am Aries
8th 7:43 pm Taurus
11th 8:26 am Gemini
13th 8:27 pm Cancer
16th 7:10 am Leo
18th 4:04 pm Virgo
20th 10:31 pm Libra
23rd 1:52 am Scorpio
25th 2:41 am Sagittarius
27th 2:33 am Capricorn
29th 3:26 am Aquarius
31st 7:23 am Pisces

January 1933
2nd 3:19 pm Aries
5th 2:38 am Taurus
7th 3:20 pm Gemini
10th 3:16 am Cancer
12th 1:25 pm Leo
14th 9:41 pm Virgo
17th 4:01 am Libra
19th 8:22 am Scorpio
21st 10:53 am Sagittarius
23rd 12:19 pm Capricorn
25th 1:60 pm Aquarius
27th 5:35 pm Pisces
30th 0:21 am Aries

February 1933
1st 10:43 am Taurus
3rd 11:05 pm Gemini
6th 11:12 am Cancer
8th 9:16 pm Leo
11th 4:42 am Virgo
13th 9:57 am Libra
15th 1:46 pm Scorpio
17th 4:42 pm Sagittarius
19th 7:23 pm Capricorn
21st 10:29 pm Aquarius
24th 2:58 am Pisces
26th 9:47 am Aries
28th 7:22 pm Taurus

March 1933
3rd 7:18 am Gemini
5th 7:42 pm Cancer
8th 6:16 am Leo
10th 1:39 pm Virgo
12th 6:02 pm Libra
14th 8:28 pm Scorpio
16th 10:19 pm Sagittarius
19th 0:48 am Capricorn
21st 4:41 am Aquarius
23rd 10:19 am Pisces
25th 5:52 pm Aries
28th 3:33 am Taurus
30th 3:15 pm Gemini

April 1933
2nd 3:49 am Cancer
4th 3:13 pm Leo
6th 11:34 pm Virgo
9th 3:60 am Libra
11th 5:31 am Scorpio
13th 5:54 am Sagittarius
15th 6:58 am Capricorn
17th 10:07 am Aquarius
19th 3:58 pm Pisces
22nd 0:13 am Aries
24th 10:32 am Taurus
26th 10:18 pm Gemini
29th 10:58 am Cancer

May 1933
1st 11:06 pm Leo
4th 8:36 am Virgo
6th 2:12 pm Libra
8th 4:04 pm Scorpio
10th 3:44 pm Sagittarius
12th 3:20 pm Capricorn
14th 4:51 pm Aquarius
16th 9:36 pm Pisces
19th 5:47 am Aries
21st 4:28 pm Taurus
24th 4:32 am Gemini
26th 5:11 pm Cancer
29th 5:31 am Leo
31st 4:03 pm Virgo

June 1933
2nd 11:15 pm Libra
5th 2:23 am Scorpio
7th 2:32 am Sagittarius
9th 1:35 am Capricorn
11th 1:43 am Aquarius
13th 4:55 am Pisces
15th 11:56 am Aries
17th 10:13 pm Taurus
20th 10:27 am Gemini
22nd 11:07 pm Cancer
25th 11:15 am Leo
27th 9:60 pm Virgo
30th 6:06 am Libra

July 1933
2nd 10:50 am Scorpio
4th 12:27 pm Sagittarius
6th 12:16 pm Capricorn
8th 12:09 pm Aquarius
10th 2:08 pm Pisces
12th 7:35 pm Aries
15th 4:52 am Taurus
17th 4:46 pm Gemini
20th 5:24 am Cancer
22nd 5:17 pm Leo
25th 3:34 am Virgo
27th 11:41 am Libra
29th 5:17 pm Scorpio
31st 8:24 pm Sagittarius

August 1933
2nd 9:40 pm Capricorn
4th 10:22 pm Aquarius
7th 0:10 am Pisces
9th 4:44 am Aries
11th 12:49 pm Taurus
13th 11:58 pm Gemini
16th 12:32 pm Cancer
19th 0:23 am Leo
21st 10:04 am Virgo
23rd 5:28 pm Libra
25th 10:44 pm Scorpio
28th 2:20 am Sagittarius
30th 4:51 am Capricorn

September 1933
1st 7:01 am Aquarius
3rd 9:46 am Pisces
5th 2:19 pm Aries
7th 9:35 pm Taurus
10th 8:03 am Gemini
12th 8:26 pm Cancer
15th 8:28 am Leo
17th 6:10 pm Virgo
20th 0:51 am Libra
22nd 4:58 am Scorpio
24th 7:48 am Sagittarius
26th 10:24 am Capricorn
28th 1:27 pm Aquarius
30th 5:28 pm Pisces

October 1933
2nd 10:50 pm Aries
5th 6:19 am Taurus
7th 4:19 pm Gemini
10th 4:29 am Cancer
12th 5:00 pm Leo
15th 3:22 am Virgo
17th 10:02 am Libra
19th 1:24 pm Scorpio
21st 2:53 pm Sagittarius
23rd 4:15 pm Capricorn
25th 6:51 pm Aquarius
27th 11:18 pm Pisces
30th 5:42 am Aries

November 1933
1st 1:54 pm Taurus
3rd 12:00 pm Gemini
6th 12:05 pm Cancer
9th 0:56 am Leo
11th 12:19 pm Virgo
13th 8:10 pm Libra
15th 11:52 pm Scorpio
18th 0:35 am Sagittarius
20th 0:24 am Capricorn
22nd 1:21 am Aquarius
24th 4:53 am Pisces
26th 11:16 am Aries
28th 8:04 pm Taurus

December 1933
1st 6:45 am Gemini
3rd 6:53 pm Cancer
6th 7:46 am Leo
8th 7:56 pm Virgo
11th 5:14 am Libra
13th 10:20 am Scorpio
15th 11:45 am Sagittarius
17th 11:09 am Capricorn
19th 10:42 am Aquarius
21st 12:21 pm Pisces
23rd 5:21 pm Aries
26th 1:45 am Taurus
28th 12:46 pm Gemini
31st 1:07 am Cancer

January 1934
2nd 1:55 pm Leo
5th 2:08 am Virgo
7th 12:15 pm Libra
9th 7:06 pm Scorpio
11th 10:16 pm Sagittarius
13th 10:37 pm Capricorn
15th 9:57 pm Aquarius
17th 10:19 pm Pisces
20th 1:30 am Aries
22nd 8:32 am Taurus
24th 6:57 pm Gemini
27th 7:25 am Cancer
29th 8:12 pm Leo

February 1934
1st 7:59 am Virgo
3rd 5:58 pm Libra
6th 1:31 am Scorpio
8th 6:11 am Sagittarius
10th 8:22 am Capricorn
12th 8:57 am Aquarius
14th 9:30 am Pisces
16th 11:44 am Aries
18th 5:08 pm Taurus
21st 2:18 am Gemini
23rd 2:24 pm Cancer
26th 3:15 am Leo
28th 2:45 pm Virgo

March 1934
3rd 0:04 am Libra
5th 6:57 am Scorpio
7th 11:56 am Sagittarius
9th 3:20 pm Capricorn
11th 5:35 pm Aquarius
13th 7:27 pm Pisces
15th 10:01 pm Aries
18th 2:48 am Taurus
20th 10:56 am Gemini
22nd 10:14 pm Cancer
25th 11:02 am Leo
27th 10:45 pm Virgo
30th 7:35 am Libra

April 1934
1st 1:34 pm Scorpio
3rd 5:37 pm Sagittarius
5th 8:46 pm Capricorn
7th 11:43 pm Aquarius
10th 2:53 am Pisces
12th 6:42 am Aries
14th 11:59 am Taurus
16th 7:44 pm Gemini
19th 6:30 am Cancer
21st 7:11 pm Leo
24th 7:18 am Virgo
26th 4:29 pm Libra
28th 10:08 pm Scorpio

May 1934
1st 1:03 am Sagittarius
3rd 2:55 am Capricorn
5th 5:08 am Aquarius
7th 8:29 am Pisces
9th 1:10 pm Aries
11th 7:26 pm Taurus
14th 3:40 am Gemini
16th 2:20 pm Cancer
19th 2:55 am Leo
21st 3:33 pm Virgo
24th 1:42 am Libra
26th 7:47 am Scorpio
28th 10:26 am Sagittarius
30th 11:13 am Capricorn

June 1934
1st 11:59 am Aquarius
3rd 2:11 pm Pisces
5th 6:35 pm Aries
8th 1:17 am Taurus
10th 10:17 am Gemini
12th 9:15 pm Cancer
15th 9:53 am Leo
17th 10:51 pm Virgo
20th 9:54 am Libra
22nd 5:20 pm Scorpio
24th 8:47 pm Sagittarius
26th 9:25 pm Capricorn
28th 9:04 pm Aquarius
30th 9:41 pm Pisces

July 1934
3rd 0:41 am Aries
5th 6:52 am Taurus
7th 3:59 pm Gemini
10th 3:22 am Cancer
12th 4:07 pm Leo
15th 5:06 am Virgo
17th 4:44 pm Libra
20th 1:28 am Scorpio
22nd 6:22 am Sagittarius
24th 8:01 am Capricorn
26th 7:44 am Aquarius
28th 7:24 am Pisces
30th 8:51 am Aries

August 1934
1st 1:32 pm Taurus
3rd 9:51 pm Gemini
6th 9:17 am Cancer
8th 10:10 pm Leo
11th 10:58 am Virgo
13th 10:33 pm Libra
16th 7:48 am Scorpio
18th 2:06 pm Sagittarius
20th 5:24 pm Capricorn
22nd 6:16 pm Aquarius
24th 6:08 pm Pisces
26th 6:46 pm Aries
28th 9:56 pm Taurus
31st 4:59 am Gemini

September 1934
2nd 3:43 pm Cancer
5th 4:33 am Leo
7th 5:15 pm Virgo
10th 4:22 am Libra
12th 1:17 pm Scorpio
14th 8:03 pm Sagittarius
17th 0:36 am Capricorn
19th 3:05 am Aquarius
21st 4:14 am Pisces
23rd 5:15 am Aries
25th 7:50 am Taurus
27th 1:38 pm Gemini
29th 11:15 pm Cancer

October 1934
2nd 11:45 am Leo
5th 0:30 am Virgo
7th 11:17 am Libra
9th 7:31 pm Scorpio
12th 1:32 am Sagittarius
14th 6:03 am Capricorn
16th 9:31 am Aquarius
18th 12:08 pm Pisces
20th 2:29 pm Aries
22nd 5:37 pm Taurus
24th 10:58 pm Gemini
27th 7:49 am Cancer
29th 7:43 pm Leo

November 1934
1st 8:34 am Virgo
3rd 7:39 pm Libra
6th 3:30 am Scorpio
8th 8:31 am Sagittarius
10th 11:56 am Capricorn
12th 2:52 pm Aquarius
14th 5:57 pm Pisces
16th 9:27 pm Aries
19th 1:47 am Taurus
21st 7:51 am Gemini
23rd 4:28 pm Cancer
26th 3:55 am Leo
28th 4:51 pm Virgo

December 1934
1st 4:36 am Libra
3rd 1:00 pm Scorpio
5th 5:50 pm Sagittarius
7th 8:08 pm Capricorn
9th 9:34 pm Aquarius
11th 11:32 pm Pisces
14th 2:53 am Aries
16th 8:00 am Taurus
18th 3:01 pm Gemini
21st 0:12 am Cancer
23rd 11:39 am Leo
26th 0:32 am Virgo
28th 12:54 pm Libra
30th 10:39 pm Scorpio

January 1935
2nd 4:23 am Sagittarius
4th 6:41 am Capricorn
6th 7:04 am Aquarius
8th 7:20 am Pisces
10th 9:08 am Aries
12th 1:31 pm Taurus
14th 8:45 pm Gemini
17th 6:40 am Cancer
19th 6:28 pm Leo
22nd 7:19 am Virgo
24th 7:57 pm Libra
27th 6:42 am Scorpio
29th 2:04 pm Sagittarius
31st 5:43 pm Capricorn

February 1935
2nd 6:23 pm Aquarius
4th 5:48 pm Pisces
6th 5:53 pm Aries
8th 8:26 pm Taurus
11th 2:39 am Gemini
13th 12:29 pm Cancer
16th 0:37 am Leo
18th 1:33 pm Virgo
21st 2:03 am Libra
23rd 1:01 pm Scorpio
25th 9:39 pm Sagittarius
28th 3:03 am Capricorn

March 1935
2nd 5:14 am Aquarius
4th 5:12 am Pisces
6th 4:43 am Aries
8th 5:48 am Taurus
10th 10:18 am Gemini
12th 6:55 pm Cancer
15th 6:50 am Leo
17th 7:52 pm Virgo
20th 8:07 am Libra
22nd 6:44 pm Scorpio
25th 3:23 am Sagittarius
27th 9:46 am Capricorn
29th 1:39 pm Aquarius
31st 3:13 pm Pisces

April 1935
2nd 3:32 pm Aries
4th 4:23 pm Taurus
6th 7:39 pm Gemini
9th 2:52 am Cancer
11th 1:55 pm Leo
14th 2:48 am Virgo
16th 3:00 pm Libra
19th 1:10 am Scorpio
21st 9:05 am Sagittarius
23rd 3:11 pm Capricorn
25th 7:42 pm Aquarius
27th 10:41 pm Pisces
30th 0:26 am Aries

May 1935
2nd 2:11 am Taurus
4th 5:30 am Gemini
6th 11:56 am Cancer
8th 9:56 pm Leo
11th 10:27 am Virgo
13th 10:48 pm Libra
16th 8:52 am Scorpio
18th 4:11 pm Sagittarius
20th 9:21 pm Capricorn
23rd 1:10 am Aquarius
25th 4:14 am Pisces
27th 6:60 am Aries
29th 10:01 am Taurus
31st 2:15 pm Gemini

June 1935
2nd 8:46 pm Cancer
5th 6:22 am Leo
7th 6:26 pm Virgo
10th 6:58 am Libra
12th 5:32 pm Scorpio
15th 0:57 am Sagittarius
17th 5:20 am Capricorn
19th 7:56 am Aquarius
21st 9:58 am Pisces
23rd 12:25 pm Aries
25th 3:57 pm Taurus
27th 9:08 pm Gemini
30th 4:29 am Cancer

July 1935
2nd 2:15 pm Leo
5th 2:10 am Virgo
7th 2:51 pm Libra
10th 2:14 am Scorpio
12th 10:22 am Sagittarius
14th 2:59 pm Capricorn
16th 4:52 pm Aquarius
18th 5:32 pm Pisces
20th 6:36 pm Aries
22nd 9:24 pm Taurus
25th 2:46 am Gemini
27th 10:47 am Cancer
29th 9:07 pm Leo

August 1935
1st 9:08 am Virgo
3rd 9:54 pm Libra
6th 9:53 am Scorpio
8th 7:21 pm Sagittarius
11th 1:08 am Capricorn
13th 3:20 am Aquarius
15th 3:19 am Pisces
17th 2:58 am Aries
19th 4:12 am Taurus
21st 8:31 am Gemini
23rd 4:22 pm Cancer
26th 3:02 am Leo
28th 3:22 pm Virgo
31st 4:08 am Libra

September 1935
2nd 4:21 pm Scorpio
5th 2:46 am Sagittarius
7th 10:03 am Capricorn
9th 1:39 pm Aquarius
11th 2:12 pm Pisces
13th 1:22 pm Aries
15th 1:15 pm Taurus
17th 3:52 pm Gemini
19th 10:29 pm Cancer
22nd 8:53 am Leo
24th 9:20 pm Virgo
27th 10:05 am Libra
29th 10:07 pm Scorpio

October 1935
2nd 8:39 am Sagittarius
4th 4:59 pm Capricorn
6th 10:19 pm Aquarius
9th 0:26 am Pisces
11th 0:19 am Aries
12th 11:54 pm Taurus
15th 1:18 am Gemini
17th 6:24 am Cancer
19th 3:38 pm Leo
22nd 3:45 am Virgo
24th 4:30 pm Libra
27th 4:14 am Scorpio
29th 2:16 pm Sagittarius
31st 10:31 pm Capricorn

November 1935
3rd 4:35 am Aquarius
5th 8:17 am Pisces
7th 9:52 am Aries
9th 10:30 am Taurus
11th 11:57 am Gemini
13th 4:01 pm Cancer
15th 11:50 pm Leo
18th 11:13 am Virgo
20th 11:52 pm Libra
23rd 11:33 am Scorpio
25th 9:08 pm Sagittarius
28th 4:27 am Capricorn
30th 9:57 am Aquarius

December 1935
2nd 2:01 pm Pisces
4th 4:52 pm Aries
6th 7:04 pm Taurus
8th 9:38 pm Gemini
11th 1:55 am Cancer
13th 9:10 am Leo
15th 7:34 pm Virgo
18th 7:57 am Libra
20th 8:00 pm Scorpio
23rd 5:41 am Sagittarius
25th 12:24 pm Capricorn
27th 4:44 pm Aquarius
29th 7:42 pm Pisces
31st 10:15 pm Aries

January 1936
3rd 1:12 am Taurus
5th 5:06 am Gemini
7th 10:32 am Cancer
9th 6:04 pm Leo
12th 4:06 am Virgo
14th 4:11 pm Libra
17th 4:36 am Scorpio
19th 3:06 pm Sagittarius
21st 10:17 pm Capricorn
24th 1:60 am Aquarius
26th 3:34 am Pisces
28th 4:37 am Aries
30th 6:40 am Taurus

February 1936
1st 10:43 am Gemini
3rd 5:02 pm Cancer
6th 1:27 am Leo
8th 11:51 am Virgo
10th 11:46 pm Libra
13th 12:23 pm Scorpio
15th 11:54 pm Sagittarius
18th 8:15 am Capricorn
20th 12:40 pm Aquarius
22nd 1:52 pm Pisces
24th 1:36 pm Aries
26th 1:55 pm Taurus
28th 4:35 pm Gemini

March 1936
1st 10:27 pm Cancer
4th 7:23 am Leo
6th 6:20 pm Virgo
9th 6:28 am Libra
11th 7:05 pm Scorpio
14th 7:03 am Sagittarius
16th 4:48 pm Capricorn
18th 10:51 pm Aquarius
21st 0:58 am Pisces
23rd 0:31 am Aries
24th 11:38 pm Taurus
27th 0:32 am Gemini
29th 4:56 am Cancer
31st 1:08 pm Leo

April 1936
3rd 0:08 am Virgo
5th 12:32 pm Libra
8th 1:06 am Scorpio
10th 1:01 pm Sagittarius
12th 11:24 pm Capricorn
15th 6:45 am Aquarius
17th 10:33 am Pisces
19th 11:18 am Aries
21st 10:39 am Taurus
23rd 10:43 am Gemini
25th 1:28 pm Cancer
27th 8:06 pm Leo
30th 6:25 am Virgo

May 1936
2nd 6:44 pm Libra
5th 7:17 am Scorpio
7th 6:55 pm Sagittarius
10th 4:55 am Capricorn
12th 12:44 pm Aquarius
14th 5:50 pm Pisces
16th 8:12 pm Aries
18th 8:49 pm Taurus
20th 9:14 pm Gemini
22nd 11:21 pm Cancer
25th 4:45 am Leo
27th 1:52 pm Virgo
30th 1:39 am Libra

June 1936
1st 2:12 pm Scorpio
4th 1:37 am Sagittarius
6th 11:01 am Capricorn
8th 6:15 pm Aquarius
10th 11:28 pm Pisces
13th 2:46 am Aries
15th 4:49 am Taurus
17th 6:32 am Gemini
19th 9:14 am Cancer
21st 2:11 pm Leo
23rd 10:17 pm Virgo
26th 9:26 am Libra
28th 9:53 pm Scorpio

July 1936
1st 9:24 am Sagittarius
3rd 6:32 pm Capricorn
6th 0:56 am Aquarius
8th 5:10 am Pisces
10th 8:11 am Aries
12th 10:48 am Taurus
14th 1:42 pm Gemini
16th 5:31 pm Cancer
18th 11:00 pm Leo
21st 6:58 am Virgo
23rd 5:33 pm Libra
26th 5:53 am Scorpio
28th 5:54 pm Sagittarius
31st 3:22 am Capricorn

August 1936
2nd 9:21 am Aquarius
4th 12:34 pm Pisces
6th 2:23 pm Aries
8th 4:15 pm Taurus
10th 7:15 pm Gemini
12th 11:53 pm Cancer
15th 6:24 am Leo
17th 2:49 pm Virgo
20th 1:18 am Libra
22nd 1:37 pm Scorpio
25th 2:09 am Sagittarius
27th 12:30 pm Capricorn
29th 7:08 pm Aquarius
31st 10:05 pm Pisces

September 1936
2nd 10:44 pm Aries
4th 11:05 pm Taurus
7th 0:55 am Gemini
9th 5:19 am Cancer
11th 12:17 pm Leo
13th 9:22 pm Virgo
16th 8:16 am Libra
18th 8:34 pm Scorpio
21st 9:24 am Sagittarius
23rd 8:51 pm Capricorn
26th 4:49 am Aquarius
28th 8:35 am Pisces
30th 9:08 am Aries

October 1936
2nd 8:28 am Taurus
4th 8:41 am Gemini
6th 11:34 am Cancer
8th 5:49 pm Leo
11th 3:02 am Virgo
13th 2:21 pm Libra
16th 2:48 am Scorpio
18th 3:38 pm Sagittarius
21st 3:37 am Capricorn
23rd 12:55 pm Aquarius
25th 6:24 pm Pisces
27th 8:06 pm Aries
29th 7:35 pm Taurus
31st 6:52 pm Gemini

November 1936
2nd 8:03 pm Cancer
5th 0:37 am Leo
7th 9:03 am Virgo
9th 8:16 pm Libra
12th 8:51 am Scorpio
14th 9:35 pm Sagittarius
17th 9:19 am Capricorn
19th 7:08 pm Aquarius
22nd 2:03 am Pisces
24th 5:33 am Aries
26th 6:28 am Taurus
28th 6:14 am Gemini
30th 6:44 am Cancer

December 1936
2nd 9:48 am Leo
4th 4:36 pm Virgo
7th 2:56 am Libra
9th 3:28 pm Scorpio
12th 4:06 am Sagittarius
14th 3:24 pm Capricorn
17th 0:43 am Aquarius
19th 7:42 am Pisces
21st 12:23 pm Aries
23rd 3:03 pm Taurus
25th 4:24 pm Gemini
27th 5:37 pm Cancer
29th 8:15 pm Leo

January 1937
1st 1:46 am Virgo
3rd 10:58 am Libra
5th 10:57 pm Scorpio
8th 11:41 am Sagittarius
10th 10:52 pm Capricorn
13th 7:22 am Aquarius
15th 1:26 pm Pisces
17th 5:47 pm Aries
19th 9:06 pm Taurus
21st 11:55 pm Gemini
24th 2:40 am Cancer
26th 6:10 am Leo
28th 11:34 am Virgo
30th 7:51 pm Libra

February 1937
2nd 7:10 am Scorpio
4th 7:57 pm Sagittarius
7th 7:30 am Capricorn
9th 3:55 pm Aquarius
11th 9:08 pm Pisces
14th 0:12 am Aries
16th 2:35 am Taurus
18th 5:24 am Gemini
20th 9:07 am Cancer
22nd 1:54 pm Leo
24th 8:06 pm Virgo
27th 4:29 am Libra

March 1937
1st 3:26 pm Scorpio
4th 4:07 am Sagittarius
6th 4:19 pm Capricorn
9th 1:34 am Aquarius
11th 6:46 am Pisces
13th 8:57 am Aries
15th 9:55 am Taurus
17th 11:22 am Gemini
19th 2:29 pm Cancer
21st 7:38 pm Leo
24th 2:45 am Virgo
26th 11:50 am Libra
28th 10:52 pm Scorpio
31st 11:34 am Sagittarius

April 1937
3rd 0:16 am Capricorn
5th 10:34 am Aquarius
7th 4:54 pm Pisces
9th 7:25 pm Aries
11th 7:39 pm Taurus
13th 7:35 pm Gemini
15th 9:04 pm Cancer
18th 1:12 am Leo
20th 8:18 am Virgo
22nd 5:54 pm Libra
25th 5:22 am Scorpio
27th 6:06 pm Sagittarius
30th 6:56 am Capricorn

May 1937
2nd 6:06 pm Aquarius
5th 1:57 am Pisces
7th 5:44 am Aries
9th 6:31 am Taurus
11th 5:58 am Gemini
13th 6:03 am Cancer
15th 8:33 am Leo
17th 2:23 pm Virgo
19th 11:35 pm Libra
22nd 11:21 am Scorpio
25th 0:10 am Sagittarius
27th 12:51 pm Capricorn
30th 0:13 am Aquarius

June 1937
1st 8:54 am Pisces
3rd 2:17 pm Aries
5th 4:34 pm Taurus
7th 4:46 pm Gemini
9th 4:34 pm Cancer
11th 5:49 pm Leo
13th 10:04 pm Virgo
16th 6:11 am Libra
18th 5:34 pm Scorpio
21st 6:26 am Sagittarius
23rd 6:58 pm Capricorn
26th 5:52 am Aquarius
28th 2:35 pm Pisces
30th 8:50 pm Aries

July 1937
3rd 0:35 am Taurus
5th 2:17 am Gemini
7th 2:55 am Cancer
9th 4:03 am Leo
11th 7:22 am Virgo
13th 2:09 pm Libra
16th 0:36 am Scorpio
18th 1:21 pm Sagittarius
21st 1:51 am Capricorn
23rd 12:17 pm Aquarius
25th 8:21 pm Pisces
28th 2:15 am Aries
30th 6:31 am Taurus

August 1937
1st 9:30 am Gemini
3rd 11:35 am Cancer
5th 1:39 pm Leo
7th 4:59 pm Virgo
9th 10:59 pm Libra
12th 8:41 am Scorpio
14th 8:59 pm Sagittarius
17th 9:36 am Capricorn
19th 8:03 pm Aquarius
22nd 3:27 am Pisces
24th 8:23 am Aries
26th 11:57 am Taurus
28th 3:03 pm Gemini
30th 6:06 pm Cancer

September 1937
1st 9:24 pm Leo
4th 1:36 am Virgo
6th 7:53 am Libra
8th 5:03 pm Scorpio
11th 5:01 am Sagittarius
13th 5:51 pm Capricorn
16th 4:48 am Aquarius
18th 12:14 pm Pisces
20th 4:28 pm Aries
22nd 6:49 pm Taurus
24th 8:46 pm Gemini
26th 11:26 pm Cancer
29th 3:17 am Leo

October 1937
1st 8:31 am Virgo
3rd 3:36 pm Libra
6th 0:57 am Scorpio
8th 12:47 pm Sagittarius
11th 1:47 am Capricorn
13th 1:35 pm Aquarius
15th 10:02 pm Pisces
18th 2:32 am Aries
20th 4:09 am Taurus
22nd 4:41 am Gemini
24th 5:49 am Cancer
26th 8:46 am Leo
28th 2:05 pm Virgo
30th 9:48 pm Libra

November 1937
2nd 7:51 am Scorpio
4th 7:48 pm Sagittarius
7th 8:51 am Capricorn
9th 9:18 pm Aquarius
12th 7:04 am Pisces
14th 12:55 pm Aries
16th 3:08 pm Taurus
18th 3:09 pm Gemini
20th 2:50 pm Cancer
22nd 4:00 pm Leo
24th 7:59 pm Virgo
27th 3:23 am Libra
29th 1:49 pm Scorpio

December 1937
2nd 2:06 am Sagittarius
4th 3:07 pm Capricorn
7th 3:40 am Aquarius
9th 2:18 pm Pisces
11th 9:53 pm Aries
14th 1:49 am Taurus
16th 2:42 am Gemini
18th 2:03 am Cancer
20th 1:50 am Leo
22nd 4:01 am Virgo
24th 9:58 am Libra
26th 7:46 pm Scorpio
29th 8:13 am Sagittarius
31st 9:17 pm Capricorn

January 1938
3rd 9:29 am Aquarius
5th 8:06 pm Pisces
8th 4:26 am Aries
10th 10:02 am Taurus
12th 12:47 pm Gemini
14th 1:20 pm Cancer
16th 1:11 pm Leo
18th 2:17 pm Virgo
20th 6:32 pm Libra
23rd 2:57 am Scorpio
25th 2:52 pm Sagittarius
28th 3:57 am Capricorn
30th 3:57 pm Aquarius

February 1938
2nd 1:57 am Pisces
4th 9:53 am Aries
6th 3:56 pm Taurus
8th 8:07 pm Gemini
10th 10:25 pm Cancer
12th 11:34 pm Leo
15th 0:57 am Virgo
17th 4:32 am Libra
19th 11:42 am Scorpio
21st 10:34 pm Sagittarius
24th 11:26 am Capricorn
26th 11:34 pm Aquarius

March 1938
1st 9:10 am Pisces
3rd 4:14 pm Aries
5th 9:29 pm Taurus
8th 1:33 am Gemini
10th 4:46 am Cancer
12th 7:24 am Leo
14th 10:07 am Virgo
16th 2:13 pm Libra
18th 8:56 pm Scorpio
21st 7:03 am Sagittarius
23rd 7:32 pm Capricorn
26th 7:52 am Aquarius
28th 5:48 pm Pisces
31st 0:33 am Aries

April 1938
2nd 4:41 am Taurus
4th 7:32 am Gemini
6th 10:08 am Cancer
8th 1:06 pm Leo
10th 4:52 pm Virgo
12th 10:03 pm Libra
15th 5:24 am Scorpio
17th 3:22 pm Sagittarius
20th 3:33 am Capricorn
22nd 4:09 pm Aquarius
25th 2:51 am Pisces
27th 10:03 am Aries
29th 1:57 pm Taurus

May 1938
1st 3:43 pm Gemini
3rd 4:50 pm Cancer
5th 6:43 pm Leo
7th 10:17 pm Virgo
10th 4:07 am Libra
12th 12:19 pm Scorpio
14th 10:41 pm Sagittarius
17th 10:52 am Capricorn
19th 11:38 pm Aquarius
22nd 11:05 am Pisces
24th 7:32 pm Aries
27th 0:17 am Taurus
29th 1:51 am Gemini
31st 1:52 am Cancer

June 1938
2nd 2:10 am Leo
4th 4:24 am Virgo
6th 9:40 am Libra
8th 6:03 pm Scorpio
11th 4:58 am Sagittarius
13th 5:22 pm Capricorn
16th 6:07 am Aquarius
18th 6:01 pm Pisces
21st 3:38 am Aries
23rd 9:44 am Taurus
25th 12:21 pm Gemini
27th 12:26 pm Cancer
29th 11:48 am Leo

July 1938
1st 12:29 pm Virgo
3rd 4:14 pm Libra
5th 11:49 pm Scorpio
8th 10:49 am Sagittarius
10th 11:23 pm Capricorn
13th 12:05 pm Aquarius
15th 11:56 pm Pisces
18th 9:60 am Aries
20th 5:28 pm Taurus
22nd 9:42 pm Gemini
24th 10:55 pm Cancer
26th 10:27 pm Leo
28th 10:19 pm Virgo
31st 0:35 am Libra

August 1938
2nd 6:54 am Scorpio
4th 5:05 pm Sagittarius
7th 5:33 am Capricorn
9th 6:14 pm Aquarius
12th 5:43 am Pisces
14th 3:33 pm Aries
16th 11:27 pm Taurus
19th 4:50 am Gemini
21st 7:38 am Cancer
23rd 8:27 am Leo
25th 8:47 am Virgo
27th 10:33 am Libra
29th 3:33 pm Scorpio

September 1938
1st 0:28 am Sagittarius
3rd 12:31 pm Capricorn
6th 1:10 am Aquarius
8th 12:26 pm Pisces
10th 9:41 pm Aries
13th 4:54 am Taurus
15th 10:22 am Gemini
17th 2:08 pm Cancer
19th 4:27 pm Leo
21st 6:03 pm Virgo
23rd 8:23 pm Libra
26th 0:59 am Scorpio
28th 9:08 am Sagittarius
30th 8:23 pm Capricorn

October 1938
3rd 8:57 am Aquarius
5th 8:27 pm Pisces
8th 5:20 am Aries
10th 11:40 am Taurus
12th 4:09 pm Gemini
14th 7:31 pm Cancer
16th 10:20 pm Leo
19th 1:10 am Virgo
21st 4:46 am Libra
23rd 10:05 am Scorpio
25th 5:59 pm Sagittarius
28th 4:42 am Capricorn
30th 5:09 pm Aquarius

November 1938
2nd 5:09 am Pisces
4th 2:32 pm Aries
6th 8:40 pm Taurus
9th 0:03 am Gemini
11th 1:59 am Cancer
13th 3:52 am Leo
15th 6:40 am Virgo
17th 11:06 am Libra
19th 5:28 pm Scorpio
22nd 1:58 am Sagittarius
24th 12:42 pm Capricorn
27th 1:01 am Aquarius
29th 1:29 pm Pisces

December 1938
2nd 0:04 am Aries
4th 6:57 am Taurus
6th 10:15 am Gemini
8th 11:07 am Cancer
10th 11:20 am Leo
12th 12:42 pm Virgo
14th 4:31 pm Libra
16th 11:14 pm Scorpio
19th 8:34 am Sagittarius
21st 7:39 pm Capricorn
24th 7:60 am Aquarius
26th 8:42 pm Pisces
29th 8:10 am Aries
31st 4:44 pm Taurus

January 1939
2nd 9:18 pm Gemini
4th 10:19 pm Cancer
6th 9:33 pm Leo
8th 9:10 pm Virgo
10th 11:12 pm Libra
13th 4:57 am Scorpio
15th 2:13 pm Sagittarius
18th 1:45 am Capricorn
20th 2:16 pm Aquarius
23rd 2:51 am Pisces
25th 2:40 pm Aries
28th 0:30 am Taurus
30th 6:45 am Gemini

February 1939
1st 9:17 am Cancer
3rd 9:05 am Leo
5th 8:06 am Virgo
7th 8:35 am Libra
9th 12:28 pm Scorpio
11th 8:26 pm Sagittarius
14th 7:43 am Capricorn
16th 8:21 pm Aquarius
19th 8:51 am Pisces
21st 8:23 pm Aries
24th 6:17 am Taurus
26th 1:44 pm Gemini
28th 6:04 pm Cancer

March 1939
2nd 7:28 pm Leo
4th 7:17 pm Virgo
6th 7:29 pm Libra
8th 10:01 pm Scorpio
11th 4:26 am Sagittarius
13th 2:38 pm Capricorn
16th 3:00 am Aquarius
18th 3:29 pm Pisces
21st 2:38 am Aries
23rd 11:55 am Taurus
25th 7:13 pm Gemini
28th 0:19 am Cancer
30th 3:14 am Leo

April 1939
1st 4:39 am Virgo
3rd 5:50 am Libra
5th 8:26 am Scorpio
7th 1:52 pm Sagittarius
9th 10:46 pm Capricorn
12th 10:33 am Aquarius
14th 11:04 pm Pisces
17th 10:10 am Aries
19th 6:53 pm Taurus
22nd 1:14 am Gemini
24th 5:41 am Cancer
26th 8:52 am Leo
28th 11:26 am Virgo
30th 2:03 pm Libra

May 1939
2nd 5:39 pm Scorpio
4th 11:11 pm Sagittarius
7th 7:37 am Capricorn
9th 6:42 pm Aquarius
12th 7:08 am Pisces
14th 6:38 pm Aries
17th 3:26 am Taurus
19th 9:02 am Gemini
21st 12:19 pm Cancer
23rd 2:33 pm Leo
25th 4:51 pm Virgo
27th 8:06 pm Libra
30th 0:47 am Scorpio

June 1939
1st 7:18 am Sagittarius
3rd 3:52 pm Capricorn
6th 2:42 am Aquarius
8th 3:05 pm Pisces
11th 3:10 am Aries
13th 12:37 pm Taurus
15th 6:28 pm Gemini
17th 9:04 pm Cancer
19th 9:57 pm Leo
21st 10:56 pm Virgo
24th 1:30 am Libra
26th 6:28 am Scorpio
28th 1:41 pm Sagittarius
30th 10:54 pm Capricorn

July 1939
3rd 9:56 am Aquarius
5th 10:17 pm Pisces
8th 10:47 am Aries
10th 9:25 pm Taurus
13th 4:17 am Gemini
15th 7:12 am Cancer
17th 7:30 am Leo
19th 7:10 am Virgo
21st 8:14 am Libra
23rd 12:08 pm Scorpio
25th 7:12 pm Sagittarius
28th 4:52 am Capricorn
30th 4:16 pm Aquarius

August 1939
2nd 4:42 am Pisces
4th 5:21 pm Aries
7th 4:45 am Taurus
9th 1:01 pm Gemini
11th 5:17 pm Cancer
13th 6:07 pm Leo
15th 5:20 pm Virgo
17th 5:08 pm Libra
19th 7:24 pm Scorpio
22nd 1:15 am Sagittarius
24th 10:36 am Capricorn
26th 10:10 pm Aquarius
29th 10:43 am Pisces
31st 11:16 pm Aries

September 1939
3rd 10:45 am Taurus
5th 8:00 pm Gemini
8th 1:51 am Cancer
10th 4:11 am Leo
12th 4:09 am Virgo
14th 3:42 am Libra
16th 4:47 am Scorpio
18th 9:08 am Sagittarius
20th 5:15 pm Capricorn
23rd 4:24 am Aquarius
25th 4:59 pm Pisces
28th 5:21 am Aries
30th 4:27 pm Taurus

October 1939
3rd 1:38 am Gemini
5th 8:14 am Cancer
7th 12:07 pm Leo
9th 1:44 pm Virgo
11th 2:18 pm Libra
13th 3:22 pm Scorpio
15th 6:40 pm Sagittarius
18th 1:24 am Capricorn
20th 11:44 am Aquarius
23rd 0:06 am Pisces
25th 12:27 pm Aries
27th 11:10 pm Taurus
30th 7:28 am Gemini

November 1939
1st 1:39 pm Cancer
3rd 5:60 pm Leo
5th 8:56 pm Virgo
7th 11:03 pm Libra
10th 1:15 am Scorpio
12th 4:46 am Sagittarius
14th 10:48 am Capricorn
16th 8:04 pm Aquarius
19th 8:02 am Pisces
21st 8:35 pm Aries
24th 7:19 am Taurus
26th 3:05 pm Gemini
28th 8:10 pm Cancer
30th 11:34 pm Leo

December 1939
3rd 2:22 am Virgo
5th 5:23 am Libra
7th 8:60 am Scorpio
9th 1:35 pm Sagittarius
11th 7:54 pm Capricorn
14th 4:47 am Aquarius
16th 4:17 pm Pisces
19th 5:02 am Aries
21st 4:30 pm Taurus
24th 0:37 am Gemini
26th 5:02 am Cancer
28th 7:05 am Leo
30th 8:30 am Virgo

January 1940
1st 10:47 am Libra
3rd 2:40 pm Scorpio
5th 8:14 pm Sagittarius
8th 3:31 am Capricorn
10th 12:46 pm Aquarius
13th 0:04 am Pisces
15th 12:56 pm Aries
18th 1:16 am Taurus
20th 10:27 am Gemini
22nd 3:30 pm Cancer
24th 5:09 pm Leo
26th 5:14 pm Virgo
28th 5:46 pm Libra
30th 8:20 pm Scorpio

February 1940
2nd 1:37 am Sagittarius
4th 9:30 am Capricorn
6th 7:23 pm Aquarius
9th 7:01 am Pisces
11th 7:49 pm Aries
14th 8:33 am Taurus
16th 7:08 pm Gemini
19th 1:47 am Cancer
21st 4:17 am Leo
23rd 4:12 am Virgo
25th 3:31 am Libra
27th 4:17 am Scorpio
29th 7:59 am Sagittarius

March 1940
2nd 3:07 pm Capricorn
5th 1:07 am Aquarius
7th 1:08 pm Pisces
10th 1:60 am Aries
12th 2:44 pm Taurus
15th 1:53 am Gemini
17th 9:53 am Cancer
19th 2:11 pm Leo
21st 3:18 pm Virgo
23rd 2:49 pm Libra
25th 2:38 pm Scorpio
27th 4:36 pm Sagittarius
29th 10:02 pm Capricorn

April 1940
1st 7:15 am Aquarius
3rd 7:11 pm Pisces
6th 8:09 am Aries
8th 8:38 pm Taurus
11th 7:29 am Gemini
13th 4:01 pm Cancer
15th 9:43 pm Leo
18th 0:34 am Virgo
20th 1:23 am Libra
22nd 1:34 am Scorpio
24th 2:50 am Sagittarius
26th 6:54 am Capricorn
28th 2:44 pm Aquarius

May 1940
1st 1:55 am Pisces
3rd 2:51 pm Aries
6th 3:11 am Taurus
8th 1:29 pm Gemini
10th 9:31 pm Cancer
13th 3:20 am Leo
15th 7:15 am Virgo
17th 9:39 am Libra
19th 11:12 am Scorpio
21st 1:03 pm Sagittarius
23rd 4:39 pm Capricorn
25th 11:21 pm Aquarius
28th 9:42 am Pisces
30th 10:18 pm Aries

June 1940
2nd 10:41 am Taurus
4th 8:46 pm Gemini
7th 3:59 am Cancer
9th 8:58 am Leo
11th 12:38 pm Virgo
13th 3:41 pm Libra
15th 6:31 pm Scorpio
17th 9:33 pm Sagittarius
20th 1:45 am Capricorn
22nd 8:19 am Aquarius
24th 5:59 pm Pisces
27th 6:14 am Aries
29th 6:51 pm Taurus

July 1940
2nd 5:11 am Gemini
4th 12:05 pm Cancer
6th 4:09 pm Leo
8th 6:43 pm Virgo
10th 9:07 pm Libra
13th 0:07 am Scorpio
15th 4:06 am Sagittarius
17th 9:19 am Capricorn
19th 4:24 pm Aquarius
22nd 1:59 am Pisces
24th 2:02 pm Aries
27th 2:54 am Taurus
29th 1:59 pm Gemini
31st 9:30 pm Cancer

August 1940
3rd 1:20 am Leo
5th 2:50 am Virgo
7th 3:51 am Libra
9th 5:48 am Scorpio
11th 9:32 am Sagittarius
13th 3:17 pm Capricorn
15th 11:07 pm Aquarius
18th 9:12 am Pisces
20th 9:14 pm Aries
23rd 10:15 am Taurus
25th 10:12 pm Gemini
28th 6:49 am Cancer
30th 11:25 am Leo

September 1940
1st 12:54 pm Virgo
3rd 12:55 pm Libra
5th 1:20 pm Scorpio
7th 3:41 pm Sagittarius
9th 8:47 pm Capricorn
12th 4:53 am Aquarius
14th 3:27 pm Pisces
17th 3:43 am Aries
19th 4:45 pm Taurus
22nd 5:03 am Gemini
24th 2:54 pm Cancer
26th 9:07 pm Leo
28th 11:42 pm Virgo
30th 11:47 pm Libra

October 1940
2nd 11:12 pm Scorpio
4th 11:53 pm Sagittarius
7th 3:31 am Capricorn
9th 10:48 am Aquarius
11th 9:18 pm Pisces
14th 9:50 am Aries
16th 10:49 pm Taurus
19th 10:57 am Gemini
21st 9:17 pm Cancer
24th 4:47 am Leo
26th 9:06 am Virgo
28th 10:35 am Libra
30th 10:26 am Scorpio

November 1940
1st 10:26 am Sagittarius
3rd 12:29 pm Capricorn
5th 6:08 pm Aquarius
8th 3:49 am Pisces
10th 4:14 pm Aries
13th 5:12 am Taurus
15th 4:58 pm Gemini
18th 2:51 am Cancer
20th 10:35 am Leo
22nd 4:07 pm Virgo
24th 7:22 pm Libra
26th 8:45 pm Scorpio
28th 9:20 pm Sagittarius
30th 10:52 pm Capricorn

December 1940
3rd 3:16 am Aquarius
5th 11:41 am Pisces
7th 11:28 pm Aries
10th 12:26 pm Taurus
13th 0:08 am Gemini
15th 9:17 am Cancer
17th 4:14 pm Leo
19th 9:34 pm Virgo
22nd 1:36 am Libra
24th 4:30 am Scorpio
26th 6:37 am Sagittarius
28th 9:02 am Capricorn
30th 1:15 pm Aquarius

January 1941
1st 8:38 pm Pisces
4th 7:38 am Aries
6th 8:29 pm Taurus
9th 8:25 am Gemini
11th 5:31 pm Cancer
13th 11:40 pm Leo
16th 3:46 am Virgo
18th 7:00 am Libra
20th 10:05 am Scorpio
22nd 1:18 pm Sagittarius
24th 5:03 pm Capricorn
26th 10:07 pm Aquarius
29th 5:38 am Pisces
31st 4:05 pm Aries

February 1941
3rd 4:41 am Taurus
5th 5:08 pm Gemini
8th 2:55 am Cancer
10th 9:05 am Leo
12th 12:20 pm Virgo
14th 2:08 pm Libra
16th 3:54 pm Scorpio
18th 6:39 pm Sagittarius
20th 10:55 pm Capricorn
23rd 5:03 am Aquarius
25th 1:21 pm Pisces
27th 11:54 pm Aries

March 1941
2nd 12:24 pm Taurus
5th 1:12 am Gemini
7th 11:59 am Cancer
9th 7:17 pm Leo
11th 10:52 pm Virgo
13th 11:52 pm Libra
16th 0:03 am Scorpio
18th 1:09 am Sagittarius
20th 4:27 am Capricorn
22nd 10:36 am Aquarius
24th 7:32 pm Pisces
27th 6:41 am Aries
29th 7:14 pm Taurus

April 1941
1st 8:05 am Gemini
3rd 7:42 pm Cancer
6th 4:23 am Leo
8th 9:17 am Virgo
10th 10:52 am Libra
12th 10:32 am Scorpio
14th 10:12 am Sagittarius
16th 11:45 am Capricorn
18th 4:36 pm Aquarius
21st 1:07 am Pisces
23rd 12:36 pm Aries
26th 1:21 am Taurus
28th 2:09 pm Gemini

May 1941
1st 1:55 am Cancer
3rd 11:29 am Leo
5th 6:02 pm Virgo
7th 9:10 pm Libra
9th 9:33 pm Scorpio
11th 8:51 pm Sagittarius
13th 9:07 pm Capricorn
16th 0:16 am Aquarius
18th 7:39 am Pisces
20th 6:36 pm Aries
23rd 7:25 am Taurus
25th 8:09 pm Gemini
28th 7:34 am Cancer
30th 5:13 pm Leo

June 1941
2nd 0:37 am Virgo
4th 5:14 am Libra
6th 7:10 am Scorpio
8th 7:23 am Sagittarius
10th 7:36 am Capricorn
12th 9:47 am Aquarius
14th 3:40 pm Pisces
17th 1:32 am Aries
19th 2:04 pm Taurus
22nd 2:43 am Gemini
24th 1:48 pm Cancer
26th 10:54 pm Leo
29th 6:00 am Virgo

July 1941
1st 11:13 am Libra
3rd 2:30 pm Scorpio
5th 4:11 pm Sagittarius
7th 5:22 pm Capricorn
9th 7:38 pm Aquarius
12th 0:43 am Pisces
14th 9:38 am Aries
16th 9:31 pm Taurus
19th 10:08 am Gemini
21st 9:13 pm Cancer
24th 5:45 am Leo
26th 12:00 pm Virgo
28th 4:39 pm Libra
30th 8:08 pm Scorpio

August 1941
1st 10:49 pm Sagittarius
4th 1:16 am Capricorn
6th 4:34 am Aquarius
8th 9:55 am Pisces
10th 6:14 pm Aries
13th 5:33 am Taurus
15th 6:09 pm Gemini
18th 5:34 am Cancer
20th 2:11 pm Leo
22nd 7:51 pm Virgo
24th 11:21 pm Libra
27th 1:49 am Scorpio
29th 4:14 am Sagittarius
31st 7:20 am Capricorn

September 1941
2nd 11:40 am Aquarius
4th 5:54 pm Pisces
7th 2:28 am Aries
9th 1:33 pm Taurus
12th 2:05 am Gemini
14th 2:06 pm Cancer
16th 11:36 pm Leo
19th 5:26 am Virgo
21st 8:14 am Libra
23rd 9:23 am Scorpio
25th 10:27 am Sagittarius
27th 12:48 pm Capricorn
29th 5:19 pm Aquarius

October 1941
2nd 0:17 am Pisces
4th 9:39 am Aries
6th 8:51 pm Taurus
9th 9:22 am Gemini
11th 9:52 pm Cancer
14th 8:25 am Leo
16th 3:31 pm Virgo
18th 6:51 pm Libra
20th 7:24 pm Scorpio
22nd 7:02 pm Sagittarius
24th 7:43 pm Capricorn
26th 11:02 pm Aquarius
29th 5:54 am Pisces
31st 3:40 pm Aries

November 1941
3rd 3:19 am Taurus
5th 3:52 pm Gemini
8th 4:24 am Cancer
10th 3:45 pm Leo
13th 0:29 am Virgo
15th 5:18 am Libra
17th 6:38 am Scorpio
19th 5:54 am Sagittarius
21st 5:15 am Capricorn
23rd 6:52 am Aquarius
25th 12:16 pm Pisces
27th 9:28 pm Aries
30th 9:19 am Taurus

December 1941
2nd 9:59 pm Gemini
5th 10:20 am Cancer
7th 9:41 pm Leo
10th 7:08 am Virgo
12th 1:41 pm Libra
14th 4:47 pm Scorpio
16th 5:08 pm Sagittarius
18th 4:30 pm Capricorn
20th 4:59 pm Aquarius
22nd 8:37 pm Pisces
25th 4:28 am Aries
27th 3:46 pm Taurus
30th 4:27 am Gemini

January 1942
1st 4:40 pm Cancer
4th 3:32 am Leo
6th 12:39 pm Virgo
8th 7:47 pm Libra
11th 0:24 am Scorpio
13th 2:30 am Sagittarius
15th 3:07 am Capricorn
17th 3:54 am Aquarius
19th 6:48 am Pisces
21st 1:14 pm Aries
23rd 11:21 pm Taurus
26th 11:45 am Gemini
29th 0:04 am Cancer
31st 10:35 am Leo

February 1942
2nd 6:56 pm Virgo
5th 1:18 am Libra
7th 5:55 am Scorpio
9th 9:06 am Sagittarius
11th 11:18 am Capricorn
13th 1:30 pm Aquarius
15th 4:55 pm Pisces
17th 10:47 pm Aries
20th 8:01 am Taurus
22nd 7:48 pm Gemini
25th 8:15 am Cancer
27th 7:05 pm Leo

March 1942
2nd 3:06 am Virgo
4th 8:21 am Libra
6th 11:49 am Scorpio
8th 2:29 pm Sagittarius
10th 5:10 pm Capricorn
12th 8:32 pm Aquarius
15th 1:10 am Pisces
17th 7:44 am Aries
19th 4:41 pm Taurus
22nd 4:02 am Gemini
24th 4:32 pm Cancer
27th 4:03 am Leo
29th 12:33 pm Virgo
31st 5:34 pm Libra

April 1942
2nd 7:55 pm Scorpio
4th 9:05 pm Sagittarius
6th 10:43 pm Capricorn
9th 1:58 am Aquarius
11th 7:21 am Pisces
13th 2:51 pm Aries
16th 0:18 am Taurus
18th 11:39 am Gemini
21st 0:10 am Cancer
23rd 12:19 pm Leo
25th 10:01 pm Virgo
28th 3:49 am Libra
30th 5:58 am Scorpio

May 1942
2nd 6:04 am Sagittarius
4th 6:09 am Capricorn
6th 8:01 am Aquarius
8th 12:48 pm Pisces
10th 8:32 pm Aries
13th 6:38 am Taurus
15th 6:16 pm Gemini
18th 6:49 am Cancer
20th 7:19 pm Leo
23rd 6:04 am Virgo
25th 1:15 pm Libra
27th 4:26 pm Scorpio
29th 4:38 pm Sagittarius
31st 3:47 pm Capricorn

June 1942
2nd 4:05 pm Aquarius
4th 7:18 pm Pisces
7th 2:14 am Aries
9th 12:18 pm Taurus
12th 0:12 am Gemini
14th 12:49 pm Cancer
17th 1:18 am Leo
19th 12:29 pm Virgo
21st 9:01 pm Libra
24th 1:49 am Scorpio
26th 3:06 am Sagittarius
28th 2:30 am Capricorn
30th 2:02 am Aquarius

July 1942
2nd 3:49 am Pisces
4th 9:16 am Aries
6th 6:25 pm Taurus
9th 6:12 am Gemini
11th 6:51 pm Cancer
14th 7:07 am Leo
16th 6:06 pm Virgo
19th 2:60 am Libra
21st 8:56 am Scorpio
23rd 11:53 am Sagittarius
25th 12:36 pm Capricorn
27th 12:39 pm Aquarius
29th 1:53 pm Pisces
31st 5:60 pm Aries

August 1942
3rd 1:49 am Taurus
5th 12:56 pm Gemini
8th 1:31 am Cancer
10th 1:37 pm Leo
13th 0:09 am Virgo
15th 8:29 am Libra
17th 2:35 pm Scorpio
19th 6:32 pm Sagittarius
21st 8:44 pm Capricorn
23rd 10:07 pm Aquarius
25th 11:55 pm Pisces
28th 3:40 am Aries
30th 10:33 am Taurus

September 1942
1st 8:41 pm Gemini
4th 9:00 am Cancer
6th 9:14 pm Leo
9th 7:28 am Virgo
11th 3:01 pm Libra
13th 8:18 pm Scorpio
15th 11:58 pm Sagittarius
18th 2:47 am Capricorn
20th 5:27 am Aquarius
22nd 8:35 am Pisces
24th 12:59 pm Aries
26th 7:35 pm Taurus
29th 5:06 am Gemini

October 1942
1st 5:04 pm Cancer
4th 5:33 am Leo
6th 4:10 pm Virgo
8th 11:33 pm Libra
11th 3:45 am Scorpio
13th 6:10 am Sagittarius
15th 8:13 am Capricorn
17th 11:03 am Aquarius
19th 3:06 pm Pisces
21st 8:36 pm Aries
24th 3:52 am Taurus
26th 1:20 pm Gemini
29th 0:59 am Cancer
31st 1:46 pm Leo

November 1942
3rd 1:18 am Virgo
5th 9:16 am Libra
7th 1:22 pm Scorpio
9th 2:45 pm Sagittarius
11th 3:19 pm Capricorn
13th 4:51 pm Aquarius
15th 8:30 pm Pisces
18th 2:32 am Aries
20th 10:39 am Taurus
22nd 8:35 pm Gemini
25th 8:17 am Cancer
27th 9:09 pm Leo
30th 9:25 am Virgo

December 1942
2nd 6:51 pm Libra
5th 0:07 am Scorpio
7th 1:32 am Sagittarius
9th 1:08 am Capricorn
11th 0:57 am Aquarius
13th 2:59 am Pisces
15th 8:09 am Aries
17th 4:20 pm Taurus
20th 2:47 am Gemini
22nd 2:47 pm Cancer
25th 3:35 am Leo
27th 4:07 pm Virgo
30th 2:41 am Libra

January 1943
1st 9:32 am Scorpio
3rd 12:28 pm Sagittarius
5th 12:33 pm Capricorn
7th 11:45 am Aquarius
9th 12:09 pm Pisces
11th 3:27 pm Aries
13th 10:24 pm Taurus
16th 8:42 am Gemini
18th 8:54 pm Cancer
21st 9:43 am Leo
23rd 10:02 pm Virgo
26th 8:44 am Libra
28th 4:46 pm Scorpio
30th 9:32 pm Sagittarius

February 1943
1st 11:14 pm Capricorn
3rd 11:11 pm Aquarius
5th 11:09 pm Pisces
8th 1:01 am Aries
10th 6:22 am Taurus
12th 3:29 pm Gemini
15th 3:25 am Cancer
17th 4:18 pm Leo
20th 4:19 am Virgo
22nd 2:28 pm Libra
24th 10:24 pm Scorpio
27th 3:58 am Sagittarius

March 1943
1st 7:17 am Capricorn
3rd 8:56 am Aquarius
5th 9:56 am Pisces
7th 11:46 am Aries
9th 3:58 pm Taurus
11th 11:39 pm Gemini
14th 10:53 am Cancer
16th 11:42 pm Leo
19th 11:41 am Virgo
21st 9:21 pm Libra
24th 4:23 am Scorpio
26th 9:22 am Sagittarius
28th 1:04 pm Capricorn
30th 3:57 pm Aquarius

April 1943
1st 6:28 pm Pisces
3rd 9:18 pm Aries
6th 1:39 am Taurus
8th 8:46 am Gemini
10th 7:04 pm Cancer
13th 7:39 am Leo
15th 7:59 pm Virgo
18th 5:19 am Libra
20th 12:01 pm Scorpio
22nd 3:55 pm Sagittarius
24th 6:40 pm Capricorn
26th 9:22 pm Aquarius
29th 0:36 am Pisces

May 1943
1st 4:40 am Aries
3rd 9:60 am Taurus
5th 5:18 pm Gemini
8th 3:19 am Cancer
10th 3:40 pm Leo
13th 4:20 am Virgo
15th 2:40 pm Libra
17th 9:18 pm Scorpio
20th 0:33 am Sagittarius
22nd 2:01 am Capricorn
24th 3:25 am Aquarius
26th 6:01 am Pisces
28th 10:20 am Aries
30th 4:26 pm Taurus

June 1943
2nd 0:31 am Gemini
4th 10:48 am Cancer
6th 11:03 pm Leo
9th 12:01 pm Virgo
11th 11:21 pm Libra
14th 6:54 am Scorpio
16th 10:32 am Sagittarius
18th 11:29 am Capricorn
20th 11:36 am Aquarius
22nd 12:42 pm Pisces
24th 3:58 pm Aries
26th 9:54 pm Taurus
29th 6:30 am Gemini

July 1943
1st 5:15 pm Cancer
4th 5:40 am Leo
6th 6:43 pm Virgo
9th 6:41 am Libra
11th 3:34 pm Scorpio
13th 8:34 pm Sagittarius
15th 10:05 pm Capricorn
17th 9:46 pm Aquarius
19th 9:32 pm Pisces
21st 11:10 pm Aries
24th 3:56 am Taurus
26th 12:08 pm Gemini
28th 11:04 pm Cancer
31st 11:44 am Leo

August 1943
3rd 0:44 am Virgo
5th 12:48 pm Libra
7th 10:39 pm Scorpio
10th 5:04 am Sagittarius
12th 8:05 am Capricorn
14th 8:34 am Aquarius
16th 8:07 am Pisces
18th 8:36 am Aries
20th 11:46 am Taurus
22nd 6:38 pm Gemini
25th 5:09 am Cancer
27th 5:49 pm Leo
30th 6:47 am Virgo

September 1943
1st 6:31 pm Libra
4th 4:19 am Scorpio
6th 11:34 am Sagittarius
8th 4:09 pm Capricorn
10th 6:15 pm Aquarius
12th 6:45 pm Pisces
14th 7:09 pm Aries
16th 9:15 pm Taurus
19th 2:43 am Gemini
21st 12:13 pm Cancer
24th 0:33 am Leo
26th 1:29 pm Virgo
29th 0:56 am Libra

October 1943
1st 10:02 am Scorpio
3rd 5:01 pm Sagittarius
5th 10:10 pm Capricorn
8th 1:39 am Aquarius
10th 3:43 am Pisces
12th 5:12 am Aries
14th 7:27 am Taurus
16th 12:11 pm Gemini
18th 8:29 pm Cancer
21st 8:13 am Leo
23rd 9:08 pm Virgo
26th 8:33 am Libra
28th 5:11 pm Scorpio
30th 11:14 pm Sagittarius

November 1943
2nd 3:36 am Capricorn
4th 7:09 am Aquarius
6th 10:15 am Pisces
8th 1:11 pm Aries
10th 4:33 pm Taurus
12th 9:31 pm Gemini
15th 5:24 am Cancer
17th 4:28 pm Leo
20th 5:20 am Virgo
22nd 5:15 pm Libra
25th 2:07 am Scorpio
27th 7:31 am Sagittarius
29th 10:41 am Capricorn

December 1943
1st 1:01 pm Aquarius
3rd 3:36 pm Pisces
5th 7:01 pm Aries
7th 11:30 pm Taurus
10th 5:34 am Gemini
12th 1:49 pm Cancer
15th 0:36 am Leo
17th 1:20 pm Virgo
20th 1:54 am Libra
22nd 11:39 am Scorpio
24th 5:39 pm Sagittarius
26th 8:22 pm Capricorn
28th 9:21 pm Aquarius
30th 10:17 pm Pisces

January 1944
2nd 0:35 am Aries
4th 5:02 am Taurus
6th 11:48 am Gemini
8th 8:49 pm Cancer
11th 7:59 am Leo
13th 8:39 pm Virgo
16th 9:26 am Libra
18th 8:24 pm Scorpio
21st 3:49 am Sagittarius
23rd 7:22 am Capricorn
25th 8:07 am Aquarius
27th 7:49 am Pisces
29th 8:18 am Aries
31st 11:13 am Taurus

February 1944
2nd 5:22 pm Gemini
5th 2:42 am Cancer
7th 2:22 pm Leo
10th 3:07 am Virgo
12th 3:53 pm Libra
15th 3:21 am Scorpio
17th 12:08 pm Sagittarius
19th 5:28 pm Capricorn
21st 7:23 pm Aquarius
23rd 7:07 pm Pisces
25th 6:33 pm Aries
27th 7:40 pm Taurus

March 1944
1st 0:06 am Gemini
3rd 8:42 am Cancer
5th 8:20 pm Leo
8th 9:19 am Virgo
10th 9:55 pm Libra
13th 9:10 am Scorpio
15th 6:29 pm Sagittarius
18th 1:12 am Capricorn
20th 4:53 am Aquarius
22nd 5:56 am Pisces
24th 5:42 am Aries
26th 6:04 am Taurus
28th 9:04 am Gemini
30th 4:04 pm Cancer

April 1944
2nd 2:56 am Leo
4th 3:49 pm Virgo
7th 4:22 am Libra
9th 3:10 pm Scorpio
12th 0:04 am Sagittarius
14th 6:54 am Capricorn
16th 11:44 am Aquarius
18th 2:26 pm Pisces
20th 3:35 pm Aries
22nd 4:31 pm Taurus
24th 7:03 pm Gemini
27th 0:49 am Cancer
29th 10:40 am Leo

May 1944
1st 11:05 pm Virgo
4th 11:38 am Libra
6th 10:18 pm Scorpio
9th 6:26 am Sagittarius
11th 12:32 pm Capricorn
13th 5:08 pm Aquarius
15th 8:34 pm Pisces
17th 11:03 pm Aries
20th 1:16 am Taurus
22nd 4:30 am Gemini
24th 10:09 am Cancer
26th 7:07 pm Leo
29th 6:59 am Virgo
31st 7:37 pm Libra

June 1944
3rd 6:29 am Scorpio
5th 2:25 pm Sagittarius
7th 7:41 pm Capricorn
9th 11:12 pm Aquarius
12th 1:60 am Pisces
14th 4:42 am Aries
16th 7:54 am Taurus
18th 12:14 pm Gemini
20th 6:32 pm Cancer
23rd 3:27 am Leo
25th 2:59 pm Virgo
28th 3:39 am Libra
30th 3:07 pm Scorpio

July 1944
2nd 11:38 pm Sagittarius
5th 4:40 am Capricorn
7th 7:13 am Aquarius
9th 8:40 am Pisces
11th 10:22 am Aries
13th 1:21 pm Taurus
15th 6:14 pm Gemini
18th 1:23 am Cancer
20th 10:55 am Leo
22nd 10:24 pm Virgo
25th 11:06 am Libra
27th 11:16 pm Scorpio
30th 8:44 am Sagittarius

August 1944
1st 2:37 pm Capricorn
3rd 5:07 pm Aquarius
5th 5:34 pm Pisces
7th 5:45 pm Aries
9th 7:23 pm Taurus
11th 11:39 pm Gemini
14th 7:07 am Cancer
16th 5:11 pm Leo
19th 5:03 am Virgo
21st 5:45 pm Libra
24th 6:11 am Scorpio
26th 4:47 pm Sagittarius
29th 0:12 am Capricorn
31st 3:42 am Aquarius

September 1944
2nd 4:13 am Pisces
4th 3:27 am Aries
6th 3:30 am Taurus
8th 6:18 am Gemini
10th 12:52 pm Cancer
12th 10:51 pm Leo
15th 11:01 am Virgo
17th 11:48 pm Libra
20th 12:11 pm Scorpio
22nd 11:17 pm Sagittarius
25th 7:51 am Capricorn
27th 1:04 pm Aquarius
29th 2:53 pm Pisces

October 1944
1st 2:28 pm Aries
3rd 1:49 pm Taurus
5th 3:05 pm Gemini
7th 7:58 pm Cancer
10th 5:04 am Leo
12th 5:05 pm Virgo
15th 5:53 am Libra
17th 6:02 pm Scorpio
20th 4:49 am Sagittarius
22nd 1:45 pm Capricorn
24th 8:17 pm Aquarius
26th 11:53 pm Pisces
29th 0:53 am Aries
31st 0:45 am Taurus

November 1944
2nd 1:29 am Gemini
4th 5:07 am Cancer
6th 12:48 pm Leo
8th 11:58 pm Virgo
11th 12:42 pm Libra
14th 0:47 am Scorpio
16th 10:60 am Sagittarius
18th 7:18 pm Capricorn
21st 1:46 am Aquarius
23rd 6:16 am Pisces
25th 8:54 am Aries
27th 10:22 am Taurus
29th 11:57 am Gemini

December 1944
1st 3:21 pm Cancer
3rd 9:53 pm Leo
6th 8:06 am Virgo
8th 8:28 pm Libra
11th 8:40 am Scorpio
13th 6:48 pm Sagittarius
16th 2:20 am Capricorn
18th 7:41 am Aquarius
20th 11:38 am Pisces
22nd 2:42 pm Aries
24th 5:25 pm Taurus
26th 8:26 pm Gemini
29th 0:43 am Cancer
31st 7:22 am Leo

January 1945
2nd 4:50 pm Virgo
5th 4:43 am Libra
7th 5:09 pm Scorpio
10th 3:51 am Sagittarius
12th 11:22 am Capricorn
14th 3:53 pm Aquarius
16th 6:26 pm Pisces
18th 8:22 pm Aries
20th 10:49 pm Taurus
23rd 2:37 am Gemini
25th 8:08 am Cancer
27th 3:35 pm Leo
30th 1:09 am Virgo

February 1945
1st 12:46 pm Libra
4th 1:20 am Scorpio
6th 12:53 pm Sagittarius
8th 9:27 pm Capricorn
11th 2:09 am Aquarius
13th 3:51 am Pisces
15th 4:13 am Aries
17th 5:07 am Taurus
19th 8:05 am Gemini
21st 1:46 pm Cancer
23rd 10:00 pm Leo
26th 8:15 am Virgo
28th 7:57 pm Libra

March 1945
3rd 8:32 am Scorpio
5th 8:43 pm Sagittarius
8th 6:32 am Capricorn
10th 12:34 pm Aquarius
12th 2:44 pm Pisces
14th 2:30 pm Aries
16th 1:57 pm Taurus
18th 3:09 pm Gemini
20th 7:35 pm Cancer
23rd 3:34 am Leo
25th 2:13 pm Virgo
28th 2:15 am Libra
30th 2:51 pm Scorpio

April 1945
2nd 3:07 am Sagittarius
4th 1:48 pm Capricorn
6th 9:28 pm Aquarius
9th 1:10 am Pisces
11th 1:37 am Aries
13th 0:39 am Taurus
15th 0:31 am Gemini
17th 3:16 am Cancer
19th 9:56 am Leo
21st 8:05 pm Virgo
24th 8:16 am Libra
26th 8:52 pm Scorpio
29th 8:55 am Sagittarius

May 1945
1st 7:39 pm Capricorn
4th 4:03 am Aquarius
6th 9:16 am Pisces
8th 11:21 am Aries
10th 11:24 am Taurus
12th 11:16 am Gemini
14th 12:57 pm Cancer
16th 6:01 pm Leo
19th 2:57 am Virgo
21st 2:43 pm Libra
24th 3:21 am Scorpio
26th 3:09 pm Sagittarius
29th 1:23 am Capricorn
31st 9:32 am Aquarius

June 1945
2nd 3:22 pm Pisces
4th 6:48 pm Aries
6th 8:22 pm Taurus
8th 9:15 pm Gemini
10th 11:03 pm Cancer
13th 3:22 am Leo
15th 11:12 am Virgo
17th 10:06 pm Libra
20th 10:35 am Scorpio
22nd 10:27 pm Sagittarius
25th 8:13 am Capricorn
27th 3:34 pm Aquarius
29th 8:51 pm Pisces

July 1945
2nd 0:30 am Aries
4th 3:04 am Taurus
6th 5:21 am Gemini
8th 8:14 am Cancer
10th 12:48 pm Leo
12th 8:01 pm Virgo
15th 6:14 am Libra
17th 6:29 pm Scorpio
20th 6:33 am Sagittarius
22nd 4:25 pm Capricorn
24th 11:17 pm Aquarius
27th 3:26 am Pisces
29th 6:09 am Aries
31st 8:31 am Taurus

August 1945
2nd 11:27 am Gemini
4th 3:26 pm Cancer
6th 8:54 pm Leo
9th 4:26 am Virgo
11th 2:24 pm Libra
14th 2:24 am Scorpio
16th 2:54 pm Sagittarius
19th 1:30 am Capricorn
21st 8:26 am Aquarius
23rd 12:02 pm Pisces
25th 1:30 pm Aries
27th 2:36 pm Taurus
29th 4:50 pm Gemini
31st 9:02 pm Cancer

September 1945
3rd 3:22 am Leo
5th 11:40 am Virgo
7th 9:51 pm Libra
10th 9:49 am Scorpio
12th 10:37 pm Sagittarius
15th 10:07 am Capricorn
17th 6:15 pm Aquarius
19th 10:17 pm Pisces
21st 11:10 pm Aries
23rd 10:53 pm Taurus
25th 11:31 pm Gemini
28th 2:40 am Cancer
30th 8:50 am Leo

October 1945
2nd 5:35 pm Virgo
5th 4:19 am Libra
7th 4:26 pm Scorpio
10th 5:18 am Sagittarius
12th 5:31 pm Capricorn
15th 3:05 am Aquarius
17th 8:27 am Pisces
19th 10:05 am Aries
21st 9:30 am Taurus
23rd 8:53 am Gemini
25th 10:15 am Cancer
27th 2:60 pm Leo
29th 11:12 pm Virgo

November 1945
1st 10:08 am Libra
3rd 10:29 pm Scorpio
6th 11:18 am Sagittarius
8th 11:36 pm Capricorn
11th 9:55 am Aquarius
13th 5:01 pm Pisces
15th 8:21 pm Aries
17th 8:46 pm Taurus
19th 8:04 pm Gemini
21st 8:15 pm Cancer
23rd 11:11 pm Leo
26th 6:02 am Virgo
28th 4:20 pm Libra

December 1945
1st 4:42 am Scorpio
3rd 5:28 pm Sagittarius
6th 5:22 am Capricorn
8th 3:31 pm Aquarius
10th 11:20 pm Pisces
13th 4:12 am Aries
15th 6:27 am Taurus
17th 7:02 am Gemini
19th 7:30 am Cancer
21st 9:35 am Leo
23rd 2:49 pm Virgo
25th 11:45 pm Libra
28th 11:43 am Scorpio
31st 0:32 am Sagittarius

January 1946
2nd 12:07 pm Capricorn
4th 9:36 pm Aquarius
7th 4:45 am Pisces
9th 9:53 am Aries
11th 1:23 pm Taurus
13th 3:42 pm Gemini
15th 5:33 pm Cancer
17th 8:05 pm Leo
20th 0:40 am Virgo
22nd 8:35 am Libra
24th 7:40 pm Scorpio
27th 8:24 am Sagittarius
29th 8:15 pm Capricorn

February 1946
1st 5:20 am Aquarius
3rd 11:28 am Pisces
5th 3:37 pm Aries
7th 6:46 pm Taurus
9th 9:46 pm Gemini
12th 1:00 am Cancer
14th 4:51 am Leo
16th 10:06 am Virgo
18th 5:38 pm Libra
21st 4:04 am Scorpio
23rd 4:39 pm Sagittarius
26th 4:58 am Capricorn
28th 2:28 pm Aquarius

March 1946
2nd 8:22 pm Pisces
4th 11:23 pm Aries
7th 1:08 am Taurus
9th 3:13 am Gemini
11th 6:31 am Cancer
13th 11:16 am Leo
15th 5:33 pm Virgo
18th 1:42 am Libra
20th 12:07 pm Scorpio
23rd 0:31 am Sagittarius
25th 1:15 pm Capricorn
27th 11:50 pm Aquarius
30th 6:20 am Pisces

April 1946
1st 9:12 am Aries
3rd 9:55 am Taurus
5th 10:27 am Gemini
7th 12:25 pm Cancer
9th 4:40 pm Leo
11th 11:19 pm Virgo
14th 8:15 am Libra
16th 7:04 pm Scorpio
19th 7:32 am Sagittarius
21st 8:27 pm Capricorn
24th 7:53 am Aquarius
26th 3:49 pm Pisces
28th 7:42 pm Aries
30th 8:29 pm Taurus

May 1946
2nd 8:04 pm Gemini
4th 8:23 pm Cancer
6th 11:05 pm Leo
9th 4:60 am Virgo
11th 1:55 pm Libra
14th 1:08 am Scorpio
16th 1:47 pm Sagittarius
19th 2:41 am Capricorn
21st 2:29 pm Aquarius
23rd 11:39 pm Pisces
26th 5:01 am Aries
28th 7:01 am Taurus
30th 6:54 am Gemini

June 1946
1st 6:31 am Cancer
3rd 7:44 am Leo
5th 12:02 pm Virgo
7th 7:59 pm Libra
10th 7:06 am Scorpio
12th 7:52 pm Sagittarius
15th 8:38 am Capricorn
17th 8:14 pm Aquarius
20th 5:40 am Pisces
22nd 12:15 pm Aries
24th 3:52 pm Taurus
26th 5:06 pm Gemini
28th 5:12 pm Cancer
30th 5:51 pm Leo

July 1946
2nd 8:48 pm Virgo
5th 3:24 am Libra
7th 1:45 pm Scorpio
10th 2:20 am Sagittarius
12th 3:04 pm Capricorn
15th 2:17 am Aquarius
17th 11:13 am Pisces
19th 5:57 pm Aries
21st 10:35 pm Taurus
24th 1:19 am Gemini
26th 2:45 am Cancer
28th 3:59 am Leo
30th 6:37 am Virgo

August 1946
1st 12:11 pm Libra
3rd 9:24 pm Scorpio
6th 9:37 am Sagittarius
8th 10:23 pm Capricorn
11th 9:20 am Aquarius
13th 5:39 pm Pisces
15th 11:39 pm Aries
18th 3:59 am Taurus
20th 7:23 am Gemini
22nd 10:07 am Cancer
24th 12:41 pm Leo
26th 3:57 pm Virgo
28th 9:17 pm Libra
31st 5:52 am Scorpio

September 1946
2nd 5:32 pm Sagittarius
5th 6:22 am Capricorn
7th 5:38 pm Aquarius
10th 1:44 am Pisces
12th 6:47 am Aries
14th 10:03 am Taurus
16th 12:47 pm Gemini
18th 3:44 pm Cancer
20th 7:15 pm Leo
22nd 11:39 pm Virgo
25th 5:44 am Libra
27th 2:17 pm Scorpio
30th 1:33 am Sagittarius

October 1946
2nd 2:29 pm Capricorn
5th 2:27 am Aquarius
7th 11:03 am Pisces
9th 4:01 pm Aries
11th 6:19 pm Taurus
13th 7:37 pm Gemini
15th 9:23 pm Cancer
18th 0:35 am Leo
20th 5:38 am Virgo
22nd 12:36 pm Libra
24th 9:43 pm Scorpio
27th 9:06 am Sagittarius
29th 9:60 pm Capricorn

November 1946
1st 10:35 am Aquarius
3rd 8:31 pm Pisces
6th 2:27 am Aries
8th 4:48 am Taurus
10th 5:08 am Gemini
12th 5:18 am Cancer
14th 6:55 am Leo
16th 11:09 am Virgo
18th 6:15 pm Libra
21st 3:59 am Scorpio
23rd 3:46 pm Sagittarius
26th 4:39 am Capricorn
28th 5:29 pm Aquarius

December 1946
1st 4:28 am Pisces
3rd 11:59 am Aries
5th 3:44 pm Taurus
7th 4:27 pm Gemini
9th 3:51 pm Cancer
11th 3:50 pm Leo
13th 6:12 pm Virgo
16th 0:08 am Libra
18th 9:46 am Scorpio
20th 9:49 pm Sagittarius
23rd 10:49 am Capricorn
25th 11:30 pm Aquarius
28th 10:41 am Pisces
30th 7:29 pm Aries

January 1947
2nd 1:05 am Taurus
4th 3:24 am Gemini
6th 3:27 am Cancer
8th 2:53 am Leo
10th 3:47 am Virgo
12th 7:59 am Libra
14th 4:19 pm Scorpio
17th 4:04 am Sagittarius
19th 5:09 pm Capricorn
22nd 5:35 am Aquarius
24th 4:21 pm Pisces
27th 1:10 am Aries
29th 7:42 am Taurus
31st 11:48 am Gemini

February 1947
2nd 1:36 pm Cancer
4th 2:01 pm Leo
6th 2:45 pm Virgo
8th 5:43 pm Libra
11th 0:27 am Scorpio
13th 11:17 am Sagittarius
16th 0:10 am Capricorn
18th 12:35 pm Aquarius
20th 10:57 pm Pisces
23rd 6:55 am Aries
25th 1:05 pm Taurus
27th 5:45 pm Gemini

March 1947
1st 8:59 pm Cancer
3rd 11:00 pm Leo
6th 0:47 am Virgo
8th 3:54 am Libra
10th 9:55 am Scorpio
12th 7:34 pm Sagittarius
15th 7:59 am Capricorn
17th 8:34 pm Aquarius
20th 6:53 am Pisces
22nd 2:18 pm Aries
24th 7:27 pm Taurus
26th 11:15 pm Gemini
29th 2:26 am Cancer
31st 5:23 am Leo

April 1947
2nd 8:32 am Virgo
4th 12:42 pm Libra
6th 6:59 pm Scorpio
9th 4:14 am Sagittarius
11th 4:09 pm Capricorn
14th 4:50 am Aquarius
16th 3:43 pm Pisces
18th 11:24 pm Aries
21st 3:53 am Taurus
23rd 6:26 am Gemini
25th 8:22 am Cancer
27th 10:45 am Leo
29th 2:17 pm Virgo

May 1947
1st 7:24 pm Libra
4th 2:37 am Scorpio
6th 12:12 pm Sagittarius
8th 11:54 pm Capricorn
11th 12:39 pm Aquarius
14th 0:19 am Pisces
16th 8:51 am Aries
18th 1:46 pm Taurus
20th 3:49 pm Gemini
22nd 4:26 pm Cancer
24th 5:19 pm Leo
26th 7:52 pm Virgo
29th 0:53 am Libra
31st 8:45 am Scorpio

June 1947
2nd 6:55 pm Sagittarius
5th 6:52 am Capricorn
7th 7:38 pm Aquarius
10th 7:44 am Pisces
12th 5:30 pm Aries
14th 11:46 pm Taurus
17th 2:32 am Gemini
19th 2:32 am Cancer
21st 2:07 am Leo
23rd 3:03 am Virgo
25th 6:55 am Libra
27th 2:21 pm Scorpio
30th 0:46 am Sagittarius

July 1947
2nd 1:03 pm Capricorn
5th 1:49 am Aquarius
7th 2:01 pm Pisces
10th 0:34 am Aries
12th 8:08 am Taurus
14th 12:12 pm Gemini
16th 1:12 pm Cancer
18th 12:35 pm Leo
20th 12:24 pm Virgo
22nd 2:39 pm Libra
24th 8:44 pm Scorpio
27th 6:42 am Sagittarius
29th 7:02 pm Capricorn

August 1947
1st 7:49 am Aquarius
3rd 7:48 pm Pisces
6th 6:18 am Aries
8th 2:40 pm Taurus
10th 8:16 pm Gemini
12th 10:49 pm Cancer
14th 11:06 pm Leo
16th 10:50 pm Virgo
19th 0:05 am Libra
21st 4:48 am Scorpio
23rd 1:39 pm Sagittarius
26th 1:31 am Capricorn
28th 2:16 pm Aquarius
31st 2:03 am Pisces

September 1947
2nd 12:01 pm Aries
4th 8:09 pm Taurus
7th 2:19 am Gemini
9th 6:11 am Cancer
11th 8:02 am Leo
13th 8:53 am Virgo
15th 10:21 am Libra
17th 2:17 pm Scorpio
19th 9:51 pm Sagittarius
22nd 8:60 am Capricorn
24th 9:36 pm Aquarius
27th 9:22 am Pisces
29th 6:56 pm Aries

October 1947
2nd 2:15 am Taurus
4th 7:42 am Gemini
6th 11:46 am Cancer
8th 2:41 pm Leo
10th 4:58 pm Virgo
12th 7:33 pm Libra
14th 11:48 pm Scorpio
17th 6:57 am Sagittarius
19th 5:17 pm Capricorn
22nd 5:39 am Aquarius
24th 5:44 pm Pisces
27th 3:30 am Aries
29th 10:13 am Taurus
31st 2:34 pm Gemini

November 1947
2nd 5:32 pm Cancer
4th 8:04 pm Leo
6th 10:55 pm Virgo
9th 2:44 am Libra
11th 8:07 am Scorpio
13th 3:38 pm Sagittarius
16th 1:39 am Capricorn
18th 1:47 pm Aquarius
21st 2:17 am Pisces
23rd 12:50 pm Aries
25th 8:04 pm Taurus
27th 11:55 pm Gemini
30th 1:31 am Cancer

December 1947
2nd 2:32 am Leo
4th 4:26 am Virgo
6th 8:17 am Libra
8th 2:27 pm Scorpio
10th 10:50 pm Sagittarius
13th 9:17 am Capricorn
15th 9:17 pm Aquarius
18th 9:59 am Pisces
20th 9:35 pm Aries
23rd 6:07 am Taurus
25th 10:42 am Gemini
27th 12:00 pm Cancer
29th 11:43 am Leo
31st 11:52 am Virgo

January 1948
2nd 2:15 pm Libra
4th 7:53 pm Scorpio
7th 4:42 am Sagittarius
9th 3:43 pm Capricorn
12th 3:55 am Aquarius
14th 4:35 pm Pisces
17th 4:42 am Aries
19th 2:38 pm Taurus
21st 8:60 pm Gemini
23rd 11:22 pm Cancer
25th 10:59 pm Leo
27th 9:58 pm Virgo
29th 10:31 pm Libra

February 1948
1st 2:29 am Scorpio
3rd 10:30 am Sagittarius
5th 9:30 pm Capricorn
8th 9:59 am Aquarius
10th 10:37 pm Pisces
13th 10:36 am Aries
15th 9:07 pm Taurus
18th 4:53 am Gemini
20th 9:04 am Cancer
22nd 10:03 am Leo
24th 9:23 am Virgo
26th 9:10 am Libra
28th 11:30 am Scorpio

March 1948
1st 5:45 pm Sagittarius
4th 3:52 am Capricorn
6th 4:14 pm Aquarius
9th 4:51 am Pisces
11th 4:31 pm Aries
14th 2:39 am Taurus
16th 10:41 am Gemini
18th 4:11 pm Cancer
20th 6:56 pm Leo
22nd 7:42 pm Virgo
24th 8:02 pm Libra
26th 9:50 pm Scorpio
29th 2:48 am Sagittarius
31st 11:37 am Capricorn

April 1948
2nd 11:18 pm Aquarius
5th 11:54 am Pisces
7th 11:27 pm Aries
10th 8:55 am Taurus
12th 4:17 pm Gemini
14th 9:39 pm Cancer
17th 1:14 am Leo
19th 3:29 am Virgo
21st 5:17 am Libra
23rd 7:53 am Scorpio
25th 12:36 pm Sagittarius
27th 8:23 pm Capricorn
30th 7:17 am Aquarius

May 1948
2nd 7:44 pm Pisces
5th 7:25 am Aries
7th 4:44 pm Taurus
9th 11:19 pm Gemini
12th 3:35 am Cancer
14th 6:37 am Leo
16th 9:14 am Virgo
18th 12:08 pm Libra
20th 3:58 pm Scorpio
22nd 9:23 pm Sagittarius
25th 5:10 am Capricorn
27th 3:33 pm Aquarius
30th 3:46 am Pisces

June 1948
1st 3:53 pm Aries
4th 1:42 am Taurus
6th 8:01 am Gemini
8th 11:24 am Cancer
10th 1:11 pm Leo
12th 2:49 pm Virgo
14th 5:35 pm Libra
16th 10:03 pm Scorpio
19th 4:29 am Sagittarius
21st 12:53 pm Capricorn
23rd 11:15 pm Aquarius
26th 11:24 am Pisces
28th 11:56 pm Aries

July 1948
1st 10:35 am Taurus
3rd 5:43 pm Gemini
5th 9:04 pm Cancer
7th 9:51 pm Leo
9th 10:04 pm Virgo
11th 11:30 pm Libra
14th 3:30 am Scorpio
16th 10:14 am Sagittarius
18th 7:15 pm Capricorn
21st 6:04 am Aquarius
23rd 6:13 pm Pisces
26th 6:55 am Aries
28th 6:31 pm Taurus
31st 2:59 am Gemini

August 1948
2nd 7:16 am Cancer
4th 8:11 am Leo
6th 7:33 am Virgo
8th 7:33 am Libra
10th 10:01 am Scorpio
12th 3:53 pm Sagittarius
15th 0:51 am Capricorn
17th 12:03 pm Aquarius
20th 0:22 am Pisces
22nd 1:04 pm Aries
25th 1:03 am Taurus
27th 10:34 am Gemini
29th 4:29 pm Cancer
31st 6:38 pm Leo

September 1948
2nd 6:20 pm Virgo
4th 5:38 pm Libra
6th 6:38 pm Scorpio
8th 10:52 pm Sagittarius
11th 6:59 am Capricorn
13th 5:59 pm Aquarius
16th 6:26 am Pisces
18th 7:02 pm Aries
21st 6:44 am Taurus
23rd 4:38 pm Gemini
25th 11:47 pm Cancer
28th 3:33 am Leo
30th 4:40 am Virgo

October 1948
2nd 4:32 am Libra
4th 5:02 am Scorpio
6th 7:60 am Sagittarius
8th 2:37 pm Capricorn
11th 0:42 am Aquarius
13th 1:04 pm Pisces
16th 1:36 am Aries
18th 12:52 pm Taurus
20th 10:14 pm Gemini
23rd 5:18 am Cancer
25th 10:07 am Leo
27th 12:51 pm Virgo
29th 2:16 pm Libra
31st 3:34 pm Scorpio

November 1948
2nd 6:15 pm Sagittarius
4th 11:42 pm Capricorn
7th 8:46 am Aquarius
9th 8:34 pm Pisces
12th 9:12 am Aries
14th 8:22 pm Taurus
17th 4:59 am Gemini
19th 11:08 am Cancer
21st 3:31 pm Leo
23rd 6:47 pm Virgo
25th 9:33 pm Libra
28th 0:19 am Scorpio
30th 3:55 am Sagittarius

December 1948
2nd 9:22 am Capricorn
4th 5:37 pm Aquarius
7th 4:48 am Pisces
9th 5:30 pm Aries
12th 5:07 am Taurus
14th 1:40 pm Gemini
16th 6:59 pm Cancer
18th 10:02 pm Leo
21st 0:19 am Virgo
23rd 2:60 am Libra
25th 6:40 am Scorpio
27th 11:31 am Sagittarius
29th 5:49 pm Capricorn

January 1949
1st 2:10 am Aquarius
3rd 1:02 pm Pisces
6th 1:41 am Aries
8th 2:01 pm Taurus
10th 11:32 pm Gemini
13th 4:54 am Cancer
15th 7:07 am Leo
17th 7:54 am Virgo
19th 9:07 am Libra
21st 12:03 pm Scorpio
23rd 5:11 pm Sagittarius
26th 0:23 am Capricorn
28th 9:30 am Aquarius
30th 8:27 pm Pisces

February 1949
2nd 9:06 am Aries
4th 9:57 pm Taurus
7th 8:35 am Gemini
9th 3:17 pm Cancer
11th 5:58 pm Leo
13th 6:05 pm Virgo
15th 5:46 pm Libra
17th 6:57 pm Scorpio
19th 10:51 pm Sagittarius
22nd 5:53 am Capricorn
24th 3:27 pm Aquarius
27th 2:55 am Pisces

March 1949
1st 3:36 pm Aries
4th 4:32 am Taurus
6th 4:01 pm Gemini
9th 0:21 am Cancer
11th 4:30 am Leo
13th 5:23 am Virgo
15th 4:41 am Libra
17th 4:28 am Scorpio
19th 6:36 am Sagittarius
21st 12:09 pm Capricorn
23rd 9:11 pm Aquarius
26th 8:50 am Pisces
28th 9:42 pm Aries
31st 10:27 am Taurus

April 1949
2nd 10:02 pm Gemini
5th 7:07 am Cancer
7th 12:55 pm Leo
9th 3:28 pm Virgo
11th 3:47 pm Libra
13th 3:29 pm Scorpio
15th 4:28 pm Sagittarius
17th 8:19 pm Capricorn
20th 4:02 am Aquarius
22nd 3:10 pm Pisces
25th 3:60 am Aries
27th 4:39 pm Taurus
30th 3:45 am Gemini

May 1949
2nd 12:40 pm Cancer
4th 7:07 pm Leo
6th 11:10 pm Virgo
9th 1:07 am Libra
11th 1:54 am Scorpio
13th 2:59 am Sagittarius
15th 6:02 am Capricorn
17th 12:24 pm Aquarius
19th 10:27 pm Pisces
22nd 11:02 am Aries
24th 11:42 pm Taurus
27th 10:22 am Gemini
29th 6:35 pm Cancer

June 1949
1st 0:35 am Leo
3rd 4:51 am Virgo
5th 7:55 am Libra
7th 10:12 am Scorpio
9th 12:25 pm Sagittarius
11th 3:43 pm Capricorn
13th 9:28 pm Aquarius
16th 6:42 am Pisces
18th 6:46 pm Aries
21st 7:28 am Taurus
23rd 6:16 pm Gemini
26th 1:60 am Cancer
28th 6:58 am Leo
30th 10:25 am Virgo

July 1949
2nd 1:21 pm Libra
4th 4:22 pm Scorpio
6th 7:45 pm Sagittarius
9th 0:02 am Capricorn
11th 6:12 am Aquarius
13th 3:04 pm Pisces
16th 2:42 am Aries
18th 3:34 pm Taurus
21st 2:55 am Gemini
23rd 10:46 am Cancer
25th 3:16 pm Leo
27th 5:35 pm Virgo
29th 7:19 pm Libra
31st 9:45 pm Scorpio

August 1949
3rd 1:26 am Sagittarius
5th 6:37 am Capricorn
7th 1:37 pm Aquarius
9th 10:47 pm Pisces
12th 10:20 am Aries
14th 11:17 pm Taurus
17th 11:19 am Gemini
19th 8:11 pm Cancer
22nd 1:07 am Leo
24th 2:55 am Virgo
26th 3:24 am Libra
28th 4:21 am Scorpio
30th 7:03 am Sagittarius

September 1949
1st 12:08 pm Capricorn
3rd 7:39 pm Aquarius
6th 5:27 am Pisces
8th 5:13 pm Aries
11th 6:11 am Taurus
13th 6:44 pm Gemini
16th 4:48 am Cancer
18th 10:59 am Leo
20th 1:30 pm Virgo
22nd 1:41 pm Libra
24th 1:23 pm Scorpio
26th 2:25 pm Sagittarius
28th 6:10 pm Capricorn

October 1949
1st 1:14 am Aquarius
3rd 11:21 am Pisces
5th 11:28 pm Aries
8th 12:25 pm Taurus
11th 1:02 am Gemini
13th 11:47 am Cancer
15th 7:32 pm Leo
17th 11:43 pm Virgo
20th 0:48 am Libra
22nd 0:19 am Scorpio
24th 0:08 am Sagittarius
26th 2:13 am Capricorn
28th 7:56 am Aquarius
30th 5:25 pm Pisces

November 1949
2nd 5:36 am Aries
4th 6:35 pm Taurus
7th 6:53 am Gemini
9th 5:33 pm Cancer
12th 1:58 am Leo
14th 7:38 am Virgo
16th 10:32 am Libra
18th 11:18 am Scorpio
20th 11:18 am Sagittarius
22nd 12:26 pm Capricorn
24th 4:30 pm Aquarius
27th 0:37 am Pisces
29th 12:21 pm Aries

December 1949
2nd 1:23 am Taurus
4th 1:27 pm Gemini
6th 11:31 pm Cancer
9th 7:25 am Leo
11th 1:27 pm Virgo
13th 5:42 pm Libra
15th 8:12 pm Scorpio
17th 9:33 pm Sagittarius
19th 11:02 pm Capricorn
22nd 2:28 am Aquarius
24th 9:26 am Pisces
26th 8:08 pm Aries
29th 8:58 am Taurus
31st 9:13 pm Gemini

January 1950
3rd 6:53 am Cancer
5th 1:55 pm Leo
7th 7:05 pm Virgo
9th 11:08 pm Libra
12th 2:28 am Scorpio
14th 5:17 am Sagittarius
16th 8:09 am Capricorn
18th 12:12 pm Aquarius
20th 6:46 pm Pisces
23rd 4:41 am Aries
25th 5:09 pm Taurus
28th 5:42 am Gemini
30th 3:47 pm Cancer

February 1950
1st 10:34 pm Leo
4th 2:36 am Virgo
6th 5:20 am Libra
8th 7:52 am Scorpio
10th 10:53 am Sagittarius
12th 2:47 pm Capricorn
14th 7:60 pm Aquarius
17th 3:14 am Pisces
19th 1:04 pm Aries
22nd 1:13 am Taurus
24th 2:02 pm Gemini
27th 1:02 am Cancer

March 1950
1st 8:27 am Leo
3rd 12:22 pm Virgo
5th 2:00 pm Libra
7th 2:57 pm Scorpio
9th 4:41 pm Sagittarius
11th 8:09 pm Capricorn
14th 1:53 am Aquarius
16th 10:02 am Pisces
18th 8:21 pm Aries
21st 8:33 am Taurus
23rd 9:28 pm Gemini
26th 9:13 am Cancer
28th 6:02 pm Leo
30th 11:01 pm Virgo

April 1950
2nd 0:42 am Libra
4th 0:37 am Scorpio
6th 0:38 am Sagittarius
8th 2:32 am Capricorn
10th 7:28 am Aquarius
12th 3:41 pm Pisces
15th 2:32 am Aries
17th 3:01 pm Taurus
20th 3:54 am Gemini
22nd 4:01 pm Cancer
25th 1:55 am Leo
27th 8:25 am Virgo
29th 11:21 am Libra

May 1950
1st 11:36 am Scorpio
3rd 10:54 am Sagittarius
5th 11:14 am Capricorn
7th 2:28 pm Aquarius
9th 9:37 pm Pisces
12th 8:21 am Aries
14th 8:59 pm Taurus
17th 9:51 am Gemini
19th 9:49 pm Cancer
22nd 8:03 am Leo
24th 3:46 pm Virgo
26th 8:24 pm Libra
28th 9:60 pm Scorpio
30th 9:44 pm Sagittarius

June 1950
1st 9:29 pm Capricorn
3rd 11:19 pm Aquarius
6th 5:02 am Pisces
8th 2:48 pm Aries
11th 3:13 am Taurus
13th 4:04 pm Gemini
16th 3:42 am Cancer
18th 1:34 pm Leo
20th 9:29 pm Virgo
23rd 3:07 am Libra
25th 6:15 am Scorpio
27th 7:24 am Sagittarius
29th 7:50 am Capricorn

July 1950
1st 9:25 am Aquarius
3rd 1:58 pm Pisces
5th 10:26 pm Aries
8th 10:16 am Taurus
10th 11:01 pm Gemini
13th 10:30 am Cancer
15th 7:51 pm Leo
18th 3:04 am Virgo
20th 8:32 am Libra
22nd 12:24 pm Scorpio
24th 2:53 pm Sagittarius
26th 4:39 pm Capricorn
28th 6:57 pm Aquarius
30th 11:19 pm Pisces

August 1950
2nd 7:06 am Aries
4th 6:08 pm Taurus
7th 6:43 am Gemini
9th 6:25 pm Cancer
12th 3:34 am Leo
14th 10:00 am Virgo
16th 2:28 pm Libra
18th 5:49 pm Scorpio
20th 8:35 pm Sagittarius
22nd 11:23 pm Capricorn
25th 2:53 am Aquarius
27th 8:05 am Pisces
29th 3:48 pm Aries

September 1950
1st 2:18 am Taurus
3rd 2:45 pm Gemini
6th 2:52 am Cancer
8th 12:29 pm Leo
10th 6:52 pm Virgo
12th 10:27 pm Libra
15th 0:26 am Scorpio
17th 2:12 am Sagittarius
19th 4:50 am Capricorn
21st 9:02 am Aquarius
23rd 3:11 pm Pisces
25th 11:31 pm Aries
28th 10:09 am Taurus
30th 10:27 pm Gemini

October 1950
3rd 10:57 am Cancer
5th 9:39 pm Leo
8th 4:50 am Virgo
10th 8:25 am Libra
12th 9:30 am Scorpio
14th 9:47 am Sagittarius
16th 10:60 am Capricorn
18th 2:31 pm Aquarius
20th 8:55 pm Pisces
23rd 5:60 am Aries
25th 5:04 pm Taurus
28th 5:22 am Gemini
30th 6:03 pm Cancer

November 1950
2nd 5:35 am Leo
4th 2:16 pm Virgo
6th 7:07 pm Libra
8th 8:27 pm Scorpio
10th 7:52 pm Sagittarius
12th 7:29 pm Capricorn
14th 9:17 pm Aquarius
17th 2:40 am Pisces
19th 11:43 am Aries
21st 11:08 pm Taurus
24th 11:38 am Gemini
27th 0:12 am Cancer
29th 11:59 am Leo

December 1950
1st 9:51 pm Virgo
4th 4:26 am Libra
6th 7:15 am Scorpio
8th 7:16 am Sagittarius
10th 6:20 am Capricorn
12th 6:40 am Aquarius
14th 10:18 am Pisces
16th 6:04 pm Aries
19th 5:12 am Taurus
21st 5:49 pm Gemini
24th 6:17 am Cancer
26th 5:43 pm Leo
29th 3:33 am Virgo
31st 11:16 am Libra

January 1951
2nd 3:53 pm Scorpio
4th 5:35 pm Sagittarius
6th 5:32 pm Capricorn
8th 5:39 pm Aquarius
10th 7:60 pm Pisces
13th 2:09 am Aries
15th 12:15 pm Taurus
18th 0:36 am Gemini
20th 1:06 pm Cancer
23rd 0:13 am Leo
25th 9:24 am Virgo
27th 4:44 pm Libra
29th 10:02 pm Scorpio

February 1951
1st 1:17 am Sagittarius
3rd 2:53 am Capricorn
5th 4:06 am Aquarius
7th 6:53 am Pisces
9th 11:48 am Aries
11th 8:37 pm Taurus
14th 8:19 am Gemini
16th 8:51 pm Cancer
19th 7:60 am Leo
21st 4:41 pm Virgo
23rd 11:01 pm Libra
26th 3:32 am Scorpio
28th 6:50 am Sagittarius

March 1951
2nd 9:30 am Capricorn
4th 12:13 pm Aquarius
6th 3:49 pm Pisces
8th 9:19 pm Aries
11th 5:35 am Taurus
13th 4:38 pm Gemini
16th 5:06 am Cancer
18th 4:43 pm Leo
21st 1:40 am Virgo
23rd 7:19 am Libra
25th 10:35 am Scorpio
27th 12:42 pm Sagittarius
29th 2:53 pm Capricorn
31st 6:05 pm Aquarius

April 1951
2nd 10:46 pm Pisces
5th 5:18 am Aries
7th 1:55 pm Taurus
10th 0:42 am Gemini
12th 1:05 pm Cancer
15th 1:18 am Leo
17th 11:03 am Virgo
19th 5:10 pm Libra
21st 7:54 pm Scorpio
23rd 8:41 pm Sagittarius
25th 9:22 pm Capricorn
27th 11:33 pm Aquarius
30th 4:15 am Pisces

May 1951
2nd 11:29 am Aries
4th 8:47 pm Taurus
7th 7:51 am Gemini
9th 8:13 pm Cancer
12th 8:48 am Leo
14th 7:42 pm Virgo
17th 3:04 am Libra
19th 6:21 am Scorpio
21st 6:43 am Sagittarius
23rd 6:10 am Capricorn
25th 6:47 am Aquarius
27th 10:12 am Pisces
29th 4:57 pm Aries

June 1951
1st 2:35 am Taurus
3rd 2:04 pm Gemini
6th 2:32 am Cancer
8th 3:10 pm Leo
11th 2:44 am Virgo
13th 11:58 am Libra
15th 4:11 pm Scorpio
17th 5:23 pm Sagittarius
19th 4:39 pm Capricorn
21st 4:09 pm Aquarius
23rd 5:54 pm Pisces
25th 11:15 pm Aries
28th 8:21 am Taurus
30th 7:53 pm Gemini

July 1951
3rd 8:28 am Cancer
5th 8:59 pm Leo
8th 8:32 am Virgo
10th 6:01 pm Libra
13th 0:17 am Scorpio
15th 3:00 am Sagittarius
17th 3:13 am Capricorn
19th 2:44 am Aquarius
21st 3:31 am Pisces
23rd 7:28 am Aries
25th 3:12 pm Taurus
28th 2:09 am Gemini
30th 2:43 pm Cancer

August 1951
2nd 3:07 am Leo
4th 2:16 pm Virgo
6th 11:34 pm Libra
9th 6:21 am Scorpio
11th 10:26 am Sagittarius
13th 12:15 pm Capricorn
15th 12:53 pm Aquarius
17th 1:55 pm Pisces
19th 5:02 pm Aries
21st 11:27 pm Taurus
24th 9:30 am Gemini
26th 9:44 pm Cancer
29th 10:08 am Leo
31st 8:60 pm Virgo

September 1951
3rd 5:31 am Libra
5th 11:47 am Scorpio
7th 4:10 pm Sagittarius
9th 7:05 pm Capricorn
11th 9:12 pm Aquarius
13th 11:21 pm Pisces
16th 2:48 am Aries
18th 8:45 am Taurus
20th 5:49 pm Gemini
23rd 5:35 am Cancer
25th 6:07 pm Leo
28th 5:03 am Virgo
30th 1:05 pm Libra

October 1951
2nd 6:21 pm Scorpio
4th 9:47 pm Sagittarius
7th 0:30 am Capricorn
9th 3:20 am Aquarius
11th 6:48 am Pisces
13th 11:21 am Aries
15th 5:39 pm Taurus
18th 2:22 am Gemini
20th 1:45 pm Cancer
23rd 2:25 am Leo
25th 1:58 pm Virgo
27th 10:24 pm Libra
30th 3:08 am Scorpio

November 1951
1st 5:19 am Sagittarius
3rd 6:41 am Capricorn
5th 8:46 am Aquarius
7th 12:26 pm Pisces
9th 5:54 pm Aries
12th 1:08 am Taurus
14th 10:17 am Gemini
16th 9:28 pm Cancer
19th 10:11 am Leo
21st 10:34 pm Virgo
24th 8:04 am Libra
26th 1:27 pm Scorpio
28th 3:17 pm Sagittarius
30th 3:23 pm Capricorn

December 1951
2nd 3:48 pm Aquarius
4th 6:12 pm Pisces
6th 11:19 pm Aries
9th 7:07 am Taurus
11th 4:56 pm Gemini
14th 4:23 am Cancer
16th 5:05 pm Leo
19th 5:50 am Virgo
21st 4:36 pm Libra
23rd 11:39 pm Scorpio
26th 2:26 am Sagittarius
28th 2:24 am Capricorn
30th 1:37 am Aquarius

January 1952
1st 2:13 am Pisces
3rd 5:47 am Aries
5th 12:49 pm Taurus
7th 10:44 pm Gemini
10th 10:36 am Cancer
12th 11:19 pm Leo
15th 11:59 am Virgo
17th 11:19 pm Libra
20th 7:39 am Scorpio
22nd 12:16 pm Sagittarius
24th 1:36 pm Capricorn
26th 1:07 pm Aquarius
28th 12:50 pm Pisces
30th 2:39 pm Aries

February 1952
1st 7:55 pm Taurus
4th 4:59 am Gemini
6th 4:46 pm Cancer
9th 5:37 am Leo
11th 6:02 pm Virgo
14th 4:58 am Libra
16th 1:42 pm Scorpio
18th 7:41 pm Sagittarius
20th 10:49 pm Capricorn
22nd 11:49 pm Aquarius
25th 0:02 am Pisces
27th 1:13 am Aries
29th 5:05 am Taurus

March 1952
2nd 12:42 pm Gemini
4th 11:40 pm Cancer
7th 12:31 pm Leo
10th 0:53 am Virgo
12th 11:15 am Libra
14th 7:20 pm Scorpio
17th 1:15 am Sagittarius
19th 5:18 am Capricorn
21st 7:54 am Aquarius
23rd 9:40 am Pisces
25th 11:37 am Aries
27th 3:10 pm Taurus
29th 9:37 pm Gemini

April 1952
1st 7:42 am Cancer
3rd 8:10 pm Leo
6th 8:40 am Virgo
8th 6:55 pm Libra
11th 2:14 am Scorpio
13th 7:07 am Sagittarius
15th 10:42 am Capricorn
17th 1:44 pm Aquarius
19th 4:41 pm Pisces
21st 7:58 pm Aries
24th 0:16 am Taurus
26th 6:44 am Gemini
28th 4:10 pm Cancer

May 1952
1st 4:14 am Leo
3rd 4:56 pm Virgo
6th 3:38 am Libra
8th 10:45 am Scorpio
10th 2:49 pm Sagittarius
12th 5:10 pm Capricorn
14th 7:15 pm Aquarius
16th 10:07 pm Pisces
19th 2:09 am Aries
21st 7:32 am Taurus
23rd 2:41 pm Gemini
26th 0:06 am Cancer
28th 12:01 pm Leo
31st 0:58 am Virgo

June 1952
2nd 12:21 pm Libra
4th 8:17 pm Scorpio
7th 0:22 am Sagittarius
9th 1:47 am Capricorn
11th 2:29 am Aquarius
13th 4:04 am Pisces
15th 7:34 am Aries
17th 1:14 pm Taurus
19th 9:05 pm Gemini
22nd 7:07 am Cancer
24th 7:03 pm Leo
27th 8:05 am Virgo
29th 8:16 pm Libra

July 1952
2nd 5:20 am Scorpio
4th 10:21 am Sagittarius
6th 12:00 pm Capricorn
8th 11:55 am Aquarius
10th 12:04 pm Pisces
12th 2:03 pm Aries
14th 6:50 pm Taurus
17th 2:40 am Gemini
19th 1:08 pm Cancer
22nd 1:21 am Leo
24th 2:24 pm Virgo
27th 2:52 am Libra
29th 12:58 pm Scorpio
31st 7:33 pm Sagittarius

August 1952
2nd 10:25 pm Capricorn
4th 10:40 pm Aquarius
6th 10:06 pm Pisces
8th 10:35 pm Aries
11th 1:47 am Taurus
13th 8:42 am Gemini
15th 6:55 pm Cancer
18th 7:21 am Leo
20th 8:23 pm Virgo
23rd 8:40 am Libra
25th 7:09 pm Scorpio
28th 2:51 am Sagittarius
30th 7:19 am Capricorn

September 1952
1st 8:60 am Aquarius
3rd 8:60 am Pisces
5th 9:01 am Aries
7th 10:53 am Taurus
9th 4:10 pm Gemini
12th 1:25 am Cancer
14th 1:40 pm Leo
17th 2:42 am Virgo
19th 2:40 pm Libra
22nd 0:43 am Scorpio
24th 8:31 am Sagittarius
26th 2:03 pm Capricorn
28th 5:21 pm Aquarius
30th 6:51 pm Pisces

October 1952
2nd 7:34 pm Aries
4th 9:06 pm Taurus
7th 1:15 am Gemini
9th 9:20 am Cancer
11th 8:50 pm Leo
14th 9:49 am Virgo
16th 9:44 pm Libra
19th 7:07 am Scorpio
21st 2:10 pm Sagittarius
23rd 7:27 pm Capricorn
25th 11:27 pm Aquarius
28th 2:22 am Pisces
30th 4:34 am Aries

November 1952
1st 6:60 am Taurus
3rd 11:07 am Gemini
5th 6:15 pm Cancer
8th 4:58 am Leo
10th 5:47 pm Virgo
13th 5:54 am Libra
15th 3:15 pm Scorpio
17th 9:32 pm Sagittarius
20th 1:39 am Capricorn
22nd 4:51 am Aquarius
24th 7:55 am Pisces
26th 11:10 am Aries
28th 2:56 pm Taurus
30th 7:55 pm Gemini

December 1952
3rd 3:10 am Cancer
5th 1:24 pm Leo
8th 1:58 am Virgo
10th 2:32 pm Libra
13th 1:39 am Scorpio
15th 6:55 am Sagittarius
17th 10:15 am Capricorn
19th 12:02 pm Aquarius
21st 1:48 pm Pisces
23rd 4:33 pm Aries
25th 8:48 pm Taurus
28th 2:50 am Gemini
30th 10:57 am Cancer

January 1953
1st 9:18 pm Leo
4th 9:42 am Virgo
6th 10:35 pm Libra
9th 9:39 am Scorpio
11th 5:09 pm Sagittarius
13th 8:53 pm Capricorn
15th 9:57 pm Aquarius
17th 10:08 pm Pisces
19th 11:11 pm Aries
22nd 2:23 am Taurus
24th 8:26 am Gemini
26th 5:10 pm Cancer
29th 4:08 am Leo
31st 4:36 pm Virgo

February 1953
3rd 5:31 am Libra
5th 5:18 pm Scorpio
8th 2:18 am Sagittarius
10th 7:27 am Capricorn
12th 9:12 am Aquarius
14th 8:58 am Pisces
16th 8:34 am Aries
18th 9:56 am Taurus
20th 2:33 pm Gemini
22nd 10:49 pm Cancer
25th 10:09 am Leo
27th 10:53 pm Virgo

March 1953
2nd 11:41 am Libra
4th 11:32 pm Scorpio
7th 9:16 am Sagittarius
9th 4:07 pm Capricorn
11th 7:35 pm Aquarius
13th 8:16 pm Pisces
15th 7:40 pm Aries
17th 7:48 pm Taurus
19th 10:37 pm Gemini
22nd 5:33 am Cancer
24th 4:18 pm Leo
27th 5:06 am Virgo
29th 5:51 pm Libra

April 1953
1st 5:19 am Scorpio
3rd 2:57 pm Sagittarius
5th 10:29 pm Capricorn
8th 3:26 am Aquarius
10th 5:48 am Pisces
12th 6:19 am Aries
14th 6:35 am Taurus
16th 8:33 am Gemini
18th 2:00 pm Cancer
20th 11:29 pm Leo
23rd 11:54 am Virgo
26th 0:42 am Libra
28th 11:50 am Scorpio
30th 8:52 pm Sagittarius

May 1953
3rd 3:55 am Capricorn
5th 9:11 am Aquarius
7th 12:45 pm Pisces
9th 2:48 pm Aries
11th 4:14 pm Taurus
13th 6:31 pm Gemini
15th 11:17 pm Cancer
18th 7:51 am Leo
20th 7:33 pm Virgo
23rd 8:16 am Libra
25th 7:31 pm Scorpio
28th 4:07 am Sagittarius
30th 10:16 am Capricorn

June 1953
1st 2:44 pm Aquarius
3rd 6:12 pm Pisces
5th 9:03 pm Aries
7th 11:41 pm Taurus
10th 3:05 am Gemini
12th 8:23 am Cancer
14th 4:31 pm Leo
17th 3:38 am Virgo
19th 4:17 pm Libra
22nd 3:56 am Scorpio
24th 12:44 pm Sagittarius
26th 6:27 pm Capricorn
28th 9:53 pm Aquarius

July 1953
1st 0:10 am Pisces
3rd 2:25 am Aries
5th 5:26 am Taurus
7th 9:46 am Gemini
9th 3:59 pm Cancer
12th 0:29 am Leo
14th 11:31 am Virgo
17th 0:04 am Libra
19th 12:14 pm Scorpio
21st 9:57 pm Sagittarius
24th 4:04 am Capricorn
26th 7:01 am Aquarius
28th 8:07 am Pisces
30th 8:59 am Aries

August 1953
1st 11:02 am Taurus
3rd 3:16 pm Gemini
5th 10:03 pm Cancer
8th 7:20 am Leo
10th 6:36 pm Virgo
13th 7:09 am Libra
15th 7:43 pm Scorpio
18th 6:27 am Sagittarius
20th 1:47 pm Capricorn
22nd 5:25 pm Aquarius
24th 6:10 pm Pisces
26th 5:47 pm Aries
28th 6:14 pm Taurus
30th 9:10 pm Gemini

September 1953
2nd 3:33 am Cancer
4th 1:09 pm Leo
7th 0:48 am Virgo
9th 1:28 pm Libra
12th 2:06 am Scorpio
14th 1:30 pm Sagittarius
16th 10:20 pm Capricorn
19th 3:28 am Aquarius
21st 5:04 am Pisces
23rd 4:31 am Aries
25th 3:47 am Taurus
27th 5:05 am Gemini
29th 10:01 am Cancer

October 1953
1st 6:57 pm Leo
4th 6:42 am Virgo
6th 7:28 pm Libra
9th 7:56 am Scorpio
11th 7:19 pm Sagittarius
14th 4:49 am Capricorn
16th 11:29 am Aquarius
18th 2:51 pm Pisces
20th 3:24 pm Aries
22nd 2:48 pm Taurus
24th 3:09 pm Gemini
26th 6:27 pm Cancer
29th 1:56 am Leo
31st 1:06 pm Virgo

November 1953
3rd 1:51 am Libra
5th 2:10 pm Scorpio
8th 1:07 am Sagittarius
10th 10:16 am Capricorn
12th 5:29 pm Aquarius
14th 10:16 pm Pisces
17th 0:34 am Aries
19th 1:14 am Taurus
21st 1:56 am Gemini
23rd 4:34 am Cancer
25th 10:45 am Leo
27th 8:43 pm Virgo
30th 9:06 am Libra

December 1953
2nd 9:30 pm Scorpio
5th 8:06 am Sagittarius
7th 4:30 pm Capricorn
9th 10:59 pm Aquarius
12th 3:44 am Pisces
14th 7:05 am Aries
16th 9:22 am Taurus
18th 11:30 am Gemini
20th 2:44 pm Cancer
22nd 8:25 pm Leo
25th 5:26 am Virgo
27th 5:11 pm Libra
30th 5:41 am Scorpio

January 1954
1st 4:37 pm Sagittarius
4th 0:45 am Capricorn
6th 6:07 am Aquarius
8th 9:42 am Pisces
10th 12:28 pm Aries
12th 3:12 pm Taurus
14th 6:31 pm Gemini
16th 11:02 pm Cancer
19th 5:27 am Leo
21st 2:16 pm Virgo
24th 1:31 am Libra
26th 2:01 pm Scorpio
29th 1:40 am Sagittarius
31st 10:21 am Capricorn

February 1954
2nd 3:34 pm Aquarius
4th 6:02 pm Pisces
6th 7:15 pm Aries
8th 8:49 pm Taurus
10th 11:55 pm Gemini
13th 5:13 am Cancer
15th 12:39 pm Leo
17th 10:02 pm Virgo
20th 9:17 am Libra
22nd 9:44 pm Scorpio
25th 9:57 am Sagittarius
27th 7:54 pm Capricorn

March 1954
2nd 2:05 am Aquarius
4th 4:29 am Pisces
6th 4:40 am Aries
8th 4:35 am Taurus
10th 6:11 am Gemini
12th 10:42 am Cancer
14th 6:20 pm Leo
17th 4:22 am Virgo
19th 3:59 pm Libra
22nd 4:27 am Scorpio
24th 4:55 pm Sagittarius
27th 3:52 am Capricorn
29th 11:32 am Aquarius
31st 3:12 pm Pisces

April 1954
2nd 3:37 pm Aries
4th 2:44 pm Taurus
6th 2:45 pm Gemini
8th 5:33 pm Cancer
11th 0:06 am Leo
13th 10:06 am Virgo
15th 9:59 pm Libra
18th 10:34 am Scorpio
20th 10:56 pm Sagittarius
23rd 10:09 am Capricorn
25th 6:60 pm Aquarius
28th 0:22 am Pisces
30th 2:08 am Aries

May 1954
2nd 1:44 am Taurus
4th 1:08 am Gemini
6th 2:33 am Cancer
8th 7:34 am Leo
10th 4:27 pm Virgo
13th 4:04 am Libra
15th 4:43 pm Scorpio
18th 4:54 am Sagittarius
20th 3:48 pm Capricorn
23rd 0:48 am Aquarius
25th 7:06 am Pisces
27th 10:28 am Aries
29th 11:33 am Taurus
31st 11:44 am Gemini

June 1954
2nd 12:51 pm Cancer
4th 4:40 pm Leo
7th 0:08 am Virgo
9th 11:01 am Libra
11th 11:30 pm Scorpio
14th 11:37 am Sagittarius
16th 10:04 pm Capricorn
19th 6:25 am Aquarius
21st 12:35 pm Pisces
23rd 4:42 pm Aries
25th 7:09 pm Taurus
27th 8:44 pm Gemini
29th 10:38 pm Cancer

July 1954
2nd 2:19 am Leo
4th 9:01 am Virgo
6th 6:57 pm Libra
9th 7:04 am Scorpio
11th 7:19 pm Sagittarius
14th 5:38 am Capricorn
16th 1:16 pm Aquarius
18th 6:33 pm Pisces
20th 10:09 pm Aries
23rd 0:54 am Taurus
25th 3:32 am Gemini
27th 6:45 am Cancer
29th 11:15 am Leo
31st 5:54 pm Virgo

August 1954
3rd 3:17 am Libra
5th 3:04 pm Scorpio
8th 3:31 am Sagittarius
10th 2:16 pm Capricorn
12th 9:53 pm Aquarius
15th 2:17 am Pisces
17th 4:39 am Aries
19th 6:29 am Taurus
21st 8:60 am Gemini
23rd 12:54 pm Cancer
25th 6:26 pm Leo
28th 1:46 am Virgo
30th 11:16 am Libra

September 1954
1st 10:50 pm Scorpio
4th 11:32 am Sagittarius
6th 11:09 pm Capricorn
9th 7:26 am Aquarius
11th 11:51 am Pisces
13th 1:21 pm Aries
15th 1:47 pm Taurus
17th 2:59 pm Gemini
19th 6:17 pm Cancer
22nd 0:06 am Leo
24th 8:14 am Virgo
26th 6:14 pm Libra
29th 5:55 am Scorpio

October 1954
1st 6:43 pm Sagittarius
4th 7:02 am Capricorn
6th 4:41 pm Aquarius
8th 10:16 pm Pisces
10th 11:58 pm Aries
12th 11:33 pm Taurus
14th 11:10 pm Gemini
17th 0:50 am Cancer
19th 5:44 am Leo
21st 1:48 pm Virgo
24th 0:12 am Libra
26th 12:12 pm Scorpio
29th 1:01 am Sagittarius
31st 1:35 pm Capricorn

November 1954
3rd 0:23 am Aquarius
5th 7:30 am Pisces
7th 10:37 am Aries
9th 10:47 am Taurus
11th 9:53 am Gemini
13th 10:05 am Cancer
15th 1:09 pm Leo
17th 7:55 pm Virgo
20th 6:03 am Libra
22nd 6:14 pm Scorpio
25th 7:01 am Sagittarius
27th 7:24 pm Capricorn
30th 6:18 am Aquarius

December 1954
2nd 2:35 pm Pisces
4th 7:33 pm Aries
6th 9:22 pm Taurus
8th 9:16 pm Gemini
10th 9:08 pm Cancer
12th 10:49 pm Leo
15th 3:57 am Virgo
17th 12:56 pm Libra
20th 0:43 am Scorpio
22nd 1:34 pm Sagittarius
25th 1:40 am Capricorn
27th 11:58 am Aquarius
29th 8:08 pm Pisces

January 1955
1st 1:55 am Aries
3rd 5:23 am Taurus
5th 7:03 am Gemini
7th 8:02 am Cancer
9th 9:45 am Leo
11th 1:48 pm Virgo
13th 9:17 pm Libra
16th 8:15 am Scorpio
18th 9:01 pm Sagittarius
21st 9:06 am Capricorn
23rd 6:55 pm Aquarius
26th 2:11 am Pisces
28th 7:19 am Aries
30th 11:05 am Taurus

February 1955
1st 2:03 pm Gemini
3rd 4:37 pm Cancer
5th 7:30 pm Leo
7th 11:42 pm Virgo
10th 6:37 am Libra
12th 4:41 pm Scorpio
15th 5:06 am Sagittarius
17th 5:32 pm Capricorn
20th 3:30 am Aquarius
22nd 10:04 am Pisces
24th 2:04 pm Aries
26th 4:46 pm Taurus
28th 7:26 pm Gemini

March 1955
2nd 10:41 pm Cancer
5th 2:51 am Leo
7th 8:12 am Virgo
9th 3:24 pm Libra
12th 1:05 am Scorpio
14th 1:14 pm Sagittarius
17th 1:60 am Capricorn
19th 12:41 pm Aquarius
21st 7:41 pm Pisces
23rd 11:08 pm Aries
26th 0:31 am Taurus
28th 1:42 am Gemini
30th 4:07 am Cancer

April 1955
1st 8:23 am Leo
3rd 2:33 pm Virgo
5th 10:35 pm Libra
8th 8:41 am Scorpio
10th 8:44 pm Sagittarius
13th 9:40 am Capricorn
15th 9:20 pm Aquarius
18th 5:24 am Pisces
20th 9:25 am Aries
22nd 10:27 am Taurus
24th 10:25 am Gemini
26th 11:12 am Cancer
28th 2:12 pm Leo
30th 7:59 pm Virgo

May 1955
3rd 4:28 am Libra
5th 3:06 pm Scorpio
8th 3:19 am Sagittarius
10th 4:19 pm Capricorn
13th 4:28 am Aquarius
15th 1:48 pm Pisces
17th 7:18 pm Aries
19th 9:10 pm Taurus
21st 8:57 pm Gemini
23rd 8:34 pm Cancer
25th 9:55 pm Leo
28th 2:17 am Virgo
30th 10:12 am Libra

June 1955
1st 8:55 pm Scorpio
4th 9:25 am Sagittarius
6th 10:21 pm Capricorn
9th 10:28 am Aquarius
11th 8:31 pm Pisces
14th 3:21 am Aries
16th 6:47 am Taurus
18th 7:36 am Gemini
20th 7:18 am Cancer
22nd 7:41 am Leo
24th 10:32 am Virgo
26th 5:01 pm Libra
29th 3:06 am Scorpio

July 1955
1st 3:36 pm Sagittarius
4th 4:30 am Capricorn
6th 4:17 pm Aquarius
9th 2:09 am Pisces
11th 9:31 am Aries
13th 2:17 pm Taurus
15th 4:42 pm Gemini
17th 5:31 pm Cancer
19th 6:07 pm Leo
21st 8:09 pm Virgo
24th 1:18 am Libra
26th 10:23 am Scorpio
28th 10:25 pm Sagittarius
31st 11:18 am Capricorn

August 1955
2nd 10:51 pm Aquarius
5th 8:02 am Pisces
7th 2:59 pm Aries
9th 8:04 pm Taurus
11th 11:34 pm Gemini
14th 1:53 am Cancer
16th 3:36 am Leo
18th 6:02 am Virgo
20th 10:40 am Libra
22nd 6:42 pm Scorpio
25th 6:05 am Sagittarius
27th 6:56 pm Capricorn
30th 6:33 am Aquarius

September 1955
1st 3:20 pm Pisces
3rd 9:24 pm Aries
6th 1:38 am Taurus
8th 4:60 am Gemini
10th 8:03 am Cancer
12th 11:05 am Leo
14th 2:37 pm Virgo
16th 7:40 pm Libra
19th 3:22 am Scorpio
21st 2:15 pm Sagittarius
24th 3:02 am Capricorn
26th 3:05 pm Aquarius
29th 0:13 am Pisces

October 1955
1st 5:45 am Aries
3rd 8:51 am Taurus
5th 10:60 am Gemini
7th 1:25 pm Cancer
9th 4:44 pm Leo
11th 9:13 pm Virgo
14th 3:16 am Libra
16th 11:29 am Scorpio
18th 10:09 pm Sagittarius
21st 10:54 am Capricorn
23rd 11:34 pm Aquarius
26th 9:33 am Pisces
28th 3:43 pm Aries
30th 6:28 pm Taurus

November 1955
1st 7:23 pm Gemini
3rd 8:13 pm Cancer
5th 10:20 pm Leo
8th 2:38 am Virgo
10th 9:19 am Libra
12th 6:15 pm Scorpio
15th 5:19 am Sagittarius
17th 6:02 pm Capricorn
20th 6:58 am Aquarius
22nd 6:08 pm Pisces
25th 1:47 am Aries
27th 5:24 am Taurus
29th 6:11 am Gemini

December 1955
1st 5:49 am Cancer
3rd 6:11 am Leo
5th 8:55 am Virgo
7th 2:53 pm Libra
9th 12:00 pm Scorpio
12th 11:36 am Sagittarius
15th 0:24 am Capricorn
17th 1:20 pm Aquarius
20th 1:02 am Pisces
22nd 10:01 am Aries
24th 3:28 pm Taurus
26th 5:31 pm Gemini
28th 5:17 pm Cancer
30th 4:39 pm Leo

January 1956
1st 5:35 pm Virgo
3rd 9:46 pm Libra
6th 6:03 am Scorpio
8th 5:35 pm Sagittarius
11th 6:33 am Capricorn
13th 7:18 pm Aquarius
16th 6:47 am Pisces
18th 4:15 pm Aries
20th 11:11 pm Taurus
23rd 3:05 am Gemini
25th 4:19 am Cancer
27th 4:07 am Leo
29th 4:21 am Virgo
31st 7:01 am Libra

February 1956
2nd 1:38 pm Scorpio
5th 0:12 am Sagittarius
7th 1:07 pm Capricorn
10th 1:51 am Aquarius
12th 12:49 pm Pisces
14th 9:49 pm Aries
17th 4:47 am Taurus
19th 9:48 am Gemini
21st 12:48 pm Cancer
23rd 2:10 pm Leo
25th 3:07 pm Virgo
27th 5:25 pm Libra
29th 10:45 pm Scorpio

March 1956
3rd 8:13 am Sagittarius
5th 8:33 pm Capricorn
8th 9:16 am Aquarius
10th 8:08 pm Pisces
13th 4:25 am Aries
15th 10:30 am Taurus
17th 3:10 pm Gemini
19th 6:47 pm Cancer
21st 9:32 pm Leo
23rd 11:53 pm Virgo
26th 3:02 am Libra
28th 8:23 am Scorpio
30th 4:60 pm Sagittarius

April 1956
2nd 4:38 am Capricorn
4th 5:23 pm Aquarius
7th 4:33 am Pisces
9th 12:42 pm Aries
11th 6:00 pm Taurus
13th 9:30 pm Gemini
16th 0:14 am Cancer
18th 3:00 am Leo
20th 6:18 am Virgo
22nd 10:39 am Libra
24th 4:48 pm Scorpio
27th 1:26 am Sagittarius
29th 12:46 pm Capricorn

May 1956
2nd 1:29 am Aquarius
4th 1:11 pm Pisces
6th 10:05 pm Aries
9th 3:22 am Taurus
11th 5:59 am Gemini
13th 7:20 am Cancer
15th 8:53 am Leo
17th 11:43 am Virgo
19th 4:27 pm Libra
21st 11:27 pm Scorpio
24th 8:49 am Sagittarius
26th 8:12 pm Capricorn
29th 8:53 am Aquarius
31st 9:09 pm Pisces

June 1956
3rd 7:01 am Aries
5th 1:16 pm Taurus
7th 4:06 pm Gemini
9th 4:41 pm Cancer
11th 4:47 pm Leo
13th 6:07 pm Virgo
15th 10:00 pm Libra
18th 5:05 am Scorpio
20th 2:59 pm Sagittarius
23rd 2:44 am Capricorn
25th 3:26 pm Aquarius
28th 3:54 am Pisces
30th 2:39 pm Aries

July 1956
2nd 10:25 pm Taurus
5th 2:24 am Gemini
7th 3:20 am Cancer
9th 2:43 am Leo
11th 2:36 am Virgo
13th 4:58 am Libra
15th 11:02 am Scorpio
17th 8:40 pm Sagittarius
20th 8:42 am Capricorn
22nd 9:28 pm Aquarius
25th 9:50 am Pisces
27th 8:53 pm Aries
30th 5:37 am Taurus

August 1956
1st 11:12 am Gemini
3rd 1:29 pm Cancer
5th 1:27 pm Leo
7th 12:53 pm Virgo
9th 1:57 pm Libra
11th 6:25 pm Scorpio
14th 3:01 am Sagittarius
16th 2:49 pm Capricorn
19th 3:38 am Aquarius
21st 3:45 pm Pisces
24th 2:30 am Aries
26th 11:21 am Taurus
28th 5:57 pm Gemini
30th 9:51 pm Cancer

September 1956
1st 11:14 pm Leo
3rd 11:22 pm Virgo
6th 0:05 am Libra
8th 3:30 am Scorpio
10th 10:51 am Sagittarius
12th 9:46 pm Capricorn
15th 10:27 am Aquarius
17th 10:33 pm Pisces
20th 8:46 am Aries
22nd 5:00 pm Taurus
24th 11:26 pm Gemini
27th 3:60 am Cancer
29th 6:48 am Leo

October 1956
1st 8:25 am Virgo
3rd 10:06 am Libra
5th 1:25 pm Scorpio
7th 7:51 pm Sagittarius
10th 5:51 am Capricorn
12th 6:10 pm Aquarius
15th 6:23 am Pisces
17th 4:33 pm Aries
20th 0:07 am Taurus
22nd 5:28 am Gemini
24th 9:22 am Cancer
26th 12:27 pm Leo
28th 3:11 pm Virgo
30th 6:12 pm Libra

November 1956
1st 10:27 pm Scorpio
4th 5:00 am Sagittarius
6th 2:30 pm Capricorn
9th 2:22 am Aquarius
11th 2:51 pm Pisces
14th 1:36 am Aries
16th 9:09 am Taurus
18th 1:43 pm Gemini
20th 4:16 pm Cancer
22nd 6:11 pm Leo
24th 8:34 pm Virgo
27th 0:11 am Libra
29th 5:37 am Scorpio

December 1956
1st 1:03 pm Sagittarius
3rd 10:38 pm Capricorn
6th 10:19 am Aquarius
8th 10:59 pm Pisces
11th 10:34 am Aries
13th 7:13 pm Taurus
16th 0:07 am Gemini
18th 1:52 am Cancer
20th 2:12 am Leo
22nd 2:58 am Virgo
24th 5:43 am Libra
26th 11:12 am Scorpio
28th 7:22 pm Sagittarius
31st 5:40 am Capricorn

January 1957
2nd 5:26 pm Aquarius
5th 6:06 am Pisces
7th 6:21 pm Aries
10th 4:24 am Taurus
12th 10:39 am Gemini
14th 1:01 pm Cancer
16th 12:50 pm Leo
18th 12:08 pm Virgo
20th 1:02 pm Libra
22nd 5:07 pm Scorpio
25th 0:54 am Sagittarius
27th 11:34 am Capricorn
29th 11:42 pm Aquarius

February 1957
1st 12:21 pm Pisces
4th 0:44 am Aries
6th 11:34 am Taurus
8th 7:32 pm Gemini
10th 11:40 pm Cancer
13th 0:19 am Leo
14th 11:18 pm Virgo
16th 10:51 pm Libra
19th 1:07 am Scorpio
21st 7:28 am Sagittarius
23rd 5:29 pm Capricorn
26th 5:42 am Aquarius
28th 6:25 pm Pisces

March 1957
3rd 6:30 am Aries
5th 5:19 pm Taurus
8th 2:02 am Gemini
10th 7:42 am Cancer
12th 10:08 am Leo
14th 10:19 am Virgo
16th 10:03 am Libra
18th 11:20 am Scorpio
20th 3:59 pm Sagittarius
23rd 0:35 am Capricorn
25th 12:18 pm Aquarius
28th 0:58 am Pisces
30th 12:52 pm Aries

April 1957
1st 11:10 pm Taurus
4th 7:28 am Gemini
6th 1:35 pm Cancer
8th 5:21 pm Leo
10th 7:12 pm Virgo
12th 8:09 pm Libra
14th 9:46 pm Scorpio
17th 1:45 am Sagittarius
19th 9:13 am Capricorn
21st 7:55 pm Aquarius
24th 8:22 am Pisces
26th 8:20 pm Aries
29th 6:15 am Taurus

May 1957
1st 1:43 pm Gemini
3rd 7:06 pm Cancer
5th 10:53 pm Leo
8th 1:36 am Virgo
10th 3:57 am Libra
12th 6:50 am Scorpio
14th 11:17 am Sagittarius
16th 6:17 pm Capricorn
19th 4:14 am Aquarius
21st 4:22 pm Pisces
24th 4:32 am Aries
26th 2:39 pm Taurus
28th 9:45 pm Gemini
31st 2:04 am Cancer

June 1957
2nd 4:45 am Leo
4th 6:59 am Virgo
6th 9:47 am Libra
8th 1:43 pm Scorpio
10th 7:11 pm Sagittarius
13th 2:38 am Capricorn
15th 12:27 pm Aquarius
18th 0:16 am Pisces
20th 12:45 pm Aries
22nd 11:39 pm Taurus
25th 7:02 am Gemini
27th 10:56 am Cancer
29th 12:30 pm Leo

July 1957
1st 1:25 pm Virgo
3rd 3:18 pm Libra
5th 7:12 pm Scorpio
8th 1:22 am Sagittarius
10th 9:37 am Capricorn
12th 7:43 pm Aquarius
15th 7:34 am Pisces
17th 8:13 pm Aries
20th 7:54 am Taurus
22nd 4:29 pm Gemini
24th 9:02 pm Cancer
26th 10:15 pm Leo
28th 9:59 pm Virgo
30th 10:21 pm Libra

August 1957
2nd 1:02 am Scorpio
4th 6:51 am Sagittarius
6th 3:25 pm Capricorn
9th 2:01 am Aquarius
11th 2:03 pm Pisces
14th 2:46 am Aries
16th 2:59 pm Taurus
19th 0:51 am Gemini
21st 6:45 am Cancer
23rd 8:47 am Leo
25th 8:27 am Virgo
27th 7:46 am Libra
29th 8:51 am Scorpio
31st 1:12 pm Sagittarius

September 1957
2nd 9:07 pm Capricorn
5th 7:51 am Aquarius
7th 8:04 pm Pisces
10th 8:45 am Aries
12th 8:57 pm Taurus
15th 7:23 am Gemini
17th 2:45 pm Cancer
19th 6:28 pm Leo
21st 7:11 pm Virgo
23rd 6:35 pm Libra
25th 6:44 pm Scorpio
27th 9:30 pm Sagittarius
30th 4:03 am Capricorn

October 1957
2nd 2:07 pm Aquarius
5th 2:18 am Pisces
7th 2:56 pm Aries
10th 2:47 am Taurus
12th 12:58 pm Gemini
14th 8:53 pm Cancer
17th 1:59 am Leo
19th 4:23 am Virgo
21st 5:04 am Libra
23rd 5:35 am Scorpio
25th 7:38 am Sagittarius
27th 12:48 pm Capricorn
29th 9:35 pm Aquarius

November 1957
1st 9:20 am Pisces
3rd 10:01 pm Aries
6th 9:36 am Taurus
8th 7:07 pm Gemini
11th 2:23 am Cancer
13th 7:34 am Leo
15th 11:05 am Virgo
17th 1:25 pm Libra
19th 3:20 pm Scorpio
21st 5:55 pm Sagittarius
23rd 10:33 pm Capricorn
26th 6:22 am Aquarius
28th 5:20 pm Pisces

December 1957
1st 5:57 am Aries
3rd 5:47 pm Taurus
6th 2:58 am Gemini
8th 9:13 am Cancer
10th 1:22 pm Leo
12th 4:28 pm Virgo
14th 7:23 pm Libra
16th 10:36 pm Scorpio
19th 2:33 am Sagittarius
21st 7:52 am Capricorn
23rd 3:23 pm Aquarius
26th 1:44 am Pisces
28th 2:14 pm Aries
31st 2:37 am Taurus

January 1958
2nd 12:18 pm Gemini
4th 6:19 pm Cancer
6th 9:21 pm Leo
8th 10:59 pm Virgo
11th 0:52 am Libra
13th 4:04 am Scorpio
15th 8:53 am Sagittarius
17th 3:16 pm Capricorn
19th 11:24 pm Aquarius
22nd 9:45 am Pisces
24th 10:04 pm Aries
27th 10:55 am Taurus
29th 9:47 pm Gemini

February 1958
1st 4:38 am Cancer
3rd 7:35 am Leo
5th 8:12 am Virgo
7th 8:28 am Libra
9th 10:08 am Scorpio
11th 2:16 pm Sagittarius
13th 8:57 pm Capricorn
16th 5:53 am Aquarius
18th 4:42 pm Pisces
21st 5:03 am Aries
23rd 6:05 pm Taurus
26th 5:50 am Gemini
28th 2:12 pm Cancer

March 1958
2nd 6:24 pm Leo
4th 7:14 pm Virgo
6th 6:37 pm Libra
8th 6:38 pm Scorpio
10th 8:59 pm Sagittarius
13th 2:38 am Capricorn
15th 11:31 am Aquarius
17th 10:42 pm Pisces
20th 11:17 am Aries
23rd 0:16 am Taurus
25th 12:17 pm Gemini
27th 9:52 pm Cancer
30th 3:44 am Leo

April 1958
1st 5:59 am Virgo
3rd 5:54 am Libra
5th 5:19 am Scorpio
7th 6:11 am Sagittarius
9th 10:07 am Capricorn
11th 5:45 pm Aquarius
14th 4:40 am Pisces
16th 5:23 pm Aries
19th 6:15 am Taurus
21st 6:01 pm Gemini
24th 3:44 am Cancer
26th 10:39 am Leo
28th 2:37 pm Virgo
30th 4:05 pm Libra

May 1958
2nd 4:14 pm Scorpio
4th 4:46 pm Sagittarius
6th 7:24 pm Capricorn
9th 1:31 am Aquarius
11th 11:30 am Pisces
13th 11:58 pm Aries
16th 12:48 pm Taurus
19th 0:13 am Gemini
21st 9:19 am Cancer
23rd 4:11 pm Leo
25th 8:58 pm Virgo
27th 11:55 pm Libra
30th 1:34 am Scorpio

June 1958
1st 2:55 am Sagittarius
3rd 5:26 am Capricorn
5th 10:40 am Aquarius
7th 7:27 pm Pisces
10th 7:22 am Aries
12th 8:12 pm Taurus
15th 7:28 am Gemini
17th 3:60 pm Cancer
19th 10:03 pm Leo
22nd 2:21 am Virgo
24th 5:41 am Libra
26th 8:30 am Scorpio
28th 11:12 am Sagittarius
30th 2:35 pm Capricorn

July 1958
2nd 7:47 pm Aquarius
5th 3:59 am Pisces
7th 3:20 pm Aries
10th 4:08 am Taurus
12th 3:43 pm Gemini
15th 0:14 am Cancer
17th 5:28 am Leo
19th 8:41 am Virgo
21st 11:12 am Libra
23rd 1:58 pm Scorpio
25th 5:26 pm Sagittarius
27th 9:53 pm Capricorn
30th 3:54 am Aquarius

August 1958
1st 12:14 pm Pisces
3rd 11:14 pm Aries
6th 12:04 pm Taurus
9th 0:16 am Gemini
11th 9:19 am Cancer
13th 2:39 pm Leo
15th 5:05 pm Virgo
17th 6:16 pm Libra
19th 7:50 pm Scorpio
21st 10:48 pm Sagittarius
24th 3:40 am Capricorn
26th 10:30 am Aquarius
28th 7:27 pm Pisces
31st 6:36 am Aries

September 1958
2nd 7:23 pm Taurus
5th 8:04 am Gemini
7th 6:19 pm Cancer
10th 0:41 am Leo
12th 3:19 am Virgo
14th 3:45 am Libra
16th 3:51 am Scorpio
18th 5:19 am Sagittarius
20th 9:17 am Capricorn
22nd 4:06 pm Aquarius
25th 1:34 am Pisces
27th 1:08 pm Aries
30th 1:58 am Taurus

October 1958
2nd 2:48 pm Gemini
5th 1:60 am Cancer
7th 9:46 am Leo
9th 1:46 pm Virgo
11th 2:42 pm Libra
13th 2:13 pm Scorpio
15th 2:13 pm Sagittarius
17th 4:28 pm Capricorn
19th 10:07 pm Aquarius
22nd 7:22 am Pisces
24th 7:12 pm Aries
27th 8:07 am Taurus
29th 8:49 pm Gemini

November 1958
1st 8:06 am Cancer
3rd 4:59 pm Leo
5th 10:44 pm Virgo
8th 1:16 am Libra
10th 1:30 am Scorpio
12th 1:04 am Sagittarius
14th 1:57 am Capricorn
16th 5:59 am Aquarius
18th 2:02 pm Pisces
21st 1:29 am Aries
23rd 2:31 pm Taurus
26th 2:59 am Gemini
28th 1:48 pm Cancer
30th 10:39 pm Leo

December 1958
3rd 5:15 am Virgo
5th 9:27 am Libra
7th 11:26 am Scorpio
9th 12:02 pm Sagittarius
11th 12:51 pm Capricorn
13th 3:45 pm Aquarius
15th 10:16 pm Pisces
18th 8:50 am Aries
20th 9:39 pm Taurus
23rd 10:07 am Gemini
25th 8:31 pm Cancer
28th 4:32 am Leo
30th 10:38 am Virgo

January 1959
1st 3:19 pm Libra
3rd 6:41 pm Scorpio
5th 8:57 pm Sagittarius
7th 10:52 pm Capricorn
10th 1:54 am Aquarius
12th 7:46 am Pisces
14th 5:13 pm Aries
17th 5:34 am Taurus
19th 6:15 pm Gemini
22nd 4:45 am Cancer
24th 12:12 pm Leo
26th 5:12 pm Virgo
28th 8:55 pm Libra
31st 0:07 am Scorpio

February 1959
2nd 3:13 am Sagittarius
4th 6:31 am Capricorn
6th 10:44 am Aquarius
8th 4:55 pm Pisces
11th 1:56 am Aries
13th 1:48 pm Taurus
16th 2:40 am Gemini
18th 1:48 pm Cancer
20th 9:38 pm Leo
23rd 2:07 am Virgo
25th 4:29 am Libra
27th 6:16 am Scorpio

March 1959
1st 8:36 am Sagittarius
3rd 12:09 pm Capricorn
5th 5:19 pm Aquarius
8th 0:26 am Pisces
10th 9:57 am Aries
12th 9:37 pm Taurus
15th 10:31 am Gemini
17th 10:27 pm Cancer
20th 7:19 am Leo
22nd 12:25 pm Virgo
24th 2:25 pm Libra
26th 2:55 pm Scorpio
28th 3:35 pm Sagittarius
30th 5:53 pm Capricorn

April 1959
1st 10:43 pm Aquarius
4th 6:25 am Pisces
6th 4:35 pm Aries
9th 4:31 am Taurus
11th 5:25 pm Gemini
14th 5:46 am Cancer
16th 3:51 pm Leo
18th 10:27 pm Virgo
21st 1:20 am Libra
23rd 1:35 am Scorpio
25th 1:01 am Sagittarius
27th 1:36 am Capricorn
29th 5:01 am Aquarius

May 1959
1st 12:04 pm Pisces
3rd 10:19 pm Aries
6th 10:39 am Taurus
8th 11:34 pm Gemini
11th 11:55 am Cancer
13th 10:39 pm Leo
16th 6:34 am Virgo
18th 11:02 am Libra
20th 12:21 pm Scorpio
22nd 11:52 am Sagittarius
24th 11:29 am Capricorn
26th 1:17 pm Aquarius
28th 6:47 pm Pisces
31st 4:21 am Aries

June 1959
2nd 4:38 pm Taurus
5th 5:35 am Gemini
7th 5:43 pm Cancer
10th 4:16 am Leo
12th 12:45 pm Virgo
14th 6:38 pm Libra
16th 9:37 pm Scorpio
18th 10:14 pm Sagittarius
20th 10:02 pm Capricorn
22nd 11:02 pm Aquarius
25th 3:12 am Pisces
27th 11:34 am Aries
29th 11:12 pm Taurus

July 1959
2nd 12:04 pm Gemini
5th 0:04 am Cancer
7th 10:05 am Leo
9th 6:13 pm Virgo
12th 0:26 am Libra
14th 4:31 am Scorpio
16th 6:39 am Sagittarius
18th 7:42 am Capricorn
20th 9:09 am Aquarius
22nd 12:46 pm Pisces
24th 7:57 pm Aries
27th 6:44 am Taurus
29th 7:23 pm Gemini

August 1959
1st 7:21 am Cancer
3rd 5:06 pm Leo
6th 0:29 am Virgo
8th 5:55 am Libra
10th 9:58 am Scorpio
12th 12:57 pm Sagittarius
14th 3:19 pm Capricorn
16th 5:55 pm Aquarius
18th 10:00 pm Pisces
21st 4:54 am Aries
23rd 3:01 pm Taurus
26th 3:18 am Gemini
28th 3:30 pm Cancer
31st 1:33 am Leo

September 1959
2nd 8:27 am Virgo
4th 12:54 pm Libra
6th 3:53 pm Scorpio
8th 6:20 pm Sagittarius
10th 9:05 pm Capricorn
13th 0:44 am Aquarius
15th 5:56 am Pisces
17th 1:19 pm Aries
19th 11:11 pm Taurus
22nd 11:16 am Gemini
24th 11:50 pm Cancer
27th 10:32 am Leo
29th 6:01 pm Virgo

October 1959
1st 10:07 pm Libra
3rd 11:53 pm Scorpio
6th 0:54 am Sagittarius
8th 2:39 am Capricorn
10th 6:14 am Aquarius
12th 12:09 pm Pisces
14th 8:21 pm Aries
17th 6:40 am Taurus
19th 6:39 pm Gemini
22nd 7:21 am Cancer
24th 7:02 pm Leo
27th 3:46 am Virgo
29th 8:37 am Libra
31st 10:11 am Scorpio

November 1959
2nd 10:03 am Sagittarius
4th 10:10 am Capricorn
6th 12:19 pm Aquarius
8th 5:39 pm Pisces
11th 2:10 am Aries
13th 1:06 pm Taurus
16th 1:15 am Gemini
18th 1:55 pm Cancer
21st 2:02 am Leo
23rd 12:03 pm Virgo
25th 6:37 pm Libra
27th 9:20 pm Scorpio
29th 9:11 pm Sagittarius

December 1959
1st 8:14 pm Capricorn
3rd 8:38 pm Aquarius
6th 0:16 am Pisces
8th 8:04 am Aries
10th 6:57 pm Taurus
13th 7:25 am Gemini
15th 8:00 pm Cancer
18th 7:56 am Leo
20th 6:27 pm Virgo
23rd 2:27 am Libra
25th 6:57 am Scorpio
27th 8:13 am Sagittarius
29th 7:39 am Capricorn
31st 7:20 am Aquarius

January 1960
2nd 9:26 am Pisces
4th 3:28 pm Aries
7th 1:24 am Taurus
9th 1:46 pm Gemini
12th 2:24 am Cancer
14th 1:59 pm Leo
17th 0:04 am Virgo
19th 8:10 am Libra
21st 1:55 pm Scorpio
23rd 4:60 pm Sagittarius
25th 5:58 pm Capricorn
27th 6:21 pm Aquarius
29th 7:59 pm Pisces

February 1960
1st 0:41 am Aries
3rd 9:21 am Taurus
5th 9:01 pm Gemini
8th 9:36 am Cancer
10th 9:09 pm Leo
13th 6:33 am Virgo
15th 1:53 pm Libra
17th 7:23 pm Scorpio
19th 11:12 pm Sagittarius
22nd 1:40 am Capricorn
24th 3:34 am Aquarius
26th 6:06 am Pisces
28th 10:42 am Aries

March 1960
1st 6:22 pm Taurus
4th 5:09 am Gemini
6th 5:36 pm Cancer
9th 5:23 am Leo
11th 2:45 pm Virgo
13th 9:19 pm Libra
16th 1:37 am Scorpio
18th 4:39 am Sagittarius
20th 7:16 am Capricorn
22nd 10:12 am Aquarius
24th 2:05 pm Pisces
26th 7:31 pm Aries
29th 3:15 am Taurus
31st 1:34 pm Gemini

April 1960
3rd 1:47 am Cancer
5th 1:59 pm Leo
8th 0:04 am Virgo
10th 6:34 am Libra
12th 9:59 am Scorpio
14th 11:38 am Sagittarius
16th 1:04 pm Capricorn
18th 3:34 pm Aquarius
20th 7:57 pm Pisces
23rd 2:23 am Aries
25th 10:53 am Taurus
27th 9:16 pm Gemini
30th 9:24 am Cancer

May 1960
2nd 9:59 pm Leo
5th 8:55 am Virgo
7th 4:26 pm Libra
9th 8:05 pm Scorpio
11th 8:55 pm Sagittarius
13th 8:53 pm Capricorn
15th 9:54 pm Aquarius
18th 1:26 am Pisces
20th 7:59 am Aries
22nd 5:02 pm Taurus
25th 3:55 am Gemini
27th 4:07 pm Cancer
30th 4:50 am Leo

June 1960
1st 4:35 pm Virgo
4th 1:30 am Libra
6th 6:16 am Scorpio
8th 7:29 am Sagittarius
10th 6:50 am Capricorn
12th 6:28 am Aquarius
14th 8:24 am Pisces
16th 1:48 pm Aries
18th 10:35 pm Taurus
21st 9:48 am Gemini
23rd 10:11 pm Cancer
26th 10:50 am Leo
28th 10:52 pm Virgo

July 1960
1st 8:41 am Libra
3rd 3:02 pm Scorpio
5th 5:37 pm Sagittarius
7th 5:32 pm Capricorn
9th 4:45 pm Aquarius
11th 5:24 pm Pisces
13th 9:10 pm Aries
16th 4:51 am Taurus
18th 3:43 pm Gemini
21st 4:09 am Cancer
23rd 4:46 pm Leo
26th 4:30 am Virgo
28th 2:30 pm Libra
30th 9:53 pm Scorpio

August 1960
2nd 2:02 am Sagittarius
4th 3:24 am Capricorn
6th 3:21 am Aquarius
8th 3:43 am Pisces
10th 6:25 am Aries
12th 12:41 pm Taurus
14th 10:30 pm Gemini
17th 10:43 am Cancer
19th 11:18 pm Leo
22nd 10:39 am Virgo
24th 8:08 pm Libra
27th 3:22 am Scorpio
29th 8:16 am Sagittarius
31st 11:06 am Capricorn

September 1960
2nd 12:34 pm Aquarius
4th 1:53 pm Pisces
6th 4:29 pm Aries
8th 9:46 pm Taurus
11th 6:33 am Gemini
13th 6:12 pm Cancer
16th 6:45 am Leo
18th 6:05 pm Virgo
21st 2:57 am Libra
23rd 9:16 am Scorpio
25th 1:41 pm Sagittarius
27th 4:53 pm Capricorn
29th 7:32 pm Aquarius

October 1960
1st 10:13 pm Pisces
4th 1:47 am Aries
6th 7:11 am Taurus
8th 3:19 pm Gemini
11th 2:19 am Cancer
13th 2:54 pm Leo
16th 2:39 am Virgo
18th 11:27 am Libra
20th 5:03 pm Scorpio
22nd 8:15 pm Sagittarius
24th 10:28 pm Capricorn
27th 0:58 am Aquarius
29th 4:27 am Pisces
31st 9:13 am Aries

November 1960
2nd 3:28 pm Taurus
4th 11:43 pm Gemini
7th 10:27 am Cancer
9th 10:59 pm Leo
12th 11:20 am Virgo
14th 9:05 pm Libra
17th 2:51 am Scorpio
19th 5:15 am Sagittarius
21st 6:03 am Capricorn
23rd 7:07 am Aquarius
25th 9:53 am Pisces
27th 2:54 pm Aries
29th 10:01 pm Taurus

December 1960
2nd 7:02 am Gemini
4th 5:53 pm Cancer
7th 6:20 am Leo
9th 7:12 pm Virgo
12th 6:05 am Libra
14th 1:07 pm Scorpio
16th 4:02 pm Sagittarius
18th 4:15 pm Capricorn
20th 3:52 pm Aquarius
22nd 4:52 pm Pisces
24th 8:37 pm Aries
27th 3:34 am Taurus
29th 1:04 pm Gemini

January 1961
1st 0:22 am Cancer
3rd 12:55 pm Leo
6th 1:47 am Virgo
8th 1:26 pm Libra
10th 10:06 pm Scorpio
13th 2:38 am Sagittarius
15th 3:39 am Capricorn
17th 2:56 am Aquarius
19th 2:33 am Pisces
21st 4:31 am Aries
23rd 9:57 am Taurus
25th 6:54 pm Gemini
28th 6:25 am Cancer
30th 7:06 pm Leo

February 1961
2nd 7:48 am Virgo
4th 7:25 pm Libra
7th 4:48 am Scorpio
9th 10:56 am Sagittarius
11th 1:46 pm Capricorn
13th 2:13 pm Aquarius
15th 1:55 pm Pisces
17th 2:45 pm Aries
19th 6:26 pm Taurus
22nd 1:54 am Gemini
24th 12:52 pm Cancer
27th 1:35 am Leo

March 1961
1st 2:11 pm Virgo
4th 1:21 am Libra
6th 10:21 am Scorpio
8th 5:01 pm Sagittarius
10th 9:18 pm Capricorn
12th 11:30 pm Aquarius
15th 0:26 am Pisces
17th 1:34 am Aries
19th 4:28 am Taurus
21st 10:38 am Gemini
23rd 8:24 pm Cancer
26th 8:49 am Leo
28th 9:31 pm Virgo
31st 8:19 am Libra

April 1961
2nd 4:35 pm Scorpio
4th 10:35 pm Sagittarius
7th 2:52 am Capricorn
9th 6:02 am Aquarius
11th 8:32 am Pisces
13th 10:57 am Aries
15th 2:20 pm Taurus
17th 7:58 pm Gemini
20th 4:53 am Cancer
22nd 4:45 pm Leo
25th 5:30 am Virgo
27th 4:33 pm Libra
30th 0:29 am Scorpio

May 1961
2nd 5:24 am Sagittarius
4th 8:40 am Capricorn
6th 11:25 am Aquarius
8th 2:24 pm Pisces
10th 5:57 pm Aries
12th 10:25 pm Taurus
15th 4:36 am Gemini
17th 1:21 pm Cancer
20th 0:45 am Leo
22nd 1:38 pm Virgo
25th 1:17 am Libra
27th 9:30 am Scorpio
29th 2:08 pm Sagittarius
31st 4:20 pm Capricorn

June 1961
2nd 5:47 pm Aquarius
4th 7:52 pm Pisces
6th 11:25 pm Aries
9th 4:39 am Taurus
11th 11:44 am Gemini
13th 8:51 pm Cancer
16th 8:17 am Leo
18th 9:11 pm Virgo
21st 9:29 am Libra
23rd 6:47 pm Scorpio
26th 0:05 am Sagittarius
28th 1:60 am Capricorn
30th 2:18 am Aquarius

July 1961
2nd 2:55 am Pisces
4th 5:16 am Aries
6th 10:06 am Taurus
8th 5:31 pm Gemini
11th 3:15 am Cancer
13th 2:58 pm Leo
16th 3:54 am Virgo
18th 4:35 pm Libra
21st 3:01 am Scorpio
23rd 9:35 am Sagittarius
25th 12:24 pm Capricorn
27th 12:40 pm Aquarius
29th 12:15 pm Pisces
31st 1:01 pm Aries

August 1961
2nd 4:25 pm Taurus
4th 11:06 pm Gemini
7th 8:59 am Cancer
9th 9:01 pm Leo
12th 10:01 am Virgo
14th 10:43 pm Libra
17th 9:41 am Scorpio
19th 5:40 pm Sagittarius
21st 10:05 pm Capricorn
23rd 11:24 pm Aquarius
25th 11:02 pm Pisces
27th 10:49 pm Aries
30th 0:37 am Taurus

September 1961
1st 5:56 am Gemini
3rd 3:04 pm Cancer
6th 3:01 am Leo
8th 4:05 pm Virgo
11th 4:32 am Libra
13th 3:21 pm Scorpio
15th 11:54 pm Sagittarius
18th 5:38 am Capricorn
20th 8:40 am Aquarius
22nd 9:34 am Pisces
24th 9:41 am Aries
26th 10:46 am Taurus
28th 2:36 pm Gemini
30th 10:19 pm Cancer

October 1961
3rd 9:44 am Leo
5th 10:45 pm Virgo
8th 11:01 am Libra
10th 9:19 pm Scorpio
13th 5:19 am Sagittarius
15th 11:21 am Capricorn
17th 3:34 pm Aquarius
19th 6:08 pm Pisces
21st 7:34 pm Aries
23rd 9:07 pm Taurus
26th 0:23 am Gemini
28th 7:06 am Cancer
30th 5:32 pm Leo

November 1961
2nd 6:16 am Virgo
4th 6:40 pm Libra
7th 4:37 am Scorpio
9th 11:47 am Sagittarius
11th 4:58 pm Capricorn
13th 8:59 pm Aquarius
16th 0:19 am Pisces
18th 3:10 am Aries
20th 6:03 am Taurus
22nd 10:01 am Gemini
24th 4:24 pm Cancer
27th 2:01 am Leo
29th 2:24 pm Virgo

December 1961
2nd 3:06 am Libra
4th 1:24 pm Scorpio
6th 8:21 pm Sagittarius
9th 0:31 am Capricorn
11th 3:12 am Aquarius
13th 5:42 am Pisces
15th 8:45 am Aries
17th 12:40 pm Taurus
19th 5:49 pm Gemini
22nd 0:49 am Cancer
24th 10:28 am Leo
26th 10:29 pm Virgo
29th 11:24 am Libra
31st 10:40 pm Scorpio

January 1962
3rd 6:19 am Sagittarius
5th 10:19 am Capricorn
7th 11:58 am Aquarius
9th 12:55 pm Pisces
11th 2:37 pm Aries
13th 6:05 pm Taurus
15th 11:42 pm Gemini
18th 7:42 am Cancer
20th 5:52 pm Leo
23rd 5:54 am Virgo
25th 6:51 pm Libra
28th 6:50 am Scorpio
30th 3:54 pm Sagittarius

February 1962
1st 9:07 pm Capricorn
3rd 10:56 pm Aquarius
5th 10:52 pm Pisces
7th 10:51 pm Aries
10th 0:36 am Taurus
12th 5:22 am Gemini
14th 1:24 pm Cancer
17th 0:04 am Leo
19th 12:28 pm Virgo
22nd 1:21 am Libra
24th 1:34 pm Scorpio
26th 11:45 pm Sagittarius

March 1962
1st 6:33 am Capricorn
3rd 9:47 am Aquarius
5th 10:14 am Pisces
7th 9:34 am Aries
9th 9:45 am Taurus
11th 12:41 pm Gemini
13th 7:30 pm Cancer
16th 5:58 am Leo
18th 6:35 pm Virgo
21st 7:28 am Libra
23rd 7:28 pm Scorpio
26th 5:48 am Sagittarius
28th 1:41 pm Capricorn
30th 6:41 pm Aquarius

April 1962
1st 8:42 pm Pisces
3rd 8:40 pm Aries
5th 8:27 pm Taurus
7th 10:02 pm Gemini
10th 3:14 am Cancer
12th 12:39 pm Leo
15th 0:57 am Virgo
17th 1:54 pm Libra
20th 1:37 am Scorpio
22nd 11:26 am Sagittarius
24th 7:19 pm Capricorn
27th 1:08 am Aquarius
29th 4:39 am Pisces

May 1962
1st 6:12 am Aries
3rd 6:50 am Taurus
5th 8:21 am Gemini
7th 12:34 pm Cancer
9th 8:39 pm Leo
12th 8:12 am Virgo
14th 9:04 pm Libra
17th 8:42 am Scorpio
19th 6:01 pm Sagittarius
22nd 1:08 am Capricorn
24th 6:30 am Aquarius
26th 10:28 am Pisces
28th 1:15 pm Aries
30th 3:17 pm Taurus

June 1962
1st 5:43 pm Gemini
3rd 9:60 pm Cancer
6th 5:26 am Leo
8th 4:14 pm Virgo
11th 4:51 am Libra
13th 4:43 pm Scorpio
16th 2:03 am Sagittarius
18th 8:28 am Capricorn
20th 12:47 pm Aquarius
22nd 3:59 pm Pisces
24th 6:44 pm Aries
26th 9:35 pm Taurus
29th 1:10 am Gemini

July 1962
1st 6:23 am Cancer
3rd 2:00 pm Leo
6th 0:22 am Virgo
8th 12:48 pm Libra
11th 1:05 am Scorpio
13th 10:55 am Sagittarius
15th 5:28 pm Capricorn
17th 9:07 pm Aquarius
19th 11:00 pm Pisces
22nd 0:35 am Aries
24th 2:60 am Taurus
26th 7:00 am Gemini
28th 1:05 pm Cancer
30th 9:24 pm Leo

August 1962
2nd 7:60 am Virgo
4th 8:18 pm Libra
7th 8:54 am Scorpio
9th 7:46 pm Sagittarius
12th 3:14 am Capricorn
14th 7:03 am Aquarius
16th 8:16 am Pisces
18th 8:27 am Aries
20th 9:24 am Taurus
22nd 12:33 pm Gemini
24th 6:38 pm Cancer
27th 3:32 am Leo
29th 2:38 pm Virgo

September 1962
1st 3:02 am Libra
3rd 3:46 pm Scorpio
6th 3:25 am Sagittarius
8th 12:15 pm Capricorn
10th 5:21 pm Aquarius
12th 6:59 pm Pisces
14th 6:33 pm Aries
16th 6:04 pm Taurus
18th 7:32 pm Gemini
21st 0:26 am Cancer
23rd 9:11 am Leo
25th 8:32 pm Virgo
28th 9:09 am Libra
30th 9:49 pm Scorpio

October 1962
3rd 9:38 am Sagittarius
5th 7:32 pm Capricorn
8th 2:19 am Aquarius
10th 5:25 am Pisces
12th 5:38 am Aries
14th 4:45 am Taurus
16th 4:54 am Gemini
18th 8:10 am Cancer
20th 3:35 pm Leo
23rd 2:31 am Virgo
25th 3:13 pm Libra
28th 3:48 am Scorpio
30th 3:18 pm Sagittarius

November 1962
2nd 1:17 am Capricorn
4th 8:58 am Aquarius
6th 1:47 pm Pisces
8th 3:42 pm Aries
10th 3:44 pm Taurus
12th 3:47 pm Gemini
14th 5:52 pm Cancer
16th 11:40 pm Leo
19th 9:36 am Virgo
21st 9:58 pm Libra
24th 10:30 am Scorpio
26th 9:41 pm Sagittarius
29th 6:58 am Capricorn

December 1962
1st 2:23 pm Aquarius
3rd 7:52 pm Pisces
5th 11:16 pm Aries
8th 0:59 am Taurus
10th 2:07 am Gemini
12th 4:24 am Cancer
14th 9:24 am Leo
16th 6:02 pm Virgo
19th 5:41 am Libra
21st 6:16 pm Scorpio
24th 5:29 am Sagittarius
26th 2:14 pm Capricorn
28th 8:41 pm Aquarius
31st 1:19 am Pisces

January 1963
2nd 4:47 am Aries
4th 7:34 am Taurus
6th 10:16 am Gemini
8th 1:44 pm Cancer
10th 7:03 pm Leo
13th 3:08 am Virgo
15th 2:06 pm Libra
18th 2:33 am Scorpio
20th 2:16 pm Sagittarius
22nd 11:23 pm Capricorn
25th 5:11 am Aquarius
27th 8:33 am Pisces
29th 10:43 am Aries
31st 12:56 pm Taurus

February 1963
2nd 4:06 pm Gemini
4th 8:42 pm Cancer
7th 3:08 am Leo
9th 11:39 am Virgo
11th 10:19 pm Libra
14th 10:37 am Scorpio
16th 10:54 pm Sagittarius
19th 8:54 am Capricorn
21st 3:18 pm Aquarius
23rd 6:13 pm Pisces
25th 7:04 pm Aries
27th 7:40 pm Taurus

March 1963
1st 9:40 pm Gemini
4th 2:09 am Cancer
6th 9:18 am Leo
8th 6:35 pm Virgo
11th 5:36 am Libra
13th 5:52 pm Scorpio
16th 6:26 am Sagittarius
18th 5:31 pm Capricorn
21st 1:19 am Aquarius
23rd 4:60 am Pisces
25th 5:35 am Aries
27th 4:58 am Taurus
29th 5:16 am Gemini
31st 8:18 am Cancer

April 1963
2nd 2:49 pm Leo
5th 0:22 am Virgo
7th 11:51 am Libra
10th 0:14 am Scorpio
12th 12:48 pm Sagittarius
15th 0:27 am Capricorn
17th 9:30 am Aquarius
19th 2:48 pm Pisces
21st 4:25 pm Aries
23rd 3:50 pm Taurus
25th 3:09 pm Gemini
27th 4:32 pm Cancer
29th 9:26 pm Leo

May 1963
2nd 6:16 am Virgo
4th 5:43 pm Libra
7th 6:16 am Scorpio
9th 6:43 pm Sagittarius
12th 6:13 am Capricorn
14th 3:48 pm Aquarius
16th 10:32 pm Pisces
19th 1:46 am Aries
21st 2:21 am Taurus
23rd 1:55 am Gemini
25th 2:31 am Cancer
27th 6:03 am Leo
29th 1:27 pm Virgo

June 1963
1st 0:10 am Libra
3rd 12:38 pm Scorpio
6th 1:02 am Sagittarius
8th 12:05 pm Capricorn
10th 9:22 pm Aquarius
13th 4:20 am Pisces
15th 8:44 am Aries
17th 10:53 am Taurus
19th 11:45 am Gemini
21st 12:51 pm Cancer
23rd 3:50 pm Leo
25th 9:58 pm Virgo
28th 7:43 am Libra
30th 7:48 pm Scorpio

July 1963
3rd 8:10 am Sagittarius
5th 7:02 pm Capricorn
8th 3:35 am Aquarius
10th 9:51 am Pisces
12th 2:15 pm Aries
14th 5:15 pm Taurus
16th 7:28 pm Gemini
18th 9:47 pm Cancer
21st 1:16 am Leo
23rd 7:11 am Virgo
25th 4:06 pm Libra
28th 3:38 am Scorpio
30th 4:06 pm Sagittarius

August 1963
2nd 3:11 am Capricorn
4th 11:22 am Aquarius
6th 4:44 pm Pisces
8th 8:07 pm Aries
10th 10:39 pm Taurus
13th 1:17 am Gemini
15th 4:41 am Cancer
17th 9:20 am Leo
19th 3:44 pm Virgo
22nd 0:27 am Libra
24th 11:41 am Scorpio
27th 0:14 am Sagittarius
29th 11:53 am Capricorn
31st 8:35 pm Aquarius

September 1963
3rd 1:37 am Pisces
5th 3:52 am Aries
7th 5:04 am Taurus
9th 6:49 am Gemini
11th 10:12 am Cancer
13th 3:33 pm Leo
15th 10:49 pm Virgo
18th 8:03 am Libra
20th 7:12 pm Scorpio
23rd 7:51 am Sagittarius
25th 8:15 pm Capricorn
28th 5:58 am Aquarius
30th 11:40 am Pisces

October 1963
2nd 1:44 pm Aries
4th 1:50 pm Taurus
6th 2:01 pm Gemini
8th 4:04 pm Cancer
10th 8:55 pm Leo
13th 4:36 am Virgo
15th 2:27 pm Libra
18th 1:53 am Scorpio
20th 2:33 pm Sagittarius
23rd 3:20 am Capricorn
25th 2:15 pm Aquarius
27th 9:35 pm Pisces
30th 0:39 am Aries

November 1963
1st 0:42 am Taurus
2nd 11:49 pm Gemini
5th 0:08 am Cancer
7th 3:26 am Leo
9th 10:17 am Virgo
11th 8:09 pm Libra
14th 7:57 am Scorpio
16th 8:41 pm Sagittarius
19th 9:22 am Capricorn
21st 8:50 pm Aquarius
24th 5:28 am Pisces
26th 10:19 am Aries
28th 11:46 am Taurus
30th 11:15 am Gemini

December 1963
2nd 10:48 am Cancer
4th 12:26 pm Leo
6th 5:30 pm Virgo
9th 2:23 am Libra
11th 2:05 pm Scorpio
14th 2:52 am Sagittarius
16th 3:20 pm Capricorn
19th 2:28 am Aquarius
21st 11:25 am Pisces
23rd 5:37 pm Aries
25th 8:55 pm Taurus
27th 9:57 pm Gemini
29th 10:08 pm Cancer
31st 11:09 pm Leo

January 1964
3rd 2:49 am Virgo
5th 10:14 am Libra
7th 9:04 pm Scorpio
10th 9:47 am Sagittarius
12th 10:12 pm Capricorn
15th 8:44 am Aquarius
17th 5:01 pm Pisces
19th 11:10 pm Aries
22nd 3:23 am Taurus
24th 6:03 am Gemini
26th 7:52 am Cancer
28th 9:47 am Leo
30th 1:13 pm Virgo

February 1964
1st 7:28 pm Libra
4th 5:14 am Scorpio
6th 5:34 pm Sagittarius
9th 6:07 am Capricorn
11th 4:35 pm Aquarius
14th 0:07 am Pisces
16th 5:08 am Aries
18th 8:44 am Taurus
20th 11:48 am Gemini
22nd 2:50 pm Cancer
24th 6:12 pm Leo
26th 10:30 pm Virgo
29th 4:49 am Libra

March 1964
2nd 1:57 pm Scorpio
5th 1:46 am Sagittarius
7th 2:32 pm Capricorn
10th 1:33 am Aquarius
12th 9:00 am Pisces
14th 1:11 pm Aries
16th 3:30 pm Taurus
18th 5:27 pm Gemini
20th 8:13 pm Cancer
23rd 0:16 am Leo
25th 5:43 am Virgo
27th 12:50 pm Libra
29th 10:04 pm Scorpio

April 1964
1st 9:42 am Sagittarius
3rd 10:37 pm Capricorn
6th 10:19 am Aquarius
8th 6:42 pm Pisces
10th 11:07 pm Aries
13th 0:36 am Taurus
15th 1:05 am Gemini
17th 2:23 am Cancer
19th 5:42 am Leo
21st 11:20 am Virgo
23rd 7:09 pm Libra
26th 5:03 am Scorpio
28th 4:47 pm Sagittarius

May 1964
1st 5:42 am Capricorn
3rd 6:04 pm Aquarius
6th 3:40 am Pisces
8th 9:11 am Aries
10th 11:05 am Taurus
12th 11:01 am Gemini
14th 10:56 am Cancer
16th 12:36 pm Leo
18th 5:06 pm Virgo
21st 0:40 am Libra
23rd 11:01 am Scorpio
25th 11:04 pm Sagittarius
28th 12:00 pm Capricorn
31st 0:32 am Aquarius

June 1964
2nd 10:57 am Pisces
4th 5:60 pm Aries
6th 9:18 pm Taurus
8th 9:49 pm Gemini
10th 9:17 pm Cancer
12th 9:37 pm Leo
15th 0:27 am Virgo
17th 6:57 am Libra
19th 4:52 pm Scorpio
22nd 5:05 am Sagittarius
24th 6:01 pm Capricorn
27th 6:20 am Aquarius
29th 4:54 pm Pisces

July 1964
2nd 0:52 am Aries
4th 5:40 am Taurus
6th 7:41 am Gemini
8th 7:57 am Cancer
10th 8:04 am Leo
12th 9:49 am Virgo
14th 2:47 pm Libra
16th 11:33 pm Scorpio
19th 11:30 am Sagittarius
22nd 0:28 am Capricorn
24th 12:28 pm Aquarius
26th 10:36 pm Pisces
29th 6:23 am Aries
31st 11:57 am Taurus

August 1964
2nd 3:27 pm Gemini
4th 5:13 pm Cancer
6th 6:12 pm Leo
8th 7:52 pm Virgo
10th 11:53 pm Libra
13th 7:36 am Scorpio
15th 6:45 pm Sagittarius
18th 7:38 am Capricorn
20th 7:37 pm Aquarius
23rd 5:11 am Pisces
25th 12:13 pm Aries
27th 5:22 pm Taurus
29th 9:17 pm Gemini

September 1964
- 1st 0:15 am Cancer
- 3rd 2:38 am Leo
- 5th 5:15 am Virgo
- 7th 9:24 am Libra
- 9th 4:24 pm Scorpio
- 12th 2:49 am Sagittarius
- 14th 3:29 pm Capricorn
- 17th 3:45 am Aquarius
- 19th 1:18 pm Pisces
- 21st 7:42 pm Aries
- 23rd 11:46 pm Taurus
- 26th 2:46 am Gemini
- 28th 5:40 am Cancer
- 30th 8:54 am Leo

October 1964
- 2nd 12:45 pm Virgo
- 4th 5:47 pm Libra
- 7th 0:59 am Scorpio
- 9th 11:06 am Sagittarius
- 11th 11:34 pm Capricorn
- 14th 12:13 pm Aquarius
- 16th 10:32 pm Pisces
- 19th 5:02 am Aries
- 21st 8:22 am Taurus
- 23rd 10:04 am Gemini
- 25th 11:39 am Cancer
- 27th 2:17 pm Leo
- 29th 6:27 pm Virgo

November 1964
- 1st 0:24 am Libra
- 3rd 8:28 am Scorpio
- 5th 6:46 pm Sagittarius
- 8th 7:08 am Capricorn
- 10th 8:09 pm Aquarius
- 13th 7:26 am Pisces
- 15th 3:05 pm Aries
- 17th 6:55 pm Taurus
- 19th 7:58 pm Gemini
- 21st 8:04 pm Cancer
- 23rd 9:00 pm Leo
- 26th 0:02 am Virgo
- 28th 5:57 am Libra
- 30th 2:34 pm Scorpio

December 1964
- 3rd 1:24 am Sagittarius
- 5th 1:55 pm Capricorn
- 8th 2:58 am Aquarius
- 10th 2:57 pm Pisces
- 13th 0:13 am Aries
- 15th 5:29 am Taurus
- 17th 7:18 am Gemini
- 19th 7:02 am Cancer
- 21st 6:34 am Leo
- 23rd 7:46 am Virgo
- 25th 12:10 pm Libra
- 27th 8:12 pm Scorpio
- 30th 7:22 am Sagittarius

January 1965
- 1st 8:06 pm Capricorn
- 4th 9:03 am Aquarius
- 6th 9:05 pm Pisces
- 9th 7:05 am Aries
- 11th 2:05 pm Taurus
- 13th 5:44 pm Gemini
- 15th 6:32 pm Cancer
- 17th 5:58 pm Leo
- 19th 5:58 pm Virgo
- 21st 8:31 pm Libra
- 24th 3:03 am Scorpio
- 26th 1:34 pm Sagittarius
- 29th 2:21 am Capricorn
- 31st 3:16 pm Aquarius

February 1965
- 3rd 2:55 am Pisces
- 5th 12:41 pm Aries
- 7th 8:22 pm Taurus
- 10th 1:36 am Gemini
- 12th 4:12 am Cancer
- 14th 4:53 am Leo
- 16th 5:08 am Virgo
- 18th 6:50 am Libra
- 20th 11:51 am Scorpio
- 22nd 8:58 pm Sagittarius
- 25th 9:16 am Capricorn
- 27th 10:13 pm Aquarius

March 1965
- 2nd 9:34 am Pisces
- 4th 6:43 pm Aries
- 7th 1:50 am Taurus
- 9th 7:12 am Gemini
- 11th 11:01 am Cancer
- 13th 1:22 pm Leo
- 15th 2:57 pm Virgo
- 17th 5:07 pm Libra
- 19th 9:34 pm Scorpio
- 22nd 5:39 am Sagittarius
- 24th 5:09 pm Capricorn
- 27th 5:56 am Aquarius
- 29th 5:28 pm Pisces

April 1965
- 1st 2:17 am Aries
- 3rd 8:25 am Taurus
- 5th 12:53 pm Gemini
- 7th 4:22 pm Cancer
- 9th 7:24 pm Leo
- 11th 10:15 pm Virgo
- 14th 1:39 am Libra
- 16th 6:45 am Scorpio
- 18th 2:35 pm Sagittarius
- 21st 1:25 am Capricorn
- 23rd 2:03 pm Aquarius
- 26th 2:00 am Pisces
- 28th 11:06 am Aries
- 30th 4:59 pm Taurus

May 1965
- 2nd 8:25 pm Gemini
- 4th 10:38 pm Cancer
- 7th 0:49 am Leo
- 9th 3:48 am Virgo
- 11th 8:05 am Libra
- 13th 2:12 pm Scorpio
- 15th 10:32 pm Sagittarius
- 18th 9:21 am Capricorn
- 20th 9:50 pm Aquarius
- 23rd 10:12 am Pisces
- 25th 8:16 pm Aries
- 28th 2:47 am Taurus
- 30th 5:56 am Gemini

June 1965
- 1st 7:04 am Cancer
- 3rd 7:48 am Leo
- 5th 9:36 am Virgo
- 7th 1:33 pm Libra
- 9th 8:05 pm Scorpio
- 12th 5:12 am Sagittarius
- 14th 4:21 pm Capricorn
- 17th 4:52 am Aquarius
- 19th 5:28 pm Pisces
- 22nd 4:27 am Aries
- 24th 12:11 pm Taurus
- 26th 4:13 pm Gemini
- 28th 5:17 pm Cancer
- 30th 4:60 pm Leo

July 1965
- 2nd 5:14 pm Virgo
- 4th 7:45 pm Libra
- 7th 1:40 am Scorpio
- 9th 10:56 am Sagittarius
- 11th 10:30 pm Capricorn
- 14th 11:07 am Aquarius
- 16th 11:44 pm Pisces
- 19th 11:09 am Aries
- 21st 8:11 pm Taurus
- 24th 1:47 am Gemini
- 26th 3:52 am Cancer
- 28th 3:37 am Leo
- 30th 2:57 am Virgo

August 1965
- 1st 3:57 am Libra
- 3rd 8:26 am Scorpio
- 5th 4:53 pm Sagittarius
- 8th 4:23 am Capricorn
- 10th 5:08 pm Aquarius
- 13th 5:37 am Pisces
- 15th 4:55 pm Aries
- 18th 2:27 am Taurus
- 20th 9:17 am Gemini
- 22nd 1:00 pm Cancer
- 24th 1:59 pm Leo
- 26th 1:38 pm Virgo
- 28th 1:57 pm Libra
- 30th 4:60 pm Scorpio

September 1965
- 1st 11:60 pm Sagittarius
- 4th 10:54 am Capricorn
- 6th 11:34 pm Aquarius
- 9th 11:55 am Pisces
- 11th 10:50 pm Aries
- 14th 7:54 am Taurus
- 16th 3:03 pm Gemini
- 18th 8:00 pm Cancer
- 20th 10:35 pm Leo
- 22nd 11:31 pm Virgo
- 25th 0:17 am Libra
- 27th 2:50 am Scorpio
- 29th 8:47 am Sagittarius

October 1965
- 1st 6:31 pm Capricorn
- 4th 6:49 am Aquarius
- 6th 7:12 pm Pisces
- 9th 5:51 am Aries
- 11th 2:15 pm Taurus
- 13th 8:39 pm Gemini
- 16th 1:26 am Cancer
- 18th 4:50 am Leo
- 20th 7:14 am Virgo
- 22nd 9:24 am Libra
- 24th 12:37 pm Scorpio
- 26th 6:14 pm Sagittarius
- 29th 3:09 am Capricorn
- 31st 2:51 pm Aquarius

November 1965
- 3rd 3:23 am Pisces
- 5th 2:19 pm Aries
- 7th 10:30 pm Taurus
- 10th 3:52 am Gemini
- 12th 7:28 am Cancer
- 14th 10:14 am Leo
- 16th 12:55 pm Virgo
- 18th 4:11 pm Libra
- 20th 8:39 pm Sqorpio
- 23rd 2:59 am Sagittarius
- 25th 11:49 am Capricorn
- 27th 11:06 pm Aquarius
- 30th 11:40 am Pisces

December 1965
- 2nd 11:23 pm Aries
- 5th 8:07 am Taurus
- 7th 1:24 pm Gemini
- 9th 3:55 pm Cancer
- 11th 5:08 pm Leo
- 13th 6:37 pm Virgo
- 15th 9:34 pm Libra
- 18th 2:42 am Scorpio
- 20th 10:04 am Sagittarius
- 22nd 7:29 pm Capricorn
- 25th 6:46 am Aquarius
- 27th 7:18 pm Pisces
- 30th 7:38 am Aries

January 1966
- 1st 5:42 pm Taurus
- 4th 0:07 am Gemini
- 6th 2:39 am Cancer
- 8th 2:50 am Leo
- 10th 2:37 am Virgo
- 12th 3:57 am Libra
- 14th 8:13 am Scorpio
- 16th 3:42 pm Sagittarius
- 19th 1:45 am Capricorn
- 21st 1:27 pm Aquarius
- 24th 1:59 am Pisces
- 26th 2:32 pm Aries
- 29th 1:41 am Taurus
- 31st 9:38 am Gemini

February 1966
- 2nd 1:35 pm Cancer
- 4th 2:11 pm Leo
- 6th 1:13 pm Virgo
- 8th 12:56 pm Libra
- 10th 3:20 pm Scorpio
- 12th 9:35 pm Sagittarius
- 15th 7:27 am Capricorn
- 17th 7:26 pm Aquarius
- 20th 8:05 am Pisces
- 22nd 8:29 pm Aries
- 25th 7:51 am Taurus
- 27th 4:59 pm Gemini

March 1966
- 1st 10:48 pm Cancer
- 4th 0:56 am Leo
- 6th 0:36 am Virgo
- 7th 11:49 pm Libra
- 10th 0:48 am Scorpio
- 12th 5:22 am Sagittarius
- 14th 1:60 pm Capricorn
- 17th 1:35 am Aquarius
- 19th 2:18 pm Pisces
- 22nd 2:33 am Aries
- 24th 1:29 pm Taurus
- 26th 10:41 pm Gemini
- 29th 5:21 am Cancer
- 31st 9:08 am Leo

April 1966
- 2nd 10:29 am Virgo
- 4th 10:41 am Libra
- 6th 11:35 am Scorpio
- 8th 2:59 pm Sagittarius
- 10th 10:03 pm Capricorn
- 13th 8:44 am Aquarius
- 15th 9:12 pm Pisces
- 18th 9:25 am Aries
- 20th 7:57 pm Taurus
- 23rd 4:24 am Gemini
- 25th 10:45 am Cancer
- 27th 3:06 pm Leo
- 29th 5:47 pm Virgo

May 1966
- 1st 7:31 pm Libra
- 3rd 9:24 pm Scorpio
- 6th 0:53 am Sagittarius
- 8th 7:17 am Capricorn
- 10th 4:54 pm Aquarius
- 13th 4:55 am Pisces
- 15th 5:13 pm Aries
- 18th 3:45 am Taurus
- 20th 11:35 am Gemini
- 22nd 4:57 pm Cancer
- 24th 8:35 pm Leo
- 26th 11:21 pm Virgo
- 29th 1:59 am Libra
- 31st 5:12 am Scorpio

June 1966
- 2nd 9:41 am Sagittarius
- 4th 4:13 pm Capricorn
- 7th 1:23 am Aquarius
- 9th 12:58 pm Pisces
- 12th 1:26 am Aries
- 14th 12:26 pm Taurus
- 16th 8:23 pm Gemini
- 19th 1:03 am Cancer
- 21st 3:27 am Leo
- 23rd 5:08 am Virgo
- 25th 7:24 am Libra
- 27th 11:06 am Scorpio
- 29th 4:33 pm Sagittarius

July 1966
- 1st 11:51 pm Capricorn
- 4th 9:16 am Aquarius
- 6th 8:40 pm Pisces
- 9th 9:15 am Aries
- 11th 9:01 pm Taurus
- 14th 5:46 am Gemini
- 16th 10:38 am Cancer
- 18th 12:24 pm Leo
- 20th 12:47 pm Virgo
- 22nd 1:41 pm Libra
- 24th 4:35 pm Scorpio
- 26th 10:06 pm Sagittarius
- 29th 6:06 am Capricorn
- 31st 4:03 pm Aquarius

August 1966
- 3rd 3:35 am Pisces
- 5th 4:14 pm Aries
- 8th 4:36 am Taurus
- 10th 2:33 pm Gemini
- 12th 8:38 pm Cancer
- 14th 10:49 pm Leo
- 16th 10:35 pm Virgo
- 18th 10:05 pm Libra
- 20th 11:23 pm Scorpio
- 23rd 3:53 am Sagittarius
- 25th 11:40 am Capricorn
- 27th 9:56 pm Aquarius
- 30th 9:48 am Pisces

September 1966
- 1st 10:27 pm Aries
- 4th 10:57 am Taurus
- 6th 9:50 pm Gemini
- 9th 5:23 am Cancer
- 11th 8:57 am Leo
- 13th 9:24 am Virgo
- 15th 8:36 am Libra
- 17th 8:38 am Scorpio
- 19th 11:27 am Sagittarius
- 21st 5:56 pm Capricorn
- 24th 3:48 am Aquarius
- 26th 3:48 pm Pisces
- 29th 4:29 am Aries

October 1966
- 1st 4:45 pm Taurus
- 4th 3:42 am Gemini
- 6th 12:08 pm Cancer
- 8th 5:21 pm Leo
- 10th 7:25 pm Virgo
- 12th 7:30 pm Libra
- 14th 7:24 pm Scorpio
- 16th 9:01 pm Sagittarius
- 19th 1:58 am Capricorn
- 21st 10:46 am Aquarius
- 23rd 10:21 pm Pisces
- 26th 11:02 am Aries
- 28th 11:04 pm Taurus
- 31st 9:25 am Gemini

November 1966
- 2nd 5:40 pm Cancer
- 4th 11:35 pm Leo
- 7th 3:08 am Virgo
- 9th 4:54 am Libra
- 11th 5:56 am Scorpio
- 13th 7:41 am Sagittarius
- 15th 11:43 am Capricorn
- 17th 7:08 pm Aquarius
- 20th 5:55 am Pisces
- 22nd 6:32 pm Aries
- 25th 6:35 am Taurus
- 27th 4:28 pm Gemini
- 29th 11:49 pm Cancer

December 1966
- 2nd 4:59 am Leo
- 4th 8:46 am Virgo
- 6th 11:42 am Libra
- 8th 2:18 pm Scorpio
- 10th 5:15 pm Sagittarius
- 12th 9:34 pm Capricorn
- 15th 4:23 am Aquarius
- 17th 2:22 pm Pisces
- 20th 2:40 am Aries
- 22nd 3:06 pm Taurus
- 25th 1:14 am Gemini
- 27th 7:55 am Cancer
- 29th 11:55 am Leo
- 31st 2:33 pm Virgo

January 1967
- 2nd 5:04 pm Libra
- 4th 8:17 pm Scorpio
- 7th 0:28 am Sagittarius
- 9th 5:55 am Capricorn
- 11th 1:10 pm Aquarius
- 13th 10:46 pm Pisces
- 16th 10:49 am Aries
- 18th 11:40 pm Taurus
- 21st 10:34 am Gemini
- 23rd 5:48 pm Cancer
- 25th 9:20 pm Leo
- 27th 10:37 pm Virgo
- 29th 11:34 pm Libra

February 1967
- 1st 1:45 am Scorpio
- 3rd 5:58 am Sagittarius
- 5th 12:14 pm Capricorn
- 7th 8:19 pm Aquarius
- 10th 6:21 am Pisces
- 12th 6:19 pm Aries
- 15th 7:18 am Taurus
- 17th 7:13 pm Gemini
- 20th 3:46 am Cancer
- 22nd 8:01 am Leo
- 24th 9:03 am Virgo
- 26th 8:47 am Libra
- 28th 9:14 am Scorpio

March 1967
- 2nd 11:58 am Sagittarius
- 4th 5:38 pm Capricorn
- 7th 2:04 am Aquarius
- 9th 12:44 pm Pisces
- 12th 0:53 am Aries
- 14th 1:54 pm Taurus
- 17th 2:18 am Gemini
- 19th 12:06 pm Cancer
- 21st 6:01 pm Leo
- 23rd 8:06 pm Virgo
- 25th 7:49 pm Libra
- 27th 7:13 pm Scorpio
- 29th 8:11 pm Sagittarius

April 1967
- 1st 0:11 am Capricorn
- 3rd 7:52 am Aquarius
- 5th 6:30 pm Pisces
- 8th 6:56 am Aries
- 10th 7:54 pm Taurus
- 13th 8:12 am Gemini
- 15th 6:33 pm Cancer
- 18th 1:53 am Leo
- 20th 5:39 am Virgo
- 22nd 6:39 am Libra
- 24th 6:20 am Scorpio
- 26th 6:31 am Sagittarius
- 28th 8:59 am Capricorn
- 30th 3:02 pm Aquarius

May 1967
- 3rd 0:48 am Pisces
- 5th 1:10 pm Aries
- 8th 2:09 am Taurus
- 10th 2:04 pm Gemini
- 13th 0:09 am Cancer
- 15th 7:46 am Leo
- 17th 12:48 pm Virgo
- 19th 3:27 pm Libra
- 21st 4:29 pm Scorpio
- 23rd 5:08 pm Sagittarius
- 25th 7:01 pm Capricorn
- 27th 11:46 pm Aquarius
- 30th 8:22 am Pisces

June 1967
- 1st 8:08 pm Aries
- 4th 9:03 am Taurus
- 6th 8:49 pm Gemini
- 9th 6:14 am Cancer
- 11th 1:16 pm Leo
- 13th 6:21 pm Virgo
- 15th 9:57 pm Libra
- 18th 0:25 am Scorpio
- 20th 2:20 am Sagittarius
- 22nd 4:48 am Capricorn
- 24th 9:15 am Aquarius
- 26th 4:53 pm Pisces
- 29th 3:54 am Aries

July 1967
- 1st 4:42 pm Taurus
- 4th 4:36 am Gemini
- 6th 1:42 pm Cancer
- 8th 7:56 pm Leo
- 11th 0:07 am Virgo
- 13th 3:19 am Libra
- 15th 6:17 am Scorpio
- 17th 9:23 am Sagittarius
- 19th 12:60 pm Capricorn
- 21st 6:01 pm Aquarius
- 24th 1:28 am Pisces
- 26th 12:02 pm Aries
- 29th 0:41 am Taurus
- 31st 12:56 pm Gemini

August 1967
- 2nd 10:30 pm Cancer
- 5th 4:23 am Leo
- 7th 7:34 am Virgo
- 9th 9:34 am Libra
- 11th 11:45 am Scorpio
- 13th 2:54 pm Sagittarius
- 15th 7:19 pm Capricorn
- 18th 1:17 am Aquarius
- 20th 9:20 am Pisces
- 22nd 7:48 pm Aries
- 25th 8:21 am Taurus
- 27th 9:07 pm Gemini
- 30th 7:30 am Cancer

September 1967
- 1st 2:02 pm Leo
- 3rd 5:04 pm Virgo
- 5th 6:02 pm Libra
- 7th 6:45 pm Scorpio
- 9th 8:41 pm Sagittarius
- 12th 0:43 am Capricorn
- 14th 7:10 am Aquarius
- 16th 3:55 pm Pisces
- 19th 2:46 am Aries
- 21st 3:19 pm Taurus
- 24th 4:19 am Gemini
- 26th 3:42 pm Cancer
- 28th 11:42 pm Leo

October 1967
- 1st 3:37 am Virgo
- 3rd 4:34 am Libra
- 5th 4:15 am Scorpio
- 7th 4:34 am Sagittarius
- 9th 7:08 am Capricorn
- 11th 12:49 pm Aquarius
- 13th 9:39 pm Pisces
- 16th 8:58 am Aries
- 18th 9:40 pm Taurus
- 21st 10:36 am Gemini
- 23rd 10:27 pm Cancer
- 26th 7:36 am Leo
- 28th 1:14 pm Virgo
- 30th 3:27 pm Libra

November 1967
- 1st 3:26 pm Scorpio
- 3rd 2:54 pm Sagittarius
- 5th 3:50 pm Capricorn
- 7th 7:49 pm Aquarius
- 10th 3:45 am Pisces
- 12th 3:01 pm Aries
- 15th 3:52 am Taurus
- 17th 4:39 pm Gemini
- 20th 4:11 am Cancer
- 22nd 1:43 pm Leo
- 24th 8:44 pm Virgo
- 27th 0:48 am Libra
- 29th 2:13 am Scorpio

December 1967
- 1st 2:11 am Sagittarius
- 3rd 2:27 am Capricorn
- 5th 5:03 am Aquarius
- 7th 11:26 am Pisces
- 9th 9:45 pm Aries
- 12th 10:32 am Taurus
- 14th 11:18 pm Gemini
- 17th 10:20 am Cancer
- 19th 7:19 pm Leo
- 22nd 2:20 am Virgo
- 24th 7:24 am Libra
- 26th 10:34 am Scorpio
- 28th 12:08 pm Sagittarius
- 30th 1:14 pm Capricorn

January 1968
- 1st 3:29 pm Aquarius
- 3rd 8:40 pm Pisces
- 6th 5:50 am Aries
- 8th 6:05 pm Taurus
- 11th 6:54 am Gemini
- 13th 5:51 pm Cancer
- 16th 2:09 am Leo
- 18th 8:10 am Virgo
- 20th 12:46 pm Libra
- 22nd 4:27 pm Scorpio
- 24th 7:25 pm Sagittarius
- 26th 9:57 pm Capricorn
- 29th 1:08 am Aquarius
- 31st 6:21 am Pisces

February 1968
- 2nd 2:44 pm Aries
- 5th 2:16 am Taurus
- 7th 3:08 pm Gemini
- 10th 2:33 am Cancer
- 12th 10:47 am Leo
- 14th 4:01 pm Virgo
- 16th 7:22 pm Libra
- 18th 10:00 pm Scorpio
- 21st 0:49 am Sagittarius
- 23rd 4:13 am Capricorn
- 25th 8:40 am Aquarius
- 27th 2:46 pm Pisces
- 29th 11:16 pm Aries

March 1968
- 3rd 10:29 am Taurus
- 5th 11:17 pm Gemini
- 8th 11:18 am Cancer
- 10th 8:26 pm Leo
- 13th 1:51 am Virgo
- 15th 4:23 am Libra
- 17th 5:34 am Scorpio
- 19th 6:57 am Sagittarius
- 21st 9:39 am Capricorn
- 23rd 2:20 pm Aquarius
- 25th 9:16 pm Pisces
- 28th 6:34 am Aries
- 30th 5:55 pm Taurus

April 1968
- 2nd 6:41 am Gemini
- 4th 7:12 pm Cancer
- 7th 5:25 am Leo
- 9th 12:00 pm Virgo
- 11th 2:58 pm Libra
- 13th 3:32 pm Scorpio
- 15th 3:26 pm Sagittarius
- 17th 4:28 pm Capricorn
- 19th 7:60 pm Aquarius
- 22nd 2:47 am Pisces
- 24th 12:34 pm Aries
- 27th 0:22 am Taurus
- 29th 1:10 pm Gemini

May 1968
- 2nd 1:50 am Cancer
- 4th 12:50 pm Leo
- 6th 8:57 pm Virgo
- 9th 1:20 am Libra
- 11th 2:29 am Scorpio
- 13th 1:54 am Sagittarius
- 15th 1:33 am Capricorn
- 17th 3:27 am Aquarius
- 19th 8:59 am Pisces
- 21st 6:18 pm Aries
- 24th 6:17 am Taurus
- 26th 7:12 pm Gemini
- 29th 7:41 am Cancer
- 31st 6:52 pm Leo

June 1968
- 3rd 3:50 am Virgo
- 5th 9:44 am Libra
- 7th 12:25 pm Scorpio
- 9th 12:40 pm Sagittarius
- 11th 12:09 pm Capricorn
- 13th 12:53 pm Aquarius
- 15th 4:49 pm Pisces
- 18th 0:51 am Aries
- 20th 12:27 pm Taurus
- 23rd 1:23 am Gemini
- 25th 1:41 pm Cancer
- 28th 0:31 am Leo
- 30th 9:22 am Virgo

July 1968
- 2nd 4:06 pm Libra
- 4th 8:18 pm Scorpio
- 6th 10:04 pm Sagittarius
- 8th 10:24 pm Capricorn
- 10th 11:04 pm Aquarius
- 13th 2:05 am Pisces
- 15th 8:57 am Aries
- 17th 7:33 pm Taurus
- 20th 8:13 am Gemini
- 22nd 8:31 pm Cancer
- 25th 6:53 am Leo
- 27th 3:07 pm Virgo
- 29th 9:31 pm Libra

August 1968
- 1st 2:10 am Scorpio
- 3rd 5:09 am Sagittarius
- 5th 6:57 am Capricorn
- 7th 8:39 am Aquarius
- 9th 11:50 am Pisces
- 11th 5:57 pm Aries
- 14th 3:37 am Taurus
- 16th 3:52 pm Gemini
- 19th 4:13 am Cancer
- 21st 2:36 pm Leo
- 23rd 10:19 pm Virgo
- 26th 3:43 am Libra
- 28th 7:37 am Scorpio
- 30th 10:40 am Sagittarius

September 1968
- 1st 1:22 pm Capricorn
- 3rd 4:20 pm Aquarius
- 5th 8:29 pm Pisces
- 8th 2:51 am Aries
- 10th 12:08 pm Taurus
- 12th 11:54 pm Gemini
- 15th 12:27 pm Cancer
- 17th 11:25 pm Leo
- 20th 7:11 am Virgo
- 22nd 11:57 am Libra
- 24th 2:37 pm Scorpio
- 26th 4:31 pm Sagittarius
- 28th 6:46 pm Capricorn
- 30th 10:11 pm Aquarius

October 1968
- 3rd 3:22 am Pisces
- 5th 10:37 am Aries
- 7th 8:07 pm Taurus
- 10th 7:44 am Gemini
- 12th 8:24 pm Cancer
- 15th 8:05 am Leo
- 17th 4:54 pm Virgo
- 19th 10:04 pm Libra
- 22nd 0:06 am Scorpio
- 24th 0:32 am Sagittarius
- 26th 1:15 am Capricorn
- 28th 3:45 am Aquarius
- 30th 8:58 am Pisces

November 1968
- 1st 4:53 pm Aries
- 4th 3:02 am Taurus
- 6th 2:48 pm Gemini
- 9th 3:26 am Cancer
- 11th 3:43 pm Leo
- 14th 1:53 am Virgo
- 16th 8:21 am Libra
- 18th 11:01 am Scorpio
- 20th 11:03 am Sagittarius
- 22nd 10:24 am Capricorn
- 24th 11:08 am Aquarius
- 26th 2:58 pm Pisces
- 28th 10:27 pm Aries

December 1968
- 1st 9:00 am Taurus
- 3rd 9:05 pm Gemini
- 6th 9:42 am Cancer
- 8th 10:02 pm Leo
- 11th 8:54 am Virgo
- 13th 5:04 pm Libra
- 15th 9:30 pm Scorpio
- 17th 10:27 pm Sagittarius
- 19th 9:33 pm Capricorn
- 21st 9:03 pm Aquarius
- 23rd 11:02 pm Pisces
- 26th 5:08 am Aries
- 28th 3:01 pm Taurus
- 31st 3:12 am Gemini

January 1969
- 2nd 3:52 pm Cancer
- 5th 3:53 am Leo
- 7th 2:39 pm Virgo
- 9th 11:32 pm Libra
- 12th 5:29 am Scorpio
- 14th 8:15 am Sagittarius
- 16th 8:38 am Capricorn
- 18th 8:20 am Aquarius
- 20th 9:27 am Pisces
- 22nd 1:50 pm Aries
- 24th 10:16 pm Taurus
- 27th 9:56 am Gemini
- 29th 10:37 pm Cancer

February 1969
- 1st 10:28 am Leo
- 3rd 8:41 pm Virgo
- 6th 4:59 am Libra
- 8th 11:16 am Scorpio
- 10th 3:20 pm Sagittarius
- 12th 5:27 pm Capricorn
- 14th 6:32 pm Aquarius
- 16th 8:05 pm Pisces
- 18th 11:49 pm Aries
- 21st 7:06 am Taurus
- 23rd 5:44 pm Gemini
- 26th 6:12 am Cancer
- 28th 6:12 pm Leo

March 1969
- 3rd 4:06 am Virgo
- 5th 11:32 am Libra
- 7th 4:55 pm Scorpio
- 9th 8:48 pm Sagittarius
- 11th 11:41 pm Capricorn
- 14th 2:10 am Aquarius
- 16th 5:07 am Pisces
- 18th 9:32 am Aries
- 20th 4:24 pm Taurus
- 23rd 2:13 am Gemini
- 25th 2:18 pm Cancer
- 28th 2:36 am Leo
- 30th 12:51 pm Virgo

April 1969
- 1st 8:02 pm Libra
- 4th 0:24 am Scorpio
- 6th 2:59 am Sagittarius
- 8th 5:05 am Capricorn
- 10th 7:49 am Aquarius
- 12th 11:44 am Pisces
- 14th 5:15 pm Aries
- 17th 0:44 am Taurus
- 19th 10:31 am Gemini
- 21st 10:17 pm Cancer
- 24th 10:50 am Leo
- 26th 9:56 pm Virgo
- 29th 5:42 am Libra

May 1969
- 1st 9:46 am Scorpio
- 3rd 11:18 am Sagittarius
- 5th 11:60 am Capricorn
- 7th 1:32 pm Aquarius
- 9th 5:08 pm Pisces
- 11th 11:09 pm Aries
- 14th 7:30 am Taurus
- 16th 5:43 pm Gemini
- 19th 5:31 am Cancer
- 21st 6:12 pm Leo
- 24th 6:04 am Virgo
- 26th 3:02 pm Libra
- 28th 8:03 pm Scorpio
- 30th 9:29 pm Sagittarius

June 1969
- 1st 9:08 pm Capricorn
- 3rd 9:07 pm Aquarius
- 5th 11:16 pm Pisces
- 8th 4:41 am Aries
- 10th 1:10 pm Taurus
- 12th 11:48 pm Gemini
- 15th 11:54 am Cancer
- 18th 0:34 am Leo
- 20th 12:51 pm Virgo
- 22nd 11:03 pm Libra
- 25th 5:27 am Scorpio
- 27th 7:55 am Sagittarius
- 29th 7:44 am Capricorn

July 1969
- 1st 6:53 am Aquarius
- 3rd 7:33 am Pisces
- 5th 11:23 am Aries
- 7th 6:58 pm Taurus
- 10th 5:33 am Gemini
- 12th 5:48 pm Cancer
- 15th 6:29 am Leo
- 17th 6:41 pm Virgo
- 20th 5:16 am Libra
- 22nd 12:58 pm Scorpio
- 24th 5:05 pm Sagittarius
- 26th 6:06 pm Capricorn
- 28th 5:35 pm Aquarius
- 30th 5:34 pm Pisces

August 1969
- 1st 7:58 pm Aries
- 4th 2:05 am Taurus
- 6th 11:53 am Gemini
- 8th 11:58 pm Cancer
- 11th 12:38 pm Leo
- 14th 0:33 am Virgo
- 16th 10:48 am Libra
- 18th 6:52 pm Scorpio
- 21st 0:12 am Sagittarius
- 23rd 2:47 am Capricorn
- 25th 3:36 am Aquarius
- 27th 4:04 am Pisces
- 29th 6:01 am Aries
- 31st 10:55 am Taurus

September 1969
- 2nd 7:26 pm Gemini
- 5th 6:57 am Cancer
- 7th 7:35 pm Leo
- 10th 7:18 am Virgo
- 12th 4:60 pm Libra
- 15th 0:25 am Scorpio
- 17th 5:40 am Sagittarius
- 19th 9:12 am Capricorn
- 21st 11:30 am Aquarius
- 23rd 1:23 pm Pisces
- 25th 3:57 pm Aries
- 27th 8:30 pm Taurus
- 30th 4:08 am Gemini

October 1969
- 2nd 2:55 pm Cancer
- 5th 3:24 am Leo
- 7th 3:19 pm Virgo
- 10th 0:48 am Libra
- 12th 7:16 am Scorpio
- 14th 11:32 am Sagittarius
- 16th 2:35 pm Capricorn
- 18th 5:22 pm Aquarius
- 20th 8:26 pm Pisces
- 23rd 0:18 am Aries
- 25th 5:34 am Taurus
- 27th 1:03 pm Gemini
- 29th 11:13 pm Cancer

November 1969
- 1st 11:35 am Leo
- 3rd 12:00 pm Virgo
- 6th 9:54 am Libra
- 8th 4:13 pm Scorpio
- 10th 7:28 pm Sagittarius
- 12th 9:09 pm Capricorn
- 14th 10:53 pm Aquarius
- 17th 1:53 am Pisces
- 19th 6:34 am Aries
- 21st 12:54 pm Taurus
- 23rd 9:00 pm Gemini
- 26th 7:12 am Cancer
- 28th 7:23 pm Leo

December 1969
- 1st 8:11 am Virgo
- 3rd 7:13 pm Libra
- 6th 2:28 am Scorpio
- 8th 5:40 am Sagittarius
- 10th 6:21 am Capricorn
- 12th 6:30 am Aquarius
- 14th 8:00 am Pisces
- 16th 12:01 pm Aries
- 18th 6:38 pm Taurus
- 21st 3:29 am Gemini
- 23rd 2:11 pm Cancer
- 26th 2:22 am Leo
- 28th 3:19 pm Virgo
- 31st 3:16 am Libra

January 1970
- 2nd 11:56 am Scorpio
- 4th 4:28 pm Sagittarius
- 6th 5:27 pm Capricorn
- 8th 4:49 pm Aquarius
- 10th 4:42 pm Pisces
- 12th 6:52 pm Aries
- 15th 0:22 am Taurus
- 17th 9:11 am Gemini
- 19th 8:15 pm Cancer
- 22nd 8:41 am Leo
- 24th 9:32 pm Virgo
- 27th 9:40 am Libra
- 29th 7:32 pm Scorpio

February 1970
- 1st 1:48 am Sagittarius
- 3rd 4:19 am Capricorn
- 5th 4:18 am Aquarius
- 7th 3:39 am Pisces
- 9th 4:21 am Aries
- 11th 8:05 am Taurus
- 13th 3:34 pm Gemini
- 16th 2:19 am Cancer
- 18th 2:56 pm Leo
- 21st 3:43 am Virgo
- 23rd 3:28 pm Libra
- 26th 1:22 am Scorpio
- 28th 8:35 am Sagittarius

March 1970
- 2nd 12:50 pm Capricorn
- 4th 2:32 pm Aquarius
- 6th 2:49 pm Pisces
- 8th 3:20 pm Aries
- 10th 5:48 pm Taurus
- 12th 11:38 pm Gemini
- 15th 9:23 am Cancer
- 17th 9:40 pm Leo
- 20th 10:29 am Virgo
- 22nd 9:57 pm Libra
- 25th 7:08 am Scorpio
- 27th 2:05 pm Sagittarius
- 29th 6:59 pm Capricorn
- 31st 10:08 pm Aquarius

April 1970
- 3rd 0:02 am Pisces
- 5th 1:33 am Aries
- 7th 4:04 am Taurus
- 9th 9:07 am Gemini
- 11th 5:37 pm Cancer
- 14th 5:16 am Leo
- 16th 6:08 pm Virgo
- 19th 5:33 am Libra
- 21st 2:13 pm Scorpio
- 23rd 8:15 pm Sagittarius
- 26th 0:27 am Capricorn
- 28th 3:43 am Aquarius
- 30th 6:38 am Pisces

May 1970
- 2nd 9:34 am Aries
- 4th 1:08 pm Taurus
- 6th 6:21 pm Gemini
- 9th 2:20 am Cancer
- 11th 1:25 pm Leo
- 14th 2:11 am Virgo
- 16th 2:00 pm Libra
- 18th 10:49 pm Scorpio
- 21st 4:10 am Sagittarius
- 23rd 7:13 am Capricorn
- 25th 9:28 am Aquarius
- 27th 12:02 pm Pisces
- 29th 3:29 pm Aries
- 31st 8:05 pm Taurus

June 1970
- 3rd 2:11 am Gemini
- 5th 10:30 am Cancer
- 7th 9:19 pm Leo
- 10th 10:02 am Virgo
- 12th 10:28 pm Libra
- 15th 7:58 am Scorpio
- 17th 1:35 pm Sagittarius
- 19th 4:03 pm Capricorn
- 21st 5:02 pm Aquarius
- 23rd 6:14 pm Pisces
- 25th 8:55 pm Aries
- 28th 1:37 am Taurus
- 30th 8:28 am Gemini

July 1970
2nd 5:25 pm Cancer
5th 4:27 am Leo
7th 5:11 pm Virgo
10th 6:01 am Libra
12th 4:36 pm Scorpio
14th 11:24 pm Sagittarius
17th 2:19 am Capricorn
19th 2:45 am Aquarius
21st 2:39 am Pisces
23rd 3:46 am Aries
25th 7:24 am Taurus
27th 1:58 pm Gemini
29th 11:15 pm Cancer

August 1970
1st 10:48 am Leo
3rd 11:36 pm Virgo
6th 12:30 pm Libra
8th 11:56 pm Scorpio
11th 8:02 am Sagittarius
13th 12:19 pm Capricorn
15th 1:28 pm Aquarius
17th 1:02 pm Pisces
19th 12:54 pm Aries
21st 2:51 pm Taurus
23rd 8:07 pm Gemini
26th 5:00 am Cancer
28th 4:40 pm Leo
31st 5:38 am Virgo

September 1970
2nd 6:25 pm Libra
5th 5:53 am Scorpio
7th 2:54 pm Sagittarius
9th 8:48 pm Capricorn
11th 11:33 pm Aquarius
13th 11:57 pm Pisces
15th 11:35 pm Aries
18th 0:20 am Taurus
20th 4:06 am Gemini
22nd 11:46 am Cancer
24th 10:54 pm Leo
27th 11:54 am Virgo
30th 0:34 am Libra

October 1970
2nd 11:34 am Scorpio
4th 8:31 pm Sagittarius
7th 3:09 am Capricorn
9th 7:23 am Aquarius
11th 9:28 am Pisces
13th 10:12 am Aries
15th 11:02 am Taurus
17th 1:48 pm Gemini
19th 8:02 pm Cancer
22nd 6:15 am Leo
24th 6:57 pm Virgo
27th 7:35 am Libra
29th 6:12 pm Scorpio

November 1970
1st 2:24 am Sagittarius
3rd 8:31 am Capricorn
5th 1:08 pm Aquarius
7th 4:31 pm Pisces
9th 6:51 pm Aries
11th 8:50 pm Taurus
13th 11:48 pm Gemini
16th 5:26 am Cancer
18th 2:39 pm Leo
21st 2:51 am Virgo
23rd 3:38 pm Libra
26th 2:23 am Scorpio
28th 9:58 am Sagittarius
30th 3:04 pm Capricorn

December 1970
2nd 6:43 pm Aquarius
4th 9:56 pm Pisces
7th 1:03 am Aries
9th 4:26 am Taurus
11th 8:36 am Gemini
13th 2:36 pm Cancer
15th 11:21 pm Leo
18th 11:06 am Virgo
21st 0:02 am Libra
23rd 11:22 am Scorpio
25th 7:23 pm Sagittarius
28th 0:02 am Capricorn
30th 2:24 am Aquarius

January 1971
1st 4:08 am Pisces
3rd 6:29 am Aries
5th 10:04 am Taurus
7th 3:11 pm Gemini
9th 10:11 pm Cancer
12th 7:27 am Leo
14th 6:58 pm Virgo
17th 7:51 am Libra
19th 8:01 pm Scorpio
22nd 5:10 am Sagittarius
24th 10:27 am Capricorn
26th 12:33 pm Aquarius
28th 1:02 pm Pisces
30th 1:39 pm Aries

February 1971
1st 3:54 pm Taurus
3rd 8:38 pm Gemini
6th 4:10 am Cancer
8th 2:10 pm Leo
11th 1:59 am Virgo
13th 2:51 pm Libra
16th 3:20 am Scorpio
18th 1:40 pm Sagittarius
20th 8:33 pm Capricorn
22nd 11:43 pm Aquarius
25th 0:05 am Pisces
26th 11:30 pm Aries
28th 11:55 pm Taurus

March 1971
3rd 3:05 am Gemini
5th 9:52 am Cancer
7th 7:58 pm Leo
10th 8:13 am Virgo
12th 9:07 pm Libra
15th 9:30 am Scorpio
17th 8:23 pm Sagittarius
20th 4:34 am Capricorn
22nd 9:24 am Aquarius
24th 11:04 am Pisces
26th 10:45 am Aries
28th 10:19 am Taurus
30th 11:50 am Gemini

April 1971
1st 4:56 pm Cancer
4th 2:07 am Leo
6th 2:19 pm Virgo
9th 3:18 am Libra
11th 3:28 pm Scorpio
14th 2:04 am Sagittarius
16th 10:35 am Capricorn
18th 4:44 pm Aquarius
20th 8:06 pm Pisces
22nd 9:09 pm Aries
24th 9:07 pm Taurus
26th 10:01 pm Gemini
29th 1:45 am Cancer

May 1971
1st 9:40 am Leo
3rd 9:05 pm Virgo
6th 9:59 am Libra
8th 10:05 pm Scorpio
11th 8:07 am Sagittarius
13th 4:09 pm Capricorn
15th 10:20 pm Aquarius
18th 2:40 am Pisces
20th 5:11 am Aries
22nd 6:32 am Taurus
24th 8:05 am Gemini
26th 11:33 am Cancer
28th 6:20 pm Leo
31st 4:51 am Virgo

June 1971
2nd 5:27 pm Libra
5th 5:35 am Scorpio
7th 3:26 pm Sagittarius
9th 10:45 pm Capricorn
12th 4:03 am Aquarius
14th 8:02 am Pisces
16th 11:06 am Aries
18th 1:40 pm Taurus
20th 4:27 pm Gemini
22nd 8:34 pm Cancer
25th 3:15 am Leo
27th 1:10 pm Virgo
30th 1:23 am Libra

July 1971
2nd 1:43 pm Scorpio
4th 11:60 pm Sagittarius
7th 7:01 am Capricorn
9th 11:25 am Aquarius
11th 2:15 pm Pisces
13th 4:35 pm Aries
15th 7:13 pm Taurus
17th 10:49 pm Gemini
20th 3:60 am Cancer
22nd 11:21 am Leo
24th 9:12 pm Virgo
27th 9:13 am Libra
29th 9:49 pm Scorpio

August 1971
1st 8:45 am Sagittarius
3rd 4:28 pm Capricorn
5th 8:45 pm Aquarius
7th 10:35 pm Pisces
9th 11:27 pm Aries
12th 0:57 am Taurus
14th 4:15 am Gemini
16th 9:54 am Cancer
18th 6:02 pm Leo
21st 4:22 am Virgo
23rd 4:24 pm Libra
26th 5:09 am Scorpio
28th 4:54 pm Sagittarius
31st 1:52 am Capricorn

September 1971
2nd 6:59 am Aquarius
4th 8:48 am Pisces
6th 8:44 am Aries
8th 8:41 am Taurus
10th 10:31 am Gemini
12th 3:26 pm Cancer
14th 11:39 pm Leo
17th 10:32 am Virgo
19th 10:49 pm Libra
22nd 11:34 am Scorpio
24th 11:44 pm Sagittarius
27th 9:49 am Capricorn
29th 4:34 pm Aquarius

October 1971
1st 7:33 pm Pisces
3rd 7:39 pm Aries
5th 6:44 pm Taurus
7th 6:56 pm Gemini
9th 10:12 pm Cancer
12th 5:34 am Leo
14th 4:18 pm Virgo
17th 4:48 am Libra
19th 5:31 pm Scorpio
22nd 5:32 am Sagittarius
24th 4:03 pm Capricorn
27th 0:11 am Aquarius
29th 4:53 am Pisces
31st 6:24 am Aries

November 1971
2nd 5:56 am Taurus
4th 5:31 am Gemini
6th 7:20 am Cancer
8th 1:02 pm Leo
10th 10:45 pm Virgo
13th 11:05 am Libra
15th 11:50 pm Scorpio
18th 11:28 am Sagittarius
20th 9:36 pm Capricorn
23rd 5:50 am Aquarius
25th 11:44 am Pisces
27th 2:60 pm Aries
29th 4:06 pm Taurus

December 1971
1st 4:26 pm Gemini
3rd 5:55 pm Cancer
5th 10:18 pm Leo
8th 6:44 am Virgo
10th 6:21 pm Libra
13th 7:00 am Scorpio
15th 6:35 pm Sagittarius
18th 4:05 am Capricorn
20th 11:30 am Aquarius
22nd 5:09 pm Pisces
24th 9:08 pm Aries
26th 11:45 pm Taurus
29th 1:38 am Gemini
31st 4:03 am Cancer

January 1972
2nd 8:26 am Leo
4th 3:54 pm Virgo
7th 2:34 am Libra
9th 3:03 pm Scorpio
12th 2:55 am Sagittarius
14th 12:21 pm Capricorn
16th 7:01 pm Aquarius
18th 11:27 pm Pisces
21st 2:36 am Aries
23rd 5:18 am Taurus
25th 8:16 am Gemini
27th 12:05 pm Cancer
29th 5:25 pm Leo

February 1972
1st 0:56 am Virgo
3rd 11:09 am Libra
5th 11:18 pm Scorpio
8th 11:33 am Sagittarius
10th 9:48 pm Capricorn
13th 4:33 am Aquarius
15th 8:07 am Pisces
17th 9:51 am Aries
19th 11:14 am Taurus
21st 1:39 pm Gemini
23rd 5:56 pm Cancer
26th 0:17 am Leo
28th 8:43 am Virgo

March 1972
1st 7:03 pm Libra
4th 7:02 am Scorpio
6th 7:36 pm Sagittarius
9th 6:46 am Capricorn
11th 2:37 pm Aquarius
13th 6:36 pm Pisces
15th 7:35 pm Aries
17th 7:29 pm Taurus
19th 8:15 pm Gemini
21st 11:27 pm Cancer
24th 5:50 am Leo
26th 2:51 pm Virgo
29th 1:44 am Libra
31st 1:51 pm Scorpio

April 1972
3rd 2:29 am Sagittarius
5th 2:18 pm Capricorn
7th 11:37 pm Aquarius
10th 4:54 am Pisces
12th 6:30 am Aries
14th 5:55 am Taurus
16th 5:20 am Gemini
18th 6:50 am Cancer
20th 11:53 am Leo
22nd 8:26 pm Virgo
25th 7:36 am Libra
27th 7:58 pm Scorpio
30th 8:32 am Sagittarius

May 1972
2nd 8:29 pm Capricorn
5th 6:32 am Aquarius
7th 1:23 pm Pisces
9th 4:31 pm Aries
11th 4:46 pm Taurus
13th 3:59 pm Gemini
15th 4:21 pm Cancer
17th 7:42 pm Leo
20th 2:59 am Virgo
22nd 1:40 pm Libra
25th 2:01 am Scorpio
27th 2:34 pm Sagittarius
30th 2:13 am Capricorn

June 1972
1st 12:13 pm Aquarius
3rd 7:51 pm Pisces
6th 0:29 am Aries
8th 2:14 am Taurus
10th 2:26 am Gemini
12th 2:48 am Cancer
14th 5:15 am Leo
16th 11:09 am Virgo
18th 8:40 pm Libra
21st 8:44 am Scorpio
23rd 9:15 pm Sagittarius
26th 8:35 am Capricorn
28th 6:01 pm Aquarius

July 1972
1st 1:19 am Pisces
3rd 6:21 am Aries
5th 9:24 am Taurus
7th 11:06 am Gemini
9th 12:33 pm Cancer
11th 3:11 pm Leo
13th 8:19 pm Virgo
16th 4:53 am Libra
18th 4:16 pm Scorpio
21st 4:46 am Sagittarius
23rd 4:08 pm Capricorn
26th 1:08 am Aquarius
28th 7:28 am Pisces
30th 11:51 am Aries

August 1972
1st 2:59 pm Taurus
3rd 5:36 pm Gemini
5th 8:21 pm Cancer
7th 11:58 pm Leo
10th 5:27 am Virgo
12th 1:32 pm Libra
15th 0:20 am Scorpio
17th 12:48 pm Sagittarius
20th 0:39 am Capricorn
22nd 9:38 am Aquarius
24th 3:26 pm Pisces
26th 6:40 pm Aries
28th 8:45 pm Taurus
30th 10:58 pm Gemini

September 1972
2nd 2:14 am Cancer
4th 6:57 am Leo
6th 1:19 pm Virgo
8th 9:39 pm Libra
11th 8:19 am Scorpio
13th 8:44 pm Sagittarius
16th 9:05 am Capricorn
18th 7:02 pm Aquarius
21st 1:09 am Pisces
23rd 3:44 am Aries
25th 4:28 am Taurus
27th 5:17 am Gemini
29th 7:42 am Cancer

October 1972
1st 12:30 pm Leo
3rd 7:34 pm Virgo
6th 4:38 am Libra
8th 3:31 pm Scorpio
11th 3:54 am Sagittarius
13th 4:44 pm Capricorn
16th 3:49 am Aquarius
18th 11:07 am Pisces
20th 2:18 pm Aries
22nd 2:36 pm Taurus
24th 2:06 pm Gemini
26th 2:49 pm Cancer
28th 6:17 pm Leo
31st 1:01 am Virgo

November 1972
2nd 10:29 am Libra
4th 9:48 pm Scorpio
7th 10:19 am Sagittarius
9th 11:11 pm Capricorn
12th 11:00 am Aquarius
14th 7:54 pm Pisces
17th 0:43 am Aries
19th 1:52 am Taurus
21st 1:06 am Gemini
23rd 0:33 am Cancer
25th 2:14 am Leo
27th 7:29 am Virgo
29th 4:19 pm Libra

December 1972
2nd 3:44 am Scorpio
4th 4:24 pm Sagittarius
7th 5:06 am Capricorn
9th 4:53 pm Aquarius
12th 2:32 am Pisces
14th 8:55 am Aries
16th 11:54 am Taurus
18th 12:22 pm Gemini
20th 11:59 am Cancer
22nd 12:40 pm Leo
24th 4:08 pm Virgo
26th 11:22 pm Libra
29th 10:13 am Scorpio
31st 10:51 pm Sagittarius

January 1973
3rd 11:29 am Capricorn
5th 10:48 pm Aquarius
8th 8:01 am Pisces
10th 2:55 pm Aries
12th 7:23 pm Taurus
14th 9:41 pm Gemini
16th 10:39 pm Cancer
18th 11:40 pm Leo
21st 2:26 am Virgo
23rd 8:21 am Libra
25th 5:55 pm Scorpio
28th 6:10 am Sagittarius
30th 6:52 pm Capricorn

February 1973
2nd 5:52 am Aquarius
4th 2:19 pm Pisces
6th 8:28 pm Aries
9th 0:53 am Taurus
11th 4:10 am Gemini
13th 6:45 am Cancer
15th 9:14 am Leo
17th 12:35 pm Virgo
19th 6:02 pm Libra
22nd 2:37 am Scorpio
24th 2:14 pm Sagittarius
27th 3:03 am Capricorn

March 1973
1st 2:18 pm Aquarius
3rd 10:30 pm Pisces
6th 3:35 am Aries
8th 6:51 am Taurus
10th 9:32 am Gemini
12th 12:31 pm Cancer
14th 4:09 pm Leo
16th 8:44 pm Virgo
19th 2:50 am Libra
21st 11:19 am Scorpio
23rd 10:26 pm Sagittarius
26th 11:15 am Capricorn
28th 11:13 pm Aquarius
31st 7:50 am Pisces

April 1973
2nd 12:43 pm Aries
4th 2:56 pm Taurus
6th 4:12 pm Gemini
8th 6:06 pm Cancer
10th 9:33 pm Leo
13th 2:47 am Virgo
15th 9:53 am Libra
17th 6:53 pm Scorpio
20th 6:04 am Sagittarius
22nd 6:50 pm Capricorn
25th 7:19 am Aquarius
27th 5:06 pm Pisces
29th 10:52 pm Aries

May 1973
2nd 1:01 am Taurus
4th 1:15 am Gemini
6th 1:35 am Cancer
8th 3:39 am Leo
10th 8:16 am Virgo
12th 3:34 pm Libra
15th 1:11 am Scorpio
17th 12:44 pm Sagittarius
20th 1:30 am Capricorn
22nd 2:16 pm Aquarius
25th 1:06 am Pisces
27th 8:09 am Aries
29th 11:24 am Taurus
31st 11:51 am Gemini

June 1973
2nd 11:23 am Cancer
4th 11:53 am Leo
6th 2:57 pm Virgo
8th 9:19 pm Libra
11th 6:54 am Scorpio
13th 6:45 pm Sagittarius
16th 7:37 am Capricorn
18th 8:19 pm Aquarius
21st 7:26 am Pisces
23rd 3:45 pm Aries
25th 8:35 pm Taurus
27th 10:17 pm Gemini
29th 10:09 pm Cancer

July 1973
1st 9:57 pm Leo
3rd 11:32 pm Virgo
6th 4:27 am Libra
8th 1:10 pm Scorpio
11th 0:49 am Sagittarius
13th 1:47 pm Capricorn
16th 2:15 am Aquarius
18th 1:06 pm Pisces
20th 9:44 pm Aries
23rd 3:39 am Taurus
25th 6:57 am Gemini
27th 8:11 am Cancer
29th 8:32 am Leo
31st 9:40 am Virgo

August 1973
2nd 1:19 pm Libra
4th 8:39 pm Scorpio
7th 7:39 am Sagittarius
9th 8:31 pm Capricorn
12th 8:51 am Aquarius
14th 7:13 pm Pisces
17th 3:17 am Aries
19th 9:13 am Taurus
21st 1:26 pm Gemini
23rd 4:08 pm Cancer
25th 5:51 pm Leo
27th 7:36 pm Virgo
29th 10:54 pm Libra

September 1973
1st 5:22 am Scorpio
3rd 3:28 pm Sagittarius
6th 4:02 am Capricorn
8th 4:28 pm Aquarius
11th 2:39 am Pisces
13th 9:53 am Aries
15th 2:59 pm Taurus
17th 6:49 pm Gemini
19th 10:02 pm Cancer
22nd 0:58 am Leo
24th 4:01 am Virgo
26th 8:05 am Libra
28th 2:25 pm Scorpio
30th 11:48 pm Sagittarius

October 1973
3rd 12:04 pm Capricorn
6th 0:50 am Aquarius
8th 11:19 am Pisces
10th 6:26 pm Aries
12th 10:36 pm Taurus
15th 1:09 am Gemini
17th 3:29 am Cancer
19th 6:26 am Leo
21st 10:21 am Virgo
23rd 3:32 pm Libra
25th 10:31 pm Scorpio
28th 8:02 am Sagittarius
30th 7:59 pm Capricorn

November 1973
2nd 8:59 am Aquarius
4th 8:26 pm Pisces
7th 4:18 am Aries
9th 8:22 am Taurus
11th 9:59 am Gemini
13th 10:48 am Cancer
15th 12:23 pm Leo
17th 3:45 pm Virgo
19th 9:17 pm Libra
22nd 5:09 am Scorpio
24th 3:15 pm Sagittarius
27th 3:15 am Capricorn
29th 4:18 pm Aquarius

December 1973
2nd 4:32 am Pisces
4th 1:46 pm Aries
6th 7:06 pm Taurus
8th 8:57 pm Gemini
10th 8:53 pm Cancer
12th 8:47 pm Leo
14th 10:23 pm Virgo
17th 2:55 am Libra
19th 10:48 am Scorpio
21st 9:22 pm Sagittarius
24th 9:43 am Capricorn
26th 10:45 pm Aquarius
29th 11:08 am Pisces
31st 9:33 pm Aries

January 1974
3rd 4:35 am Taurus
5th 7:57 am Gemini
7th 8:26 am Cancer
9th 7:44 am Leo
11th 7:47 am Virgo
13th 10:28 am Libra
15th 4:59 pm Scorpio
18th 3:14 am Sagittarius
20th 3:48 pm Capricorn
23rd 4:49 am Aquarius
25th 4:59 pm Pisces
28th 3:31 am Aries
30th 11:37 am Taurus

February 1974
1st 4:51 pm Gemini
3rd 7:04 pm Cancer
5th 7:11 pm Leo
7th 6:53 pm Virgo
9th 8:14 pm Libra
12th 0:59 am Scorpio
14th 10:05 am Sagittarius
16th 10:16 pm Capricorn
19th 11:20 am Aquarius
21st 11:15 pm Pisces
24th 9:11 am Aries
26th 5:10 pm Taurus
28th 11:10 pm Gemini

March 1974
3rd 2:60 am Cancer
5th 4:49 am Leo
7th 5:35 am Virgo
9th 6:56 am Libra
11th 10:46 am Scorpio
13th 6:24 pm Sagittarius
16th 5:42 am Capricorn
18th 6:37 pm Aquarius
21st 6:30 am Pisces
23rd 3:59 pm Aries
25th 11:09 pm Taurus
28th 4:32 am Gemini
30th 8:38 am Cancer

April 1974
1st 11:40 am Leo
3rd 1:57 pm Virgo
5th 4:25 pm Libra
7th 8:28 pm Scorpio
10th 3:30 am Sagittarius
12th 1:60 pm Capricorn
15th 2:34 am Aquarius
17th 2:41 pm Pisces
20th 0:20 am Aries
22nd 6:50 am Taurus
24th 11:08 am Gemini
26th 2:17 pm Cancer
28th 5:04 pm Leo
30th 7:60 pm Virgo

May 1974
2nd 11:39 pm Libra
5th 4:45 am Scorpio
7th 12:09 pm Sagittarius
9th 10:16 pm Capricorn
12th 10:36 am Aquarius
14th 11:04 pm Pisces
17th 9:15 am Aries
19th 4:07 pm Taurus
21st 7:52 pm Gemini
23rd 9:45 pm Cancer
25th 11:12 pm Leo
28th 1:26 am Virgo
30th 5:17 am Libra

June 1974
1st 11:13 am Scorpio
3rd 7:24 pm Sagittarius
6th 5:50 am Capricorn
8th 6:04 pm Aquarius
11th 6:43 am Pisces
13th 5:50 pm Aries
16th 1:45 am Taurus
18th 5:55 am Gemini
20th 7:19 am Cancer
22nd 7:30 am Leo
24th 8:15 am Virgo
26th 11:02 am Libra
28th 4:43 pm Scorpio

July 1974
1st 1:22 am Sagittarius
3rd 12:22 pm Capricorn
6th 0:41 am Aquarius
8th 1:25 pm Pisces
11th 1:10 am Aries
13th 10:17 am Taurus
15th 3:50 pm Gemini
17th 5:53 pm Cancer
19th 5:43 pm Leo
21st 5:12 pm Virgo
23rd 6:23 pm Libra
25th 10:47 pm Scorpio
28th 7:03 am Sagittarius
30th 6:12 pm Capricorn

August 1974
2nd 6:47 am Aquarius
4th 7:26 pm Pisces
7th 7:14 am Aries
9th 5:10 pm Taurus
12th 0:16 am Gemini
14th 3:47 am Cancer
16th 4:26 am Leo
18th 3:45 am Virgo
20th 3:48 am Libra
22nd 6:43 am Scorpio
24th 1:40 pm Sagittarius
27th 0:16 am Capricorn
29th 12:53 pm Aquarius

September 1974
1st 1:30 am Pisces
3rd 12:56 pm Aries
5th 10:51 pm Taurus
8th 6:34 am Gemini
10th 11:37 am Cancer
12th 1:52 pm Leo
14th 2:13 pm Virgo
16th 2:22 pm Libra
18th 4:20 pm Scorpio
20th 9:48 pm Sagittarius
23rd 7:26 am Capricorn
25th 7:39 pm Aquarius
28th 8:13 am Pisces
30th 7:25 pm Aries

October 1974
3rd 4:38 am Taurus
5th 11:59 am Gemini
7th 5:28 pm Cancer
9th 9:02 pm Leo
11th 10:57 pm Virgo
14th 0:12 am Libra
16th 2:27 am Scorpio
18th 7:21 am Sagittarius
20th 3:50 pm Capricorn
23rd 3:22 am Aquarius
25th 3:57 pm Pisces
28th 3:12 am Aries
30th 11:57 am Taurus

November 1974
1st 6:22 pm Gemini
3rd 11:01 pm Cancer
6th 2:30 am Leo
8th 5:19 am Virgo
10th 8:01 am Libra
12th 11:28 am Scorpio
14th 4:44 pm Sagittarius
17th 0:45 am Capricorn
19th 11:43 am Aquarius
22nd 0:14 am Pisces
24th 11:57 am Aries
26th 9:04 pm Taurus
29th 2:57 am Gemini

December 1974
1st 6:21 am Cancer
3rd 8:32 am Leo
5th 10:42 am Virgo
7th 1:45 pm Libra
9th 6:16 pm Scorpio
12th 0:35 am Sagittarius
14th 9:09 am Capricorn
16th 7:52 pm Aquarius
19th 8:14 am Pisces
21st 8:36 pm Aries
24th 6:42 am Taurus
26th 1:12 pm Gemini
28th 4:13 pm Cancer
30th 5:05 pm Leo

January 1975
1st 5:35 pm Virgo
3rd 7:25 pm Libra
5th 11:39 pm Scorpio
8th 6:43 am Sagittarius
10th 4:01 pm Capricorn
13th 3:04 am Aquarius
15th 3:26 pm Pisces
18th 4:04 am Aries
20th 3:17 pm Taurus
22nd 11:23 pm Gemini
25th 3:20 am Cancer
27th 3:60 am Leo
29th 3:16 am Virgo
31st 3:17 am Libra

February 1975
2nd 5:58 am Scorpio
4th 12:16 pm Sagittarius
6th 9:44 pm Capricorn
9th 9:18 am Aquarius
11th 9:47 pm Pisces
14th 10:22 am Aries
16th 10:09 pm Taurus
19th 7:31 am Gemini
21st 1:14 pm Cancer
23rd 3:09 pm Leo
25th 2:36 pm Virgo
27th 1:43 pm Libra

March 1975
1st 2:40 pm Scorpio
3rd 7:10 pm Sagittarius
6th 3:41 am Capricorn
8th 3:11 pm Aquarius
11th 3:49 am Pisces
13th 4:18 pm Aries
16th 3:53 am Taurus
18th 1:40 pm Gemini
20th 8:47 pm Cancer
23rd 0:31 am Leo
25th 1:21 am Virgo
27th 0:53 am Libra
29th 1:10 am Scorpio
31st 4:13 am Sagittarius

April 1975
2nd 11:13 am Capricorn
4th 9:45 pm Aquarius
7th 10:16 am Pisces
9th 10:44 pm Aries
12th 9:51 am Taurus
14th 7:13 pm Gemini
17th 2:27 am Cancer
19th 7:11 am Leo
21st 9:40 am Virgo
23rd 10:41 am Libra
25th 11:43 am Scorpio
27th 2:25 pm Sagittarius
29th 8:12 pm Capricorn

May 1975
2nd 5:36 am Aquarius
4th 5:35 pm Pisces
7th 6:01 am Aries
9th 5:00 pm Taurus
12th 1:43 am Gemini
14th 8:05 am Cancer
16th 12:35 pm Leo
18th 3:44 pm Virgo
20th 6:04 pm Libra
22nd 8:26 pm Scorpio
24th 11:51 pm Sagittarius
27th 5:35 am Capricorn
29th 2:14 pm Aquarius

June 1975
1st 1:33 am Pisces
3rd 2:01 pm Aries
6th 1:19 am Taurus
8th 9:45 am Gemini
10th 3:17 pm Cancer
12th 6:43 pm Leo
14th 9:10 pm Virgo
16th 11:40 pm Libra
19th 2:59 am Scorpio
21st 7:37 am Sagittarius
23rd 1:59 pm Capricorn
25th 10:34 pm Aquarius
28th 9:35 am Pisces
30th 10:03 pm Aries

July 1975
3rd 9:51 am Taurus
5th 6:55 pm Gemini
8th 0:22 am Cancer
10th 2:49 am Leo
12th 3:56 am Virgo
14th 5:24 am Libra
16th 8:26 am Scorpio
18th 1:35 pm Sagittarius
20th 8:46 pm Capricorn
23rd 5:58 am Aquarius
25th 4:60 pm Pisces
28th 5:27 am Aries
30th 5:53 pm Taurus

August 1975
2nd 3:60 am Gemini
4th 10:11 am Cancer
6th 12:40 pm Leo
8th 12:53 pm Virgo
10th 12:54 pm Libra
12th 2:34 pm Scorpio
14th 7:02 pm Sagittarius
17th 2:26 am Capricorn
19th 12:11 pm Aquarius
21st 11:32 pm Pisces
24th 12:02 pm Aries
27th 0:44 am Taurus
29th 11:49 am Gemini
31st 7:33 pm Cancer

September 1975
2nd 11:08 pm Leo
4th 11:30 pm Virgo
6th 10:38 pm Libra
8th 10:47 pm Scorpio
11th 1:41 am Sagittarius
13th 8:15 am Capricorn
15th 5:53 pm Aquarius
18th 5:32 am Pisces
20th 6:08 pm Aries
23rd 6:43 am Taurus
25th 6:12 pm Gemini
28th 3:05 am Cancer
30th 8:16 am Leo

October 1975
2nd 10:00 am Virgo
4th 9:41 am Libra
6th 9:13 am Scorpio
8th 10:42 am Sagittarius
10th 3:35 pm Capricorn
13th 0:10 am Aquarius
15th 11:42 am Pisces
18th 0:20 am Aries
20th 12:42 pm Taurus
22nd 11:52 pm Gemini
25th 8:54 am Cancer
27th 3:16 pm Leo
29th 6:44 pm Virgo
31st 7:55 pm Libra

November 1975
2nd 8:10 pm Scorpio
4th 9:13 pm Sagittarius
7th 0:47 am Capricorn
9th 8:06 am Aquarius
11th 6:45 pm Pisces
14th 7:17 am Aries
16th 7:37 pm Taurus
19th 6:12 am Gemini
21st 2:33 pm Cancer
23rd 8:47 pm Leo
26th 1:05 am Virgo
28th 3:47 am Libra
30th 5:38 am Scorpio

December 1975
2nd 7:37 am Sagittarius
4th 11:04 am Capricorn
6th 5:18 pm Aquarius
9th 2:55 am Pisces
11th 3:09 pm Aries
14th 3:40 am Taurus
16th 2:10 pm Gemini
18th 9:49 pm Cancer
21st 2:53 am Leo
23rd 6:27 am Virgo
25th 9:27 am Libra
27th 12:29 pm Scorpio
29th 3:55 pm Sagittarius
31st 8:19 pm Capricorn

January 1976
3rd 2:35 am Aquarius
5th 11:40 am Pisces
7th 11:22 pm Aries
10th 12:09 pm Taurus
12th 11:21 pm Gemini
15th 6:57 am Cancer
17th 11:13 am Leo
19th 1:25 pm Virgo
21st 3:12 pm Libra
23rd 5:50 pm Scorpio
25th 9:52 pm Sagittarius
28th 3:25 am Capricorn
30th 10:38 am Aquarius

February 1976
1st 7:50 pm Pisces
4th 7:20 am Aries
6th 8:14 pm Taurus
9th 8:13 am Gemini
11th 4:55 pm Cancer
13th 9:31 pm Leo
15th 10:60 pm Virgo
17th 11:15 pm Libra
20th 0:15 am Scorpio
22nd 3:20 am Sagittarius
24th 8:58 am Capricorn
26th 4:50 pm Aquarius
29th 2:44 am Pisces

March 1976
2nd 2:24 pm Aries
5th 3:19 am Taurus
7th 3:55 pm Gemini
10th 1:58 am Cancer
12th 7:52 am Leo
14th 9:56 am Virgo
16th 9:45 am Libra
18th 9:22 am Scorpio
20th 10:39 am Sagittarius
22nd 2:54 pm Capricorn
24th 10:20 pm Aquarius
27th 8:35 am Pisces
29th 8:38 pm Aries

April 1976
1st 9:34 am Taurus
3rd 10:15 pm Gemini
6th 9:04 am Cancer
8th 4:33 pm Leo
10th 8:15 pm Virgo
12th 8:54 pm Libra
14th 8:16 pm Scorpio
16th 8:18 pm Sagittarius
18th 10:45 pm Capricorn
21st 4:51 am Aquarius
23rd 2:31 pm Pisces
26th 2:36 am Aries
28th 3:36 pm Taurus

May 1976
1st 4:02 am Gemini
3rd 2:51 pm Cancer
5th 11:08 pm Leo
8th 4:18 am Virgo
10th 6:37 am Libra
12th 7:03 am Scorpio
14th 7:06 am Sagittarius
16th 8:37 am Capricorn
18th 1:10 pm Aquarius
20th 9:30 pm Pisces
23rd 9:09 am Aries
25th 10:08 pm Taurus
28th 10:19 am Gemini
30th 8:37 pm Cancer

June 1976
2nd 4:35 am Leo
4th 10:17 am Virgo
6th 1:56 pm Libra
8th 3:57 pm Scorpio
10th 5:07 pm Sagittarius
12th 6:47 pm Capricorn
14th 10:32 pm Aquarius
17th 5:49 am Pisces
19th 4:35 pm Aries
22nd 5:22 am Taurus
24th 5:35 pm Gemini
27th 3:27 am Cancer
29th 10:36 am Leo

July 1976
1st 3:44 pm Virgo
3rd 7:33 pm Libra
5th 10:32 pm Scorpio
8th 1:06 am Sagittarius
10th 3:50 am Capricorn
12th 7:57 am Aquarius
14th 2:41 pm Pisces
17th 0:40 am Aries
19th 1:11 pm Taurus
22nd 1:40 am Gemini
24th 11:35 am Cancer
26th 6:16 pm Leo
28th 10:22 pm Virgo
31st 1:13 am Libra

August 1976
2nd 3:56 am Scorpio
4th 7:04 am Sagittarius
6th 10:56 am Capricorn
8th 3:59 pm Aquarius
10th 11:00 pm Pisces
13th 8:52 am Aries
15th 9:06 pm Taurus
18th 9:52 am Gemini
20th 8:31 pm Cancer
23rd 3:28 am Leo
25th 7:01 am Virgo
27th 8:42 am Libra
29th 10:06 am Scorpio
31st 12:32 pm Sagittarius

September 1976
2nd 4:32 pm Capricorn
4th 10:20 pm Aquarius
7th 6:14 am Pisces
9th 4:20 pm Aries
12th 4:31 am Taurus
14th 5:31 pm Gemini
17th 5:03 am Cancer
19th 1:06 pm Leo
21st 5:13 pm Virgo
23rd 6:27 pm Libra
25th 6:34 pm Scorpio
27th 7:24 pm Sagittarius
29th 10:15 pm Capricorn

October 1976
2nd 3:51 am Aquarius
4th 12:12 pm Pisces
6th 10:51 pm Aries
9th 11:12 am Taurus
12th 0:14 am Gemini
14th 12:21 pm Cancer
16th 9:49 pm Leo
19th 3:23 am Virgo
21st 5:24 am Libra
23rd 5:17 am Scorpio
25th 4:52 am Sagittarius
27th 5:60 am Capricorn
29th 10:11 am Aquarius
31st 5:56 pm Pisces

November 1976
3rd 4:47 am Aries
5th 5:23 pm Taurus
8th 6:20 am Gemini
10th 6:27 pm Cancer
13th 4:34 am Leo
15th 11:40 am Virgo
17th 3:30 pm Libra
19th 4:29 pm Scorpio
21st 4:06 pm Sagittarius
23rd 4:09 pm Capricorn
25th 6:36 pm Aquarius
28th 0:50 am Pisces
30th 11:06 am Aries

December 1976
2nd 11:42 pm Taurus
5th 12:36 pm Gemini
8th 0:21 am Cancer
10th 10:09 am Leo
12th 5:53 pm Virgo
14th 11:13 pm Libra
17th 2:02 am Scorpio
19th 2:54 am Sagittarius
21st 3:14 am Capricorn
23rd 4:53 am Aquarius
25th 9:43 am Pisces
27th 6:37 pm Aries
30th 6:45 am Taurus

January 1977
1st 7:43 pm Gemini
4th 7:10 am Cancer
6th 4:19 pm Leo
8th 11:24 pm Virgo
11th 4:47 am Libra
13th 8:43 am Scorpio
15th 11:18 am Sagittarius
17th 1:04 pm Capricorn
19th 3:17 pm Aquarius
21st 7:35 pm Pisces
24th 3:24 am Aries
26th 2:43 pm Taurus
29th 3:38 am Gemini
31st 3:18 pm Cancer

February 1977
3rd 0:13 am Leo
5th 6:17 am Virgo
7th 10:36 am Libra
9th 2:04 pm Scorpio
11th 5:12 pm Sagittarius
13th 8:15 pm Capricorn
15th 11:46 pm Aquarius
18th 4:49 am Pisces
20th 12:28 pm Aries
22nd 11:06 pm Taurus
25th 11:51 am Gemini
28th 0:04 am Cancer

March 1977
2nd 9:22 am Leo
4th 3:16 pm Virgo
6th 6:35 pm Libra
8th 8:39 pm Scorpio
10th 10:43 pm Sagittarius
13th 1:42 am Capricorn
15th 6:03 am Aquarius
17th 12:09 pm Pisces
19th 8:25 pm Aries
22nd 7:08 am Taurus
24th 7:40 pm Gemini
27th 8:15 am Cancer
29th 6:38 pm Leo

April 1977
1st 1:25 am Virgo
3rd 4:39 am Libra
5th 5:41 am Scorpio
7th 6:12 am Sagittarius
9th 7:45 am Capricorn
11th 11:28 am Aquarius
13th 5:52 pm Pisces
16th 2:54 am Aries
18th 2:04 pm Taurus
21st 2:38 am Gemini
23rd 3:24 pm Cancer
26th 2:43 am Leo
28th 10:48 am Virgo
30th 3:09 pm Libra

May 1977
2nd 4:22 pm Scorpio
4th 4:01 pm Sagittarius
6th 3:59 pm Capricorn
8th 6:05 pm Aquarius
10th 11:29 pm Pisces
13th 8:33 am Aries
15th 8:05 pm Taurus
18th 8:50 am Gemini
20th 9:35 pm Cancer
23rd 9:10 am Leo
25th 6:27 pm Virgo
28th 0:29 am Libra
30th 2:55 am Scorpio

June 1977
1st 2:54 am Sagittarius
3rd 2:09 am Capricorn
5th 2:47 am Aquarius
7th 6:42 am Pisces
9th 2:40 pm Aries
12th 1:57 am Taurus
14th 2:51 pm Gemini
17th 3:28 am Cancer
19th 2:50 pm Leo
22nd 0:28 am Virgo
24th 7:30 am Libra
26th 11:36 am Scorpio
28th 12:58 pm Sagittarius
30th 12:48 pm Capricorn

July 1977
2nd 1:01 pm Aquarius
4th 3:38 pm Pisces
6th 10:06 pm Aries
9th 8:37 am Taurus
11th 9:15 pm Gemini
14th 9:48 am Cancer
16th 8:51 pm Leo
19th 5:56 am Virgo
21st 1:06 pm Libra
23rd 6:10 pm Scorpio
25th 9:03 pm Sagittarius
27th 10:14 pm Capricorn
29th 11:04 pm Aquarius

August 1977
1st 1:26 am Pisces
3rd 6:59 am Aries
5th 4:21 pm Taurus
8th 4:30 am Gemini
10th 5:03 pm Cancer
13th 3:55 am Leo
15th 12:24 pm Virgo
17th 6:48 pm Libra
19th 11:36 pm Scorpio
22nd 3:03 am Sagittarius
24th 5:29 am Capricorn
26th 7:41 am Aquarius
28th 10:50 am Pisces
30th 4:15 pm Aries

September 1977
2nd 0:51 am Taurus
4th 12:28 pm Gemini
7th 1:02 am Cancer
9th 12:10 pm Leo
11th 8:33 pm Virgo
14th 2:07 am Libra
16th 5:45 am Scorpio
18th 8:29 am Sagittarius
20th 11:05 am Capricorn
22nd 2:14 pm Aquarius
24th 6:32 pm Pisces
27th 0:41 am Aries
29th 9:24 am Taurus

October 1977
1st 8:34 pm Gemini
4th 9:09 am Cancer
6th 8:57 pm Leo
9th 5:55 am Virgo
11th 11:25 am Libra
13th 2:09 pm Scorpio
15th 3:28 pm Sagittarius
17th 4:53 pm Capricorn
19th 7:38 pm Aquarius
22nd 0:25 am Pisces
24th 7:37 am Aries
26th 4:54 pm Taurus
29th 4:07 am Gemini
31st 4:41 pm Cancer

November 1977
3rd 5:01 am Leo
5th 3:12 pm Virgo
7th 9:50 pm Libra
10th 0:42 am Scorpio
12th 1:04 am Sagittarius
14th 0:52 am Capricorn
16th 2:02 am Aquarius
18th 6:02 am Pisces
20th 1:17 pm Aries
22nd 11:09 pm Taurus
25th 10:49 am Gemini
27th 11:20 pm Cancer
30th 11:51 am Leo

December 1977
2nd 11:03 pm Virgo
5th 7:13 am Libra
7th 11:27 am Scorpio
9th 12:18 pm Sagittarius
11th 11:28 am Capricorn
13th 11:06 am Aquarius
15th 1:16 pm Pisces
17th 7:16 pm Aries
20th 4:57 am Taurus
22nd 4:53 pm Gemini
25th 5:29 am Cancer
27th 5:51 pm Leo
30th 5:11 am Virgo

January 1978
1st 2:27 pm Libra
3rd 8:32 pm Scorpio
5th 11:02 pm Sagittarius
7th 10:54 pm Capricorn
9th 10:06 pm Aquarius
11th 10:52 pm Pisces
14th 3:09 am Aries
16th 11:37 am Taurus
18th 11:08 pm Gemini
21st 11:51 am Cancer
24th 0:04 am Leo
26th 10:54 am Virgo
28th 8:07 pm Libra
31st 3:02 am Scorpio

February 1978
2nd 7:11 am Sagittarius
4th 8:48 am Capricorn
6th 9:06 am Aquarius
8th 9:52 am Pisces
10th 1:03 pm Aries
12th 7:54 pm Taurus
15th 6:27 am Gemini
17th 6:56 pm Cancer
20th 7:09 am Leo
22nd 5:39 pm Virgo
25th 2:03 am Libra
27th 8:27 am Scorpio

March 1978
1st 1:00 pm Sagittarius
3rd 3:57 pm Capricorn
5th 5:51 pm Aquarius
7th 7:47 pm Pisces
9th 11:10 pm Aries
12th 5:21 am Taurus
14th 2:52 pm Gemini
17th 2:50 am Cancer
19th 3:11 pm Leo
22nd 1:50 am Virgo
24th 9:40 am Libra
26th 3:00 pm Scorpio
28th 6:38 pm Sagittarius
30th 9:25 pm Capricorn

April 1978
2nd 0:05 am Aquarius
4th 3:21 am Pisces
6th 7:55 am Aries
8th 2:25 pm Taurus
10th 11:29 pm Gemini
13th 11:01 am Cancer
15th 11:32 pm Leo
18th 10:41 am Virgo
20th 6:51 pm Libra
22nd 11:41 pm Scorpio
25th 2:01 am Sagittarius
27th 3:30 am Capricorn
29th 5:31 am Aquarius

May 1978
1st 9:03 am Pisces
3rd 2:29 pm Aries
5th 9:53 pm Taurus
8th 7:22 am Gemini
10th 6:44 pm Cancer
13th 7:16 am Leo
15th 7:14 pm Virgo
18th 4:22 am Libra
20th 9:35 am Scorpio
22nd 11:28 am Sagittarius
24th 11:43 am Capricorn
26th 12:15 pm Aquarius
28th 2:42 pm Pisces
30th 7:56 pm Aries

June 1978
2nd 3:52 am Taurus
4th 1:56 pm Gemini
7th 1:31 am Cancer
9th 2:08 pm Leo
12th 2:34 am Virgo
14th 12:51 pm Libra
16th 7:24 pm Scorpio
18th 9:60 pm Sagittarius
20th 9:52 pm Capricorn
22nd 9:11 pm Aquarius
24th 9:59 pm Pisces
27th 1:56 am Aries
29th 9:26 am Taurus

July 1978
1st 7:40 pm Gemini
4th 7:35 am Cancer
6th 8:13 pm Leo
9th 8:42 am Virgo
11th 7:46 pm Libra
14th 3:43 am Scorpio
16th 7:44 am Sagittarius
18th 8:30 am Capricorn
20th 7:44 am Aquarius
22nd 7:31 am Pisces
24th 9:52 am Aries
26th 3:56 pm Taurus
29th 1:33 am Gemini
31st 1:30 pm Cancer

August 1978
3rd 2:11 am Leo
5th 2:28 pm Virgo
8th 1:28 am Libra
10th 10:07 am Scorpio
12th 3:38 pm Sagittarius
14th 5:59 pm Capricorn
16th 6:14 pm Aquarius
18th 6:07 pm Pisces
20th 7:32 pm Aries
23rd 0:06 am Taurus
25th 8:36 am Gemini
27th 7:59 pm Cancer
30th 8:39 am Leo

September 1978
1st 8:47 pm Virgo
4th 7:14 am Libra
6th 3:36 pm Scorpio
8th 9:38 pm Sagittarius
11th 1:19 am Capricorn
13th 3:08 am Aquarius
15th 4:10 am Pisces
17th 5:52 am Aries
19th 9:47 am Taurus
21st 4:60 pm Gemini
24th 3:33 am Cancer
26th 4:01 pm Leo
29th 4:10 am Virgo

October 1978
1st 2:14 pm Libra
3rd 9:47 pm Scorpio
6th 3:06 am Sagittarius
8th 6:51 am Capricorn
10th 9:42 am Aquarius
12th 12:13 pm Pisces
14th 3:06 pm Aries
16th 7:23 pm Taurus
19th 2:05 am Gemini
21st 11:55 am Cancer
24th 0:04 am Leo
26th 12:29 pm Virgo
28th 10:51 pm Libra
31st 5:49 am Scorpio

November 1978
2nd 10:02 am Sagittarius
4th 12:40 pm Capricorn
6th 3:04 pm Aquarius
8th 6:07 pm Pisces
10th 10:12 pm Aries
13th 3:36 am Taurus
15th 10:48 am Gemini
17th 8:16 pm Cancer
20th 8:10 am Leo
22nd 8:56 pm Virgo
25th 8:03 am Libra
27th 3:33 pm Scorpio
29th 7:20 pm Sagittarius

December 1978
1st 8:44 pm Capricorn
3rd 9:36 pm Aquarius
5th 11:36 pm Pisces
8th 3:41 am Aries
10th 9:53 am Taurus
12th 5:57 pm Gemini
15th 3:51 am Cancer
17th 3:38 pm Leo
20th 4:32 am Virgo
22nd 4:35 pm Libra
25th 1:30 am Scorpio
27th 6:03 am Sagittarius
29th 7:13 am Capricorn
31st 6:55 am Aquarius

January 1979
2nd 7:12 am Pisces
4th 9:47 am Aries
6th 3:23 pm Taurus
8th 11:43 pm Gemini
11th 10:16 am Cancer
13th 10:17 pm Leo
16th 11:10 am Virgo
18th 11:40 pm Libra
21st 9:45 am Scorpio
23rd 4:02 pm Sagittarius
25th 6:23 pm Capricorn
27th 6:11 pm Aquarius
29th 5:27 pm Pisces
31st 6:15 pm Aries

February 1979
2nd 10:05 pm Taurus
5th 5:37 am Gemini
7th 4:08 pm Cancer
10th 4:28 am Leo
12th 5:18 pm Virgo
15th 5:35 am Libra
17th 4:09 pm Scorpio
19th 11:51 pm Sagittarius
22nd 3:58 am Capricorn
24th 5:10 am Aquarius
26th 4:53 am Pisces
28th 4:57 am Aries

March 1979
2nd 7:14 am Taurus
4th 1:04 pm Gemini
6th 10:36 pm Cancer
9th 10:49 am Leo
11th 11:44 pm Virgo
14th 11:40 am Libra
16th 9:50 pm Scorpio
19th 5:36 am Sagittarius
21st 10:53 am Capricorn
23rd 1:50 pm Aquarius
25th 3:04 pm Pisces
27th 3:49 pm Aries
29th 5:40 pm Taurus
31st 10:09 pm Gemini

April 1979
3rd 6:27 am Cancer
5th 5:59 pm Leo
8th 6:52 am Virgo
10th 6:45 pm Libra
13th 4:15 am Scorpio
15th 11:16 am Sagittarius
17th 4:22 pm Capricorn
19th 8:01 pm Aquarius
21st 10:41 pm Pisces
24th 0:52 am Aries
26th 3:30 am Taurus
28th 7:53 am Gemini
30th 3:16 pm Cancer

May 1979
3rd 1:57 am Leo
5th 2:41 pm Virgo
8th 2:48 am Libra
10th 12:07 pm Scorpio
12th 6:23 pm Sagittarius
14th 10:27 pm Capricorn
17th 1:26 am Aquarius
19th 4:19 am Pisces
21st 7:31 am Aries
23rd 11:22 am Taurus
25th 4:31 pm Gemini
27th 11:51 pm Cancer
30th 10:11 am Leo

June 1979
1st 10:41 pm Virgo
4th 11:08 am Libra
6th 9:03 pm Scorpio
9th 3:14 am Sagittarius
11th 6:23 am Capricorn
13th 8:08 am Aquarius
15th 9:59 am Pisces
17th 12:56 pm Aries
19th 5:21 pm Taurus
21st 11:24 pm Gemini
24th 7:27 am Cancer
26th 5:50 pm Leo
29th 6:15 am Virgo

July 1979
1st 7:06 pm Libra
4th 5:53 am Scorpio
6th 12:50 pm Sagittarius
8th 4:04 pm Capricorn
10th 4:59 pm Aquarius
12th 5:26 pm Pisces
14th 7:00 pm Aries
16th 10:45 pm Taurus
19th 5:03 am Gemini
21st 1:44 pm Cancer
24th 0:32 am Leo
26th 1:02 pm Virgo
29th 2:05 am Libra
31st 1:42 pm Scorpio

August 1979
2nd 10:03 pm Sagittarius
5th 2:21 am Capricorn
7th 3:27 am Aquarius
9th 3:06 am Pisces
11th 3:12 am Aries
13th 5:26 am Taurus
15th 10:47 am Gemini
17th 7:21 pm Cancer
20th 6:32 am Leo
22nd 7:13 pm Virgo
25th 8:13 am Libra
27th 8:11 pm Scorpio
30th 5:36 am Sagittarius

September 1979
1st 11:28 am Capricorn
3rd 1:55 pm Aquarius
5th 2:02 pm Pisces
7th 1:31 pm Aries
9th 2:17 pm Taurus
11th 5:59 pm Gemini
14th 1:27 am Cancer
16th 12:28 pm Leo
19th 1:15 am Virgo
21st 2:10 pm Libra
24th 1:55 am Scorpio
26th 11:33 am Sagittarius
28th 6:36 pm Capricorn
30th 10:48 pm Aquarius

October 1979
3rd 0:23 am Pisces
5th 0:27 am Aries
7th 0:45 am Taurus
9th 3:09 am Gemini
11th 9:14 am Cancer
13th 7:13 pm Leo
16th 7:51 am Virgo
18th 8:44 pm Libra
21st 8:00 am Scorpio
23rd 5:07 pm Sagittarius
26th 0:11 am Capricorn
28th 5:15 am Aquarius
30th 8:26 am Pisces

November 1979
1st 10:08 am Aries
3rd 11:16 am Taurus
5th 1:30 pm Gemini
7th 6:27 pm Cancer
10th 3:16 am Leo
12th 3:21 pm Virgo
15th 4:15 am Libra
17th 3:26 pm Scorpio
19th 11:56 pm Sagittarius
22nd 6:00 am Capricorn
24th 10:35 am Aquarius
26th 2:16 pm Pisces
28th 5:16 pm Aries
30th 7:54 pm Taurus

December 1979
2nd 11:02 pm Gemini
5th 4:03 am Cancer
7th 12:13 pm Leo
9th 11:32 pm Virgo
12th 12:27 pm Libra
15th 0:08 am Scorpio
17th 8:32 am Sagittarius
19th 1:51 pm Capricorn
21st 5:12 pm Aquarius
23rd 7:50 pm Pisces
25th 10:40 pm Aries
28th 2:08 am Taurus
30th 6:34 am Gemini

January 1980
1st 12:33 pm Cancer
3rd 8:49 pm Leo
6th 7:50 am Virgo
8th 8:37 pm Libra
11th 8:50 am Scorpio
13th 6:12 pm Sagittarius
15th 11:51 pm Capricorn
18th 2:25 am Aquarius
20th 3:33 am Pisces
22nd 4:54 am Aries
24th 7:36 am Taurus
26th 12:14 pm Gemini
28th 7:05 pm Cancer
31st 4:11 am Leo

February 1980
2nd 3:23 pm Virgo
5th 4:04 am Libra
7th 4:43 pm Scorpio
10th 3:15 am Sagittarius
12th 10:06 am Capricorn
14th 1:14 pm Aquarius
16th 1:52 pm Pisces
18th 1:45 pm Aries
20th 2:39 pm Taurus
22nd 6:03 pm Gemini
25th 0:36 am Cancer
27th 10:14 am Leo
29th 9:54 pm Virgo

March 1980
3rd 10:40 am Libra
5th 11:24 pm Scorpio
8th 10:35 am Sagittarius
10th 6:59 pm Capricorn
12th 11:46 pm Aquarius
15th 1:10 am Pisces
17th 0:41 am Aries
19th 0:13 am Taurus
21st 1:49 am Gemini
23rd 7:00 am Cancer
25th 4:02 pm Leo
28th 3:53 am Virgo
30th 4:49 pm Libra

April 1980
2nd 5:21 am Scorpio
4th 4:34 pm Sagittarius
7th 1:41 am Capricorn
9th 7:56 am Aquarius
11th 11:03 am Pisces
13th 11:39 am Aries
15th 11:12 am Taurus
17th 11:47 am Gemini
19th 3:18 pm Cancer
21st 10:54 pm Leo
24th 10:14 am Virgo
26th 11:11 pm Libra
29th 11:34 am Scorpio

May 1980
1st 10:23 pm Sagittarius
4th 7:13 am Capricorn
6th 2:01 pm Aquarius
8th 6:31 pm Pisces
10th 8:44 pm Aries
12th 9:25 pm Taurus
14th 10:09 pm Gemini
17th 0:53 am Cancer
19th 7:19 am Leo
21st 5:35 pm Virgo
24th 6:12 am Libra
26th 6:37 pm Scorpio
29th 5:04 am Sagittarius
31st 1:13 pm Capricorn

June 1980
2nd 7:28 pm Aquarius
5th 0:10 am Pisces
7th 3:23 am Aries
9th 5:30 am Taurus
11th 7:25 am Gemini
13th 10:35 am Cancer
15th 4:26 pm Leo
18th 1:49 am Virgo
20th 1:56 pm Libra
23rd 2:27 am Scorpio
25th 12:58 pm Sagittarius
27th 8:45 pm Capricorn
30th 2:03 am Aquarius

July 1980
2nd 5:48 am Pisces
4th 8:48 am Aries
6th 11:32 am Taurus
8th 2:36 pm Gemini
10th 6:48 pm Cancer
13th 1:04 am Leo
15th 10:15 am Virgo
17th 9:55 pm Libra
20th 10:32 am Scorpio
22nd 9:40 pm Sagittarius
25th 5:42 am Capricorn
27th 10:32 am Aquarius
29th 1:10 pm Pisces
31st 2:55 pm Aries

August 1980
2nd 4:58 pm Taurus
4th 8:12 pm Gemini
7th 1:14 am Cancer
9th 8:28 am Leo
11th 5:58 pm Virgo
14th 5:33 am Libra
16th 6:14 pm Scorpio
19th 6:04 am Sagittarius
21st 3:06 pm Capricorn
23rd 8:30 pm Aquarius
25th 10:42 pm Pisces
27th 11:12 pm Aries
29th 11:42 pm Taurus

September 1980
1st 1:53 am Gemini
3rd 6:44 am Cancer
5th 2:26 pm Leo
8th 0:32 am Virgo
10th 12:24 pm Libra
13th 1:07 am Scorpio
15th 1:26 pm Sagittarius
17th 11:45 pm Capricorn
20th 6:26 am Aquarius
22nd 9:22 am Pisces
24th 9:36 am Aries
26th 8:55 am Taurus
28th 9:25 am Gemini
30th 12:51 pm Cancer

October 1980
2nd 7:59 pm Leo
5th 6:20 am Virgo
7th 6:31 pm Libra
10th 7:15 am Scorpio
12th 7:38 pm Sagittarius
15th 6:34 am Capricorn
17th 2:49 pm Aquarius
19th 7:28 pm Pisces
21st 8:40 pm Aries
23rd 7:55 pm Taurus
25th 7:19 pm Gemini
27th 9:02 pm Cancer
30th 2:40 am Leo

November 1980
1st 12:21 pm Virgo
4th 0:30 am Libra
6th 1:18 pm Scorpio
9th 1:25 am Sagittarius
11th 12:13 pm Capricorn
13th 9:08 pm Aquarius
16th 3:18 am Pisces
18th 6:18 am Aries
20th 6:48 am Taurus
22nd 6:29 am Gemini
24th 7:23 am Cancer
26th 11:28 am Leo
28th 7:40 pm Virgo

December 1980
1st 7:14 am Libra
3rd 7:59 pm Scorpio
6th 7:55 am Sagittarius
8th 6:09 pm Capricorn
11th 2:34 am Aquarius
13th 8:60 am Pisces
15th 1:18 pm Aries
17th 3:33 pm Taurus
19th 4:40 pm Gemini
21st 6:05 pm Cancer
23rd 9:35 pm Leo
26th 4:35 am Virgo
28th 3:06 pm Libra
31st 3:34 am Scorpio

January 1981
2nd 3:38 pm Sagittarius
5th 1:39 am Capricorn
7th 9:09 am Aquarius
9th 2:39 pm Pisces
11th 6:42 pm Aries
13th 9:45 pm Taurus
16th 0:17 am Gemini
18th 3:09 am Cancer
20th 7:24 am Leo
22nd 2:06 pm Virgo
24th 11:44 pm Libra
27th 11:48 am Scorpio
30th 0:10 am Sagittarius

February 1981
1st 10:31 am Capricorn
3rd 5:51 pm Aquarius
5th 10:20 pm Pisces
8th 1:02 am Aries
10th 3:12 am Taurus
12th 5:53 am Gemini
14th 9:46 am Cancer
16th 3:14 pm Leo
18th 10:34 pm Virgo
21st 8:14 am Libra
23rd 7:55 pm Scorpio
26th 8:26 am Sagittarius
28th 7:43 pm Capricorn

March 1981
3rd 3:47 am Aquarius
5th 8:07 am Pisces
7th 9:45 am Aries
9th 10:23 am Taurus
11th 11:46 am Gemini
13th 3:10 pm Cancer
15th 9:05 pm Leo
18th 5:22 am Virgo
20th 3:33 pm Libra
23rd 3:15 am Scorpio
25th 3:51 pm Sagittarius
28th 3:51 am Capricorn
30th 1:09 pm Aquarius

April 1981
1st 6:37 pm Pisces
3rd 8:22 pm Aries
5th 8:03 pm Taurus
7th 7:50 pm Gemini
9th 9:35 pm Cancer
12th 2:39 am Leo
14th 10:59 am Virgo
16th 9:38 pm Libra
19th 9:40 am Scorpio
21st 10:15 pm Sagittarius
24th 10:30 am Capricorn
26th 8:56 pm Aquarius
29th 3:54 am Pisces

May 1981
1st 6:53 am Aries
3rd 6:58 am Taurus
5th 6:03 am Gemini
7th 6:22 am Cancer
9th 9:46 am Leo
11th 4:59 pm Virgo
14th 3:25 am Libra
16th 3:39 pm Scorpio
19th 4:14 am Sagittarius
21st 4:19 pm Capricorn
24th 2:59 am Aquarius
26th 11:01 am Pisces
28th 3:39 pm Aries
30th 5:08 pm Taurus

June 1981
1st 4:49 pm Gemini
3rd 4:43 pm Cancer
5th 6:47 pm Leo
8th 0:26 am Virgo
10th 9:59 am Libra
12th 9:55 pm Scorpio
15th 10:32 am Sagittarius
17th 10:21 pm Capricorn
20th 8:34 am Aquarius
22nd 4:42 pm Pisces
24th 10:18 pm Aries
27th 1:16 am Taurus
29th 2:22 am Gemini

July 1981
1st 2:59 am Cancer
3rd 4:51 am Leo
5th 9:32 am Virgo
7th 5:45 pm Libra
10th 5:02 am Scorpio
12th 5:35 pm Sagittarius
15th 5:18 am Capricorn
17th 2:60 pm Aquarius
19th 10:25 pm Pisces
22nd 3:44 am Aries
24th 7:18 am Taurus
26th 9:42 am Gemini
28th 11:43 am Cancer
30th 2:25 pm Leo

August 1981
1st 6:58 pm Virgo
4th 2:26 am Libra
6th 1:01 pm Scorpio
9th 1:23 am Sagittarius
11th 1:17 pm Capricorn
13th 10:56 pm Aquarius
16th 5:32 am Pisces
18th 9:48 am Aries
20th 12:45 pm Taurus
22nd 3:20 pm Gemini
24th 6:18 pm Cancer
26th 10:12 pm Leo
29th 3:35 am Virgo
31st 11:07 am Libra

September 1981
2nd 9:13 pm Scorpio
5th 9:24 am Sagittarius
7th 9:48 pm Capricorn
10th 7:54 am Aquarius
12th 2:29 pm Pisces
14th 5:53 pm Aries
16th 7:30 pm Taurus
18th 9:01 pm Gemini
20th 11:40 pm Cancer
23rd 4:11 am Leo
25th 10:32 am Virgo
27th 6:43 pm Libra
30th 4:56 am Scorpio

October 1981
2nd 5:01 pm Sagittarius
5th 5:47 am Capricorn
7th 4:57 pm Aquarius
10th 0:32 am Pisces
12th 3:59 am Aries
14th 4:43 am Taurus
16th 4:43 am Gemini
18th 5:55 am Cancer
20th 9:39 am Leo
22nd 4:07 pm Virgo
25th 0:56 am Libra
27th 11:40 am Scorpio
29th 11:50 pm Sagittarius

November 1981
1st 12:46 pm Capricorn
4th 0:50 am Aquarius
6th 9:46 am Pisces
8th 2:33 pm Aries
10th 3:41 pm Taurus
12th 3:00 pm Gemini
14th 2:40 pm Cancer
16th 4:36 pm Leo
18th 9:55 pm Virgo
21st 6:34 am Libra
23rd 5:38 pm Scorpio
26th 6:01 am Sagittarius
28th 6:52 pm Capricorn

December 1981
1st 7:07 am Aquarius
3rd 5:13 pm Pisces
5th 11:49 pm Aries
8th 2:29 am Taurus
10th 2:29 am Gemini
12th 1:42 am Cancer
14th 2:09 am Leo
16th 5:41 am Virgo
18th 1:03 pm Libra
20th 11:38 pm Scorpio
23rd 12:11 pm Sagittarius
26th 0:58 am Capricorn
28th 12:51 pm Aquarius
30th 11:01 pm Pisces

January 1982
2nd 6:29 am Aries
4th 10:57 am Taurus
6th 12:46 pm Gemini
8th 1:01 pm Cancer
10th 1:24 pm Leo
12th 3:42 pm Virgo
14th 9:19 pm Libra
17th 6:48 am Scorpio
19th 6:60 pm Sagittarius
22nd 7:49 am Capricorn
24th 7:22 pm Aquarius
27th 4:47 am Pisces
29th 11:55 am Aries
31st 5:02 pm Taurus

February 1982
2nd 8:19 pm Gemini
4th 10:17 pm Cancer
6th 11:50 pm Leo
9th 2:16 am Virgo
11th 7:05 am Libra
13th 3:20 pm Scorpio
16th 2:44 am Sagittarius
18th 3:34 pm Capricorn
21st 3:11 am Aquarius
23rd 12:04 pm Pisces
25th 6:14 pm Aries
27th 10:32 pm Taurus

March 1982
2nd 1:49 am Gemini
4th 4:49 am Cancer
6th 7:51 am Leo
8th 11:29 am Virgo
10th 4:37 pm Libra
13th 0:17 am Scorpio
15th 11:05 am Sagittarius
17th 11:46 pm Capricorn
20th 11:48 am Aquarius
22nd 8:57 pm Pisces
25th 2:35 am Aries
27th 5:38 am Taurus
29th 7:44 am Gemini
31st 10:10 am Cancer

April 1982
2nd 1:39 pm Leo
4th 6:20 pm Virgo
7th 0:26 am Libra
9th 8:37 am Scorpio
11th 7:08 pm Sagittarius
14th 7:42 am Capricorn
16th 8:16 pm Aquarius
19th 6:15 am Pisces
21st 12:17 pm Aries
23rd 2:55 pm Taurus
25th 3:48 pm Gemini
27th 4:44 pm Cancer
29th 7:10 pm Leo

May 1982
1st 11:44 pm Virgo
4th 6:34 am Libra
6th 3:26 pm Scorpio
9th 2:18 am Sagittarius
11th 2:51 pm Capricorn
14th 3:44 am Aquarius
16th 2:42 pm Pisces
18th 10:03 pm Aries
21st 1:20 am Taurus
23rd 1:54 am Gemini
25th 1:38 am Cancer
27th 2:28 am Leo
29th 5:46 am Virgo
31st 12:06 pm Libra

June 1982
2nd 9:12 pm Scorpio
5th 8:33 am Sagittarius
7th 9:11 pm Capricorn
10th 10:06 am Aquarius
12th 9:43 pm Pisces
15th 6:16 am Aries
17th 11:01 am Taurus
19th 12:31 pm Gemini
21st 12:13 pm Cancer
23rd 11:60 am Leo
25th 1:41 pm Virgo
27th 6:34 pm Libra
30th 3:03 am Scorpio

July 1982
2nd 2:27 pm Sagittarius
5th 3:15 am Capricorn
7th 4:01 pm Aquarius
10th 3:33 am Pisces
12th 12:45 pm Aries
14th 6:56 pm Taurus
16th 10:03 pm Gemini
18th 10:46 pm Cancer
20th 10:36 pm Leo
22nd 11:21 pm Virgo
25th 2:47 am Libra
27th 10:04 am Scorpio
29th 8:49 pm Sagittarius

August 1982
1st 9:36 am Capricorn
3rd 10:17 pm Aquarius
6th 9:21 am Pisces
8th 6:20 pm Aries
11th 1:00 am Taurus
13th 5:21 am Gemini
15th 7:39 am Cancer
17th 8:42 am Leo
19th 9:44 am Virgo
21st 12:27 pm Libra
23rd 6:25 pm Scorpio
26th 4:13 am Sagittarius
28th 4:41 pm Capricorn
31st 5:22 am Aquarius

September 1982
2nd 4:07 pm Pisces
5th 0:24 am Aries
7th 6:26 am Taurus
9th 10:57 am Gemini
11th 2:18 pm Cancer
13th 4:46 pm Leo
15th 6:60 pm Virgo
17th 10:05 pm Libra
20th 3:36 am Scorpio
22nd 12:35 pm Sagittarius
25th 0:32 am Capricorn
27th 1:19 pm Aquarius
30th 0:19 am Pisces

October 1982
2nd 8:02 am Aries
4th 1:07 pm Taurus
6th 4:38 pm Gemini
8th 7:40 pm Cancer
10th 10:45 pm Leo
13th 2:10 am Virgo
15th 6:26 am Libra
17th 12:26 pm Scorpio
19th 9:05 pm Sagittarius
22nd 8:41 am Capricorn
24th 9:36 pm Aquarius
27th 9:08 am Pisces
29th 5:21 pm Aries
31st 10:03 pm Taurus

November 1982
3rd 0:23 am Gemini
5th 1:58 am Cancer
7th 4:12 am Leo
9th 7:43 am Virgo
11th 12:48 pm Libra
13th 7:44 pm Scorpio
16th 4:55 am Sagittarius
18th 4:23 pm Capricorn
21st 5:21 am Aquarius
23rd 5:41 pm Pisces
26th 3:04 am Aries
28th 8:28 am Taurus
30th 10:34 am Gemini

December 1982
2nd 10:58 am Cancer
4th 11:29 am Leo
6th 1:37 pm Virgo
8th 6:14 pm Libra
11th 1:35 am Scorpio
13th 11:30 am Sagittarius
15th 11:16 pm Capricorn
18th 12:13 pm Aquarius
21st 0:56 am Pisces
23rd 11:30 am Aries
25th 6:33 pm Taurus
27th 9:48 pm Gemini
29th 10:12 pm Cancer
31st 9:33 pm Leo

January 1983
2nd 9:51 pm Virgo
5th 0:45 am Libra
7th 7:20 am Scorpio
9th 5:16 pm Sagittarius
12th 5:27 am Capricorn
14th 6:26 pm Aquarius
17th 7:01 am Pisces
19th 6:05 pm Aries
22nd 2:34 am Taurus
24th 7:36 am Gemini
26th 9:24 am Cancer
28th 9:09 am Leo
30th 8:38 am Virgo

February 1983
1st 9:53 am Libra
3rd 2:37 pm Scorpio
5th 11:29 pm Sagittarius
8th 11:35 am Capricorn
11th 0:41 am Aquarius
13th 12:60 pm Pisces
15th 11:46 pm Aries
18th 8:28 am Taurus
20th 2:48 pm Gemini
22nd 6:29 pm Cancer
24th 7:46 pm Leo
26th 7:49 pm Virgo
28th 8:31 pm Libra

March 1983
2nd 11:51 pm Scorpio
5th 7:18 am Sagittarius
7th 6:30 pm Capricorn
10th 7:29 am Aquarius
12th 7:44 pm Pisces
15th 5:58 am Aries
17th 2:02 pm Taurus
19th 8:18 pm Gemini
22nd 0:53 am Cancer
24th 3:43 am Leo
26th 5:19 am Virgo
28th 6:50 am Libra
30th 10:02 am Scorpio

April 1983
1st 4:24 pm Sagittarius
4th 2:30 am Capricorn
6th 3:06 pm Aquarius
9th 3:29 am Pisces
11th 1:32 pm Aries
13th 8:56 pm Taurus
16th 2:12 am Gemini
18th 6:12 am Cancer
20th 9:25 am Leo
22nd 12:11 pm Virgo
24th 3:04 pm Libra
26th 7:07 pm Scorpio
29th 1:29 am Sagittarius

May 1983
1st 11:04 am Capricorn
3rd 11:09 pm Aquarius
6th 11:41 am Pisces
8th 10:14 pm Aries
11th 5:33 am Taurus
13th 9:59 am Gemini
15th 12:45 pm Cancer
17th 3:00 pm Leo
19th 5:37 pm Virgo
21st 9:12 pm Libra
24th 2:18 am Scorpio
26th 9:30 am Sagittarius
28th 7:09 pm Capricorn
31st 7:01 am Aquarius

June 1983
2nd 7:42 pm Pisces
5th 6:55 am Aries
7th 2:59 pm Taurus
9th 7:34 pm Gemini
11th 9:30 pm Cancer
13th 10:21 pm Leo
15th 11:37 pm Virgo
18th 2:38 am Libra
20th 8:02 am Scorpio
22nd 3:57 pm Sagittarius
25th 2:09 am Capricorn
27th 2:07 pm Aquarius
30th 2:51 am Pisces

July 1983
2nd 2:44 pm Aries
5th 0:05 am Taurus
7th 5:37 am Gemini
9th 7:47 am Cancer
11th 7:53 am Leo
13th 7:45 am Virgo
15th 9:15 am Libra
17th 1:43 pm Scorpio
19th 9:32 pm Sagittarius
22nd 8:12 am Capricorn
24th 8:26 pm Aquarius
27th 9:10 am Pisces
29th 9:21 pm Aries

August 1983
1st 7:33 am Taurus
3rd 2:38 pm Gemini
5th 6:06 pm Cancer
7th 6:35 pm Leo
9th 5:50 pm Virgo
11th 5:55 pm Libra
13th 8:46 pm Scorpio
16th 3:36 am Sagittarius
18th 2:01 pm Capricorn
21st 2:26 am Aquarius
23rd 3:09 pm Pisces
26th 3:07 am Aries
28th 1:35 pm Taurus
30th 9:47 pm Gemini

September 1983
2nd 2:51 am Cancer
4th 4:45 am Leo
6th 4:36 am Virgo
8th 4:16 am Libra
10th 5:54 am Scorpio
12th 11:14 am Sagittarius
14th 8:35 pm Capricorn
17th 8:45 am Aquarius
19th 9:29 pm Pisces
22nd 9:09 am Aries
24th 7:11 pm Taurus
27th 3:23 am Gemini
29th 9:21 am Cancer

October 1983
1st 12:52 pm Leo
3rd 2:14 pm Virgo
5th 2:44 pm Libra
7th 4:11 pm Scorpio
9th 8:24 pm Sagittarius
12th 4:33 am Capricorn
14th 4:03 pm Aquarius
17th 4:40 am Pisces
19th 4:16 pm Aries
22nd 1:46 am Taurus
24th 9:07 am Gemini
26th 2:45 pm Cancer
28th 6:49 pm Leo
30th 9:32 pm Virgo

November 1983
1st 11:32 pm Libra
4th 1:55 am Scorpio
6th 6:14 am Sagittarius
8th 1:37 pm Capricorn
11th 0:12 am Aquarius
13th 12:41 pm Pisces
16th 0:37 am Aries
18th 10:04 am Taurus
20th 4:42 pm Gemini
22nd 9:09 pm Cancer
25th 0:19 am Leo
27th 3:03 am Virgo
29th 5:57 am Libra

December 1983
1st 9:44 am Scorpio
3rd 2:60 pm Sagittarius
5th 10:30 pm Capricorn
8th 8:44 am Aquarius
10th 8:54 pm Pisces
13th 9:15 am Aries
15th 7:31 pm Taurus
18th 2:23 am Gemini
20th 6:00 am Cancer
22nd 7:43 am Leo
24th 9:03 am Virgo
26th 11:22 am Libra
28th 3:29 pm Scorpio
30th 9:44 pm Sagittarius

January 1984
2nd 6:11 am Capricorn
4th 4:32 pm Aquarius
7th 4:35 am Pisces
9th 5:15 pm Aries
12th 4:34 am Taurus
14th 12:35 pm Gemini
16th 4:43 pm Cancer
18th 5:48 pm Leo
20th 5:37 pm Virgo
22nd 6:11 pm Libra
24th 9:07 pm Scorpio
27th 3:14 am Sagittarius
29th 12:15 pm Capricorn
31st 11:10 pm Aquarius

February 1984
3rd 11:23 am Pisces
6th 0:04 am Aries
8th 12:03 pm Taurus
10th 9:37 pm Gemini
13th 3:19 am Cancer
15th 5:07 am Leo
17th 4:32 am Virgo
19th 3:42 am Libra
21st 4:48 am Scorpio
23rd 9:28 am Sagittarius
25th 5:52 pm Capricorn
28th 5:03 am Aquarius

March 1984
1st 5:30 pm Pisces
4th 6:07 am Aries
6th 6:08 pm Taurus
9th 4:28 am Gemini
11th 11:43 am Cancer
13th 3:17 pm Leo
15th 3:44 pm Virgo
17th 2:54 pm Libra
19th 2:54 pm Scorpio
21st 5:46 pm Sagittarius
24th 0:36 am Capricorn
26th 11:10 am Aquarius
28th 11:36 pm Pisces
31st 12:12 pm Aries

April 1984
2nd 11:54 pm Taurus
5th 10:01 am Gemini
7th 5:56 pm Cancer
9th 11:01 pm Leo
12th 1:10 am Virgo
14th 1:30 am Libra
16th 1:42 am Scorpio
18th 3:46 am Sagittarius
20th 9:16 am Capricorn
22nd 6:30 pm Aquarius
25th 6:26 am Pisces
27th 7:00 pm Aries
30th 6:27 am Taurus

May 1984
2nd 3:59 pm Gemini
4th 11:25 pm Cancer
7th 4:41 am Leo
9th 7:58 am Virgo
11th 9:52 am Libra
13th 11:24 am Scorpio
15th 1:54 pm Sagittarius
17th 6:46 pm Capricorn
20th 2:57 am Aquarius
22nd 2:10 pm Pisces
25th 2:38 am Aries
27th 2:10 pm Taurus
29th 11:21 pm Gemini

June 1984
1st 5:50 am Cancer
3rd 10:16 am Leo
5th 1:25 pm Virgo
7th 4:02 pm Libra
9th 6:48 pm Scorpio
11th 10:26 pm Sagittarius
14th 3:51 am Capricorn
16th 11:45 am Aquarius
18th 10:19 pm Pisces
21st 10:40 am Aries
23rd 10:37 pm Taurus
26th 7:59 am Gemini
28th 2:04 pm Cancer
30th 5:27 pm Leo

July 1984
2nd 7:26 pm Virgo
4th 9:26 pm Libra
7th 0:28 am Scorpio
9th 5:04 am Sagittarius
11th 11:25 am Capricorn
13th 7:43 pm Aquarius
16th 6:12 am Pisces
18th 6:26 pm Aries
21st 6:51 am Taurus
23rd 5:06 pm Gemini
25th 11:44 pm Cancer
28th 2:39 am Leo
30th 3:28 am Virgo

August 1984
1st 4:04 am Libra
3rd 6:07 am Scorpio
5th 10:33 am Sagittarius
7th 5:27 pm Capricorn
10th 2:26 am Aquarius
12th 1:14 pm Pisces
15th 1:27 am Aries
17th 2:11 pm Taurus
20th 1:30 am Gemini
22nd 9:14 am Cancer
24th 12:55 pm Leo
26th 1:31 pm Virgo
28th 12:59 pm Libra
30th 1:27 pm Scorpio

September 1984
1st 4:34 pm Sagittarius
3rd 10:55 pm Capricorn
6th 8:13 am Aquarius
8th 7:25 pm Pisces
11th 7:46 am Aries
13th 8:32 pm Taurus
16th 8:22 am Gemini
18th 5:32 pm Cancer
20th 10:47 pm Leo
23rd 0:19 am Virgo
24th 11:41 pm Libra
26th 11:04 pm Scorpio
29th 0:31 am Sagittarius

October 1984
1st 5:31 am Capricorn
3rd 2:07 pm Aquarius
6th 1:18 am Pisces
8th 1:50 pm Aries
11th 2:27 am Taurus
13th 2:12 pm Gemini
15th 12:00 pm Cancer
18th 6:38 am Leo
20th 9:52 am Virgo
22nd 10:31 am Libra
24th 10:11 am Scorpio
26th 10:49 am Sagittarius
28th 2:11 pm Capricorn
30th 9:16 pm Aquarius

November 1984
2nd 7:52 am Pisces
4th 8:21 pm Aries
7th 8:52 am Taurus
9th 8:09 pm Gemini
12th 5:28 am Cancer
14th 12:30 pm Leo
16th 5:04 pm Virgo
18th 7:28 pm Libra
20th 8:31 pm Scorpio
22nd 9:35 pm Sagittarius
25th 0:19 am Capricorn
27th 6:12 am Aquarius
29th 3:38 pm Pisces

December 1984
2nd 3:43 am Aries
4th 4:20 pm Taurus
7th 3:23 am Gemini
9th 11:53 am Cancer
11th 6:06 pm Leo
13th 10:35 pm Virgo
16th 1:52 am Libra
18th 4:27 am Scorpio
20th 7:00 am Sagittarius
22nd 10:24 am Capricorn
24th 3:52 pm Aquarius
27th 0:20 am Pisces
29th 11:52 am Aries

January 1985
1st 0:36 am Taurus
3rd 11:57 am Gemini
5th 8:16 pm Cancer
8th 1:28 am Leo
10th 4:40 am Virgo
12th 7:14 am Libra
14th 10:09 am Scorpio
16th 1:50 pm Sagittarius
18th 6:31 pm Capricorn
21st 0:39 am Aquarius
23rd 9:06 am Pisces
25th 8:06 pm Aries
28th 8:53 am Taurus
30th 9:00 pm Gemini

February 1985
2nd 5:56 am Cancer
4th 10:58 am Leo
6th 1:08 pm Virgo
8th 2:13 pm Libra
10th 3:52 pm Scorpio
12th 7:12 pm Sagittarius
15th 0:27 am Capricorn
17th 7:39 am Aquarius
19th 4:40 pm Pisces
22nd 3:45 am Aries
24th 4:28 pm Taurus
27th 5:09 am Gemini

March 1985
1st 3:19 pm Cancer
3rd 9:27 pm Leo
5th 11:44 pm Virgo
7th 11:49 pm Libra
9th 11:47 pm Scorpio
12th 1:31 am Sagittarius
14th 5:58 am Capricorn
16th 1:14 pm Aquarius
18th 10:50 pm Pisces
21st 10:21 am Aries
23rd 11:07 pm Taurus
26th 12:01 pm Gemini
28th 11:13 pm Cancer
31st 6:47 am Leo

April 1985
2nd 10:21 am Virgo
4th 10:53 am Libra
6th 10:13 am Scorpio
8th 10:22 am Sagittarius
10th 1:03 pm Capricorn
12th 7:06 pm Aquarius
15th 4:32 am Pisces
17th 4:19 pm Aries
20th 5:11 am Taurus
22nd 5:59 pm Gemini
25th 5:23 am Cancer
27th 2:06 pm Leo
29th 7:21 pm Virgo

May 1985
1st 9:21 pm Libra
3rd 9:17 pm Scorpio
5th 8:58 pm Sagittarius
7th 10:13 pm Capricorn
10th 2:41 am Aquarius
12th 10:60 am Pisces
14th 10:26 pm Aries
17th 11:23 am Taurus
19th 12:00 pm Gemini
22nd 11:01 am Cancer
24th 7:50 pm Leo
27th 2:04 am Virgo
29th 5:37 am Libra
31st 7:05 am Scorpio

June 1985
2nd 7:34 am Sagittarius
4th 8:37 am Capricorn
6th 11:58 am Aquarius
8th 6:51 pm Pisces
11th 5:26 am Aries
13th 6:12 pm Taurus
16th 6:43 am Gemini
18th 5:19 pm Cancer
21st 1:31 am Leo
23rd 7:29 am Virgo
25th 11:44 am Libra
27th 2:34 pm Scorpio
29th 4:29 pm Sagittarius

July 1985
1st 6:23 pm Capricorn
3rd 9:38 pm Aquarius
6th 3:44 am Pisces
8th 1:24 pm Aries
11th 1:44 am Taurus
13th 2:21 pm Gemini
16th 0:53 am Cancer
18th 8:22 am Leo
20th 1:26 pm Virgo
22nd 5:09 pm Libra
24th 8:16 pm Scorpio
26th 11:12 pm Sagittarius
29th 2:21 am Capricorn
31st 6:28 am Aquarius

August 1985
2nd 12:37 pm Pisces
4th 9:44 pm Aries
7th 9:42 am Taurus
9th 10:31 pm Gemini
12th 9:24 am Cancer
14th 4:53 pm Leo
16th 9:14 pm Virgo
18th 11:43 pm Libra
21st 1:51 am Scorpio
23rd 4:37 am Sagittarius
25th 8:26 am Capricorn
27th 1:33 pm Aquarius
29th 8:25 pm Pisces

September 1985
1st 5:43 am Aries
3rd 5:28 pm Taurus
6th 6:26 am Gemini
8th 6:07 pm Cancer
11th 2:25 am Leo
13th 6:49 am Virgo
15th 8:33 am Libra
17th 9:17 am Scorpio
19th 10:43 am Sagittarius
21st 1:52 pm Capricorn
23rd 7:13 pm Aquarius
26th 2:51 am Pisces
28th 12:44 pm Aries

October 1985
1st 0:34 am Taurus
3rd 1:35 pm Gemini
6th 1:58 am Cancer
8th 11:28 am Leo
10th 5:05 pm Virgo
12th 7:10 pm Libra
14th 7:12 pm Scorpio
16th 7:07 pm Sagittarius
18th 8:37 pm Capricorn
21st 0:55 am Aquarius
23rd 8:31 am Pisces
25th 6:48 pm Aries
28th 6:60 am Taurus
30th 7:58 pm Gemini

November 1985
2nd 8:29 am Cancer
4th 7:01 pm Leo
7th 2:17 am Virgo
9th 5:48 am Libra
11th 6:30 am Scorpio
13th 5:54 am Sagittarius
15th 5:57 am Capricorn
17th 8:32 am Aquarius
19th 2:48 pm Pisces
22nd 0:44 am Aries
24th 1:08 pm Taurus
27th 2:07 am Gemini
29th 2:20 pm Cancer

December 1985
2nd 0:59 am Leo
4th 9:09 am Virgo
6th 2:28 pm Libra
8th 4:54 pm Scorpio
10th 5:12 pm Sagittarius
12th 5:02 pm Capricorn
14th 6:20 pm Aquarius
16th 10:52 pm Pisces
19th 7:42 am Aries
21st 7:42 pm Taurus
24th 8:44 am Gemini
26th 8:42 pm Cancer
29th 6:42 am Leo
31st 2:40 pm Virgo

January 1986
2nd 8:43 pm Libra
5th 0:44 am Scorpio
7th 2:47 am Sagittarius
9th 3:43 am Capricorn
11th 5:05 am Aquarius
13th 8:45 am Pisces
15th 4:09 pm Aries
18th 3:16 am Taurus
20th 4:12 pm Gemini
23rd 4:14 am Cancer
25th 1:45 pm Leo
27th 8:51 pm Virgo
30th 2:09 am Libra

February 1986
1st 6:18 am Scorpio
3rd 9:31 am Sagittarius
5th 12:02 pm Capricorn
7th 2:38 pm Aquarius
9th 6:36 pm Pisces
12th 1:22 am Aries
14th 11:42 am Taurus
17th 0:18 am Gemini
19th 12:38 pm Cancer
21st 10:25 pm Leo
24th 4:58 am Virgo
26th 9:07 am Libra
28th 12:06 pm Scorpio

March 1986
2nd 2:53 pm Sagittarius
4th 5:57 pm Capricorn
6th 9:43 pm Aquarius
9th 2:50 am Pisces
11th 10:07 am Aries
13th 8:06 pm Taurus
16th 8:24 am Gemini
18th 9:05 pm Cancer
21st 7:35 am Leo
23rd 2:36 pm Virgo
25th 6:22 pm Libra
27th 8:06 pm Scorpio
29th 9:22 pm Sagittarius
31st 11:26 pm Capricorn

April 1986
3rd 3:13 am Aquarius
5th 9:06 am Pisces
7th 5:14 pm Aries
10th 3:37 am Taurus
12th 3:52 pm Gemini
15th 4:42 am Cancer
17th 4:06 pm Leo
20th 0:25 am Virgo
22nd 4:48 am Libra
24th 6:15 am Scorpio
26th 6:18 am Sagittarius
28th 6:45 am Capricorn
30th 9:11 am Aquarius

May 1986
2nd 2:35 pm Pisces
4th 11:01 pm Aries
7th 10:00 am Taurus
9th 10:25 pm Gemini
12th 11:17 am Cancer
14th 11:14 pm Leo
17th 8:41 am Virgo
19th 2:36 pm Libra
21st 4:59 pm Scorpio
23rd 4:55 pm Sagittarius
25th 4:18 pm Capricorn
27th 5:05 pm Aquarius
29th 8:58 pm Pisces

June 1986
1st 4:46 am Aries
3rd 3:48 pm Taurus
6th 4:26 am Gemini
8th 5:14 pm Cancer
11th 5:09 am Leo
13th 3:14 pm Virgo
15th 10:37 pm Libra
18th 2:34 am Scorpio
20th 3:34 am Sagittarius
22nd 3:00 am Capricorn
24th 2:53 am Aquarius
26th 5:18 am Pisces
28th 11:41 am Aries
30th 9:55 pm Taurus

July 1986
3rd 10:33 am Gemini
5th 11:20 pm Cancer
8th 10:52 am Leo
10th 8:47 pm Virgo
13th 4:37 am Libra
15th 9:53 am Scorpio
17th 12:30 pm Sagittarius
19th 1:08 pm Capricorn
21st 1:20 pm Aquarius
23rd 3:03 pm Pisces
25th 8:06 pm Aries
28th 5:14 am Taurus
30th 5:20 pm Gemini

August 1986
2nd 6:03 am Cancer
4th 5:24 pm Leo
7th 2:44 am Virgo
9th 10:02 am Libra
11th 3:34 pm Scorpio
13th 7:14 pm Sagittarius
15th 9:21 pm Capricorn
17th 10:44 pm Aquarius
20th 0:52 am Pisces
22nd 5:30 am Aries
24th 1:40 pm Taurus
27th 1:01 am Gemini
29th 1:38 pm Cancer

September 1986
1st 1:07 am Leo
3rd 10:02 am Virgo
5th 4:32 pm Libra
7th 9:11 pm Scorpio
10th 0:41 am Sagittarius
12th 3:27 am Capricorn
14th 6:07 am Aquarius
16th 9:29 am Pisces
18th 2:36 pm Aries
20th 10:25 pm Taurus
23rd 9:15 am Gemini
25th 9:44 pm Cancer
28th 9:36 am Leo
30th 6:55 pm Virgo

October 1986
3rd 1:03 am Libra
5th 4:34 am Scorpio
7th 6:48 am Sagittarius
9th 8:54 am Capricorn
11th 11:47 am Aquarius
13th 4:05 pm Pisces
15th 10:14 pm Aries
18th 6:37 am Taurus
20th 5:15 pm Gemini
23rd 5:36 am Cancer
25th 6:00 pm Leo
28th 4:18 am Virgo
30th 11:00 am Libra

November 1986
1st 2:16 pm Scorpio
3rd 3:18 pm Sagittarius
5th 3:51 pm Capricorn
7th 5:31 pm Aquarius
9th 9:30 pm Pisces
12th 4:16 am Aries
14th 1:26 pm Taurus
17th 0:26 am Gemini
19th 12:46 pm Cancer
22nd 1:24 am Leo
24th 12:41 pm Virgo
26th 8:57 pm Libra
29th 1:13 am Scorpio

December 1986
1st 2:07 am Sagittarius
3rd 1:29 am Capricorn
5th 1:24 am Aquarius
7th 3:52 am Pisces
9th 9:55 am Aries
11th 7:12 pm Taurus
14th 6:42 am Gemini
16th 7:09 pm Cancer
19th 7:43 am Leo
21st 7:28 pm Virgo
24th 4:60 am Libra
26th 11:00 am Scorpio
28th 1:14 pm Sagittarius
30th 12:53 pm Capricorn

January 1987
1st 11:58 am Aquarius
3rd 12:43 pm Pisces
5th 4:57 pm Aries
8th 1:16 am Taurus
10th 12:42 pm Gemini
13th 1:19 am Cancer
15th 1:45 pm Leo
18th 1:14 am Virgo
20th 11:05 am Libra
22nd 6:28 pm Scorpio
24th 10:35 pm Sagittarius
26th 11:42 pm Capricorn
28th 11:17 pm Aquarius
30th 11:26 pm Pisces

February 1987
2nd 2:12 am Aries
4th 8:60 am Taurus
6th 7:26 pm Gemini
9th 7:56 am Cancer
11th 8:22 pm Leo
14th 7:25 am Virgo
16th 4:43 pm Libra
19th 0:05 am Scorpio
21st 5:08 am Sagittarius
23rd 7:55 am Capricorn
25th 9:08 am Aquarius
27th 10:09 am Pisces

March 1987
1st 12:41 pm Aries
3rd 6:16 pm Taurus
6th 3:28 am Gemini
8th 3:25 pm Cancer
11th 3:55 am Leo
13th 2:53 pm Virgo
15th 11:36 pm Libra
18th 5:56 am Scorpio
20th 10:30 am Sagittarius
22nd 1:47 pm Capricorn
24th 4:18 pm Aquarius
26th 6:47 pm Pisces
28th 10:13 pm Aries
31st 3:49 am Taurus

April 1987
2nd 12:20 pm Gemini
4th 11:34 pm Cancer
7th 12:02 pm Leo
9th 11:29 pm Virgo
12th 8:02 am Libra
14th 1:39 pm Scorpio
16th 5:01 pm Sagittarius
18th 7:22 pm Capricorn
20th 9:45 pm Aquarius
23rd 1:03 am Pisces
25th 5:42 am Aries
27th 12:08 pm Taurus
29th 8:45 pm Gemini

May 1987
2nd 7:41 am Cancer
4th 8:07 pm Leo
7th 8:05 am Virgo
9th 5:26 pm Libra
11th 11:09 pm Scorpio
14th 1:42 am Sagittarius
16th 2:38 am Capricorn
18th 3:45 am Aquarius
20th 6:27 am Pisces
22nd 11:27 am Aries
24th 6:41 pm Taurus
27th 3:56 am Gemini
29th 3:01 pm Cancer

June 1987
1st 3:27 am Leo
3rd 3:54 pm Virgo
6th 2:22 am Libra
8th 9:01 am Scorpio
10th 11:49 am Sagittarius
12th 12:04 pm Capricorn
14th 11:49 am Aquarius
16th 1:00 pm Pisces
18th 5:02 pm Aries
21st 0:10 am Taurus
23rd 9:58 am Gemini
25th 9:22 pm Cancer
28th 9:52 am Leo
30th 10:33 pm Virgo

July 1987
3rd 9:50 am Libra
5th 5:58 pm Scorpio
7th 10:03 pm Sagittarius
9th 10:42 pm Capricorn
11th 9:50 pm Aquarius
13th 9:38 pm Pisces
16th 0:02 am Aries
18th 6:09 am Taurus
20th 3:36 pm Gemini
23rd 3:14 am Cancer
25th 3:50 pm Leo
28th 4:25 am Virgo
30th 3:56 pm Libra

August 1987
2nd 1:08 am Scorpio
4th 6:42 am Sagittarius
6th 8:47 am Capricorn
8th 8:36 am Aquarius
10th 8:04 am Pisces
12th 9:14 am Aries
14th 1:44 pm Taurus
16th 10:01 pm Gemini
19th 9:21 am Cancer
21st 9:58 pm Leo
24th 10:23 am Virgo
26th 9:35 pm Libra
29th 6:47 am Scorpio
31st 1:20 pm Sagittarius

September 1987
2nd 5:00 pm Capricorn
4th 6:19 pm Aquarius
6th 6:37 pm Pisces
8th 7:36 pm Aries
10th 10:57 pm Taurus
13th 5:59 am Gemini
15th 4:25 pm Cancer
18th 4:50 am Leo
20th 5:13 pm Virgo
23rd 3:57 am Libra
25th 12:28 pm Scorpio
27th 6:48 pm Sagittarius
29th 11:08 pm Capricorn

October 1987
2nd 1:50 am Aquarius
4th 3:39 am Pisces
6th 5:36 am Aries
8th 8:60 am Taurus
10th 3:07 pm Gemini
13th 0:30 am Cancer
15th 12:34 pm Leo
18th 1:06 am Virgo
20th 11:47 am Libra
22nd 7:39 pm Scorpio
25th 0:57 am Sagittarius
27th 4:32 am Capricorn
29th 7:27 am Aquarius
31st 10:20 am Pisces

November 1987
2nd 1:41 pm Aries
4th 6:04 pm Taurus
7th 0:15 am Gemini
9th 9:12 am Cancer
11th 8:45 pm Leo
14th 9:28 am Virgo
16th 8:46 pm Libra
19th 4:43 am Scorpio
21st 9:13 am Sagittarius
23rd 11:31 am Capricorn
25th 1:13 pm Aquarius
27th 3:43 pm Pisces
29th 7:38 pm Aries

December 1987
2nd 1:06 am Taurus
4th 8:16 am Gemini
6th 5:22 pm Cancer
9th 4:40 am Leo
11th 5:29 pm Virgo
14th 5:36 am Libra
16th 2:35 pm Scorpio
18th 7:29 pm Sagittarius
20th 9:06 pm Capricorn
22nd 9:21 pm Aquarius
24th 10:12 pm Pisces
27th 1:07 am Aries
29th 6:40 am Taurus
31st 2:32 pm Gemini

January 1988
3rd 0:18 am Cancer
5th 11:49 am Leo
8th 0:35 am Virgo
10th 1:13 pm Libra
12th 11:39 pm Scorpio
15th 5:53 am Sagittarius
17th 8:10 am Capricorn
19th 8:02 am Aquarius
21st 7:31 am Pisces
23rd 8:37 am Aries
25th 12:43 pm Taurus
27th 8:06 pm Gemini
30th 6:14 am Cancer

February 1988
1st 6:08 pm Leo
4th 6:54 am Virgo
6th 7:35 pm Libra
9th 6:38 am Scorpio
11th 2:30 pm Sagittarius
13th 6:32 pm Capricorn
15th 7:23 pm Aquarius
17th 6:44 pm Pisces
19th 6:38 pm Aries
21st 8:54 pm Taurus
24th 2:45 am Gemini
26th 12:16 pm Cancer
29th 0:12 am Leo

March 1988
2nd 1:07 pm Virgo
5th 1:33 am Libra
7th 12:25 pm Scorpio
9th 8:58 pm Sagittarius
12th 2:29 am Capricorn
14th 5:06 am Aquarius
16th 5:42 am Pisces
18th 5:47 am Aries
20th 7:09 am Taurus
22nd 11:27 am Gemini
24th 7:30 pm Cancer
27th 6:55 am Leo
29th 7:50 pm Virgo

April 1988
1st 8:04 am Libra
3rd 6:25 pm Scorpio
6th 2:29 am Sagittarius
8th 8:17 am Capricorn
10th 12:08 pm Aquarius
12th 2:23 pm Pisces
14th 3:47 pm Aries
16th 5:33 pm Taurus
18th 9:12 pm Gemini
21st 4:08 am Cancer
23rd 2:38 pm Leo
26th 3:17 am Virgo
28th 3:36 pm Libra

May 1988
1st 1:39 am Scorpio
3rd 8:50 am Sagittarius
5th 1:53 pm Capricorn
7th 5:36 pm Aquarius
9th 8:40 pm Pisces
11th 11:24 pm Aries
14th 2:23 am Taurus
16th 6:35 am Gemini
18th 1:10 pm Cancer
20th 10:53 pm Leo
23rd 11:13 am Virgo
25th 11:50 pm Libra
28th 10:02 am Scorpio
30th 4:54 pm Sagittarius

June 1988
1st 8:59 pm Capricorn
3rd 11:35 pm Aquarius
6th 2:02 am Pisces
8th 5:06 am Aries
10th 9:05 am Taurus
12th 2:18 pm Gemini
14th 9:22 pm Cancer
17th 7:00 am Leo
19th 7:04 pm Virgo
22nd 7:56 am Libra
24th 6:56 pm Scorpio
27th 2:15 am Sagittarius
29th 5:57 am Capricorn

July 1988
1st 7:31 am Aquarius
3rd 8:36 am Pisces
5th 10:42 am Aries
7th 2:31 pm Taurus
9th 8:18 pm Gemini
12th 4:12 am Cancer
14th 2:15 pm Leo
17th 2:18 am Virgo
19th 3:20 pm Libra
22nd 3:11 am Scorpio
24th 11:36 am Sagittarius
26th 4:02 pm Capricorn
28th 5:22 pm Aquarius
30th 5:24 pm Pisces

August 1988
1st 5:57 pm Aries
3rd 8:28 pm Taurus
6th 1:45 am Gemini
8th 9:56 am Cancer
10th 8:29 pm Leo
13th 8:48 am Virgo
15th 9:52 pm Libra
18th 10:08 am Scorpio
20th 7:52 pm Sagittarius
23rd 1:47 am Capricorn
25th 4:02 am Aquarius
27th 4:01 am Pisces
29th 3:31 am Aries
31st 4:25 am Taurus

September 1988
2nd 8:17 am Gemini
4th 3:41 pm Cancer
7th 2:16 am Leo
9th 2:49 pm Virgo
12th 3:51 am Libra
14th 4:05 pm Scorpio
17th 2:25 am Sagittarius
19th 9:40 am Capricorn
21st 1:38 pm Aquarius
23rd 2:47 pm Pisces
25th 2:30 pm Aries
27th 2:32 pm Taurus
29th 4:47 pm Gemini

October 1988
1st 10:39 pm Cancer
4th 8:33 am Leo
6th 9:01 pm Virgo
9th 10:03 am Libra
11th 9:57 pm Scorpio
14th 7:57 am Sagittarius
16th 3:42 pm Capricorn
18th 9:03 pm Aquarius
20th 11:58 pm Pisces
23rd 0:58 am Aries
25th 1:22 am Taurus
27th 2:56 am Gemini
29th 7:33 am Cancer
31st 4:08 pm Leo

November 1988
3rd 4:02 am Virgo
5th 5:03 pm Libra
8th 4:44 am Scorpio
10th 2:03 pm Sagittarius
12th 9:11 pm Capricorn
15th 2:35 am Aquarius
17th 6:32 am Pisces
19th 9:11 am Aries
21st 11:02 am Taurus
23rd 1:15 pm Gemini
25th 5:24 pm Cancer
28th 0:52 am Leo
30th 12:02 pm Virgo

December 1988
3rd 0:57 am Libra
5th 12:47 pm Scorpio
7th 9:53 pm Sagittarius
10th 4:05 am Capricorn
12th 8:25 am Aquarius
14th 11:52 am Pisces
16th 3:03 pm Aries
18th 6:12 pm Taurus
20th 9:44 pm Gemini
23rd 2:36 am Cancer
25th 10:01 am Leo
27th 8:28 pm Virgo
30th 9:09 am Libra

January 1989
1st 9:33 pm Scorpio
4th 7:07 am Sagittarius
6th 1:09 pm Capricorn
8th 4:29 pm Aquarius
10th 6:31 pm Pisces
12th 8:37 pm Aries
14th 11:38 pm Taurus
17th 3:59 am Gemini
19th 10:01 am Cancer
21st 6:05 pm Leo
24th 4:34 am Virgo
26th 5:02 pm Libra
29th 5:46 am Scorpio
31st 4:24 pm Sagittarius

February 1989
2nd 11:28 pm Capricorn
5th 2:48 am Aquarius
7th 3:52 am Pisces
9th 4:19 am Aries
11th 5:48 am Taurus
13th 9:28 am Gemini
15th 3:45 pm Cancer
18th 0:33 am Leo
20th 11:37 am Virgo
23rd 0:06 am Libra
25th 12:56 pm Scorpio
28th 0:29 am Sagittarius

March 1989
2nd 8:53 am Capricorn
4th 1:31 pm Aquarius
6th 2:56 pm Pisces
8th 2:36 pm Aries
10th 2:29 pm Taurus
12th 4:22 pm Gemini
14th 9:29 pm Cancer
17th 6:17 am Leo
19th 5:42 pm Virgo
22nd 6:24 am Libra
24th 7:11 pm Scorpio
27th 6:52 am Sagittarius
29th 4:22 pm Capricorn
31st 10:45 pm Aquarius

April 1989
3rd 1:36 am Pisces
5th 1:50 am Aries
7th 1:07 am Taurus
9th 1:32 am Gemini
11th 5:02 am Cancer
13th 12:35 pm Leo
15th 11:40 pm Virgo
18th 12:33 pm Libra
21st 1:14 am Scorpio
23rd 12:38 pm Sagittarius
25th 10:16 pm Capricorn
28th 5:31 am Aquarius
30th 10:00 am Pisces

May 1989
2nd 11:49 am Aries
4th 11:55 am Taurus
6th 12:08 pm Gemini
8th 2:27 pm Cancer
10th 8:27 pm Leo
13th 6:33 am Virgo
15th 7:09 pm Libra
18th 7:47 am Scorpio
20th 6:51 pm Sagittarius
23rd 3:54 am Capricorn
25th 10:59 am Aquarius
27th 4:10 pm Pisces
29th 7:25 pm Aries
31st 8:60 pm Taurus

June 1989
2nd 10:04 pm Gemini
5th 0:19 am Cancer
7th 5:33 am Leo
9th 2:35 pm Virgo
12th 2:32 am Libra
14th 3:11 pm Scorpio
17th 2:12 am Sagittarius
19th 10:39 am Capricorn
21st 4:56 pm Aquarius
23rd 9:37 pm Pisces
26th 1:08 am Aries
28th 3:47 am Taurus
30th 6:10 am Gemini

July 1989
2nd 9:23 am Cancer
4th 2:43 pm Leo
6th 11:06 pm Virgo
9th 10:32 am Libra
11th 11:10 pm Scorpio
14th 10:28 am Sagittarius
16th 6:59 pm Capricorn
19th 0:36 am Aquarius
21st 4:07 am Pisces
23rd 6:42 am Aries
25th 9:13 am Taurus
27th 12:19 pm Gemini
29th 4:35 pm Cancer
31st 10:43 pm Leo

August 1989
3rd 7:22 am Virgo
5th 6:30 pm Libra
8th 7:04 am Scorpio
10th 7:00 pm Sagittarius
13th 4:13 am Capricorn
15th 9:54 am Aquarius
17th 12:43 pm Pisces
19th 1:59 pm Aries
21st 3:14 pm Taurus
23rd 5:43 pm Gemini
25th 10:15 pm Cancer
28th 5:16 am Leo
30th 2:33 pm Virgo

September 1989
2nd 1:49 am Libra
4th 2:24 pm Scorpio
7th 2:50 am Sagittarius
9th 1:08 pm Capricorn
11th 7:59 pm Aquarius
13th 11:06 pm Pisces
15th 11:38 pm Aries
17th 11:23 pm Taurus
20th 0:17 am Gemini
22nd 3:53 am Cancer
24th 10:48 am Leo
26th 8:35 pm Virgo
29th 8:17 am Libra

October 1989
1st 8:54 pm Scorpio
4th 9:29 am Sagittarius
6th 8:43 pm Capricorn
9th 5:02 am Aquarius
11th 9:32 am Pisces
13th 10:38 am Aries
15th 9:53 am Taurus
17th 9:23 am Gemini
19th 11:15 am Cancer
21st 4:52 pm Leo
24th 2:16 am Virgo
26th 2:12 pm Libra
29th 2:56 am Scorpio
31st 3:23 pm Sagittarius

November 1989
3rd 2:47 am Capricorn
5th 12:06 pm Aquarius
7th 6:21 pm Pisces
9th 9:06 pm Aries
11th 9:08 pm Taurus
13th 8:19 pm Gemini
15th 8:54 pm Cancer
18th 0:46 am Leo
20th 8:58 am Virgo
22nd 8:27 pm Libra
25th 9:12 am Scorpio
27th 9:30 pm Sagittarius
30th 8:25 am Capricorn

December 1989
2nd 5:40 pm Aquarius
5th 0:48 am Pisces
7th 5:09 am Aries
9th 6:56 am Taurus
11th 7:15 am Gemini
13th 7:53 am Cancer
15th 10:47 am Leo
17th 5:24 pm Virgo
20th 3:47 am Libra
22nd 4:18 pm Scorpio
25th 4:35 am Sagittarius
27th 3:08 pm Capricorn
29th 11:38 pm Aquarius

January 1990
1st 6:09 am Pisces
3rd 10:54 am Aries
5th 2:03 pm Taurus
7th 4:01 pm Gemini
9th 5:54 pm Cancer
11th 9:04 pm Leo
14th 2:60 am Virgo
16th 12:21 pm Libra
19th 0:16 am Scorpio
21st 12:41 pm Sagittarius
23rd 11:27 pm Capricorn
26th 7:22 am Aquarius
28th 12:48 pm Pisces
30th 4:32 pm Aries

February 1990
1st 7:28 pm Taurus
3rd 10:13 pm Gemini
6th 1:28 am Cancer
8th 5:55 am Leo
10th 12:17 pm Virgo
12th 9:10 pm Libra
15th 8:35 am Scorpio
17th 9:05 pm Sagittarius
20th 8:25 am Capricorn
22nd 4:48 pm Aquarius
24th 9:48 pm Pisces
27th 0:16 am Aries

March 1990
1st 1:44 am Taurus
3rd 3:39 am Gemini
5th 7:06 am Cancer
7th 12:28 pm Leo
9th 7:49 pm Virgo
12th 5:11 am Libra
14th 4:27 pm Scorpio
17th 4:56 am Sagittarius
19th 4:59 pm Capricorn
22nd 2:28 am Aquarius
24th 8:03 am Pisces
26th 10:11 am Aries
28th 10:27 am Taurus
30th 10:46 am Gemini

April 1990
1st 12:55 pm Cancer
3rd 5:53 pm Leo
6th 1:43 am Virgo
8th 11:46 am Libra
10th 11:18 pm Scorpio
13th 11:49 am Sagittarius
16th 0:16 am Capricorn
18th 10:48 am Aquarius
20th 5:53 pm Pisces
22nd 8:56 pm Aries
24th 9:01 pm Taurus
26th 8:13 pm Gemini
28th 8:42 pm Cancer

May 1990
1st 0:09 am Leo
3rd 7:21 am Virgo
5th 5:30 pm Libra
8th 5:24 am Scorpio
10th 5:56 pa Sagittarius
13th 6:21 am Capricorn
15th 5:28 pm Aquarius
18th 1:53 am Pisces
20th 6:28 am Aries
22nd 7:40 am Taurus
24th 7:01 am Gemini
26th 6:38 am Cancer
28th 8:35 am Leo
30th 2:13 pm Virgo

June 1990
1st 11:31 pm Libra
4th 11:24 am Scorpio
6th 12:00 pm Sagittarius
9th 12:11 pm Capricorn
11th 11:09 pm Aquarius
14th 7:57 am Pisces
16th 1:51 pm Aries
18th 4:40 pm Taurus
20th 5:14 pm Gemini
22nd 5:12 pm Cancer
24th 6:29 pm Leo
26th 10:43 pm Virgo
29th 6:51 am Libra

July 1990
1st 6:02 pm Scorpio
4th 6:35 am Sagittarius
6th 6:39 pm Capricorn
9th 5:05 am Aquarius
11th 1:28 pm Pisces
13th 7:35 pm Aries
15th 11:29 pm Taurus
18th 1:32 am Gemini
20th 2:46 am Cancer
22nd 4:33 am Leo
24th 8:23 am Virgo
26th 3:24 pm Libra
29th 1:40 am Scorpio
31st 1:59 pm Sagittarius

August 1990
3rd 2:08 am Capricorn
5th 12:16 pm Aquarius
7th 7:54 pm Pisces
10th 1:15 am Aries
12th 4:56 am Taurus
14th 7:43 am Gemini
16th 10:14 am Cancer
18th 1:15 pm Leo
20th 5:37 pm Virgo
23rd 0:19 am Libra
25th 9:60 am Scorpio
27th 9:59 pm Sagittarius
30th 10:21 am Capricorn

September 1990
1st 8:49 pm Aquarius
4th 4:03 am Pisces
6th 8:21 am Aries
8th 10:56 am Taurus
10th 1:07 pm Gemini
12th 3:56 pm Cancer
14th 7:55 pm Leo
17th 1:20 am Virgo
19th 8:38 am Libra
21st 6:09 pm Scorpio
24th 5:54 am Sagittarius
26th 6:37 pm Capricorn
29th 5:51 am Aquarius

October 1990
1st 1:37 pm Pisces
3rd 5:38 pm Aries
5th 7:05 pm Taurus
7th 7:48 pm Gemini
9th 9:31 pm Cancer
12th 1:17 am Leo
14th 7:24 am Virgo
16th 3:30 pm Libra
19th 1:25 am Scorpio
21st 1:13 pm Sagittarius
24th 2:04 am Capricorn
26th 2:11 pm Aquarius
28th 11:23 pm Pisces
31st 4:11 am Aries

November 1990
2nd 5:30 am Taurus
4th 5:07 am Gemini
6th 5:10 am Cancer
8th 7:28 am Leo
10th 12:52 pm Virgo
12th 9:10 pm Libra
15th 7:42 am Scorpio
17th 7:40 pm Sagittarius
20th 8:33 am Capricorn
22nd 9:08 pm Aquarius
25th 7:27 am Pisces
27th 2:00 pm Aries
29th 4:33 pm Taurus

December 1990
1st 4:21 pm Gemini
3rd 3:30 pm Cancer
5th 4:05 pm Leo
7th 7:42 pm Virgo
10th 3:02 am Libra
12th 1:29 pm Scorpio
15th 1:43 am Sagittarius
17th 2:35 pm Capricorn
20th 2:59 am Aquarius
22nd 1:45 pm Pisces
24th 9:43 pm Aries
27th 2:07 am Taurus
29th 3:24 am Gemini
31st 3:04 am Cancer

January 1991
2nd 2:57 am Leo
4th 5:01 am Virgo
6th 10:39 am Libra
8th 8:01 pm Scorpio
11th 8:07 am Sagittarius
13th 8:59 pm Capricorn
16th 9:02 am Aquarius
18th 7:22 pm Pisces
21st 3:27 am Aries
23rd 8:57 am Taurus
25th 12:04 pm Gemini
27th 1:23 pm Cancer
29th 2:05 pm Leo
31st 3:48 pm Virgo

February 1991
2nd 8:05 pm Libra
5th 4:03 am Scorpio
7th 3:24 pm Sagittarius
10th 4:14 am Capricorn
12th 4:13 pm Aquarius
15th 1:58 am Pisces
17th 9:09 am Aries
19th 2:23 pm Taurus
21st 6:09 pm Gemini
23rd 8:56 pm Cancer
25th 11:13 pm Leo
28th 1:52 am Virgo

March 1991
2nd 6:06 am Libra
4th 1:13 pm Scorpio
6th 11:34 pm Sagittarius
9th 12:13 pm Capricorn
12th 0:29 am Aquarius
14th 10:05 am Pisces
16th 4:34 pm Aries
18th 8:39 pm Taurus
20th 11:36 pm Gemini
23rd 2:28 am Cancer
25th 5:44 am Leo
27th 9:43 am Virgo
29th 2:52 pm Libra
31st 10:02 pm Scorpio

April 1991
3rd 8:02 am Sagittarius
5th 8:21 pm Capricorn
8th 8:57 am Aquarius
10th 7:14 pm Pisces
13th 1:48 am Aries
15th 5:03 am Taurus
17th 6:42 am Gemini
19th 8:18 am Cancer
21st 11:06 am Leo
23rd 3:32 pm Virgo
25th 9:36 pm Libra
28th 5:36 am Scorpio
30th 3:46 pm Sagittarius

May 1991
3rd 3:56 am Capricorn
5th 4:50 pm Aquarius
8th 4:01 am Pisces
10th 11:29 am Aries
12th 3:03 pm Taurus
14th 3:60 pm Gemini
16th 4:15 pm Cancer
18th 5:33 pm Leo
20th 9:02 pm Virgo
23rd 3:10 am Libra
25th 11:44 am Scorpio
27th 10:21 pm Sagittarius
30th 10:42 am Capricorn

June 1991
1st 11:42 pm Aquarius
4th 11:34 am Pisces
6th 8:22 pm Aries
9th 1:12 am Taurus
11th 2:35 am Gemini
13th 2:16 am Cancer
15th 2:12 am Leo
17th 4:05 am Virgo
19th 9:06 am Libra
21st 5:21 pm Scorpio
24th 4:18 am Sagittarius
26th 4:50 pm Capricorn
29th 5:46 am Aquarius

July 1991
1st 5:48 pm Pisces
4th 3:31 am Aries
6th 9:48 am Taurus
8th 12:38 pm Gemini
10th 1:02 pm Cancer
12th 12:37 pm Leo
14th 1:17 pm Virgo
16th 4:39 pm Libra
18th 11:41 pm Scorpio
21st 10:19 am Sagittarius
23rd 10:57 pm Capricorn
26th 11:48 am Aquarius
28th 11:34 pm Pisces
31st 9:18 am Aries

August 1991
2nd 4:29 pm Taurus
4th 8:53 pm Gemini
6th 10:48 pm Cancer
8th 11:10 pm Leo
10th 11:36 pm Virgo
13th 1:54 am Libra
15th 7:39 am Scorpio
17th 5:14 pm Sagittarius
20th 5:34 am Capricorn
22nd 6:27 pm Aquarius
25th 5:49 am Pisces
27th 2:59 pm Aries
29th 10:00 pm Taurus

September 1991
1st 3:03 am Gemini
3rd 6:19 am Cancer
5th 8:14 am Leo
7th 9:39 am Virgo
9th 11:57 am Libra
11th 4:48 pm Scorpio
14th 1:17 am Sagittarius
16th 1:05 pm Capricorn
19th 1:56 am Aquarius
21st 1:17 pm Pisces
23rd 9:56 pm Aries
26th 3:59 am Taurus
28th 8:25 am Gemini
30th 11:57 am Cancer

October 1991
2nd 2:60 pm Leo
4th 5:46 pm Virgo
6th 9:03 pm Libra
9th 2:03 am Scorpio
11th 10:03 am Sagittarius
13th 9:12 pm Capricorn
16th 10:04 am Aquarius
18th 9:52 pm Pisces
21st 6:30 am Aries
23rd 11:53 am Taurus
25th 3:08 pm Gemini
27th 5:37 pm Cancer
29th 8:21 pm Leo
31st 11:48 pm Virgo

November 1991
3rd 4:14 am Libra
5th 10:13 am Scorpio
7th 6:26 pm Sagittarius
10th 5:20 am Capricorn
12th 6:08 pm Aquarius
15th 6:31 am Pisces
17th 4:04 pm Aries
19th 9:49 pm Taurus
22nd 0:23 am Gemini
24th 1:26 am Cancer
26th 2:38 am Leo
28th 5:14 am Virgo
30th 9:50 am Libra

December 1991
2nd 4:36 pm Scorpio
5th 1:34 am Sagittarius
7th 12:45 pm Capricorn
10th 1:28 am Aquarius
12th 2:18 pm Pisces
15th 1:06 am Aries
17th 8:05 am Taurus
19th 11:18 am Gemini
21st 11:54 am Cancer
23rd 11:41 am Leo
25th 12:28 pm Virgo
27th 3:42 pm Libra
29th 10:05 pm Scorpio

January 1992
1st 7:33 am Sagittarius
3rd 7:11 pm Capricorn
6th 8:00 am Aquarius
8th 8:52 pm Pisces
11th 8:19 am Aries
13th 4:57 pm Taurus
15th 9:54 pm Gemini
17th 11:26 pm Cancer
19th 10:57 pm Leo
21st 10:23 pm Virgo
23rd 11:43 pm Libra
26th 4:35 am Scorpio
28th 1:23 pm Sagittarius
31st 1:07 am Capricorn

Index